SQL Server 2012

Programming

Kalman Toth

SQL Server 2012 Programming

Copyright © 2012 by Kalman Toth

SQL Server 2012 Programming

Contents at a Glance

About the Author

Kalman Toth has been working with relational database technology since 1990 when one day his boss, at a commodity brokerage firm in Greenwich, Connecticut, had to leave early and gave his SQL Server login & password to Kalman along with a small SQL task. Kalman was a C/C++ developer fascinated by SQL, therefore, he studied a Transact-SQL manual 3 times from start to end "dry", without any server access. His boss was satisfied with the execution of SQL task and a few days later Kalman's dream came true: he got his very own SQL Server login. His relational database career since then includes database design, database development, database administration, OLAP architecture and Business Intelligence development. Applications included enterprise-level general ledger & financial accounting, bond funds auditing, international stock market feeds processing, broker-dealer firm risk management, derivative instruments analytics, consumer ecommerce database management for online dating, personal finance, physical fitness, diet and health. Currently he is Principal Trainer at www.sqlusa.com. His MSDN forum participation in the Transact-SQL and SQL Server Tools was rewarded with the Microsoft Community Contributor award. Kalman has a Master of Arts degree in Physics from Columbia University and a Master of Philosophy degree in Computing Science also from Columbia. Microsoft certifications in database administration, development and Business Intelligence. The dream SQL career took him across United States & Canada as well as South America & Europe. SQL also involved him in World History. At one time he worked for Deloitte & Touche on the 96th floor of World Trade Center North. On September 11, 2001, he was an RDBMS consultant at Citibank on 111 Wall Street. After escaping at 10:30 on that fateful Tuesday morning in the heavy dirt smoke, it took 10 days before he could return to his relational database development job just 1/2 mile from the nearly three thousand victims buried under steel. What Kalman loves about SQL is that the same friendly, yet powerful, commands can process 2 records or 2 million records or 200 million records the same easy way. His current interest is Artificial Intelligence. He is convinced that machine intelligence will not only replace human intelligence but surpass it million times in the near future. His hobby is flying gliders & vintage fighter planes. Accessibility: @dbdesign1 at Twitter; http://twitter.com/dbdesign1, http://twitter.com/sqlusa, http://www.sqlusa.com/contact2005/.

IV

V

CONTENTS

INTRODUCTION

Developers across the world are facing database issues daily. While they are immersed in procedural languages with loops , RDBMS forces them to think in terms of sets without loops. It takes transition. It takes training. It takes experience. Developers are exposed also to Excel worksheets or spreadsheets as they were called in the not so distant past. So if you know worksheets how hard databases can be? After all worksheets look pretty much like database tables? The big difference is connections among well-designed tables. A database is a set of connected tables which represent entities in the real world. A database can be 100 connected tables or 3000. The connection is very simple: row A in table Alpha has affiliated data with row B in table Beta. But even with 200 tables and 300 connections (FOREIGN KEY references), it takes a good amount of time to familiarize to the point of acceptable working knowledge.

"The Cemetery of Computer Languages" is expanding. You can see tombstones like PL/1, Forth, Ada, Pascal, LISP, RPG, APL, SNOBOL, JOVIAL, Algol and the list goes on. For some, the future is in question: PowerBuilder, ColdFusion, FORTRAN & COBOL. SQL on the other hand running strong after 3 decades of glorious existence. What is the difference? The basic difference is that SQL can handle large datasets in a consistent manner based on mathematical foundations. You can throw together a computer language easy: assignment statements, looping, if-then conditional, 300 library functions, and voila! Here is the new language: Mars/1, named after the red planet to be fashionable with NASA's new Mars robot. But can Mars/1 JOIN a table of 1 million rows with a table of 10 million rows in a second? The success of SQL language is so compelling that other technologies are tagged onto it like XML/XQuery which deals with semi-structured information objects.

In SQL you are thinking at a high level. In C# or Java, you are dealing with details, lots of them. That is the big difference. Why is so much of the book dedicated to database design? Why not plunge into SQL coding and sooner or later the developer will get a hang of the design? Because high level thinking requires thinking at the database design level. A farmer has 6 mules, how do we model it in the database? We design the Farmer and FarmAnimal tables, then connect them with FarmerID FOREIGN KEY in FarmAnimal referencing the FarmerID PRIMARY KEY in the Farmer table. What is the big deal about it, looks so simple? In fact, how about just calling the tables Table1 & Table2 to be more generic? Ouch... meaningful naming is the very basis of good database design. Relational database design is truly simple for simple well-understood models. The challenge starts in modeling complex objects such as financial derivative instruments, airplane passenger scheduling or social network website. When you need to add 5 new tables to a 1000 tables database and hook them in (define FOREIGN KEY references) correctly, it is a huge challenge. To begin with, some of the 5 new tables may already be redundant, but you don't know that until you understand what the 1000 tables are really storing. Frequently, learning the application area is the biggest challenge for a developer when starting a new job.

The SQL language is simple to program and read even if when touching 10 tables. Complexities are abound though. The very first one: does the SQL statement touch the right data set? 999 records and 1000 or 998? T-SQL statements are turned into Transact-SQL scripts, stored procedures, user-defined functions and triggers, server-side database objects. They can be 5 statements or 1000 statements long programs. The style of Transact-SQL programming is different from the style in procedural programming languages. There are no arrays, only tables or table variables. Typically there is no looping, only set-based operations. Error control is different. Testing & debugging is relatively simple in Transact-SQL due to the interactive environment and the magic of selecting & executing a part without recompiling the whole.

WHO THIS BOOK IS FOR

Developers, programmers and systems analysts who are new to relational database technology. Also developers, designers and administrators, who know some SQL programming and database design, wish to expand their RDBMS design & development technology horizons. Familiarity with other computer language is assumed. The book has lots of queries, lots of T-SQL scripts, plenty to learn. The best way to learn it is to type in the query in your own SQL Server copy and test it, examine it, change it. Wouldn't it be easier just to copy & paste it? It would but the learning value would diminish. You need to feel the SQL language in your fingers. SQL queries must "pour" out from your fingers into the keyboard. Why is that so important? After everything can be found on the web and just copy & paste? Well not exactly. If you want to be an expert, it has to be in your head not on the web. Second, when your supervisor is looking over your shoulder, "Charlie, can you tell me what is the total revenue for March?", you have to be able to type in the query without SQL forum search and provide the results to your superior promptly.

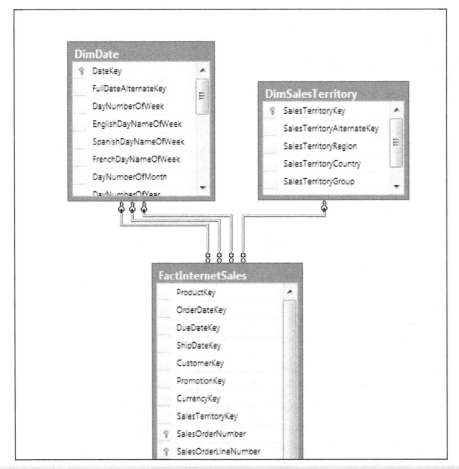

ABOUT THIS BOOK

Beginning relational database design and beginning Transact-SQL programming. It is not a reference manual, rather learn by examples: there are over 1,100 SELECT queries in the book. Instead of imaginary tables, the book uses the SQL Server sample databases for explanations and examples: pubs (PRIMARY KEYs 9, FOREIGN KEYs 10) , Northwind (PRIMARY KEYs 13, FOREIGN KEYs 13) and the AdventureWorks family. Among them: AdventureWorks, AdventureWorks2008, AdventureWorks2012 (PRIMARY KEYs 71, FOREIGN KEYs 90), & AdventureWorksDW2012 (PRIMARY KEYs 27, FOREIGN KEYs 44). The book introduces relational database design concepts, then reinforces them again and again, not to bore the reader, rather indoctrinate with relational database design principles. Light weight SQL starts at the beginning of the book, because working with database metadata (not the content of the database, rather data which describes the database) is essential for understanding database design. By the time the reader gets to T-SQL programming, already knows basic SQL programming from the database design section of the book. The book was designed to be readable in any environment, even on the beach laptop around or no laptop in sight at all. All queries are followed by results row count and /or full/partial results listing in tabular (grid) format. For full benefits though, the reader should try out the T-SQL queries and scripts as he progresses from page to page, topic to topic. Example for SQL Server 2012 T-SQL query and results presentation.

```
SELECT          V.Name                                   AS Vendor,
                FORMAT(SUM(POH.TotalDue), 'c', 'en-US')  AS [Total Purchase],
                FORMAT(AVG(POH.TotalDue), 'c', 'en-US')  AS [Average Purchase]
FROM AdventureWorks.Purchasing.Vendor AS V
    INNER JOIN AdventureWorks.Purchasing.PurchaseOrderHeader AS POH
        ON V.VendorID = POH.VendorID
GROUP BY V.Name  ORDER BY Vendor;
-- (79 row(s) affected) - Partial results.
```

Vendor	Total Purchase	Average Purchase
Advanced Bicycles	$28,502.09	$558.86
Allenson Cycles	$498,589.59	$9,776.27
American Bicycles and Wheels	$9,641.01	$189.04
American Bikes	$1,149,489.84	$22,539.02

CONVENTIONS USED IN THIS BOOK

The Transact-SQL queries and scripts (sequence of statements) are shaded.

The number of resulting rows is displayed as a comment line: -- (79 row(s) affected) .

The results of the queries is usually displayed in grid format.

Less frequently the results are enclosed in comment markers: /*...... */ .

When a query is a trivial variation of a previous query, no result is displayed.

While the intention of the book is database design & database development, SQL Server installation and some database administration tasks are included.

"Apparatus Intelligentia

vincet

Humanum Intelligentia"

Dedicated to the Pioneers of
Microcomputer Revolution

This page is intentionally left blank.

CHAPTER 1: SQL Server Sample & System Databases

AdventureWorks Series of OLTP Databases

AdventureWorks sample On Line Transaction Processing (OLTP) database has been introduced with SQL Server 2005 to replace the previous sample database Northwind, a fictional gourmet food items distributor. The intent of the AdventureWorks sample database is to support the business operations of AdventureWorks Cycles, a fictitious mountain, touring and road bike manufacturer. The company sells through dealer network and online on the web. In addition to bikes, it sells frames and parts as well as accessories such as helmets, biking clothes and water bottles. The AdventureWorks2012 database image of Touring-1000 Blue, 50 bike in Production.ProductPhoto table.

T-SQL query to generate the list of tables of AdventureWorks2012 in 5 columns. The core query is simple. Presenting the results in 5 columns instead of 1 column adds a bit of complexity.

```
;WITH cteTableList AS (        SELECT CONCAT(SCHEMA_NAME(schema_id), '.', name)           AS  TableName,
  (( ROW_NUMBER() OVER( ORDER BY CONCAT(SCHEMA_NAME(schema_id),'.', name)) ) % 5)      AS  Remainder,
  (( ROW_NUMBER() OVER( ORDER BY CONCAT(SCHEMA_NAME(schema_id),'.', name)) - 1 )/ 5)   AS  Quotient
                      FROM AdventureWorks2012.sys.tables),
CTE AS (SELECT TableName, CASE WHEN Remainder=0 THEN 5 ELSE Remainder END AS Remainder, Quotient
        FROM cteTableList)
SELECT    MAX(CASE WHEN Remainder = 1 THEN TableName END),
          MAX(CASE WHEN Remainder = 2 THEN TableName END),
          MAX(CASE WHEN Remainder = 3 THEN TableName END),
          MAX(CASE WHEN Remainder = 4 THEN TableName END),
          MAX(CASE WHEN Remainder = 5 THEN TableName END)
FROM  CTE GROUP  BY Quotient ORDER  BY Quotient;
GO
```

The query result set in grid format: tables in AdventureWorks2012

dbo.AWBuildVersion	dbo.DatabaseLog	dbo.ErrorLog	HumanResources.Dep artment	HumanResources.E mployee
HumanResources.Employe eDepartmentHistory	HumanResources.EmployeePa yHistory	HumanResources. JobCandidate	HumanResources.Shif t	Person.Address
Person.AddressType	Person.BusinessEntity	Person.BusinessE ntityAddress	Person.BusinessEntity Contact	Person.ContactTyp e
Person.CountryRegion	Person.EmailAddress	Person.Password	Person.Person	Person.PersonPhon e
Person.PhoneNumberType	Person.StateProvince	Production.BillOf Materials	Production.Culture	Production.Docum ent
Production.Illustration	Production.Location	Production.Produ ct	Production.ProductCa tegory	Production.Product CostHistory
Production.ProductDescrip tion	Production.ProductDocument	Production.Produ ctInventory	Production.ProductLis tPriceHistory	Production.Product Model
Production.ProductModelIl lustration	Production.ProductModelProd uctDescriptionCulture	Production.Produ ctPhoto	Production.ProductPr oductPhoto	Production.Product Review
Production.ProductSubcate gory	Production.ScrapReason	Production.Transa ctionHistory	Production.Transactio nHistoryArchive	Production.UnitMe asure
Production.WorkOrder	Production.WorkOrderRouting	Purchasing.Produ ctVendor	Purchasing.PurchaseO rderDetail	Purchasing.Purchas eOrderHeader
Purchasing.ShipMethod	Purchasing.Vendor	Sales.CountryRegi onCurrency	Sales.CreditCard	Sales.Currency
Sales.CurrencyRate	Sales.Customer	Sales.PersonCredi tCard	Sales.SalesOrderDetai l	Sales.SalesOrderHe ader
Sales.SalesOrderHeaderSal esReason	Sales.SalesPerson	Sales.SalesPerson QuotaHistory	Sales.SalesReason	Sales.SalesTaxRate
Sales.SalesTerritory	Sales.SalesTerritoryHistory	Sales.ShoppingCar tItem	Sales.SpecialOffer	Sales.SpecialOfferP roduct
Sales.Store	NULL	NULL	NULL	NULL

CHAPTER 1: SQL Server Sample & System Databases

Diagram of Person.Person & Related Tables

Database diagram displays the Person.Person and related tables. PRIMARY KEYs are marked with a gold (in color display) key. The "oo------->" line is interpreted as many-to-one relationship. For example a person (one) can have one or more (many) credit cards. The "oo" side is the table with **FOREIGN KEY** referencing the gold key side table with the **PRIMARY KEY**.

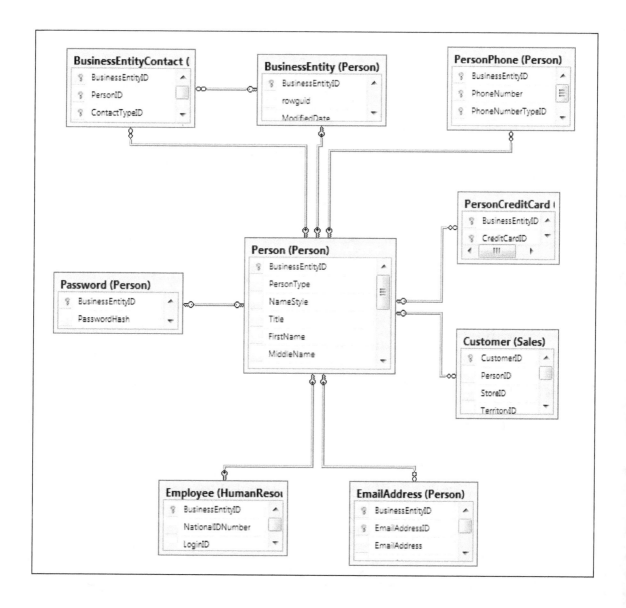

Diagram of Sales.SalesOrderHeader and Related Tables

Database diagram displays Sales.SalesOrderHeader and all tables related with **FOREIGN KEY** constraints. The SalesOrderHeader table stores the general information about each order. Line items, e.g. 5 Helmets at $30 each, are stored in the SalesOrderDetail table.

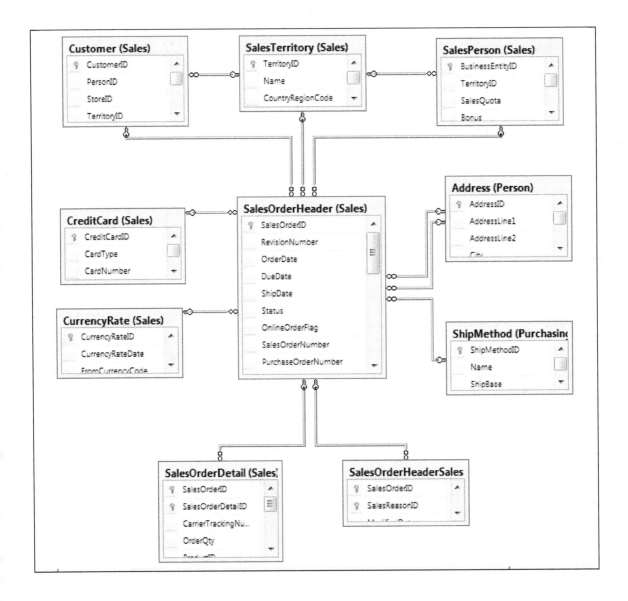

SELECT Query Basics

We have to use "light-weight" SQL (Structured Query Language) in the database design lessons. The reason is that rather difficult to discuss any database related topic without demonstration T-SQL scripts, in fact it would not make sense. **Relational database** and the **SQL language** are "married" to each other forever and ever.

The Simplest SELECT Statement

The simplest SELECT statement is "SELECT * FROM TableNameX" as demonstrated following. The "*" means wildcard inclusion of all columns in the table. Since there is no any other clause in the SELECT statement, it means also to retrieve all rows in the **table in no particular order**. Small tables which were populated in order are usually retrieved in order even though there is no ORDER BY clause. But this behaviour is purely coincidental. **Only ORDER BY clause can guarantee a sorted output.**

```
SELECT * FROM AdventureWorks2012.HumanResources.Department;
-- (16 row(s) affected)
```

DepartmentID	Name	GroupName	ModifiedDate
1	Engineering	Research and Development	2002-06-01 00:00:00.000
2	Tool Design	Research and Development	2002-06-01 00:00:00.000
3	Sales	Sales and Marketing	2002-06-01 00:00:00.000
4	Marketing	Sales and Marketing	2002-06-01 00:00:00.000
5	Purchasing	Inventory Management	2002-06-01 00:00:00.000
6	Research and Development	Research and Development	2002-06-01 00:00:00.000
7	Production	Manufacturing	2002-06-01 00:00:00.000
8	Production Control	Manufacturing	2002-06-01 00:00:00.000
9	Human Resources	Executive General and Administration	2002-06-01 00:00:00.000
10	Finance	Executive General and Administration	2002-06-01 00:00:00.000
11	Information Services	Executive General and Administration	2002-06-01 00:00:00.000
12	Document Control	Quality Assurance	2002-06-01 00:00:00.000
13	Quality Assurance	Quality Assurance	2002-06-01 00:00:00.000
14	Facilities and Maintenance	Executive General and Administration	2002-06-01 00:00:00.000
15	Shipping and Receiving	Inventory Management	2002-06-01 00:00:00.000
16	Executive	Executive General and Administration	2002-06-01 00:00:00.000

When tables are JOINed, SELECT * returns all the columns with all the data in the participant tables.

```
SELECT TOP 3 * FROM Sales.SalesOrderHeader H
          INNER JOIN Sales.SalesOrderDetail D
              ON H.SalesOrderID = D.SalesOrderID;
-- 121,317 rows in the JOIN
```

CHAPTER 1: SQL Server Sample & System Databases

Query Result Set In Text Format
If no grid format available, text format can be used. While it works, it is a challenge to read it, but computer geeks are used to this kind of data dump.

```
/* SalesOrderID RevisionNumber OrderDate        DueDate         ShipDate         Status
OnlineOrderFlag SalesOrderNumber       PurchaseOrderNumber     AccountNumber CustomerID
SalesPersonID TerritoryID BillToAddressID ShipToAddressID ShipMethodID CreditCardID
CreditCardApprovalCode CurrencyRateID SubTotal        TaxAmt          Freight        TotalDue
Comment                                                          rowguid
ModifiedDate        SalesOrderID SalesOrderDetailID CarrierTrackingNumber   OrderQty ProductID
SpecialOfferID UnitPrice        UnitPriceDiscount   LineTotal        rowguid          ModifiedDate
----------- -------------- ----------------------- ----------------------- ----------------------- ------ --------------- --------------------
------ ----------------------- ----------- ------------------------ --------------- ------------- -----------
- ----------------------- ----------------------- ---------------- --------------- ------------ -----------
--------------------------------------------------------------------------------------------------------------
---------- -------------------- ----------- ------------------------ -------- ----------- ------------- -----------
-------- -------------------- ---------------------------------------------------------------- ----------------------

43735    3       2005-07-10 00:00:00.000 2005-07-22 00:00:00.000 2005-07-17 00:00:00.000 5    1
SO43735           NULL            10-4030-016522 16522    NULL    9     25384       25384
1      6526    1034619Vi33896      119     3578.27         286.2616        89.4568
3953.9884       NULL                                                98F80245-
C398-4562-BDAF-EA3E9A0DDFAC 2005-07-17 00:00:00.000 43735       391     NULL            1
749    1       3578.27         0.00        3578.270000         74838EF7-FDEB-4EB3-8978-
BA310FBA82E6 2005-07-10 00:00:00.000
43736    3       2005-07-10 00:00:00.000 2005-07-22 00:00:00.000 2005-07-17 00:00:00.000 5    1
SO43736           NULL            10-4030-011002 11002    NULL    9     20336       20336
1      1416    1135092Vi7270       119     3399.99         271.9992        84.9998
3756.989        NULL                                                C14E29E7-
DB11-44EF-943E-143925A5A9AE 2005-07-17 00:00:00.000 43736       392     NULL            1
773    1       3399.99         0.00        3399.990000         3A0229FA-0A03-4126-
97CE-C3425968B670 2005-07-10 00:00:00.000
43737    3       2005-07-11 00:00:00.000 2005-07-23 00:00:00.000 2005-07-18 00:00:00.000 5    1
SO43737           NULL            10-4030-013261 13261    NULL    8     29772       29772
1      NULL    NULL            136     3578.27         286.2616        89.4568       3953.9884
NULL                                                0B3E274D-E5A8-4E8C-A417-
0EAFABCFF162 2005-07-18 00:00:00.000 43737       393     NULL            1     750    1
3578.27        0.00        3578.270000         65AFCCE8-CA28-41C4-9A07-0265FB2DA5C8
2005-07-11 00:00:00.000         (3 row(s) affected)  */
```

```
SELECT MatchingRows = COUNT(*) FROM AdventureWorks2012.Sales.SalesOrderHeader H
  INNER JOIN AdventureWorks2012.Sales.SalesOrderDetail D
      ON H.SalesOrderID = D.SalesOrderID;    -- INNER JOIN MatchingRows 121317
```

```
SELECT AllRowsInDetail = COUNT(*) FROM AdventureWorks2012.Sales.SalesOrderDetail
-- AllRowsInDetail 121317
```

CHAPTER 1: SQL Server Sample & System Databases

SELECT Query with WHERE Clause Predicate

Query to demonstrate how can we be selective with columns, furthermore, filter returned rows (WHERE clause) and sort them (ORDER BY clause).

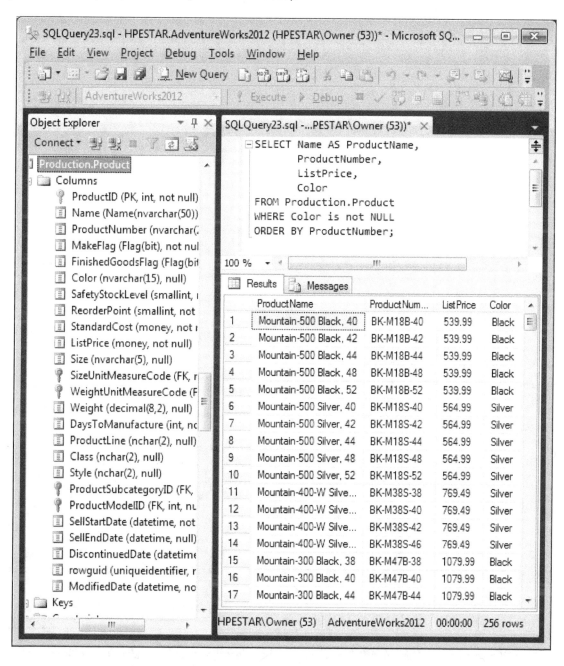

Aggregating Data with GROUP BY Query

The second basic query is GROUP BY aggregation which creates a **summary** of detail data.
GROUP BY query can be used to preview, review, survey , assess, and analyze data at a high
level.

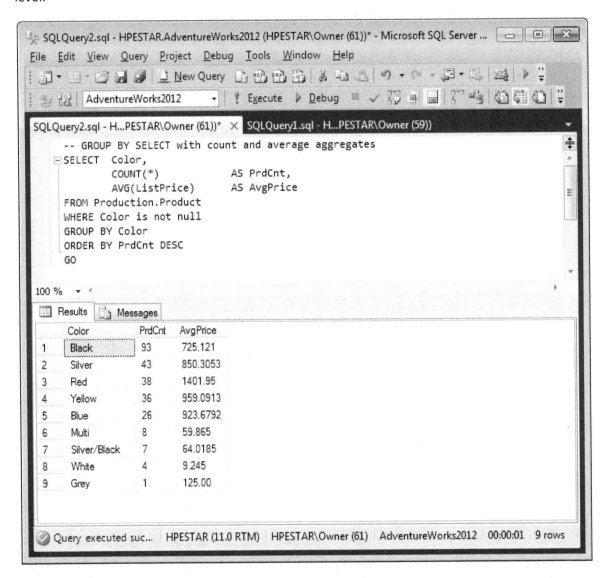

NOTE
GROUP BY aggregate queries can efficiently "fingerprint" (profile) data in tables, even millions of rows.
GROUP BY aggregates form the computational base of Business Intelligence.

GROUP BY Query with 2 Tables & ORDER BY for Sorting

JOINing two tables on matching KEYs, FOREIGN KEY to PRIMARY KEY, to combine the data
contents in a consistent fashion.

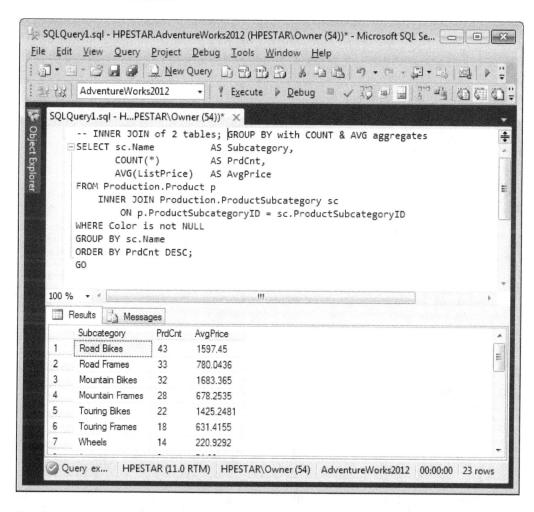

LEN(), DATALENGTH(), LTRIM() & RTRIM() Functions

The LEN() function counts characters without the trailing spaces. DATALENGTH() counts storage
bytes including trailing spaces. LTRIM() trims leading spaces, RTRIM() trims trailing spaces.

```
DECLARE @W varchar(32)= CHAR(32)+'Denver'+CHAR(32);
DECLARE @UW nvarchar(32) = CHAR(32)+N'MEGŐRZÉSE'+CHAR(32);  -- UNICODE 2 bytes per character
SELECT Length=LEN(@W), DLength=DATALENGTH (@W);                              -- 7  8
SELECT Length=LEN(@UW), DLength=DATALENGTH (@UW);                           -- 10 22
SELECT Length=LEN(LTRIM(RTRIM(@W))), DLength=DATALENGTH (LTRIM(RTRIM(@W)));  -- 6  6
SELECT Length=LEN(LTRIM(RTRIM(@UW))), DLength=DATALENGTH (LTRIM(RTRIM(@UW))); -- 9 18
```

CHAPTER 1: SQL Server Sample & System Databases

Finding All Accessories in Production.Product Table
Query to list all accessories (a category) for sale.

USE AdventureWorks2012;

```
SELECT          UPPER(PC.Name) AS Category, PSC.Name              AS Subcategory,
                P.Name AS Product, FORMAT(ListPrice, 'c', 'en-US')      AS ListPrice,
                FORMAT(StandardCost, 'c', 'en-US')            AS StandardCost
FROM Production.Product AS P
   INNER JOIN Production.ProductSubcategory AS PSC
          ON PSC.ProductSubcategoryID = P.ProductSubcategoryID
   INNER JOIN Production.ProductCategory AS PC
          ON PC.ProductCategoryID = PSC.ProductCategoryID
WHERE PC.Name = 'Accessories'
ORDER BY Category, Subcategory, Product;
```

Category	Subcategory	Product	ListPrice	StandardCost
ACCESSORIES	Bike Racks	Hitch Rack - 4-Bike	$120.00	$44.88
ACCESSORIES	Bike Stands	All-Purpose Bike Stand	$159.00	$59.47
ACCESSORIES	Bottles and Cages	Mountain Bottle Cage	$9.99	$3.74
ACCESSORIES	Bottles and Cages	Road Bottle Cage	$8.99	$3.36
ACCESSORIES	Bottles and Cages	Water Bottle - 30 oz.	$4.99	$1.87
ACCESSORIES	Cleaners	Bike Wash - Dissolver	$7.95	$2.97
ACCESSORIES	Fenders	Fender Set - Mountain	$21.98	$8.22
ACCESSORIES	Helmets	Sport-100 Helmet, Black	$34.99	$13.09
ACCESSORIES	Helmets	Sport-100 Helmet, Blue	$34.99	$13.09
ACCESSORIES	Helmets	Sport-100 Helmet, Red	$34.99	$13.09
ACCESSORIES	Hydration Packs	Hydration Pack - 70 oz.	$54.99	$20.57
ACCESSORIES	Lights	Headlights - Dual-Beam	$34.99	$14.43
ACCESSORIES	Lights	Headlights - Weatherproof	$44.99	$18.56
ACCESSORIES	Lights	Taillights - Battery-Powered	$13.99	$5.77
ACCESSORIES	Locks	Cable Lock	$25.00	$10.31
ACCESSORIES	Panniers	Touring-Panniers, Large	$125.00	$51.56
ACCESSORIES	Pumps	Minipump	$19.99	$8.25
ACCESSORIES	Pumps	Mountain Pump	$24.99	$10.31
ACCESSORIES	Tires and Tubes	HL Mountain Tire	$35.00	$13.09
ACCESSORIES	Tires and Tubes	HL Road Tire	$32.60	$12.19
ACCESSORIES	Tires and Tubes	LL Mountain Tire	$24.99	$9.35
ACCESSORIES	Tires and Tubes	LL Road Tire	$21.49	$8.04
ACCESSORIES	Tires and Tubes	ML Mountain Tire	$29.99	$11.22
ACCESSORIES	Tires and Tubes	ML Road Tire	$24.99	$9.35
ACCESSORIES	Tires and Tubes	Mountain Tire Tube	$4.99	$1.87
ACCESSORIES	Tires and Tubes	Patch Kit/8 Patches	$2.29	$0.86
ACCESSORIES	Tires and Tubes	Road Tire Tube	$3.99	$1.49
ACCESSORIES	Tires and Tubes	Touring Tire	$28.99	$10.84
ACCESSORIES	Tires and Tubes	Touring Tire Tube	$4.99	$1.87

How Can SQL Work without Looping?

Looping is implicit in the SQL language. The commands are set oriented and carried out for each member of the set be it 5 or 500 millions in an unordered manner.

SELECT * FROM AdventureWorks2012.Sales.SalesOrderDetail;   (121317 row(s) affected)

SQL Server database engine looped through internally on all rows in SalesOrderDetail table in an unordered way. In fact the database engine may have used some ordering for efficiency, but that behaviour is a blackbox as far as programming concerned. Implicit looping makes SQL statements so simple, yet immensely powerful for information access from low level to high level.

Single-Valued SQL Queries

Single-valued SQL queries are very important because **we can use them where ever the T-SQL syntax requires a single value just by enclosing the query in parenthesis**. The next T-SQL query returns a single value, a cell from the table which is the intersection of a row and a column.

SELECT ListPrice FROM AdventureWorks2012.Production.Product WHERE ProductID = 800;
-- (1 row(s) affected)

ListPrice
1120.49

The ">" comparison operator requires a single value on the right hand side so we plug in the single-valued query. The WHERE condition is evaluated for each row (implicit looping).

SELECT ProductID, Name AS ProductName, ListPrice
FROM AdventureWorks2012.Production.Product   -- 504 rows
WHERE ListPrice > 2 * (
            SELECT ListPrice FROM AdventureWorks2012.Production.Product
            WHERE ProductID = 800
)
ORDER BY ListPrice DESC, ProductName;   -- (35 row(s) affected) - Partial results.

ProductID	ProductName	ListPrice
750	Road-150 Red, 44	3578.27
751	Road-150 Red, 48	3578.27
752	Road-150 Red, 52	3578.27
753	Road-150 Red, 56	3578.27
749	Road-150 Red, 62	3578.27
771	Mountain-100 Silver, 38	3399.99

CHAPTER 1: SQL Server Sample & System Databases

Data Dictionary Description of Tables in the Sales Schema

It is not easy to understand a database with 70 tables, even harder with 2,000 tables. Documentation is very helpful, if not essential, for any database. SQL Server provides Data Dictionary facility for documenting tables and other objects in the database. Data which describes the design & structure of a database is called **metadata**. Here is the high level documentation of tables in the Sales schema using the fn_listextendedproperty system function.

```
SELECT
        CONCAT('Sales.', objname COLLATE DATABASE_DEFAULT)       AS TableName,
        value                                                    AS [Description]
FROM fn_listextendedproperty (NULL, 'schema', 'Sales', 'table', default, NULL, NULL)
ORDER BY TableName;
```

TableName	Description
Sales.ContactCreditCard	Cross-reference table mapping customers in the Contact table to their credit card information in the CreditCard table.
Sales.CountryRegionCurrency	Cross-reference table mapping ISO currency codes to a country or region.
Sales.CreditCard	Customer credit card information.
Sales.Currency	Lookup table containing standard ISO currencies.
Sales.CurrencyRate	Currency exchange rates.
Sales.Customer	Current customer information. Also see the Individual and Store tables.
Sales.CustomerAddress	Cross-reference table mapping customers to their address(es).
Sales.Individual	Demographic data about customers that purchase Adventure Works products online.
Sales.SalesOrderDetail	Individual products associated with a specific sales order. See SalesOrderHeader.
Sales.SalesOrderHeader	General sales order information.
Sales.SalesOrderHeaderSalesReason	Cross-reference table mapping sales orders to sales reason codes.
Sales.SalesPerson	Sales representative current information.
Sales.SalesPersonQuotaHistory	Sales performance tracking.
Sales.SalesReason	Lookup table of customer purchase reasons.
Sales.SalesTaxRate	Tax rate lookup table.
Sales.SalesTerritory	Sales territory lookup table.
Sales.SalesTerritoryHistory	Sales representative transfers to other sales territories.
Sales.ShoppingCartItem	Contains online customer orders until the order is submitted or cancelled.
Sales.SpecialOffer	Sale discounts lookup table.
Sales.SpecialOfferProduct	Cross-reference table mapping products to special offer discounts.
Sales.Store	Customers (resellers) of Adventure Works products.
Sales.StoreContact	Cross-reference table mapping stores and their employees.

NULL Values in Tables & Query Results

NULL means no value. If so why do we capitalize it? We don't have to. Somehow, it became a custom in the RDBMS industry, nobody knows anymore how it started. Since the U.S. default collation for server and databases are case insensitive, we can just use "null" as well. **NULL value is different from empty string (") or 0 (zero) which can be tested by the "=" or "!=" operators.** If a database table does not have a value in a cell for whatever reason, it is marked (flagged) as NULL by the database engine. When a value is entered, the NULL marking goes away. **NULL values can be tested by "IS NULL" or "IS NOT NULL" operators, but not the "=" or "!=" operators.**

The likelihood is high that the color attribute is not applicable to items like tire tube, that is the reason that some cell values were left unassigned (null).

```
SELECT TOP 5    Name                              AS ProductName,
                ProductNumber,
                ListPrice,
                Color
FROM AdventureWorks2012.Production.Product
WHERE Color IS NULL  ORDER BY ProductName DESC;
```

ProductName	ProductNumber	ListPrice	Color
Water Bottle - 30 oz.	WB-H098	4.99	NULL
Touring Tire Tube	TT-T092	4.99	NULL
Touring Tire	TI-T723	28.99	NULL
Touring Rim	RM-T801	0.00	NULL
Touring End Caps	EC-T209	0.00	NULL

We can do random selection as well and get a mix of products with color and null value.

```
SELECT TOP 5    Name AS ProductName,
                ProductNumber,
                ListPrice,
                Color
FROM AdventureWorks2012.Production.Product  ORDER BY NEWID();    -- Random sort
```

ProductName	ProductNumber	ListPrice	Color
Touring-1000 Yellow, 46	BK-T79Y-46	2384.07	Yellow
HL Spindle/Axle	SD-9872	0.00	NULL
ML Mountain Tire	TI-M602	29.99	NULL
Road-650 Red, 60	BK-R50R-60	782.99	Red
Pinch Bolt	PB-6109	0.00	NULL

CHAPTER 1: SQL Server Sample & System Databases

NULL Values Generated by Queries

NULL values can be generated by queries as well. Typically, LEFT JOIN, RIGHT JOIN and some functions generate NULLs. The meaning of OUTER JOINs: include no-match rows from the left or right table in addition to the matching rows.

```
SELECT TOP 5
            PS.Name                    AS Category,
            P.Name                     AS ProductName,
            ProductNumber,
            ListPrice,
            Color
FROM AdventureWorks2012.Production.Product P
   RIGHT JOIN AdventureWorks2012.Production.ProductSubcategory PS
        ON    PS.ProductSubcategoryID = P.ProductSubcategoryID
              AND ListPrice >= 3500.0
ORDER BY newid();
GO
```

Category	ProductName	ProductNumber	ListPrice	Color
Road Bikes	Road-150 Red, 62	BK-R93R-62	3578.27	Red
Road Bikes	Road-150 Red, 52	BK-R93R-52	3578.27	Red
Bib-Shorts	NULL	NULL	NULL	NULL
Socks	NULL	NULL	NULL	NULL
Cranksets	NULL	NULL	NULL	NULL

Some system functions, like the brand new TRY_CONVERT(), can generate NULL values as well. If the PostalCode cannot be converted into an integer, TRY_CONVERT() returns NULL.

```
SELECT TOP 5   ConvertedZip = TRY_CONVERT(INT, PostalCode),
            AddressLine1,
            City,
            PostalCode
FROM Person.Address  ORDER by newid();
```

ConvertedZip	AddressLine1	City	PostalCode
91945	5979 El Pueblo	Lemon Grove	91945
NULL	7859 Green Valley Road	London	W1V 5RN
3220	6004 Peabody Road	Geelong	3220
NULL	6713 Eaker Way	Burnaby	V3J 6Z3
NULL	5153 Hackamore Lane	Shawnee	V8Z 4N5

The SOUNDEX() Function to Check Sound Alikes

The soundex() function is very interesting for testing different spelling of words such as names.

```
USE AdventureWorks2012;
GO

SELECT DISTINCT LastName
FROM Person.Person
WHERE soundex(LastName) = soundex('Steel');
GO
```

LastName
Seidel
Sotelo
Stahl
Steel
Steele

```
SELECT DISTINCT LastName
FROM Person.Person
WHERE soundex(LastName) = soundex('Brown');
```

LastName
Bourne
Brian
Brown
Browne
Bruno

```
SELECT DISTINCT FirstName FROM Person.Person
WHERE soundex(FirstName) = soundex('Mary');
```

FirstName
Mari
Maria
María
Mariah
Marie
Mario
Mary
Mary Lou
Mayra

Building an FK-PK Diagram in AdventureWorks2012

The **FOREIGN KEY - PRIMARY KEY** diagram of AdventureWorks2012 database with over 70 tables can be built just by adding the tables to the diagram. The FK-PK lines are automatically drawn. An FK-PK line represents a predefined referential constraint.

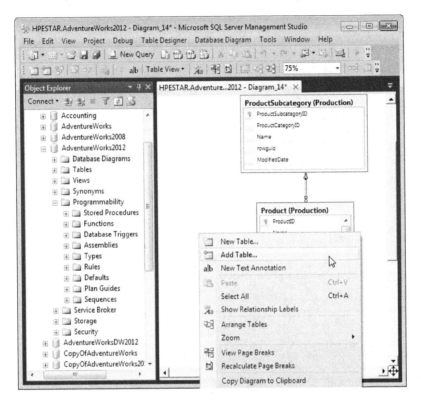

While all tables are important in a database, tables with the most connections play central roles, in a way analogous to the Sun with planets around it.

```
-- PRIMARY KEY tables with the most FOREIGN KEY references
SELECT          schema_name(schema_id)          AS SchemaName,
                o.name                          AS PKTable,
                count(*)                        AS FKCount
FROM sys.sysforeignkeys s    INNER JOIN sys.objects o      ON s.rkeyid = o.object_id
GROUP BY schema_id, o.name    HAVING count(*) >= 5    ORDER BY FKCount DESC;
```

SchemaName	PKTable	FKCount
Production	Product	14
Person	Person	7
HumanResources	Employee	6
Person	BusinessEntity	5
Sales	SalesTerritory	5

CHAPTER 1: SQL Server Sample & System Databases

AdventureWorksDW2012 Data Warehouse Database

AdventureWorksDW series contain second hand data only since they are Data Warehouse databases. All data originates from other sources such as the AdventureWorks OLTP database & Excel worksheets. Tables in the data warehousing database are divided into two groups: dimension tables & fact tables.

Simple data warehouse query.

```
SELECT          D.CalendarYear AS [Year], C.SalesTerritoryCountry AS [Country],
                FORMAT(SUM(S.SalesAmount),'c0','en-US') AS TotalSales
FROM FactInternetSales AS S  INNER JOIN DimDate AS D ON S.OrderDateKey = D.DateKey
        INNER JOIN DimSalesTerritory AS C ON S.SalesTerritoryKey = C.SalesTerritoryKey
GROUP BY D.CalendarYear, C.SalesTerritoryCountry  ORDER BY Year DESC, SUM(S.SalesAmount) DESC;
```

Year	Country	TotalSales
2008	United States	$3,324,031
2008	Australia	$2,563,884
2008	United Kingdom	$1,210,286
2008	Germany	$1,076,891
2008	France	$922,179

Diagram of a Star Schema in AdventureWorksDW2012

The high level star schema diagram in AdventureWorksDW2012 Data Warehouse database with FactResellerSales fact table and related dimension tables. The temporal dimension table DimDate plays a central role in Business Intelligence data analytics.

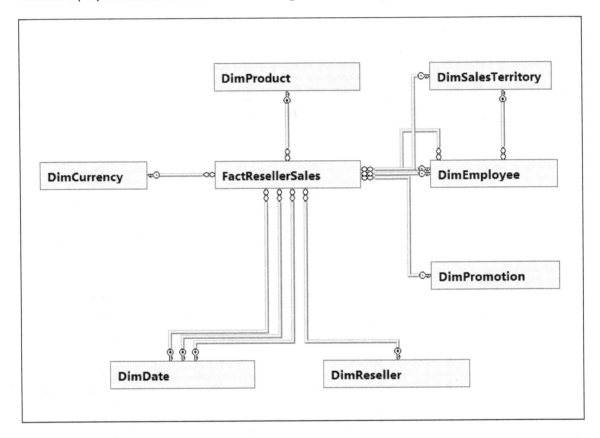

Distribution of **PRIMARY KEY - FOREIGN KEY** relationships can be generated from metadata (system views) for the entire Data Warehouse.

```
SELECT   schema_name(schema_id) AS SchemaName, o.name AS PKTable,  count(*) AS FKCount
FROM sys.sysforeignkeys s   INNER JOIN sys.objects o    ON s.rkeyid = o.object_id
GROUP BY schema_id, o.name  HAVING COUNT(*) > 2 ORDER BY FKCount DESC;
```

SchemaName	PKTable	FKCount
dbo	DimDate	12
dbo	DimCurrency	4
dbo	DimSalesTerritory	4
dbo	DimEmployee	3
dbo	DimProduct	3

AdventureWorks2008 Sample Database

There were substantial changes made from the prior version of the sample database. Among them demonstration use of the **hierarchyid** data type which has been introduced with SS 2008 to support sophisticated tree hierarchy processing. In addition employee, customer and dealer PRIMARY KEYs are pooled together and called BusinessEntityID.

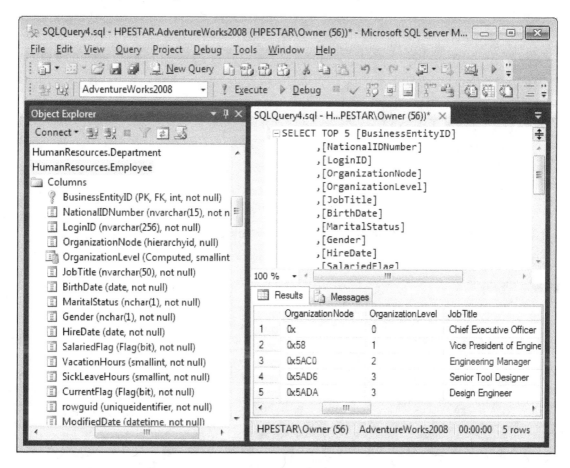

AdventureWorks2012 Sample Database

There were no apparent design changes made from the prior version of the sample database. A significant content change: dates were advanced 4 years. An OrderDate (Sales.SalesOrderHeader table) of 2004-02-01 in previous versions is now 2008-02-01.

The OrderDate statistics in the two sample databases.

```
SELECT [Year]          = YEAR(OrderDate),     OrderCount     = COUNT(*)
FROM AdventureWorks2008.Sales.SalesOrderHeader GROUP BY YEAR(OrderDate)
ORDER BY [Year];
```

Year	OrderCount
2001	1379
2002	3692
2003	12443
2004	13951

```
SELECT [Year]          = YEAR(OrderDate),     OrderCount     = COUNT(*)
FROM AdventureWorks2012.Sales.SalesOrderHeader GROUP BY YEAR(OrderDate)
ORDER BY [Year];
```

Year	OrderCount
2005	1379
2006	3692
2007	12443
2008	13951

Starting with SQL Server 2012, numeric figures, among others, can be formatted with the FORMAT function.

```
SELECT [Year]          = YEAR(OrderDate),
       OrderCount      = FORMAT(COUNT(*), '###,###')
FROM AdventureWorks2012.Sales.SalesOrderHeader
GROUP BY YEAR(OrderDate)  ORDER BY [Year];
```

Year	OrderCount
2005	1,379
2006	3,692
2007	12,443
2008	13,951

Production.Product and Related Tables

The Product table is the "center" of the database. The reason is that AdventureWorks Cycles is a product base company selling through dealers and directly to consumers through the internet. You may wonder why are we pushing **FOREIGN KEY - PRIMARY KEY** relationship so vehemently? Because there is nothing else to a database just **well-designed tables and their connections which are FK-PK constraints.**

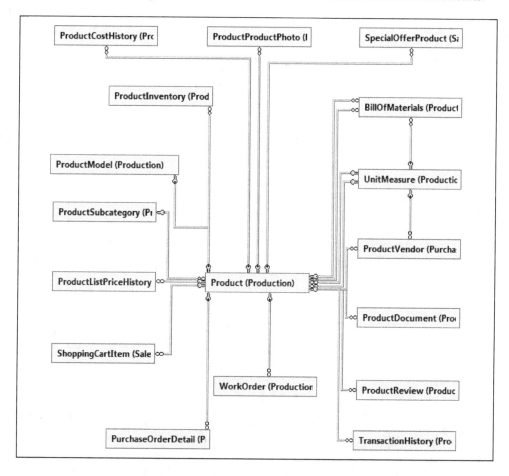

Simple OLTP query.

```
SELECT Color, WOCount=COUNT(*)  FROM Production.WorkOrder W
      INNER JOIN Production.Product P    ON W.ProductID = P.ProductID  WHERE Color != ''
GROUP BY Color ORDER BY WOCount DESC;
```

Color	WOCount
Black	18952
Silver	6620
Yellow	5231
Red	4764
Blue	2319

CHAPTER 1: SQL Server Sample & System Databases

Descriptions of Columns in Production.Product Table

Queries to list the description of table and columns from Extended Property (data dictionary).

```
USE AdventureWorks2012;
SELECT          objname AS TableName, value   AS [Description]
FROM fn_listextendedproperty( NULL, 'schema', 'Production', 'table', 'Product', NULL, NULL);
```

TableName	Description
Product	Products sold or used in the manfacturing of sold products.

```
SELECT          'Production.Product'          AS TableName,          -- String literal
                objname                       AS ColumnName,
                value                         AS [Description]
FROM fn_listextendedproperty( NULL, 'schema', 'Production', 'table',
                'Product', 'column', default);
```

TableName	ColumnName	Description
Production.Product	ProductID	Primary key for Product records.
Production.Product	Name	Name of the product.
Production.Product	ProductNumber	Unique product identification number.
Production.Product	MakeFlag	0 = Product is purchased, 1 = Product is manufactured in-house.
Production.Product	FinishedGoodsFlag	0 = Product is not a salable item. 1 = Product is salable.
Production.Product	Color	Product color.
Production.Product	SafetyStockLevel	Minimum inventory quantity.
Production.Product	ReorderPoint	Inventory level that triggers a purchase order or work order.
Production.Product	StandardCost	Standard cost of the product.
Production.Product	ListPrice	Selling price.
Production.Product	Size	Product size.
Production.Product	SizeUnitMeasureCode	Unit of measure for Size column.
Production.Product	WeightUnitMeasureCode	Unit of measure for Weight column.
Production.Product	Weight	Product weight.
Production.Product	DaysToManufacture	Number of days required to manufacture the product.
Production.Product	ProductLine	R = Road, M = Mountain, T = Touring, S = Standard
Production.Product	Class	H = High, M = Medium, L = Low
Production.Product	Style	W = Womens, M = Mens, U = Universal
Production.Product	ProductSubcategoryID	Product is a member of this product subcategory. Foreign key to ProductSubCategory.ProductSubCategoryID.
Production.Product	ProductModelID	Product is a member of this product model. Foreign key to ProductModel.ProductModelID.
Production.Product	SellStartDate	Date the product was available for sale.
Production.Product	SellEndDate	Date the product was no longer available for sale.
Production.Product	DiscontinuedDate	Date the product was discontinued.
Production.Product	rowguid	ROWGUIDCOL number uniquely identifying the record. Used to support a merge replication sample.
Production.Product	ModifiedDate	Date and time the record was last updated.

Mountain Bikes in Production.Product Table

Query to list all mountain bikes offered for sale by AdventureWorks Cycles with category, subcategory, list price and standard cost information.

```
USE AdventureWorks2012;
SELECT  UPPER(PC.Name) AS Category, PSC.Name AS Subcategory,
        P.Name AS Product, FORMAT(ListPrice, 'c', 'en-US') AS ListPrice,
        FORMAT(StandardCost, 'c', 'en-US') AS StandardCost
FROM Production.Product AS P
   INNER JOIN Production.ProductSubcategory AS PSC
            ON PSC.ProductSubcategoryID = P.ProductSubcategoryID
   INNER JOIN Production.ProductCategory AS PC
            ON PC.ProductCategoryID = PSC.ProductCategoryID
WHERE PSC.Name = 'Mountain Bikes'
ORDER BY Category, Subcategory, Product;
```

Category	Subcategory	Product	ListPrice	StandardCost
BIKES	Mountain Bikes	Mountain-100 Black, 38	$3,374.99	$1,898.09
BIKES	Mountain Bikes	Mountain-100 Black, 42	$3,374.99	$1,898.09
BIKES	Mountain Bikes	Mountain-100 Black, 44	$3,374.99	$1,898.09
BIKES	Mountain Bikes	Mountain-100 Black, 48	$3,374.99	$1,898.09
BIKES	Mountain Bikes	Mountain-100 Silver, 38	$3,399.99	$1,912.15
BIKES	Mountain Bikes	Mountain-100 Silver, 42	$3,399.99	$1,912.15
BIKES	Mountain Bikes	Mountain-100 Silver, 44	$3,399.99	$1,912.15
BIKES	Mountain Bikes	Mountain-100 Silver, 48	$3,399.99	$1,912.15
BIKES	Mountain Bikes	Mountain-200 Black, 38	$2,294.99	$1,251.98
BIKES	Mountain Bikes	Mountain-200 Black, 42	$2,294.99	$1,251.98
BIKES	Mountain Bikes	Mountain-200 Black, 46	$2,294.99	$1,251.98
BIKES	Mountain Bikes	Mountain-200 Silver, 38	$2,319.99	$1,265.62
BIKES	Mountain Bikes	Mountain-200 Silver, 42	$2,319.99	$1,265.62
BIKES	Mountain Bikes	Mountain-200 Silver, 46	$2,319.99	$1,265.62
BIKES	Mountain Bikes	Mountain-300 Black, 38	$1,079.99	$598.44
BIKES	Mountain Bikes	Mountain-300 Black, 40	$1,079.99	$598.44
BIKES	Mountain Bikes	Mountain-300 Black, 44	$1,079.99	$598.44
BIKES	Mountain Bikes	Mountain-300 Black, 48	$1,079.99	$598.44
BIKES	Mountain Bikes	Mountain-400-W Silver, 38	$769.49	$419.78
BIKES	Mountain Bikes	Mountain-400-W Silver, 40	$769.49	$419.78
BIKES	Mountain Bikes	Mountain-400-W Silver, 42	$769.49	$419.78
BIKES	Mountain Bikes	Mountain-400-W Silver, 46	$769.49	$419.78
BIKES	Mountain Bikes	Mountain-500 Black, 40	$539.99	$294.58
BIKES	Mountain Bikes	Mountain-500 Black, 42	$539.99	$294.58
BIKES	Mountain Bikes	Mountain-500 Black, 44	$539.99	$294.58
BIKES	Mountain Bikes	Mountain-500 Black, 48	$539.99	$294.58
BIKES	Mountain Bikes	Mountain-500 Black, 52	$539.99	$294.58
BIKES	Mountain Bikes	Mountain-500 Silver, 40	$564.99	$308.22
BIKES	Mountain Bikes	Mountain-500 Silver, 42	$564.99	$308.22
BIKES	Mountain Bikes	Mountain-500 Silver, 44	$564.99	$308.22
BIKES	Mountain Bikes	Mountain-500 Silver, 48	$564.99	$308.22
BIKES	Mountain Bikes	Mountain-500 Silver, 52	$564.99	$308.22

Prior SQL Server Sample Databases

There are two other sample databases used in the releases of SQL Server: **Northwind** and **pubs**.
Northwind has been introduced with SQL Server 7.0 in 1998. That SQL Server version had very
short lifetime, replaced with SQL Server 2000 in year 2000. The pubs sample database originates
from the time Microsoft & Sybase worked jointly on the database server project around 1990.
Despite the relative simplicity of pre-2005 sample databases, they were good enough to
demonstrate basic RDBMS SQL queries.

Book sales summary GROUP BY aggregation query.

```
USE pubs;
SELECT pub_name           AS Publisher,
     au_lname             AS Author,
     title                AS Title,
     SUM(qty)             AS SoldQty
FROM   authors
     INNER JOIN titleauthor
          ON authors.au_id = titleauthor.au_id
     INNER JOIN titles
          ON titles.title_id = titleauthor.title_id
     INNER JOIN publishers
          ON publishers.pub_id = titles.pub_id
     INNER JOIN sales
          ON sales.title_id = titles.title_id
GROUP  BY      pub_name,
               au_lname,
               title
ORDER BY Publisher, Author, Title;
-- (23 row(s) affected) - Partial results.
```

Publisher	Author	Title
Algodata Infosystems	Bennet	The Busy Executive's Database Guide
Algodata Infosystems	Carson	But Is It User Friendly?
Algodata Infosystems	Dull	Secrets of Silicon Valley
Algodata Infosystems	Green	The Busy Executive's Database Guide
Algodata Infosystems	Hunter	Secrets of Silicon Valley
Algodata Infosystems	MacFeather	Cooking with Computers: Surreptitious Balance Sheets
Algodata Infosystems	O'Leary	Cooking with Computers: Surreptitious Balance Sheets
Algodata Infosystems	Straight	Straight Talk About Computers
Binnet & Hardley	Blotchet-Halls	Fifty Years in Buckingham Palace Kitchens
Binnet & Hardley	DeFrance	The Gourmet Microwave

Northwind Sample Database

The Northwind database contains well-prepared sales data for a fictitious company called Northwind Traders, which imports & exports specialty gourmet foods & drinks from wholesale suppliers around the world. The company's sales offices are located in Seattle & London. Among gourmet food item products: Carnarvon Tigers, Teatime Chocolate Biscuits, Sir Rodney's Marmalade, Sir Rodney's Scones, Gustaf's Knäckebröd, Tunnbröd & Guaraná Fantástica.

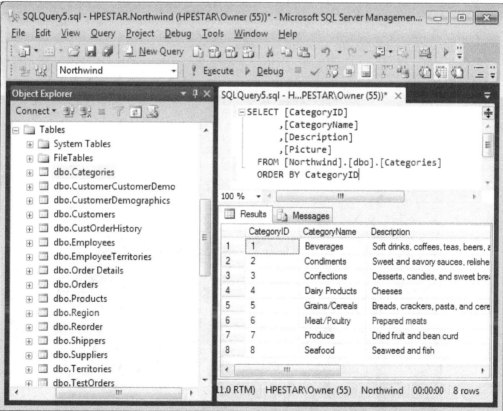

Diagram of Northwind Database

The basic diagram of Northwind database excluding a few ancillary tables. The Orders table is central since the business is wholesale distribution (reselling) of high-end food products.

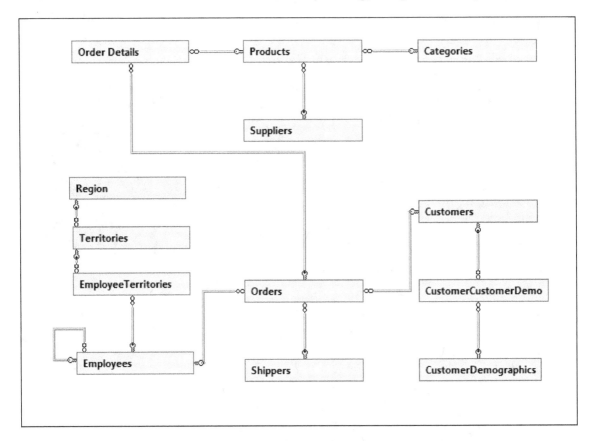

pubs Sample Database

The pubs database is a very small and simple publishing database, yet it demonstrates the main features of database design such as PRIMARY KEYs, FOREIGN KEYs, and junction table reflecting many-to-many relationship. The main entities (tables) are: (book) titles, authors, titleauthor (junction table), publishers, sales & royalties.

Book Titles in pubs Database

The titles table has the most interesting content in the pubs database as demonstrated by the following T-SQL query.

```
SELECT  TOP 4 title_id AS TitleID, title AS Title, type                    AS Type,
        pub_id AS PubID, FORMAT(price, 'c','en-US')                        AS Price,
        FORMAT(advance, 'c','en-US')                                       AS  Advance,
        FORMAT(royalty/100.0, 'p') AS Royalty, FORMAT(ytd_sales, 'c', 'en-US')   AS YTDSales,
        Notes
FROM pubs.dbo.titles
ORDER BY title;
```

TitleID	Title	Type	PubID	Price	Advance	Royalty	YTDSales	Notes
PC1035	But Is It User Friendly?	popular_comp	1389	$22.95	$7,000.00	16.00 %	$8,780.00	A survey of software for the naive user, focusing on the 'friendliness' of each.
PS1372	Computer Phobic AND Non-Phobic Individuals: Behavior Variations	psychology	0877	$21.59	$7,000.00	10.00 %	$375.00	A must for the specialist, this book examines the difference between those who hate and fear computers and those who don't.
BU1111	Cooking with Computers: Surreptitious Balance Sheets	business	1389	$11.95	$5,000.00	10.00 %	$3,876.00	Helpful hints on how to use your electronic resources to the best advantage.
PS7777	Emotional Security: A New Algorithm	psychology	0736	$7.99	$4,000.00	10.00 %	$3,336.00	Protecting yourself and your loved ones from undue emotional stress in the modern world. Use of computer and nutritional aids emphasized.

Diagram of pubs Database

Since pubs is a small database, the diagram conveniently fits on a page.

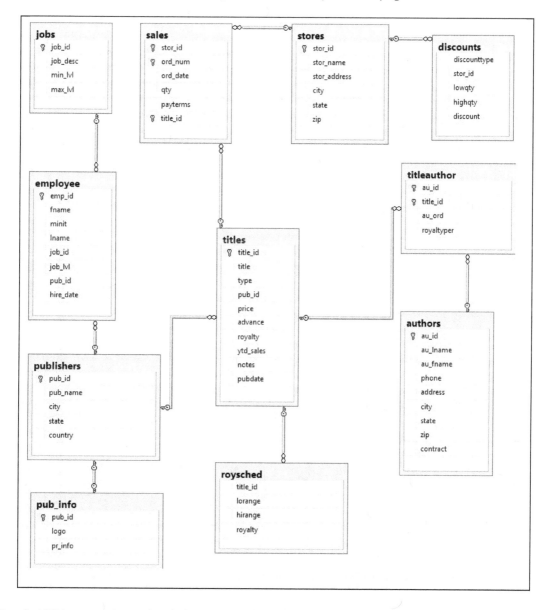

Simple JOIN on non-key columns.

```
USE pubs; SELECT p.*, a.* FROM authors AS a
INNER JOIN publishers AS p ON a.city = p.city ORDER BY p.city, a.au_lname;
```

pub_id	pub_name	city	state	country	au_id	au_lname	au_fname	phone	address	city	state	zip	contract
1389	Algodata Infosystems	Berkeley	CA	USA	409-56-7008	Bennet	Abraham	415 658-9932	6223 Bateman St.	Berkeley	CA	94705	1
1389	Algodata Infosystems	Berkeley	CA	USA	238-95-7766	Carson	Cheryl	415 548-7723	589 Darwin Ln.	Berkeley	CA	94705	1

SQL Server System Databases

The master, model, tempdb and msdb are system databases for special database server operations purposes. SSMS Object Explorer drill-down listing of system databases.

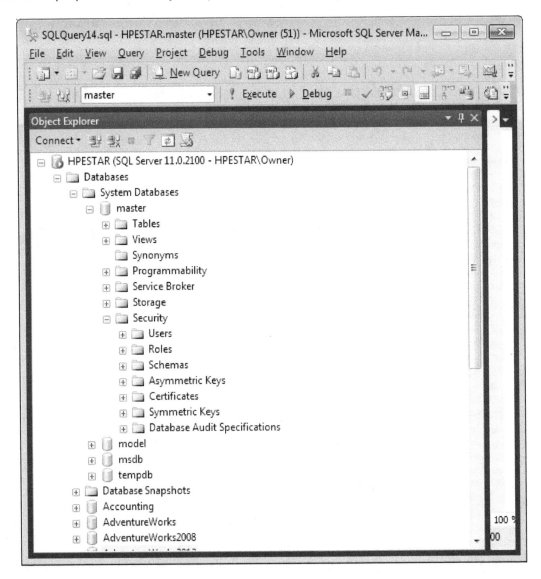

Query to create a new table in tempdb for development purposes.

```
SELECT * INTO tempdb.dbo.Product
FROM AdventureWorks2012.Production.Product
WHERE ListPrice > 0.0;
-- (304 row(s) affected)
```

The master Database

The master system database is the nerve center of SQL Server. It contains tables and db objects essential for server operations. System tables are accessible only through read-only views. System tables cannot be changed by users. A subset of the system views are called Dynamic Management Views (DMV) which return server state information for monitoring the operational aspects of a SQL Server instance, diagnosing problems, and performance tuning. Dynamic Management Functions (DMF) are applied in conjunction with DMVs.

```
SELECT TOP 5     ST.text,
                 EQS.*
FROM master.sys.dm_exec_query_stats AS EQS                  -- DMV
CROSS APPLY master.sys.dm_exec_sql_text(EQS.sql_handle) as ST     -- DMF
ORDER BY last_worker_time DESC;
```

SQL Server Management Studio Object Explorer display of some objects in the master database and a query listing all databases.

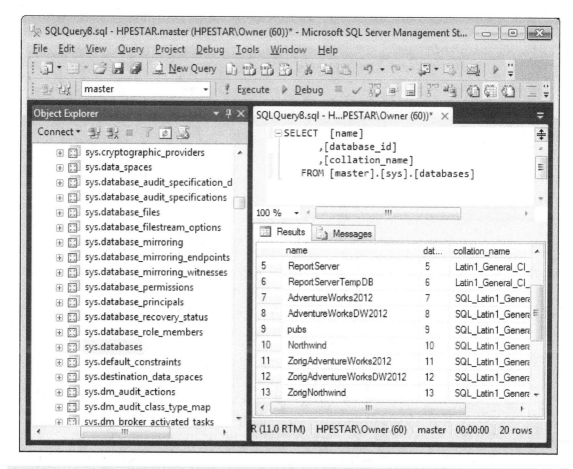

An Important System View In master Database: sys.databases

```
SELECT TOP (10) name, database_id
FROM master.sys.databases
ORDER BY database_id;
```

name	database_id
master	1
tempdb	2
model	3
msdb	4
ReportServer	5
ReportServerTempDB	6
AdventureWorks2012	7
AdventureWorksDW2012	8
pubs	9
Northwind	10

spt_values table in master database can be used for integer sequence with a range of 0 - 2047.

```
-- End of the range - BOTTOM
SELECT TOP 5 number FROM master.dbo.spt_values WHERE TYPE='P'
ORDER BY number DESC;
```

number
2047
2046
2045
2044
2043

Example for using the sequence in spt_values to generate DATE and MONTH sequences.

```
SELECT TOP 5 number,  dateadd(day, number, '20000101')      AS "Date",
                      dateadd(mm, number, '20000101')       AS "Month"
FROM master.dbo.spt_values  WHERE type = 'P'  ORDER BY number;
```

number	Date	Month
0	2000-01-01 00:00:00.000	2000-01-01 00:00:00.000
1	2000-01-02 00:00:00.000	2000-02-01 00:00:00.000
2	2000-01-03 00:00:00.000	2000-03-01 00:00:00.000
3	2000-01-04 00:00:00.000	2000-04-01 00:00:00.000
4	2000-01-05 00:00:00.000	2000-05-01 00:00:00.000

The model Database

The model database serves as prototype for a new database. The model database is also the prototype for tempdb when the SQL Server instance started. Upon server shutdown or restart everything is wiped out of tempdb, it starts with a clean slate as a copy of the model database. Therefore we should only place objects into the tempdb can be purged any time.

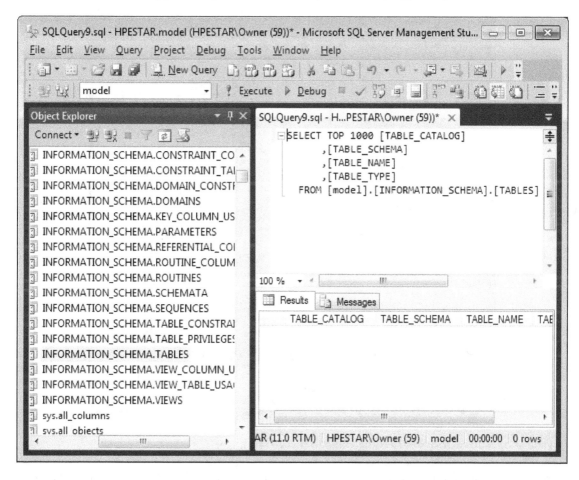

CHAPTER 1: SQL Server Sample & System Databases

The msdb Database

The msdb database is used for server internal operations such as support for SQL Server Agent job scheduling facility or keeping track of database the all important backups and restores.

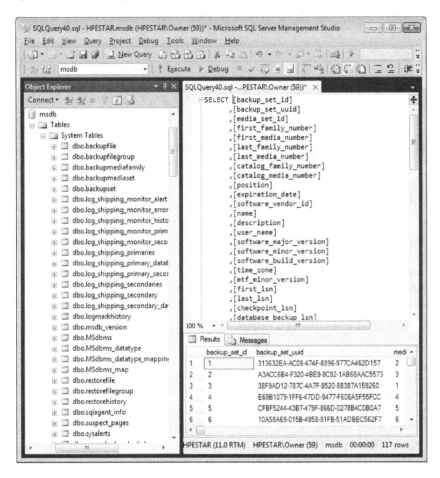

Database backup history query using table in msdb database.

```
SELECT  s.name AS Name, CONVERT(DATE,MAX(b.backup_finish_date)) AS LastGoodBackup,
        b.type AS Type
FROM master.dbo.sysdatabases AS s
LEFT OUTER JOIN msdb.dbo.backupset AS b ON s.name = b.database_name
GROUP BY s.name, b.type ORDER BY Name, Type;
```

Name	LastGoodBackup	Type
Accounting	2016-11-29	D
AdventureWorks	2016-11-29	D
AdventureWorks2008	2016-11-29	D
AdventureWorks2012	2016-11-29	D

The tempdb Database

The tempdb serves as temporary database for system operations such as sorting. Temporary tables (#temp1) and global temporary tables (##globaltemp1) are stored in the tempdb as well. "Permanent" tables can be created in tempdb with a short lifetime which lasts till shutdown or restart.

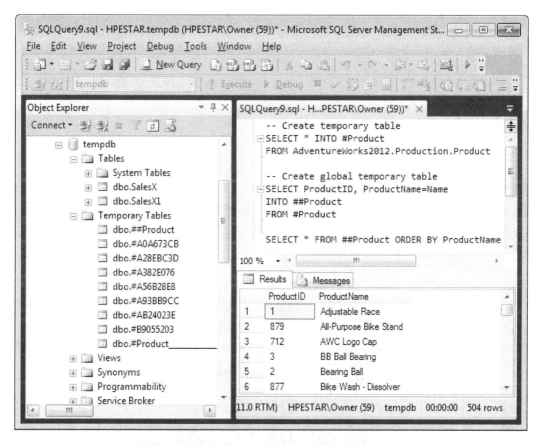

CHAPTER 1: SQL Server Sample & System Databases

Sudden Death in tempdb When Server Restarts

Even though a temporary table and a global temporary table are created and queried in the context setting for AdventureWorks2012 database, they are placed into tempdb automatically. Same consideration when a temporary table is created from a stored procedure which is compiled in an application database. Upon server restart everything is wiped out of tempdb, rebirth follows as a copy of model db. We should not place anything into tempdb we cannot afford to lose. tempdb is also used by SQL Server engine for operations such as version control, sorting and more.

> Instead of GUI & mouse use T-SQL scripts which can be saved as .sql disk files.

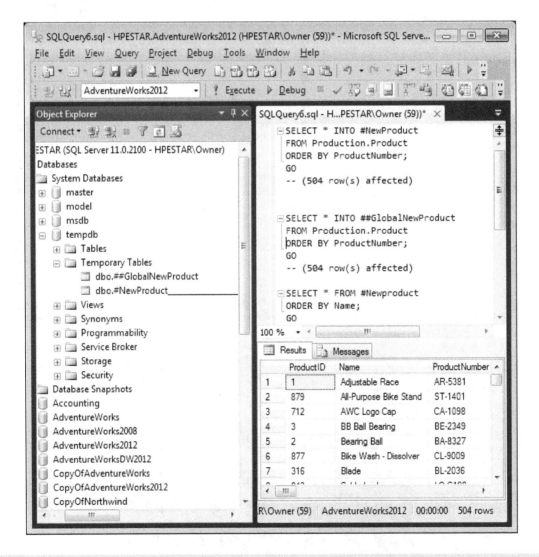

CHAPTER 2: Installing SQL Server 2012

SQL Server 2012 Express Edition Installation

The **Express Edition** is free. It can be installed from the following webpage.

http://www.microsoft.com/sqlserver/en/us/editions/2012-editions/express.aspx

Installation instructions provided.

SQL Server 2012 Evaluation Edition Installation

The **Evaluation Edition** is free for a certain time period like 6 months. It can be installed from the following webpage.

http://www.microsoft.com/en-us/download/details.aspx?id=29066

Installation instructions provided.

SQL Server 2012 Pay Edition Installation

The installation process from the distribution DVD is fairly automatic. Product key (4 x 5 alphanumeric) entry is required near the beginning of the installation.

Planning tab has the preparation steps.

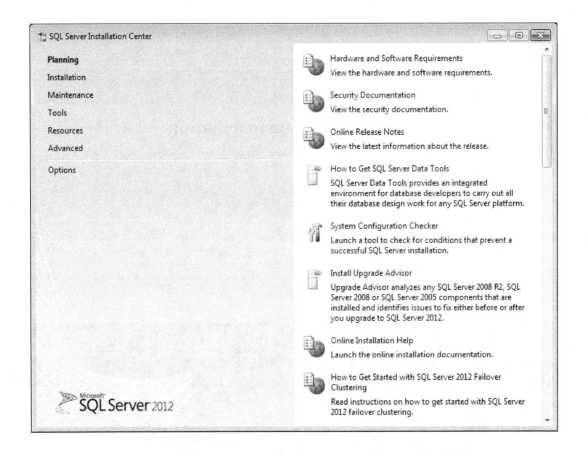

The Installation tab has the SQL Server and Client Tools (SS Management Studio is a client tool) install options.

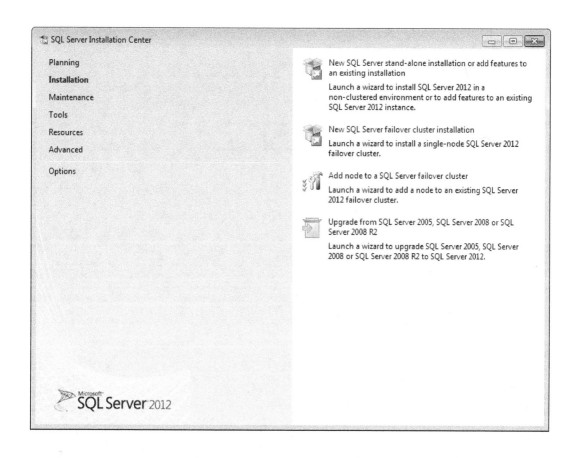

Setup Support Rules page shows the results of preliminary checks for installation readiness. Failed issues require fix.

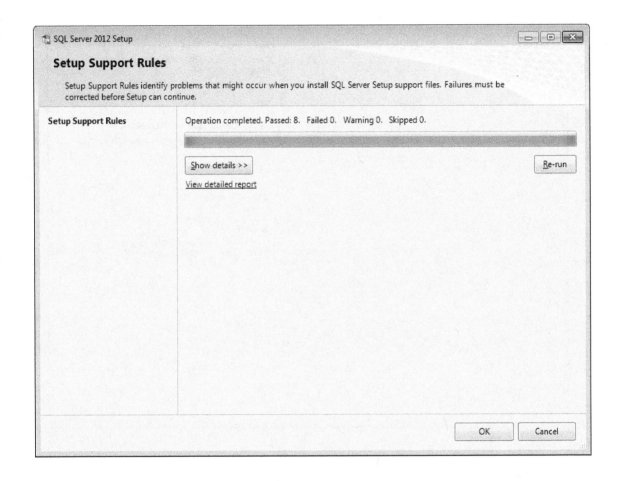

Product Updates page checks the web for latest updates.

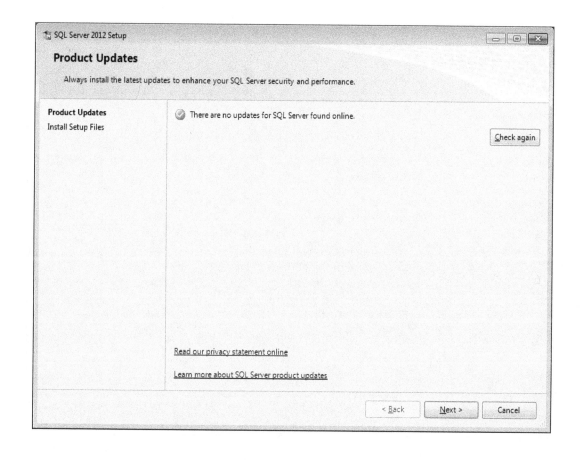

Setup Support Rules page performs a number of internal system checks.

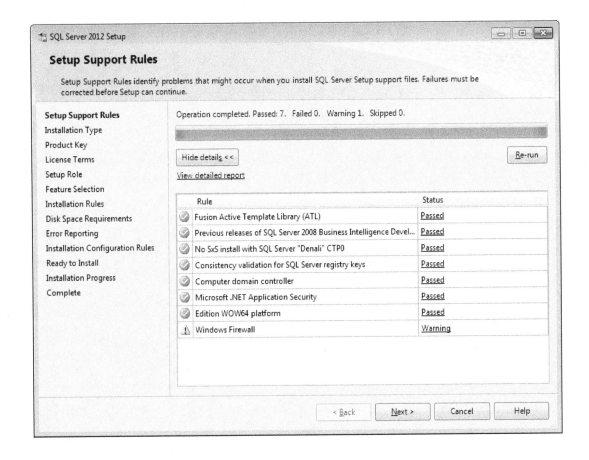

Installation Type page displays currently installed SQL Server products.

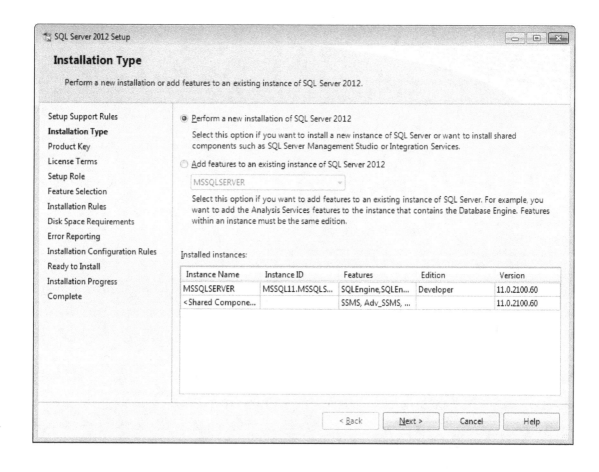

Product Key page requests key entry from packaging box inside cover.

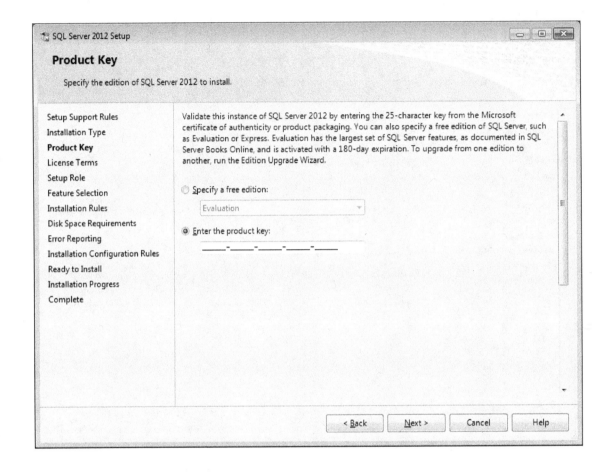

License terms page requires acceptance checkmark.

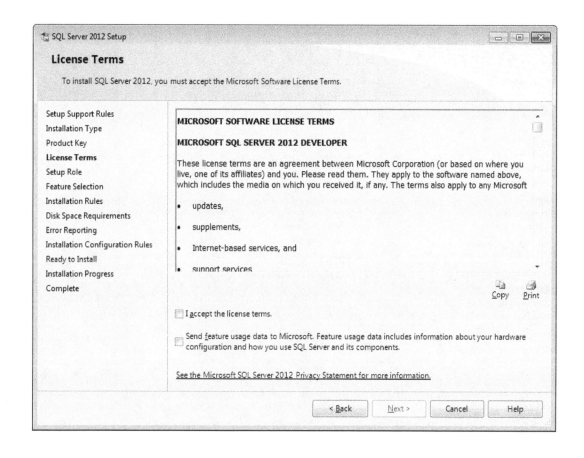

Setup Role page lists installation options. "All Features with Defaults" is the easiest to install.

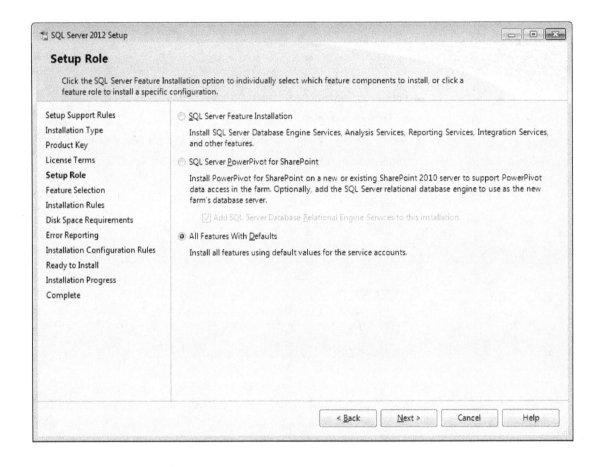

Feature Selection page can be used to pick & choose features.

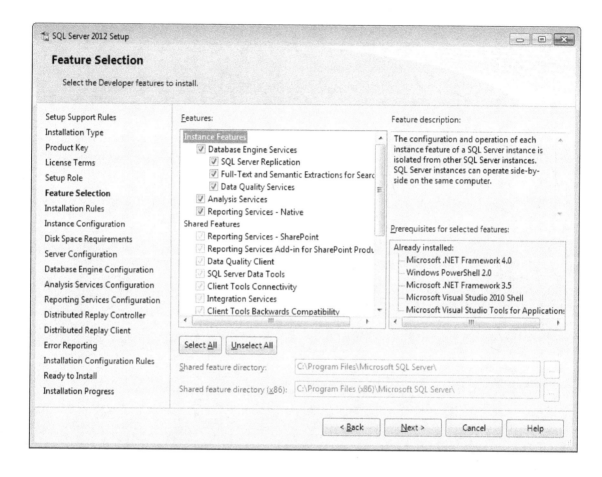

Installation Rules page performs further internal system checks.

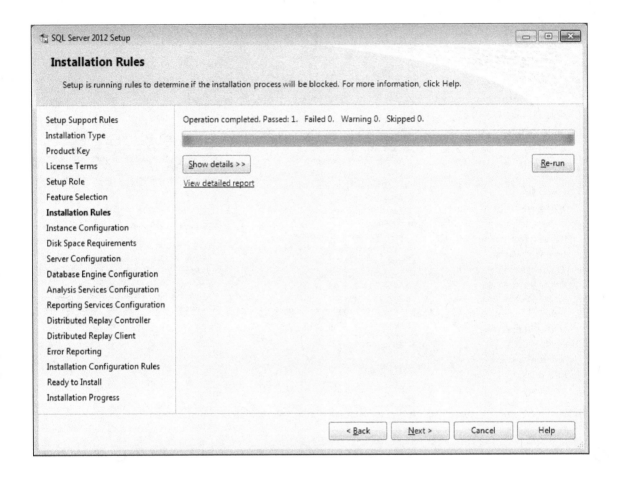

Instance Configuration page requires name entrance for the named instance since the default instance is already installed.

The SQL Server reference is [YOURSERVER] for the default instance and [YOURSERVER\INSTANCENAME] for the named instance.

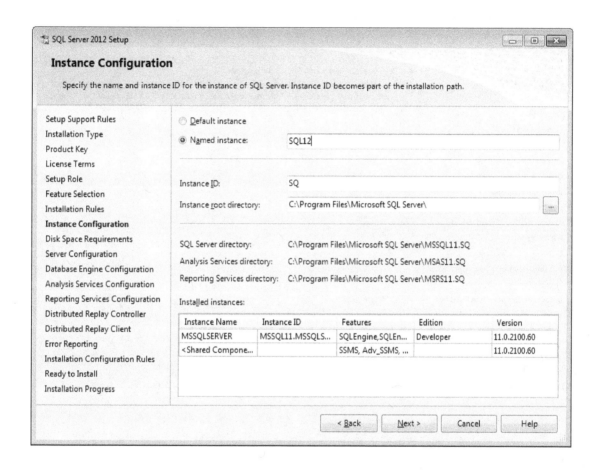

Disk Space Requirements page checks for available disk space.

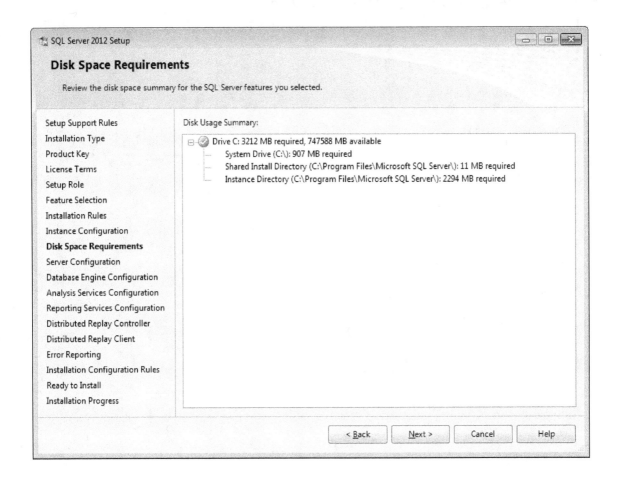

The Server Configuration page covers accounts, startup type and collation.

For example, SQL Server Agent (job management) can be set to automatic instead of manual startup.

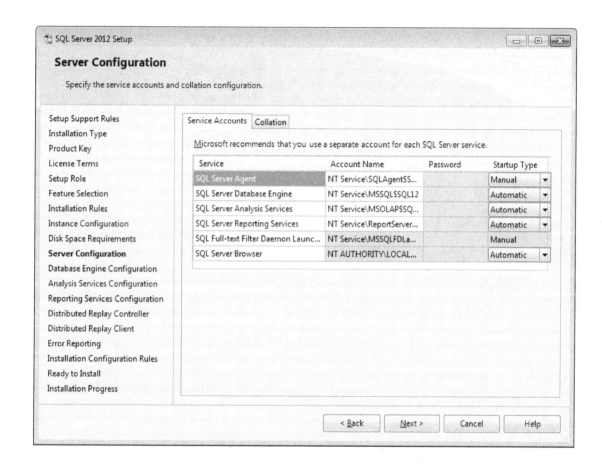

The collation page offers choosing a different collation from the default. Note: selecting collation requires quite an expertise, safest choice is the default.

The "_CI_AS" suffix in the collation name means Case Insensitive, Accent Sensitive (foreign word with accent marks on E & O: PÉNZSZERZŐ).

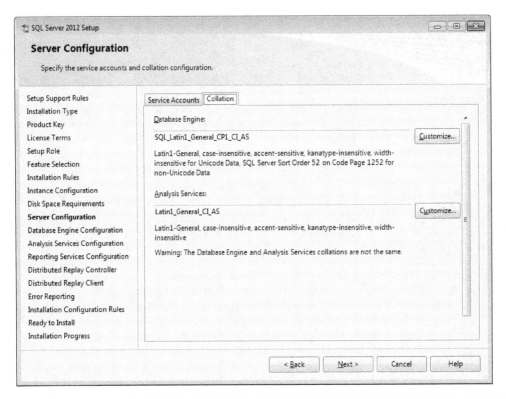

-- Case Insensitive, Accent Sensitive sort
DECLARE @Words TABLE ([Foreign] nvarchar(32)); INSERT @Words VALUES
(N'PÉNZSZERZŐ'),(N'Pénzszerző'), (N'PENZSZERZŐ'), (N'pÉNZSZERZŐ'), (N'PÉNZSZERZŐ'), (N'pENZSZERZŐ'),
(N'pénzszerző'), (N'péNZSZERZŐ') ;
SELECT * FROM @Words ORDER BY [Foreign];

Foreign
PENZSZERZŐ
pENZSZERZŐ
pénzszerző
péNZSZERZŐ
pÉNZSZERZŐ
PÉNZSZERZŐ
PÉNZSZERZŐ
Pénzszerző

The Database Engine Configuration page offers administrator accounts, data directories and FILESTREAM setup options.

FILESTREAM is required for FileTable, a new feature of SQL Server 2012.

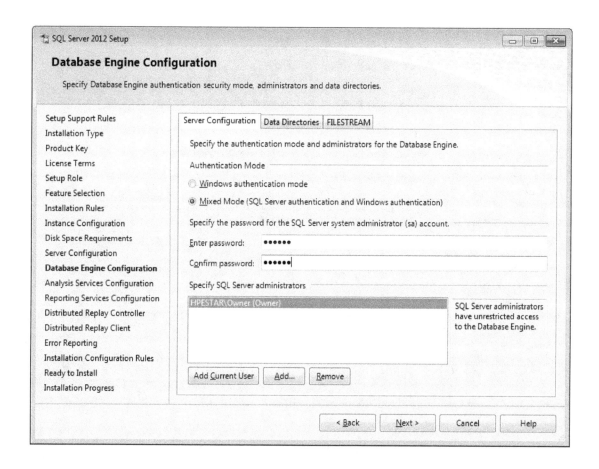

Error Reporting page has checkmark option to report errors automatically.

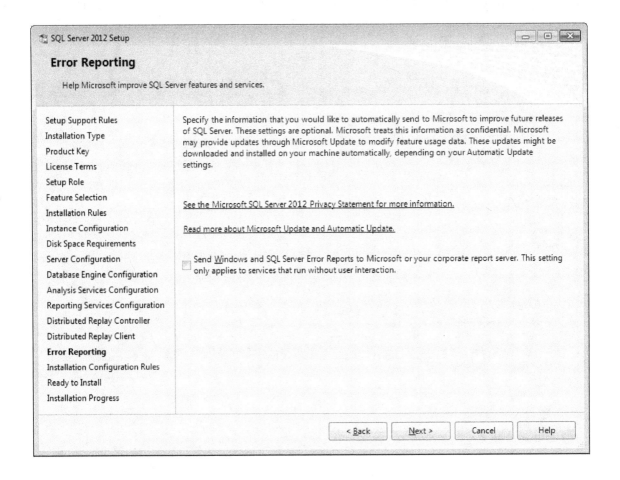

Installation Configuration Rules page performs a final check.

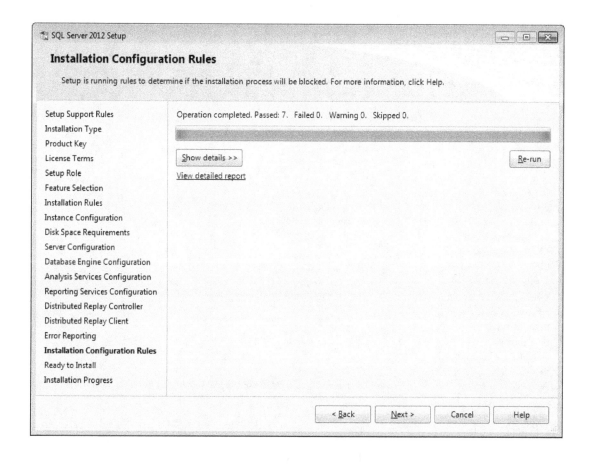

Ready to Install page shows the action plan.

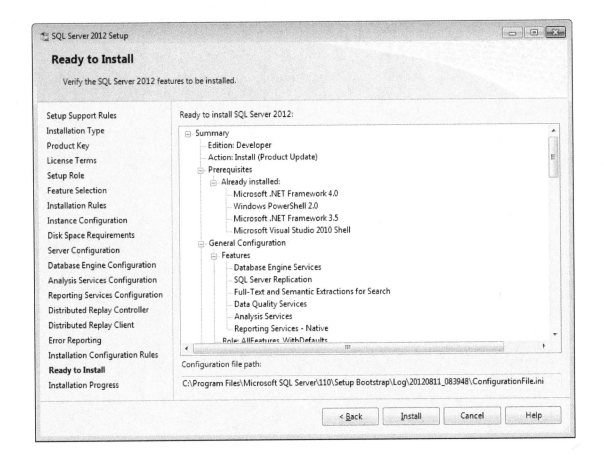

Installation Progress page displays progress messages (this part will take a few minutes).

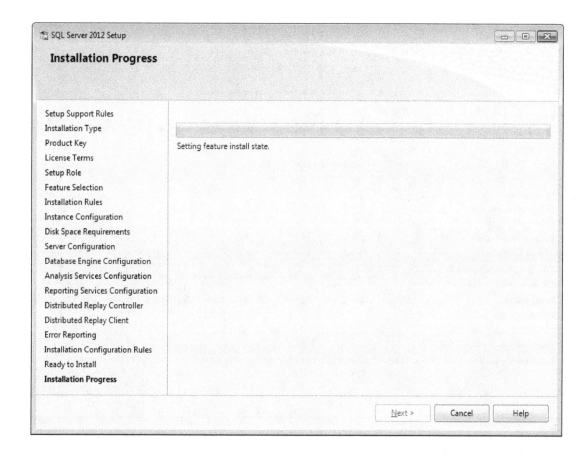

The Complete page displays successful installation information or failure.

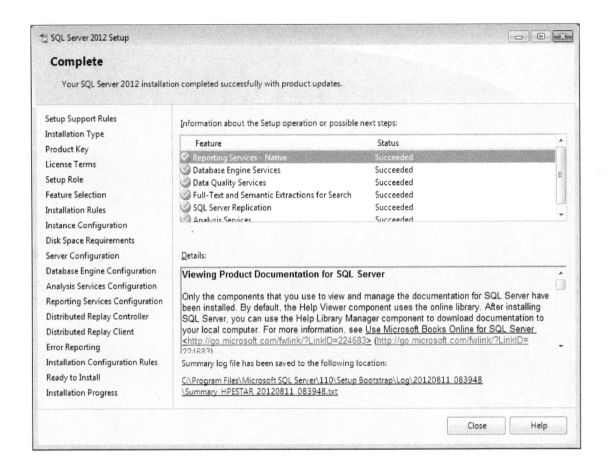

Start Menu for SQL Server 2012

The Start Menu has all the components related to SQL Server including Management Studio and SQL Server Data Tools for Business Intelligence (SSAS, SSIS & SSRS) application design.

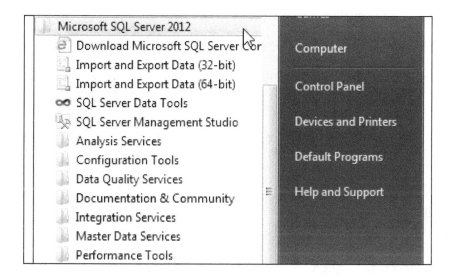

Creating Shortcut for Management Studio on Desktop

Management Studio can also be pinned to the Start Menu or Taskbar from the right-click drop-down menu.

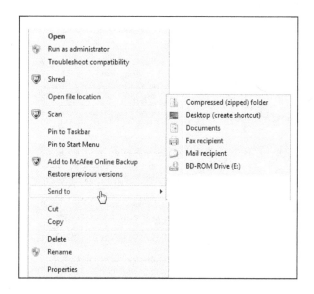

Launching SQL Server Configuration Manager

Expand (left click) the Configuration Tools tab on the Start Menu and click on SQL Server Configuration Manager.

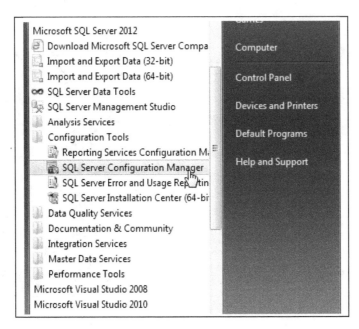

SQL Server should be running by itself after installation, if not, it can be started and/or reconfigured.

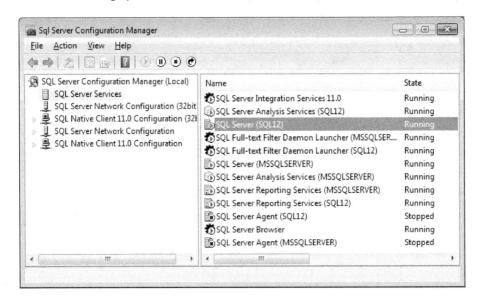

Starting, Restarting & Stopping SQL Server

Right click on the server name in Configuration Manager launches the control menu. To start the server, click on Start.

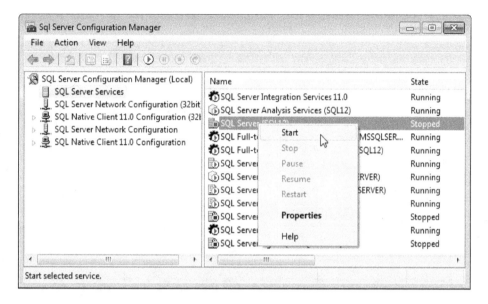

Message window pops up.

To stop a running server or restart it, click on the menu item respectively.

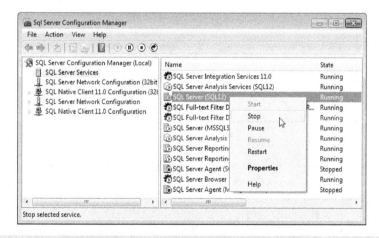

Connecting to the New Named SQL Server Instance

The newly installed SS instance is ready for use. Here is how we can connect to it from SSMS Object
Explorer. NOTE: on your computer you will see YOURCOMPUTERNAME instead of "HPESTAR".

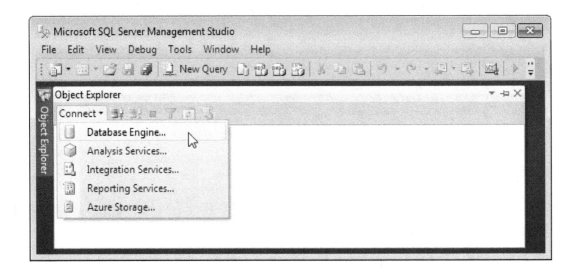

Investigating the New SQL Server Instance

We can start discovering the new SQL Server instance in Query Editor & Object Explorer.

SELECT @@version;
-- Microsoft SQL Server 2012 - 11.0.2100.60 (X64)

SELECT @@SERVERNAME;
-- YOURSERVERNAME\SQL12;

-- SS Version, Level (service pack), Edition
SELECT   CONCAT ('Microsoft SQL Server ',convert(varchar, SERVERPROPERTY('ProductVersion')), ' -- ',
        convert(varchar, SERVERPROPERTY('ProductLevel')), ' -- ',convert(varchar,
SERVERPROPERTY('Edition')));
-- Microsoft SQL Server 11.0.2100.60 -- RTM -- Developer Edition (64-bit)

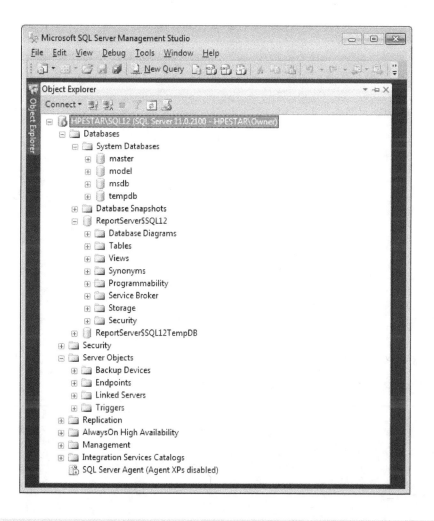

Connecting to 2 SQL Server Instances Simultaneously

SSMS Object Explorer support multiple SS instances connections. Warning: **Production, QA and Development SS instances may look similar, an opportunity to get confused and carry out actions on the wrong server**. Best prevention: **take regular database backups and connect only to one SQL Server instance at one time**.

The first connection is the named instance, the second is the default instance.

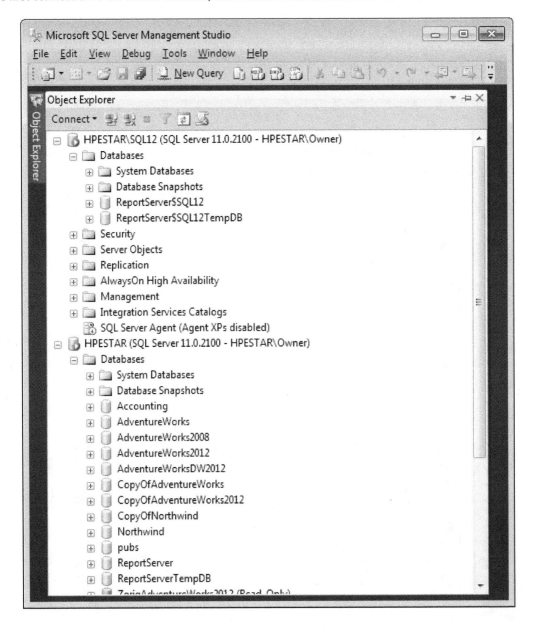

BACKUP DATABASE Command

Database backup command; the backup filename can be changed at will to reflect the backup date.

```
BACKUP DATABASE [AdventureWorks2012] TO  DISK = N'F:\data\backup\AW20161023.bak';
```

```
-- Dynamic backup filename with datestamp
DECLARE @Filename nvarchar(64) = CONCAT(N'F:\data\backup\AW', CONVERT(varchar, CONVERT(DATE, getdate())),'.bak');
BACKUP DATABASE [AdventureWorks2012] TO  DISK = @Filename;
-- AW2018-08-23.bak
```

Installing Books Online - BOL

Books Online can be installed from the web or from the distribution DVD. Select Manage Help Settings from the Help menu in Management Studio.

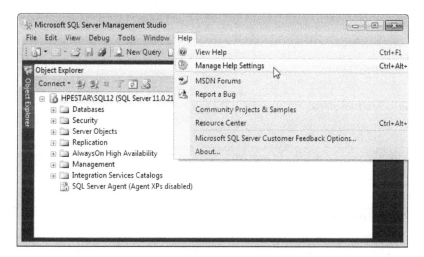

Select **Install content from online** from the pop-up panel.

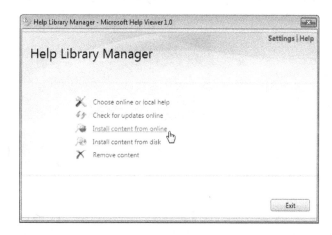

Add Books Online to the to do list on the dialog box.

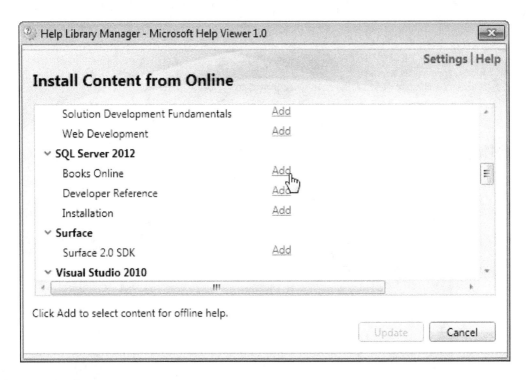

Click on UPDATE button.

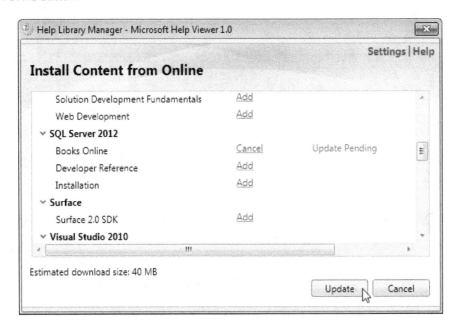

Updating will take a few minutes.

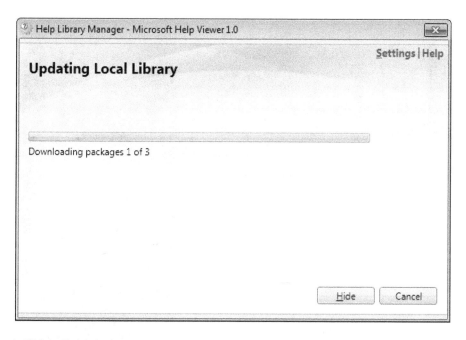

Finish panel. Click in Finish button.

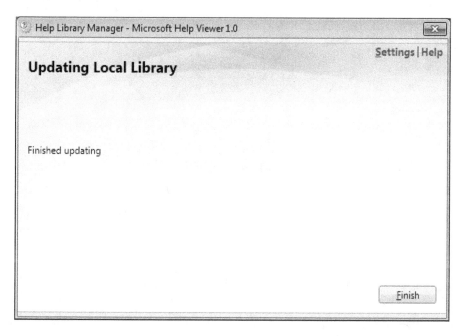

Creating Shortcut for Books Online on Desktop.

Follow the usual process for shortcut creation, start with right click on SQL Server Documentation.

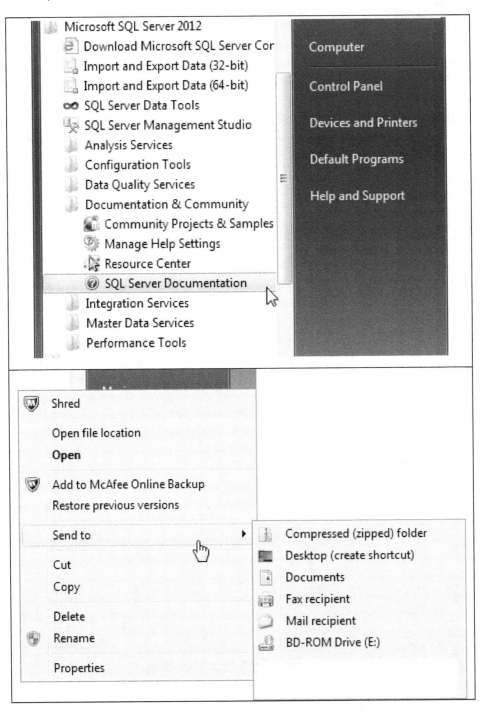

Installing Developer Reference

To install Developer Reference follow the same process as for Book Online.

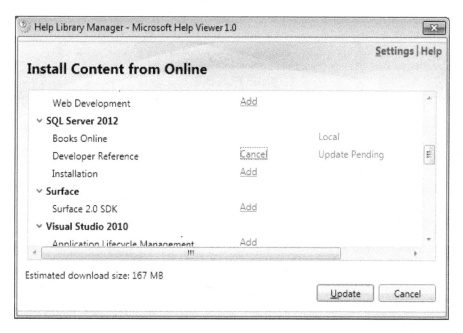

Click on Update button. Update will take a few minutes.

Developer Reference will install into Books Online.

Desktop segment with SSMS, SSDT and Books Online (includes Developer Reference).

Searching Books Online Contents Mode

Books Online is the complete reference tool for SQL Server. The implementation in Microsoft Help Viewer is new to SQL Server 2012. In the Contents mode, you drill-down in the left pane and read the article in the right pane.

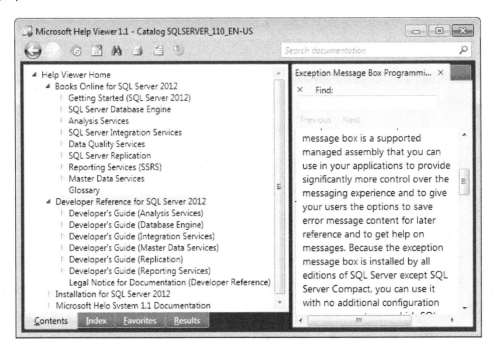

When you click on a Contents item, the corresponding article pops up in the right pane.

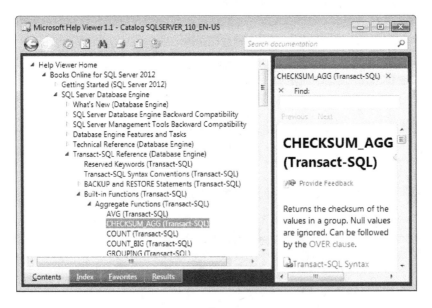

Searching Books Online Index Mode

In the Index Mode, items are listed alphabetically. When you click on an item, the corresponding article pops up in the right pane.

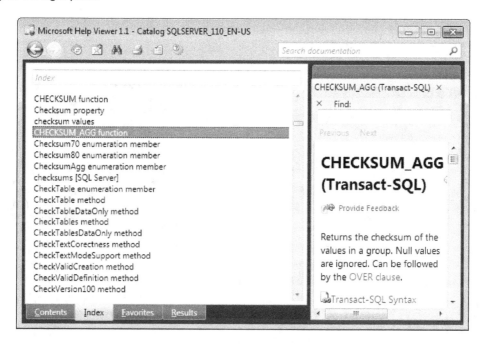

Searching the Web for SQL Server MSDN Articles

When searching the web for SS documentation use the prefix "SQL SERVER" or "T-SQL" before the keyword.

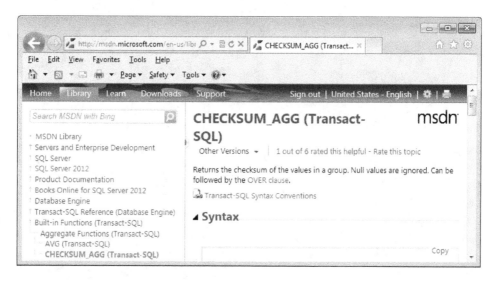

Installing AdventureWorks2012 Sample Database

AdventureWorks2012 and other related databases can be installed from the following webpage:
http://msftdbprodsamples.codeplex.com/releases/view/55330

Community Projects & Samples from the Start Menu will bring up the following site:
http://sqlserversamples.codeplex.com/

Installing Northwind & pubs Sample Databases

Here is the download website with instructions. http://www.microsoft.com/en-
us/download/details.aspx?displaylang=en&id=23654

CHAPTER 3: Structure of the SELECT Statement

The SELECT Clause

The SELECT clause is the only required clause in a SELECT statement, all the other clauses are optional. The SELECT columns can be literals (constants), expressions, table columns and even subqueries. Lines can be commented with "--".

```
SELECT 15 * 15;                                          -- 225
```

```
SELECT Today = convert(DATE, getdate());                 -- 2016-07-27    -- getdate() T-
SQL only
SELECT Today = convert(DATE, CURRENT_TIMESTAMP);         -- 2016-07-27    -- ANSI SQL
```

```
SELECT          Color,
                ProdCnt                  = COUNT(*),
                AvgPrice                 = FORMAT(AVG(ListPrice),'c','en-US')
FROM AdventureWorks2012.Production.Product p
WHERE Color is not null
GROUP BY Color
        HAVING count(*) > 10
ORDER BY AvgPrice DESC;
```

Color	ProdCnt	AvgPrice
Yellow	36	$959.09
Blue	26	$923.68
Silver	43	$850.31
Black	93	$725.12
Red	38	$1,401.95

```
-- Equivalent with column aliases on the right
SELECT          Color,
                COUNT(*)                              AS ProdCnt,
                FORMAT(AVG(ListPrice),'c','en-US')    AS AvgPrice
FROM AdventureWorks2012.Production.Product p  WHERE Color is not null
GROUP BY Color HAVING count(*) > 10  ORDER BY AvgPrice DESC;
GO
```

SELECT with Search Expression

SELECT statement can have complex expressions for text or numbers as demonstrated in the next T-SQL query for finding the street name in AddressLine1 column.

```
SELECT  AddressID,
        SUBSTRING(AddressLine1, CHARINDEX(' ', AddressLine1+' ', 1) +1,
        CHARINDEX(' ', AddressLine1+' ', CHARINDEX(' ', AddressLine1+' ', 1) +1) -
        CHARINDEX(' ', AddressLine1+' ', 1) -1)                               AS StreetName,
        AddressLine1,
        City
FROM AdventureWorks2012.Person.Address
WHERE ISNUMERIC (LEFT(AddressLine1,1))=1
   AND City = 'Seattle'
ORDER BY AddressLine1;
-- -- (141 row(s) affected)- Partial results.
```

AddressID	StreetName	AddressLine1	City
13079	boulevard	081, boulevard du Montparnasse	Seattle
859	Oak	1050 Oak Street	Seattle
110	Slow	1064 Slow Creek Road	Seattle
113	Ravenwood	1102 Ravenwood	Seattle
95	Bradford	1220 Bradford Way	Seattle
32510	Steven	1349 Steven Way	Seattle
118	Balboa	136 Balboa Court	Seattle
32519	Mazatlan	137 Mazatlan	Seattle
25869	Calle	1386 Calle Verde	Seattle
114	Yorba	1398 Yorba Linda	Seattle
15657	Book	151 Book Ct	Seattle
105	Stillman	1619 Stillman Court	Seattle
18002	Carmel	1635 Carmel Dr	Seattle
19813	Acardia	1787 Acardia Pl.	Seattle
16392	Orchid	1874 Orchid Ct	Seattle
18053	Green	1883 Green View Court	Seattle
13035	Mt.	1887 Mt. Diablo St	Seattle
29864	Valley	1946 Valley Crest Drive	Seattle
13580	Hill	2030 Hill Drive	Seattle
106	San	2144 San Rafael	Seattle

```
-- Search for Crest in the middle of AddessLine1
SELECT * FROM AdventureWorks2012.Person.Address
WHERE AddressLine1 LIKE '% Crest %';
-- (21 row(s) affected)
```

CHAPTER 3: Structure of the SELECT Statement

SELECT Statement with Subquery

Two Northwind category images, Beverages & Dairy Products, from the dbo.Categories table.

The following SELECT statement involves a subquery which is called a derived table. It also demonstrates that INNER JOIN can be performed with a GROUP BY subquery as well not only with another table or view.

```
USE Northwind;
SELECT          c.CategoryName                    AS Category,
                cnum.NoOfProducts                 AS CatProdCnt,
                p.ProductName                     AS Product,
                FORMAT(p.UnitPrice,'c', 'en-US')  AS UnitPrice
FROM    Categories c
                INNER JOIN Products p       ON c.CategoryID = p.CategoryID
                INNER JOIN (    SELECT          c.CategoryID,
                                                NoOfProducts = count(* )
                        FROM    Categories c
                                INNER JOIN Products p
                                ON c.CategoryID = p.CategoryID
                        GROUP BY c.CategoryID
                ) cnum                                    -- derived table
                ON c.CategoryID = cnum.CategoryID
ORDER BY Category, Product;       -- (77 row(s) affected) - Partial results.
```

Category	CatProdCnt	Product	UnitPrice
Dairy Products	10	Mozzarella di Giovanni	$34.80
Dairy Products	10	Queso Cabrales	$21.00
Dairy Products	10	Queso Manchego La Pastora	$38.00
Dairy Products	10	Raclette Courdavault	$55.00
Grains/Cereals	7	Filo Mix	$7.00
Grains/Cereals	7	Gnocchi di nonna Alice	$38.00
Grains/Cereals	7	Gustaf's Knäckebröd	$21.00
Grains/Cereals	7	Ravioli Angelo	$19.50
Grains/Cereals	7	Singaporean Hokkien Fried Mee	$14.00
Grains/Cereals	7	Tunnbröd	$9.00

Creating Delimited String List (CSV) with XML PATH

The XML PATH clause , the text() function and correlated subquery is used to create a comma delimited string within the SELECT columns. Note: it cannot be done using traditional (without XML) SQL single statement, it can be done with multiple SQL statements only. STUFF() string function is applied to replace the leading comma with an empty string.

```
USE AdventureWorks;

SELECT Territory        = st.[Name],
       SalesYTD =  FORMAT(floor(SalesYTD), 'c', 'en-US'), -- currency format
       SalesStaffAssignmentHistory =

       STUFF((SELECT CONCAT(', ', c.FirstName, SPACE(1), c.LastName)       AS [text()]
              FROM   Person.Contact c
              INNER JOIN Sales.SalesTerritoryHistory sth
              ON c.ContactID = sth.SalesPersonID
              WHERE  sth.TerritoryID =   st.TerritoryID
              ORDER  BY StartDate
              FOR XML Path ('')), 1, 1, SPACE(0))

FROM   Sales.SalesTerritory st
ORDER  BY SalesYTD DESC;
GO
```

Territory	SalesYTD	SalesStaffAssignmentHistory
Southwest	$8,351,296.00	Shelley Dyck, Jauna Elson
Canada	$6,917,270.00	Carla Eldridge, Michael Emanuel, Gail Erickson
Northwest	$5,767,341.00	Shannon Elliott, Terry Eminhizer, Martha Espinoza
Central	$4,677,108.00	Linda Ecoffey, Maciej Dusza
France	$3,899,045.00	Mark Erickson
Northeast	$3,857,163.00	Maciej Dusza, Linda Ecoffey
United Kingdom	$3,514,865.00	Michael Emanuel
Southeast	$2,851,419.00	Carol Elliott
Germany	$2,481,039.00	Janeth Esteves
Australia	$1,977,474.00	Twanna Evans

```
-- Comma delimited list of column names
SELECT CONCAT(',', c.name) AS [text()]
FROM  sys.columns c   WHERE c.[object_id] = OBJECT_ID('Purchasing.PurchaseOrderDetail')
ORDER BY column_id FOR XML PATH('');
```

CHAPTER 3: Structure of the SELECT Statement

Logical Processing Order of the SELECT Statement

The results from the previous step will be available to the next step. The logical processing order for a SELECT statement is the following. Actual processing by the database engine may be different due to performance and other considerations.

1.	FROM
2.	ON
3.	JOIN
4.	WHERE
5.	GROUP BY
6.	WITH CUBE or WITH ROLLUP
7.	HAVING
8.	SELECT
9.	DISTINCT
10.	ORDER BY
11.	TOP

As an example, it is logical to filter with the WHERE clause prior to applying GROUP BY. It is also logical to sort when the final result set is available.

SELECT Color, COUNT(*) AS ColorCount FROM AdventureWorks2012.Production.Product
WHERE Color is not NULL GROUP BY Color ORDER BY ColorCount DESC;

Color	ColorCount
Black	93
Silver	43
Red	38
Yellow	36
Blue	26
Multi	8
Silver/Black	7
White	4
Grey	1

CHAPTER 3: Structure of the SELECT Statement

The TOP Clause

The TOP clause filters results according the sorting specified in an ORDER BY clause, otherwise random filtering takes place.

Simple TOP usage to return 10 rows only.

SELECT TOP 10 SalesOrderID, OrderDate, TotalDue
FROM AdventureWorks2012.Sales.SalesOrderHeader ORDER BY TotalDue DESC;

SalesOrderID	OrderDate	TotalDue
51131	2007-07-01 00:00:00.000	187487.825
55282	2007-10-01 00:00:00.000	182018.6272
46616	2006-07-01 00:00:00.000	170512.6689
46981	2006-08-01 00:00:00.000	166537.0808
47395	2006-09-01 00:00:00.000	165028.7482
47369	2006-09-01 00:00:00.000	158056.5449
47355	2006-09-01 00:00:00.000	145741.8553
51822	2007-08-01 00:00:00.000	145454.366
44518	2005-11-01 00:00:00.000	142312.2199
51858	2007-08-01 00:00:00.000	140042.1209

TOP function usage: not known in advance how many rows will be returned due to "TIES".

SELECT   TOP 1 WITH TIES coalesce(Color, 'N/A')   AS Color,
            FORMAT(ListPrice, 'c', 'en-US')   AS ListPrice,
            Name   AS ProductName,
            ProductID
FROM   AdventureWorks2012.Production.Product
ORDER BY ROW_NUMBER() OVER(PARTITION BY Color ORDER BY ListPrice DESC);

Color	ListPrice	ProductName	ProductID
N/A	$229.49	HL Fork	804
Black	$3,374.99	Mountain-100 Black, 38	775
Red	$3,578.27	Road-150 Red, 62	749
Silver	$3,399.99	Mountain-100 Silver, 38	771
Blue	$2,384.07	Touring-1000 Blue, 46	966
Grey	$125.00	Touring-Panniers, Large	842
Multi	$89.99	Men's Bib-Shorts, S	855
Silver/Black	$80.99	HL Mountain Pedal	937
White	$9.50	Mountain Bike Socks, M	709
Yellow	$2,384.07	Touring-1000 Yellow, 46	954

The DISTINCT Clause to Omit Duplicates

The DISTINCT clause returns only unique results, omitting duplicates in the result set.

```
USE AdventureWorks2012;
SELECT DISTINCT Color FROM Production.Product
WHERE Color is not NULL
ORDER BY Color;
GO
```

Color
Black
Blue
Grey
Multi
Red
Silver
Silver/Black
White
Yellow

```
SELECT DISTINCT ListPrice
FROM Production.Product
 WHERE ListPrice > 0.0
ORDER BY ListPrice DESC;
GO
-- (102 row(s) affected) - Partial results.
```

ListPrice
3578.27
3399.99
3374.99
2443.35

```
-- Using DISTINCT in COUNT - NULL is counted
SELECT          COUNT(*)                      AS TotalRows,
                COUNT(DISTINCT Color)         AS ProductColors,
                COUNT(DISTINCT Size)          AS ProductSizes
FROM AdventureWorks2012.Production.Product;
```

TotalRows	ProductColors	ProductSizes
504	9	18

CHAPTER 3: Structure of the SELECT Statement

The CASE Conditional Expression

The CASE conditional expression evaluates to a **single value of the same data type**, therefore **it can be used anywhere in a query where a single value is required.**

```
SELECT          CASE ProductLine
                    WHEN 'R' THEN 'Road'
                    WHEN 'M' THEN 'Mountain'
                    WHEN 'T' THEN 'Touring'
                    WHEN 'S' THEN 'Other'
                    ELSE 'Parts'
                END                     AS Category,
                Name                    AS ProductName,
                ProductNumber
FROM AdventureWorks2012.Production.Product
ORDER BY ProductName;
GO
-- (504 row(s) affected) - Partial results.
```

Category	ProductName	ProductNumber
Touring	Touring-3000 Blue, 62	BK-T18U-62
Touring	Touring-3000 Yellow, 44	BK-T18Y-44
Touring	Touring-3000 Yellow, 50	BK-T18Y-50
Touring	Touring-3000 Yellow, 54	BK-T18Y-54
Touring	Touring-3000 Yellow, 58	BK-T18Y-58
Touring	Touring-3000 Yellow, 62	BK-T18Y-62
Touring	Touring-Panniers, Large	PA-T100
Other	Water Bottle - 30 oz.	WB-H098
Mountain	Women's Mountain Shorts, L	SH-W890-L

Query to return different result sets for repeated execution due to newid().

```
SELECT  TOP 3 CompanyName,   City=CONCAT(City, ', ', Country),          PostalCode,
        [IsNumeric] =  CASE    WHEN PostalCode like '[0-9][0-9][0-9][0-9][0-9]'
                               THEN '5-Digit Numeric'   ELSE 'Other'  END
FROM    Northwind.dbo.Suppliers
ORDER BY NEWID();                       -- random sort
GO
```

CompanyName	City	PostalCode	IsNumeric
PB Knäckebröd AB	Göteborg, Sweden	S-345 67	Other
Gai pâturage	Annecy, France	74000	5-Digit Numeric
Heli Süßwaren GmbH & Co. KG	Berlin, Germany	10785	5-Digit Numeric

Same query as above expanded with ROW_NUMBER() and another CASE expression column.

```
SELECT          ROW_NUMBER() OVER (ORDER BY Name)                    AS RowNo,
                CASE ProductLine
                  WHEN 'R' THEN 'Road'
                  WHEN 'M' THEN 'Mountain'
                  WHEN 'T' THEN 'Touring'
                  WHEN 'S' THEN 'Other'
                  ELSE 'Parts'
                END                             AS Category,
                Name                            AS ProductName,
                CASE WHEN Color is null THEN 'N/A'
                        ELSE Color END          AS Color,
                ProductNumber
FROM Production.Product    ORDER BY ProductName;
-- (504 row(s) affected) - Partial results.
```

RowNo	Category	ProductName	Color	ProductNumber
1	Parts	Adjustable Race	N/A	AR-5381
2	Mountain	All-Purpose Bike Stand	N/A	ST-1401
3	Other	AWC Logo Cap	Multi	CA-1098
4	Parts	BB Ball Bearing	N/A	BE-2349
5	Parts	Bearing Ball	N/A	BA-8327
6	Other	Bike Wash - Dissolver	N/A	CL-9009
7	Parts	Blade	N/A	BL-2036
8	Other	Cable Lock	N/A	LO-C100
9	Parts	Chain	Silver	CH-0234
10	Parts	Chain Stays	N/A	CS-2812

Testing PostalCode with ISNUMERIC and generating a flag with CASE expression.

```
SELECT  TOP (4) AddressID,   City,    PostalCode                       AS Zip,
        CASE WHEN ISNUMERIC(PostalCode) = 1 THEN 'Y'  ELSE 'N'  END    AS IsZipNumeric
FROM    AdventureWorks2008.Person.Address  ORDER BY NEWID();
```

AddressID	City	Zip	IsZipNumeric
16704	Paris	75008	Y
26320	Grossmont	91941	Y
27705	Matraville	2036	Y
18901	Kirkby	KB9	N

CHAPTER 3: Structure of the SELECT Statement

The OVER Clause

The OVER clause defines the partitioning and sorting of a rowset (intermediate result set) preceding the application of an associated window function, such as ranking. Window functions are also dubbed as ranking functions.

```
USE AdventureWorks2012;
-- Query with three different OVER clauses
SELECT   ROW_NUMBER() OVER ( ORDER BY SalesOrderID, ProductID)              AS RowNum
         ,SalesOrderID, ProductID, OrderQty
         ,RANK() OVER(PARTITION BY SalesOrderID ORDER BY OrderQty DESC)     AS Ranking
         ,SUM(OrderQty) OVER(PARTITION BY SalesOrderID)                     AS TotalQty
         ,AVG(OrderQty) OVER(PARTITION BY SalesOrderID)                     AS AvgQty
         ,COUNT(OrderQty) OVER(PARTITION BY SalesOrderID)  AS "Count"  -- T-SQL keyword, use "" or []
         ,MIN(OrderQty) OVER(PARTITION BY SalesOrderID)                     AS "Min"
         ,MAX(OrderQty) OVER(PARTITION BY SalesOrderID)                     AS "Max"
FROM Sales.SalesOrderDetail
WHERE SalesOrderID BETWEEN 61190 AND 61199
ORDER BY RowNum;
-- (143 row(s) affected) - Partial results.
```

RowNum	SalesOrderID	ProductID	OrderQty	Ranking	TotalQty	AvgQty	Count	Min	Max
1	61190	707	4	13	159	3	40	1	17
2	61190	708	3	18	159	3	40	1	17
3	61190	711	5	8	159	3	40	1	17
4	61190	712	12	2	159	3	40	1	17
5	61190	714	3	18	159	3	40	1	17
6	61190	715	5	8	159	3	40	1	17
7	61190	716	5	8	159	3	40	1	17
8	61190	858	4	13	159	3	40	1	17
9	61190	859	7	6	159	3	40	1	17
10	61190	864	8	4	159	3	40	1	17
11	61190	865	3	18	159	3	40	1	17
12	61190	870	9	3	159	3	40	1	17
13	61190	876	4	13	159	3	40	1	17
14	61190	877	5	8	159	3	40	1	17
15	61190	880	1	34	159	3	40	1	17
16	61190	881	5	8	159	3	40	1	17
17	61190	883	2	26	159	3	40	1	17
18	61190	884	17	1	159	3	40	1	17
19	61190	885	3	18	159	3	40	1	17
20	61190	886	1	34	159	3	40	1	17
21	61190	889	2	26	159	3	40	1	17
22	61190	892	4	13	159	3	40	1	17
23	61190	893	3	18	159	3	40	1	17
24	61190	895	1	34	159	3	40	1	17

FROM Clause: Specifies the Data Source

The FROM clause specifies the source data sets for the query such as tables, views, derived tables and table-valued functions. Typically the tables are JOINed together. The most common JOIN is INNER JOIN which is based on equality between FOREIGN KEY and PRIMARY KEY values in the two tables.

PERFORMANCE NOTE
All FOREIGN KEYs should be indexed. PRIMARY KEYs are indexed automatically with unique index.

```
USE AdventureWorks2012;
GO
SELECT
  ROW_NUMBER() OVER(ORDER BY SalesYTD DESC)                          AS RowNo,
  ROW_NUMBER() OVER(PARTITION BY PostalCode ORDER BY SalesYTD DESC)    AS SeqNo,
            CONCAT(p.FirstName, SPACE(1), p.LastName)        AS SalesStaff,
            FORMAT(s.SalesYTD,'c','en-US')                   AS YTDSales,
            City,
            a.PostalCode                                     AS ZipCode
FROM Sales.SalesPerson AS s
  INNER JOIN Person.Person AS p
    ON s.BusinessEntityID = p.BusinessEntityID
  INNER JOIN Person.Address AS a
    ON a.AddressID = p.BusinessEntityID
WHERE TerritoryID IS NOT NULL   AND SalesYTD <> 0 ORDER BY ZipCode, SeqNo;
```

RowNo	SeqNo	SalesStaff	YTDSales	City	ZipCode
1	1	Linda Mitchell	$4,251,368.55	Issaquah	98027
3	2	Michael Blythe	$3,763,178.18	Issaquah	98027
4	3	Jillian Carson	$3,189,418.37	Issaquah	98027
8	4	Tsvi Reiter	$2,315,185.61	Issaquah	98027
12	5	Garrett Vargas	$1,453,719.47	Issaquah	98027
14	6	Pamela Ansman-Wolfe	$1,352,577.13	Issaquah	98027
2	1	Jae Pak	$4,116,871.23	Renton	98055
5	2	Ranjit Varkey Chudukatil	$3,121,616.32	Renton	98055
6	3	José Saraiva	$2,604,540.72	Renton	98055
7	4	Shu Ito	$2,458,535.62	Renton	98055
9	5	Rachel Valdez	$1,827,066.71	Renton	98055
10	6	Tete Mensa-Annan	$1,576,562.20	Renton	98055
11	7	David Campbell	$1,573,012.94	Renton	98055
13	8	Lynn Tsoflias	$1,421,810.92	Renton	98055

The WHERE Clause to Filter Records (Rows)

The WHERE clause filters the rows generated by the query. Only rows satisfying (TRUE) the WHERE clause predicates are returned.

PERFORMANCE NOTE
All columns in WHERE clause should be indexed.

USE AdventureWorks2012;

String equal match predicate - equal is TRUE, not equal is FALSE.

SELECT ProductID, Name, ListPrice, Color
FROM Production.Product WHERE Name = 'Mountain-100 Silver, 38' ;

ProductID	Name	ListPrice	Color
771	Mountain-100 Silver, 38	3399.99	Silver

-- Function equality predicate
SELECT * FROM Sales.SalesOrderHeader WHERE YEAR(OrderDate) = 2008;
-- (13951 row(s) affected)

PERFORMANCE NOTE
When a column is used as a parameter in a function (e.g. YEAR(OrderDate)), index (if any) usage is voided. Instead of random SEEK, all rows are SCANned in the table. The predicate is not SARGable.

-- String wildcard match predicate
SELECT ProductID, Name, ListPrice, Color
FROM Production.Product WHERE Name LIKE ('%touring%');

-- Integer range predicate
SELECT ProductID, Name, ListPrice, Color
FROM Production.Product WHERE ProductID >= 997 ;

-- Double string wildcard match predicate
SELECT ProductID, Name, ListPrice, Color
FROM Production.Product WHERE Name LIKE ('%bike%') AND Name LIKE ('%44%');

-- String list match predicate
SELECT ProductID, Name, ListPrice, Color FROM Production.Product
WHERE Name IN ('Mountain-100 Silver, 44', 'Mountain-100 Black, 44');

CHAPTER 3: Structure of the SELECT Statement

85

The GROUP BY Clause to Aggregate Results

The GROUP BY clause is applied to partition the rows and calculate aggregate values. An extremely powerful way of looking at the data from a summary point of view.

```
SELECT
        V.Name                                  AS Vendor,
        FORMAT(SUM(TotalDue), 'c', 'en-US')     AS TotalPurchase,
        A.City,
        SP.Name                                 AS State,
        CR.Name                                 AS Country
FROM Purchasing.Vendor AS V
   INNER JOIN Purchasing.VendorAddress AS VA
           ON VA.VendorID = V.VendorID
   INNER JOIN Person.Address AS A
           ON A.AddressID = VA.AddressID
   INNER JOIN Person.StateProvince AS SP
           ON SP.StateProvinceID = A.StateProvinceID
   INNER JOIN Person.CountryRegion AS CR
           ON CR.CountryRegionCode = SP.CountryRegionCode
   INNER JOIN Purchasing.PurchaseOrderHeader POH
           ON POH.VendorID = V.VendorID
GROUP BY V.Name, A.City, SP.Name, CR.Name
ORDER BY SUM(TotalDue) DESC, Vendor;  -- TotalPurchase does a string sort instead of numeric
GO
-- (79 row(s) affected) - Partial results.
```

Vendor	TotalPurchase	City	State	Country
Superior Bicycles	$5,034,266.74	Lynnwood	Washington	United States
Professional Athletic Consultants	$3,379,946.32	Burbank	California	United States
Chicago City Saddles	$3,347,165.20	Daly City	California	United States
Jackson Authority	$2,821,333.52	Long Beach	California	United States
Vision Cycles, Inc.	$2,777,684.91	Glendale	California	United States
Sport Fan Co.	$2,675,889.22	Burien	Washington	United States
Proseware, Inc.	$2,593,901.31	Lebanon	Oregon	United States
Crowley Sport	$2,472,770.05	Chicago	Illinois	United States
Greenwood Athletic Company	$2,472,770.05	Lemon Grove	Arizona	United States
Mitchell Sports	$2,424,284.37	Everett	Washington	United States
First Rate Bicycles	$2,304,231.55	La Mesa	New Mexico	United States
Signature Cycles	$2,236,033.80	Coronado	California	United States
Electronic Bike Repair & Supplies	$2,154,773.37	Tacoma	Washington	United States
Vista Road Bikes	$2,090,857.52	Salem	Oregon	United States
Victory Bikes	$2,052,173.62	Issaquah	Washington	United States
Bicycle Specialists	$1,952,375.30	Lake Oswego	Oregon	United States

The HAVING Clause to Filter Aggregates

The HAVING clause is similar to the WHERE clause filtering but applies to GROUP BY aggregates.

```
USE AdventureWorks;
SELECT
            V.Name                              AS Vendor,
            FORMAT(SUM(TotalDue), 'c', 'en-US')  AS TotalPurchase,
            A.City,
            SP.Name                             AS State,
            CR.Name                             AS Country
FROM Purchasing.Vendor AS V
   INNER JOIN Purchasing.VendorAddress AS VA
            ON VA.VendorID = V.VendorID
   INNER JOIN Person.Address AS A
            ON A.AddressID = VA.AddressID
   INNER JOIN Person.StateProvince AS SP
            ON SP.StateProvinceID =  A.StateProvinceID
   INNER JOIN Person.CountryRegion AS CR
            ON CR.CountryRegionCode = SP.CountryRegionCode
   INNER JOIN Purchasing.PurchaseOrderHeader POH
            ON POH.VendorID = V.VendorID
GROUP BY  V.Name, A.City, SP.Name, CR.Name
HAVING SUM(TotalDue) < $26000    -- HAVING clause predicate
ORDER BY SUM(TotalDue) DESC,  Vendor;
```

Vendor	TotalPurchase	City	State	Country
Speed Corporation	$25,732.84	Anacortes	Washington	United States
Gardner Touring Cycles	$25,633.64	Altadena	California	United States
National Bike Association	$25,513.90	Sedro Woolley	Washington	United States
Australia Bike Retailer	$25,060.04	Bellingham	Washington	United States
WestAmerica Bicycle Co.	$25,060.04	Houston	Texas	United States
Ready Rentals	$23,635.06	Kirkland	Washington	United States
Morgan Bike Accessories	$23,146.99	Albany	New York	United States
Continental Pro Cycles	$22,960.07	Long Beach	California	United States
American Bicycles and Wheels	$9,641.01	West Covina	California	United States
Litware, Inc.	$8,553.32	Santa Cruz	California	United States
Business Equipment Center	$8,497.80	Everett	Montana	United States
Bloomington Multisport	$8,243.95	West Covina	California	United States
International	$8,061.10	Salt Lake City	Utah	United States
Wide World Importers	$8,025.60	Concord	California	United States
Midwest Sport, Inc.	$7,328.72	Detroit	Michigan	United States
Wood Fitness	$6,947.58	Philadelphia	Pennsylvania	United States
Metro Sport Equipment	$6,324.53	Lebanon	Oregon	United States
Burnett Road Warriors	$5,779.99	Corvallis	Oregon	United States
Lindell	$5,412.57	Lebanon	Oregon	United States
Consumer Cycles	$3,378.17	Torrance	California	United States
Northern Bike Travel	$2,048.42	Anacortes	Washington	United States

The ORDER BY Clause to Sort Results

The ORDER BY clause sorts the result set. It guarantees ordering according to the columns or expressions listed from major to minor keys. Unique ordering requires a set of keys which generate unique data rows. The major key, YEAR(HireDate), in the first example is not sufficient for uniqueness.

```
USE AdventureWorks2012;            -- Sort on 2 keys
SELECT BusinessEntityID AS EmployeeID, JobTitle, HireDate
FROM HumanResources.Employee  ORDER BY YEAR(HireDate) DESC, EmployeeID;
-- (290 row(s) affected) - Partial results.
```

EmployeeID	JobTitle	HireDate
285	Pacific Sales Manager	2007-04-15
286	Sales Representative	2007-07-01
288	Sales Representative	2007-07-01

```
-- Sort on CASE conditional expression
SELECT   BusinessEntityID AS SalesStaffID, CONCAT(LastName, ', ', FirstName) AS FullName,
         CASE CountryRegionName WHEN 'United States' THEN TerritoryName
             ELSE '' END AS TerritoryName, CountryRegionName
FROM Sales.vSalesPerson   WHERE TerritoryName IS NOT NULL        -- view
ORDER BY CASE WHEN CountryRegionName != 'United States' THEN  CountryRegionName
         ELSE TerritoryName  END;
```

SalesStaffID	FullName	TerritoryName	CountryRegionName
286	Tsoflias, Lynn		Australia
278	Vargas, Garrett		Canada
282	Saraiva, José		Canada

The EXCEPT & INTERSECT Set Operators

The EXCEPT operator & the INTERSECT operator require the column lists are compatible for the comparison.

```
USE tempdb; -- Prepare two tables with 400 random(newid()) picks from the Product table
SELECT TOP (400) * INTO Prod1 FROM AdventureWorks2012.Production.Product ORDER BY NEWID();
SELECT TOP (400) * INTO Prod2 FROM AdventureWorks2012.Production.Product ORDER BY NEWID();

-- EXCEPT SET OPERATOR - no match rows
SELECT * FROM PROD1 EXCEPT SELECT * FROM PROD2;  -- (81 row(s) affected)

-- INTERSECT SET OPERATOR - matching rows
SELECT * FROM PROD1 INTERSECT SELECT * FROM PROD2;  -- (319 row(s) affected)
```

CHAPTER 3: Structure of the SELECT Statement

CTE - Common Table Expression

CTE helps with structured programming by the definition of named subqueries at the beginning of the query. It supports nesting and recursion.

```
USE AdventureWorks;
-- Testing CTE
WITH CTE (SalesPersonID, NumberOfOrders, MostRecentOrderDate)
    AS  (        SELECT SalesPersonID, COUNT(*), CONVERT(date, MAX(OrderDate))
                 FROM Sales.SalesOrderHeader
                 GROUP BY SalesPersonID   )
SELECT * FROM CTE;
-- (18 row(s) affected) - Partial results.
```

SalesPersonID	NumberOfOrders	MostRecentOrderDate
284	39	2004-05-01
278	234	2004-06-01
281	242	2004-06-01

```
-- Using CTE in a query
;WITH CTE (SalesPersonID, NumberOfOrders, MostRecentOrderDate)
    AS ( SELECT SalesPersonID, COUNT(*), CONVERT(date, MAX(OrderDate))
         FROM Sales.SalesOrderHeader   GROUP BY SalesPersonID        )
-- Start of outer (main) query
 SELECT         E.EmployeeID,
                OE.NumberOfOrders                AS EmpOrders,
                OE.MostRecentOrderDate           AS EmpLastOrder,
                E.ManagerID,
                OM.NumberOfOrders                AS MgrOrders,
                OM.MostRecentOrderDate           AS MgrLastOrder
 FROM   HumanResources.Employee AS E
        INNER JOIN CTE AS OE             ON E.EmployeeID = OE.SalesPersonID
        LEFT OUTER JOIN CTE AS OM        ON E.ManagerID = OM.SalesPersonID
ORDER BY EmployeeID;
-- (17 row(s) affected) - Partial results.
```

EmployeeID	EmpOrders	EmpLastOrder	ManagerID	MgrOrders	MgrLastOrder
268	48	2004-06-01	273	NULL	NULL
275	450	2004-06-01	268	48	2004-06-01
276	418	2004-06-01	268	48	2004-06-01
277	473	2004-06-01	268	48	2004-06-01
278	234	2004-06-01	268	48	2004-06-01

Combining Results of Multiple Queries with UNION

UNION and UNION ALL (no duplicates elimination) operators can be used to **stack result sets from two or more queries into a single result set**.

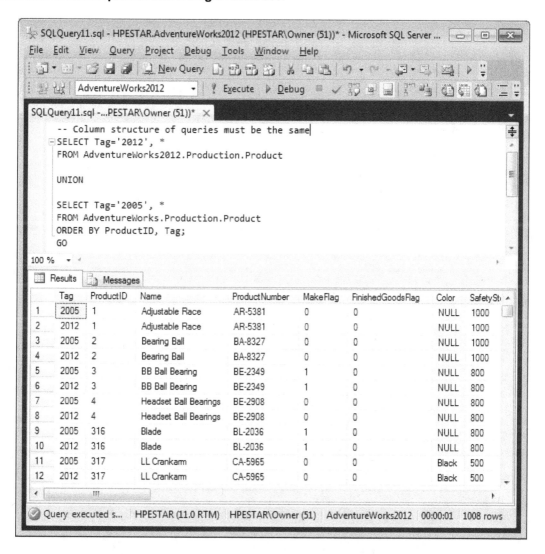

```
-- Combining data from OLTP & data warehouse databases
SELECT FirstName,LastName, 0 AS TotalChildren
FROM AdventureWorks2012.Person.Person
UNION ALL
SELECT FirstName,LastName, TotalChildren
FROM AdventureWorksDW2012..DimCustomer;
```

CHAPTER 3: Structure of the SELECT Statement

TOP n by Group Query with OVER PARTITION BY

OVER PARTITION BY method is very convenient for TOP n by group selection. List of top 3 orders placed by resellers (customers of AdventureWorks Cycles).

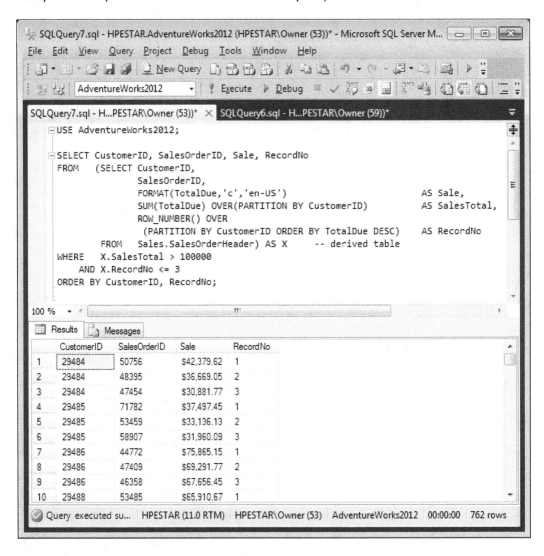

```
-- Row numbering by partitioning view results
SELECT ROW_NUMBER() OVER(PARTITION BY PhoneNumberType ORDER BY SalesYTD DESC) RN,
       CONCAT(FirstName, ' ', LastName) as Name, ROUND(SalesYTD,2,1) AS YTDSales,
       PhoneNumberType
FROM AdventureWorks2012.Sales.vSalesPerson
ORDER BY PhoneNumberType, RN;
```

CHAPTER 4: SQL Server Management Studio

SQL Server Programming, Administration & Management Tool

SQL Server Management Studio (SSMS) is a GUI (Graphical User Interface) tool for accessing, configuring, managing, administering, and developing all major components of SQL Server with the exception of Business Intelligence components: SSAS (Analysis Services), SSRS (Reporting Services) & SSIS (Integration Services). The two main environments in SSMS: Object Explorer and Query Editor. Object Explorer is used to access servers, databases and db objects. Query Editor is to develop and execute queries. SSMS is used by a DBA (Data Base Administrator) for administrative and programming functions. SSMS can also be used by a database developer to develop application related db objects such as stored procedures, functions and triggers. Some developers prefer to stay in Visual Studio environment which has features to support database development albeit not as extensive as Management Studio. A typical screen display of Management Studio.

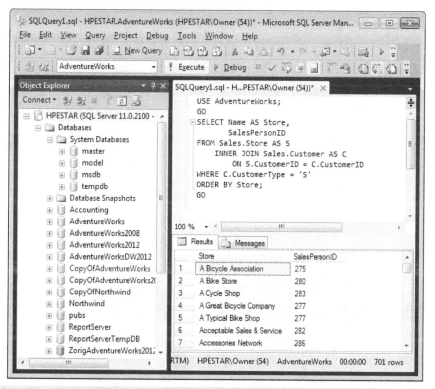

CHAPTER 4: SQL Server Management Studio

Query Editor

The Query Editor is used to type in queries, edit them and submit them for execution by the server. Queries can also be loaded from a disk file, typically with .sql extension. In addition to textual query development, a number of special tools available such as graphical query designer, debugger, execution plan display and query analysis by the Database Engine Tuning Advisor. IntelliSense provides contextual assistance with SQL syntax checking and guessing object names in a drop-down menu based on the typed prefix.

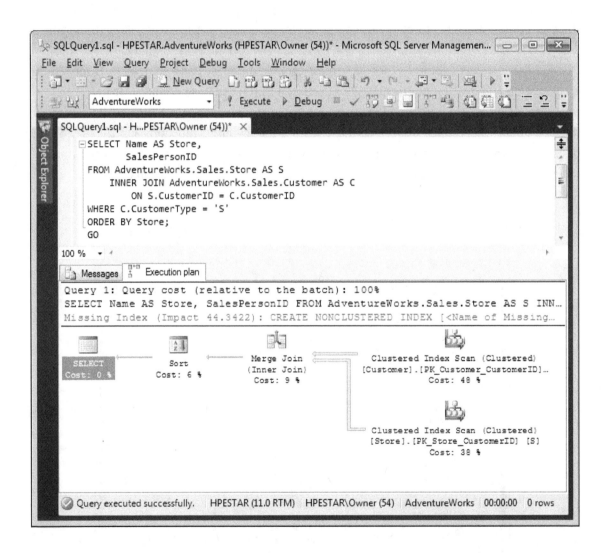

Execute All Batches in Query Editor

The entire content of the Query Editor is executed when we click on the Execute button.
Batches typically separated by "GO" on a separate line.

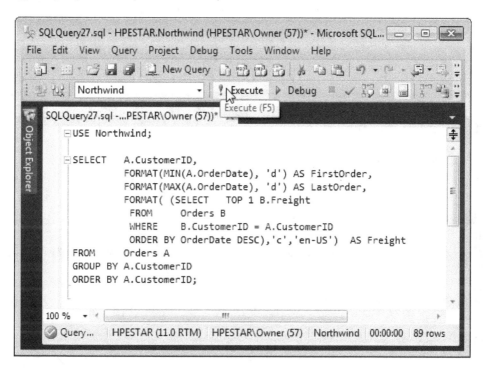

The Significance of GO in T-SQL Scripts

"GO" is not transmitted to SQL Server. "GO" indicates the end of batch to the client software
such as SSMS. "GO" also indicates the end of a logical unit to the human reader. Certain
statements must be the first line, or have "GO" preceding them.

```
USE AdventureWorks2012;
CREATE FUNCTION Z () RETURNS TABLE AS
RETURN  SELECT * FROM Production.ProductSubcategory;
GO    /* Msg 111, Level 15, State 1, Line 2   'CREATE FUNCTION' must be the first statement in a
query batch. */
```

```
USE AdventureWorks2012;
GO
CREATE FUNCTION Z () RETURNS TABLE AS RETURN SELECT * FROM
Production.ProductSubcategory;
GO
-- Command(s) completed successfully.
```

The Results Pane contains the result rows of the query. It is currently set to Grid format.

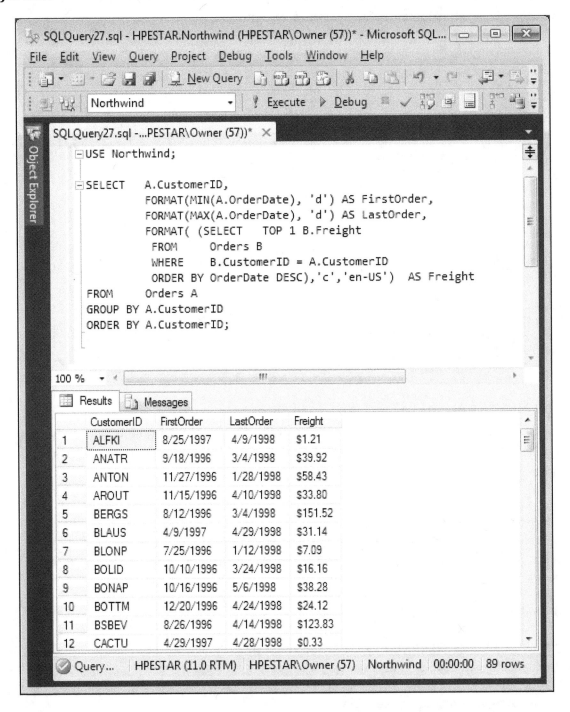

The Messages Pane gets the row count values, warning & error messages as well as the output of the PRINT & RAISERROR statements if any.

The client software also gets the same messages following query execution.

Routing Results to Grid, Text or File

Results can be routed to Grid, Text or File from the right-click menu or the Query drop-down menu.

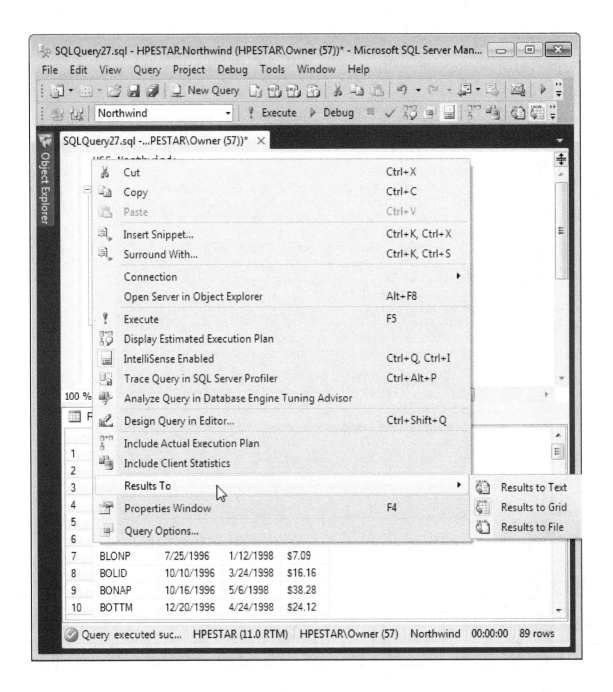

Routing Results to Text

The following screen window image displays results in text format. Messages also come to the Results window, following the results rows.

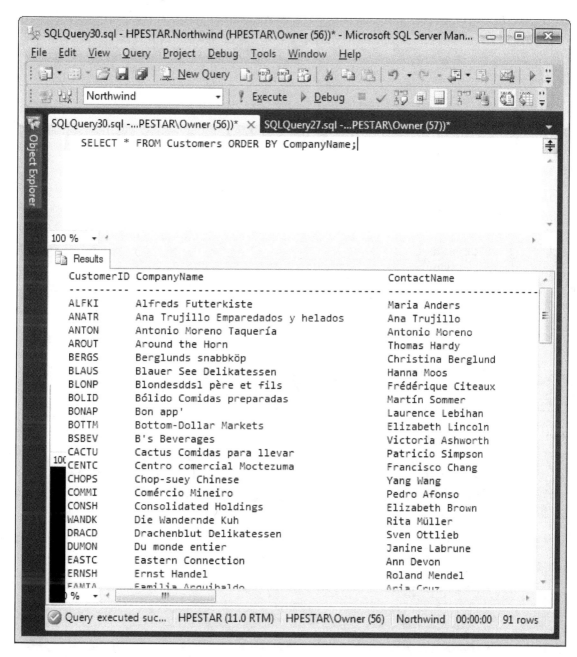

Routing Results to File

When the routing option is file, the file save window pops up upon query execution.

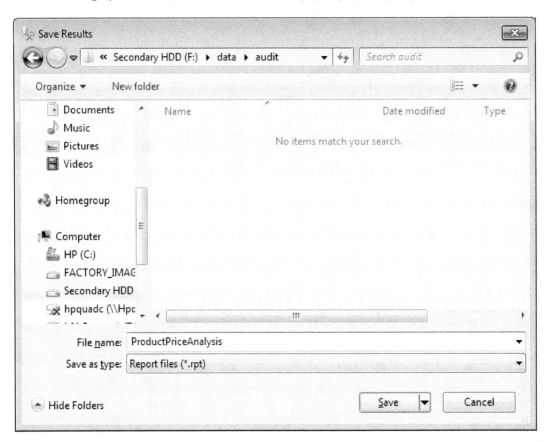

Part of the file in Notepad.

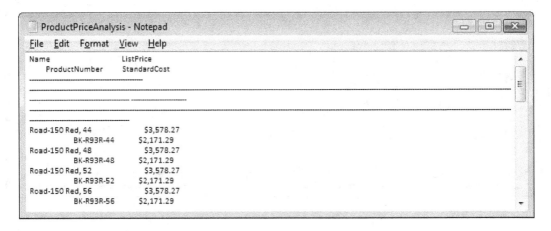

Saving Results in CSV Flat File Format

Results can also be saved in CSV (comma separated values) format which can be read by Excel and other software.

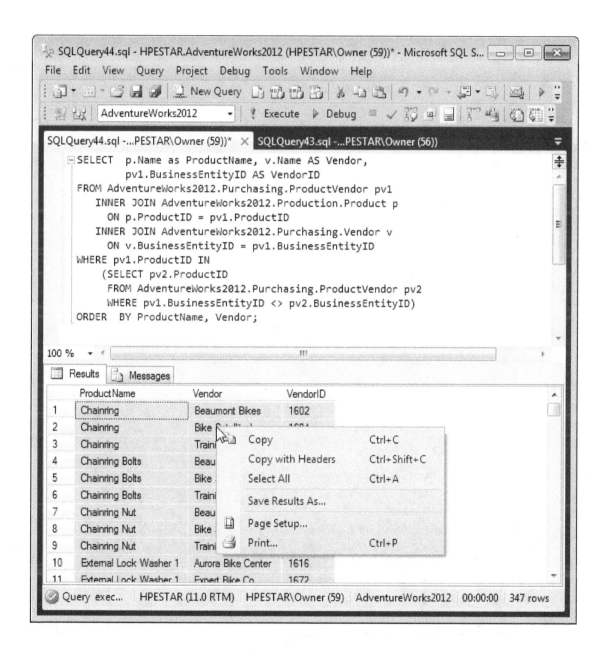

The saving file dialog box is configured automatically to csv saving.

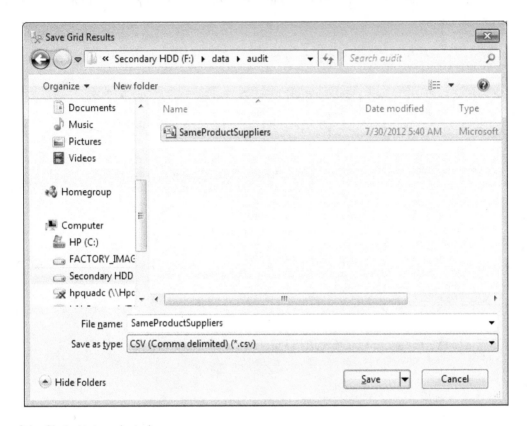

Part of the file in Notepad window.

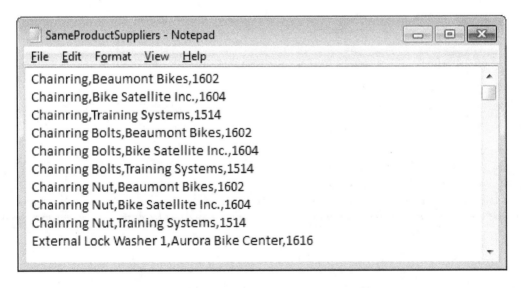

Copy & Paste Results to Excel

Using the copy / copy with headers option in SSMS result window, the query results can simply be pasted into an Excel worksheet. Excel may do implicit conversions on some columns.

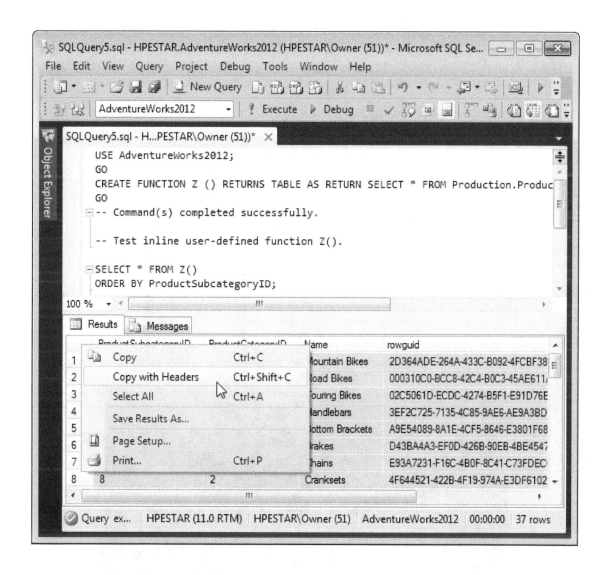

After pasting into an Excel worksheet some formatting may be necessary such as for datetime columns.

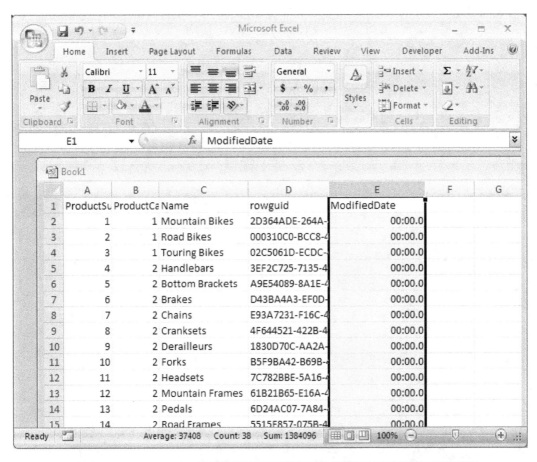

Error Handling & Debugging

Error handling and debugging is a major part of database development work. When there is an error, it is displayed in the Messages area (or returned to the application client software) which automatically becomes active. In the following example, we introduced an invalid column name which resulted in error. The error message line reference starts with the top line of the batch which is the first line after the first "GO" which indicates a new batch. The red wave-underlining comes from optional IntelliSense and not related to the execution attempt error message. IntelliSense gives warning ahead of time if it detects a potential error. Simple errors can be corrected with help from the error message. Complex errors may required web search and/or examining the query in parts.

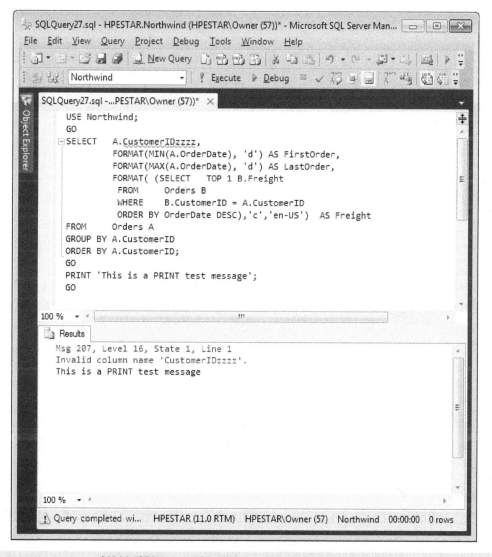

Locating the Error Line in a Query

Position the cursor on the error and double click. The error line will be highlighted. This method does not work for all errors.

Error Message Pointing to the Wrong Line

For some errors, the first line of the query (3) is returned by the database engine not the actual error line (13). The error message is still very helpful though in this instance.

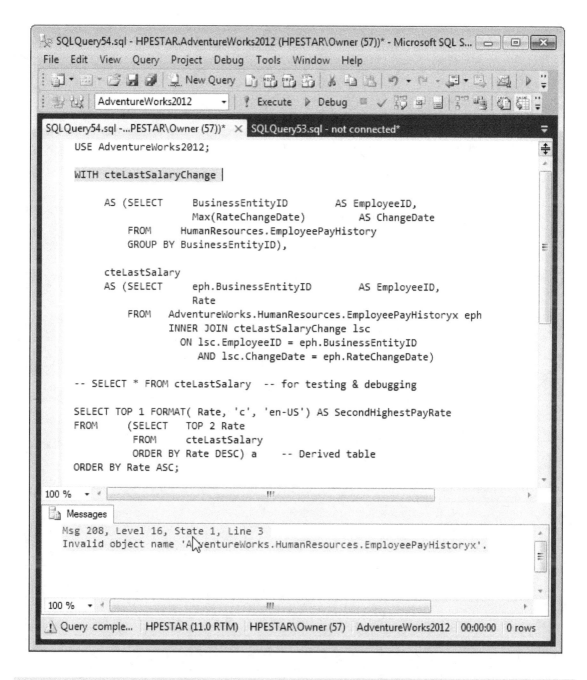

Parsing a Query for Syntax Errors

A query (or one or more batches) can be parsed for syntax errors. Parsing catches syntax errors such as using "ORDER" instead of "ORDER BY" for sorting.

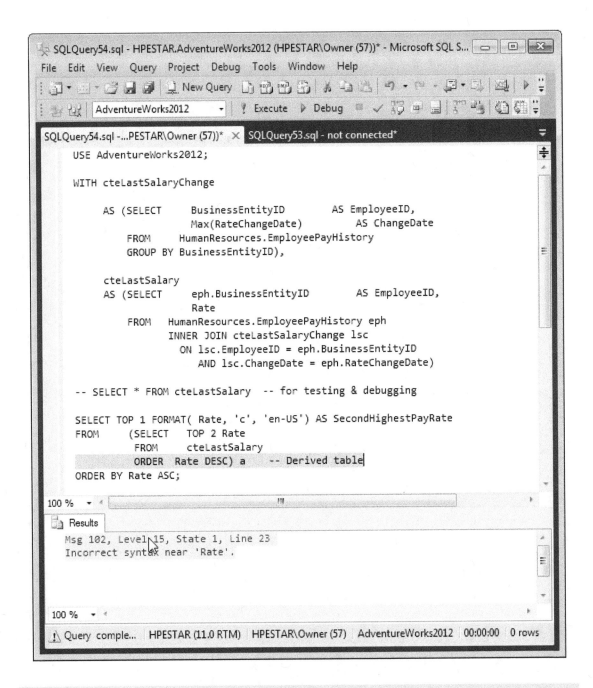

Deferred Name Resolution Process

Deferred Name Resolution Process: Only syntax errors are caught when parsed, not execution (runtime) errors as shown in the following demo which has an invalid table reference (EmployeePayHistoryx). Similarly, **stored procedures can be compiled without errors with invalid table references**. A table need not exist for stored procedure compilation, only for execution.

Executing Single Batch Only

A single batch can be executed by selecting (highlighting) it and clicking on Execute.

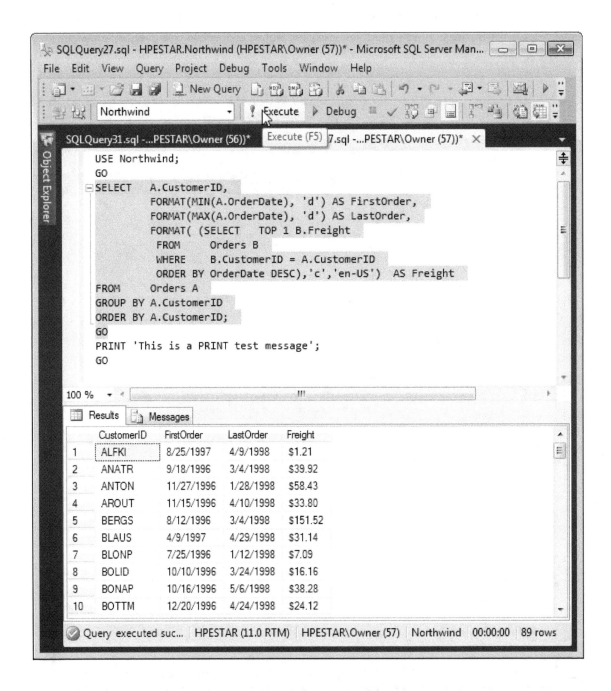

Executing Part of a Query

A part of a query can be executed as long as it is a valid query, otherwise error results. The query part has to be selected (highlighted) and the Execute button has to be pushed. The selected part of the query is considered a batch which is sent to the server. In this example, we executed the subquery (inner query) in the WHERE clause predicate.

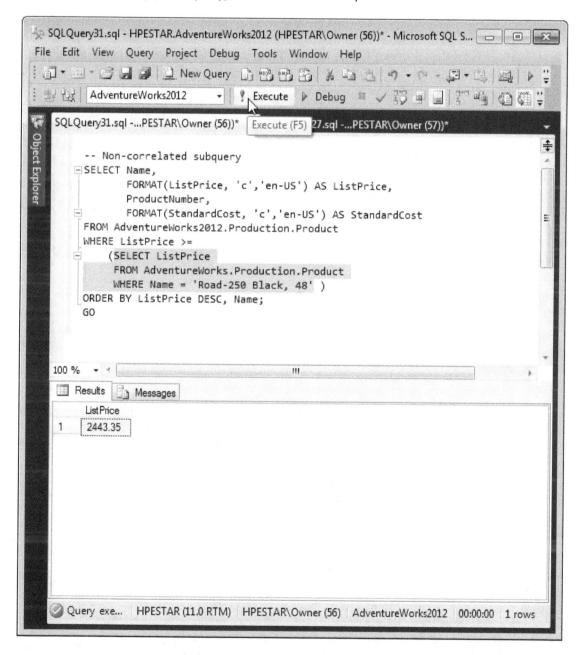

Object Explorer

SSMS Object Explorer functions as:

- ➢ A tree-based directory of all database objects
- ➢ A launching base for graphical user-interface tools
- ➢ An access way to object properties

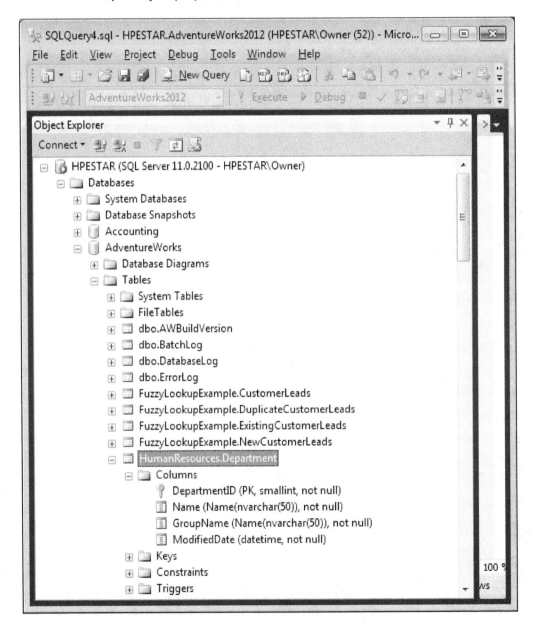

Context-Sensitive Right-Click Menu

Based on what object the cursor is on, right-click menu changes accordingly, it is context-sensitive. In the following demo the cursor is on table object when we right click on the mouse.

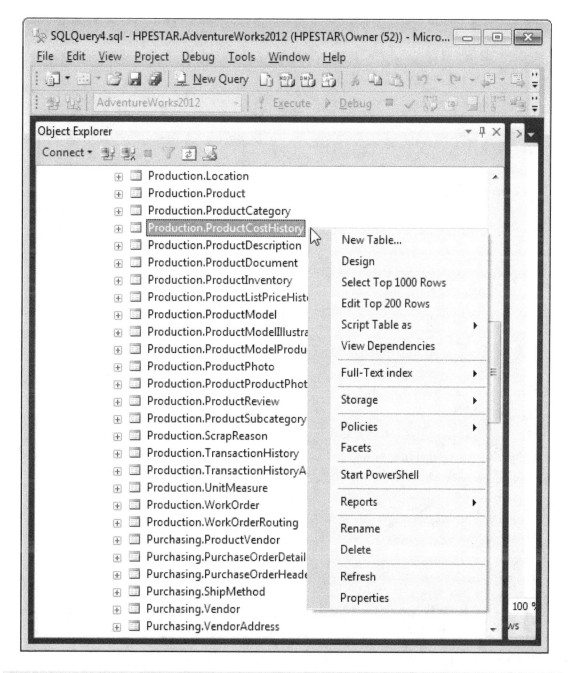

Server Administration & Management Tools

All the available SQL Server administration and management tools can be accessed from the Object Explorer. Usually the Database Administrator (DBA) uses these tools.

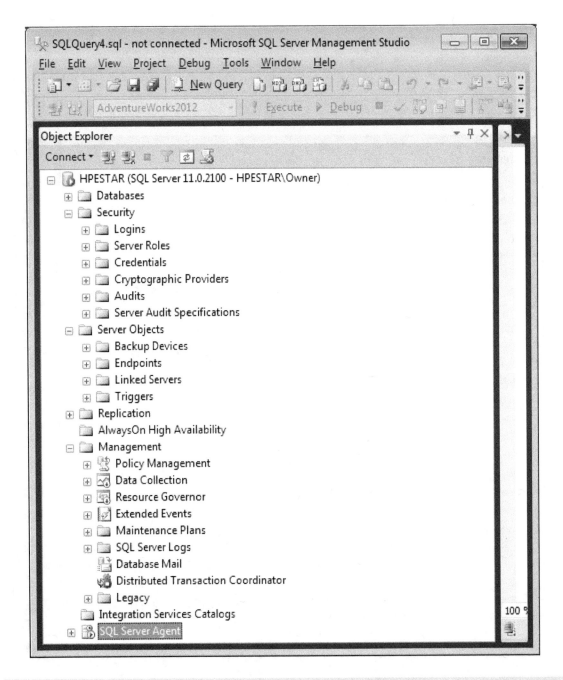

SQL Server Agent Jobs to Automate Administration Tasks

SQL Server Agent is a job creation and scheduling facility with notification features. For example, database backup job can be scheduled to execute 2:15AM every night as shown on the following dialog box. Stored procedure execution can also be setup as a job and scheduled for periodic execution.

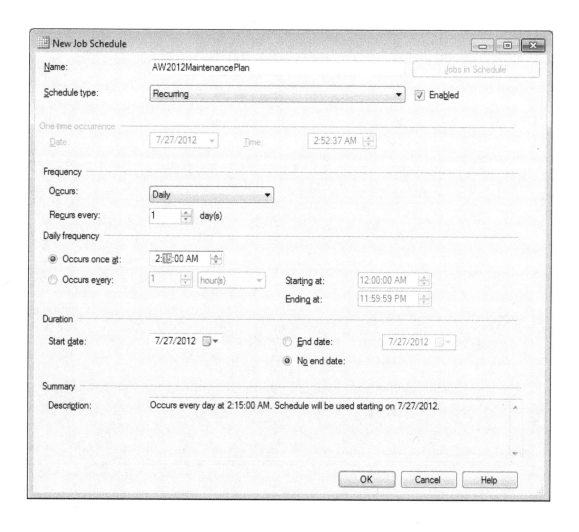

Job properties panel can be used to create and manage jobs with multiple job steps and multiple schedules.

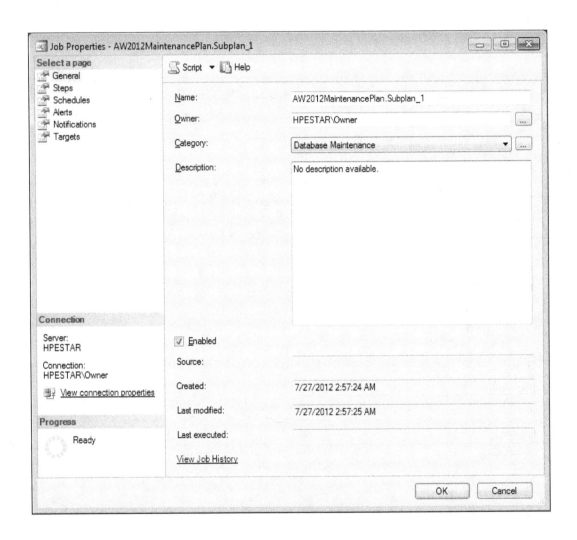

Graphical Query Designer

The Design Query in Editor entry on the Query drop-down menu launches the graphical Query Designer which can be used to design the query with GUI method and the T-SQL SELECT code will be generated automatically upon completion.

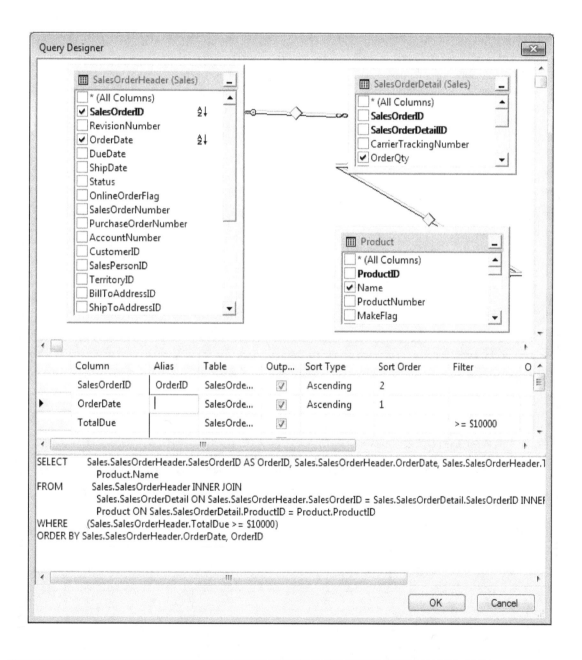

Designing a GROUP BY Query in Query Designer

Query Designer can be used to design from simple to complex queries. It can also serve as a starter query for a more complex query. It is really easy to get the tables JOINs graphically.

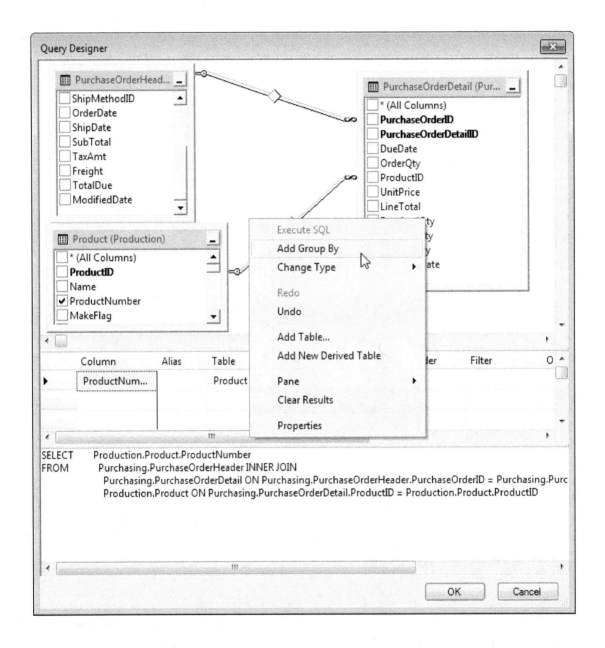

The Production.Product.Name column will also be configured as GROUP BY (drop-down default).

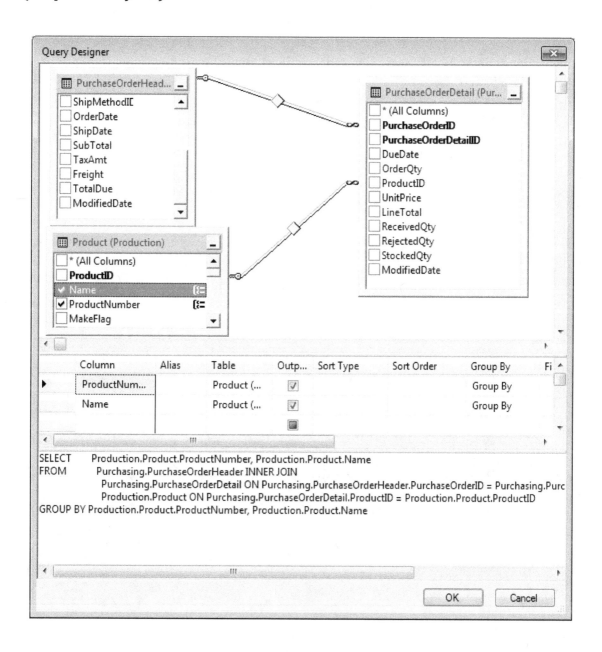

We add the TotalDue column and change the summary function to "SUM" from "Group by" and configure sorting on the first column.

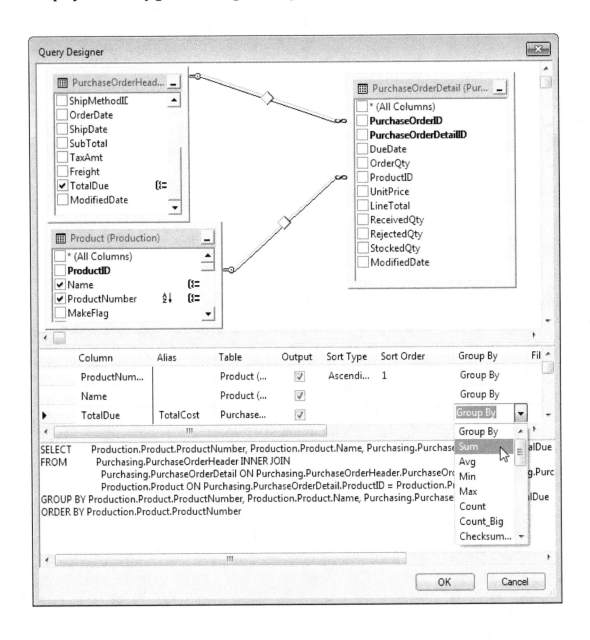

After pressing OK, the query is moved into the Query Editor window. Frequently it requires reformatting.

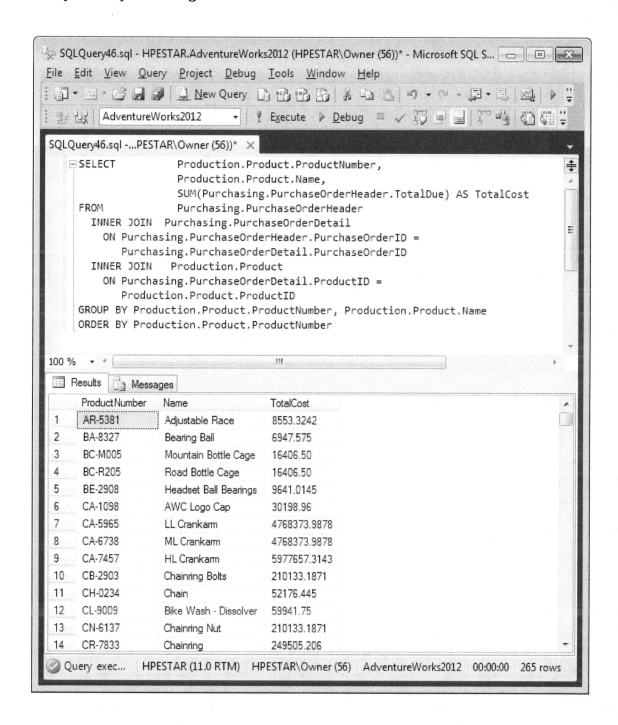

The only remaining issue with the query is the 3-part column references which is hard to read. We can change the query for readability improvement by using table aliases.

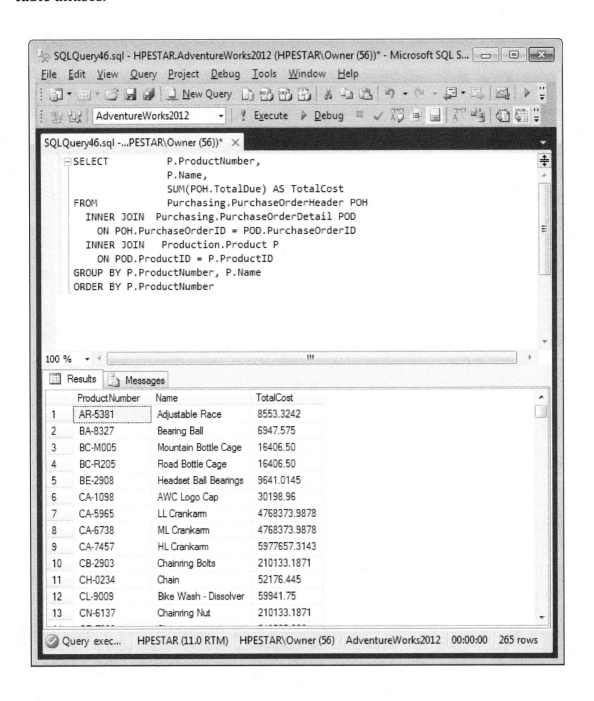

Graphically Editing of an Existing Query

An existing query, exception certain complex queries, can be uploaded into the Graphical Query Designer the following way: select (highlight) the query and right-click for the drop-down menu; click on Design Query in Editor.

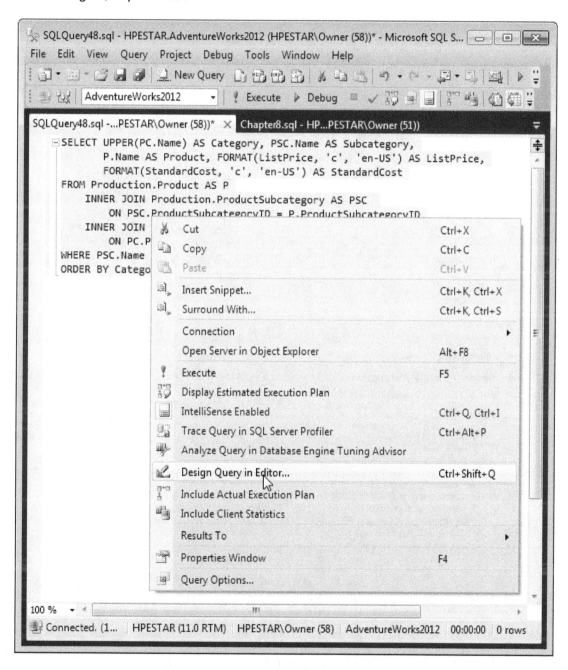

Following screen image shows the query in the Graphical Query Designer after some manual beautifying such as moving the tables for better display.

The query can be edited graphically and upon clicking on "OK", the query text is updated in the Query Editor window.

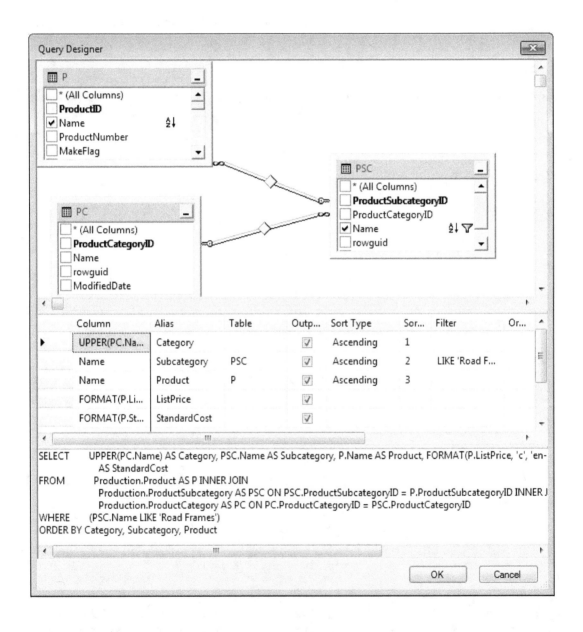

Configuring Line Numbers in Query Editor

Line numbering is an option which is off by default. Line numbers are helpful to find errors in large queries or T-SQL scripts (a sequence of T-SQL statements) when the error references a line number. Following is an example an error which includes the line number.

The Display Line Numbers option in the query editor can be activated from Options.

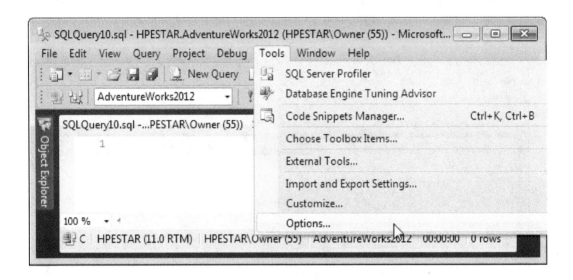

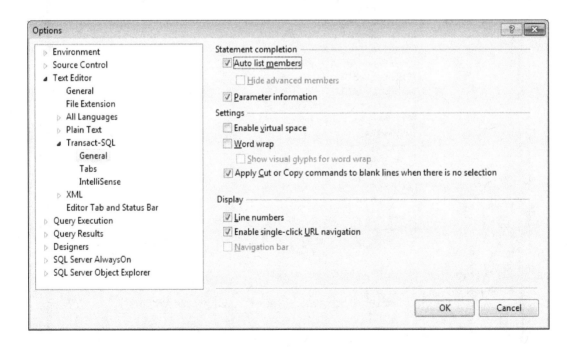

IntelliSense - Your Smart Assistant

IntelliSense is a smart agent in Query Editor. It helps completing long object names and pointing out potential errors by red wave-lining (squiggly) them.

The Options configuration screen for IntelliSense.

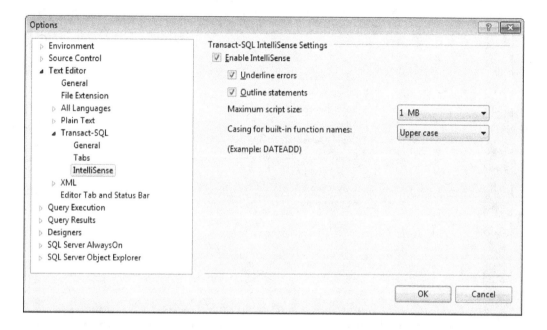

Underlining with red wave-line potential errors such as misspelling of a column name.

```
SELECT TOP 1000 [BillOfMaterialsID]
      ,[ProductAssemblyID]
      ,[ComponentID]
      ,[StartDate]
      ,[EndDate]
      ,[UnitMeasureCodex]
      ,[BOMLevel]
      ,[PerAssemblyQty]
      ,[ModifiedDate]
  FROM [AdventureWorks2012].[Production].[BillOfMaterials]
```

IntelliSense Guessing and Completing Object Names

Screenshots show IntelliSense in action when typing queries.

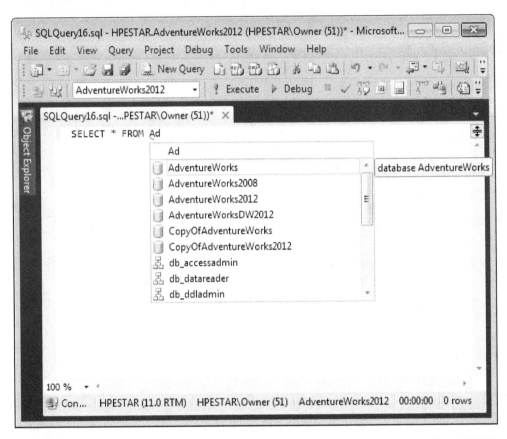

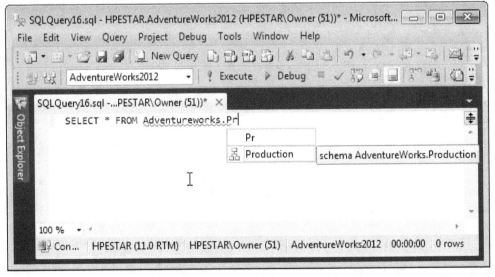

CHAPTER 4: SQL Server Management Studio

IntelliSense drop-down menu for "Prod".

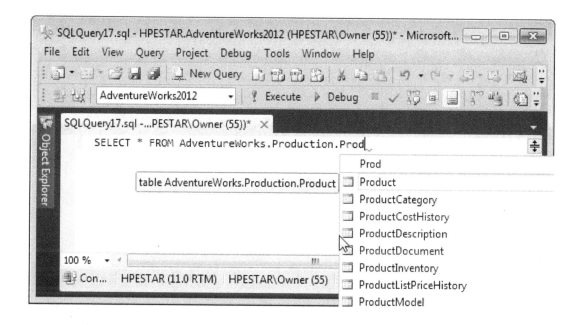

IntelliSense drop-down menu for "ProductS".

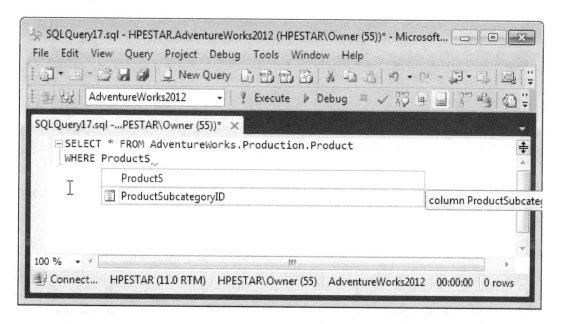

CHAPTER 4: SQL Server Management Studio

IntelliSense completion assistance for "ProductN"

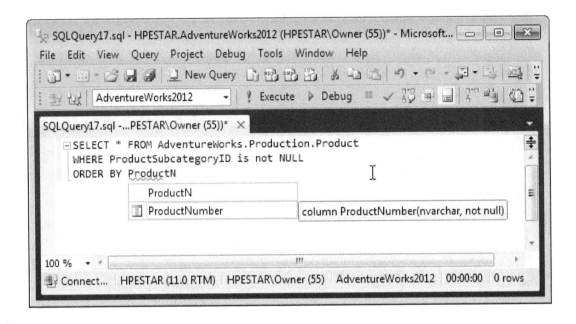

IntelliSense completion assistance for "Produ"

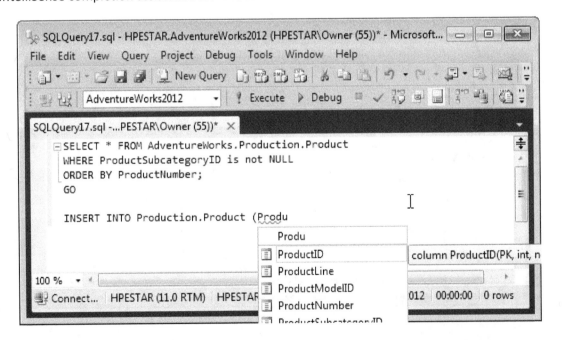

CHAPTER 4: SQL Server Management Studio

IntelliSense Assisting with User-Defined Objects

IntelliSense helps out with a user-defined stored procedure execution.

```
SQLQuery75.sql - HPESTAR.AdventureWorks2012 (HPESTAR\Owner (58))* - Microsoft SQL S...
File  Edit  View  Query  Project  Debug  Tools  Window  Help
New Query
AdventureWorks2012          Execute    Debug

SQLQuery75.sql -...PESTAR\Owner (58))*  ×

    USE AdventureWorks2012;
    GO
  CREATE PROCEDURE sprocProductPaging
    (
      @PageNumber int,
      @RowsPerPage int
    )
    AS
  BEGIN
  SELECT  ProductNumber,
          Name            AS ProductName,
          ListPrice,
          Color
    FROM Production.Product p
    WHERE ProductSubcategoryID is not NULL
    ORDER BY ProductNumber
    OFFSET (@PageNumber-1) * @RowsPerPage ROWS
    FETCH NEXT @RowsPerPage ROWS ONLY;
  END;
    GO
    -- Command(s) completed successfully.

    EXEC sprocProductPaging 10
    AdventureWorks2012.dbo.sprocProductPaging @PageNumber int, @RowsPerPage int
    Stored procedures always return INT.

100 %
  Query ex...  HPESTAR (11.0 RTM)  HPESTAR\Owner (58)  AdventureWorks2012  00:00:00  20 rows
```

IntelliSense Smart Guessing Partial Word in Middle of Object Names

You don't have to remember how an object name starts. You just have to remember some part of the name. Looking for the system view associated with "waits".

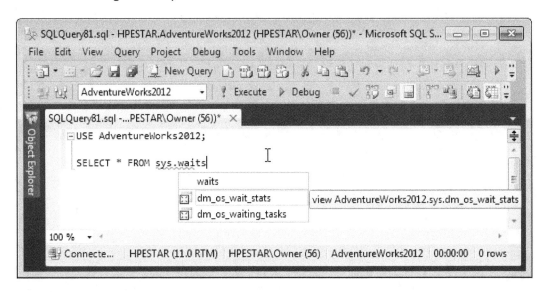

Looking for the SalesOrderHeader table but only remembering "head".

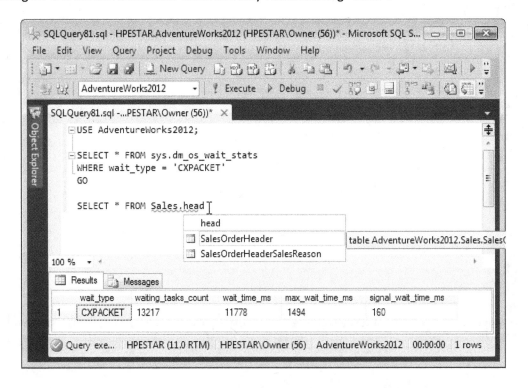

Hovering over Red Squiggly Underline Errors for Explanation

IntelliSense red wave (squiggly) underlining of errors which is caused, actually, by a single invalid table reference.

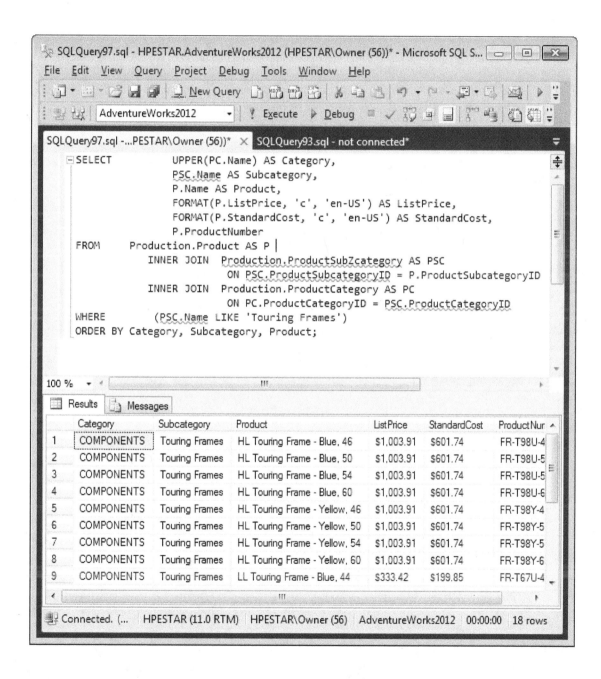

Common Error: The multi-part identifier "abc" could not be bound.

Hovering over the first error results in an explanation pop-up. This is a distant error, the kind usually the hardest to solve, because, actually, it is a secondary error caused by the primary error which is located on a different line. In this instance, there are few lines difference only, but in a large stored procedure the difference can be 200 lines as an example.

```
PSC.Name AS Subcategory,
```
The multi-part identifier "PSC.Name" could not be bound.

Hovering over the second error yields the cause of all errors: "ProductSubZcategory".

```
Production.ProductSubZcategory AS PSC
```
Invalid object name 'Production.ProductSubZcategory'.

The remaining error messages are all "multi-part..." caused by the solitary invalid table reference.

```
PSC.ProductSubcategoryID = P.ProductSubcategoryID
```
The multi-part identifier "PSC.ProductSubcategoryID" could not be bound.

After fixing the table name, all errors are gone.

```
SELECT          UPPER(PC.Name)                      AS Category,
                PSC.Name                            AS Subcategory,
                P.Name                              AS Product,
                FORMAT(P.ListPrice, 'c', 'en-US')   AS ListPrice,
                FORMAT(P.StandardCost, 'c', 'en-US') AS StandardCost,
                P.ProductNumber
FROM       Production.Product AS P
            INNER JOIN  Production.ProductSubcategory AS PSC
                    ON PSC.ProductSubcategoryID = P.ProductSubcategoryID
            INNER JOIN  Production.ProductCategory AS PC
                    ON PC.ProductCategoryID = PSC.ProductCategoryID
WHERE       (PSC.Name LIKE 'Touring Frames')
ORDER BY Category, Subcategory, Product;
```

Refreshing IntelliSense Cache for New DB Objects

IntelliSense cache is not updated real-time. If new objects are created in another connection (session), they will not be seen until exit SSMS/reenter or IntelliSense cache is updated. No red-wave underline for the **newly created object SOD** in the same connection.

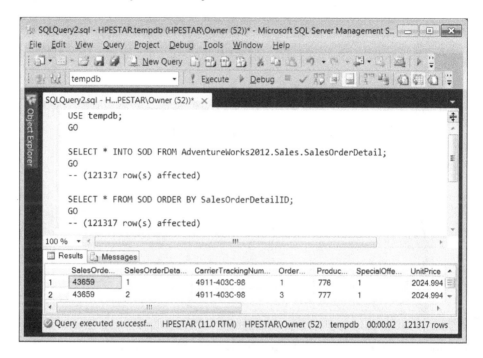

In another connection, the query works, but there are red squiggly underlining for the new table & column.

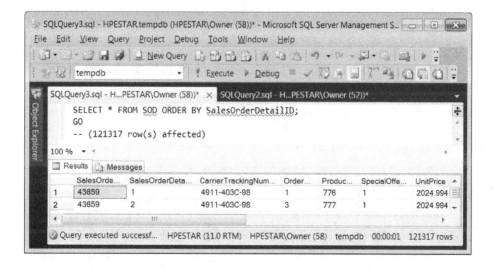

Refreshing IntelliSense Local Cache

Squiggly red line goes away in all connections for the new database objects.

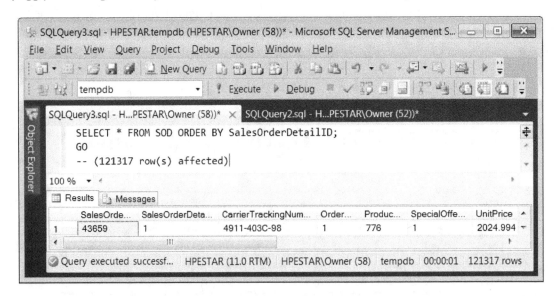

CHAPTER 5: Basic Concepts of Client-Server Computing

Client - Server Relational Database Management System

The "server" is SQL Server, operating on a powerful hardware platform, managing databases and related items. The client is application software. The real client is naturally a human user who runs the application software. Automated software which uses the database for one thing or another is also considered a "client". The client computer, in the next room or thousands of miles away, is connected to the server through communications link. The client software sends a request, a query, to SQL Server, after execution the server returns the results to the client. An example for a query sent by the client to the server:

SELECT ListPrice FROM AdventureWorks2012.Production.Product WHERE ProductID = 800;

SQL Server executes the query and returns "1120.49" to the client with a flag indicating successful query execution. A tempting analogy is a restaurant: kitchen is the server, patrons are the clients and the communications / delivery done by waiters & waitresses.

Screenshot displays SQL Server (highlighted) along with other related software such as SQL Server Agent (job scheduling facility) , SSIS (data transformation & transfer), SSRS (Reporting), SSAS (OLAP Cube) and other auxiliary software.

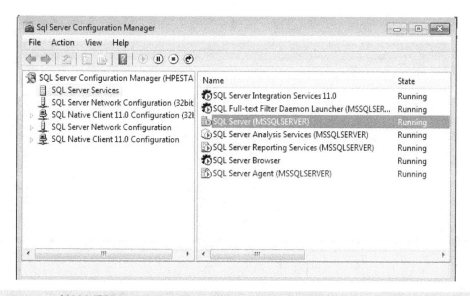

Database Objects on Server-Side

Screenshot of Object Explorer displays almost all important database objects with the exception of constraints, triggers and indexes.

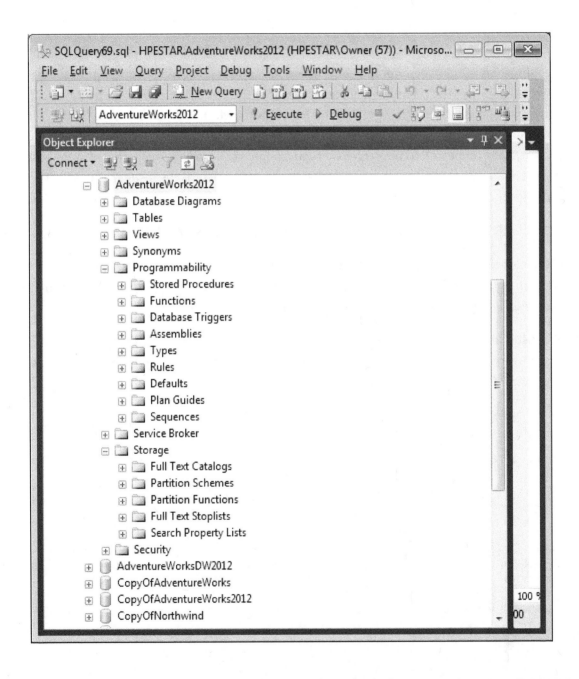

Database Related Items on Client-Side

On the client side the following items:

> ➤ SQL Server client libraries to access the server and database
> ➤ SQL queries imbedded in application programs
> ➤ Stored procedure calls imbedded in application software

Queries by themselves are not database object. To make them database objects we have to build stored procedures, functions or views around them.

The following code segment illustrates database connection and query from ASP to Inventory database. In ANSI SQL terminology catalog means database.

```
' Connect
<%
Dim StrConnInventory
Dim ConnInventory

StrConnInventory = "Provider=SQLOLEDB.1;Data Source=LONDONHEADOFFICE;Initial
Catalog=Inventory;User ID=finance;Password=fa$nAnCe#9*"

Set ConnInventory = Server.CreateObject("ADODB.Connection")

ConnInventory.ConnectionTimeout = 4000
ConnInventory.CommandTimeout = 4000
ConnInventory.Open StrConnInventory

' Query
Dim YourQuery As String = "SELECT Name, Price FROM Product"
 Dim YourCommand As New SqlCommand(YourQuery)
 YourCommand.Connection = ConnInventory
 YourConnection.Open()
 YourCommand.ExecuteNonQuery()
 Response.Write(YourCommand)
 YourCommand.Connection.Close()
%>
' Disconnect
<%
ConnInventory.Close
Set ConnInventory = Nothing
%>
```

SQL Server Profiler to Monitor Client-Server Communications

SQL Server Profiler, a tool in SSMS, has two modes of operations: interactive GUI and silent T-SQL script based operation. The simplest use of the Profiler is to check what queries are sent to the server (SQL Server) from the client and how long does processing take (duration). The client software sending the queries is SSMS. Even though SSMS appears as the "face of SQL Server", it is only a client software.

```
USE pubs;
GO
SELECT * FROM titles;
GO


USE Northwind;
GO
SELECT * FROM Products ORDER BY ProductName;
GO


USE AdventureWorks2012;
GO
SELECT * FROM Sales.SalesOrderHeader WHERE OrderDate='20080201';
GO
```

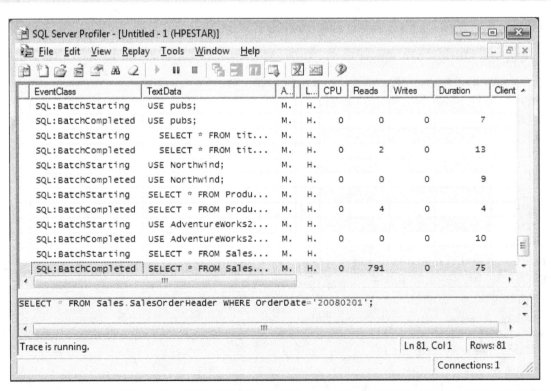

Table - Database Object

A database table holds data in tabular format by rows and columns. The main method of connecting tables is FOREIGN KEY referencing PRIMARY KEY. A set of connected tables makes up the database. Screenshot displays the structure and partial content of Northwind database Products table.

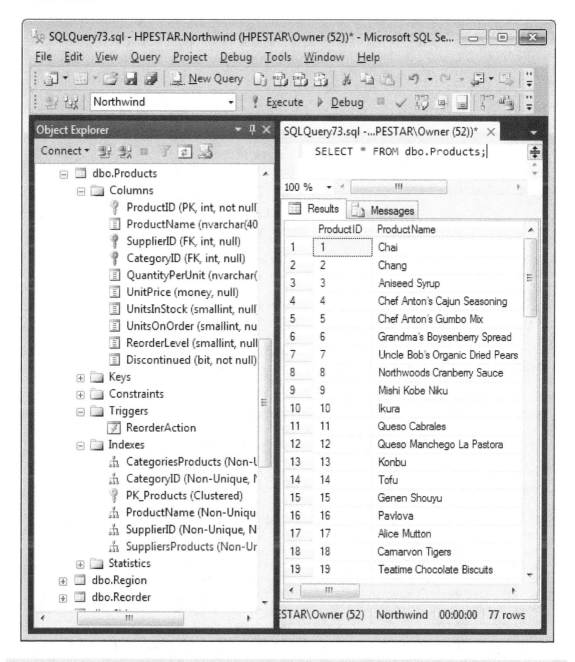

Tables in Production Schema

The listing and data dictionary description of tables in AdventureWorks2012 Production schema.

```
USE AdventureWorks2012;

SELECT  CONCAT('Production.', objname COLLATE DATABASE_DEFAULT) AS TableName,
        value                                           AS [Description]
FROM fn_listextendedproperty (          NULL,
                         'schema', 'Production',
                         'table', default,
                         NULL, NULL)
ORDER BY TableName;
```

TableName	Description
Production.BillOfMaterials	Items required to make bicycles and bicycle subassemblies. It identifies the hierarchical relationship between a parent product and its components.
Production.Culture	Lookup table containing the languages in which some AdventureWorks data is stored.
Production.Document	Product maintenance documents.
Production.Illustration	Bicycle assembly diagrams.
Production.Location	Product inventory and manufacturing locations.
Production.Product	Products sold or used in the manfacturing of sold products.
Production.ProductCategory	High-level product categorization.
Production.ProductCostHistory	Changes in the cost of a product over time.
Production.ProductDescription	Product descriptions in several languages.
Production.ProductDocument	Cross-reference table mapping products to related product documents.
Production.ProductInventory	Product inventory information.
Production.ProductListPriceHistory	Changes in the list price of a product over time.
Production.ProductModel	Product model classification.
Production.ProductModelIllustration	Cross-reference table mapping product models and illustrations.
Production.ProductModelProductDescriptionCulture	Cross-reference table mapping product descriptions and the language the description is written in.
Production.ProductPhoto	Product images.
Production.ProductProductPhoto	Cross-reference table mapping products and product photos.
Production.ProductReview	Customer reviews of products they have purchased.
Production.ProductSubcategory	Product subcategories. See ProductCategory table.
Production.ScrapReason	Manufacturing failure reasons lookup table.
Production.TransactionHistory	Record of each purchase order, sales order, or work order transaction year to date.
Production.TransactionHistoryArchive	Transactions for previous years.
Production.UnitMeasure	Unit of measure lookup table.
Production.WorkOrder	Manufacturing work orders.
Production.WorkOrderRouting	Work order details.

Index - Database Object

An index on a table is a B-tree based structure which speeds up random searches. **Typically PRIMARY KEY (automatic), FOREIGN KEY and WHERE clause columns have indexes.** If the index is constructed on more than one column, it is called **composite index**. If all the columns in a query are in the index, it is called **covering index**. Properties dialog box displays the PRIMARY KEY composite index of the EmployeeDepartmentHistory table.

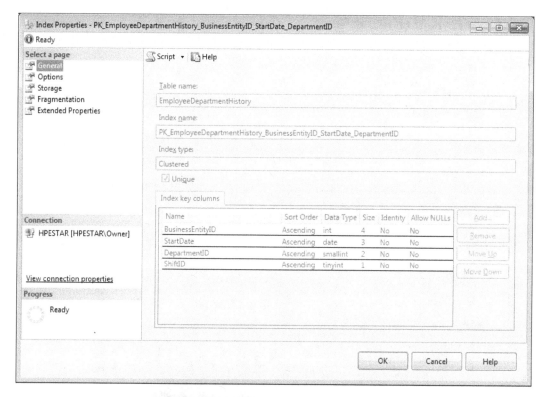

Diagram of EmployeeDepartmentHistory and Related Tables

EmployeeDepartmentHistory is a simple junction table with three FOREIGN KEYs to the Employee, Shift and Department tables respectively.

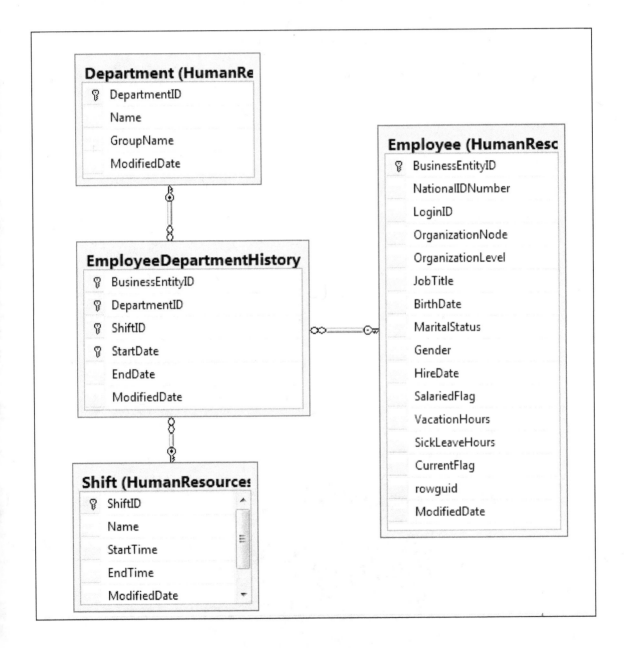

Index Description in Data Dictionary

The indexes listing for Product, SalesOrderHeader & SalesOrderDetail tables.

USE AdventureWorks2012;

```
SELECT   objtype                          AS ObjectType,
         'Sales.SalesOrderHeader'         AS TableName,
         objname                          AS ObjectName,
         value                            AS [Description]
FROM fn_listextendedproperty (NULL, 'schema', 'Sales', 'table', 'SalesOrderHeader', 'index', default)

UNION

SELECT objtype, 'Sales.SalesOrderDetail', objname, value
FROM fn_listextendedproperty (NULL, 'schema', 'Sales', 'table', 'SalesOrderDetail', 'index', default)

UNION

SELECT objtype, 'Production.Product', objname,  value
FROM fn_listextendedproperty (NULL, 'schema', 'Production', 'table', 'Product', 'index', default)
ORDER BY TableName;
GO
```

ObjectType	TableName	ObjectName	Description
INDEX	Production.Product	AK_Product_Name	Unique nonclustered index.
INDEX	Production.Product	AK_Product_ProductNumber	Unique nonclustered index.
INDEX	Production.Product	AK_Product_rowguid	Unique nonclustered index. Used to support replication samples.
INDEX	Production.Product	PK_Product_ProductID	Clustered index created by a primary key constraint.
INDEX	Sales.SalesOrderDetail	AK_SalesOrderDetail_rowguid	Unique nonclustered index. Used to support replication samples.
INDEX	Sales.SalesOrderDetail	IX_SalesOrderDetail_ProductID	Nonclustered index.
INDEX	Sales.SalesOrderDetail	PK_SalesOrderDetail_SalesOrderID_SalesOrderDetailID	Clustered index created by a primary key constraint.
INDEX	Sales.SalesOrderHeader	AK_SalesOrderHeader_rowguid	Unique nonclustered index. Used to support replication samples.
INDEX	Sales.SalesOrderHeader	AK_SalesOrderHeader_SalesOrderNumber	Unique nonclustered index.
INDEX	Sales.SalesOrderHeader	IX_SalesOrderHeader_CustomerID	Nonclustered index.
INDEX	Sales.SalesOrderHeader	IX_SalesOrderHeader_SalesPersonID	Nonclustered index.
INDEX	Sales.SalesOrderHeader	PK_SalesOrderHeader_SalesOrderID	Clustered index created by a primary key constraint.

Constraint - Database Object

The **PRIMARY KEY constraint ensures that each row has a unique ID. The FOREIGN KEY constraint ensures that the FK points to (references) a valid PK. CHECK constraint enforces formulas (check clauses) defined for a column such as OrderQty > 0.** If the formula evaluates to TRUE, the CHECK constraint satisfied, otherwise ERROR condition is generated by the database engine. SSMS screenshot shows a CHECK constraints listing query and results in the Northwind database.

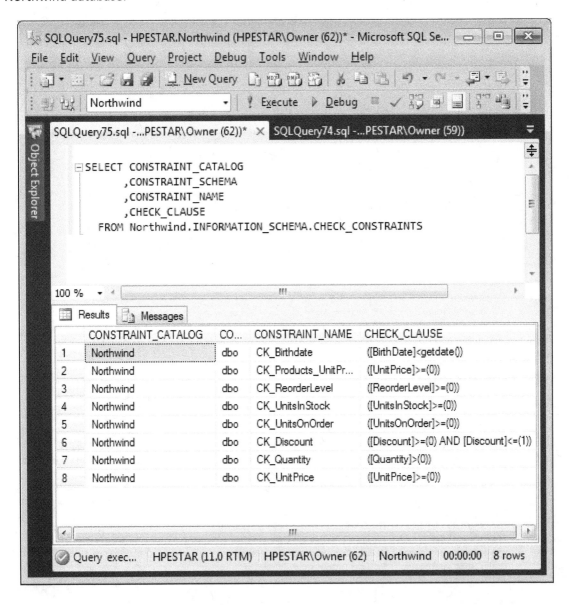

PRIMARY KEY & FOREIGN KEY Constraint Descriptions in Data Dictionary

Query to retrieve constraint descriptions (extended properties) for Product, SalesOrderHeader & SalesOrderDetail tables. Note: *description* not definition.

```
USE AdventureWorks2012;

-- UNION of 3 result sets
SELECT objtype AS ObjectType, 'Sales.SalesOrderHeader' AS TableName,
        objname as ObjectName, value AS [Description]
FROM fn_listextendedproperty (NULL, 'schema', 'Sales', 'table', 'SalesOrderHeader', 'constraint', default)
WHERE left(convert(varchar,value),7)='Foreign' or left(convert(varchar,value),7)='Primary'
UNION
SELECT objtype, 'Sales.SalesOrderDetail', objname,  value
FROM fn_listextendedproperty (NULL, 'schema', 'Sales', 'table', 'SalesOrderDetail', 'constraint', default)
WHERE left(convert(varchar,value),7)='Foreign' or left(convert(varchar,value),7)='Primary'
UNION
SELECT objtype, 'Production.Product', objname,  value
FROM fn_listextendedproperty (NULL, 'schema', 'Production', 'table', 'Product', 'constraint', default)
WHERE left(convert(varchar,value),7)='Foreign' or left(convert(varchar,value),7)='Primary'
ORDER BY TableName, ObjectName DESC;
GO
```

ObjectType	TableName	ObjectName	Description
CONSTRAINT	Production.Product	PK_Product_ProductID	Primary key (clustered) constraint
CONSTRAINT	Production.Product	FK_Product_UnitMeasure_WeightUnitMeasureCode	Foreign key constraint referencing UnitMeasure.UnitMeasureCode.
CONSTRAINT	Production.Product	FK_Product_UnitMeasure_SizeUnitMeasureCode	Foreign key constraint referencing UnitMeasure.UnitMeasureCode.
CONSTRAINT	Production.Product	FK_Product_ProductSubcategory_ProductSubcategoryID	Foreign key constraint referencing ProductSubcategory.ProductSubcategoryID.
CONSTRAINT	Production.Product	FK_Product_ProductModel_ProductModelID	Foreign key constraint referencing ProductModel.ProductModelID.
CONSTRAINT	Sales.SalesOrderDetail	PK_SalesOrderDetail_SalesOrderID_SalesOrderDetailID	Primary key (clustered) constraint
CONSTRAINT	Sales.SalesOrderDetail	FK_SalesOrderDetail_SpecialOfferProduct_SpecialOfferIDProductID	Foreign key constraint referencing SpecialOfferProduct.SpecialOfferIDProductID.
CONSTRAINT	Sales.SalesOrderDetail	FK_SalesOrderDetail_SalesOrderHeader_SalesOrderID	Foreign key constraint referencing SalesOrderHeader.PurchaseOrderID.
CONSTRAINT	Sales.SalesOrderHeader	PK_SalesOrderHeader_SalesOrderID	Primary key (clustered) constraint
CONSTRAINT	Sales.SalesOrderHeader	FK_SalesOrderHeader_ShipMethod_ShipMethodID	Foreign key constraint referencing ShipMethod.ShipMethodID.
CONSTRAINT	Sales.SalesOrderHeader	FK_SalesOrderHeader_SalesTerritory_TerritoryID	Foreign key constraint referencing SalesTerritory.TerritoryID.
CONSTRAINT	Sales.SalesOrderHeader	FK_SalesOrderHeader_SalesPerson_SalesPersonID	Foreign key constraint referencing SalesPerson.SalesPersonID.
CONSTRAINT	Sales.SalesOrderHeader	FK_SalesOrderHeader_Customer_CustomerID	Foreign key constraint referencing Customer.CustomerID.
CONSTRAINT	Sales.SalesOrderHeader	FK_SalesOrderHeader_CurrencyRate_CurrencyRateID	Foreign key constraint referencing CurrencyRate.CurrencyRateID.
CONSTRAINT	Sales.SalesOrderHeader	FK_SalesOrderHeader_CreditCard_CreditCardID	Foreign key constraint referencing CreditCard.CreditCardID.
CONSTRAINT	Sales.SalesOrderHeader	FK_SalesOrderHeader_Address_ShipToAddressID	Foreign key constraint referencing Address.AddressID.
CONSTRAINT	Sales.SalesOrderHeader	FK_SalesOrderHeader_Address_BillToAddressID	Foreign key constraint referencing Address.AddressID.

View - Database Object

A SELECT query, with some restrictions, can be repackaged as view and thus become a server-side object, a coveted status, from "homeless" to "mansion". The creation of view is very simple, basically a name assignment is required as shown in the following demonstration. As soon as the CREATE VIEW statement is executed successfully the query, unknown to the SQL Server so far, becomes an "official" SQL Server database object, stored in the database. A view, a virtual table, can be used just like a table in SELECT queries. A note about the query: **the column aliases FirstAuthor and SecondAuthor cannot be used in the WHERE clause, only in the ORDER BY clause if present.**

SELECT results from views require ORDER BY if sorting is desired. There is no way around it.

```
USE pubs;
GO
```

```
CREATE VIEW vAuthorsInSameCity
AS
SELECT          FirstAuthor        = CONCAT(au1.au_fname,' ', au1.au_lname),
                SecondAuthor       = CONCAT(au2.au_fname,' ', au2.au_lname),
                FirstCity          = au1.city,
                SecondCity         = au2.city
FROM    authors au1
     INNER JOIN authors au2
      ON au1.city = au2.city
WHERE   CONCAT(au1.au_fname,' ', au1.au_lname) < CONCAT(au2.au_fname,' ', au2.au_lname)
GO
```

```
SELECT * FROM vAuthorsInSameCity
ORDER BY FirstAuthor, SecondAuthor
GO
-- (13 row(s) affected) - Partial results.
```

FirstAuthor	SecondAuthor	FirstCity	SecondCity
Abraham Bennet	Cheryl Carson	Berkeley	Berkeley
Albert Ringer	Anne Ringer	Salt Lake City	Salt Lake City
Ann Dull	Sheryl Hunter	Palo Alto	Palo Alto
Dean Straight	Dirk Stringer	Oakland	Oakland
Dean Straight	Livia Karsen	Oakland	Oakland
Dean Straight	Marjorie Green	Oakland	Oakland
Dean Straight	Stearns MacFeather	Oakland	Oakland
Dirk Stringer	Livia Karsen	Oakland	Oakland

View Descriptions in Data Dictionary

Query to list view descriptions in selected schemas.

```
USE AdventureWorks2012;
SELECT   CONCAT('Sales.', objname COLLATE DATABASE_DEFAULT)               AS ViewName,
         value                                                           AS [Description]
FROM fn_listextendedproperty (NULL, 'schema', 'Sales', 'view', default, NULL, NULL)
UNION
SELECT   CONCAT('Production.', objname COLLATE DATABASE_DEFAULT),  value
FROM fn_listextendedproperty (NULL, 'schema', 'Production', 'view', default, NULL, NULL)
UNION
SELECT   CONCAT('HumanResources.', objname COLLATE DATABASE_DEFAULT),  value
FROM fn_listextendedproperty (NULL, 'schema', 'HumanResources', 'view', default, NULL, NULL)
UNION
SELECT   CONCAT('Person.', objname COLLATE DATABASE_DEFAULT),   value
FROM fn_listextendedproperty (NULL, 'schema', 'Person', 'view', default, NULL, NULL)
ORDER BY ViewName;  -- (18 row(s) affected) - Partial results.
```

ViewName	Description
HumanResources.vEmployee	Employee names and addresses.
HumanResources.vEmployeeDepartment	Returns employee name, title, and current department.
HumanResources.vEmployeeDepartmentHistory	Returns employee name and current and previous departments.
HumanResources.vJobCandidate	Job candidate names and resumes.

CREATE Indexed View for Business Critical Queries

An indexed view is stored like a table unlike a standard view which is a virtual table with a query that is evaluated upon view invocation. Performance is the main benefit of an indexed view, but it comes at a cost: it slows down INSERTs and other operations in the underlying tables.

```
IF OBJECT_ID ('Sales.vSalesByDateByProduct', 'V') IS NOT NULL DROP VIEW Sales.vSalesByDateByProduct ;
GO
CREATE VIEW Sales.vSalesByDateByProduct WITH SCHEMABINDING  AS
   SELECT OrderDate, ProductNumber, SUM(LineTotal) AS TotalSales, COUNT_BIG(*) AS Items
   FROM Sales.SalesOrderDetail AS sod INNER JOIN Sales.SalesOrderHeader AS soh
     ON soh.SalesOrderID = sod.SalesOrderID   INNER JOIN Production.Product p ON sod.ProductID=p.ProductID
       GROUP BY OrderDate, ProductNumber;
GO
CREATE UNIQUE CLUSTERED INDEX idxVSalesCI ON Sales.vSalesByDateByProduct (OrderDate, ProductNumber);
GO
SELECT * FROM Sales.vSalesByDateByProduct ORDER BY OrderDate, ProductNumber;
GO  -- (26878 row(s) affected) - Partial results.
```

OrderDate	ProductNumber	TotalSales	Items
2005-07-01 00:00:00.000	BK-M82B-38	44549.868000	7
2005-07-01 00:00:00.000	BK-M82B-42	32399.904000	8
2005-07-01 00:00:00.000	BK-M82B-44	46574.862000	7

Graphical View Designer

A view can be designed graphically or an existing view altered by using the Design option on the View drop-down menu in SSMS Object Explorer. First we create a view, then enter the graphical view designer to take a look.

```
USE [Northwind];
GO
CREATE VIEW [dbo].[ListOfProducts] AS
SELECT Categories.CategoryName as Category, ProductName, CompanyName AS Supplier
FROM Categories          INNER JOIN Products  ON Categories.CategoryID = Products.CategoryID
                         INNER JOIN Suppliers  ON Suppliers.SupplierID = Products.SupplierID
WHERE (((Products.Discontinued)=0));
GO
```

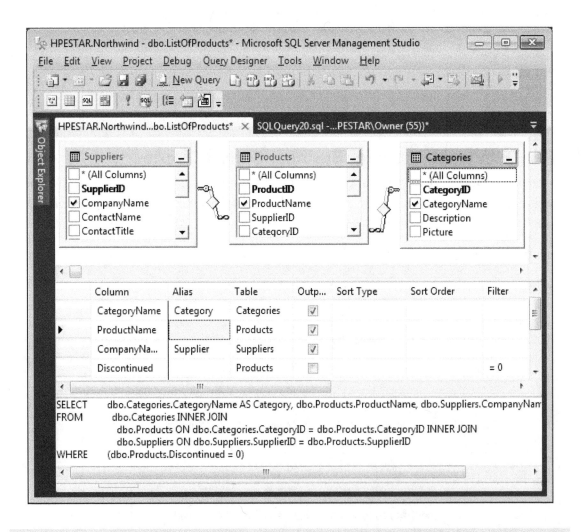

Stored Procedure: Server-Side Program

Stored procedures are T-SQL programs with optional input/output parameters. They vary from very simply to extremely complex. Following is the query which we will transform into a stored procedure, a server-side database object. Typical stored procedure returns table-like results to the client application software just like a SELECT query. That is though not a requirement.

```
USE AdventureWorks2012;
GO
SELECT      P.Name                  AS Product,
            L.Name                  AS [Inventory Location],
            SUM(PI.Quantity)        AS [Qty Available]
FROM Production.Product AS P
   INNER JOIN Production.ProductInventory AS PI
            ON P.ProductID = PI.ProductID
   INNER JOIN Production.Location AS L
            ON PI.LocationID = L.LocationID
   INNER JOIN Production.ProductSubcategory SC
            ON P.ProductSubcategoryID = SC.ProductSubcategoryID
WHERE SC.Name = 'Touring Bikes'
GROUP BY P.Name, L.Name
ORDER BY P.Name;
GO
-- (44 row(s) affected) - Partial results.
```

Product	Inventory Location	Qty Available
Touring-1000 Blue, 46	Final Assembly	86
Touring-1000 Blue, 46	Finished Goods Storage	99
Touring-1000 Blue, 50	Final Assembly	81
Touring-1000 Blue, 50	Finished Goods Storage	67
Touring-1000 Blue, 54	Final Assembly	60
Touring-1000 Blue, 54	Finished Goods Storage	73
Touring-1000 Blue, 60	Final Assembly	99
Touring-1000 Blue, 60	Finished Goods Storage	30
Touring-1000 Yellow, 46	Final Assembly	83
Touring-1000 Yellow, 46	Finished Goods Storage	65
Touring-1000 Yellow, 50	Final Assembly	62
Touring-1000 Yellow, 50	Finished Goods Storage	75
Touring-1000 Yellow, 54	Final Assembly	40
Touring-1000 Yellow, 54	Finished Goods Storage	35
Touring-1000 Yellow, 60	Final Assembly	100

Stored Procedure with Input Parameters

To make the stored procedure even more useful, we replace the literal 'Touring Bikes' with an input parameter.

```
CREATE PROC uspProductInventoryLocation @Subcategory nvarchar(50)
AS
BEGIN
SELECT          P.Name                          AS Product,
                L.Name                          AS [Inventory Location],
                SUM(PI.Quantity)                AS [Qty Available]
FROM Production.Product AS P
    INNER JOIN Production.ProductInventory AS PI
            ON P.ProductID = PI.ProductID
    INNER JOIN Production.Location AS L
            ON PI.LocationID = L.LocationID
    INNER JOIN Production.ProductSubcategory SC
            ON P.ProductSubcategoryID = SC.ProductSubcategoryID
WHERE SC.Name = @Subcategory
GROUP BY P.Name, L.Name
ORDER BY P.Name;
END
GO
```

```
-- Execute stored procedure with parameter
EXEC uspProductInventoryLocation 'Touring Bikes';
-- (44 row(s) affected)

EXEC uspProductInventoryLocation 'Mountain Bikes';        -- (64 row(s) affected) - Partial results.
```

Product	Inventory Location	Qty Available
Mountain-100 Black, 38	Final Assembly	56
Mountain-100 Black, 38	Finished Goods Storage	99
Mountain-100 Black, 42	Final Assembly	116
Mountain-100 Black, 42	Finished Goods Storage	78
Mountain-100 Black, 44	Final Assembly	100
Mountain-100 Black, 44	Finished Goods Storage	49
Mountain-100 Black, 48	Final Assembly	65
Mountain-100 Black, 48	Finished Goods Storage	88
Mountain-100 Silver, 38	Final Assembly	100
Mountain-100 Silver, 38	Finished Goods Storage	49
Mountain-100 Silver, 42	Final Assembly	65
Mountain-100 Silver, 42	Finished Goods Storage	88
Mountain-100 Silver, 44	Final Assembly	75
Mountain-100 Silver, 44	Finished Goods Storage	83
Mountain-100 Silver, 48	Final Assembly	102

Stored Procedure Descriptions in Data Dictionary

Query to list stored procedure descriptions in selected schemas.

```
USE AdventureWorks2012;

SELECT
        CONCAT('dbo.', objname COLLATE DATABASE_DEFAULT)              AS SprocName,
        value                                                         AS [Description]
FROM fn_listextendedproperty (NULL, 'schema', 'dbo', 'procedure', default, NULL, NULL)
WHERE LEN(convert(nvarchar(max),value)) > 4
UNION
SELECT
        CONCAT('dbo.', objname COLLATE DATABASE_DEFAULT),
        value
FROM fn_listextendedproperty (NULL, 'schema', 'HumanResources', 'procedure', default, NULL, NULL)
ORDER BY SprocName;
```

SprocName	Description
dbo.uspGetBillOfMaterials	Stored procedure using a recursive query to return a multi-level bill of material for the specified ProductID.
dbo.uspGetEmployeeManagers	Stored procedure using a recursive query to return the direct and indirect managers of the specified employee.
dbo.uspGetManagerEmployees	Stored procedure using a recursive query to return the direct and indirect employees of the specified manager.
dbo.uspGetWhereUsedProductID	Stored procedure using a recursive query to return all components or assemblies that directly or indirectly use the specified ProductID.
dbo.uspLogError	Logs error information in the ErrorLog table about the error that caused execution to jump to the CATCH block of a TRY...CATCH construct. Should be executed from within the scope of a CATCH block otherwise it will return without inserting error information.
dbo.uspPrintError	Prints error information about the error that caused execution to jump to the CATCH block of a TRY...CATCH construct. Should be executed from within the scope of a CATCH block otherwise it will return without printing any error information.
dbo.uspUpdateEmployeeHireInfo	Updates the Employee table and inserts a new row in the EmployeePayHistory table with the values specified in the input parameters.
dbo.uspUpdateEmployeeLogin	Updates the Employee table with the values specified in the input parameters for the given BusinessEntityID.
dbo.uspUpdateEmployeePersonalInfo	Updates the Employee table with the values specified in the input parameters for the given EmployeeID.

Trigger: Event Fired Server-Side Program

Trigger is like a stored procedure with four differences:

> ➢ Trigger is fired by an event such as table insert not by a call like a stored procedure.
> ➢ Trigger has the deleted (old row copy) and inserted (new row copy) tables available.
> ➢ Trigger does not have input/output parameter option.
> ➢ Trigger never returns table-like results.

Trigger to synchronize data in StateTaxFreeBondArchive table if data is inserted or updated in the StateTaxFreeBond table.

```
CREATE TRIGGER trgFillInMissingCouponRate

ON [dbo].StateTaxFreeBond

FOR INSERT,UPDATE

AS

BEGIN

    UPDATE StateTaxFreeBondArchive

        SET CouponRate = isnull(i.CouponRate,m.CouponRate)

    FROM StateTaxFreeBondArchive m

        INNER JOIN inserted i

            ON m.MBCID = i.MBCID

END
GO
```

Once a trigger is compiled, it is active and working silently in the background whenever insert, update or delete event fires it up.

It is important to note that there is a downside to the trigger "stealth" operation: if a trigger is dropped , it may not be noticed as part of the day-to-day operation. This behaviour is unlike stored procedure whereby if dropped, it causes error in the calling application software which can be noticed by users.

Function: Read-Only Server-Side Program

A user-defined function is also a program like a stored procedure, however, **no database change can be performed within a function, read only**. The database can be changed both in a trigger and a stored procedure. The following T-SQL script demonstrates the creation and use of a table-valued user-defined function. The other function type is scalar-valued, returns only a single value.

```
CREATE FUNCTION dbo.ufnSplitCommaDelimitedIntegerString (@NumberList nvarchar(max))
RETURNS @SplitList TABLE ( Element INT )
AS
 BEGIN
   DECLARE @Pointer   int,
       @Element nvarchar(32)
   SET @NumberList = LTRIM(RTRIM(@NumberList))
   IF ( RIGHT(@NumberList, 1) != ',' )
    SET @NumberList=@NumberList + ','
   SET @Pointer = CHARINDEX(',', @NumberList, 1)
   IF REPLACE(@NumberList, ',', '') <> ''
    BEGIN
      WHILE ( @Pointer > 0 )
      BEGIN
        SET @Element = LTRIM(RTRIM(LEFT(@NumberList, @Pointer - 1)))
        IF ( @Element <> '' )
         INSERT INTO @SplitList
         VALUES    (CONVERT(int, @Element))
        SET @NumberList = RIGHT(@NumberList,
              LEN(@NumberList) - @Pointer  )
        SET @Pointer = CHARINDEX(',', @NumberList, 1)
      END
    END
   RETURN
 END;
GO
SELECT * FROM  dbo.ufnSplitCommaDelimitedIntegerString ('1, 2, 4, 8, 16, 32, 64, 128, 256');
```

Element
1
2
4
8
16
32
64
128
256

User-Defined Function Descriptions in Data Dictionary

Query to list user-defined function descriptions in the default "dbo" schema. "dbo" stands for database owner, a database role.

```
USE AdventureWorks2012;
GO

SELECT
        CONCAT('dbo.', objname COLLATE DATABASE_DEFAULT)              AS UDFName,
        value                                                        AS [Description]
FROM fn_listextendedproperty (NULL, 'schema', 'dbo', 'function', default, NULL, NULL)
WHERE LEN(convert(nvarchar(max),value)) > 4
ORDER BY UDFName;
GO
```

UDFName	Description
dbo.ufnGetAccountingEndDate	Scalar function used in the uSalesOrderHeader trigger to set the starting account date.
dbo.ufnGetAccountingStartDate	Scalar function used in the uSalesOrderHeader trigger to set the ending account date.
dbo.ufnGetContactInformation	Table value function returning the first name, last name, job title and contact type for a given contact.
dbo.ufnGetDocumentStatusText	Scalar function returning the text representation of the Status column in the Document table.
dbo.ufnGetProductDealerPrice	Scalar function returning the dealer price for a given product on a particular order date.
dbo.ufnGetProductListPrice	Scalar function returning the list price for a given product on a particular order date.
dbo.ufnGetProductStandardCost	Scalar function returning the standard cost for a given product on a particular order date.
dbo.ufnGetPurchaseOrderStatusText	Scalar function returning the text representation of the Status column in the PurchaseOrderHeader table.
dbo.ufnGetSalesOrderStatusText	Scalar function returning the text representation of the Status column in the SalesOrderHeader table.
dbo.ufnGetStock	Scalar function returning the quantity of inventory in LocationID 6 (Miscellaneous Storage)for a specified ProductID.
dbo.ufnLeadingZeros	Scalar function used by the Sales.Customer table to help set the account number

Sequence - Database Object

The INT IDENTITY(1,1) function commonly used as **SURROGATE PRIMARY KEY** is limited to the host table. Sequence object, new in SQL Server 2012, can be shared by tables and programs. T-SQL script to demonstrate how two tables can share an integer sequence.

```
USE AdventureWorks2012;
GO
CREATE SEQUENCE CustomerSequence as INT
START WITH 1  INCREMENT BY 1;
GO
CREATE TABLE LONDONCustomer
(
        CustomerID      INT PRIMARY KEY,
        Name            NVARCHAR(64) UNIQUE,
        ModifiedDate    DATE default (CURRENT_TIMESTAMP)    );
GO
CREATE TABLE NYCCustomer
(
        CustomerID      INT PRIMARY KEY,
        Name            NVARCHAR(64) UNIQUE,
        ModifiedDate    DATE default (CURRENT_TIMESTAMP)    );
GO
INSERT NYCCustomer (CustomerID, Name)
VALUES
        (NEXT VALUE FOR CustomerSequence, 'Richard Blackstone'),
        (NEXT VALUE FOR CustomerSequence, 'Anna Smithfield');
GO
SELECT * FROM NYCCustomer;
```

CustomerID	Name	ModifiedDate
1	Richard Blackstone	2016-07-18
2	Anna Smithfield	2016-07-18

```
INSERT LONDONCustomer (CustomerID, Name)
VALUES
        (NEXT VALUE FOR CustomerSequence, 'Kevin Lionheart'),
        (NEXT VALUE FOR CustomerSequence, 'Linda Wakefield');
GO

SELECT * FROM LONDONCustomer;
```

CustomerID	Name	ModifiedDate
3	Kevin Lionheart	2016-07-18
4	Linda Wakefield	2016-07-18

ROW_NUMBER() and Ranking Functions

Ranking functions (window functions), introduced with SQL Server 2005, provide sequencing and ranking items in a partition or all. ROW_NUMBER() (sequence) function is the most used.

```
SELECT  CustomerID,
        CONVERT(date, OrderDate)                     AS OrderDate,
        RANK() OVER (    PARTITION BY CustomerID
                         ORDER BY OrderDate DESC)    AS RankNo
FROM   AdventureWorks2012.Sales.SalesOrderHeader
ORDER  BY CustomerID,  RankNo;
GO
-- (31465 row(s) affected) - Partial results.
```

CustomerID	OrderDate	RankNo
11014	2007-11-01	1
11014	2007-09-24	2
11015	2007-07-22	1
11016	2007-08-13	1
11017	2008-04-16	1
11017	2007-07-05	2
11017	2005-07-15	3
11018	2008-04-26	1
11018	2007-07-20	2
11018	2005-07-20	3
11019	2008-07-15	1
11019	2008-07-14	2
11019	2008-06-12	3
11019	2008-06-02	4
11019	2008-06-01	5
11019	2008-04-28	6
11019	2008-04-19	7
11019	2008-03-22	8
11019	2008-03-11	9
11019	2008-02-23	10
11019	2008-01-24	11
11019	2007-11-26	12
11019	2007-11-09	13
11019	2007-10-30	14
11019	2007-09-14	15
11019	2007-09-05	16
11019	2007-08-16	17
11020	2007-07-02	1

Partition data by CustomerID and rank it OrderDate DESC (most recent orders first).

```
SELECT *
FROM   (SELECT CustomerID,
           CONVERT(date, OrderDate)        AS OrderDate,
           RANK()  OVER (
               PARTITION BY CustomerID
               ORDER BY OrderDate DESC)      AS RankNo
       FROM   AdventureWorks2012.Sales.SalesOrderHeader)  x -- derived table
WHERE  RankNo  BETWEEN 1 AND 4
ORDER  BY CustomerID;
GO
-- (29383 row(s) affected)  - Partial results.
```

CustomerID	OrderDate	RankNo
11675	2007-08-13	1
11675	2006-04-27	2
11676	2008-06-11	1
11676	2008-02-21	2
11677	2008-06-02	1
11677	2008-03-24	2
11677	2008-03-17	3
11677	2008-03-07	4
11678	2007-08-09	1
11678	2006-04-12	2
11679	2008-06-01	1
11679	2008-04-15	2
11680	2008-07-22	1
11680	2008-03-04	2
11681	2008-05-28	1
11681	2007-09-08	2
11682	2008-06-11	1
11682	2008-03-08	2
11683	2007-08-11	1
11683	2006-04-07	2
11684	2008-06-14	1
11684	2008-01-02	2
11685	2008-06-15	1
11685	2007-09-12	2
11686	2007-10-26	1
11686	2007-09-09	2
11687	2007-12-23	1
11687	2007-10-14	2
11688	2007-08-18	1
11688	2006-04-04	2
11689	2008-03-05	1
11689	2008-02-27	2

Query to compare RANK, DENSE_RANK and NTILE.

```
USE AdventureWorks;

SELECT c.AccountNumber                       AS CustAccount,
    FLOOR(h.SubTotal / 1000)                 AS [SubTotal (Thousands $)],
    ROW_NUMBER() OVER(
        ORDER BY FLOOR(h.SubTotal /1000) DESC)  AS RowNumber,
    RANK() OVER(
        ORDER BY FLOOR(h.SubTotal /1000) DESC)  AS Rank,
    DENSE_RANK() OVER(
        ORDER BY FLOOR(h.SubTotal /1000) DESC)  AS DenseRank,
    NTILE(5) OVER(
        ORDER BY FLOOR(h.SubTotal /1000) DESC)  AS NTile
FROM  Sales.Customer c
    INNER JOIN Sales.SalesOrderHeader h
        ON c.CustomerID = h.CustomerID
    INNER JOIN Sales.SalesTerritory t
        ON h.TerritoryID = t.TerritoryID
WHERE  t.Name = 'Germany'
        AND OrderDate >= '20040101' AND OrderDate < DATEADD(yy, 1, '20040101' )
        AND SubTotal >= 4000.0
ORDER  BY RowNumber;
```

CustAccount	SubTotal (Thousands $)	RowNumber	Rank	DenseRank	NTile
AW00000230	100.00	1	1	1	1
AW00000230	88.00	2	2	2	1
AW00000302	77.00	3	3	3	1
AW00000320	68.00	4	4	4	1
AW00000536	68.00	5	4	4	1
AW00000536	64.00	6	6	5	1
AW00000266	58.00	7	7	6	1
AW00000302	44.00	8	8	7	2
AW00000687	43.00	9	9	8	2
AW00000482	36.00	10	10	9	2
AW00000176	36.00	11	10	9	2
AW00000464	35.00	12	12	10	2
AW00000320	35.00	13	12	10	2
AW00000176	34.00	14	14	11	2
AW00000464	34.00	15	14	11	3

Dynamic SQL To Soar Beyond the Limits of Static SQL

Static (regular) T-SQL syntax does not accept variables at all places in a query. With dynamic SQL we can overcome the limitation. Dynamic SQL script uses table list metadata from the INFORMATION_SCHEMA.TABLES system view to build a COUNT() query for all tables. COUNT(*) returns 4 bytes integer. For large values COUNT_BIG() returns an 8 bytes integer.

```
DECLARE @SQL nvarchar(max) = '', @Schema sysname, @Table sysname;
SELECT TOP 20 @SQL = CONCAT(@SQL , 'SELECT ''',QUOTENAME(TABLE_SCHEMA),'.',
        QUOTENAME(TABLE_NAME),'''',
        '= COUNT(*) FROM ', QUOTENAME(TABLE_SCHEMA),'.',QUOTENAME(TABLE_NAME) , ';',
CHAR(10))
FROM AdventureWorks2012.INFORMATION_SCHEMA.TABLES
WHERE TABLE_TYPE='BASE TABLE';
PRINT @SQL;          -- Test & debug - Partial results.
```

```
SELECT '[Production].[ScrapReason]'= COUNT(*) FROM [Production].[ScrapReason];
SELECT '[HumanResources].[Shift]'= COUNT(*) FROM [HumanResources].[Shift];
SELECT '[Production].[ProductCategory]'= COUNT(*) FROM [Production].[ProductCategory];
SELECT '[Purchasing].[ShipMethod]'= COUNT(*) FROM [Purchasing].[ShipMethod];
SELECT '[Production].[ProductCostHistory]'= COUNT(*) FROM [Production].[ProductCostHistory];
SELECT '[Production].[ProductDescription]'= COUNT(*) FROM [Production].[ProductDescription];
SELECT '[Sales].[ShoppingCartItem]'= COUNT(*) FROM [Sales].[ShoppingCartItem];
SELECT '[Production].[ProductDocument]'= COUNT(*) FROM [Production].[ProductDocument];
SELECT '[dbo].[DatabaseLog]'= COUNT(*) FROM [dbo].[DatabaseLog];
SELECT '[Production].[ProductInventory]'= COUNT(*) FROM [Production].[ProductInventory];
```

```
EXEC sp_executesql @SQL   -- Dynamic SQL query execution
-- Partial results.
```

[Production].[ScrapReason]
16

[HumanResources].[Shift]
3

[Production].[ProductCategory]
4

[Purchasing].[ShipMethod]
5

Built-in System Functions

SQL Server T-SQL language has a large collection of system functions such as date & time, string and math function. The nested REPLACE string function can be used to remove unwanted characters from a string.

```
DECLARE @text nvarchar(128) = '#1245! $99^@';
SELECT REPLACE(REPLACE(REPLACE(REPLACE(REPLACE(REPLACE(REPLACE(REPLACE(REPLACE(@text,
       '!',''),'@',''),'#',''),'$',''),'%',''),'^',''),'&',''),'*',''),' ',''); 	 -- 124599
```

All the system function are listed in SSMS Object Explorer under the Programmability tab.

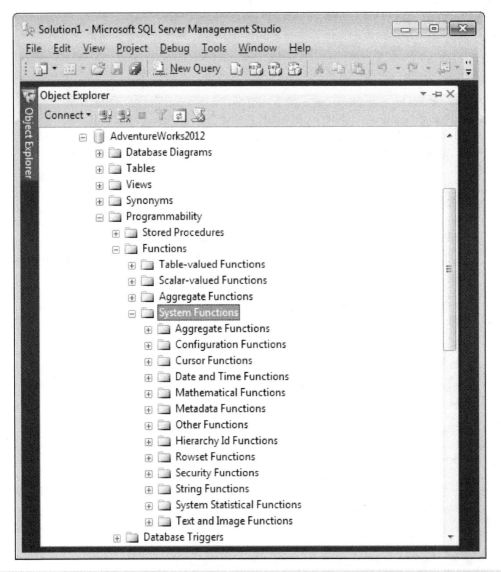

Local Variables & Table Variables in T-SQL

Local variables with different data types have scope of a batch or a stored procedure/trigger/function. Note that a "GO" in T-SQL script indicates end of batch, therefore the end of scope for local variables. Table variable is a virtual table with similar scope to local variable. Script to demonstrate local and table variables.

```
DECLARE @i INT;  SET @i = 999;

SELECT @i + @i;
-- 1998

SELECT @i = 555;  -- assignment
SELECT @i + @i;
GO
-- 1110
```

```
DECLARE @i INT = 999;              -- new in SQL Server 2008
SET @i += 1;                       -- new in SQL Server 2008

SELECT @i;
GO
-- 1000
```

```
DECLARE @OrderShipperJunction TABLE                    -- Table variable
  (
    ShipperID              SMALLINT IDENTITY ( 1, 1 ) PRIMARY KEY,
    ShipperName            NVARCHAR(64),
    PurchaseOrderID        INT,
    ShipDate               DATE DEFAULT (CURRENT_TIMESTAMP),
    FreightCost            SMALLMONEY
  );
INSERT @OrderShipperJunction
    (ShipperName,
     PurchaseOrderID,
     FreightCost)
VALUES('Custom Motor Bike Distributor',     11111,     177.34)

SELECT * FROM  @OrderShipperJunction
GO
```

ShipperID	ShipperName	PurchaseOrderID	ShipDate	FreightCost
1	Custom Motor Bike Distributor	11111	2016-07-18	177.34

CHAPTER 5: Basic Concepts of Client-Server Computing

Metadata Visibility Through System Views

The system views provide SQL Server and database metadata which can be used just for viewing in SSMS Object Explorer or programmatically in T-SQL scripts. The system views are based on system tables which are no longer accessible since SQL Server 2005. The system view sys.objects contains all the basic info on each and every user objects in the database with the exception of indexes. Query to retrieve partial data form sys.objects system view.

```
select
    s.name                  as [Schema],
    o.name                  as [Name],
    o.type_desc             as [Type],
    o.create_date           as CreateDate
from    sys.objects o
        inner join sys.schemas s
            on s.schema_id = o.schema_id
where is_ms_shipped = 0
order by [Type], [Schema], [Name]
-- (722 row(s) affected)  -  Partial results.
```

Schema	Name	Type	CreateDate
HumanResources	Department	USER_TABLE	2012-03-14 13:14:19.267
HumanResources	Employee	USER_TABLE	2012-03-14 13:14:19.303
HumanResources	EmployeeDepartmentHistory	USER_TABLE	2012-03-14 13:14:19.313
HumanResources	EmployeePayHistory	USER_TABLE	2012-03-14 13:14:19.320
HumanResources	JobCandidate	USER_TABLE	2012-03-14 13:14:19.337
HumanResources	Shift	USER_TABLE	2012-03-14 13:14:19.593
Person	Address	USER_TABLE	2012-03-14 13:14:19.140
Person	AddressType	USER_TABLE	2012-03-14 13:14:19.150
Person	BusinessEntity	USER_TABLE	2012-03-14 13:14:19.183
Person	BusinessEntityAddress	USER_TABLE	2012-03-14 13:14:19.190
Person	BusinessEntityContact	USER_TABLE	2012-03-14 13:14:19.197
Person	ContactType	USER_TABLE	2012-03-14 13:14:19.207
Person	CountryRegion	USER_TABLE	2012-03-14 13:14:19.220
Person	EmailAddress	USER_TABLE	2012-03-14 13:14:19.290
Person	Password	USER_TABLE	2012-03-14 13:14:19.350
Person	Person	USER_TABLE	2012-03-14 13:14:19.357
Person	PersonPhone	USER_TABLE	2012-03-14 13:14:19.370
Person	PhoneNumberType	USER_TABLE	2012-03-14 13:14:19.377
Person	StateProvince	USER_TABLE	2012-03-14 13:14:19.623
Production	BillOfMaterials	USER_TABLE	2012-03-14 13:14:19.170
Production	Culture	USER_TABLE	2012-03-14 13:14:19.237

Constructing T-SQL Identifiers

Identifiers are the names given to SQL Server & database objects such as linked servers, tables, views or stored procedures.

Very simple rule: **do not include any special character in an identifier other than single underscore (_). Double underscore in an identifier inevitably leads to confusion, loss of database developer productivity.**

Creating good identifiers helps with productivity in database development, administration and maintenance. Using names AccountsPayable1 and AccountsPayable2 as variations for AccountsPayable is not good because the 1,2 suffixes are meaningless. On the other hand AccountsPayableLondon & AccountsPayableNYC are good, meaningful names. The list of identifiers can be enumerated from AdventureWorks2012.sys.objects.

SELECT name FROM AdventureWorks2012.sys.objects ORDER BY name; -- (820 row(s) affected)

Selected results with comments.

Identifier(name)	Style Comment
Account	single word
AddressType	double words CamelCase style
BillOfMaterials	CamelCase (also known as Pascal case)
BusinessEntityContact	CamelCase
CK__ImageStore__67152DD3	double underscore separator, CK prefix for CHECK CONSTRAINT
CK_Document_Status	single underscore separator
CK_EmployeeDepartmentHistory_EndDate	mixed - CamelCase and underscore
DF__ImageStor__is_sy__75634D2A	database engine (system) generated name
sp_creatediagram	old-fashioned, sp prefix for system procedure
syscscolsegments	old-fashioned with abbreviations
ufnGetProductDealerPrice	Hungarian naming, ufn stands for user(-defined) function
vSalesPersonSalesByFiscalYears	Hungarian naming, v prefix is for view

CHAPTER 5: Basic Concepts of Client-Server Computing

The Use of [] - Square Brackets in Identifiers

Each identifier can be enclosed in square brackets, but not required. If the identifier is the same as a T-SQL reserved keyword, then it is required. Square brackets are also required when the identifier includes a special character such as space. Double quotes can be used also but that becomes very confusing when single quotes are present. The use of brackets is demonstrated in the following T-SQL script.

```
USE Northwind;

-- Syntax error without brackets since table name has space
SELECT * FROM Order Details;
/* ERROR
Msg 156, Level 15, State 1, Line 3
Incorrect syntax near the keyword 'Order'.
*/

-- Valid statement with brackets around table name
SELECT * FROM [Order Details];
-- (2155 row(s) affected)

-- Create and populate table with SELECT INTO
-- Error since ORDER is a reserved keyword
SELECT * INTO Order FROM Orders;
/* ERROR
Msg 156, Level 15, State 1, Line 1
Incorrect syntax near the keyword 'Order'.
*/

-- With brackets, query is valid
SELECT * INTO [Order] FROM Orders;
-- (830 row(s) affected)
```

When a database object is scripted out in SSMS Object Explore, the identifiers are surrounded with square brackets even when not needed as shown in the following demonstration.

```
CREATE TABLE [dbo].[Order Details](
        [OrderID] [int] NOT NULL,
        [ProductID] [int] NOT NULL,
        [UnitPrice] [money] NOT NULL,
        [Quantity] [smallint] NOT NULL,
        [Discount] [real] NOT NULL,
 CONSTRAINT [PK_Order_Details] PRIMARY KEY CLUSTERED
(       [OrderID] ASC,
        [ProductID] ASC));
```

CHAPTER 6: New Programming Features in SS 2012

PARSE() Function

T-SQL script to demonstrate the use of the PARSE() function. The culture parameter provides support for languages & countries beyond the CONVERT() function available in past versions.

```
-- PARSE() returns the result of expression translated to requested data type - String to datetime
SELECT PARSE('SAT, 13 December 2014' AS datetime USING 'en-US') AS [Date&Time];
-- 2014-12-13 00:00:00.000

SELECT PARSE('Saturday, 13 December 2014' AS datetime USING 'en-US') AS [Date&Time];
-- 2014-12-13 00:00:00.000

SELECT PARSE('Saturday 13 December 2014' AS datetime USING 'en-US') AS [Date&Time];
-- 2014-12-13 00:00:00.000

SELECT PARSE('Saturday December 13 2014' AS datetime USING 'en-US') AS [Date&Time];
-- 2014-12-13 00:00:00.000

SELECT PARSE('Saturday December 13, 2014' AS datetime USING 'en-US') AS [Date&Time];
-- 2014-12-13 00:00:00.000

-- Inconsistent string date
SELECT PARSE('Monday, 13 December 2014' AS datetime USING 'en-US') AS [Date&Time];
/*Msg 9819, Level 16, State 1, Line 1
Error converting string value 'Monday, 13 December 2014' into data type datetime using culture 'en-US'*/

-- German culture
SELECT PARSE('Samstag December 13, 2014' AS datetime USING 'DE') AS [Date&Time];
-- 2014-12-13 00:00:00.000

-- Spanish
SELECT PARSE('Sábado December 13, 2014' AS datetime USING 'ES') AS [Date&Time];
-- 2014-12-13 00:00:00.000

-- Hungarian
SELECT PARSE('Szombat December 13, 2014' AS datetime USING 'HU') AS [Date&Time];
-- 2014-12-13 00:00:00.000

SELECT PARSE('Cumartesi December 13, 2014' AS datetime USING 'TR') AS [Date&Time];  -- Turkish
```

PARSE() Function Usage for Currency Conversion

```
-- German culture - Euro currency conversion
SELECT PARSE('€9999,95' AS money USING 'DE') AS Currency;
-- 9999.95


SELECT PARSE('€9999,95' AS money USING 'de-DE') AS Currency;
-- 9999.95


-- Italian culture - Euro currency conversion
SELECT PARSE('€9999,95' AS money USING 'IT') AS Currency;
-- 9999.95

-- Netherland culture - Euro currency conversion
SELECT PARSE('€9999,95' AS money USING 'NL') AS Currency;
-- 9999.95

-- Slovakian culture - Euro currency conversion
SELECT PARSE('€9999,95' AS money USING 'SK') AS Currency;
-- 9999.95


-- United States - Euro is not US currency
SELECT PARSE('€9999,95' AS money USING 'US') AS Currency;
/*
Msg 9818, Level 16, State 1, Line 1
The culture parameter 'US' provided in the function call is not supported.
*/


-- Italian
SELECT CONVERT(DECIMAL (12,0), PARSE('€99999,95' AS money USING 'IT')) AS DecimalValue;
-- 100000


-- PARSE with variable parameters
DECLARE @AMOUNT AS VARCHAR(12) = '$9999.00';   DECLARE @CULTURE AS CHAR(5) = 'EN-US';
SELECT DOLLAR = PARSE(@AMOUNT AS MONEY USING @CULTURE) ;
GO
-- 9999.00


-- PARSE invalid data
DECLARE @AMOUNT AS VARCHAR(12) = '$9999A.00';   DECLARE @CULTURE AS CHAR(5) = 'EN-US';
SELECT DOLLAR = PARSE(@AMOUNT AS MONEY USING @CULTURE);
GO
/*
Msg 9819, Level 16, State 1, Line 4
Error converting string value '$9999A.00' into data type money using culture 'EN-US'.
*/
```

TRY_CONVERT() Function

The TRY_CONVERT() function augments the CONVERT function to handle invalid data without giving an error. **It is a revolutionary new feature which makes invalid data handling significantly easier in T-SQL.**

```
-- CONVERT returns error on invalid data
SELECT [City]
        ,[PostalCode]
        ,CONVERT(INT, PostalCode)
 FROM AdventureWorks2012.Person.Address
 ORDER BY PostalCode;
/* Msg 245, Level 16, State 1, Line 1
Conversion failed when converting the nvarchar value '7L' to data type int.
*/
```

```
--  TRY_CONVERT() returns NULL for invalid data
SELECT DISTINCT [City]
        ,[PostalCode]
        ,TRY_CONVERT(INT, PostalCode) AS INTValue
 FROM AdventureWorks2012.Person.Address
 ORDER BY PostalCode;
```

City	PostalCode	INTValue
Union Gap	98903	98903
Ellensburg	98926	98926
Spokane	99202	99202
Kennewick	99337	99337
Walla Walla	99362	99362
Stoke-on-Trent	AS23	NULL
Birmingham	B29 6SL	NULL
Cambridge	BA5 3HX	NULL
W. York	BD1 4SJ	NULL
London	C2H 7AU	NULL
Cambridge	CB4 4BZ	NULL
Billericay	CM11	NULL

```
-- String date conversion to date data type
SET DATEFORMAT dmy;  -- US date format
SELECT TRY_CONVERT(date, '31/12/2016') AS Result;
-- 2016-12-31
```

```
-- Invalid date
SELECT TRY_CONVERT(date, '12/31/2016') AS Result;
-- NULL
GO
```

CHAPTER 6: New Programming Features in SS 2012

TRY_CONVERT() Usage in Adding Column to Table

Add new column as sequential row number (rowid) to table using the identity(int,1,1) function.

NOTE
The IDENTITY values usually follow the ORDER BY specifications sequentially, but there is no guarantee. If ordering is important, create an empty table first with IDENTITY column and populate it with INSERT SELECT ORDER BY.

```
 USE tempdb;

SELECT TRY_CONVERT(int, [SalesOrderID]) AS [NewSalesOrderID],   -- disable IDENTITY inheritance
    *
INTO  SOH
FROM  AdventureWorks.Sales.SalesOrderHeader  ORDER  BY OrderDate,  CustomerID;
GO
-- (31465 row(s) affected)


-- Take out duplicate SalesOrderID with the IDENTITY property
ALTER TABLE SOH DROP COLUMN SalesOrderID;
GO


-- Rename NewSalesOrderID to SalesOrderID
EXEC sp_rename 'dbo.SOH.NewSalesOrderID', 'SalesOrderID';
GO


-- Add IDENTITY function as new first column  for sequence generation - sequential ID
SELECT RowNumber = IDENTITY(INT, 1, 1),     *
INTO  #SOH  FROM  SOH  ORDER  BY OrderDate, CustomerID;
GO


 SELECT * INTO  SalesOrderHeader  FROM  #SOH ;  -- Create a permanent table
GO
SELECT TOP (5) *  FROM  SalesOrderHeader  ORDER  BY RowNumber ;
GO
```

RowNumber	SalesOrderID	RevisionNumber	OrderDate	DueDate	ShipDate
1	43676	1	2001-07-01 00:00:00.000	2001-07-13 00:00:00.000	2001-07-08 00:00:00.000
2	43695	1	2001-07-01 00:00:00.000	2001-07-13 00:00:00.000	2001-07-08 00:00:00.000
3	43674	1	2001-07-01 00:00:00.000	2001-07-13 00:00:00.000	2001-07-08 00:00:00.000
4	43660	1	2001-07-01 00:00:00.000	2001-07-13 00:00:00.000	2001-07-08 00:00:00.000
5	43672	1	2001-07-01 00:00:00.000	2001-07-13 00:00:00.000	2001-07-08 00:00:00.000

```
DROP TABLE SOH ;
DROP TABLE #SOH ;
DROP TABLE tempdb.dbo.SalesOrderHeader ;
```

TRY_PARSE() Function

The TRY_PARSE() function returns NULL instead of error in case of invalid data. T-SQL script to demonstrate the various uses of TRY_PARSE.

```
--  TRY_PARSE() parses or returns NULL if cast fails
SELECT TRY_PARSE('Monday, 13 December 2014' AS datetime USING 'en-US') AS [Date&Time];
-- NULL

SELECT TRY_PARSE('SAT, 13 December 2014' AS datetime USING 'en-US') AS [Date&Time];
-- 2014-12-13 00:00:00.000

-- Using the new feature with CASE Conditional.
SELECT CASE WHEN TRY_PARSE('Monday, 13 December 2014' AS datetime USING 'en-US') is NULL
        THEN (SELECT CONVERT(datetime, '19000101'))
    ELSE  (SELECT PARSE('Monday, 13 December 2014' AS datetime USING 'en-US')) END;
-- 1900-01-01 00:00:00.000

-- TRY_PARSE with variable parameters and IIF conditional
DECLARE @AMOUNT AS VARCHAR(12) = '$9999.00', @CULTURE AS CHAR(5) = 'EN-US';

SELECT RESULT = IIF(TRY_PARSE(@AMOUNT AS MONEY USING @CULTURE) IS NOT NULL
                            ,PARSE(@AMOUNT AS MONEY USING @CULTURE) ,-1.0);
-- 9999.0000

DECLARE @AMOUNT AS VARCHAR(12) = '$9999A.00'; DECLARE @CULTURE AS CHAR(5) = 'EN-US';

SELECT RESULT = IIF(TRY_PARSE(@AMOUNT AS MONEY USING @CULTURE) IS NOT NULL
                            ,PARSE(@AMOUNT AS MONEY USING @CULTURE) ,-1.0);
-- -1.0000

DECLARE @AMOUNT AS VARCHAR(12) = '$9999A.00', @CULTURE AS CHAR(5) = 'EN-US';

SELECT RESULT = IIF(TRY_PARSE(@AMOUNT AS MONEY USING @CULTURE) IS NOT NULL
                            ,PARSE(@AMOUNT AS MONEY USING @CULTURE) ,NULL);
GO
-- NULL

-- Note the multiplication by 100 using the German culture
DECLARE @AMOUNT AS VARCHAR(12) = '€77777.00'; DECLARE @CULTURE AS CHAR(5) = 'de-DE';

SELECT RESULT = IIF(TRY_PARSE(@AMOUNT AS MONEY USING @CULTURE) IS NOT NULL
                            ,PARSE(@AMOUNT AS MONEY USING @CULTURE) ,NULL);
GO
-- 7777700.00
```

FORMAT() Function

FORMAT() function is borrowed from the .NET languages. It augments the CONVERT function. T-SQL scripts to demonstrate some of the functionalities.

SELECT FORMAT(1111.22,'c','en-us');	$1,111.22
SELECT FORMAT(1111.22,'c','en-gb');	£1,111.22
SELECT FORMAT(1111.22,'c','de');	1.111,22 €
SELECT FORMAT(1111.22,'c','it');	€ 1.111,22
SELECT FORMAT(1111.22,'c','hu');	1 111,22 Ft
SELECT FORMAT(1111.22,'c','tr');	1.111,22 TL
SELECT FORMAT(1111.22,'c','es');	1.111,22 €
SELECT FORMAT(1111.22,'c','nl');	1.111,22 €
SELECT FORMAT(1111.22,'c','pl');	1 111,22 zł
SELECT FORMAT(1111.22,'c','ru');	1 111,22p.
SELECT FORMAT(1111.22,'c','se');	kr 1 111,22

DECLARE @culture char(2)='fr' ; SELECT FORMAT(1111.22, 'c', @culture); -- 1 111,22 €

SELECT FORMAT(1111.22,'c','gr');   /* Msg 9818, Level 16, State 1, Line 1
The culture parameter 'gr' provided in the function call is not supported.   */

SELECT FORMAT (getdate(), 'yyyy/MM/dd hh:mm:ss tt', 'en-US')';   -- 2016/06/03 09:56:44 AM
SELECT FORMAT (getdate(), 'MMM dd, yyyy hh:mm:ss tt', 'en-US');   -- Jun 03, 2016 09:57:45 AM

SELECT FORMAT (getdate(), 'y', 'en-US') ;   -- July, 2016
SELECT FORMAT (getdate(), 'M', 'en-US') ;   -- July 10
SELECT FORMAT (getdate(), 'd', 'en-US') ;   -- 7/10/2016

-- Percent formatting
SELECT TOP (4) ProductNumber, ListPrice, StandardCost, Markup = FORMAT(ListPrice / StandardCost, 'p', 'en-us')
FROM AdventureWorks2012.Production.Product WHERE ListPrice > 0.0 ORDER BY ProductNumber;

ProductNumber	ListPrice	StandardCost	Markup
BB-7421	53.99	23.9716	225.22 %
BB-8107	101.24	44.9506	225.22 %
BB-9108	121.49	53.9416	225.22 %
BC-M005	9.99	3.7363	267.37 %

CHAPTER 6: New Programming Features in SS 2012

CONCAT() Function

The CONCAT() function concatenates two or more strings. Previously the + operator was the only available way to concatenate. **NOTE: CONCAT treats NULL as an empty string, this is different from the + operator concatenation.** T-SQL scripts to demonstrate usage.

```
-- Using + string concatenation operator
SELECT  'New'+SPACE(1)+'York'+SPACE(1)+'City' ;        -- New York City
```

```
-- Using the new CONCAT() function
SELECT  CONCAT('New', SPACE(1),'York', SPACE(1), 'City'); -- New York City
```

```
-- Concatenating string columns with CONCAT()
SELECT CONCAT(FirstName, ' ',  LastName) AS FullName
FROM AdventureWorks2012.Person.Person
ORDER by FullName;
/* FullName
...
Blake Wright
Blake Young
Bob Alan
Bob Chapman
Bob Fernandez ... /
```

CHOOSE() Function

The CHOOSE() function returns an item from a list of values as specified by an index. T-SQL scripts to demonstrate usage.

```
SELECT CHOOSE ( 3, 'NYC', 'LA', 'Chicago', 'Houston' ) AS City;
-- Chicago
```

```
SELECT CHOOSE ( 3, 'one', 'two', 'three', 'four', 'five' ) AS Number;
-- three
```

```
DECLARE @weekday as tinyint=6;
SELECT CHOOSE(@weekday, 'Sunday', 'Monday', 'Tuesday', 'Wednesday', 'Thursday', 'Friday', 'Saturday');
-- Friday
```

```
-- Random weekday selection using newid() and rand() functions
DECLARE @weekday as tinyint=Round(Rand(Cast(Newid() AS VARBINARY)) * 6+1,0);
SELECT CHOOSE(@weekday, 'Sunday', 'Monday', 'Tuesday', 'Wednesday', 'Thursday', 'Friday', 'Saturday');
GO 10
-- Friday  Sunday  Tuesday .....
```

THROW Statement

The THROW statement passes the error incurred in TRY - CATCH to the application.
Demonstration T-SQL script follows.

```
CREATE TABLE Alpha
(
        ID INT PRIMARY KEY
);
GO
```

```
BEGIN TRY
   INSERT Alpha(ID) VALUES(7);
   INSERT Alpha(ID) VALUES(7); -- Force error by attempting duplicate insert
END TRY
BEGIN CATCH
   PRINT 'In CATCH';
  -- The error message encountered will be passed down to the client software application
   THROW;
END CATCH;
/*
In CATCH

Msg 2627, Level 14, State 1, Line 7
Violation of PRIMARY KEY constraint 'PK__Alpha__3214EC272A076B44'. Cannot insert
duplicate key in object 'dbo.Alpha'. The duplicate key value is (1).
*/
```

```
-- No THROW catch  - Error message not materialized
BEGIN TRY
   INSERT Alpha(ID) VALUES(7);
END TRY
BEGIN CATCH
   PRINT 'In CATCH';
END CATCH;
/*
(0 row(s) affected)
In CATCH.
*/
```

```
-- Cleanup
DROP TABLE Alpha
GO
```

IIF() Function

The IIF() function returns one of two values based on a condition. Here is a T-SQL demonstration script.

```
SELECT TOP 10  ProductID, ListPrice,
              IIF ( Color is not null, Color, 'N/A' ) AS [Color]
FROM AdventureWorks2012.Production.Product
ORDER BY ProductID DESC;
GO
```

ProductID	ListPrice	Color
999	539.99	Black
998	539.99	Black
997	539.99	Black
996	121.49	N/A
995	101.24	N/A
994	53.99	N/A
993	539.99	Black
992	539.99	Black
991	539.99	Black
990	539.99	Black

DATEFROMPARTS() & DATETIMEFROMPARTS() Functions

The DATEFROMPARTS() & DATETIMEFROMPARTS() functions generate date / datetime value from date parts. Demonstration T-SQL script.

```
SELECT DATEFROMPARTS ( 2016, 10, 23 ) AS RealDate;
GO
-- 2016-10-23
```

```
SELECT DATETIMEFROMPARTS ( 2016, 10, 23, 10, 10, 10, 500 ) AS RealDateTime;
GO
-- 2016-10-23 10:10:10.500
```

```
DECLARE @Year smallint = 2016, @Month tinyint = 10, @Day tinyint = 23;
SELECT DATEFROMPARTS(@Year, @Month, @Day);
GO
-- 2016-10-23
```

EOMONTH() Function

The EOMONTH() function returns the last day of the month for the given input date parameter.
T-SQL script to demonstrate usage.

```
SELECT EOMONTH('20140201') -- 2014-02-28
```

```
SELECT EOMONTH('20160201') -- 2016-02-29
GO
```

```
-- Future/past months optional parameter
DECLARE    @anydate DATE = '20161023';
SELECT
        CurrentMonthEnd      = EOMONTH(@anydate),
        NextMonthEnd         = EOMONTH(@anydate, 1),
        PrevMonthEnd         = EOMONTH(@anydate, -1);
GO
```

CurrentMonthEnd	NextMonthEnd	PrevMonthEnd
2016-10-31	2016-11-30	2016-09-30

```
-- Span 12 months of last day of month by using the sequence from spt_values
DECLARE    @anydate DATE = '20161023';
SELECT  TOP 12   LastDayOfMonth= EOMONTH(@anydate, number)
FROM master.dbo.spt_values WHERE type = 'P'  ORDER BY number;
GO
```

LastDayOfMonth
2016-10-31
2016-11-30
2016-12-31
2017-01-31
2017-02-28
2017-03-31
2017-04-30
2017-05-31
2017-06-30
2017-07-31
2017-08-31
2017-09-30

Result Set Paging with OFFSET & FETCH NEXT

Frequently a query produces a large results set. On the client side usually it has to be presented in small segments such as 20 lines at a time.

USE AdventureWorks2012;

SELECT ProductNumber, Name, ListPrice, Color
FROM Production.Product ORDER BY ProductNumber
        OFFSET 0 ROWS   FETCH NEXT 10 ROWS ONLY;
-- (10 row(s) affected)

ProductNumber	Name	ListPrice	Color
AR-5381	Adjustable Race	0.00	NULL
BA-8327	Bearing Ball	0.00	NULL
BB-7421	LL Bottom Bracket	53.99	NULL
BB-8107	ML Bottom Bracket	101.24	NULL
BB-9108	HL Bottom Bracket	121.49	NULL
BC-M005	Mountain Bottle Cage	9.99	NULL
BC-R205	Road Bottle Cage	8.99	NULL
BE-2349	BB Ball Bearing	0.00	NULL
BE-2908	Headset Ball Bearings	0.00	NULL
BK-M18B-40	Mountain-500 Black, 40	539.99	Black

SELECT ProductNumber, Name, ListPrice, Color
FROM Production.Product ORDER BY ProductNumber
        OFFSET 10 ROWS   FETCH NEXT 10 ROWS ONLY;
-- (10 row(s) affected)

ProductNumber	Name	ListPrice	Color
BK-M18B-42	Mountain-500 Black, 42	539.99	Black
BK-M18B-44	Mountain-500 Black, 44	539.99	Black
BK-M18B-48	Mountain-500 Black, 48	539.99	Black
BK-M18B-52	Mountain-500 Black, 52	539.99	Black
BK-M18S-40	Mountain-500 Silver, 40	564.99	Silver
BK-M18S-42	Mountain-500 Silver, 42	564.99	Silver
BK-M18S-44	Mountain-500 Silver, 44	564.99	Silver
BK-M18S-48	Mountain-500 Silver, 48	564.99	Silver
BK-M18S-52	Mountain-500 Silver, 52	564.99	Silver
BK-M38S-38	Mountain-400-W Silver, 38	769.49	Silver

SELECT ProductNumber, Name, ListPrice, Color
FROM Production.Product   ORDER BY ProductNumber OFFSET 500 ROWS   FETCH NEXT 10 ROWS ONLY;
-- (4 row(s) affected)

ProductNumber	Name	ListPrice	Color
VE-C304-L	Classic Vest, L	63.50	Blue
VE-C304-M	Classic Vest, M	63.50	Blue
VE-C304-S	Classic Vest, S	63.50	Blue
WB-H098	Water Bottle - 30 oz.	4.99	NULL

Result Paging Stored Procedure
The OFFSET FETCH functionality can be wrapped into a stored procedure.

```
USE AdventureWorks2012;
GO
```

```
CREATE PROCEDURE sprocProductPaging  (   @PageNumber int,   @RowsPerPage int  )
AS
BEGIN
SELECT            ProductNumber,
                  Name AS ProductName,
                  ListPrice,
                  Color
  FROM Production.Product p
  WHERE ProductSubcategoryID is not NULL
  ORDER BY ProductNumber
  OFFSET (@PageNumber-1) * @RowsPerPage ROWS
   FETCH NEXT @RowsPerPage ROWS ONLY;
END;
GO
-- Command(s) completed successfully.
```

```
EXEC sprocProductPaging 10, 20
GO
-- (20 row(s) affected)
```

ProductNumber	ProductName	ListPrice	Color
FR-T67Y-44	LL Touring Frame - Yellow, 44	333.42	Yellow
FR-T67Y-50	LL Touring Frame - Yellow, 50	333.42	Yellow
FR-T67Y-54	LL Touring Frame - Yellow, 54	333.42	Yellow
FR-T67Y-58	LL Touring Frame - Yellow, 58	333.42	Yellow
FR-T67Y-62	LL Touring Frame - Yellow, 62	333.42	Yellow
FR-T98U-46	HL Touring Frame - Blue, 46	1003.91	Blue
FR-T98U-50	HL Touring Frame - Blue, 50	1003.91	Blue
FR-T98U-54	HL Touring Frame - Blue, 54	1003.91	Blue
FR-T98U-60	HL Touring Frame - Blue, 60	1003.91	Blue
FR-T98Y-46	HL Touring Frame - Yellow, 46	1003.91	Yellow
FR-T98Y-50	HL Touring Frame - Yellow, 50	1003.91	Yellow
FR-T98Y-54	HL Touring Frame - Yellow, 54	1003.91	Yellow
FR-T98Y-60	HL Touring Frame - Yellow, 60	1003.91	Yellow
FW-M423	LL Mountain Front Wheel	60.745	Black
FW-M762	ML Mountain Front Wheel	209.025	Black
FW-M928	HL Mountain Front Wheel	300.215	Black
FW-R623	LL Road Front Wheel	85.565	Black
FW-R762	ML Road Front Wheel	248.385	Black
FW-R820	HL Road Front Wheel	330.06	Black
FW-T905	Touring Front Wheel	218.01	Black

LEAD() & LAG() Functions

THE LEAD() & LAG() analytical functions belong to the **OVER** family of functions.

```
USE AdventureWorks2012;
GO
 SELECT
        SalesOrderID,
        OrderQty,
        FORMAT(LineTotal, 'c', 'en-US')                                    AS LineTotal,
        LEAD(SalesOrderDetailID) OVER (ORDER BY SalesOrderDetailID )       AS [LEAD],
        SalesOrderDetailID                                                 AS SODID,
        LAG(SalesOrderDetailID) OVER (ORDER BY SalesOrderDetailID  )       AS [LAG]
 FROM Sales.SalesOrderDetail sod
 WHERE SalesOrderID IN    (SELECT SalesOrderID FROM Sales.SalesOrderHeader
                    WHERE TotalDue >= 180000)
 ORDER BY SalesOrderDetailID;
 --(111 row(s) affected) - Partial results.
```

SalesOrderID	OrderQty	LineTotal	LEAD	SODID	LAG
51131	11	$337.57	36817	36816	NULL
51131	12	$368.25	36818	36817	36816
51131	9	$5,421.11	36819	36818	36817
51131	2	$400.10	36820	36819	36818
51131	15	$200.76	36821	36820	36819
51131	2	$567.90	36822	36821	36820
51131	6	$8,582.65	36823	36822	36821
51131	4	$1,135.80	36824	36823	36822
51131	16	$12,206.44	36825	36824	36823
51131	8	$4,818.77	36826	36825	36824

.....

SalesOrderID	OrderQty	LineTotal	LEAD	SODID	LAG
55282	2	$76.20	55443	55442	55441
55282	4	$1,781.64	55444	55443	55442
55282	10	$146.94	55445	55444	55443
55282	3	$600.16	55446	55445	55444
55282	3	$1,807.04	55447	55446	55445
55282	28	$800.10	55448	55447	55446
55282	15	$18,685.15	55449	55448	55447
55282	8	$239.95	55450	55449	55448
55282	3	$1,336.23	55451	55450	55449
55282	7	$33.39	NULL	55451	55450

FIRST_VALUE() & LAST_VALUE() Analytic Functions

The FIRST_VALUE() and LAST_VALUE() analytic functions can be applied in conjunction with the OVER clause.

```
USE AdventureWorks2012;
GO
;WITH CTE AS
        (SELECT   PSC.Name AS Subcategory,
  FIRST_VALUE(P.Name) OVER (PARTITION BY PSC.Name ORDER BY ListPrice ASC) AS LeastExpensive,
        MIN(ListPrice) OVER (PARTITION BY PSC.Name ORDER BY ListPrice ASC)        AS LowPrice,
  LAST_VALUE(P.Name)  OVER (PARTITION BY PSC.Name ORDER BY ListPrice ASC) AS MostExpensive,
        MAX(ListPrice) OVER (PARTITION BY PSC.Name ORDER BY ListPrice ASC)        AS HighPrice,
        ROW_NUMBER() OVER (PARTITION BY PSC.Name ORDER BY ListPrice DESC)    AS RN
        FROM Production.Product P
        INNER JOIN Production.ProductSubcategory PSC
            ON P.ProductSubcategoryID = PSC.ProductSubcategoryID)
SELECT * FROM CTE WHERE RN = 1 ORDER BY Subcategory;
```

Subcategory	LeastExpensive	LowPrice	MostExpensive	HighPrice	RN
Bib-Shorts	Men's Bib-Shorts, S	89.99	Men's Bib-Shorts, L	89.99	1
Bike Racks	Hitch Rack - 4-Bike	120.00	Hitch Rack - 4-Bike	120.00	1
Bike Stands	All-Purpose Bike Stand	159.00	All-Purpose Bike Stand	159.00	1
Bottles and Cages	Water Bottle - 30 oz.	4.99	Mountain Bottle Cage	9.99	1
Bottom Brackets	LL Bottom Bracket	53.99	HL Bottom Bracket	121.49	1
Brakes	Rear Brakes	106.50	Front Brakes	106.50	1
Caps	AWC Logo Cap	8.99	AWC Logo Cap	8.99	1
Chains	Chain	20.24	Chain	20.24	1
Cleaners	Bike Wash - Dissolver	7.95	Bike Wash - Dissolver	7.95	1
Cranksets	LL Crankset	175.49	HL Crankset	404.99	1
Derailleurs	Front Derailleur	91.49	Rear Derailleur	121.46	1
Fenders	Fender Set - Mountain	21.98	Fender Set - Mountain	21.98	1
Forks	LL Fork	148.22	HL Fork	229.49	1
Gloves	Half-Finger Gloves, S	24.49	Full-Finger Gloves, L	37.99	1
Handlebars	LL Road Handlebars	44.54	HL Mountain Handlebars	120.27	1
Headsets	LL Headset	34.20	HL Headset	124.73	1
Helmets	Sport-100 Helmet, Blue	34.99	Sport-100 Helmet, Black	34.99	1
Hydration Packs	Hydration Pack - 70 oz.	54.99	Hydration Pack - 70 oz.	54.99	1
Jerseys	Long-Sleeve Logo Jersey, S	49.99	Short-Sleeve Classic Jersey, XL	53.99	1
Lights	Taillights - Battery-Powered	13.99	Headlights - Weatherproof	44.99	1
Locks	Cable Lock	25.00	Cable Lock	25.00	1
Mountain Bikes	Mountain-500 Black, 40	539.99	Mountain-100 Silver, 48	3399.99	1
Mountain Frames	LL Mountain Frame - Black, 40	249.79	HL Mountain Frame - Silver, 46	1364.50	1
Panniers	Touring-Panniers, Large	125.00	Touring-Panniers, Large	125.00	1
Pedals	LL Mountain Pedal	40.49	Touring Pedal	80.99	1
Pumps	Minipump	19.99	Mountain Pump	24.99	1
Road Bikes	Road-750 Black, 44	539.99	Road-150 Red, 56	3578.27	1
Road Frames	LL Road Frame - Black, 44	337.22	HL Road Frame - Red, 58	1431.50	1
Saddles	LL Mountain Seat/Saddle	27.12	HL Touring Seat/Saddle	52.64	1
Shorts	Men's Sports Shorts, S	59.99	Women's Mountain Shorts, L	69.99	1
Socks	Racing Socks, M	8.99	Mountain Bike Socks, L	9.50	1
Tights	Women's Tights, S	74.99	Women's Tights, L	74.99	1
Tires and Tubes	Patch Kit/8 Patches	2.29	HL Mountain Tire	35.00	1
Touring Bikes	Touring-3000 Blue, 44	742.35	Touring-1000 Blue, 60	2384.07	1
Touring Frames	LL Touring Frame - Blue, 50	333.42	HL Touring Frame - Yellow, 60	1003.91	1
Vests	Classic Vest, S	63.50	Classic Vest, L	63.50	1
Wheels	LL Mountain Front Wheel	60.745	HL Road Rear Wheel	357.06	1

CUME_DIST() & PERCENT_RANK() Analytic Functions

CUME_DIST() and PERCENT_RANK() analytic functions work in conjunction with the OVER clause.

```
SELECT   Department,
         CONCAT(LastName,', ', FirstName)                                    AS FullName,
         Rate,
         FORMAT(CUME_DIST () OVER (PARTITION BY Department ORDER BY Rate),'p')   AS CumuDist,
         FORMAT(PERCENT_RANK()  OVER (PARTITION BY Department ORDER BY Rate ),'p') AS PctRnk
FROM HumanResources.vEmployeeDepartmentHistory AS edh  -- view
   INNER JOIN HumanResources.EmployeePayHistory AS e
             ON e.BusinessEntityID = edh.BusinessEntityID
ORDER BY Department, Rate DESC;
-- (334 row(s) affected) - Partial results.
```

Department	FullName	Rate	CumuDist	PctRnk
Facilities and Maintenance	Altman, Gary	24.0385	100.00 %	100.00 %
Facilities and Maintenance	Kleinerman, Christian	20.4327	85.71 %	83.33 %
Facilities and Maintenance	Hedlund, Magnus	9.75	71.43 %	66.67 %
Facilities and Maintenance	Penor, Lori	9.25	57.14 %	0.00 %
Facilities and Maintenance	Macrae, Stuart	9.25	57.14 %	0.00 %
Facilities and Maintenance	Berry, Jo	9.25	57.14 %	0.00 %
Facilities and Maintenance	Coleman, Pat	9.25	57.14 %	0.00 %
Finance	Norman, Laura	60.0962	100.00 %	100.00 %
Finance	Norman, Laura	48.5577	92.31 %	91.67 %
Finance	Kahn, Wendy	43.2692	84.62 %	83.33 %
Finance	Norman, Laura	39.06	76.92 %	75.00 %
Finance	Liu, David	34.7356	69.23 %	66.67 %
Finance	Moreland, Barbara	26.4423	61.54 %	50.00 %
Finance	Seamans, Mike	26.4423	61.54 %	50.00 %
Finance	Tomic, Dragan	19.00	46.15 %	8.33 %
Finance	Sheperdigian, Janet	19.00	46.15 %	8.33 %
Finance	Poe, Deborah	19.00	46.15 %	8.33 %
Finance	Spoon, Candy	19.00	46.15 %	8.33 %
Finance	Walton, Bryan	19.00	46.15 %	8.33 %
Finance	Barber, David	13.4615	7.69 %	0.00 %
Human Resources	Barreto de Mattos, Paula	27.1394	100.00 %	100.00 %
Human Resources	Johnson, Willis	18.2692	83.33 %	60.00 %
Human Resources	Luthra, Vidur	18.2692	83.33 %	60.00 %
Human Resources	Martin, Mindy	16.5865	50.00 %	40.00 %
Human Resources	Culbertson, Grant	13.9423	33.33 %	0.00 %
Human Resources	Chen, Hao	13.9423	33.33 %	0.00 %

EXEC New Option: WITH RESULT SETS

The WITH RESULT SETS clause can be used to remap the result set of a stored procedure or system procedure execution.

```
EXEC sp_who;
GO
```
-- (145 row(s) affected) - Partial results.

spid	ecid	status	loginame	hostname	blk	dbname	cmd	request_id
1	0	background	sa		0	NULL	LOG WRITER	0
2	0	background	sa		0	NULL	RECOVERY WRITER	0
3	0	background	sa		0	NULL	LAZY WRITER	0
4	0	background	sa		0	master	SIGNAL HANDLER	0
5	0	background	sa		0	NULL	LOCK MONITOR	0

```
EXEC sp_who
 WITH RESULT SETS
 (
 (
 SPID INT,
 ECID INT,
 STATUS VARCHAR(32),
 LOGINAME SYSNAME,
 HOSTNAME SYSNAME,
 BLK TINYINT,
 DBNAME SYSNAME,
 CMD VARCHAR(64),
 REQUESTID INT
 )
 );
```
-- (145 row(s) affected) - Partial results.

SPID	ECID	STATUS	LOGINAME	HOSTNAME	BLK	DBNAME	CMD	REQUESTID
47	0	background	sa		0	master	BRKR TASK	0
48	0	background	sa		0	master	BRKR TASK	0
51	0	sleeping	HPESTAR\Owner	HPESTAR	0	master	AWAITING COMMAND	0
52	0	sleeping	HPESTAR\Owner	HPESTAR	0	master	AWAITING COMMAND	0
53	0	sleeping	HPESTAR\Owner	HPESTAR	0	AdventureWorks2012	AWAITING COMMAND	0
54	0	sleeping	HPESTAR\Owner	HPESTAR	0	AdventureWorks2008	AWAITING COMMAND	0
55	0	sleeping	HPESTAR\Owner	HPESTAR	0	AdventureWorks2008	AWAITING COMMAND	0
56	0	sleeping	NT SERVICE\ReportServer	HPESTAR	0	ReportServer	AWAITING COMMAND	0
57	0	sleeping	HPESTAR\Owner	HPESTAR	0	AdventureWorks2008	AWAITING COMMAND	0
58	0	runnable	HPESTAR\Owner	HPESTAR	0	AdventureWorks2012	SELECT	0
59	0	sleeping	NT SERVICE\ReportServer	HPESTAR	0	ReportServer	AWAITING COMMAND	0
60	0	runnable	HPESTAR\Owner	HPESTAR	0	master	SELECT	0

CHAPTER 7: JOINing Tables with INNER & OUTER JOINs

SELECT with INNER JOIN

The SELECT statement is used to retrieve data from table(s). An INNER JOIN is a join in which the values in the columns being joined are compared using a comparison operator. Inner join also known as equi-join when equality condition is applied. Equi-join: PRIMARY KEY (table a) = FOREIGN KEY (table b).

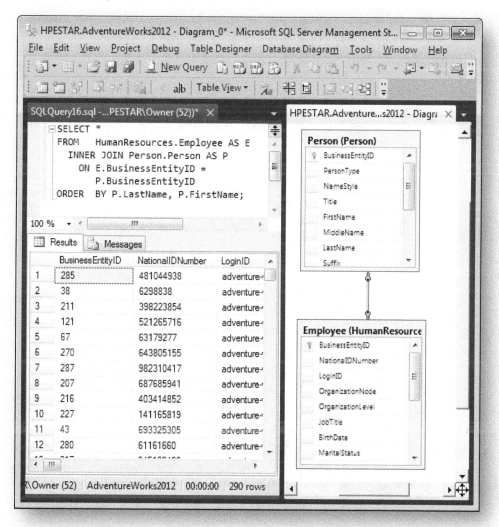

FOREIGN KEY Constraint as Base for INNER JOIN

The INNER JOIN is based on HumanResources.Employee.BusinessEntityID (PRIMARY KEY) is a
FOREIGN KEY to Person.Person.BusinessEntityID. The Employee table is in one-to-one
relationship with a subset of the Person table.

Diagram of Person.Person and Related Tables

The population of Person.Person includes all employees, contacts, and customers, therefore a key table in the database.

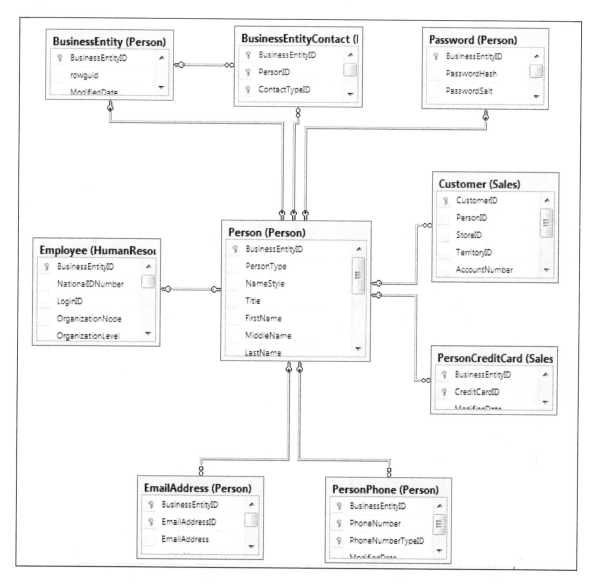

```
-- INNER JOIN ON PRIMARY KEY & FOREIGN KEY
SELECT * FROM Person.Person AS P
        INNER JOIN Person.PersonPhone AS PH
            ON P.BusinessEntityID = PH.BusinessEntityID;
-- (19972 row(s) affected)
```

CHAPTER 7: JOINing Tables with INNER & OUTER JOINs

EQUI-JOIN BETWEEN FOREIGN KEY & PRIMARY KEY

EQUI JOIN means the equality operator is used to match the left and right keys. The reason for the popularity: the goal of most query is to gather information from related tables records (rows). Query to demonstrate why are 3 tables necessary to get a meaningful business report with just a few columns.

```
USE AdventureWorks;
GO


SELECT          CONCAT(LastName, ', ', FirstName)        AS Consumer,
                EmailAddress,
                Phone,
                CU.AccountNumber,
                C.ContactID,
                I.CustomerID
FROM Person.Contact AS C
   INNER JOIN Sales.Individual AS I
     ON C.ContactID = I.ContactID
   INNER JOIN Sales.Customer AS CU
     ON I.CustomerID = CU.CustomerID
WHERE CU.CustomerType = 'I'
ORDER BY LastName, FirstName ;
GO
-- (18484 row(s) affected) - Partial results.
```

Consumer	EmailAddress	Phone	AccountNumber	ContactID	CustomerID
Pal, Yolanda	yolanda11@adventure-works.com	1 (11) 500 555-0110	AW00023748	2837	23748
Palit, Punya	punya0@adventure-works.com	164-555-0118	AW00017574	14759	17574
Parker, Adam	adam29@adventure-works.com	808-555-0157	AW00018228	14771	18228
Parker, Alex	alex26@adventure-works.com	613-555-0123	AW00029252	14783	29252
Parker, Alexandra	alexandra50@adventure-works.com	974-555-0142	AW00016866	8977	16866
Parker, Allison	allison30@adventure-works.com	750-555-0124	AW00026501	9021	26501
Parker, Amanda	amanda51@adventure-works.com	978-555-0167	AW00018081	8985	18081
Parker, Amber	amber7@adventure-works.com	1 (11) 500 555-0198	AW00023959	8999	23959
Parker, Andrea	andrea23@adventure-works.com	612-555-0113	AW00020091	8461	20091
Parker, Angel	angel21@adventure-works.com	815-555-0120	AW00014273	14779	14273
Parker, Bailey	bailey28@adventure-works.com	604-555-0112	AW00019529	9007	19529
Parker, Blake	blake44@adventure-works.com	432-555-0151	AW00015008	3413	15008
Parker, Caleb	caleb28@adventure-works.com	593-555-0116	AW00026318	14760	26318
Parker, Carlos	carlos25@adventure-works.com	937-555-0143	AW00020676	14778	20676
Parker, Charles	charles43@adventure-works.com	266-555-0118	AW00021267	4105	21267
Parker, Chloe	chloe5@adventure-works.com	360-555-0121	AW00027480	8965	27480
Parker, Connor	connor28@adventure-works.com	936-555-0177	AW00028839	14763	28839
Parker, Courtney	courtney5@adventure-works.com	266-555-0176	AW00017612	9002	17612
Parker, Dalton	dalton42@adventure-works.com	535-555-0190	AW00013064	3722	13064
Parker, Devin	devin40@adventure-works.com	897-555-0155	AW00011684	4192	11684
Parker, Eduardo	eduardo41@adventure-works.com	131-555-0192	AW00012939	4269	12939

Diagram of Sales.Customer and Related Tables

Customer is the source of revenue for any business. Therefore, proper table design is paramount.

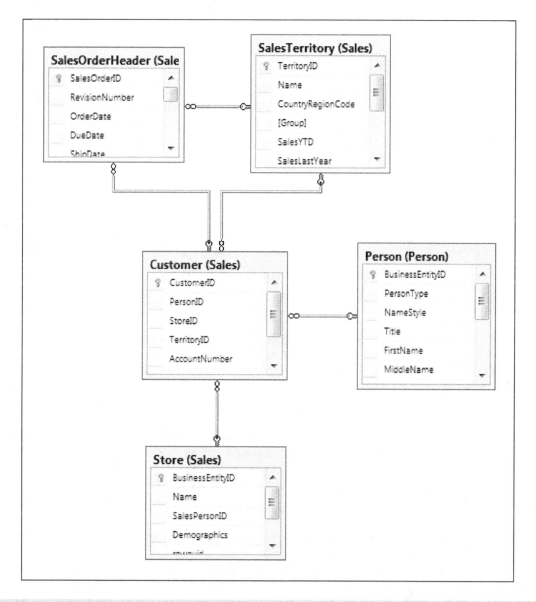

-- INNER JOIN ON PRIMARY KEY & FOREIGN KEY - NOTE: PK & FK named differently
SELECT * FROM Sales.Store AS S
          INNER JOIN Sales.Customer AS C   ON S.BusinessEntityID = C.StoreID;
-- (1336 row(s) affected)

Extracting All or Partial Data from JOINed Tables

T-SQL scripts to demonstrate how to JOIN two tables and extract all or subset of the
information.

USE AdventureWorks2012;

```
-- SELECT all columns from the JOINed tables
SELECT *
FROM   HumanResources.Employee              AS E    -- E is a table alias
    INNER JOIN Person.Person                AS P    -- P is a table alias
        ON E.BusinessEntityID = P.BusinessEntityID
ORDER  BY P.LastName;
-- (290 row(s) affected)  - Partial results.
```

FirstName	MiddleName	LastName
Syed	E	Abbas
Kim	B	Abercrombie
Hazem	E	Abolrous
Pilar	G	Ackerman
Jay	G	Adams

```
SELECT E.*                    -- SELECT Employee columns from the JOINed tables
FROM   HumanResources.Employee AS E
    INNER JOIN Person.Person AS P    ON E.BusinessEntityID = P.BusinessEntityID
ORDER  BY P.LastName;
-- Partial results.
```

JobTitle	BirthDate	MaritalStatus	Gender
Pacific Sales Manager	1969-02-11	M	M
Production Technician - WC60	1961-01-14	M	F
Quality Assurance Manager	1971-11-27	S	M
Shipping and Receiving Supervisor	1966-10-11	S	M

```
-- SELECT Person columns from the JOINed tables
SELECT P.* FROM   HumanResources.Employee AS E
            INNER JOIN Person.Person AS P      ON E.BusinessEntityID = P.BusinessEntityID
ORDER  BY P.LastName;
-- Partial results.
```

BusinessEntityID	PersonType
285	SP
38	EM
211	EM

SELECT All Columns From The Joined Tables Using Table Alias And Wildcard

```
SELECT E.*, P.*
FROM   HumanResources.Employee              AS E    -- E is a table alias
    INNER JOIN Person.Person                AS P    -- P is a table alias
        ON E.BusinessEntityID = P.BusinessEntityID
ORDER  BY P.LastName;
-- Same results as SELECT * FROM
```

```
-- Count JOINed rows
SELECT count(*)
FROM   HumanResources.Employee AS E
    INNER JOIN Person.Person AS P
        ON E.BusinessEntityID = P.BusinessEntityID
-- 290
```

```
-- Vertically output reduction: eliminate columns from the available pool
SELECT   E.BusinessEntityID            AS EmployeeID,    -- column alias
         E.JobTitle,
         P.FirstName,
         P.LastName
FROM   HumanResources.Employee AS E
    INNER JOIN Person.Person AS P    ON E.BusinessEntityID = P.BusinessEntityID
ORDER  BY P.LastName;
-- (290 row(s) affected) - Partial results.
```

EmployeeID	JobTitle	FirstName	LastName
285	Pacific Sales Manager	Syed	Abbas
38	Production Technician - WC60	Kim	Abercrombie
211	Quality Assurance Manager	Hazem	Abolrous
121	Shipping and Receiving Supervisor	Pilar	Ackerman

```
-- Create a new output column from the available pool of columns
SELECT   E.BusinessEntityID                  AS EmployeeID,
         E.JobTitle,
         CONCAT(P.FirstName, ' ', P.LastName)     AS NAME
FROM   HumanResources.Employee AS E
    INNER JOIN Person.Person AS P    ON E.BusinessEntityID = P.BusinessEntityID
ORDER  BY P.LastName;
-- (290 row(s) affected) - Partial results.
```

EmployeeID	JobTitle	NAME
285	Pacific Sales Manager	Syed Abbas
38	Production Technician - WC60	Kim Abercrombie
211	Quality Assurance Manager	Hazem Abolrous
121	Shipping and Receiving Supervisor	Pilar Ackerman

CHAPTER 7: JOINing Tables with INNER & OUTER JOINs

Table Aliases for Readability

The table alias serves as shorthand for table name to improve the **readability of queries**. It should be as short as possible and as meaningful as possible when we have to use a few letters. The next T-SQL query applies four table aliases: c, soh, sod, p.

```
USE AdventureWorks;
SELECT DISTINCT SalesPerson = CONCAT(c.FirstName,SPACE(1), c.LastName)
FROM   Person.Contact c
    INNER JOIN Sales.SalesOrderHeader soh
    ON soh.SalesPersonId = c.ContactID
    INNER JOIN Sales.SalesOrderDetail sod
    ON soh.SalesOrderId = sod.SalesOrderId
    INNER JOIN Production.Product p
    ON sod.ProductID = p.ProductID    AND p.Name LIKE ('%Touring Frame%');
GO /*    SalesPerson
         Carla Eldridge
         Carol Elliott
         Gail Erickson  ....*/
```

Column Aliases for Readability & Presentation

The column alias serves as a meaningful column name either replacing a column name or filling in when there is no column name. In the previous example the = sign was used to establish the column alias. Alternate setting follows applying "AS" (it can be skipped) after the column. If the alias has spaces it has to be included in square brackets like [Bond Sales] or double quotes.

```
USE AdventureWorks;
SELECT DISTINCT  CONCAT(c.FirstName,' ', c.LastName)                AS SalesPerson
FROM   Person.Contact c
    INNER JOIN Sales.SalesOrderHeader soh
    ON soh.SalesPersonId = c.ContactID
    INNER JOIN Sales.SalesOrderDetail sod
    ON soh.SalesOrderId = sod.SalesOrderId
    INNER JOIN Production.Product p
    ON sod.ProductID = p.ProductID   AND p.Name LIKE ('%Touring Frame%');
-- (17 row(s) affected) - Partial results.
```

SalesPerson
Carla Eldridge
Carol Elliott
Gail Erickson
Gary Drury
Janeth Esteves
Jauna Elson
John Emory

Derived Table Alias with a List of Column Aliases

Optionally column alias list can be specified for derived tables just like in CTE definition. T-SQL query demonstrates nested derived tables with table-column aliases (P & J).

```
SELECT DISTINCT ProdID, ProdName, ProdPrice, OrderQuantity
FROM    (
                SELECT    ID, ProductName, Price,           -- Derived table columns
                          OrderQty                          -- SOD column
                FROM AdventureWorks2012.Sales.SalesOrderDetail SOD
                INNER JOIN
                        (SELECT ProductID, Name, ListPrice
                         FROM AdventureWorks2012.Production.Product
                        ) P(ID, ProductName, Price)         -- inner derived table
                ON SOD.ProductID = P.ID
        ) J (ProdID, ProdName, ProdPrice, OrderQuantity)    -- outer derived table
ORDER BY ProdPrice DESC, ProdName;
-- (2667 row(s) affected) - Partial results.
```

ProdID	ProdName	ProdPrice	OrderQuantity
750	Road-150 Red, 44	3578.27	3
750	Road-150 Red, 44	3578.27	6
750	Road-150 Red, 44	3578.27	1
750	Road-150 Red, 44	3578.27	4
750	Road-150 Red, 44	3578.27	2
750	Road-150 Red, 44	3578.27	5
751	Road-150 Red, 48	3578.27	6
751	Road-150 Red, 48	3578.27	3
751	Road-150 Red, 48	3578.27	2
751	Road-150 Red, 48	3578.27	5
751	Road-150 Red, 48	3578.27	4
751	Road-150 Red, 48	3578.27	1
752	Road-150 Red, 52	3578.27	5
752	Road-150 Red, 52	3578.27	3
752	Road-150 Red, 52	3578.27	6
752	Road-150 Red, 52	3578.27	1
752	Road-150 Red, 52	3578.27	4
752	Road-150 Red, 52	3578.27	2
753	Road-150 Red, 56	3578.27	6
753	Road-150 Red, 56	3578.27	3

INNER JOIN with Additional Conditions

The ON clause of a JOIN can include additional conditions as the following demonstration shows. The INNER JOIN is still based on FOREIGN KEY relationship, but only a subset of records (rows) returned due to the additional conditions, or JOIN predicates. The first query returns the distinct set of cases where the Selling Price was below the ListPrice for ProductID 800 which is a yellow road bike. The second query covers the remaining range where the Selling Price was equal or above the ListPrice.

```
USE AdventureWorks2012;
SELECT DISTINCT( P.ProductID ),
        ProductName = P.Name,          -- column alias
        P.ListPrice,
        SOD.UnitPrice AS 'Selling Price'   -- column alias
FROM   Sales.SalesOrderDetail AS SOD       -- table alias
    INNER JOIN  Production.Product AS P    -- table alias
    ON SOD.ProductID = P.ProductID
      AND SOD.UnitPrice < P.ListPrice          -- JOIN predicate
      AND  P.ProductID = 800;                  -- JOIN predicate
```

ProductID	ProductName	ListPrice	Selling Price
800	Road-550-W Yellow, 44	1120.49	600.2625
800	Road-550-W Yellow, 44	1120.49	672.294
800	Road-550-W Yellow, 44	1120.49	1000.4375

```
SELECT DISTINCT( P.ProductID ),
        ProductName = P.Name,
        P.ListPrice,
        SOD.UnitPrice AS 'Selling Price'
FROM   Sales.SalesOrderDetail AS SOD
    INNER JOIN  Production.Product AS P
    ON SOD.ProductID = P.ProductID
      AND SOD.UnitPrice >= P.ListPrice
      AND  P.ProductID BETWEEN 800 AND 900
ORDER BY ProductName;
-- (26 row(s) affected) - Partial results.
```

ProductID	ProductName	ListPrice	Selling Price
879	All-Purpose Bike Stand	159.00	159.00
877	Bike Wash - Dissolver	7.95	7.95
866	Classic Vest, L	63.50	63.50
865	Classic Vest, M	63.50	63.50
864	Classic Vest, S	63.50	63.50
878	Fender Set - Mountain	21.98	21.98
860	Half-Finger Gloves, L	24.49	24.49
859	Half-Finger Gloves, M	24.49	24.49
858	Half-Finger Gloves, S	24.49	24.49
876	Hitch Rack - 4-Bike	120.00	120.00

Counting Rows in JOINs

As the T-SQL script following shows, the basic FOREIGN KEY based JOIN returns 121,317 rows which is all the rows in Sales.SalesOrderDetail table. The additional condition P.ProductID = 800 selects a subset of 495 rows which is then divided between the < and >= conditions.

```
USE AdventureWorks2012;
SELECT Rows = count(*)
FROM   Sales.SalesOrderDetail AS SOD
     INNER JOIN  Production.Product AS P     ON SOD.ProductID = P.ProductID
-- 121317
```

```
SELECT Rows = count(*)
FROM   Sales.SalesOrderDetail AS SOD
     INNER JOIN  Production.Product AS P   ON SOD.ProductID = P.ProductID   AND P.ProductID = 800;
-- 495
```

```
SELECT Rows = count(*)
FROM   Sales.SalesOrderDetail AS SOD
    INNER JOIN  Production.Product AS P
     ON SOD.ProductID = P.ProductID
       AND SOD.UnitPrice < P.ListPrice
       AND P.ProductID = 800;
-- 285
```

```
SELECT Rows = count(*)
FROM   Sales.SalesOrderDetail AS SOD
    INNER JOIN  Production.Product AS P
     ON SOD.ProductID = P.ProductID
       AND SOD.UnitPrice >= P.ListPrice
       AND P.ProductID = 800;
-- 210
```

```
SELECT COUNT(P.ProductID)
FROM   Sales.SalesOrderDetail AS SOD
    INNER JOIN  Production.Product AS P
     ON SOD.ProductID = P.ProductID
       AND SOD.UnitPrice >= P.ListPrice
       AND  P.ProductID BETWEEN 800 AND 900;
-- 21085
```

```
SELECT COUNT(DISTINCT P.ProductID)
FROM   Sales.SalesOrderDetail AS SOD
    INNER JOIN  Production.Product AS P
     ON SOD.ProductID = P.ProductID   AND SOD.UnitPrice >= P.ListPrice
       AND  P.ProductID BETWEEN 800 AND 900;
```

INNER JOIN with 3 Tables

T-SQL query to demonstrate JOINing three tables. Due to the application of the FORMAT function, column name is lost. Therefore we have to alias the formatted column with the original column name or something else. Both INNER JOINs are based on FOREIGN KEY relationships. PV.ProductID is an FK to the Production.Product table, and the PV.VendorID is an FK to the Purchasing.Vendor table. The Purchasing.ProductVendor table is a junction table representing many-to-many relationships between products and vendors: a vendor may supply many products (see Beaumont Bikes in results) and a product may be supplied by many vendors (see Chainring in results).

```
USE AdventureWorks;
GO
SELECT          P.ProductNumber,
                P.Name                          AS Product,
                V.Name                          AS Vendor,
                FORMAT (PV.LastReceiptCost, 'c', 'en-US')   AS LastReceiptCost
FROM Production.Product AS P
  INNER JOIN Purchasing.ProductVendor AS PV
        ON P.ProductID = PV.ProductID
  INNER JOIN Purchasing.Vendor AS V
        ON V.VendorID = PV.VendorID
ORDER BY Product;
GO
-- (406 row(s) affected) - Partial results.
```

ProductNumber	Product	Vendor	LastReceiptCost
AR-5381	Adjustable Race	Litware, Inc.	$50.26
BA-8327	Bearing Ball	Wood Fitness	$41.92
CH-0234	Chain	Varsity Sport Co.	$15.74
CR-7833	Chainring	Beaumont Bikes	$25.42
CR-7833	Chainring	Bike Satellite Inc.	$26.37
CR-7833	Chainring	Training Systems	$28.70
CB-2903	Chainring Bolts	Beaumont Bikes	$47.47
CB-2903	Chainring Bolts	Bike Satellite Inc.	$45.37
CB-2903	Chainring Bolts	Training Systems	$49.64
CN-6137	Chainring Nut	Beaumont Bikes	$42.80
CN-6137	Chainring Nut	Bike Satellite Inc.	$40.49
CN-6137	Chainring Nut	Training Systems	$44.32
RA-7490	Cone-Shaped Race	Midwest Sport, Inc.	$44.22
CR-9981	Crown Race	Business Equipment Center	$50.26
RA-2345	Cup-Shaped Race	Bloomington Multisport	$48.76
DC-8732	Decal 1	SUPERSALES INC.	$0.21
DC-9824	Decal 2	SUPERSALES INC.	$0.21
LE-6000	External Lock Washer 1	Pro Sport Industries	$41.24
LE-6000	External Lock Washer 1	Aurora Bike Center	$43.27
LE-6000	External Lock Washer 1	Expert Bike Co	$41.17

T-SQL Query To Return All Road Frames Offered For Sale By AdventureWorks Cycles

```
USE AdventureWorks2012;
SELECT          UPPER(PC.Name)          AS Category,  PSC.Name              AS Subcategory,
                P.Name          AS Product,   FORMAT(ListPrice, 'c', 'en-US')    AS ListPrice,
                FORMAT(StandardCost, 'c', 'en-US')                               AS StandardCost
FROM Production.Product AS P
   INNER JOIN Production.ProductSubcategory AS PSC
           ON PSC.ProductSubcategoryID = P.ProductSubcategoryID
   INNER JOIN Production.ProductCategory AS PC
           ON PC.ProductCategoryID = PSC.ProductCategoryID
WHERE PSC.Name like 'Road Frames'  ORDER BY Category, Subcategory, Product;
```

Category	Subcategory	Product	ListPrice	StandardCost
COMPONENTS	Road Frames	HL Road Frame - Black, 44	$1,431.50	$868.63
COMPONENTS	Road Frames	HL Road Frame - Black, 48	$1,431.50	$868.63
COMPONENTS	Road Frames	HL Road Frame - Black, 52	$1,431.50	$868.63
COMPONENTS	Road Frames	HL Road Frame - Black, 58	$1,431.50	$1,059.31
COMPONENTS	Road Frames	HL Road Frame - Black, 62	$1,431.50	$868.63
COMPONENTS	Road Frames	HL Road Frame - Red, 44	$1,431.50	$868.63
COMPONENTS	Road Frames	HL Road Frame - Red, 48	$1,431.50	$868.63
COMPONENTS	Road Frames	HL Road Frame - Red, 52	$1,431.50	$868.63
COMPONENTS	Road Frames	HL Road Frame - Red, 56	$1,431.50	$868.63
COMPONENTS	Road Frames	HL Road Frame - Red, 58	$1,431.50	$1,059.31
COMPONENTS	Road Frames	HL Road Frame - Red, 62	$1,431.50	$868.63
COMPONENTS	Road Frames	LL Road Frame - Black, 44	$337.22	$204.63
COMPONENTS	Road Frames	LL Road Frame - Black, 48	$337.22	$204.63
COMPONENTS	Road Frames	LL Road Frame - Black, 52	$337.22	$204.63
COMPONENTS	Road Frames	LL Road Frame - Black, 58	$337.22	$204.63
COMPONENTS	Road Frames	LL Road Frame - Black, 60	$337.22	$204.63
COMPONENTS	Road Frames	LL Road Frame - Black, 62	$337.22	$204.63
COMPONENTS	Road Frames	LL Road Frame - Red, 44	$337.22	$187.16
COMPONENTS	Road Frames	LL Road Frame - Red, 48	$337.22	$187.16
COMPONENTS	Road Frames	LL Road Frame - Red, 52	$337.22	$187.16
COMPONENTS	Road Frames	LL Road Frame - Red, 58	$337.22	$187.16
COMPONENTS	Road Frames	LL Road Frame - Red, 60	$337.22	$187.16
COMPONENTS	Road Frames	LL Road Frame - Red, 62	$337.22	$187.16
COMPONENTS	Road Frames	ML Road Frame - Red, 44	$594.83	$352.14
COMPONENTS	Road Frames	ML Road Frame - Red, 48	$594.83	$352.14
COMPONENTS	Road Frames	ML Road Frame - Red, 52	$594.83	$352.14
COMPONENTS	Road Frames	ML Road Frame - Red, 58	$594.83	$352.14
COMPONENTS	Road Frames	ML Road Frame - Red, 60	$594.83	$352.14
COMPONENTS	Road Frames	ML Road Frame-W - Yellow, 38	$594.83	$360.94
COMPONENTS	Road Frames	ML Road Frame-W - Yellow, 40	$594.83	$360.94
COMPONENTS	Road Frames	ML Road Frame-W - Yellow, 42	$594.83	$360.94
COMPONENTS	Road Frames	ML Road Frame-W - Yellow, 44	$594.83	$360.94
COMPONENTS	Road Frames	ML Road Frame-W - Yellow, 48	$594.83	$360.94

INNER JOIN with Junction Table

Three tables INNER JOIN includes the titleauthor junction table which represent many-to-many relationship. All JOINs are EQUI-JOINs with FOREIGN KEYs and PRIMARY KEYs.

```
USE pubs;

SELECT         FORMAT(ytd_sales, 'c', 'en-US')                              AS YTDSales,
               CONCAT(au.au_fname, ' ', au.au_lname)                        AS Author,
               FORMAT((ytd_sales * royalty) / 100,'c','en-US')              AS AuthorRev,
               FORMAT((ytd_sales - (ytd_sales * royalty) / 100),'c','en-US') AS PublisherRev
FROM titles t
     INNER JOIN titleauthor ta
          ON t.title_id = ta.title_id
     INNER JOIN authors au
          ON ta.au_id = au.au_id
ORDER BY       YTDSales DESC,          -- Major sort key
               Author ASC;             -- Minor sort key
GO
```

YTDSales	Author	AuthorRev	PublisherRev
$8,780.00	Cheryl Carson	$1,404.00	$7,376.00
$4,095.00	Abraham Bennet	$409.00	$3,686.00
$4,095.00	Akiko Yokomoto	$409.00	$3,686.00
$4,095.00	Ann Dull	$409.00	$3,686.00
$4,095.00	Burt Gringlesby	$409.00	$3,686.00
$4,095.00	Dean Straight	$409.00	$3,686.00
$4,095.00	Marjorie Green	$409.00	$3,686.00
$4,095.00	Michael O'Leary	$409.00	$3,686.00
$4,095.00	Sheryl Hunter	$409.00	$3,686.00
$4,072.00	Johnson White	$407.00	$3,665.00
$375.00	Livia Karsen	$37.00	$338.00
$375.00	Stearns MacFeather	$37.00	$338.00
$375.00	Sylvia Panteley	$37.00	$338.00
$3,876.00	Michael O'Leary	$387.00	$3,489.00
$3,876.00	Stearns MacFeather	$387.00	$3,489.00
$3,336.00	Charlene Locksley	$333.00	$3,003.00
$22,246.00	Anne Ringer	$5,339.00	$16,907.00
$22,246.00	Michel DeFrance	$5,339.00	$16,907.00
$2,045.00	Albert Ringer	$245.00	$1,800.00
$2,045.00	Anne Ringer	$245.00	$1,800.00
$2,032.00	Innes del Castillo	$243.00	$1,789.00
$18,722.00	Marjorie Green	$4,493.00	$14,229.00
$15,096.00	Reginald Blotchet-Halls	$2,113.00	$12,983.00
$111.00	Albert Ringer	$11.00	$100.00
NULL	Charlene Locksley	NULL	NULL

NON-EQUI JOINs for Data Analytics

We can use not equal operators in JOIN predicates as demonstrated in the next query. The second predicate in the JOIN is less than JOIN.

```
USE AdventureWorks2012;
GO
-- List of "red" products sold at a discount
SELECT DISTINCT         p.ProductNumber,
                        p.Name                                  AS ProductName,
                        FORMAT(p.ListPrice,'c','en-US')         AS ListPrice,
                        FORMAT(sod.UnitPrice,'c','en-US')       AS SellPrice
FROM Sales.SalesOrderDetail AS sod
    INNER JOIN Production.Product AS p
        ON sod.ProductID = p.ProductID
        AND sod.UnitPrice < p.ListPrice
WHERE Color = 'Red'
ORDER BY p.ProductNumber;
--(86 row(s) affected) - Partial results.
```

ProductNumber	ProductName	ListPrice	SellPrice
BK-R50R-44	Road-650 Red, 44	$782.99	$234.90
BK-R50R-44	Road-650 Red, 44	$782.99	$419.46
BK-R50R-44	Road-650 Red, 44	$782.99	$430.64
BK-R50R-44	Road-650 Red, 44	$782.99	$454.13
BK-R50R-44	Road-650 Red, 44	$782.99	$469.79
BK-R50R-44	Road-650 Red, 44	$782.99	$563.75
BK-R50R-44	Road-650 Red, 44	$782.99	$699.10
BK-R50R-48	Road-650 Red, 48	$782.99	$419.46
BK-R50R-48	Road-650 Red, 48	$782.99	$430.64
BK-R50R-48	Road-650 Red, 48	$782.99	$454.13
BK-R50R-48	Road-650 Red, 48	$782.99	$469.79
BK-R50R-48	Road-650 Red, 48	$782.99	$563.75

To resolve the duplicate issue which makes DISTINCT usage necessary, we have to include the SalesOrderID column.

```
SELECT                  p.ProductNumber,
                        p.Name                                  AS ProductName,
                        FORMAT(p.ListPrice,'c','en-US')         AS ListPrice,
                        FORMAT(sod.UnitPrice,'c','en-US')       AS SellPrice,
                        sod.SalesOrderID
FROM Sales.SalesOrderDetail AS sod
    INNER JOIN Production.Product AS p
        ON sod.ProductID = p.ProductID
        AND sod.UnitPrice < p.ListPrice
WHERE Color = 'Red'   ORDER BY p.ProductNumber;
-- (8408 row(s) affected)
```

CHAPTER 7: JOINing Tables with INNER & OUTER JOINs

Interchangeability of ON & WHERE Predicates in INNER JOINs

We can freely place the predicates to either the ON clause or the WHERE clause in an INNER JOIN. This is not true for OUTER JOINs such as LEFT JOINs.

```
USE AdventureWorks2012;
-- List of "blue" products sold at a discount
SELECT DISTINCT  p.ProductNumber, p.Name                    AS ProductName,
                 FORMAT(p.ListPrice,'c','en-US')            AS ListPrice,
                 FORMAT(sod.UnitPrice,'c','en-US')          AS SellPrice
FROM Sales.SalesOrderDetail AS sod
   INNER JOIN Production.Product AS p
        ON sod.ProductID = p.ProductID
        AND sod.UnitPrice < p.ListPrice
WHERE Color = 'Blue'  ORDER BY p.ProductNumber;
--(57 row(s) affected)
```

```
SELECT DISTINCT  p.ProductNumber, p.Name                    AS ProductName,
                 FORMAT(p.ListPrice,'c','en-US')            AS ListPrice,
                 FORMAT(sod.UnitPrice,'c','en-US')          AS SellPrice
FROM Sales.SalesOrderDetail AS sod
   INNER JOIN Production.Product AS p
        ON sod.ProductID = p.ProductID
        AND sod.UnitPrice < p.ListPrice
        AND Color = 'Blue'
ORDER BY p.ProductNumber;
--(57 row(s) affected)
```

```
SELECT DISTINCT  p.ProductNumber, p.Name                    AS ProductName,
                 FORMAT(p.ListPrice,'c','en-US')            AS ListPrice,
                 FORMAT(sod.UnitPrice,'c','en-US')          AS SellPrice
FROM Sales.SalesOrderDetail AS sod
   INNER JOIN Production.Product AS p
   ON sod.ProductID = p.ProductID
WHERE sod.UnitPrice < p.ListPrice   AND Color = 'Blue'  ORDER BY p.ProductNumber;
--(57 row(s) affected)
```

```
-- Old-style INNER JOIN with table list and WHERE clause
SELECT DISTINCT  p.ProductNumber, p.Name                    AS ProductName,
                 FORMAT(p.ListPrice,'c','en-US')            AS ListPrice,
                 FORMAT(sod.UnitPrice,'c','en-US')          AS SellPrice
FROM Sales.SalesOrderDetail AS sod,  Production.Product AS p
WHERE sod.ProductID = p.ProductID
        AND sod.UnitPrice < p.ListPrice
        AND Color = 'Blue'
ORDER BY p.ProductNumber;          --(57 row(s) affected)
```

SELF-JOIN for Analytics Within a Table

When a table is JOINed to itself, it is a called a self-join. The purpose of such a JOIN is to examine data relations within the table. The Production.Product table is self-joined to itself on the ProductSubcategoryID FOREIGN KEY(not on a PRIMARY KEY), a many-to-many JOIN. Subsequently, we made the query "friendlier" by using subcategory names as opposed to ID-s.

```
SELECT DISTINCT  P1.ProductSubcategoryID,
                 P1.ListPrice                    AS ListPrice1,
                 P2.ListPrice                    AS ListPrice2
FROM   Production.Product P1
  INNER JOIN Production.Product P2
   ON P1.ProductSubcategoryID = P2.ProductSubcategoryID
   AND P1.ListPrice < P2.ListPrice
   AND P1.ListPrice < $15
   AND P2.ListPrice < $15;
```

ProductSubcategoryID	ListPrice1	ListPrice2
23	8.99	9.50
28	4.99	8.99
28	4.99	9.99
28	8.99	9.99
37	2.29	3.99
37	2.29	4.99
37	3.99	4.99

```
SELECT DISTINCT  PS.Name AS Subcategory,
                 P1.ListPrice      AS ListPrice1,
                 P2.ListPrice      AS ListPrice2
FROM   Production.ProductSubcategory PS
    INNER JOIN Production.Product P1
        ON PS.ProductSubcategoryID = P1.ProductSubcategoryID
    INNER JOIN Production.Product P2
        ON P1.ProductSubcategoryID = P2.ProductSubcategoryID
        AND P1.ListPrice < P2.ListPrice              -- To prevent duplicate processing
        AND P1.ListPrice < $15
        AND P2.ListPrice < $15;
```

Subcategory	ListPrice1	ListPrice2
Bottles and Cages	4.99	8.99
Bottles and Cages	4.99	9.99
Bottles and Cages	8.99	9.99
Socks	8.99	9.50
Tires and Tubes	2.29	3.99
Tires and Tubes	2.29	4.99
Tires and Tubes	3.99	4.99

T-SQL SELF-JOIN Query Lists The Competing Suppliers For Each Product Purchased From Vendor

Since the ProductID in the ProductVendor table is part of a composite PRIMARY KEY, we can conclude that it is a many-to-many JOIN.

```
SELECT DISTINCT
            Vendor = V.[Name],
            P1.BusinessEntityID,
            Product = P.[Name],
            P1.ProductID
FROM   Production.Product P
   INNER JOIN Purchasing.ProductVendor P1
      ON P.ProductID = P1.ProductID
   INNER JOIN Purchasing.Vendor V
      ON P1.BusinessEntityID = V.BusinessEntityID
   INNER JOIN Purchasing.ProductVendor P2
      ON P1.ProductID = P2.ProductID
WHERE  P1.BusinessEntityID <> P2.BusinessEntityID
ORDER  BY Product, Vendor
-- (347 row(s) affected) - Partial results.
```

Vendor	BusinessEntityID	Product	ProductID
Beaumont Bikes	1602	Chainring	322
Bike Satellite Inc.	1604	Chainring	322
Training Systems	1514	Chainring	322
Beaumont Bikes	1602	Chainring Bolts	320
Bike Satellite Inc.	1604	Chainring Bolts	320
Training Systems	1514	Chainring Bolts	320
Beaumont Bikes	1602	Chainring Nut	321
Bike Satellite Inc.	1604	Chainring Nut	321
Training Systems	1514	Chainring Nut	321
Aurora Bike Center	1616	External Lock Washer 1	409
Expert Bike Co	1672	External Lock Washer 1	409
Pro Sport Industries	1686	External Lock Washer 1	409
Aurora Bike Center	1616	External Lock Washer 2	411
Pro Sport Industries	1686	External Lock Washer 2	411
Aurora Bike Center	1616	External Lock Washer 3	403
Expert Bike Co	1672	External Lock Washer 3	403
Pro Sport Industries	1686	External Lock Washer 3	403
Aurora Bike Center	1616	External Lock Washer 4	404
Expert Bike Co	1672	External Lock Washer 4	404
Pro Sport Industries	1686	External Lock Washer 4	404
Aurora Bike Center	1616	External Lock Washer 5	406
Expert Bike Co	1672	External Lock Washer 5	406
Pro Sport Industries	1686	External Lock Washer 5	406
Aurora Bike Center	1616	External Lock Washer 6	408
Expert Bike Co	1672	External Lock Washer 6	408

Applying SELF-JOIN for Numbering Result Lines

T-SQL script to demonstrate how SELF-JOIN can be used for numbering lines in query results. Note that in these days we would use **ROW_NUMBER()** function which has been introduced with SQL Server 2005.

```
USE Northwind ;
GO


SELECT   OD.OrderID,
              SeqNo                                    AS LineItem,
              OD.ProductID,
              FORMAT(UnitPrice,'c','en-US')            AS UnitPrice,
              Quantity,
              FORMAT(Discount, 'p')                    AS Discount
FROM    [Order Details] OD
  INNER JOIN (SELECT  count(* )  AS SeqNo,
              a.OrderID,
              a.ProductID
        FROM    [Order Details] A
            INNER JOIN [Order Details] B
              ON A.ProductID >= B.ProductID             -- Prevent duplicates
              AND A.OrderID = B.OrderID
        GROUP BY A.OrderID,   A.ProductID) a
      ON OD.OrderID = a.OrderID
        AND OD.ProductID = a.ProductID
WHERE   OD.OrderID < 10400
ORDER BY        OD.OrderID,
              LineItem
-- (405 row(s) affected) - Partial results.
```

Vendor	AddressLine1	AddressLine2	City	State	Country
A. Datum Corporation	2596 Big Canyon Road		New York	New York	United States
Advanced Bicycles	7995 Edwards Ave.		Lynnwood	Washington	United States
Allenson Cycles	4659 Montoya		Altadena	California	United States
American Bicycles and Wheels	1667 Warren Street		West Covina	California	United States
American Bikes	7179 Montana		Torrance	California	United States
Anderson's Custom Bikes	9 Guadalupe Dr.		Burbank	California	United States
Aurora Bike Center	65 Park Glen Court		Port Orchard	Washington	United States
Australia Bike Retailer	28 San Marino Ct.		Bellingham	Washington	United States
Beaumont Bikes	2472 Alexander Place		West Covina	Idaho	United States
Bergeron Off-Roads	9830 May Way		Mill Valley	Montana	United States
Bicycle Specialists	1286 Cincerto Circle		Lake Oswego	Oregon	United States
Bike Satellite Inc.	2141 Delaware Ct.		Downey	Tennessee	United States
Bloomington Multisport	218 Fall Creek Road		West Covina	California	United States
Burnett Road Warriors	5807 Churchill Dr.		Corvallis	Oregon	United States
Business Equipment Center	6061 St. Paul Way		Everett	Montana	United States
Capital Road Cycles	628 Muir Road		Los Angeles	California	United States
Carlson Specialties	2313 B Southampton Rd		Missoula	Montana	United States
Chicago City Saddles	3 Gehringer Drive		Daly City	California	United States
Chicago Rent-All	15 Pear Dr.		Newport Beach	California	United States
Circuit Cycles	1 Mt. Dell Drive		Portland	Oregon	United States

INNER JOIN with 5 Tables

It takes accessing five tables to get the vendor name & address information in AdventureWorks. In fact this is the main complaint against 3NF relational database design: too many JOINs required to extract data. True, but the benefits of 3NF design are overwhelming. A way to overcome the "too many JOINs" issue is creating views which are pre-canned SELECT queries.

```
USE AdventureWorks;
GO
```

```
SELECT V.Name                AS Vendor,
    A.AddressLine1,
    isnull(A.AddressLine2, '')    AS AddressLine2,
    A.City,
    SP.Name                AS State,
    CR.Name            AS Country
FROM   Purchasing.Vendor AS V
    INNER JOIN Purchasing.VendorAddress AS VA
        ON VA.VendorID = V.VendorID
    INNER JOIN Person.Address AS A
        ON A.AddressID = VA.AddressID
    INNER JOIN Person.StateProvince AS SP
        ON SP.StateProvinceID = A.StateProvinceID
    INNER JOIN Person.CountryRegion AS CR
        ON CR.CountryRegionCode = SP.CountryRegionCode
ORDER  BY Vendor;
GO
-- (104 row(s) affected) - Partial results.
```

Vendor	AddressLine1	AddressLine2	City	State	Country
A. Datum Corporation	2596 Big Canyon Road		New York	New York	United States
Advanced Bicycles	7995 Edwards Ave.		Lynnwood	Washington	United States
Allenson Cycles	4659 Montoya		Altadena	California	United States
American Bicycles and Wheels	1667 Warren Street		West Covina	California	United States
American Bikes	7179 Montana		Torrance	California	United States
Anderson's Custom Bikes	9 Guadalupe Dr.		Burbank	California	United States
Aurora Bike Center	65 Park Glen Court		Port Orchard	Washington	United States
Australia Bike Retailer	28 San Marino Ct.		Bellingham	Washington	United States
Beaumont Bikes	2472 Alexander Place		West Covina	Idaho	United States
Bergeron Off-Roads	9830 May Way		Mill Valley	Montana	United States
Bicycle Specialists	1286 Cincerto Circle		Lake Oswego	Oregon	United States
Bike Satellite Inc.	2141 Delaware Ct.		Downey	Tennessee	United States
Bloomington Multisport	218 Fall Creek Road		West Covina	California	United States
Burnett Road Warriors	5807 Churchill Dr.		Corvallis	Oregon	United States
Business Equipment Center	6061 St. Paul Way		Everett	Montana	United States
Capital Road Cycles	628 Muir Road		Los Angeles	California	United States

Creating View as Workaround for "Too Many JOINs"

It is so simple to create a view, that counterproductive if not done for queries which are used again and again. Given that large database systems may have a great number of views, meaningful long names are paremount.

```
-- No implicit ORDER BY can be included in a view - no trick around it either
CREATE VIEW vVendorAddress  AS
SELECT V.Name                    AS Vendor,
    A.AddressLine1,
    isnull(A.AddressLine2, '')        AS AddressLine2,
    A.City,
    SP.Name                    AS State,
    CR.Name                AS Country
FROM   Purchasing.Vendor AS V
    INNER JOIN Purchasing.VendorAddress AS VA      ON VA.VendorID = V.VendorID
    INNER JOIN Person.Address AS A                 ON A.AddressID = VA.AddressID
    INNER JOIN Person.StateProvince AS SP          ON SP.StateProvinceID = A.StateProvinceID
    INNER JOIN Person.CountryRegion AS CR          ON CR.CountryRegionCode = SP.CountryRegionCode
ORDER  BY Vendor;
GO  /* Msg 1033, Level 15, State 1, Procedure vVendorAddress, Line 18
The ORDER BY clause is invalid in views, inline functions, derived tables, subqueries, and common table
expressions, unless TOP, OFFSET or FOR XML is also specified.  */
```

```
CREATE VIEW vVendorAddress  AS
SELECT V.Name                    AS Vendor,
    A.AddressLine1,
    isnull(A.AddressLine2, '')        AS AddressLine2,
    A.City,
    SP.Name                    AS State,
    CR.Name                AS Country
FROM   Purchasing.Vendor AS V
    INNER JOIN Purchasing.VendorAddress AS VA      ON VA.VendorID = V.VendorID
    INNER JOIN Person.Address AS A                 ON A.AddressID = VA.AddressID
    INNER JOIN Person.StateProvince AS SP          ON SP.StateProvinceID = A.StateProvinceID
    INNER JOIN Person.CountryRegion AS CR          ON CR.CountryRegionCode = SP.CountryRegionCode
GO
```

```
SELECT TOP 5 * FROM vVendorAddress ORDER BY Vendor;
```

Vendor	AddressLine1	AddressLine2	City	State	Country
A. Datum Corporation	2596 Big Canyon Road		New York	New York	United States
Advanced Bicycles	7995 Edwards Ave.		Lynnwood	Washington	United States
Allenson Cycles	4659 Montoya		Altadena	California	United States
American Bicycles and Wheels	1667 Warren Street		West Covina	California	United States
American Bikes	7179 Montana		Torrance	California	United States

CHAPTER 7: JOINing Tables with INNER & OUTER JOINs

Non-Key INNER JOIN for Analytics

So far we have seen INNER JOINs based on FOREIGN KEY to PRIMARY equality relationships. The next INNER JOIN is based on the equality of the first 5 letters of last names. It is also a SELF-JOIN. In addition to the last name part equality, two more conditions are reducing the result set. The < condition is intended to reduce duplicates and the first letter of last name is 'S' limits the query results further. This is a many-to-many JOIN.

```
USE AdventureWorks2012;

SELECT  DISTINCT
    CONCAT( A.FirstName, space(1), A.LastName)      AS Person,
    CONCAT( B.FirstName, space(1), B.LastName)      AS LastNameNeighbor
FROM   Person.Person A
    INNER JOIN  Person.Person B
      ON LEFT(A.LastName, 5) = LEFT(B.LastName, 5)
        AND A.LastName < B.LastName
        AND LEFT(A.LastName, 1) = 'S'
ORDER  BY        Person,
                 LastNameNeighbor;
-- (169 row(s) affected) - Partial results.
```

Person	LastNameNeighbor
Abigail Smith	Lorrin Smith-Bates
Adriana Smith	Lorrin Smith-Bates
Alexander Smith	Lorrin Smith-Bates
Alexandra Smith	Lorrin Smith-Bates
Alexis Smith	Lorrin Smith-Bates
Allen Smith	Lorrin Smith-Bates
Alyssa Smith	Lorrin Smith-Bates
Andre Smith	Lorrin Smith-Bates
Andrew Smith	Lorrin Smith-Bates
Arthur Smith	Lorrin Smith-Bates
Ashley Smith	Lorrin Smith-Bates
Austin Smith	Lorrin Smith-Bates
Barry Srini	Sethu Srinivasan
Ben Smith	Lorrin Smith-Bates
Benjamin Smith	Lorrin Smith-Bates
Beth Srini	Sethu Srinivasan
Brandon Smith	Lorrin Smith-Bates
Brandy Srini	Sethu Srinivasan
Brett Srini	Sethu Srinivasan
Brianna Smith	Lorrin Smith-Bates

JOINing Tables without Relationship for Combinatorics

SQL Server will execute such a JOIN on any pair of compatible columns as demonstrated by the next T-SQL query. Note this is only a demo, there is no business meaning to it unless the combinatorial results are useful for some application. A more practical example in the pubs database matching author city with publisher city using a JOIN.

```
USE Northwind;   -- Cross database JOIN query
SELECT   P.ProductID,
         P.ProductName        AS NorthwindProduct,
         PP.Name              AS AWProduct
FROM dbo.Products P
        INNER JOIN AdventureWorks2008.Production.Product PP      ON P.ProductID = PP.ProductID
ORDER BY P.ProductID;
```

ProductID	NorthwindProduct	AWProduct
1	Chai	Adjustable Race
2	Chang	Bearing Ball
3	Aniseed Syrup	BB Ball Bearing
4	Chef Anton's Cajun Seasoning	Headset Ball Bearings

Cartesian Product

When all rows in one table combined with all rows of another table it is called a Cartesian product. The cardinality of such a JOIN is (Table 1 Rows) x (Table 2 Rows).

```
-- Old-fashioned no JOIN predicate 2-table query - Cardinality 4x4 = 16
SELECT Category1 = A.Name, Category2 = B.Name
FROM Production.ProductCategory A, Production.ProductCategory B ORDER BY Category1, Category2;
```

```
-- Equivalent CROSS JOIN
SELECT Category1 = A.Name, Category2 = B.Name
FROM Production.ProductCategory A  CROSS JOIN Production.ProductCategory B
ORDER BY Category1, Category2;
```

Category1	Category2
Accessories	Accessories
Accessories	Bikes
Accessories	Clothing
Accessories	Components
Bikes	Accessories
Bikes	Bikes
Bikes	Clothing
Bikes	Components
Clothing	Accessories
Clothing	Bikes
Clothing	Clothing
Clothing	Components
Components	Accessories
Components	Bikes
Components	Clothing
Components	Components

SQL OUTER JOIN for Inclusion of Unmatched Rows

We have seen that INNER JOINs return rows only when there is at least one row from both tables that satisfies the join condition or conditions such as FOREIGN KEY matching the referenced PRIMARY KEY. Inner join queries do not return the rows that do not meet the ON condition with a row from the other table.

OUTER JOINs, however, return all rows from one or both tables in the JOIN. All rows are returned from the left table in a LEFT OUTER JOIN (including non-matching rows), and all rows are returned from the right table in a RIGHT OUTER JOIN. All rows from both tables are returned in a FULL OUTER JOIN. LEFT OUTER JOIN is totally equivalent to RIGHT OUTER JOIN. LEFT OUTER JOIN is mostly used by programmers in countries where the writing is left to right. **RIGHT OUTER JOIN is typically used by developers in countries where the writing is right to left**. **The non-matching rows in an OUTER JOIN are returned with NULL value fields**, therefore, they can be distinquished from the matching rows with a null test.

The following are synonyms:

LEFT JOIN - LEFT OUTER JOIN

RIGHT JOIN - RIGHT OUTER JOIN

FULL JOIN - FULL OUTER JOIN

The legacy syntax for outer joins *= (left join) or =* (right join) is not supported anymore. T-SQL example script lists products (left table) even if they are not being sold such as assembly parts.

```
USE AdventureWorks2012;
SELECT          P.Name,          SOD.SalesOrderID,
                CASE     WHEN SalesOrderID is null THEN 'Non-matching'
                         ELSE 'Matching' END               AS JoinInfo
FROM   Production.Product P
    LEFT OUTER JOIN Sales.SalesOrderDetail SOD     ON P.ProductID = SOD.ProductID
ORDER  BY P.Name;   -- (121555 row(s) affected) - Partial results.
```

Name	SalesOrderID	JoinInfo
Adjustable Race	NULL	Non-matching
All-Purpose Bike Stand	51179	Matching
All-Purpose Bike Stand	51488	Matching
All-Purpose Bike Stand	51520	Matching
All-Purpose Bike Stand	51558	Matching
All-Purpose Bike Stand	51882	Matching
All-Purpose Bike Stand	51903	Matching
All-Purpose Bike Stand	51970	Matching
All-Purpose Bike Stand	52010	Matching
All-Purpose Bike Stand	52032	Matching

LEFT JOIN: Include Unmatched Rows from Left Table

In the LEFT JOIN example, the Vendor table is LEFT JOINed to the PurchaseOrderHeader table to find out which vendors did not supply anything. The LEFT JOIN is based on FOREIGN KEY relationship.

```
USE AdventureWorks2012;

SELECT Vendor = V.Name
FROM   Purchasing.Vendor V
    LEFT JOIN Purchasing.PurchaseOrderHeader POH
        ON V.BusinessEntityID = POH.VendorID
WHERE  POH.VendorID IS NULL          -- Test if POH columns are null
ORDER by Vendor;   -- (18 row(s) affected) - Partial results.
```

Vendor
A. Datum Corporation
Cycling Master
Electronic Bike Co.
GMA Ski & Bike
Holiday Skate & Cycle
Illinois Trek & Clothing

T-SQL query to check which pedal products for sale were reviewed and which ones not.

```
SELECT   p.Name           AS ProductName,
         ProductNumber,
         pr.ProductReviewID,
         pr.ReviewerName,
         pr.Rating
FROM Production.Product p
  LEFT JOIN Production.ProductReview pr
        ON p.ProductID = pr.ProductID
WHERE p.ProductSubcategoryID is not null   AND p.Name like '%pedal%'  ORDER BY ProductNumber;
-- (8 row(s) affected)
```

ProductName	ProductNumber	ProductReviewID	ReviewerName	Rating
LL Mountain Pedal	PD-M282	NULL	NULL	NULL
ML Mountain Pedal	PD-M340	NULL	NULL	NULL
HL Mountain Pedal	PD-M562	2	David	4
HL Mountain Pedal	PD-M562	3	Jill	2
LL Road Pedal	PD-R347	NULL	NULL	NULL
ML Road Pedal	PD-R563	NULL	NULL	NULL
HL Road Pedal	PD-R853	NULL	NULL	NULL
Touring Pedal	PD-T852	NULL	NULL	NULL

RIGHT JOIN - Same as LEFT with Tables Switched

The RIGHT JOIN is totally equivalent, including performance, to the corresponding LEFT JOIN.
RIGHT JOIN is more frequently used in countries where they write right to left.

```
USE AdventureWorks2012;

SELECT Vendor = V.Name
FROM   Purchasing.PurchaseOrderHeader POH
    RIGHT JOIN Purchasing.Vendor V
     ON V.BusinessEntityID = POH.VendorID
WHERE  POH.VendorID IS NULL
ORDER by Vendor;
-- (18 row(s) affected) - Partial results.
```

Vendor
A. Datum Corporation
Cycling Master
Electronic Bike Co.
GMA Ski & Bike
Holiday Skate & Cycle

T-SQL RIGHT JOIN examples progress toward a query to provide users with a good report.

```
USE AdventureWorks2012;

SELECT ST.Name AS  Territory,
    SP.BusinessEntityID
FROM   Sales.SalesTerritory ST
    RIGHT OUTER JOIN Sales.SalesPerson SP
     ON ST.TerritoryID = SP.TerritoryID;
-- (17 row(s) affected)
```

```
SELECT   isnull(ST.Name, ' ')                    AS Territory,
        SP.BusinessEntityID,
        CONCAT (C.FirstName, ' ', C.LastName)      AS Name
FROM   Sales.SalesTerritory ST
    RIGHT OUTER JOIN Sales.SalesPerson SP
     ON ST.TerritoryID = SP.TerritoryID
    INNER JOIN Person.Person C
     ON SP.BusinessEntityID = C.BusinessEntityID;
-- (17 row(s) affected)
```

Add a WHERE condition filter on Sales.SalesPerson SalesYTD column
The NULLs indicate the no match rows in the RIGHT OUTER JOIN.

```
SELECT   ST.CountryRegionCode,
         ST.Name                                  AS Territory,
         SP.BusinessEntityID                       AS EmployeeID,
         CONCAT(C.FirstName, ' ', C.LastName )     AS Name
FROM   Sales.SalesTerritory ST
     RIGHT OUTER JOIN Sales.SalesPerson SP
      ON ST.TerritoryID = SP.TerritoryID
     INNER JOIN Person.Person C
      ON SP.BusinessEntityID = C.BusinessEntityID
WHERE SP.SalesYTD > 1000.0
ORDER BY        CountryRegionCode,
                Territory;
GO
-- (17 row(s) affected)
```

CountryRegionCode	Territory	EmployeeID	Name
NULL	NULL	274	Stephen Jiang
NULL	NULL	285	Syed Abbas
NULL	NULL	287	Amy Alberts
AU	Australia	286	Lynn Tsoflias
CA	Canada	278	Garrett Vargas
CA	Canada	282	José Saraiva
DE	Germany	288	Rachel Valdez
FR	France	290	Ranjit Varkey Chudukatil
GB	United Kingdom	289	Jae Pak
US	Central	277	Jillian Carson
US	Northeast	275	Michael Blythe
US	Northwest	283	David Campbell
US	Northwest	284	Tete Mensa-Annan
US	Northwest	280	Pamela Ansman-Wolfe
US	Southeast	279	Tsvi Reiter
US	Southwest	276	Linda Mitchell
US	Southwest	281	Shu Ito

```
-- Counting the RIGHT JOIN  match rows using a ProductSubcategory column
SELECT COUNT( S.Name)
FROM Production.ProductSubcategory S RIGHT JOIN Production.Product P
   ON S.ProductSubcategoryID = P.ProductSubcategoryID;
-- 295
```

CHAPTER 7: JOINing Tables with INNER & OUTER JOINs

Cardinality of OUTER JOINs

The number of rows returned in an OUTER JOIN is equal to the matching rows plus the non-matching rows from either or both tables. **To identify the non-matching rows (the ones with the NULLs) in an outer join we have to choose a not-nullable column like the PRIMARY KEY column.** T-SQL script demonstrates the cardinality involved with a LEFT JOIN.

```
USE AdventureWorks2012;

-- Rows in LEFT JOIN
SELECT Rows = count(*)
FROM   Production.Product P
    LEFT OUTER JOIN Sales.SalesOrderDetail SOD
         ON P.ProductID = SOD.ProductID
-- 121555

-- Rows in right table
SELECT Rows = count(*)
FROM Sales.SalesOrderDetail
-- 121317

-- Non-matching rows in left table
SELECT Rows = count(*)
FROM   Production.Product P
    LEFT OUTER JOIN Sales.SalesOrderDetail SOD
         ON P.ProductID = SOD.ProductID
WHERE SalesOrderID is NULL
-- 238

-- Right table rows + non-matching left table rows = rows returned by left join
SELECT 121317 + 238
-- 121555
```

Since the count queries are single valued, we can do the following summation.

```
SELECT (SELECT Rows = count(*)  FROM Sales.SalesOrderDetail )
+
(SELECT Rows = count(*)
FROM   Production.Product P
    LEFT OUTER JOIN Sales.SalesOrderDetail SOD
         ON P.ProductID = SOD.ProductID
WHERE SalesOrderID is NULL);
GO  -- 121555
```

LEFT JOIN & RIGHT JOIN on the Same Table

LEFT JOIN & RIGHT JOIN can be combined on the same table to keep all rows from that table even if they don't match the other two tables. The Production.Product table has a FOREIGN KEY referencing the ProductSubcategory table and another FOREIGN KEY referencing the UnitMeasure table.

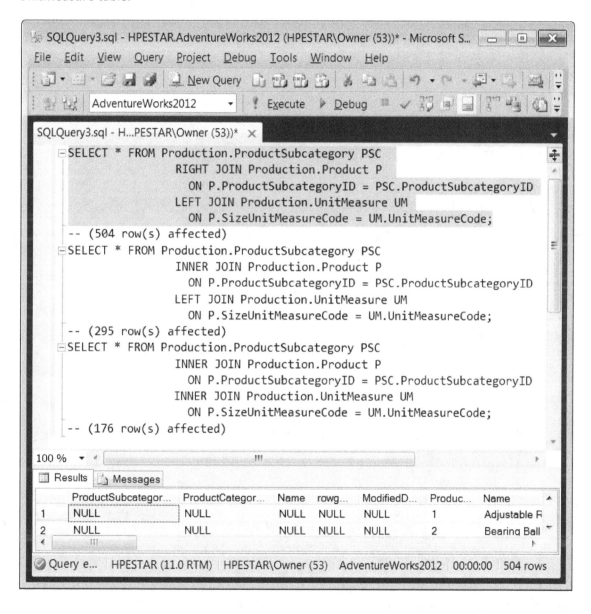

FULL JOIN to Include All Unmatched Rows

The operation FULL JOIN combines LEFT JOIN and RIGHT JOIN, therefore it does not matter which is the left table or right table, it is a fully symmetrical set operation. T-SQL script demonstrates FULL OUTER JOIN.

```
USE tempdb;
-- Create tables for demo
SELECT distinct Color INTO Color
FROM AdventureWorks2012.Production.Product
WHERE Color is not null;
GO
```

```
SELECT ID=IDENTITY(int, 1, 1), * INTO NormalColor
FROM Color;
SELECT ID=IDENTITY(int, 1, 1), Color=CONCAT('Light', Color)  INTO LightColor
FROM Color;
```

```
DELETE NormalColor WHERE Color = 'Red';
```

```
DELETE LightColor WHERE Color = 'LightBlue';
```

```
-- Demo tables ready - full join query
SELECT   NormalColor     = n.Color,
         LightColor      = l.Color
FROM   NormalColor n     FULL OUTER JOIN LightColor l    ON n.ID = l.ID
ORDER BY NormalColor;
```

NormalColor	LightColor
NULL	LightRed
Black	LightBlack
Blue	NULL
Grey	LightGrey
Multi	LightMulti
Silver	LightSilver
Silver/Black	LightSilver/Black
White	LightWhite
Yellow	LightYellow

```
DROP TABLE  tempdb.dbo.Color;  DROP TABLE tempdb.dbo.NormalColor;
DROP TABLE tempdb.dbo.LightColor;
GO
```

CROSS JOIN for Cartesian Product

A CROSS JOIN with no connecting columns for joining produces a Cartesian product: combines all rows of the left table with all rows of the right tables. If the left table has x rows and the right table y rows, the CROSS JOIN is going to have x*y rows. That is called Cartesian explosion as it happens sometimes unintentionally in database development. In fact, a huge CROSS JOIN can bring SQL Server "to its knees", overwhelming CPU and disk resources. On the same note, no matter how powerful is the hardware platform, a bad runaway query can make SQL Server unresponsive to normal queries from other connections. T-SQL script to demonstrate CROSS JOIN.

```
USE AdventureWorks2012;

-- Cardinality of CROSS JOIN
SELECT count(*) from HumanResources.Employee;          -- 290
SELECT count(*) from HumanResources.Department;        -- 16
SELECT 16 * 290;                                       -- 4640

SELECT          E.BusinessEntityID             AS EMPLOYEEID,
                D.Name                         AS DEPARTMENT
FROM   HumanResources.Employee E   CROSS JOIN HumanResources.Department D
ORDER  BY       EMPLOYEEID,        DEPARTMENT;
-- (4640 row(s) affected) - Partial results.
```

EMPLOYEEID	DEPARTMENT
1	Production Control
1	Purchasing
1	Quality Assurance
1	Research and Development
1	Sales
1	Shipping and Receiving
1	Tool Design
2	Document Control
2	Engineering
2	Executive
2	Facilities and Maintenance
2	Finance
2	Human Resources
2	Information Services
2	Marketing
2	Production

CROSS JOIN Generated Multiplication Table

A CROSS JOIN can be used to create combinatorical results. In the next example, a multiplication table is created using a CROSS JOIN which is also a SELF-JOIN. CTE stands for Common Table Expression, which can be used as a table in SELECT and other queries. The master database spt_values table is used to get a sequence of numbers. The ".." in the table reference means: use the default schema which is "dbo".

```
; WITH cteNumber                          -- cte for numbers 1 to 10
    AS (SELECT NUMBER
       FROM   master..spt_values
       WHERE  TYPE = 'P'
           AND NUMBER BETWEEN 1 AND 10)
SELECT MULTIPLICATION=CONCAT( ltrim(str(B.NUMBER)) , ' * '
            , ltrim(str(A.NUMBER)) , ' = '
            , ltrim(str(A.NUMBER * B.NUMBER)) )
FROM   cteNumber A   CROSS JOIN cteNumber B;
-- (100 row(s) affected) - Partial results.
```

MULTIPLICATION
1 * 1 = 1
1 * 2 = 2
1 * 3 = 3
1 * 4 = 4
1 * 5 = 5
1 * 6 = 6
1 * 7 = 7
1 * 8 = 8
1 * 9 = 9
1 * 10 = 10
2 * 1 = 2
2 * 2 = 4
2 * 3 = 6
2 * 4 = 8
2 * 5 = 10
2 * 6 = 12
2 * 7 = 14
2 * 8 = 16
2 * 9 = 18
2 * 10 = 20
3 * 1 = 3
3 * 2 = 6
3 * 3 = 9
3 * 4 = 12
3 * 5 = 15

INNER JOIN with 7 Tables

 T-SQL query lists AdventureWorks Cycles retail (web) customers with total purchase amount and order dates. The name & address displays multiple times if a customer did multiple purchases. Generally, that is undesirable, and requires end-user report design considerations how to resolve it. The sorting uses Sales.SalesOrderHeader OrderDate which is datetime data type, instead of the mdy format string report date. mdy string format dates do not sort in chronological order.

```
USE AdventureWorks;
GO

SELECT CONCAT(C.LastName, ', ', C.FirstName)           AS CustomerName,
       A.City,
       SP.Name                                         AS State,
       CR.Name                                         AS Country,
       A.PostalCode,
       FORMAT(SOH.TotalDue, 'c','en-US')               AS SalesAmount,
       FORMAT(SOH.OrderDate,'d')                       AS OrderDate
FROM Person.Contact AS C
  INNER JOIN Sales.Individual AS I
        ON C.ContactID = I.ContactID
  INNER JOIN Sales.CustomerAddress AS CA
        ON CA.CustomerID = I.CustomerID
  INNER JOIN Person.Address AS A
        ON A.AddressID = CA.AddressID
  INNER JOIN Person.StateProvince SP
        ON SP.StateProvinceID = A.StateProvinceID
  INNER JOIN Person.CountryRegion CR
        ON CR.CountryRegionCode = SP.CountryRegionCode
  INNER JOIN Sales.SalesOrderHeader SOH
        ON C.ContactID = SOH.CustomerID
ORDER BY CustomerName, soh.OrderDate ;
-- (16493 row(s) affected)  - Partial results.
```

CustomerName	City	State	Country	PostalCode	SalesAmount	OrderDate
Adams, Aaron	Downey	California	United States	90241	$734.70	3/4/2004
Adams, Adam	Newport Beach	California	United States	92625	$2,566.12	4/16/2004
Adams, Alex	Lake Oswego	Oregon	United States	97034	$2,410.63	3/18/2003
Adams, Alex	Lake Oswego	Oregon	United States	97034	$1,293.38	12/9/2003
Adams, Alex	Lake Oswego	Oregon	United States	97034	$2,643.12	2/1/2004
Adams, Angel	Burlingame	California	United States	94010	$865.20	5/24/2003
Adams, Angel	Burlingame	California	United States	94010	$2,597.81	3/1/2004
Adams, Carlos	Langford	British Columbia	Canada	V9	$44.18	6/28/2004
Adams, Connor	Westminster	British Columbia	Canada	V3L 1H4	$183.74	4/14/2004
Adams, Elijah	Seattle	Washington	United States	98104	$8.04	11/2/2003

INNER JOIN with GROUP BY Subquery

We have to make the GROUP BY subquery into a derived table first. Subsequently, we can apply it just like any other table in a query.

```
USE AdventureWorks2012;
GO

SELECT  Subcategory = Name,
        Color,
        ColorCount,
        AvgListPrice
FROM  (
        SELECT ProductSubcategoryID,              -- grouping column
        Color = COALESCE(Color, 'N/A'),           -- grouping column with transformation
        ColorCount = COUNT(*),                     -- aggregate function
        AvgListPrice = AVG(COALESCE(ListPrice, 0.0))  -- aggregate function
        FROM   AdventureWorks2008.Production.Product
        GROUP  BY      ProductSubcategoryID,
                       Color) x                    -- derived table (subquery)
    INNER JOIN Production.ProductSubcategory psc
        ON psc.ProductSubcategoryID = x.ProductSubcategoryID
ORDER  BY Subcategory,
        Color;
GO
-- (48 row(s) affected) - Partial results.
```

Subcategory	Color	ColorCount	AvgListPrice
Bib-Shorts	Multi	3	89.990000
Bike Racks	N/A	1	120.000000
Bike Stands	N/A	1	159.000000
Bottles and Cages	N/A	3	7.990000
Bottom Brackets	N/A	3	92.240000
Brakes	Silver	2	106.500000
Caps	Multi	1	8.990000
Chains	Silver	1	20.240000
Cleaners	N/A	1	7.950000
Cranksets	Black	3	278.990000
Derailleurs	Silver	2	106.475000
Fenders	N/A	1	21.980000

Making Queries Readable & Results Presentable

A database developer has to make a query readable for productivity gain in development and ease of maintenance. At the same time the results must be readable to the user. The next query with results demonstrates how to achieve both objectives.

```
USE AdventureWorks2012;
GO

SELECT  PC.Name                          AS Category,
        PSC.Name                         AS Subcategory,
        PM.Name                          AS Model,
        P.Name                           AS ProductName,
        FORMAT(ListPrice,'c','en-US')    AS Price
FROM Production.Product AS P
   INNER JOIN Production.ProductModel AS PM
        ON PM.ProductModelID = P.ProductModelID
   INNER JOIN Production.ProductSubcategory AS PSC
        ON PSC.ProductSubcategoryID = P.ProductSubcategoryID
   INNER JOIN Production.ProductCategory AS PC
        ON PC.ProductCategoryID = PSC.ProductCategoryID
ORDER BY Category, Subcategory, ProductName;
GO
-- (295 row(s) affected) - Partial results.
```

The confusing 4 "Name" columns are clarified by well-chosen column aliases. The meaningful column aliases are used in the ORDER BY clause even though not required. To help the user, the list price is currency formatted.

Category	Subcategory	Model	ProductName	Price
Accessories	Bike Racks	Hitch Rack - 4-Bike	Hitch Rack - 4-Bike	$120.00
Accessories	Bike Stands	All-Purpose Bike Stand	All-Purpose Bike Stand	$159.00
Accessories	Bottles and Cages	Mountain Bottle Cage	Mountain Bottle Cage	$9.99
Accessories	Bottles and Cages	Road Bottle Cage	Road Bottle Cage	$8.99
Accessories	Bottles and Cages	Water Bottle	Water Bottle - 30 oz.	$4.99
Accessories	Cleaners	Bike Wash	Bike Wash - Dissolver	$7.95
Accessories	Fenders	Fender Set - Mountain	Fender Set - Mountain	$21.98
Accessories	Helmets	Sport-100	Sport-100 Helmet, Black	$34.99
Accessories	Helmets	Sport-100	Sport-100 Helmet, Blue	$34.99
Accessories	Helmets	Sport-100	Sport-100 Helmet, Red	$34.99

A 12 Tables JOIN Query

The next query JOINs 11 tables, some of the tables occur more than once in the query.

```
USE AdventureWorks;

DECLARE         @Year  int,
                @Month int

SET @Year     = 2004;
SET @Month    = 1;

SELECT SOH.SalesOrderNumber                       AS SON,
    SOH.PurchaseOrderNumber                       AS PO,
    S.Name                                        AS Store,
    CONVERT(VARCHAR, SOH.OrderDate, 110)          AS OrderDate,
    CONVERT(VARCHAR, SOH.ShipDate, 110)           AS ShipDate,
    FORMAT(TotalDue,'c','en-US')                  AS [Total Due],
    CONCAT(C.FirstName,' ',C.LastName)            AS SalesStaff,
    SM.Name                                       AS ShpngMethod,
    BA.AddressLine1                               AS BlngAddress1,
    Isnull(BA.AddressLine2, '')                   AS BlngAddress2,
    BA.City                                       AS BlngCity,
    BSP.Name                                      AS BlngStateProvince,
    BA.PostalCode                                 AS BlngPostalCode,
    BCR.Name                                      AS BlngCountryRegion,
    SA.AddressLine1                               AS ShpngAddress1,
    Isnull(SA.AddressLine2, '')                   AS ShpngAddress2,
    SA.City                                       AS ShpngCity,
    SSP.Name                                      AS ShpngStateProvince,
    SA.PostalCode                                 AS ShpngPostalCode,
    SCR.Name                                      AS ShpngCountryRegion,
    CONCAT(CC.FirstName,' ',CC.LastName)          AS CustomerContact,
    CC.Phone                                      AS CustomerPhone,
    SOH.AccountNumber
FROM   Person.Address SA
    INNER JOIN Person.StateProvince SSP
        ON SA.StateProvinceID = SSP.StateProvinceID
    INNER JOIN Person.CountryRegion SCR
        ON SSP.CountryRegionCode = SCR.CountryRegionCode
    INNER JOIN Sales.SalesOrderHeader SOH
        INNER JOIN Person.Contact CC
            ON SOH.ContactID = CC.ContactID
        INNER JOIN Person.Address BA
            INNER JOIN Person.StateProvince BSP
                ON BA.StateProvinceID = BSP.StateProvinceID
            INNER JOIN Person.CountryRegion BCR
```

```
-- T-SQL query continued

                    ON BSP.CountryRegionCode =
                         BCR.CountryRegionCode
                  ON SOH.BillToAddressID = BA.AddressID
              ON SA.AddressID = SOH.ShipToAddressID
          INNER JOIN Person.Contact C
                INNER JOIN HumanResources.Employee E
                    ON C.ContactID = E.ContactID
              ON SOH.SalesPersonID = E.EmployeeID
          INNER JOIN Purchasing.ShipMethod SM
              ON SOH.ShipMethodID = SM.ShipMethodID
          INNER JOIN Sales.Store S
              ON SOH.CustomerID = S.CustomerID
WHERE  SOH.OrderDate >= datefromparts(@Year, @month, 1)
    AND  SOH.OrderDate < dateadd(mm,1,datefromparts(@Year, @month, 1))
ORDER  BY Store,  OrderDate DESC;
GO
-- (96 row(s) affected) - Partial results.
```

SON	PO	Store	OrderDate	ShipDate	Total Due	SalesStaff	ShpngMethod	BlngAddress1
SO61257	PO3741176337	Activity Center	01-01-2004	01-08-2004	$12,764.08	Tsvi Reiter	CARGO TRANSPORT 5	Factory Stores Of America
SO61256	PO1421187796	All Cycle Shop	01-01-2004	01-08-2004	$201.08	Tete Mensa-Annan	CARGO TRANSPORT 5	25111 228th St Sw
SO61251	PO6380165323	All Seasons Sports Supply	01-01-2004	01-08-2004	$2,863.30	Michael Blythe	CARGO TRANSPORT 5	Ohms Road
SO61263	PO5452121402	Amalgamated Parts Shop	01-01-2004	01-08-2004	$39,103.04	Rachel Valdez	CARGO TRANSPORT 5	Brunnenstr 422
SO61227	PO10730172247	Area Bike Accessories	01-01-2004	01-08-2004	$75,916.89	Shu Ito	CARGO TRANSPORT 5	6900 Sisk Road
SO61187	PO13978135025	Basic Bike Company	01-01-2004	01-08-2004	$72.92	David Campbell	CARGO TRANSPORT 5	15 East Main
SO61190	PO12441157171	Best Cycle Store	01-01-2004	01-08-2004	$49,337.61	Rachel Valdez	CARGO TRANSPORT 5	Berliner Platz 45
SO61221	PO15399128383	Best o' Bikes	01-01-2004	01-08-2004	$5,872.73	Michael Blythe	CARGO TRANSPORT 5	250880 Baur Blvd
SO61173	PO522171689	Better Bike Shop	01-01-2004	01-08-2004	$38,511.29	Tsvi Reiter	CARGO TRANSPORT 5	42525 Austell Road
SO61254	PO4872176154	Bicycle Exporters	01-01-2004	01-08-2004	$10,665.06	Rachel Valdez	CARGO TRANSPORT 5	Hellweg 4934
SO61243	PO7859152962	Bike Dealers Association	01-01-2004	01-08-2004	$18,976.48	Shu Ito	CARGO TRANSPORT 5	9952 E. Lohman Ave.
SO61250	PO4930183869	Bikes for Kids and Adults	01-01-2004	01-08-2004	$3,852.87	Jae Pak	CARGO TRANSPORT 5	9900 Ronson Drive
SO61209	PO11484136165	Casual Bicycle Store	01-01-2004	01-08-2004	$37,314.33	Jillian Carson	CARGO TRANSPORT 5	Westside Plaza
SO61204	PO15312134209	Citywide Service and Repair	01-01-2004	01-08-2004	$29,797.18	Jae Pak	CARGO TRANSPORT 5	Box 99354 300 Union Street
SO61192	PO10092119585	Classic Cycle Store	01-01-2004	01-08-2004	$3,691.57	Jillian Carson	CARGO TRANSPORT 5	630 Oldgate Lane

Order of Tables or Predicates Does Not Matter

Frequent question: does the order of tables matter in a JOIN? Should I put BETWEEN predicate before LIKE predicate? Valid syntax variations do not matter. The database engine translates the query to an internal form prior to creating an execution plan. Thus the different variations get translated to the same internal form. The only way we have some control over the database engine if we rewrite a single statement complex query to a multi-statements script.

Nondeterministic CTE

CTE is evaluated for every reference, therefore it may return different results if certain functions are used such as newid(), thus yielding a nondeterministic CTE.

```
;WITH CTE AS (SELECT Random = NEWID()),
CTE1 AS (SELECT * FROM CTE),
CTE2 AS (SELECT * FROM CTE),
CTE3 AS (SELECT * FROM CTE),
CTE4 AS (SELECT * FROM CTE),
CTE5 AS (SELECT * FROM CTE)
SELECT * FROM CTE1
UNION ALL
SELECT * FROM CTE2
UNION ALL
SELECT * FROM CTE3
UNION ALL
SELECT * FROM CTE4
UNION ALL
SELECT * FROM CTE5
UNION ALL
SELECT * FROM CTE
UNION ALL
SELECT * FROM CTE
UNION ALL
SELECT * FROM CTE;
```

Random
08D45FE2-52C6-4E15-83A3-0B2F27837887
D6A094E6-0C8A-43E4-B6C4-8821F6EE8E73
281A5852-3D9A-4F2A-99FA-F60EE28FD2E0
C327ED19-5C03-4D9B-A8E8-6ACABAA08F1C
80DDE508-A6AA-4F2B-AB2F-CEEF7EC5E163
5F611B03-46F4-4EED-A8E0-76020527899D
FF8DAE17-65F6-4D80-8AF5-29EBAEBD2FEB
CF342DC9-4CF9-46FD-87F0-3213106C447D

The CROSS APPLY Operator

The APPLY (CROSS APPLY & OUTER APPLY) operators were introduced with SQL Server 2005. The CROSS APPLY operator merges rows from tables (or views) with rows from table-valued function, a form of JOIN.

```
USE AdventureWorks2012;
SELECT
        q.last_execution_time               AS LastRun,
        t.TEXT                              AS QueryText,
        q.sql_handle                        AS SQLHandle
FROM    sys.dm_exec_query_stats AS q                   -- system view
            CROSS APPLY
            sys.dm_exec_sql_text(q.sql_handle) AS t    -- table-valued system function
WHERE LEFT(t.TEXT,8)='SELECT *'  ORDER BY LastRun DESC;
```

LastRun	QueryText
2016-08-01 14:46:12.537	SELECT * FROM Sales.SalesOrderHeader
2016-08-01 14:44:54.257	SELECT * FROM Production.Product
2016-08-01 13:29:25.213	SELECT * FROM sys.dm_os_wait_stats
2016-08-01 09:36:57.980	select * from sys.sysforeignkeys s
2016-08-01 09:36:39.077	select * from sysforeignkeys s

```
-- Return the top N purchase order by amount - inline table-valued function
CREATE FUNCTION dbo.ufnGetTopNPurchases(@VendorID AS INT, @N AS INT)
RETURNS TABLE  AS
RETURN
 SELECT TOP ( @N ) *   FROM Purchasing.PurchaseOrderHeader
  WHERE VendorID = @VendorID   ORDER BY TotalDue DESC;
GO   -- Command(s) completed successfully.
```

```
-- List the top 5 highest purchases from vendors
SELECT  V.VendorID,
        P.PurchaseOrderID,
        FORMAT(P.TotalDue, 'c','en-US')     AS TotalDue
FROM    Purchasing.Vendor AS V  CROSS APPLY  dbo.ufnGetTopNPurchases(V.VendorID, 5) AS P
ORDER BY  V.VendorID, TotalDue DESC
-- (395 row(s) affected) - Partial results.
```

VendorID	PurchaseOrderID	TotalDue
74	325	$1,654.75
74	1727	$855.22
74	2517	$855.22
74	3307	$855.22
74	167	$785.61

Using CROSS APPLY with Columns Specified Table Alias

A regular table alias would result in error in the following delimited string list query. Table alias with column(s) specifications "o(list)" works, the table alias is "o", it has one column "list".

CHAPTER 8: Basic SELECT Statement Syntax & Examples

Simple SELECT Statement Variations

SELECT is the most famous statement in the SQL language. It is used to query tables, and generate reports for users. Although SQL Server Reporting Services and other 3rd party packages available for reporting purposes, frequently reports are generated straight from the database with SELECT queries. The next query returns all rows, all columns sorted on DepartmentID.

```
USE AdventureWorks2012;
```

```
SELECT * FROM  HumanResources.Department  ORDER BY DepartmentID;
-- (16 row(s) affected)
```

DepartmentID	Name	GroupName	ModifiedDate
1	Engineering	Research and Development	1998-06-01 00:00:00.000
2	Tool Design	Research and Development	1998-06-01 00:00:00.000
3	Sales	Sales and Marketing	1998-06-01 00:00:00.000
4	Marketing	Sales and Marketing	1998-06-01 00:00:00.000
5	Purchasing	Inventory Management	1998-06-01 00:00:00.000
6	Research and Development	Research and Development	1998-06-01 00:00:00.000
7	Production	Manufacturing	1998-06-01 00:00:00.000
8	Production Control	Manufacturing	1998-06-01 00:00:00.000
9	Human Resources	Executive General and Administration	1998-06-01 00:00:00.000
10	Finance	Executive General and Administration	1998-06-01 00:00:00.000
11	Information Services	Executive General and Administration	1998-06-01 00:00:00.000
12	Document Control	Quality Assurance	1998-06-01 00:00:00.000
13	Quality Assurance	Quality Assurance	1998-06-01 00:00:00.000
14	Facilities and Maintenance	Executive General and Administration	1998-06-01 00:00:00.000
15	Shipping and Receiving	Inventory Management	1998-06-01 00:00:00.000
16	Executive	Executive General and Administration	1998-06-01 00:00:00.000

Since the time part of ModifiedDate is not being used, and that makes business sense, we can format it just as date.

```
SELECT TOP (3) DepartmentID, Name, GroupName, CONVERT(DATE, ModifiedDate) AS ModifiedDate
FROM  HumanResources.Department  ORDER BY DepartmentID;
-- (16 row(s) affected)
```

DepartmentID	Name	GroupName	ModifiedDate
1	Engineering	Research and Development	1998-06-01
2	Tool Design	Research and Development	1998-06-01
3	Sales	Sales and Marketing	1998-06-01

SELECT query with sort on EnglishProductName in DESCending order
ASCending sort is the default.

```
USE AdventureWorksDW2012
GO
```

```
SELECT  *
FROM    DimProduct
ORDER BY EnglishProductName DESC
GO
-- (606 row(s) affected) - Partial results.
```

EnglishProductName	SpanishProductName	FrenchProductName	StandardCost
Women's Tights, S	Mallas para mujer, P	Collants pour femmes, taille S	30.9334
Women's Tights, M	Mallas para mujer, M	Collants pour femmes, taille M	30.9334
Women's Tights, L	Mallas para mujer, G	Collants pour femmes, taille L	30.9334
Women's Mountain Shorts, S			26.1763
Women's Mountain Shorts, M			26.1763
Women's Mountain Shorts, L			26.1763
Water Bottle - 30 oz.			1.8663
Touring-Panniers, Large	Cesta de paseo, grande	Sacoches de vélo de randonnée, grande capacité	51.5625
Touring-3000 Yellow, 62	Paseo: 3000, amarilla, 62	Vélo de randonnée 3000 jaune, 62	461.4448
Touring-3000 Yellow, 58	Paseo: 3000, amarilla, 58	Vélo de randonnée 3000 jaune, 58	461.4448

The next query sorts on the SpanishProductName column in ascending order.

```
SELECT  *
FROM    DimProduct
ORDER BY SpanishProductName ASC
GO
-- (606 row(s) affected) - Partial results.
```

EnglishProductName	SpanishProductName
HL Crankset	Bielas GA
LL Crankset	Bielas GB
ML Crankset	Bielas GM
Mountain Pump	Bomba de montaña
Cable Lock	Cable antirrobo
Chain	Cadena
Mountain Bike Socks,	Calcetines para bicicleta de montaña, G

Sorting on FrenchProductName, if empty, use EnglishProductName.

```
SELECT  * FROM    DimProduct ORDER BY FrenchProductName, EnglishProductName;
GO
```

Using the TOP Clause in SELECT Queries

The TOP clause limits the number of rows returned as specified in the TOP expression according the sorted order if any. In the following query, the sorting is based on a major key (LastName) and a minor key (FirstName).

```
USE AdventureWorks2012
GO
```

```
SELECT  TOP 100 *
FROM    Person.Person ORDER BY LastName, FirstName
-- (100 row(s) affected) - Partial results.
```

BusinessEntityID	PersonType	Title	FirstName	LastName	EmailPromotion
285	SP	Mr.	Syed	Abbas	0
293	SC	Ms.	Catherine	Abel	1
295	SC	Ms.	Kim	Abercrombie	0
2170	GC	NULL	Kim	Abercrombie	2
38	EM	NULL	Kim	Abercrombie	2
211	EM	NULL	Hazem	Abolrous	0
2357	GC	NULL	Sam	Abolrous	1
297	SC	Sr.	Humberto	Acevedo	2
291	SC	Mr.	Gustavo	Achong	2
299	SC	Sra.	Pilar	Ackerman	0

The total population of the Person.Person table is 19,972 rows.

```
SELECT * FROM   Person.Person ORDER BY LastName, FirstName
-- (19972 row(s) affected)
```

We can also count the rows applying the COUNT function.

```
SELECT  RowsCount = count(*) FROM   Person.Person
-- 19972
```

When counting, it is safe to count the PRIMARY KEY (ProductID) values.

```
SELECT  RowsCount = count(ProductID)  FROM   Production.Product;
-- 504
```

```
SELECT  RowsCount = count(Color)  FROM   Production.Product;    -- 256
```

Using the WHERE Clause in SELECT Queries

The WHERE clause filters the rows to be returned according the one or more predicates. The next T-SQL scripts demonstrate simple WHERE clause predicates, including multiple WHERE conditions.

```
-- Last name starts with S
SELECT *
FROM    Person.Person
WHERE   LEFT(LastName,1) = 'S'
ORDER BY LastName;
-- (2130 row(s) affected)
```

```
-- First name is Shelly
SELECT  *
FROM    Person.Person
WHERE   FirstName = 'Shelly'
ORDER BY LastName;
-- (1 row(s) affected)
```

```
-- First name is John
SELECT  *
FROM    Person.Person
WHERE   FirstName = 'John'
ORDER BY LastName;
-- (58 row(s) affected)
```

```
-- First name John, last name starts with S - Multiple WHERE conditions
SELECT  *
FROM    Person.Person
WHERE   FirstName = 'John'
     AND LEFT(LastName,1) = 'S'
ORDER BY LastName ;
-- (2 row(s) affected)
```

```
-- Last name starts with S OR first name starts with J
SELECT  *
FROM    Person.Person
WHERE   LEFT(FirstName,1) = 'J'  OR LEFT(LastName,1) = 'S'
ORDER BY LastName;
-- (4371 row(s) affected)
```

```
-- Last name starts with S AND first name starts with J
SELECT  *
FROM    Person.Person  WHERE    LEFT(FirstName,1) = 'J'    AND LEFT(LastName,1) = 'S'
ORDER BY LastName;    -- (221 row(s) affected)
```

Using Literals in SELECT Queries

Literals or constants are used commonly in T-SQL queries, also as defaults for columns, local variables, and parameters. The format of a literal depends on the data type of the value it represents. The database engine may perform implicit conversion to match data types. Explicit conversion of literals can be achieved with the CONVERT or CAST functions. T-SQL scripts demonstrate literal use in WHERE clause predicates.

```
USE AdventureWorks2012;
-- Integer literal  in WHERE clause predicate
SELECT * FROM Production.Product
WHERE ProductID = 800;
-- (1 row(s) affected)
```

```
-- String literal in WHERE clause predicate
SELECT * FROM Production.Product WHERE Color = 'Blue';
-- (26 row(s) affected)
```

```
USE AdventureWorksDW2012;
-- UNICODE (2 bytes per character) string literal
SELECT * FROM DimProduct
WHERE SpanishProductName = N'Jersey clásico de manga corta, G';
-- (1 row(s) affected)
```

```
-- UNICODE string literal
SELECT * FROM DimProduct
WHERE FrenchProductName = N'Roue arrière de vélo de randonnée';
-- (1 row(s) affected)
```

```
USE AdventureWorks2012;
-- Money literal in WHERE clause predicate
SELECT * FROM Production.Product
WHERE ListPrice > = $2000.0;
-- (35 row(s) affected)
```

```
-- Floating point literal with implicit conversion to MONEY
SELECT * FROM Production.Product  WHERE ListPrice > = 2.000E+3;
-- (35 row(s) affected)
```

```
-- Hex (binary) literal
SELECT * FROM Production.Product  WHERE rowguid >= 0x23D89CEE9F444F3EB28963DE6BA2B737
-- (302 row(s) affected)
```

```
-- The rest of the 504 products
SELECT * FROM Production.Product  WHERE rowguid < 0x23D89CEE9F444F3EB28963DE6BA2B737
-- (202 row(s) affected)
```

Date & Time Literals in SELECT Queries

Date and time literals appear to come from an infinite pool. Every country has tens of string date & time variations. Despite the many external string representation, **date, datetime, datetime, time, smalldatetime** and other temporal data types have unique, well-defined representation within the database engine.

ymd date literal format is the cleanest. There is eternal confusion about the North American mdy string date format and the European dmy string date format. The date and time format with "T" separator (last one) is the ISO date time format literal. ANSI Date literal - YYYYMMDD - the best choice since it work in any country.

CONVERT or CAST Date Time Literal	Result
SELECT [Date] = CAST('20160228' AS date)	2016-02-28
SELECT [Datetime] = CAST('20160228' AS datetime)	2016-02-28 00:00:00.000
SELECT [SmallDatetime] = CAST('20160228' AS smalldatetime)	2016-02-28 00:00:00
SELECT [Datetime] = CONVERT(datetime,'2016-02-28')	2016-02-28 00:00:00.000
SELECT [Datetime2] = CONVERT(datetime2,'2016-02-28')	2016-02-28 00:00:00.0000000
SELECT [Datetime] = CONVERT(datetime, '20160228')	2016-02-28 00:00:00.000
SELECT [Datetime2] = CONVERT(datetime2,'20160228')	2016-02-28 00:00:00.0000000
SELECT [Datetime] = CAST('Mar 15, 2016' AS datetime)	2016-03-15 00:00:00.000
SELECT [Datetime2] = CAST('Mar 15, 2016' AS datetime2)	2016-03-15 00:00:00.0000000
SELECT [Date] = CAST('Mar 15, 2016' AS date)	2016-03-15
SELECT CAST('16:40:31' AS datetime)	1900-01-01 16:40:31.000
SELECT CAST('16:40:31' AS time)	16:40:31.0000000
SELECT [Datetime] = CAST('Mar 15, 2016 12:07:34.444' AS datetime)	2016-03-15 12:07:34.443
SELECT [Datetime2] = CAST('Mar 15, 2016 12:07:34.4445555' AS datetime2)	2016-03-15 12:07:34.4445555
SELECT [Datetime] = CAST('2016-03-15T12:07:34.513' AS datetime)	2016-03-15 12:07:34.513

ymd, dmy & mdy String Date Format Literals

Date and time string literals are the least understood part of the T-SQL language by database developers. It is a constant source of confusion and frustration, in addition huge economic cost of lost programmer's productivity. ymd, dmy & mdy are the main string date formats. Some countries use ydm format. Setting dateformat overrides the implicit setting by language.

The basic principles:

> **There is only one DATETIME data type internal format**, independent where SQL Server is operated: New York, London, Amsterdam, Berlin, Moscow, Hong Kong, Singapore, Tokyo, Melbourne or Rio de Janeiro.
> There are hundreds of national string date & time formats which have nothing to do with SQL Server.
> String date must be properly converted to DATETIME format.

```
SET DATEFORMAT ymd
SELECT convert(datetime,'16/05/08')              -- 2016-05-08 00:00:00.000


-- Setting DATEFORMAT to UK-Style (European)
SET DATEFORMAT dmy
SELECT convert(datetime,'20/05/16')              -- 2016-05-20 00:00:00.000


-- Setting DATEFORMAT to US-Style
SET DATEFORMAT mdy
SELECT convert(datetime,'05/20/16')              -- 2016-05-20 00:00:00.000
SELECT convert(datetime,'05/20/2016')            -- 2016-05-20 00:00:00.000
```
Interestingly we can achieve the same implicit conversion action by setting language.

```
-- Setting DATEFORMAT ymd  via language
SET LANGUAGE Japanese;  SELECT convert(datetime,'16/05/08') ;        -- 2016-05-08 00:00:00.000


-- Setting DATEFORMAT to UK-Style (European) via language
SET LANGUAGE British;  SELECT convert(datetime,'20/05/16');          -- 2016-05-20 00:00:00.000
SELECT convert(datetime,'05/20/16');
/* Msg 242, Level 16, State 3, Line 3
The conversion of a varchar data type to a datetime data type resulted in an out-of-range value.  */


-- Setting DATEFORMAT to US-Style via language
SET LANGUAGE English;  SELECT convert(datetime,'05/20/16');          -- 2016-05-20 00:00:00.000
SELECT convert(datetime,'05/20/2016');            -- 2016-05-20 00:00:00.000
SELECT convert(datetime,'20/05/2016');
/* Msg 242, Level 16, State 3, Line 4
The conversion of a varchar data type to a datetime data type resulted in an out-of-range value.  */
```

CHAPTER 8: Basic SELECT Statement Syntax & Examples

Setting DATEFIRST with Literal

DATEFIRST indicates the first day of the week which may vary by country, culture or business. The next T-SQL script demonstrates how it can be set by integer literal 1-7. It overrides the implicit setting by language. @@DATEFIRST is a system (SQL Server database engine) variable.

```
SET DATEFIRST 7 -- Sunday as first day of the week
SELECT DATEPART(dw, '20160315');          -- 3
SELECT DATENAME(dw, '20160315');          -- Tuesday
SELECT @@DATEFIRST                        -- 7


SET DATEFIRST 1 -- Monday as first day of the week
SELECT DATEPART(dw, '20160315');          -- 2
SELECT DATENAME(dw, '20160315');          -- Tuesday
SELECT @@DATEFIRST                        -- 1
```

Language Setting - SET LANGUAGE

DATEFIRST is tied to the language setting, just the like the date format (ymd, dmy, or mdy).

```
SET LANGUAGE us_english
SELECT DATEPART(dw, '20160315');          -- 3
SELECT DATENAME(dw, '20160315');          -- Tuesday
SELECT @@DATEFIRST                        -- 7


SET LANGUAGE german
SELECT DATEPART(dw, '20160315');          -- 2
SELECT DATENAME(dw, '20160315');          -- Dienstag
SELECT @@DATEFIRST                        -- 1


SET LANGUAGE british
SELECT DATEPART(dw, '20160315');          -- 2
SELECT DATENAME(dw, '20160315');          -- Tuesday
SELECT @@DATEFIRST                        -- 1


SET LANGUAGE hungarian
SELECT DATEPART(dw, '20160315');          -- 2
SELECT DATENAME(dw, '20160315');          -- kedd
SELECT @@DATEFIRST                        -- 1


SET LANGUAGE spanish
SELECT DATEPART(dw, '20160315');          -- 2
SELECT DATENAME(dw, '20160315');          -- Martes
SELECT @@DATEFIRST                        -- 1
```

The sys.syslanguages System View

The syslanguages table contains not only language related information, but date related settings as well.

```
SELECT
        langid,
        dateformat,
        datefirst,
        name                          AS native_language,
        alias                         AS english,
        left(shortmonths, 15)         AS shortmonths,
        left(days,15)                 AS days
FROM AdventureWorks2012.sys.syslanguages
ORDER BY langid;
GO
-- (34 row(s) affected)  -  Partial results.
```

langid	dateformat	datefirst	native_language	english	shortmonths	days
0	mdy	7	us_english	English	Jan,Feb,Mar,Apr	Monday,Tuesday,
1	dmy	1	Deutsch	German	Jan,Feb,Mär,Apr	Montag,Dienstag
2	dmy	1	Français	French	janv,févr,mars,	lundi,mardi,mer
3	ymd	7	日本語	Japanese	01,02,03,04,05,	月曜日,火曜日,水曜日,木曜日
4	dmy	1	Dansk	Danish	jan,feb,mar,apr	mandag,tirsdag,
5	dmy	1	Español	Spanish	Ene,Feb,Mar,Abr	Lunes,Martes,Mi
6	dmy	1	Italiano	Italian	gen,feb,mar,apr	lunedì,martedì,
7	dmy	1	Nederlands	Dutch	jan,feb,mrt,apr	maandag,dinsdag
8	dmy	1	Norsk	Norwegian	jan,feb,mar,apr	mandag,tirsdag,
9	dmy	7	Português	Portuguese	jan,fev,mar,abr	segunda-feira,t
10	dmy	1	Suomi	Finnish	tammi,helmi,maa	maanantai,tiist
11	ymd	1	Svenska	Swedish	jan,feb,mar,apr	måndag,tisdag,o
12	dmy	1	čeština	Czech	I,II,III,IV,V,V	pondělí,úterý,s
13	ymd	1	magyar	Hungarian	jan,febr,márc,á	hétfő,kedd,szer
14	dmy	1	polski	Polish	I,II,III,IV,V,V	poniedziałek,wt
15	dmy	1	română	Romanian	Ian,Feb,Mar,Apr	luni,marţi,mier
16	ymd	1	hrvatski	Croatian	sij,vel,ožu,tra	ponedjeljak,uto
17	dmy	1	slovenčina	Slovak	I,II,III,IV,V,V	pondelok,utorok
18	dmy	1	slovenski	Slovenian	jan,feb,mar,apr	ponedeljek,tore
19	dmy	1	ελληνικά	Greek	Ιαν,Φεβ,Μαρ,Απρ	Δευτέρα,Τρίτη,Τ
20	dmy	1	български	Bulgarian	януари,февруари	понеделник,втор
21	dmy	1	русский	Russian	янв,фев,мар,апр	понедельник,вто
22	dmy	1	Türkçe	Turkish	Oca,Şub,Mar,Nis	Pazartesi,Salı,
23	dmy	1	British	British English	Jan,Feb,Mar,Apr	Monday,Tuesday,
24	dmy	1	eesti	Estonian	jaan,veebr,märt	esmaspäev,teisi
25	ymd	1	latviešu	Latvian	jan,feb,mar,apr	pirmdiena,otrdi
26	ymd	1	lietuvių	Lithuanian	sau,vas,kov,bal	pirmadienis,ant
27	dmy	7	Português (Brasil)	Brazilian	Jan,Fev,Mar,Abr	Segunda-Feira,T
28	ymd	7	繁體中文	Traditional Chinese	01,02,03,04,05,	星期一,星期二,星期三,星期四
29	ymd	7	한국어	Korean	01,02,03,04,05,	월요일,화요일,수요일,목요일
30	ymd	7	简体中文	Simplified Chinese	01,02,03,04,05,	星期一,星期二,星期三,星期四
31	dmy	1	Arabic	Arabic	Jan,Feb,Mar,Apr	Monday,Tuesday,
32	dmy	7	ไทย	Thai	ม.ค.,ก.พ.,มี.ค.	จันทร์,อังคาร,พ
33	dmy	1	norsk (bokmål)	Bokmål	jan,feb,mar,apr	mandag,tirsdag,

DBCC USEROPTIONS

The DBCC USEROPTIONS command displays some of the connection (session) settings. As we have seen these settings play an important part on how date literals are interpreted by the system such as dateformat.

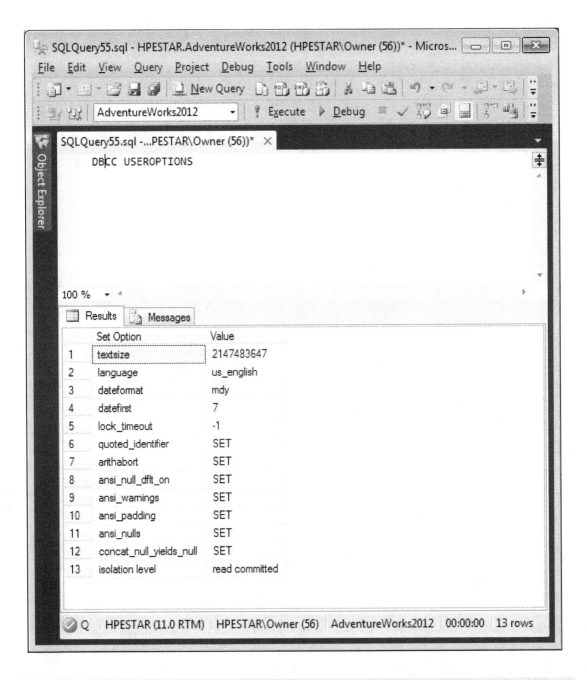

Easy SELECT Queries for Fun & Learning

T-SQL scripts to demonstrate simple, easy-to-read SELECT query variations. Important note: alias column names cannot be reused in successive computed columns by expressions or anywhere else in the query except the ORDER BY clause.

```
-- Datetime range with string literal date
SELECT  * FROM    Person.Person
WHERE   ModifiedDate <= '2002-08-09 00:00:00.000'  ORDER BY LastName;
-- (38 row(s) affected)
```

> **NOTE**
> The string literal above looks like datetime, but it is not. It is only a string literal. The database engine will try to convert it to datetime data type at runtime (implicit conversion), and if successful the query will be executed.
> The syntax of the following query is OK, however, it will fail at execution time.
> SELECT * FROM   Person.Person WHERE   ModifiedDate <= 'New York City' ORDER BY LastName;
> /* Msg 241, Level 16, State 1, Line 1 Conversion failed when converting date and/or time from character string. */

```
-- Complimentary (remaining) datetime range specified again with string literal
SELECT * FROM    Person.Person  WHERE   ModifiedDate > '2002-08-09 00:00:00.000'  ORDER BY
LastName;
-- (19934 row(s) affected)
```

```
-- Total rows in Person.Person
SELECT ( 38 + 19934 ) AS TotalRows;    -- 19972
```

```
SELECT count(* ) FROM   Person.Person -- 19972
```

```
SELECT TableRows = count(* ),  Calc = 38 + 19934  FROM   Person.Person;  -- 19972     19972
```

```
-- Get prefix left of comma or entire string if there is no comma present
SELECT TOP 4                                                     ProductNumber,
        LEFT(Name, COALESCE(NULLIF(CHARINDEX(',',Name)-1,-1),LEN(Name)))  AS NamePrefix,
        Name                                                     AS ProductName
FROM AdventureWorks2012.Production.Product   WHERE CHARINDEX(',',Name) > 0
ORDER BY ProductName;
```

ProductNumber	NamePrefix	ProductName
VE-C304-L	Classic Vest	Classic Vest, L
VE-C304-M	Classic Vest	Classic Vest, M
VE-C304-S	Classic Vest	Classic Vest, S
GL-F110-L	Full-Finger Gloves	Full-Finger Gloves, L

CHAPTER 8: Basic SELECT Statement Syntax & Examples

NULL refers to no information available. Note: "=" and "!=" operators are not used with NULL; "IS" or "IS NOT" operators are applicable.

```
SELECT *
FROM    Person.Person
WHERE   AdditionalContactInfo IS NOT NULL
ORDER BY LastName;
-- (10 row(s) affected)
```

```
SELECT *
FROM    Person.Person
WHERE   AdditionalContactInfo IS NULL
ORDER BY LastName;
-- (19962 row(s) affected)
```

```
SELECT   DISTINCT FirstName
FROM     Person.Person
ORDER BY FirstName;     -- (1018 row(s) affected)
```

```
-- Summary revenue by product, interesting sort
USE AdventureWorks2012;
GO
SELECT  TOP 10 p.Name                                  AS ProductName,
  FORMAT(SUM(((OrderQty * UnitPrice) * (1.0 - UnitPriceDiscount))),'c','en-US') AS SubTotal
FROM Production.Product AS p
INNER JOIN Sales.SalesOrderDetail AS sod
ON p.ProductID = sod.ProductID
GROUP BY p.Name
ORDER BY REVERSE(p.Name);
```

ProductName	SubTotal
Water Bottle - 30 oz.	$28,654.16
Hydration Pack - 70 oz.	$105,826.42
LL Mountain Frame - Black, 40	$1,198.99
ML Mountain Frame - Black, 40	$14,229.41
Mountain-300 Black, 40	$501,648.88
Mountain-500 Black, 40	$101,734.12
LL Mountain Frame - Silver, 40	$69,934.28
ML Mountain Frame-W - Silver, 40	$195,826.39
Mountain-500 Silver, 40	$145,089.43
Mountain-400-W Silver, 40	$323,703.82

CHAPTER 8: Basic SELECT Statement Syntax & Examples

DISTINCT & GROUP BY operations are generally "expensive".

SELECT   DISTINCT LastName FROM   Person.Person ORDER BY LastName; -- (1206 row(s) affected)

-- LastName popularity descending
SELECT LastName,   Frequency = count(*)
FROM   Person.Person
GROUP BY LastName
ORDER BY Frequency DESC;
GO

LastName	Frequency
Diaz	211
Hernandez	188
Sanchez	175
Martinez	173
Torres	172
Martin	171
Perez	170
Gonzalez	169
Lopez	168
Rodriguez	166

-- Sort on column not in SELECT list - Note: demo only, confusing to end user
SELECT   LastName
FROM   Person.Person
ORDER BY FirstName;
-- (19972 row(s) affected)

-- Sort on column not in SELECT list
SELECT   Name = CONCAT(LastName, ', ', FirstName)
FROM   Person.Person
ORDER BY LastName;
-- (19972 row(s) affected)

-- Sort on column alias
SELECT   Name = CONCAT(LastName, ', ', FirstName)
FROM   Person.Person
ORDER BY Name;
-- (19972 row(s) affected)

SELECT   CONCAT(LastName, ', ', FirstName) AS FullName
FROM   Person.Person
WHERE   LastName >= 'K' ORDER BY LastName;
-- (12057 row(s) affected)

CHAPTER 8: Basic SELECT Statement Syntax & Examples

The NULLIF Function Actually Creates A NULL

```
SELECT  CONCAT(LastName, ', ', FirstName ) AS FullName
FROM    Person.Person  WHERE   LastName < 'K'  ORDER BY LastName;
-- (7915 row(s) affected)
```

```
-- Cardinality check
SELECT Difference= ((count(*)) - (12057 + 7915)) FROM  Person.Person; -- 0
```

```
-- Using the NULLIF function in counting
-- Count of all list prices - no NULLs in column
SELECT COUNT(ListPrice) FROM   AdventureWorks2012.Production.Product
-- 504
```

```
-- Counts only when ListPrice != 0 - does not count NULLs (ListPrice = 0.0)
SELECT COUNT(NULLIF(ListPrice,0.0)) FROM   AdventureWorks2012.Production.Product
-- 304
```

```
SELECT COUNT(ListPrice)  FROM  AdventureWorks2012.Production.Product  WHERE ListPrice = 0;
-- 200
```

Cardinality of DISTINCT & GROUP BY Clauses

The cardinality of DISTINCT and the cardinality of GROUP BY are the same with the same column(s).

```
-- FirstName by popularity descending
SELECT FirstName,
       Freq = count(* )
FROM   Person.Person
GROUP BY FirstName
ORDER BY Freq DESC;
-- (1018 row(s) affected)
```

FirstName	Freq
Richard	103
Katherine	99
Marcus	97
James	97
Jennifer	96
Dalton	93
Lucas	93
Alexandra	93
Morgan	92
Seth	92

```
SELECT  DISTINCT FirstName  FROM    Person.Person  ORDER BY FirstName;  -- (1018 row(s) affected)
```

CHAPTER 8: Basic SELECT Statement Syntax & Examples

Column Alias Can only Be Used in ORDER BY

Column aliases cannot be used in other computed columns (expressions), neither in the WHERE clause or GROUP BY clause.

```
SELECT  TableRows = count(* ),
        Calculated = 38 + 19934,
        Difference = (count(*) - 38 - 19934)
FROM  Person.Person;
```

TableRows	Calculated	Difference
19972	19972	0

Workarounds for Column Alias Use Restriction

There is a simple workaround for recycling column aliases in other clauses than just the ORDER BY: make the query into a derived table (x) and include it in an outer query. Similarly, CTEs can be used instead of derived tables.

```
-- Derived table workaround
SELECT TableRows, Calculated, Difference = TableRows - Calculated
FROM (
        SELECT  TableRows = count(* ),     Calculated = 38 + 19934,
        FROM   Person.Person
        ) x ;  -- Derived table
GO
```

TableRows	Calculated	Difference
19972	19972	0

```
-- CTE workaround
;WITH CTE AS (
        SELECT  TableRows = count(* ),     Calculated = 38 + 19934
        FROM   Person.Person)
-- Outer query
SELECT TableRows, Calculated, Difference = TableRows - Calculated
FROM CTE;
```

TableRows	Calculated	Difference
19972	19972	0

When the Clock Strikes Midnight: datetime Behaviour

This is one of the most troublesome issues in T-SQL programming (midnight bug, Cinderella syndrom): the predicate YYYYMMDD (date string literal) = DatetimeColumn does not include the entire day, only records with time at midnight: 00:00:00.000 .

```
USE AdventureWorks2012;

-- Note: only midnight 2003-08-09 included
-- Even a second after midnight is not included like 2003-08-09 00:00:01.000
SELECT  *
FROM    Person.Person
WHERE       ModifiedDate BETWEEN '2002-08-09 00:00:00.000'
            AND '2003-08-09 00:00:00.000'
ORDER BY LastName;
GO
-- (396 row(s) affected)
```

```
-- Entire day of 2003-08-09 included
-- The count same as before because no records after midnight 2003-08-09
SELECT  *
FROM    Person.Person
WHERE       ModifiedDate >= '2002-08-09 00:00:00.000'
            AND ModifiedDate < '2003-08-10 00:00:00.000'
ORDER BY LastName;
GO
-- (396 row(s) affected)
```

LEFT(), RIGHT() & SUBSTRING() String Functions

```
SELECT   FirstCharOfFirstName = LEFT(FirstName,1),          -- column alias
         FirstCharOfLastName  = LEFT(LastName,1),           -- column alias
         LastCharOfLastName  = RIGHT(LastName,1),           -- column alias
         FullName = CONCAT(FirstName, SPACE(1), LastName) ,  -- column alias
         *                                                  -- wild card, all columns
FROM    Person.Person
WHERE   SUBSTRING(FirstName,1,1) = 'J'
    AND SUBSTRING (LastName,1,1) = 'S'
    AND (RIGHT(LastName,1) = 'H' OR RIGHT(LastName,1) = 'Z')
ORDER BY LastName;
-- (59 row(s) affected) - Partial result.
```

FirstCharOfFirstName	FirstCharOfLastName	LastCharOfLastName	FullName	BusinessEntityID
J	S	z	Jacqueline Sanchez	8975
J	S	z	Jada Sanchez	9499
J	S	z	Jade Sanchez	9528
J	S	z	Janelle Sanchez	18590
J	S	z	Jared Sanchez	15266
J	S	z	Jarrod Sanchez	2948
J	S	z	Jay Sanchez	10298
J	S	z	Jennifer Sanchez	20440
J	S	z	Jeremiah Sanchez	15292
J	S	z	Jermaine Sanchez	8040

```
-- Sort on first column
SELECT BusinessEntityID, JobTitle, SUBSTRING(JobTitle, 5, 7)  AS MiddleOfJobTitle
FROM   HumanResources.Employee
WHERE  BirthDate <= '1960/12/31'    -- date literal (constant)
ORDER BY 1;
-- (27 row(s) affected) - Partial results.
```

BusinessEntityID	JobTitle	MiddleOfJobTitle
5	Design Engineer	gn Engi
6	Design Engineer	gn Engi
12	Tool Designer	Design
15	Design Engineer	gn Engi
23	Marketing Specialist	eting S
27	Production Supervisor - WC60	uction

```
-- String functions usage in formatting
DECLARE @SSN char(9) = '123456789';
SELECT SSN=CONCAT(LEFT(@SSN,3),'-', SUBSTRING(@SSN,4,2),'-', RIGHT(@SSN,4));
-- 123-45-6789
```

CHAPTER 8: Basic SELECT Statement Syntax & Examples

ASCII value range is 0-127. Extended ASCII: 128-255. Size is 8-bit, one byte.

```
SELECT TOP 5      ProductNumber,
                  SUBSTRING(ProductNumber,9,1)          AS MiddleSubstring,
                  ASCII(SUBSTRING(ProductNumber,9,1))   AS ASCIIValue
FROM AdventureWorks2008.Production.Product
WHERE LEN(ProductNumber) > 8
ORDER BY Name;                          - OK syntax, but does not make sense
```

ProductNumber	MiddleSubstring	ASCIIValue
VE-C304-L	L	76
VE-C304-M	M	77
VE-C304-S	S	83
GL-F110-L	L	76
GL-F110-M	M	77

NOTE
Table columns and columns by expressions (computed) can be mixed in a query at will.

```
-- Computed (expressions) & table columns
SELECT FirstCharOfFirstName = LEFT(FirstName,1),          -- string expression
       FirstCharOfLastName  = LEFT(LastName,1),           -- string expression
       FullName = CONCAT(LastName, ', ', FirstName ),     -- string expression
       SquareOfID = SQUARE(BusinessEntityID),             -- math expression
       *                                                  -- wild card, all table columns
FROM    Person.Person
WHERE   LEFT(FirstName,1) = 'J'
    AND LEFT(LastName,2) = 'Sm'
ORDER BY FullName;
-- (14 row(s) affected)   - Partial results.
```

FirstCharOfFirstName	FirstCharOfLastName	FullName	SquareOfID	BusinessEntityID
J	S	Smith, Jacob	348680929	18673
J	S	Smith, James	308986084	17578
J	S	Smith, Jasmine	129572689	11383
J	S	Smith, Jeff	3139984	1772
J	S	Smith, Jennifer	122699929	11077
J	S	Smith, Jeremiah	20511841	4529
J	S	Smith, Jessica	145829776	12076
J	S	Smith, John	332041284	18222
J	S	Smith, Jonathan	312228900	17670
J	S	Smith, Jose	300710281	17341
J	S	Smith, Joseph	357474649	18907
J	S	Smith, Joshua	351825049	18757
J	S	Smith, Julia	121616784	11028
J	S	Smith, Justin	324900625	18025

CHAPTER 8: Basic SELECT Statement Syntax & Examples

Transact-SQL Reserved Keywords

List of reserved keywords in SQL Server 2012 Transact-SQL. Keywords can only be used as delimited identifiers such as [Inner] or "Order".

ADD	EXTERNAL	PROCEDURE
ALL	FETCH	PUBLIC
ALTER	FILE	RAISERROR
AND	FILLFACTOR	READ
ANY	FOR	READTEXT
AS	FOREIGN	RECONFIGURE
ASC	FREETEXT	REFERENCES
AUTHORIZATION	FREETEXTTABLE	REPLICATION
BACKUP	FROM	RESTORE
BEGIN	FULL	RESTRICT
BETWEEN	FUNCTION	RETURN
BREAK	GOTO	REVERT
BROWSE	GRANT	REVOKE
BULK	GROUP	RIGHT
BY	HAVING	ROLLBACK
CASCADE	HOLDLOCK	ROWCOUNT
CASE	IDENTITY	ROWGUIDCOL
CHECK	IDENTITY_INSERT	RULE
CHECKPOINT	IDENTITYCOL	SAVE
CLOSE	IF	SCHEMA
CLUSTERED	IN	SECURITYAUDIT
COALESCE	INDEX	SELECT
COLLATE	INNER	SEMANTICKEYPHRASETABLE
COLUMN	INSERT	SEMANTICSIMILARITYDETAILSTABLE
COMMIT	INTERSECT	SEMANTICSIMILARITYTABLE
COMPUTE	INTO	SESSION_USER
CONSTRAINT	IS	SET
CONTAINS	JOIN	SETUSER
CONTAINSTABLE	KEY	SHUTDOWN
CONTINUE	KILL	SOME
CONVERT	LEFT	STATISTICS
CREATE	LIKE	SYSTEM_USER
CROSS	LINENO	TABLE
CURRENT	LOAD	TABLESAMPLE
CURRENT_DATE	MERGE	TEXTSIZE
CURRENT_TIME	NATIONAL	THEN
CURRENT_TIMESTAMP	NOCHECK	TO
CURRENT_USER	NONCLUSTERED	TOP
CURSOR	NOT	TRAN
DATABASE	NULL	TRANSACTION
DBCC	NULLIF	TRIGGER
DEALLOCATE	OF	TRUNCATE
DECLARE	OFF	TRY_CONVERT
DEFAULT	OFFSETS	TSEQUAL
DELETE	ON	UNION
DENY	OPEN	UNIQUE
DESC	OPENDATASOURCE	UNPIVOT
DISK	OPENQUERY	UPDATE
DISTINCT	OPENROWSET	UPDATETEXT
DISTRIBUTED	OPENXML	USE
DOUBLE	OPTION	USER
DROP	OR	VALUES
DUMP	ORDER	VARYING
ELSE	OUTER	VIEW
END	OVER	WAITFOR
ERRLVL	PERCENT	WHEN
ESCAPE	PIVOT	WHERE
EXCEPT	PLAN	WHILE
EXEC	PRECISION	WITH
EXECUTE	PRIMARY	WITHIN GROUP
EXISTS	PRINT	WRITETEXT
EXIT	PROC	

Case Sensitive Sort with Latin1_General_CS_AI

For case sensitive sort on a column with case insensitive collation, we have use a case sensitive (CS) collation such as Latin1_General_CS_AI.

```
-- CASE INSENSITIVE sort using default collation
SELECT lname FROM
        (SELECT TOP 5 UPPER (LastName) AS lname FROM Person.Person ORDER BY FirstName) x
UNION ALL   SELECT lname FROM
        (SELECT TOP 5 LOWER (LastName) AS lname FROM Person.Person ORDER BY FirstName) y
ORDER BY lname;
-- ADAMS, adams, alexander, ALEXANDER, leonetti, LEONETTI, WRIGHT, WRIGHT, wright, wright
```

```
-- CASE SENSITIVE sort using %CS% collation
SELECT lname FROM ( SELECT lname FROM
   (SELECT TOP 5 UPPER (LastName) AS lname FROM Person.Person ORDER BY FirstName) x
   UNION ALL  SELECT lname FROM
   (SELECT TOP 5 LOWER (LastName) AS lname FROM Person.Person ORDER BY FirstName) y  ) z
ORDER BY lname COLLATE Latin1_General_CS_AI;
-- adams,ADAMS,alexander,ALEXANDER,leonetti,LEONETTI,wright,wright,WRIGHT,WRIGHT
```

CHAPTER 8: Basic SELECT Statement Syntax & Examples

The ORDER BY Clause for Sorting Query Results

The ORDER BY clause is located at the very end of the query. In fact the sorting itself takes place after the query executed and generated **an unordered result set**. Although frequently, especially for small sets, the results appear to be sorted, **only an ORDER BY clause can guarantee proper sorting**. INSERT, UPDATE, DELETE & MERGE statement do not support sorting, **the database engine performs all set operations unordered**. T-SQL scripts demonstrate the many variations of the ORDER BY clause.

```
USE AdventureWorks2012;
GO
```

```
-- A column can be used for sorting even though not explicitly used in the SELECT list
SELECT *
FROM   Production.Product
ORDER  BY Name ASC;
GO
```

```
-- Sort on the second column, whatever it may be
SELECT *
FROM   Production.Product
ORDER  BY 2 DESC;
GO
```

```
-- ASCending is the default sort order, it is not necessary to use
SELECT  Name AS ProductName,
             *
FROM   Production.Product
ORDER  BY ProductName ASC;
GO
```

```
SELECT  TOP (10) Name AS ProductName,            *
FROM   Production.Product   ORDER  BY 1 ASC;
```

ProductName	ProductID	Name	ProductNumber	MakeFlag	FinishedGoodsFlag	Color	SafetyStockLevel
Adjustable Race	1	Adjustable Race	AR-5381	0	0	NULL	1000
All-Purpose Bike Stand	879	All-Purpose Bike Stand	ST-1401	0	1	NULL	4
AWC Logo Cap	712	AWC Logo Cap	CA-1098	0	1	Multi	4
BB Ball Bearing	3	BB Ball Bearing	BE-2349	1	0	NULL	800
Bearing Ball	2	Bearing Ball	BA-8327	0	0	NULL	1000
Bike Wash - Dissolver	877	Bike Wash - Dissolver	CL-9009	0	1	NULL	4
Blade	316	Blade	BL-2036	1	0	NULL	800
Cable Lock	843	Cable Lock	LO-C100	0	1	NULL	4
Chain	952	Chain	CH-0234	0	1	Silver	500
Chain Stays	324	Chain Stays	CS-2812	1	0	NULL	1000

Using Column Alias in the ORDER BY Clause

Column alias can be used in an ORDER BY clause. In fact, it should be used to make the query more readable.

```
-- ProductName is a column alias, it can only be used in the ORDER BY clause, not anywhere before
SELECT ProductName = Name, *
FROM Production.Product
WHERE ProductName like '%glove%'
ORDER BY ProductName ASC ;
GO
/* ERROR
Msg 207, Level 16, State 1, Line 3
Invalid column name 'ProductName'.
*/
```

```
-- The TOP clause uses the ORDER BY sorting to select the 5 rows
SELECT TOP (5) ProductName = Name, *
FROM Production.Product
WHERE Name like '%glove%'
ORDER BY ProductName ASC ;
```

ProductName	ProductID	Name	ProductNumber	MakeFlag	FinishedGoodsFlag	Color	SafetyStockLevel
Full-Finger Gloves, L	863	Full-Finger Gloves, L	GL-F110-L	0	1	Black	4
Full-Finger Gloves, M	862	Full-Finger Gloves, M	GL-F110-M	0	1	Black	4
Full-Finger Gloves, S	861	Full-Finger Gloves, S	GL-F110-S	0	1	Black	4
Half-Finger Gloves, L	860	Half-Finger Gloves, L	GL-H102-L	0	1	Black	4
Half-Finger Gloves, M	859	Half-Finger Gloves, M	GL-H102-M	0	1	Black	4

```
-- Descending sort on name which is string data type
SELECT TOP (10) ProductName = Name, *
FROM Production.Product
WHERE Name like '%road%'
ORDER BY ProductName DESC ;
```

ProductName	ProductID	Name	ProductNumber	MakeFlag	FinishedGoodsFlag	Color	SafetyStockLevel
Road-750 Black, 58	977	Road-750 Black, 58	BK-R19B-58	1	1	Black	100
Road-750 Black, 52	999	Road-750 Black, 52	BK-R19B-52	1	1	Black	100
Road-750 Black, 48	998	Road-750 Black, 48	BK-R19B-48	1	1	Black	100
Road-750 Black, 44	997	Road-750 Black, 44	BK-R19B-44	1	1	Black	100
Road-650 Red, 62	761	Road-650 Red, 62	BK-R50R-62	1	1	Red	100
Road-650 Red, 60	760	Road-650 Red, 60	BK-R50R-60	1	1	Red	100
Road-650 Red, 58	759	Road-650 Red, 58	BK-R50R-58	1	1	Red	100
Road-650 Red, 52	764	Road-650 Red, 52	BK-R50R-52	1	1	Red	100
Road-650 Red, 48	763	Road-650 Red, 48	BK-R50R-48	1	1	Red	100
Road-650 Red, 44	762	Road-650 Red, 44	BK-R50R-44	1	1	Red	100

Using Table Alias in the ORDER BY Clause

Unlike the column alias, table alias can be used anywhere in the query within the scope of the alias.

```
-- Using table alias in ORDER BY
SELECT P.*
FROM   Production.Product P
ORDER  BY P.Name ASC;
GO
```

ProductID	Name	ProductNumber	MakeFlag	FinishedGoodsFlag	Color	SafetyStockLevel
958	Touring-3000 Blue, 54	BK-T18U-54	1	1	Blue	100
959	Touring-3000 Blue, 58	BK-T18U-58	1	1	Blue	100
960	Touring-3000 Blue, 62	BK-T18U-62	1	1	Blue	100
961	Touring-3000 Yellow, 44	BK-T18Y-44	1	1	Yellow	100
962	Touring-3000 Yellow, 50	BK-T18Y-50	1	1	Yellow	100
963	Touring-3000 Yellow, 54	BK-T18Y-54	1	1	Yellow	100
964	Touring-3000 Yellow, 58	BK-T18Y-58	1	1	Yellow	100
965	Touring-3000 Yellow, 62	BK-T18Y-62	1	1	Yellow	100
842	Touring-Panniers, Large	PA-T100	0	1	Grey	4
870	Water Bottle - 30 oz.	WB-H098	0	1	NULL	4
869	Women's Mountain Shorts, L	SH-W890-L	0	1	Black	4
868	Women's Mountain Shorts, M	SH-W890-M	0	1	Black	4
867	Women's Mountain Shorts, S	SH-W890-S	0	1	Black	4
854	Women's Tights, L	TG-W091-L	0	1	Black	4
853	Women's Tights, M	TG-W091-M	0	1	Black	4
852	Women's Tights, S	TG-W091-S	0	1	Black	4

```
-- Specific column list instead of all (*)
SELECT   Name,
         ProductNumber,
         ListPrice AS PRICE
FROM   Production.Product  P
ORDER  BY P.Name ASC;
GO
```

```
SELECT          Name,
                ProductNumber,
                ListPrice AS PRICE
FROM   Production.Product  P
ORDER  BY P.ListPrice DESC;
```

```
-- Equivalent to above with column alias usage
SELECT          Name,
                ProductNumber,
                ListPrice AS PRICE
FROM   Production.Product  P ORDER  BY PRICE DESC;
```

CHAPTER 8: Basic SELECT Statement Syntax & Examples

Easy ORDER BY Queries for Exercises

T-SQL scripts demonstrate easily readable queries with sorted result sets.

```
USE pubs ;
```

```
SELECT TYPE,  AvgPrice=FORMAT(AVG(price) , 'c', 'en-US')
FROM  titles WHERE  royalty = 10 GROUP  BY TYPE ORDER  BY TYPE ;
```

TYPE	AvgPrice
business	$17.31
popular_comp	$20.00
psychology	$14.14
trad_cook	$17.97

```
SELECT          type = type,
                AvgPrice = FORMAT(AVG(price),'c', 'en-US')
FROM  titles  WHERE  royalty = 10  GROUP  BY type  ORDER  BY AvgPrice;
```

type	AvgPrice
psychology	$14.14
business	$17.31
trad_cook	$17.97
popular_comp	$20.00

```
SELECT   type                          AS [type],
         FORMAT(AVG(price),'c', 'en-US')    AS AvgPrice
FROM  titles  GROUP  BY [type]  ORDER  BY [type] desc;
```

type	AvgPrice
UNDECIDED	NULL
trad_cook	$15.96
psychology	$13.50
popular_comp	$21.48
mod_cook	$11.49
business	$13.73

An Aggregate Function Can Be Used in an ORDER BY Clause

The NULL related warning message can be turned off: SET ANSI_WARNINGS OFF; alternately ISNULL function can be used in the query.

```
SELECT TYPE, AVG(price) Avg FROM titles  GROUP  BY TYPE ORDER  BY AVG(price);
/* Warning: Null value is eliminated by an aggregate or other SET operation.
(6 row(s) affected) */
```

CHAPTER 8: Basic SELECT Statement Syntax & Examples

Eliminate NULL in result with COALESCE or ISNULL functions

```
SELECT [type] = type,
       AvgPrice = COALESCE(FORMAT(AVG(price),'c', 'en-US') ,'')
FROM  titles  GROUP  BY [type]  ORDER  BY [type] desc;
```

type	AvgPrice
UNDECIDED	
trad_cook	$15.96
psychology	$13.50
popular_comp	$21.48
mod_cook	$11.49
business	$13.73

```
SELECT           pub_name                        Publisher,
                 FORMAT(AVG(price),'c', 'en-US')  AvgPrice
FROM   titles
    INNER JOIN publishers
     ON  titles.pub_id = publishers.pub_id
GROUP  BY pub_name
ORDER  BY pub_name;
```

Publisher	AvgPrice
Algodata Infosystems	$18.98
Binnet & Hardley	$15.41
New Moon Books	$9.78

```
SELECT TOP(3) * FROM  titles ORDER  BY title;
```

title_id	title	type	pub_id	price	advance	royalty	ytd_sales	notes	pubdate
PC1035	But Is It User Friendly?	popular_comp	1389	22.95	7000.00	16	8780	A survey of software for the naive user, focusing on the 'friendliness' of each.	1991-06-30 00:00:00.000
PS1372	Computer Phobic AND Non-Phobic Individuals: Behavior Variations	psychology	0877	21.59	7000.00	10	375	A must for the specialist, this book examines the difference between those who hate and fear computers and those who don't.	1991-10-21 00:00:00.000
BU1111	Cooking with Computers: Surreptitious Balance Sheets	business	1389	11.95	5000.00	10	3876	Helpful hints on how to use your electronic resources to the best advantage.	1991-06-09 00:00:00.000

```
SELECT TOP(3) * FROM  publishers ORDER  BY pub_name;
```

pub_id	pub_name	city	state	country
1389	Algodata Infosystems	Berkeley	CA	USA
0877	Binnet & Hardley	Washington	DC	USA
1622	Five Lakes Publishing	Chicago	IL	USA

CHAPTER 8: Basic SELECT Statement Syntax & Examples

Sorting Products by Attributes

```
USE Northwind;

SELECT          UnitsInStock,
                ProductID,
                ProductName,
                QuantityPerUnit,
                FORMAT( UnitPrice, 'c', 'en-US') AS UnitPrice  -- Column alias is same as column
FROM   Northwind.dbo.Products WHERE  UnitsInStock BETWEEN 15 AND 25  ORDER  BY
UnitsInStock;
```

UnitsInStock	ProductID	ProductName	QuantityPerUnit	UnitPrice
15	7	Uncle Bob's Organic Dried Pears	12 - 1 lb pkgs.	$30.00
15	26	Gumbär Gummibärchen	100 - 250 g bags	$31.23
15	48	Chocolade	10 pkgs.	$12.75
15	70	Outback Lager	24 - 355 ml bottles	$15.00
17	38	Côte de Blaye	12 - 75 cl bottles	$263.50
17	43	Ipoh Coffee	16 - 500 g tins	$46.00
17	62	Tarte au sucre	48 pies	$49.30
17	2	Chang	24 - 12 oz bottles	$19.00
19	60	Camembert Pierrot	15 - 300 g rounds	$34.00
20	24	Guaraná Fantástica	12 - 355 ml cans	$4.50
20	35	Steeleye Stout	24 - 12 oz bottles	$18.00
20	51	Manjimup Dried Apples	50 - 300 g pkgs.	$53.00
21	54	Tourtière	16 pies	$7.45
21	56	Gnocchi di nonna Alice	24 - 250 g pkgs.	$38.00
22	11	Queso Cabrales	1 kg pkg.	$21.00
22	64	Wimmers gute Semmelknödel	20 bags x 4 pieces	$33.25
24	13	Konbu	2 kg box	$6.00
24	63	Vegie-spread	15 - 625 g jars	$43.90
25	19	Teatime Chocolate Biscuits	10 boxes x 12 pieces	$9.20

```
-- A second key is necessary for unique ordering
SELECT  TOP(8)  UnitsInStock,
                ProductID,
                ProductName,
                QuantityPerUnit,
                FORMAT( UnitPrice, 'c', 'en-US') AS UnitPrice
FROM   Northwind.dbo.Products
WHERE  UnitsInStock BETWEEN 15 AND 25 ORDER  BY UnitsInStock, ProductName;
```

UnitsInStock	ProductID	ProductName	QuantityPerUnit	UnitPrice
15	48	Chocolade	10 pkgs.	$12.75
15	26	Gumbär Gummibärchen	100 - 250 g bags	$31.23
15	70	Outback Lager	24 - 355 ml bottles	$15.00
15	7	Uncle Bob's Organic Dried Pears	12 - 1 lb pkgs.	$30.00
17	2	Chang	24 - 12 oz bottles	$19.00
17	38	Côte de Blaye	12 - 75 cl bottles	$263.50
17	43	Ipoh Coffee	16 - 500 g tins	$46.00
17	62	Tarte au sucre	48 pies	$49.30

Changing WHERE condition changes the cardinality of result set

```
SELECT        UnitsInStock,
              ProductID,
              ProductName,
              QuantityPerUnit,
              FORMAT( UnitPrice, 'c', 'en-US')          AS UnitPrice
FROM   Northwind.dbo.Products
WHERE  UnitsInStock = 15 or UnitsInStock =  25  -- same as UnitsInStock IN (15, 25)
ORDER  BY UnitsInStock, ProductName;
```

UnitsInStock	ProductID	ProductName	QuantityPerUnit	UnitPrice
15	48	Chocolade	10 pkgs.	$12.75
15	26	Gumbär Gummibärchen	100 - 250 g bags	$31.23
15	70	Outback Lager	24 - 355 ml bottles	$15.00
15	7	Uncle Bob's Organic Dried Pears	12 - 1 lb pkgs.	$30.00
25	19	Teatime Chocolate Biscuits	10 boxes x 12 pieces	$9.20

```
SELECT  TOP(7)  UnitsInStock,
                ProductID,
                ProductName,
                QuantityPerUnit,
                FORMAT( UnitPrice, 'c', 'en-US')          AS UnitPrice
FROM   Northwind.dbo.Products  ORDER  BY UnitsInStock DESC, ProductName ASC;
```

UnitsInStock	ProductID	ProductName	QuantityPerUnit	UnitPrice
125	75	Rhönbräu Klosterbier	24 - 0.5 l bottles	$7.75
123	40	Boston Crab Meat	24 - 4 oz tins	$18.40
120	6	Grandma's Boysenberry Spread	12 - 8 oz jars	$25.00
115	55	Pâté chinois	24 boxes x 2 pies	$24.00
113	61	Sirop d'érable	24 - 500 ml bottles	$28.50
112	33	Geitost	500 g	$2.50
112	36	Inlagd Sill	24 - 250 g jars	$19.00

```
SELECT  TOP(5)  UnitsInStock, ProductID, ProductName,        QuantityPerUnit,
                FORMAT( UnitPrice, 'c', 'en-US') AS UnitPrice
FROM   Northwind.dbo.Products
WHERE  UnitsInStock > 15  AND UnitsInStock < 25  ORDER  BY UnitsInStock DESC, ProductName ASC;
```

UnitsInStock	ProductID	ProductName	QuantityPerUnit	UnitPrice
24	13	Konbu	2 kg box	$6.00
24	63	Vegie-spread	15 - 625 g jars	$43.90
22	11	Queso Cabrales	1 kg pkg.	$21.00
22	64	Wimmers gute Semmelknödel	20 bags x 4 pieces	$33.25
21	56	Gnocchi di nonna Alice	24 - 250 g pkgs.	$38.00

CHAPTER 8: Basic SELECT Statement Syntax & Examples

The "Tricky" BETWEEN & NOT BETWEEN Operators
They are very English-like, but results should be verified to make sure they work as intended.

```
SELECT  TOP(5)  UnitsInStock, ProductID, ProductName,        QuantityPerUnit,
            FORMAT( UnitPrice, 'c', 'en-US') AS UnitPrice
FROM   Northwind.dbo.Products
WHERE  UnitsInStock BETWEEN 15 AND 25
ORDER  BY UnitsInStock DESC, ProductName ASC;
GO
```

UnitsInStock	ProductID	ProductName	QuantityPerUnit	UnitPrice
25	19	Teatime Chocolate Biscuits	10 boxes x 12 pieces	$9.20
24	13	Konbu	2 kg box	$6.00
24	63	Vegie-spread	15 - 625 g jars	$43.90
22	11	Queso Cabrales	1 kg pkg.	$21.00
22	64	Wimmers gute Semmelknödel	20 bags x 4 pieces	$33.25

```
SELECT  TOP(5)  UnitsInStock, ProductID, ProductName,        QuantityPerUnit,
            FORMAT( UnitPrice, 'c', 'en-US') AS UnitPrice
FROM   Northwind.dbo.Products
WHERE  UnitsInStock NOT BETWEEN 15 AND 25
ORDER  BY UnitsInStock DESC, ProductName ASC;
```

UnitsInStock	ProductID	ProductName	QuantityPerUnit	UnitPrice
125	75	Rhönbräu Klosterbier	24 - 0.5 l bottles	$7.75
123	40	Boston Crab Meat	24 - 4 oz tins	$18.40
120	6	Grandma's Boysenberry Spread	12 - 8 oz jars	$25.00
115	55	Pâté chinois	24 boxes x 2 pies	$24.00
113	61	Sirop d'érable	24 - 500 ml bottles	$28.50

```
SELECT          Orders.OrderID,
            Shippers.*
FROM   Shippers
    INNER JOIN Orders
      ON ( Shippers.ShipperID = Orders.ShipVia )
ORDER  BY Orders.OrderID;
GO
-- (830 row(s) affected) - Partial results.
```

OrderID	ShipperID	CompanyName	Phone
10248	3	Federal Shipping	(503) 555-9931
10249	1	Speedy Express	(503) 555-9831
10250	2	United Package	(503) 555-3199
10251	1	Speedy Express	(503) 555-9831
10252	2	United Package	(503) 555-3199
10253	2	United Package	(503) 555-3199

A second key is frequently required in sorting exception is PRIMARY KEY column.

```
SELECT   OrderID,
         ProductID,
         FORMAT( UnitPrice, 'c', 'en-US')              AS UnitPrice,
         Quantity,
         Discount
FROM  [Order Details]  ORDER  BY OrderID ASC, ProductID ASC;
GO
-- (2155 row(s) affected) - Partial results.
```

OrderID	ProductID	UnitPrice	Quantity	Discount
10248	11	$14.00	12	0
10248	42	$9.80	10	0
10248	72	$34.80	5	0
10249	14	$18.60	9	0
10249	51	$42.40	40	0
10250	41	$7.70	10	0
10250	51	$42.40	35	0.15
10250	65	$16.80	15	0.15

```
-- Sort keys are different from expression column EmployeeName
SELECT   CONCAT(LastName,', ', FirstName)  AS EmployeeName ,
         Title, City, Country
FROM   Northwind.dbo.Employees ORDER  BY LastName,  FirstName ASC;
```

EmployeeName	Title	City	Country
Buchanan, Steven	Sales Manager	London	UK
Callahan, Laura	Inside Sales Coordinator	Seattle	USA
Davolio, Nancy	Sales Representative	Seattle	USA
Dodsworth, Anne	Sales Representative	London	UK
Fuller, Andrew	Vice President, Sales	Tacoma	USA
King, Robert	Sales Representative	London	UK
Leverling, Janet	Sales Representative	Kirkland	USA
Peacock, Margaret	Sales Representative	Redmond	USA
Suyama, Michael	Sales Representative	London	UK

```
-- Equivalent sort
SELECT TOP(3)    CONCAT(LastName,', ', FirstName) AS EmployeeName ,    Title, City, Country
FROM   Northwind.dbo.Employees  ORDER  BY EmployeeName ASC;
```

EmployeeName	Title	City	Country
Buchanan, Steven	Sales Manager	London	UK
Callahan, Laura	Inside Sales Coordinator	Seattle	USA
Davolio, Nancy	Sales Representative	Seattle	USA

CHAPTER 8: Basic SELECT Statement Syntax & Examples

Using Multiple Keys in the ORDER BY Clause

If a single sort key does not result in unique ordering, multiple keys can be used. In the next example the Price (major) key is based on a column which is not unique. If we add Name as a second (minor) key, unique ordering will be guaranteed since Name is a unique column, it has a unique index and not null. It's worth noting if Name would allow nulls, we would need a third key for unique ordering.

```
-- Single key sort
SELECT   P.Name,
         P.ProductNumber,
         P.ListPrice              AS PRICE
FROM   Production.Product P
WHERE   P.ProductLine = 'R'   AND P.DaysToManufacture < 4    ORDER  BY  P. ListPrice DESC;
```

Name	ProductNumber	PRICE
HL Road Frame - Black, 58	FR-R92B-58	1431.50
HL Road Frame - Red, 58	FR-R92R-58	1431.50
HL Road Frame - Red, 62	FR-R92R-62	1431.50
HL Road Frame - Red, 44	FR-R92R-44	1431.50
HL Road Frame - Red, 48	FR-R92R-48	1431.50
HL Road Frame - Red, 52	FR-R92R-52	1431.50
HL Road Frame - Red, 56	FR-R92R-56	1431.50
HL Road Frame - Black, 62	FR-R92B-62	1431.50
HL Road Frame - Black, 44	FR-R92B-44	1431.50
HL Road Frame - Black, 48	FR-R92B-48	1431.50
HL Road Frame - Black, 52	FR-R92B-52	1431.50
ML Road Frame-W - Yellow, 40	FR-R72Y-40	594.83

```
-- Double key sort - PRICE is the major key, Name is the minor key
SELECT   P.Name,
         P.ProductNumber,
         P.ListPrice              AS PRICE
FROM   Production.Product P
WHERE   P.ProductLine = 'R'   AND P.DaysToManufacture < 4   ORDER  BY  PRICE DESC, Name;
```

Name	ProductNumber	PRICE
HL Road Frame - Black, 44	FR-R92B-44	1431.50
HL Road Frame - Black, 48	FR-R92B-48	1431.50
HL Road Frame - Black, 52	FR-R92B-52	1431.50
HL Road Frame - Black, 58	FR-R92B-58	1431.50
HL Road Frame - Black, 62	FR-R92B-62	1431.50
HL Road Frame - Red, 44	FR-R92R-44	1431.50
HL Road Frame - Red, 48	FR-R92R-48	1431.50
HL Road Frame - Red, 52	FR-R92R-52	1431.50
HL Road Frame - Red, 56	FR-R92R-56	1431.50
HL Road Frame - Red, 58	FR-R92R-58	1431.50
HL Road Frame - Red, 62	FR-R92R-62	1431.50
ML Road Frame - Red, 44	FR-R72R-44	594.83

ORDER BY in Complex Queries

An ORDER BY can be in a complex query and/or ORDER BY can be complex itself. T-SQL scripts demonstrate complex ORDER BY usage.

```
-- We cannot tell just by query inspection if the second key is sufficient for unique ordering or not
-- If we inspect the result set it becomes obvious that we need a third key at least (SalesOrderID unsorted)
SELECT   ProductName            = P.Name,
         NonDiscountSales       = ( OrderQty * UnitPrice ),
         Discounts              = ( ( OrderQty * UnitPrice ) * UnitPriceDiscount ) ,
         SalesOrderID
FROM   Production.Product P
   INNER JOIN Sales.SalesOrderDetail SOD
      ON P.ProductID = SOD.ProductID
ORDER  BY        ProductName DESC,
                 NonDiscountSales DESC;
GO
```

ProductName	NonDiscountSales	Discounts	SalesOrderID
Women's Tights, S	1049.86	104.986	47355
Women's Tights, S	824.89	41.2445	46987
Women's Tights, S	783.6455	39.1823	47400
Women's Tights, S	742.401	37.1201	50206
Women's Tights, S	701.1565	35.0578	46993
Women's Tights, S	701.1565	35.0578	46671
Women's Tights, S	701.1565	35.0578	50688
Women's Tights, S	701.1565	35.0578	49481
Women's Tights, S	659.912	32.9956	48295
Women's Tights, S	659.912	32.9956	46967
Women's Tights, S	618.6675	30.9334	46652
Women's Tights, S	608.9188	12.1784	46672
Women's Tights, S	608.9188	12.1784	47365
Women's Tights, S	565.4246	11.3085	47004
Women's Tights, S	565.4246	11.3085	50663

NOTE

Even though SELECT DISTINCT results may appear to be sorted, **only ORDER BY clause can guarantee sort**. This holds true for any kind of SELECT statement, simple or complex.

```
SELECT DISTINCT JobTitle   FROM   HumanResources.Employee ;
```

```
SELECT DISTINCT JobTitle   FROM   HumanResources.Employee ORDER  BY JobTitle;
```

CHAPTER 8: Basic SELECT Statement Syntax & Examples

ORDER BY with ROW_NUMBER()

T-SQL queries demonstrate sorting with not matching and matching ROW_NUMBER() sequence number.

```
SELECT
   ROW_NUMBER()  OVER( PARTITION BY CountryRegionName  ORDER BY SalesYTD ASC) AS SeqNo,
   CountryRegionName AS Country,  FirstName, LastName,  JobTitle,
   FORMAT(SalesYTD, 'c', 'en-US') AS SalesYTD,
   FORMAT(SalesLastYear, 'c', 'en-US') AS SalesLastYear
FROM  Sales.vSalesPerson          ORDER  BY JobTitle,   SalesYTD DESC;
```

SeqNo	Country	FirstName	LastName	JobTitle	SalesYTD	SalesLastYear
2	United States	Amy	Alberts	European Sales Manager	$519,905.93	$0.00
3	United States	Stephen	Jiang	North American Sales Manager	$559,697.56	$0.00
1	United States	Syed	Abbas	Pacific Sales Manager	$172,524.45	$0.00
11	United States	Linda	Mitchell	Sales Representative	$4,251,368.55	$1,439,156.03
1	United Kingdom	Jae	Pak	Sales Representative	$4,116,871.23	$1,635,823.40
10	United States	Michael	Blythe	Sales Representative	$3,763,178.18	$1,750,406.48
9	United States	Jillian	Carson	Sales Representative	$3,189,418.37	$1,997,186.20
1	France	Ranjit	Varkey Chudukatil	Sales Representative	$3,121,616.32	$2,396,539.76
2	Canada	José	Saraiva	Sales Representative	$2,604,540.72	$2,038,234.65
8	United States	Shu	Ito	Sales Representative	$2,458,535.62	$2,073,506.00
7	United States	Tsvi	Reiter	Sales Representative	$2,315,185.61	$1,849,640.94
1	Germany	Rachel	Valdez	Sales Representative	$1,827,066.71	$1,307,949.79
6	United States	Tete	Mensa-Annan	Sales Representative	$1,576,562.20	$0.00
5	United States	David	Campbell	Sales Representative	$1,573,012.94	$1,371,635.32
1	Canada	Garrett	Vargas	Sales Representative	$1,453,719.47	$1,620,276.90
1	Australia	Lynn	Tsoflias	Sales Representative	$1,421,810.92	$2,278,548.98
4	United States	Pamela	Ansman-Wolfe	Sales Representative	$1,352,577.13	$1,927,059.18

```
-- ROW_NUMBER() ORDER BY in synch with sort ORDER BY
SELECT  ROW_NUMBER()  OVER( ORDER BY JobTitle, SalesYTD DESC) AS SeqNo,
    CountryRegionName AS Country,  FirstName, LastName,  JobTitle,
    FORMAT(SalesYTD, 'c', 'en-US') AS SalesYTD, FORMAT(SalesLastYear, 'c', 'en-US') AS SalesLastYear
FROM  Sales.vSalesPerson ORDER  BY         SeqNo;
```

SeqNo	Country	FirstName	LastName	JobTitle	SalesYTD	SalesLastYear
1	United States	Amy	Alberts	European Sales Manager	$519,905.93	$0.00
2	United States	Stephen	Jiang	North American Sales Manager	$559,697.56	$0.00
3	United States	Syed	Abbas	Pacific Sales Manager	$172,524.45	$0.00
4	United States	Linda	Mitchell	Sales Representative	$4,251,368.55	$1,439,156.03
5	United Kingdom	Jae	Pak	Sales Representative	$4,116,871.23	$1,635,823.40
6	United States	Michael	Blythe	Sales Representative	$3,763,178.18	$1,750,406.48
7	United States	Jillian	Carson	Sales Representative	$3,189,418.37	$1,997,186.20
8	France	Ranjit	Varkey Chudukatil	Sales Representative	$3,121,616.32	$2,396,539.76
9	Canada	José	Saraiva	Sales Representative	$2,604,540.72	$2,038,234.65
10	United States	Shu	Ito	Sales Representative	$2,458,535.62	$2,073,506.00
11	United States	Tsvi	Reiter	Sales Representative	$2,315,185.61	$1,849,640.94
12	Germany	Rachel	Valdez	Sales Representative	$1,827,066.71	$1,307,949.79
13	United States	Tete	Mensa-Annan	Sales Representative	$1,576,562.20	$0.00
14	United States	David	Campbell	Sales Representative	$1,573,012.94	$1,371,635.32
15	Canada	Garrett	Vargas	Sales Representative	$1,453,719.47	$1,620,276.90
16	Australia	Lynn	Tsoflias	Sales Representative	$1,421,810.92	$2,278,548.98
17	United States	Pamela	Ansman-Wolfe	Sales Representative	$1,352,577.13	$1,927,059.18

ORDER BY Clause with CASE Conditional Expression

Sort by LastName, MiddleName if exists else FirstName, and FirstName in case MiddleName is used.

```
USE AdventureWorks;

SELECT        FirstName,
              COALESCE(MiddleName, '')         AS MName,  -- ISNULL can also be used
              LastName,
              AddressLine1,
              COALESCE(AddressLine2, '')       AS Addr2,
              City,
              SP.Name                          AS [State],
              CR.Name                          AS Country,
              I.CustomerID
FROM   Person.Contact AS C
    INNER JOIN Sales.Individual AS I
        ON C.ContactID = I.ContactID
    INNER JOIN Sales.CustomerAddress AS CA
        ON CA.CustomerID = I.CustomerID
    INNER JOIN Person.[Address] AS A
        ON A.AddressID = CA.AddressID
    INNER JOIN Person.StateProvince SP
        ON SP.StateProvinceID = A.StateProvinceID
    INNER JOIN Person.CountryRegion CR
        ON CR.CountryRegionCode = SP.CountryRegionCode
ORDER  BY LastName,
    CASE
    WHEN MiddleName != '' THEN MiddleName
    ELSE FirstName
    END,
    FirstName;
-- (18508 row(s) affected) -Partial results.
```

FirstName	MName	LastName	AddressLine1	Addr2	City	State	Country	CustomerID
Chloe	A	Adams	3001 N. 48th Street		Marysville	Washington	United States	19410
Eduardo	A	Adams	4283 Meaham Drive		San Diego	California	United States	25292
Kaitlyn	A	Adams	3815 Berry Dr.		Westminster	British Columbia	Canada	11869
Mackenzie	A	Adams	9639 Ida Drive		Langford	British Columbia	Canada	14640
Sara	A	Adams	7503 Hill Drive		Milwaukie	Oregon	United States	16986
Adam		Adams	9381 Bayside Way		Newport Beach	California	United States	13323
Amber		Adams	9720 Morning Glory Dr.		Brisbane	Queensland	Australia	26746
Angel		Adams	9556 Lyman Rd.		Burlingame	California	United States	18504
Aaron	B	Adams	4116 Stanbridge Ct.		Downey	California	United States	28866
Noah	B	Adams	6738 Wallace Dr.		El Cajon	California	United States	16977
Bailey		Adams	1817 Adobe Drive		Kirkland	Washington	United States	13280
Ben		Adams	1534 Land Ave		Bremerton	Washington	United States	28678
Alex	C	Adams	237 Bellwood Dr.		Lake Oswego	Oregon	United States	21139
Courtney	C	Adams	6089 Santa Fe Dr.		Torrance	California	United States	18075
Ian	C	Adams	7963 Elk Dr	#4	Versailles	Yveline	France	29422

Special Sorting, Like United States On Top Of The Country Pop-Up List
It requires CASE or IIF conditional expression.

```
-- Major sort key is Color if not null, else product name
-- Minor sort on ProductNumber
SELECT ProductID,
    ProductNumber,
    Name AS ProductName,
    FORMAT(ListPrice, 'c', 'en-US') AS ListPrice,
    Color
FROM   Production.Product
WHERE  Name LIKE ( '%Road%' )
ORDER  BY        CASE
                    WHEN Color IS NULL THEN Name
                    ELSE Color
            END,
            ProductNumber DESC;
-- (103 row(s) affected) - Partial results.
```

ProductID	ProductNumber	ProductName	ListPrice	Color
768	BK-R50B-44	Road-650 Black, 44	$782.99	Black
977	BK-R19B-58	Road-750 Black, 58	$539.99	Black
999	BK-R19B-52	Road-750 Black, 52	$539.99	Black
998	BK-R19B-48	Road-750 Black, 48	$539.99	Black
997	BK-R19B-44	Road-750 Black, 44	$539.99	Black
813	HB-R956	HL Road Handlebars	$120.27	NULL
512	RM-R800	HL Road Rim	$0.00	NULL
519	SA-R522	HL Road Seat Assembly	$196.92	NULL
913	SE-R995	HL Road Seat/Saddle	$52.64	NULL
933	TI-R982	HL Road Tire	$32.60	NULL
811	HB-R504	LL Road Handlebars	$44.54	NULL
510	RM-R436	LL Road Rim	$0.00	NULL
517	SA-R127	LL Road Seat Assembly	$133.34	NULL
911	SE-R581	LL Road Seat/Saddle	$27.12	NULL
931	TI-R092	LL Road Tire	$21.49	NULL
812	HB-R720	ML Road Handlebars	$61.92	NULL
511	RM-R600	ML Road Rim	$0.00	NULL
518	SA-R430	ML Road Seat Assembly	$147.14	NULL
912	SE-R908	ML Road Seat/Saddle	$39.14	NULL
932	TI-R628	ML Road Tire	$24.99	NULL
717	FR-R92R-62	HL Road Frame - Red, 62	$1,431.50	Red
706	FR-R92R-58	HL Road Frame - Red, 58	$1,431.50	Red
721	FR-R92R-56	HL Road Frame - Red, 56	$1,431.50	Red

T-SQL queries demonstrate complex sorting with the CASE expression usage.
CASE expression returns a SINGLE SCALAR VALUE of the same data type.

```
SELECT   SellStartDate,
         SellEndDate,
         *
FROM   Production.Product
WHERE   Name LIKE ( '%mountain%' )
ORDER  BY CASE
                WHEN SellEndDate IS NULL THEN SellStartDate
                ELSE SellEndDate
           END DESC, Name;
GO
-- (94 row(s) affected) -Partial results.
```

SellStartDate	SellEndDate	ProductID	Name	ProductNumber
2007-07-01 00:00:00.000	NULL	986	Mountain-500 Silver, 44	BK-M18S-44
2007-07-01 00:00:00.000	NULL	987	Mountain-500 Silver, 48	BK-M18S-48
2007-07-01 00:00:00.000	NULL	988	Mountain-500 Silver, 52	BK-M18S-52
2007-07-01 00:00:00.000	NULL	869	Women's Mountain Shorts, L	SH-W890-L
2007-07-01 00:00:00.000	NULL	868	Women's Mountain Shorts, M	SH-W890-M
2007-07-01 00:00:00.000	NULL	867	Women's Mountain Shorts, S	SH-W890-S
2006-07-01 00:00:00.000	2007-06-30 00:00:00.000	817	HL Mountain Front Wheel	FW-M928
2006-07-01 00:00:00.000	2007-06-30 00:00:00.000	825	HL Mountain Rear Wheel	RW-M928
2006-07-01 00:00:00.000	2007-06-30 00:00:00.000	815	LL Mountain Front Wheel	FW-M423
2006-07-01 00:00:00.000	2007-06-30 00:00:00.000	823	LL Mountain Rear Wheel	RW-M423
2006-07-01 00:00:00.000	2007-06-30 00:00:00.000	814	ML Mountain Frame - Black, 38	FR-M63B-38
2006-07-01 00:00:00.000	2007-06-30 00:00:00.000	830	ML Mountain Frame - Black, 40	FR-M63B-40

```
-- 2 keys descending sort
SELECT          PRODUCTNAME   = P.Name,
                SALETOTAL     = ( OrderQty * UnitPrice ),
                NETSALETOTAL  = ( ( OrderQty - RejectedQty ) * UnitPrice )
FROM   Production.Product P
    INNER JOIN Purchasing.PurchaseOrderDetail SOD
       ON P.ProductID = SOD.ProductID
ORDER  BY PRODUCTNAME  DESC,  SALETOTAL DESC;

-- Column alias sorting of GROUP BY aggregation results
SELECT [YEAR]=YEAR(OrderDate), Orders = COUNT(*)
FROM AdventureWorks2012.Sales.SalesOrderHeader
GROUP BY YEAR(OrderDate)  ORDER BY [YEAR];
```

YEAR	Orders
2005	1379
2006	3692
2007	12443
2008	13951

CHAPTER 8: Basic SELECT Statement Syntax & Examples

ORDER BY Clause with IIF Conditional Function

Sort by LastName, MiddleName if exists else FirstName, and FirstName in case MiddleName is used.

```
USE AdventureWorks;

SELECT          FirstName,
                COALESCE(MiddleName, '')        AS MName,  -- ISNULL can also be used
                LastName,
                AddressLine1,
                COALESCE(AddressLine2, '')      AS Addr2,
                City,
                SP.Name                         AS [State],
                CR.Name                         AS Country,
                I.CustomerID
FROM   Person.Contact AS C
    INNER JOIN Sales.Individual AS I
        ON C.ContactID = I.ContactID
    INNER JOIN Sales.CustomerAddress AS CA
        ON CA.CustomerID = I.CustomerID
    INNER JOIN Person.[Address] AS A
        ON A.AddressID = CA.AddressID
    INNER JOIN Person.StateProvince SP
        ON SP.StateProvinceID = A.StateProvinceID
    INNER JOIN Person.CountryRegion CR
        ON CR.CountryRegionCode = SP.CountryRegionCode
ORDER  BY       LastName,
                IIF( MiddleName != '',
                        MiddleName,             -- TRUE condition return value
                        FirstName),             -- FALSE condition return value
                FirstName;
GO
-- (18508 row(s) affected) -Partial results.
```

FirstName	MName	LastName	AddressLine1	Addr2	City	State	Country	CustomerID
Chloe	A	Adams	3001 N. 48th Street		Marysville	Washington	United States	19410
Eduardo	A	Adams	4283 Meaham Drive		San Diego	California	United States	25292
Kaitlyn	A	Adams	3815 Berry Dr.		Westminster	British Columbia	Canada	11869
Mackenzie	A	Adams	9639 Ida Drive		Langford	British Columbia	Canada	14640
Sara	A	Adams	7503 Hill Drive		Milwaukie	Oregon	United States	16986
Adam		Adams	9381 Bayside Way		Newport Beach	California	United States	13323
Amber		Adams	9720 Morning Glory Dr.		Brisbane	Queensland	Australia	26746
Angel		Adams	9556 Lyman Rd.		Burlingame	California	United States	18504
Aaron	B	Adams	4116 Stanbridge Ct.		Downey	California	United States	28866
Noah	B	Adams	6738 Wallace Dr.		El Cajon	California	United States	16977
Bailey		Adams	1817 Adobe Drive		Kirkland	Washington	United States	13280
Ben		Adams	1534 Land Ave		Bremerton	Washington	United States	28678
Alex	C	Adams	237 Bellwood Dr.		Lake Oswego	Oregon	United States	21139
Courtney	C	Adams	6089 Santa Fe Dr.		Torrance	California	United States	18075
Ian	C	Adams	7963 Elk Dr	#4	Versailles	Yveline	France	29422

ORDER BY Clause with the RANK() Function

T-SQL query demonstrates the combination of CASE expression and RANK() function in an ORDER BY clause. Note that while such a complex sort is technically impressive, ultimately it has to make sense to the user, the Business Intelligence consumer.

```
-- SQL complex sorting
USE AdventureWorks;

SELECT          ContactID,
                FirstName,
                LastName,
                COALESCE(Title, '')  AS Title
FROM   Person.Contact
WHERE  LEFT(FirstName, 1) = 'M'
ORDER  BY CASE
                WHEN LEFT(LastName, 1) = 'A' THEN RANK()
                            OVER( ORDER BY CONCAT(FirstName, SPACE(1), LastName))
                WHEN LEFT(LastName, 1) = 'M' THEN RANK()
                            OVER( ORDER BY CONCAT(LastName,', ', FirstName), Title)
                WHEN LEFT(LastName, 1) = 'U' THEN RANK()
                            OVER(  ORDER BY CONCAT(LastName,', ', FirstName)  DESC)
                ELSE RANK()
                            OVER( ORDER BY LastName ASC, FirstName DESC)
        END;
```

ContactID	FirstName	LastName	Title
9500	Mackenzie	Adams	
10144	Mackenzie	Allen	
10128	Madeline	Allen	
11708	Madison	Alexander	
11527	Madison	Anderson	
19872	Morgan	Bailey	
8059	Michelle	Bailey	
8080	Melissa	Bailey	
18291	Megan	Bailey	
8070	Mariah	Bailey	
2432	Maria	Bailey	
14378	Marcus	Bailey	
8063	Makayla	Bailey	
8032	Mackenzie	Bailey	
9521	Morgan	Baker	
3320	Miguel	Baker	
15437	Mason	Baker	
9546	Mary	Baker	
1082	Mary	Baker	
9539	Maria	Baker	

ORDER BY Clause with Custom Mapped Sort Sequence

Typically we rely on alphabets or numbers for sorting. What if, for example, we don't want United States way down on a website drop-down menu, rather than on the top with Canada and United Kingdom just above "lucky" Australia? We have to do custom mapping for such a sort in the ORDER BY clause.

```
USE AdventureWorks;
SELECT          AddressLine1,
                City,
                SP.StateProvinceCode            AS State,
                PostalCode,
                CR.Name                         AS  Country
FROM   Person.[Address] A
    INNER JOIN Person.StateProvince SP          ON A.StateProvinceID = SP.StateProvinceID
    INNER JOIN Person.CountryRegion CR          ON SP.CountryRegionCode = CR.CountryRegionCode
ORDER  BY (      CASE    WHEN CR.Name = 'United States' THEN 0
                         WHEN CR.Name = 'Canada' THEN 1
                         WHEN CR.Name = 'United Kingdom' THEN 2   ELSE 3  END ),
                Country,
                City
                AddressLine1;
-- (19614 row(s) affected) - Partial results.
```

AddressLine1	City	State	PostalCode	Country
9355 Armstrong Road	York	ENG	YO15	United Kingdom
939 Vista Del Diablo	York	ENG	YO15	United Kingdom
9458 Flame Drive	York	ENG	YO15	United Kingdom
9557 Steven Circle	York	ENG	Y03 4TN	United Kingdom

Sorting on the Last Word of a String

```
USE tempdb;
SELECT BusinessEntityID, FULLNAME = CONCAT(FirstName , SPACE(1), LastName )
INTO   People FROM   AdventureWorks2012.Person.Person ORDER  BY BusinessEntityID ;

SELECT *  FROM   People
ORDER  BY REVERSE(LEFT(REVERSE(FullName), charindex(' ', REVERSE(FullName) + ' ' ) - 1)),
       FullName ;
GO -- (19972 row(s) affected) - Partial results.
```

BusinessEntityID	FULLNAME
285	Syed Abbas
293	Catherine Abel
295	Kim Abercrombie

ORDER BY Clause with Custom Alphanumeric Sort Sequence

A frequent requirement is custom sorting on alphanumeric field (column). The next T-SQL query demonstrates special alphanumeric sorting.

```
USE AdventureWorks;

SELECT AddressLine1,
            isnull(AddressLine2, '')     AS Addressline2,
            City,
            SP.StateProvinceCode    AS State,
            PostalCode,
            CR.Name                  AS Country
FROM  Person.[Address] A
    INNER JOIN Person.StateProvince SP
    ON A.StateProvinceID = SP.StateProvinceID
    INNER JOIN Person.CountryRegion CR
    ON SP.CountryRegionCode = CR.CountryRegionCode
ORDER  BY (      CASE
                WHEN Ascii([AddressLine1]) BETWEEN 65 AND 90 THEN 0 -- Upper case alpha
                WHEN Ascii([AddressLine1]) BETWEEN 48 AND 57 THEN 1 -- Digits
                ELSE 2
            END ),
            AddressLine1,
            City;
GO
-- (19614 row(s) affected) - Partial results.
```

AddressLine1	Addressline2	City	State	PostalCode	Country
Zur Lindung 46		Leipzig	NW	04139	Germany
Zur Lindung 6		Saarlouis	SL	66740	Germany
Zur Lindung 6		Solingen	NW	42651	Germany
Zur Lindung 609		Sulzbach Taunus	SL	66272	Germany
Zur Lindung 7		Berlin	HE	14129	Germany
Zur Lindung 7		Neunkirchen	SL	66578	Germany
Zur Lindung 764		Paderborn	HH	33041	Germany
Zur Lindung 78		Berlin	HH	10791	Germany
Zur Lindung 787		München	NW	80074	Germany
00, rue Saint-Lazare		Dunkerque	59	59140	France
02, place de Fontenoy		Verrieres Le Buisson	91	91370	France
035, boulevard du Montparnasse		Verrieres Le Buisson	91	91370	France
081, boulevard du Montparnasse		Saint-Denis	93	93400	France
081, boulevard du Montparnasse		Seattle	WA	98104	United States
084, boulevard du Montparnasse		Les Ulis	91	91940	France
1 Corporate Center Drive		Miami	FL	33127	United States
1 Mt. Dell Drive		Portland	OR	97205	United States
1 Smiling Tree Court	Space 55	Los Angeles	CA	90012	United States
1, allée des Princes		Courbevoie	92	92400	France

Working with Synonyms

A synonym is a shorthand name for a longer name including multi-part names. **While prefix like "sn" or "syn" is not required, it is a good practice since otherwise a synonym can be confused with a (real) table for example, leading to loss of DBA or developer productivity.**

```
USE tempdb;
GO


-- Create synonyms for a 3-part names
CREATE SYNONYM snCustomerAW  FOR AdventureWorks.Sales.Customer;
CREATE SYNONYM snCustomerAW12  FOR AdventureWorks2012.Sales.Customer;


-- Create a synonym for 4-part name linked server
CREATE SYNONYM snCustomerLDNAW12  FOR
       [LONDONPROD8].AdventureWorks2012.Sales.Customer;
GO -- Command(s) completed successfully.


-- Query the Customer tables by using the synonyms
SELECT * FROM snCustomerAW ORDER BY AccountNumber;     -- (19185 row(s) affected)
SELECT * FROM snCustomerAW12 ORDER BY AccountNumber;  -- (19820 row(s) affected)
GO


-- Delete a synonym
DROP SYNONYM snCustomerAW;  -- Command(s) completed successfully.
GO


-- Enumerating all synonyms in database
SELECT  name                            AS "Name"
       ,base_object_name                AS "Definition"
       ,PARSENAME(base_object_name, 4)  AS "Server"
       ,PARSENAME(base_object_name, 3)  AS "Database"
       ,PARSENAME(base_object_name, 2)  AS "Schema"
       ,PARSENAME(base_object_name, 1)  AS "Object"
  FROM sys.synonyms ORDER BY Definition;
```

Name	Definition	Server	Database	Schema	Object
CustomerAW12	[AdventureWorks2012].[Sales].[Customer]	NULL	AdventureWorks2012	Sales	Customer
CustomerLNDAW12	[LONDONPROD8].[AdventureWorks2012].[Sales].[Customer]	LONDONPROD8	AdventureWorks2012	Sales	Customer

Date & Time Conversion To / From String

While there are only a few internal representation of date and time, string representations are many, even not deterministic since they may change from one country to another such as weekday and month names.   T-SQL scripts demonstrate the myriad of date and time conversion possibilities.

The CONVERT() Function with Style Number Parameter

```
-- String source  format: mon dd yyyy hh:mmAM (or PM)
-- 100 is the style number parameter for CONVERT
SELECT [Date&Time] = convert(datetime, 'Oct 23 2020 11:01AM', 100)
```

Date&Time
2020-10-23 11:01:00.000

```
-- Default without style number
SELECT convert(datetime, 'Oct 23 2020 11:01AM')                    -- 2020-10-23 11:01:00.000
```

```
-- Without century (yy) string date conversion with style number 0
-- Input format: mon dd yy hh:mmAM (or PM)
SELECT [Date&Time] = convert(datetime, 'Oct 23 20 11:01AM', 0)
```

Date&Time
2020-10-23 11:01:00.000

```
-- Default without style number
SELECT convert(datetime, 'Oct 23 20 11:01AM')                      -- 2020-10-23 11:01:00.000
```

Convert string date & time to datetime (8-bytes internal representation) data type.

```
SELECT convert(datetime, '10/23/2016', 101)           -- mm/dd/yyyy
```

```
SELECT convert(datetime, '2016.10.23', 102)           -- yyyy.mm.dd ANSI date with century
```

```
SELECT convert(datetime, '23/10/2016', 103)           -- dd/mm/yyyy
```

```
SELECT convert(datetime, '23.10.2016', 104)-- dd.mm.yyyy
```

```
SELECT convert(datetime, '23-10-2016', 105)           -- dd-mm-yyyy
```

```
-- mon (month) types are nondeterministic conversions, dependent on language setting.
SELECT convert(datetime, '23 OCT 2016', 106)          -- dd mon yyyy
```

CHAPTER 8: Basic SELECT Statement Syntax & Examples

String Datetime Formats With "Mon" Are Nondeterministic, Language Dependent

SELECT [Date&Time] = convert(datetime, 'Oct 23, 2016', 107) -- mon dd, yyyy

> Date&Time
> 2016-10-23 00:00:00.000

SELECT [Date&Time]=convert(datetime, '20:10:44', 108)   -- hh:mm:ss

> Date&Time
> 1900-01-01 20:10:44.000

SELECT [Date&Time]=convert(datetime, 'Oct 23 2016 11:02:44:013AM', 109) -- mon dd yyyy hh:mm:ss:mmmAM (or PM)

> Date&Time
> 2016-10-23 11:02:44.013

SELECT convert(datetime, '10-23-2016', 110)   -- mm-dd-yyyy
SELECT convert(datetime, '2016/10/23', 111)   -- yyyy/mm/dd

-- YYYYMMDD ISO date format works at any language setting - international standard
SELECT [Date&Time]=convert(datetime, '20161023')

> Date&Time
> 2016-10-23 00:00:00.000

SELECT [Date&Time]=convert(datetime, '20161023', 112)   -- ISO yyyymmdd

> Date&Time
> 2016-10-23 00:00:00.000

SELECT [Date&Time]=convert(datetime, '23 Oct 2016 11:02:07:577', 113) -- dd mon yyyy hh:mm:ss:mmm

> Date&Time
> 2016-10-23 11:02:07.577

SELECT [Date&Time]=convert(datetime, '20:10:25:300', 114)   -- hh:mm:ss:mmm(24h)

> Date&Time
> 1900-01-01 20:10:25.300

SELECT [Date&Time]=convert(datetime, '2016-10-23 20:44:11', 120)   -- yyyy-mm-dd hh:mm:ss(24h)
> Date&Time
> 2016-10-23 20:44:11.000

CHAPTER 8: Basic SELECT Statement Syntax & Examples

Style 126 Is ISO 8601 Format: International Standard; Works With Any Language Setting

SELECT [Date&Time]=convert(datetime, '2018-10-23T18:52:47.513', 126) -- yyyy-mm-ddThh:mm:ss(.mmm)

> Date&Time
> 2018-10-23 18:52:47.513

SELECT [Date&Time]=convert(datetime, '2016-10-23 20:44:11.500', 121)   -- yyyy-mm-dd hh:mm:ss.mmm

> Date&Time
> 2016-10-23 20:44:11.500

-- Islamic / Hijri date conversion

SELECT CONVERT(nvarchar(32), convert(datetime,'2016-10-23'), 130);
-- 22 محرم 1438 12:00:00:000AM

SELECT [Date&Time]=convert(datetime, N'23 شوال 1441 6:52:47:513PM', 130)

> Date&Time
> 2020-06-14 18:52:47.513

SELECT [Date&Time]=convert(datetime, '23/10/1441 6:52:47:513PM',   131)

> Date&Time
> 2020-06-14 18:52:47.513

-- Convert DDMMYYYY format to datetime with intermediate conversion using STUFF().

SELECT STUFF(STUFF('31012016',3,0,'-'),6,0,'-');
-- 31-01-2016

SELECT [Date&Time]=convert(datetime, STUFF(STUFF('31012016',3,0,'-'),6,0,'-'), 105)

> Date&Time
> 2016-01-31 00:00:00.000

-- Equivalent
SELECT STUFF(STUFF('31012016',3,0,'/'),6,0,'/');   -- 31/01/2016
SELECT [Date&Time]=convert(datetime, STUFF(STUFF('31012016',3,0,'/'),6,0,'/'), 103)

CHAPTER 8: Basic SELECT Statement Syntax & Examples

String to Datetime Conversion Without Century

String to datetime conversion without century - some exceptions.   Nondeterministic means language setting (also regional setting) dependent such as Mar/Mär/mars/márc .

SELECT [Date&Time]=convert(datetime, 'Oct 23 16 11:02:44AM')   -- Default

Date&Time
2016-10-23 11:02:44.000

SELECT convert(datetime, '10/23/16', 1)	mm/dd/yy	U.S.
SELECT convert(datetime, '16.10.23', 2)	yy.mm.dd	ANSI
SELECT convert(datetime, '23/10/16', 3)	dd/mm/yy	UK/FR
SELECT convert(datetime, '23.10.16', 4)	dd.mm.yy	German
SELECT convert(datetime, '23-10-16', 5)	dd-mm-yy	Italian
SELECT convert(datetime, '23 OCT 16', 6)	dd mon yy	non-det.
SELECT convert(datetime, 'Oct 23, 16', 7)	mon dd, yy	non-det.
SELECT convert(datetime, '20:10:44', 8)	hh:mm:ss	
SELECT convert(datetime, 'Oct 23 16 11:02:44:013AM', 9)	Default with msec	
SELECT convert(datetime, '10-23-16', 10)	mm-dd-yy	U.S.
SELECT convert(datetime, '16/10/23', 11)	yy/mm/dd	Japan
SELECT convert(datetime, '161023', 12)	yymmdd	ISO
SELECT convert(datetime, '23 Oct 16 11:02:07:577', 13)	dd mon yy hh:mm:ss:mmm EU dflt	
SELECT convert(datetime, '20:10:25:300', 14)	hh:mm:ss:mmm(24h)	
SELECT convert(datetime, '2016-10-23 20:44:11',20)	yyyy-mm-dd hh:mm:ss(24h) ODBC can.	
SELECT convert(datetime, '2016-10-23 20:44:11.500', 21)	yyyy-mm-dd hh:mm:ss.mmm ODBC	

Combine Date & Time String into Datetime

```
DECLARE @DateTimeValue varchar(32), @DateValue char(8), @TimeValue char(6)
 SELECT @DateValue = '20200718',           @TimeValue = '211920'
SELECT          @DateTimeValue =
                CONCAT(
                convert(varchar, convert(datetime, @DateValue), 111),
                ' ', substring(@TimeValue, 1, 2) , ':', substring(@TimeValue, 3, 2) , ':',
substring(@TimeValue, 5, 2)  )

SELECT  DateInput = @DateValue, TimeInput = @TimeValue,  DateTimeOutput = @DateTimeValue;
GO
```

DateInput	TimeInput	DateTimeOutput
20200718	211920	2020/07/18 21:19:20

```
SELECT DATETIMEFROMPARTS (2020, 07, 1, 21, 01, 20, 700)          -- New in SQL Server 2012
```

Date and Time Internal Storage Format

DATETIME 8 bytes internal storage structure:

- ➢ 1st 4 bytes: number of days after the base date 1900-01-01
- ➢ 2nd 4 bytes: number of clock-ticks (3.33 milliseconds) since midnight

```
SELECT CONVERT(binary(8), CURRENT_TIMESTAMP);
```

Hex
0x0000A09C00F23CE1

DATE 3 bytes internal storage structure:

- ➢ 3 bytes integer: number of days after the first date 0001-01-01
- ➢ Note: hex byte order reversed

SMALLDATETIME 4 bytes internal storage structure

- ➢ 1st 2 bytes: number of days after the base date 1900-01-01
- ➢ 2nd 2 bytes: number of minutes since midnight

```
SELECT Hex=CONVERT(binary(4), convert(smalldatetime, getdate()));
```

Hex
0xA09C0375

CHAPTER 8: Basic SELECT Statement Syntax & Examples

Date & Time Operations Using System Operators & Functions

```
-- Conversion from hex (binary) to datetime value
DECLARE @dtHex binary(8)= 0x00009966002d3344;  DECLARE @dt datetime = @dtHex;
SELECT @dt;   -- 2007-07-09 02:44:34.147
```

```
-- SQL convert seconds to HH:MM:SS -
DECLARE @Seconds INT;  SET @Seconds = 20000 ;
SELECT HH = @Seconds / 3600, MM = (@Seconds%3600) / 60, SS = (@Seconds%60) ;
```

HH	MM	SS
5	33	20

Extract Date Only from DATETIME Data Type

```
DECLARE @Now datetime = CURRENT_TIMESTAMP -- getdate()

SELECT  DateAndTime      = @Now     -- Date portion and Time portion
        ,DateString           = REPLACE(LEFT(CONVERT (varchar, @Now, 112),10),' ','-')
        ,[Date]               = CONVERT(DATE, @Now)  -- SQL Server 2008 and on - date part
        ,Midnight1            = dateadd(day, datediff(day,0, @Now), 0)
        ,Midnight2            = CONVERT(DATETIME,CONVERT(int, @Now))
        ,Midnight3            = CONVERT(DATETIME,CONVERT(BIGINT,@Now) &
(POWER(Convert(bigint,2),32)-1));
```

DateAndTime	DateString	Date	Midnight1	Midnight2	Midnight3
2020-07-28 15:01:51.960	20200728	2020-07-28	2020-07-28 00:00:00.000	2020-07-29 00:00:00.000	2020-07-29 00:00:00.000

```
-- Compare today with database dates
SELECT          TOP (10)  OrderDate = CONVERT(date, OrderDate),
                Today = CONVERT(date, getdate()),
                DeltaDays = DATEDIFF(DD, OrderDate, getdate())
FROM AdventureWorks2012.Sales.SalesOrderHeader  ORDER BY NEWID(); -- random sort
```

OrderDate	Today	DeltaDays
2008-01-15	2012-08-10	1669
2006-07-14	2012-08-10	2219
2008-07-05	2012-08-10	1497
2008-03-01	2012-08-10	1623
2007-10-01	2012-08-10	1775
2007-01-15	2012-08-10	2034
2008-05-27	2012-08-10	1536
2008-04-18	2012-08-10	1575
2008-04-25	2012-08-10	1568
2006-12-17	2012-08-10	2063

String Date Formats Without Time

```
-- String date format yyyy/mm/dd from datetime
SELECT CONVERT(VARCHAR(10), GETDATE(), 111) AS [YYYY/MM/DD] ;
```

YYYY/MM/DD
2012/07/28

```
SELECT CONVERT(VARCHAR(10), GETDATE(), 112) AS [YYYYMMDD];
```

YYYYMMDD
20120728

```
SELECT REPLACE(CONVERT(VARCHAR(10), GETDATE(), 111),'/',' ') AS [YYYY MM DD];
```

YYYY MM DD
2020 07 28

```
-- Converting to special (non-standard) date formats: DD-MMM-YY
SELECT UPPER(REPLACE(CONVERT(VARCHAR,GETDATE(),6),' ','-')) AS CustomDate;
```

CustomDate
28-JUL-20

```
-- SQL convert date string to datetime - time set to 00:00:00.000 or 12:00AM

PRINT CONVERT(datetime,'07-10-2020',110) ;        -- Jul 10 2020 12:00AM
PRINT CONVERT(datetime,'2020/07/10',111) ;        -- Jul 10 2020 12:00AM
PRINT CONVERT(datetime,'20200710', 112);          -- Jul 10 2020 12:00AM
GO
```

```
-- SQL Server cast string to date / datetime
DECLARE @DateValue char(8) = '20200718'

SELECT [Date] = CAST (@DateValue AS datetime);
GO
```

Date
2020-07-18 00:00:00.000

CHAPTER 8: Basic SELECT Statement Syntax & Examples

String date to string date conversion with nested CONVERT

```
SELECT CONVERT(varchar, CONVERT(datetime, '20140508'), 100) AS StringDate;
```

StringDate
May 8 2014 12:00AM

```
-- T-SQL convert date to integer
DECLARE @Date datetime;  SET @Date = getdate();
SELECT DateAsInteger = CAST (CONVERT(varchar,@Date,112) as INT);
GO
```

DateAsInteger
20120728

```
-- SQL Server convert integer to datetime
DECLARE @iDate int = 20151225;
SELECT IntegerToDatetime = CAST(convert(varchar,@iDate) as datetime)
GO
```

IntegerToDatetime
2015-12-25 00:00:00.000

```
-- Alternates: date-only datetime values

SELECT [DATE-ONLY]=CONVERT(DATETIME, FLOOR(CONVERT(FLOAT, GETDATE())));

SELECT [DATE-ONLY]=CONVERT(DATETIME, FLOOR(CONVERT(MONEY, GETDATE())));

SELECT [DATE-ONLY]=CONVERT(DATETIME, CONVERT(DATE, GETDATE()));
```

```
-- CAST string to datetime
-- String date preparation, length is 10 characters
SELECT CONVERT(varchar, GETDATE(), 101), LEN (CONVERT(varchar, GETDATE(), 101))
--      07/28/2018     10
```

```
SELECT [DATE-ONLY]=CAST(CONVERT(varchar, GETDATE(), 101) AS DATETIME);
```

DATE-ONLY
2018-07-28 00:00:00.000

CHAPTER 8: Basic SELECT Statement Syntax & Examples

DATEADD() and DATEDIFF() Functions

```
-- T-SQL strip time from date
SELECT getdate() AS [DateTime], dateadd(dd, datediff(dd, 0, getdate()), 0) [DateOnly];
```

DateTime	DateOnly
2012-07-28 17:24:07.300	2012-07-28 00:00:00.000

```
-- First day of current month
SELECT dateadd(month, datediff(month, 0, getdate()), 0)  AS FirstDayOfCurrentMonth;
SELECT dateadd(dd,1, EOMONTH(getdate(),-1));  -- New to SQL Server 2012
```

FirstDayOfCurrentMonth
2020-07-01 00:00:00.000

```
-- 15th day of current month
SELECT dateadd(day,14,dateadd(month, datediff(month,0,getdate()),0))
                                                  AS MiddleOfCurrentMonth;
SELECT dateadd(dd,15, EOMONTH(getdate(),-1));  -- New to SQL Server 2012
```

MiddleOfCurrentMonth
2012-07-15 00:00:00.000

```
-- First Monday of current month
SELECT  dateadd(day, (9-datepart(weekday,
        dateadd(month, datediff(month, 0, getdate()), 0)))%7,
        dateadd(month, datediff(month, 0, getdate()), 0)) AS [First Monday Of Current Month];
GO
```

First Monday Of Current Month
2012-07-02 00:00:00.000

```
-- Next Monday calculation from the reference date which was a Monday
DECLARE @Now datetime = GETDATE();
DECLARE @NextMonday datetime = dateadd(dd, ((datediff(dd, '19000101', @Now)
                / 7) * 7) + 7, '19000101');
SELECT [Now]=@Now, [Next Monday]=@NextMonday;
GO
```

Now	Next Monday
2012-07-28 17:35:29.657	2012-07-30 00:00:00.000

Last Date & First Date Calculations

```
-- Last Friday of current month

SELECT   dateadd(day, -7+(6-datepart(weekday,

         dateadd(month, datediff(month, 0, getdate())+1, 0)))%7,

         dateadd(month, datediff(month, 0, getdate())+1, 0)) ;

-- First day of next month

SELECT dateadd(month, datediff(month, 0, getdate())+1, 0) ;

-- 15th of next month

SELECT dateadd(day,14, dateadd(month, datediff(month, 0, getdate())+1, 0));

-- First Monday of next month

SELECT   dateadd(day, (9-datepart(weekday,
         dateadd(month, datediff(month, 0, getdate())+1, 0)))%7,
         dateadd(month, datediff(month, 0, getdate())+1, 0));


-- Next 12 months start & end - EOMONTH is new to SQL Server 2012
SELECT TOP 12
         DATEADD(DD,1, EOMONTH(getdate(),number-1))     AS Start,
         EOMONTH(getdate(),number)                      AS [End]
FROM master.dbo.spt_values  -- get integer sequence
WHERE type='P'  ORDER BY number;
GO
```

Start	End
2016-08-01	2016-08-31
2016-09-01	2016-09-30
2016-10-01	2016-10-31
2016-11-01	2016-11-30
2016-12-01	2016-12-31
2017-01-01	2017-01-31
2017-02-01	2017-02-28
2017-03-01	2017-03-31
2017-04-01	2017-04-30
2017-05-01	2017-05-31
2017-06-01	2017-06-30
2017-07-01	2017-07-31

BETWEEN Operator for Date Range

Date time range SELECT using the using >= and < operators. Count Sales Orders for date range 2007 OCT-NOV.

```
DECLARE  @StartDate DATETIME,  @EndDate DATETIME
SET @StartDate = convert(DATETIME,'10/01/2007',101)
SET @EndDate  = convert(DATETIME,'11/30/2007',101)
SELECT @StartDate, @EndDate
-- 2007-10-01 00:00:00.000  2007-11-30 00:00:00.000
SELECT dateadd(DAY,1,@EndDate),    dateadd(ms,-3,dateadd(DAY,1,@EndDate))
-- 2007-12-01 00:00:00.000  2007-11-30 23:59:59.997

SELECT [Sales Orders for 2007 OCT-NOV] = COUNT(* )
FROM   AdventureWorks2012.Sales.SalesOrderHeader
WHERE  OrderDate >= @StartDate
       AND OrderDate < dateadd(DAY,1,@EndDate)
```

Sales Orders for 2007 OCT-NOV
3668

Equivalent date range query using BETWEEN comparison. It requires a bit of trick programming. 23.59.59.997 is the last available time in a day.

```
SELECT [Sales Orders for 2007 OCT-NOV] = COUNT(* )
FROM   AdventureWorks2012.Sales.SalesOrderHeader
WHERE   OrderDate BETWEEN @StartDate
        AND dateadd(ms,-3, dateadd(DAY, 1, @EndDate))
GO
```

Sales Orders for 2007 OCT-NOV
3668

The BETWEEN operator can be used with string dates as well. Note: anything after midnight on 2004-02-10 is not included.

```
USE AdventureWorks;
SELECT POs=COUNT(*) FROM Purchasing.PurchaseOrderHeader
WHERE OrderDate BETWEEN '20040201' AND '20040210'
GO
```

POs
108

CHAPTER 8: Basic SELECT Statement Syntax & Examples

22222222

BETWEEN Dates Without Time: Entire 2004-02-10 Day Included This Fashion

```
SELECT POs=COUNT(*) FROM Purchasing.PurchaseOrderHeader
WHERE datediff(dd,0,OrderDate)
        BETWEEN datediff(dd,0,'20040201 12:11:39') AND datediff(dd,0,'20040210 14:33:19')
```

POs
108

The datetime range BETWEEN is equivalent to >=...AND....<= operators.

```
SELECT POs=COUNT(*) FROM Purchasing.PurchaseOrderHeader
WHERE OrderDate  BETWEEN '2004-02-01 00:00:00.000' AND '2004-02-10  00:00:00.000'
```

POs
108

Orders with datetime OrderDate-s of

'2004-02-10 00:00:01.000'	1 second after midnight (start of day at 12:00AM)
'2004-02-10 00:01:00.000'	1 minute after midnight
'2004-02-10 01:00:00.000'	1 hour after midnight
'2004-02-10 23:00:00.000'	23 hours after midnight

would not included in the preceding two queries. Only datetime OrderDate of '2004-02-10 00:00:00.000' would be included. That would be OK if the time part is not used. But even in that case and order can be entered accidentally with a time part, that would throw off the count.

To include the entire day of 2004-02-10, move the day up by one and use the < operator:

```
SELECT POs=COUNT(*) FROM Purchasing.PurchaseOrderHeader
WHERE OrderDate >= '20040201' AND OrderDate < '20040211';
```

POs
108

The reason we cannot detect a difference is due to lack of data passed midnight on 2004-02-11.

```
SELECT  [PurchaseOrderID], [RevisionNumber], [Status],
        [EmployeeID], [VendorID], [ShipMethodID], [OrderDate]
FROM [AdventureWorks].[Purchasing].[PurchaseOrderHeader] WHERE PurchaseOrderID = 1665;
```

PurchaseOrderID	RevisionNumber	Status	EmployeeID	VendorID	ShipMethodID	OrderDate
1665	0	4	261	43	5	2004-02-10 00:00:00.000

Advance the datetime one second from midnight, the BETWEEN datetime query is not going to count it

```
UPDATE [AdventureWorks].[Purchasing].[PurchaseOrderHeader]
      SET OrderDate = '2004-02-10 00:00:01.000'
WHERE PurchaseOrderID = 1665;  -- (1 row(s) affected)
```

This is the current value for OrderDate datetime.

PurchaseOrderID	RevisionNumber	Status	EmployeeID	VendorID	ShipMethodID	OrderDate
1665	0	4	261	43	5	2004-02-10 00:00:01.000

The following queries are not going to count this passed midnight record any more.

```
SELECT POs=COUNT(*) FROM Purchasing.PurchaseOrderHeader
WHERE OrderDate BETWEEN '2004-02-01 00:00:00.000' AND '2004-02-10  00:00:00.000'
```

POs
107

```
USE AdventureWorks; SELECT POs=COUNT(*) FROM Purchasing.PurchaseOrderHeader
WHERE OrderDate BETWEEN '20040201' AND '20040210'
```

POs
107

While the query we designed specifically for a case like this will count it correctly.

```
SELECT POs=COUNT(*) FROM Purchasing.PurchaseOrderHeader
WHERE OrderDate >= '20040201' AND OrderDate < '20040211'
```

POs
108

We restore the data to its original value.

```
UPDATE [AdventureWorks].[Purchasing].[PurchaseOrderHeader]
      SET OrderDate = '2004-02-10 00:00:00.000'
WHERE PurchaseOrderID = 1665;    -- (1 row(s) affected)
```

CHAPTER 8: Basic SELECT Statement Syntax & Examples

Date Validation Function ISDATE()

```
DECLARE @StringDate varchar(32);
SET @StringDate = '2011-03-15 18:50';
IF EXISTS( SELECT * WHERE ISDATE(@StringDate) = 1)
  PRINT 'VALID DATE: ' + @StringDate
ELSE
  PRINT 'INVALID DATE: ' + @StringDate;
```

> VALID DATE: 2011-03-15 18:50

```
DECLARE @StringDate varchar(32) ;
SET @StringDate = '20112-03-15 18:50';
IF EXISTS( SELECT * WHERE ISDATE(@StringDate) = 1)
  PRINT 'VALID DATE: ' + @StringDate
ELSE  PRINT 'INVALID DATE: ' + @StringDate;
GO
```

> INVALID DATE: 20112-03-15 18:50

First and Last Day of Date Periods

Calculating date periods markers is a very important task in T-SQL programming, especially related to reporting queries.

```
DECLARE @Date DATE = '20161023';  SELECT ReferenceDate  = @Date;

SELECT FirstDayOfYear = CONVERT(DATE, dateadd(yy, datediff(yy,0, @Date),0));

SELECT LastDayOfYear  = CONVERT(DATE, dateadd(yy, datediff(yy,0, @Date)+1,-1));

SELECT FDofSemester = CONVERT(DATE, dateadd(qq,((datediff(qq,0,@Date)/2)*2),0));

SELECT LastDayOfSemester  = CONVERT(DATE, dateadd(qq,((datediff(qq,0,@Date)/2)*2)+2,-1));

SELECT FirstDayOfQuarter  = CONVERT(DATE, dateadd(qq, datediff(qq,0, @Date),0));

SELECT LastDayOfQuarter = CONVERT(DATE, dateadd(qq, datediff(qq,0,@Date)+1,-1));
```

LastDayOfQuarter
2016-12-31

The brand-new EOMonth() function simplifies month start/end formulas

```
SELECT LastDayOfMonth = EOMonth (@Date);  -- New in SQL Server 2012

SELECT FirstDayOfMonth = CONVERT(DATE, dateadd(mm, datediff(mm,0, @Date),0));

SELECT LastDayOfMonth = CONVERT(DATE, dateadd(mm, datediff(mm,0, @Date)+1,-1));

SELECT FirstDayOfWeek = CONVERT(DATE, dateadd(wk, datediff(wk,0, @Date),0));

SELECT LastDayOfWeek = CONVERT(DATE, dateadd(wk, datediff(wk,0, @Date)+1,-1));
GO
```

Month Sequence Generator

Sometimes date based data may have gaps missing months. For reporting purposes we may want to include all months from start date to end date. To do that we have to generate a continuous sequence of months, and use it to fill in the gaps. Calendar table can also be used for such a task.

```
DECLARE @Date date = '2000-01-01'
SELECT MonthStart=dateadd(MM, number, @Date)
FROM  master.dbo.spt_values
WHERE type='P' AND  dateadd(MM, number, @Date) <= CURRENT_TIMESTAMP
ORDER BY MonthStart;   -- (151 row(s) affected) - Partial results.
```

MonthStart
2000-01-01
2000-02-01
2000-03-01
2000-04-01
2000-05-01
2000-06-01
2000-07-01
2000-08-01
2000-09-01
2000-10-01
2000-11-01
2000-12-01
2001-01-01
2001-02-01
2001-03-01
2001-04-01

Selected U.S. & International Date Styles

The U.S. date style is m/d/y.

```
DECLARE @DateTimeValue varchar(32) = '10/23/2016';

SELECT StringDate=@DateTimeValue,  [SSMS-Style] = CONVERT(datetime, @DatetimeValue);

SELECT @DateTimeValue = '10/23/2016 23:01:05';

SELECT StringDate = @DateTimeValue, [SSMS-Style] = CONVERT(datetime, @DatetimeValue);
GO
```

StringDate	SSMS-Style
10/23/2016	2016-10-23 00:00:00.000

StringDate	SSMS-Style
10/23/2016 23:01:05	2016-10-23 23:01:05.000

The UK or British/French style is dmy.

```
DECLARE @DateTimeValue varchar(32) = '23/10/16 23:01:05';

SELECT StringDate = @DateTimeValue,  [SSMS-Style] = CONVERT(datetime, @DatetimeValue, 3);

 SELECT @DateTimeValue = '23/10/2016 04:01 PM';

SELECT StringDate = @DateTimeValue,  [SSMS-Style] = CONVERT(datetime, @DatetimeValue, 103);
GO
```

The German style is dmy as well with a new twist to it: period instead of slash.

```
DECLARE @DateTimeValue varchar(32)  = '23.10.16 23:01:05';
SELECT StringDate = @DateTimeValue, [SSMS -Style] = CONVERT(datetime, @DatetimeValue, 4);
 SELECT @DateTimeValue = '23.10.2016 04:01 PM';
SELECT StringDate = @DateTimeValue, [SSMS -Style] = CONVERT(datetime, @DatetimeValue, 104);
GO
```

```
-- Nondeterministic month name (mon)
SET LANGUAGE Spanish; SELECT CONVERT(varchar, getdate(), 100);          -- Ago 10 2018  4:43PM
SET LANGUAGE Turkish; SELECT CONVERT(varchar, getdate(), 100);          -- Agu 10 2018  4:44PM
SET LANGUAGE Polish; SELECT CONVERT(varchar, getdate(), 100);           -- VIII 10 2018  4:46PM
SET LANGUAGE Hungarian; SELECT CONVERT(varchar, getdate(), 100);        -- aug 10 2018  4:46PM
SET LANGUAGE Russian; SELECT CONVERT(nvarchar, getdate(), 100);         -- авг 10 2018  4:47PM
```

CHAPTER 8: Basic SELECT Statement Syntax & Examples

The DATEPART() Function to Decompose a Date

The DATEPART() function returns a part of a date.

```
DECLARE @dt datetime = getdate();
SELECT DATEPART(YEAR, @dt)              AS YYYY,
       DATEPART(MONTH, @dt)             AS MM,
       DATEPART(DAY, @dt)               AS DD;
```

YYYY	MM	DD
2016	7	29

```
SELECT * FROM Northwind.dbo.Orders
WHERE DATEPART(YEAR, OrderDate)         = '1996' AND
      DATEPART(MONTH,OrderDate)         = '07'   AND
      DATEPART(DAY, OrderDate)          = '10'
```

```
/*OrderID     CustomerID    EmployeeID    OrderDate         RequiredDate        ShippedDate
      ShipVia Freight ShipName      Shipaddress       ShipCity ShipRegion      ShipPostalCode
      ShipCountry
10253  HANAR  3       1996-07-10 00:00:00.000 1996-07-24 00:00:00.000 1996-07-16 00:00:00.000
       2      58.17   Hanari Carnes    Rua do Paço, 67  Rio de Janeiro   RJ       05454-876
       Brazil */
```

Alternate syntax for DATEPART.

```
SELECT * FROM Northwind.dbo.Orders
WHERE          YEAR(OrderDate)   = 1996       AND
               MONTH(OrderDate)  = 07         AND
               DAY(OrderDate)    = 10
GO
```

```
-- Additional datepart parameters including Julian date
DECLARE @dt datetime = getdate();
SELECT DATEPART(DAY, @dt)               AS DD,
       DATEPART(WEEKDAY, @dt)           AS WD,
       DATEPART(DAYOFYEAR, @dt)         AS JulianDate,
       DATEPART(WEEK, @dt)              AS Week,
       DATEPART(ISO_WEEK, @dt)          AS ISOWeek,
       DATEPART(HOUR, @dt)              AS HH;
```

DD	WD	JulianDate	Week	ISOWeek	HH
10	5	223	33	32	17

CHAPTER 8: Basic SELECT Statement Syntax & Examples

The DATENAME() Function to Get Date Part Names

The DATENAME() function can be used to find out the words for months and weekdays.

```
SELECT DayName=DATENAME(weekday, OrderDate), SalesPerWeekDay = COUNT(*)
FROM AdventureWorks2008.Sales.SalesOrderHeader
GROUP BY DATENAME(weekday, OrderDate), DATEPART(weekday,OrderDate)
ORDER BY DATEPART(weekday,OrderDate);
```

DayName	SalesPerWeekDay
Sunday	4482
Monday	4591
Tuesday	4346
Wednesday	4244
Thursday	4483
Friday	4444
Saturday	4875

DATENAME application for month names

```
SELECT MonthName=DATENAME(month, OrderDate), SalesPerMonth = COUNT(*)
FROM AdventureWorks2008.Sales.SalesOrderHeader
GROUP BY DATENAME(month, OrderDate), MONTH(OrderDate) ORDER BY MONTH(OrderDate);
```

MonthName	SalesPerMonth
January	2483
February	2686
March	2750
April	2740
May	3154
June	3079
July	2094
August	2411
September	2298
October	2282
November	2474
December	3014

```
SELECT DATENAME(MM,dateadd(MM,7,-1))  -- July  - Month name from month number
```

Extract Date from Text with PATINDEX Pattern Matching

```
USE tempdb;
go

CREATE TABLE InsiderTransaction (
    InsiderTransactionID int identity primary key,
    TradeDate datetime,
    TradeMsg varchar(256),
    ModifiedDate datetime default (getdate())  );

-- Populate table with dummy data
INSERT InsiderTransaction (TradeMsg)
VALUES ('INSIDER TRAN QABC Hammer, Bruce D. CSO 09-02-08 Buy 2,000 6.10');
INSERT InsiderTransaction (TradeMsg)
VALUES ('INSIDER TRAN QABC Schmidt, Steven CFO 08-25-08 Buy 2,500 6.70') ;
INSERT InsiderTransaction (TradeMsg)
VALUES ('INSIDER TRAN QABC  Hammer, Bruce D. CSO  08-20-08 Buy 3,000 8.59');
INSERT InsiderTransaction (TradeMsg)
VALUES ('INSIDER TRAN QABC Walters,  Jeff CTO 08-15-08  Sell 5,648 8.49');
INSERT InsiderTransaction (TradeMsg)
VALUES  ('INSIDER TRAN  QABC  Walters, Jeff CTO   08-15-08 Option Exercise 5,648 2.15');
INSERT InsiderTransaction (TradeMsg)
VALUES('INSIDER TRAN QABC Hammer, Bruce D. CSO 07-31-08  Buy 5,000 8.05');
INSERT InsiderTransaction (TradeMsg)
VALUES('INSIDER TRAN QABC Lennot, Mark  Director  08-31-07 Buy 1,500 9.97');
INSERT InsiderTransaction (TradeMsg)
VALUES('INSIDER TRAN QABC  O''Neal, Linda COO  08-01-08 Sell 5,000 6.50');
```

Pattern match for MM-DD-YY using the PATINDEX string function to extract dates from stock trade message text.

```
SELECT  InsiderTransactionID ,      substring(TradeMsg,
        patindex('%[01][0-9]-[0123][0-9]-[0-9][0-9]%', TradeMsg),8) AS TradeDate
FROM InsiderTransaction  WHERE  patindex('%[01][0-9]-[0123][0-9]-[0-9][0-9]%', TradeMsg) > 0;
```

InsiderTransactionID	TradeDate
1	09-02-08
2	08-25-08
3	08-20-08
4	08-15-08
5	08-15-08
6	07-31-08
7	08-31-07
8	08-01-08

Valid Ranges for Date & Time Data Types

> DATE (3 bytes) date range:

> January 1, 1 through December 31, 9999 A.D.

> SMALLDATETIME (4 bytes) date range:

> January 1, 1900 through June 6, 2079

> DATETIME (8 bytes) date range:

> January 1, 1753 through December 31, 9999

> DATETIME2 (6-8 bytes) date range:

> January 1, 1 A.D. through December 31, 9999 A.D.

Smalldatetime has limited range. The statement below will give a date range error.

```
SELECT CONVERT(smalldatetime, '2110-01-01')
/* Msg 242, Level 16, State 3, Line 1
The conversion of a varchar data type to a smalldatetime data type
resulted in an out-of-range value. */
```

```
-- Date Columbus discovers America
SELECT CONVERT(datetime, '14921012');
/* Msg 242, Level 16, State 3, Line 2
The conversion of a varchar data type to a datetime data type resulted in an out-of-range value. */
```

```
SELECT CONVERT(datetime2, '14921012');   -- 1492-10-10 00:00:00.0000000
```

```
SELECT CONVERT(date, '14921012');              -- 1492-10-12
```

CHAPTER 8: Basic SELECT Statement Syntax & Examples

Last Week Calculations

```
-- SQL last Friday - Implied string to datetime conversions in dateadd & datediff
DECLARE @BaseFriday CHAR(8), @LastFriday datetime, @LastMonday datetime;
SET @BaseFriday = '19000105';
SELECT  @LastFriday = dateadd(dd,
        (datediff (dd, @BaseFriday, CURRENT_TIMESTAMP) / 7) * 7, @BaseFriday) ;
SELECT [Last Friday] = @LastFriday ;
```

Last Friday
2012-07-27 00:00:00.000

```
-- Last Monday (last week's Monday)
SELECT  @LastMonday=dateadd(dd,  (datediff (dd, @BaseFriday,
        CURRENT_TIMESTAMP) / 7) * 7 - 4, @BaseFriday)
SELECT [Last Monday]= @LastMonday;
```

Last Monday
2012-07-23 00:00:00.000

```
-- Last week - SUN - SAT
SELECT          [Last Week] = CONCAT(CONVERT(varchar,dateadd(day, -1, @LastMonday), 101), ' - ',
                CONVERT(varchar, dateadd(day, 1,  @LastFriday), 101))
```

Last Week
07/22/2012 - 07/28/2012

```
-- Next 10 weeks including this one; SUN - SAT
SELECT  TOP 10  [ Week] = CONCAT(CONVERT(varchar,dateadd(day, -1+number*7, @LastMonday), 101),
        ' - ',      CONVERT(varchar, dateadd(day, 1+number*7,  @LastFriday), 101))
FROM master.dbo.spt_values  WHERE type = 'P';
```

Week
08/05/2012 - 08/11/2012
08/12/2012 - 08/18/2012
08/19/2012 - 08/25/2012
08/26/2012 - 09/01/2012
09/02/2012 - 09/08/2012
09/09/2012 - 09/15/2012
09/16/2012 - 09/22/2012
09/23/2012 - 09/29/2012
09/30/2012 - 10/06/2012
10/07/2012 - 10/13/2012

Specific Day Calculations

```
-- First day of current month
SELECT dateadd(month, datediff(month, 0, getdate()), 0);
```

```
-- 15th day of current month
SELECT dateadd(day,14,dateadd(month,datediff(month,0,getdate()),0));
```

```
-- First Monday of current month
SELECT   dateadd(day, (9-datepart(weekday,
         dateadd(month, datediff(month, 0, getdate()), 0)))%7,
         dateadd(month, datediff(month, 0, getdate()), 0)) ;
```

```
-- Next Monday calculation from the reference date which was a Monday
DECLARE @Now datetime = GETDATE();
DECLARE @NextMonday datetime = dateadd(dd, ((datediff(dd, '19000101', @Now) / 7) * 7) + 7,
'19000101');
SELECT [Now]=@Now, [Next Monday]=@NextMonday;
```

```
-- Last Friday of current month
SELECT   dateadd(day, -7+(6-datepart(weekday,
         dateadd(month, datediff(month, 0, getdate())+1, 0)))%7,
         dateadd(month, datediff(month, 0, getdate())+1, 0)) ;
```

```
-- First day of next month
SELECT dateadd(month, datediff(month, 0, getdate())+1, 0);
```

```
-- 15th of next month
SELECT dateadd(day,14, dateadd(month, datediff(month, 0, getdate())+1, 0));
```

```
-- First Monday of next month
SELECT   dateadd(day, (9-datepart(weekday,
         dateadd(month, datediff(month, 0, getdate())+1, 0)))%7,
          dateadd(month, datediff(month, 0, getdate())+1, 0))  AS NextMonthMonday;
```

NextMonthMonday
2012-08-06 00:00:00.000

CHAPTER 8: Basic SELECT Statement Syntax & Examples

CHAPTER 9: Subqueries in SELECT Statements

Subqueries

Subquery ("inner query") is query within a query which is called the "outer query".

When a subquery involves columns form the outer query, it is called correlated subquery.

When a subquery has a table alias, it is called a derived table.

With SQL Server 2005 a new kind of subquery was introduced: Common Table Expression (CTE). A query can have one or more CTEs. If they are related, they are called nested CTEs. CTEs support recursion.

Correlated subquery is used to retrieve the last freight cost for the customer.

```
-- Correlated subquery - it has reference to an outer query column: A.CustomerID
USE Northwind;

SELECT  A.CustomerID,
      FORMAT(MIN(A.OrderDate), 'd')                         AS FirstOrder,
      FORMAT(MAX(A.OrderDate), 'd')                         AS LastOrder,
      FORMAT( (SELECT  TOP 1 B.Freight
            FROM    Orders B
            WHERE   B.CustomerID = A.CustomerID
            ORDER BY OrderDate DESC),'c','en-US')           AS LastFreight
FROM    Orders A
GROUP BY A.CustomerID ORDER BY A.CustomerID;  -- (89 row(s) affected) - Partial results.
```

CustomerID	FirstOrder	LastOrder	LastFreight
ALFKI	8/25/1997	4/9/1998	$1.21
ANATR	9/18/1996	3/4/1998	$39.92
ANTON	11/27/1996	1/28/1998	$58.43
AROUT	11/15/1996	4/10/1998	$33.80
BERGS	8/12/1996	3/4/1998	$151.52
BLAUS	4/9/1997	4/29/1998	$31.14
BLONP	7/25/1996	1/12/1998	$7.09
BOLID	10/10/1996	3/24/1998	$16.16
BONAP	10/16/1996	5/6/1998	$38.28
BOTTM	12/20/1996	4/24/1998	$24.12
BSBEV	8/26/1996	4/14/1998	$123.83
CACTU	4/29/1997	4/28/1998	$0.33

Non-Correlated Subqueries

In the next query, the inner query is not linked to the outer query at all (no outer column is used in the inner query). The implication is that the inner query can be executed by itself. The inner query needs to return a single value in this instance due to the ">=" operator. If it were to return multiple values, error would result.

```
-- Non-correlated subquery
SELECT          Name,
                FORMAT(ListPrice, 'c','en-US')          AS ListPrice,
                ProductNumber,
                FORMAT(StandardCost, 'c','en-US')       AS StandardCost
FROM AdventureWorks2012.Production.Product
WHERE ListPrice >=
                (SELECT ListPrice
                 FROM AdventureWorks.Production.Product
                 WHERE Name = 'Road-250 Black, 48' )

ORDER BY ListPrice DESC, Name;
GO
```

Name	ListPrice	ProductNumber	StandardCost
Road-150 Red, 44	$3,578.27	BK-R93R-44	$2,171.29
Road-150 Red, 48	$3,578.27	BK-R93R-48	$2,171.29
Road-150 Red, 52	$3,578.27	BK-R93R-52	$2,171.29
Road-150 Red, 56	$3,578.27	BK-R93R-56	$2,171.29
Road-150 Red, 62	$3,578.27	BK-R93R-62	$2,171.29
Mountain-100 Silver, 38	$3,399.99	BK-M82S-38	$1,912.15
Mountain-100 Silver, 42	$3,399.99	BK-M82S-42	$1,912.15
Mountain-100 Silver, 44	$3,399.99	BK-M82S-44	$1,912.15
Mountain-100 Silver, 48	$3,399.99	BK-M82S-48	$1,912.15
Mountain-100 Black, 38	$3,374.99	BK-M82B-38	$1,898.09
Mountain-100 Black, 42	$3,374.99	BK-M82B-42	$1,898.09
Mountain-100 Black, 44	$3,374.99	BK-M82B-44	$1,898.09
Mountain-100 Black, 48	$3,374.99	BK-M82B-48	$1,898.09
Road-250 Black, 44	$2,443.35	BK-R89B-44	$1,554.95
Road-250 Black, 48	$2,443.35	BK-R89B-48	$1,554.95
Road-250 Black, 52	$2,443.35	BK-R89B-52	$1,554.95
Road-250 Black, 58	$2,443.35	BK-R89B-58	$1,554.95
Road-250 Red, 44	$2,443.35	BK-R89R-44	$1,518.79
Road-250 Red, 48	$2,443.35	BK-R89R-48	$1,518.79
Road-250 Red, 52	$2,443.35	BK-R89R-52	$1,518.79
Road-250 Red, 58	$2,443.35	BK-R89R-58	$1,554.95

Subquery returned more than 1 value Error

The following query fails. The reason: the ">=" requires a single value on the right side. The subquery returns 46 values.

```
-- Non-correlated subquery
SELECT          Name,
                FORMAT(ListPrice, 'c','en-US')                  AS ListPrice,
                ProductNumber,
                FORMAT(StandardCost, 'c','en-US')               AS StandardCost
FROM AdventureWorks2012.Production.Product
WHERE ListPrice >=
   (SELECT ListPrice
    FROM AdventureWorks.Production.Product
    WHERE Name LIKE 'Road%' )
ORDER BY ListPrice DESC, Name;
GO
/* Msg 512, Level 16, State 1, Line 3
Subquery returned more than 1 value. This is not permitted when the subquery follows =, !=, <, <= , >, >=
or when the subquery is used as an expression. */
```

If we change the WHERE clause predicate operator from ">=" to "IN" then the query will execute correctly since the IN operator works with a set of values on the right side.

```
-- Non-correlated subquery
SELECT   Name,
         FORMAT(ListPrice, 'c','en-US')                  AS ListPrice,
         ProductNumber,
         FORMAT(StandardCost, 'c','en-US')               AS StandardCost
FROM AdventureWorks2012.Production.Product
WHERE ListPrice IN
         (SELECT ListPrice
          FROM AdventureWorks.Production.Product  WHERE Name LIKE 'Road%' )
ORDER BY ListPrice DESC, Name;
-- (253 row(s) affected)  -- Partial results.
```

Name	ListPrice	ProductNumber	StandardCost
AWC Logo Cap	$8.99	CA-1098	$6.92
Racing Socks, L	$8.99	SO-R809-L	$3.36
Racing Socks, M	$8.99	SO-R809-M	$3.36
Road Bottle Cage	$8.99	BC-R205	$3.36
Road-650 Black, 44	$782.99	BK-R50B-44	$486.71
Road-650 Black, 48	$782.99	BK-R50B-48	$486.71
Road-650 Black, 52	$782.99	BK-R50B-52	$486.71

Correlated Subqueries

In a correlated subquery there is a reference to an outer query column. In other words, the subquery by itself cannot be executed due to the correlation. In the next query, the inner query references soh.SalesOrderID column from the outer query in the WHERE clause predicate which is like an EQUI-JOIN.

```
SELECT          soh.SalesOrderID,
                FORMAT (soh.OrderDate, 'yyyy-MM-dd')                      AS OrderDate,


                ( SELECT FORMAT(MAX(sod.UnitPrice),'c','en-US')
                  FROM   AdventureWorks2012.Sales.SalesOrderDetail AS sod
                  WHERE  soh.SalesOrderID = sod.SalesOrderID )            AS MaxUnitPrice,


                FORMAT(TotalDue, 'c', 'en-US')                           AS TotalDue
FROM    AdventureWorks2012.Sales.SalesOrderHeader AS soh
ORDER BY MaxUnitPrice DESC, SalesOrderID;     -- (31465 row(s) affected) - Partial results.
```

SalesOrderID	OrderDate	MaxUnitPrice	TotalDue
51087	2007-07-01	$953.63	$2,721.27
51099	2007-07-01	$953.63	$5,276.64
51119	2007-07-01	$953.63	$2,040.14
51173	2007-07-01	$953.63	$1,457.54
51701	2007-08-01	$953.63	$2,634.93
51798	2007-08-01	$953.63	$907.09
51805	2007-08-01	$953.63	$907.09
51808	2007-08-01	$953.63	$1,827.45
51861	2007-08-01	$953.63	$11,762.43
53489	2007-09-01	$953.63	$1,814.18

The next query with correlated subquery list sales staff with 0.015 commission rate.

```
SELECT CONCAT(p.LastName,', ', p.FirstName) AS SalesPerson, e.BusinessEntityID AS EmployeeID
FROM AdventureWorks2012.Person.Person AS p
            INNER JOIN AdventureWorks2012.HumanResources.Employee AS e
            ON e.BusinessEntityID = p.BusinessEntityID
WHERE 0.015 IN (SELECT CommissionPct  FROM AdventureWorks2012.Sales.SalesPerson sp
            WHERE e.BusinessEntityID = sp.BusinessEntityID)  ORDER BY SalesPerson;
```

SalesPerson	EmployeeID
Carson, Jillian	277
Mitchell, Linda	276
Saraiva, José	282

CHAPTER 9: Subqueries in SELECT Statements

Single-Valued Correlated Subqueries
The query syntax determines if we can use a single-valued subquery or multiple-valued. A subquery can be the argument of a function.

```
USE AdventureWorks2012;
```

```
-- Single value subquery in SELECT list
SELECT  SOH.SalesOrderID                              AS SOID,
        CONVERT(DATE,SOH.OrderDate)                   AS OrderDate,
        FORMAT(SOH.Subtotal,'c0','en-US')             AS Subtotal,
        (SELECT MAX(SOD.UnitPrice)
         FROM Sales.SalesOrderDetail AS SOD
         WHERE SOH.SalesOrderID=SOD.SalesOrderID)      AS MaxUnitPrice
FROM Sales.SalesOrderHeader SOH    ORDER BY SOID;
--(31467 row(s) affected) - Partial results.
```

SOID	OrderDate	Subtotal	MaxUnitPrice
43659	2005-07-01	$20,566	2039.994
43660	2005-07-01	$1,294	874.794

```
-- Make the subquery the argument of the FORMAT function
SELECT  TOP (10)        SOH.SalesOrderID              AS SOID,
                        CONVERT(DATE,SOH.OrderDate)   AS OrderDate,
                        FORMAT(SOH.Subtotal,'c0','en-US')  AS Subtotal,
                        FORMAT(
    (SELECT MAX(SOD.UnitPrice)
    FROM Sales.SalesOrderDetail AS SOD
    WHERE SOH.SalesOrderID=SOD.SalesOrderID)
                        ,'c2','en-US')                AS MaxUnitPrice
FROM Sales.SalesOrderHeader SOH   ORDER BY SOID;
```

SOID	OrderDate	Subtotal	MaxUnitPrice
43659	2005-07-01	$20,566	$2,039.99
43660	2005-07-01	$1,294	$874.79
43661	2005-07-01	$32,726	$2,039.99
43662	2005-07-01	$28,833	$2,146.96
43663	2005-07-01	$419	$419.46
43664	2005-07-01	$24,433	$2,039.99
43665	2005-07-01	$14,353	$2,039.99
43666	2005-07-01	$5,056	$2,146.96
43667	2005-07-01	$6,107	$2,039.99
43668	2005-07-01	$35,944	$2,146.96

CHAPTER 9: Subqueries in SELECT Statements

Correlated Subqueries with Same Table

In a correlated subquery, we can use a table from the outer query. In such a case table alias usage is required. In the next query with correlated subquery which lists same part suppliers, the ProductVendor table is referenced by both the outer query and inner query, therefore table alias is required.

```
SELECT          p.Name                          AS ProductName,
                v.Name                          AS Vendor,
                pv1.BusinessEntityID            AS VendorID
FROM AdventureWorks2012.Purchasing.ProductVendor pv1
   INNER JOIN AdventureWorks2012.Production.Product p ON p.ProductID = pv1.ProductID
   INNER JOIN AdventureWorks2012.Purchasing.Vendor v  ON v.BusinessEntityID = pv1.BusinessEntityID
WHERE pv1.ProductID IN      (      SELECT pv2.ProductID
                                   FROM AdventureWorks2012.Purchasing.ProductVendor pv2
                                   WHERE pv1.BusinessEntityID <> pv2.BusinessEntityID)
ORDER  BY ProductName, Vendor;           -- (347 row(s) affected) - Partial results.
```

ProductName	Vendor	VendorID
Internal Lock Washer 7	Aurora Bike Center	1616
Internal Lock Washer 7	Pro Sport Industries	1686
Internal Lock Washer 8	Aurora Bike Center	1616
Internal Lock Washer 8	Pro Sport Industries	1686
Internal Lock Washer 9	Aurora Bike Center	1616
Internal Lock Washer 9	Pro Sport Industries	1686
LL Crankarm	Proseware, Inc.	1678

CROSS APPLY with Correlated Subquery

The CROSS APPLY operator can connect tables with correlated subqueries as demonstrated following, INNER JOIN would not work in this case.

```
USE AdventureWorks;      DECLARE  @Year  INT = 2003, @Month INT = 2;
SELECT   s.Name                                          AS Customer,
         FORMAT(SalesAmount.OrderTotal,'c','en-US')       AS [Total Sales]
FROM     Sales.Customer AS c  INNER JOIN Sales.Store AS s   ON s.CustomerID = c.CustomerID
    CROSS APPLY  (      SELECT   soh.CustomerId,   Sum(sod.LineTotal) AS OrderTotal
                   FROM    Sales.SalesOrderHeader AS soh
               INNER JOIN Sales.SalesOrderDetail AS sod   ON sod.SalesOrderId = soh.SalesOrderId
                   WHERE soh.CustomerId = c.CustomerId
               AND OrderDate > = DATEFROMPARTS(@Year, @Month, 1)
               AND OrderDate <  DATEADD(mm, 1, DATEFROMPARTS(@Year, @Month, 1))
                   GROUP BY soh.CustomerId)               AS SalesAmount
ORDER BY Customer;       -- (132 row(s) affected) - Partial results.
```

Customer	Total Sales
Ace Bicycle Supply	$647.99
Affordable Sports Equipment	$50,953.32
Alpine Ski House	$939.59
Basic Sports Equipment	$159.56

Derived Tables: SELECT from SELECT

A non-correlated subquery can be made into a derived table by enclosing it in parenthesis and assigning a table alias, such as "CAT" in the following example. It can then be used like a regular table for example in JOINs.

```
USE Northwind;

SELECT   c.CategoryName  AS Category,
         p.ProductName,   p.UnitPrice,    CAT.NoOfProducts
FROM     Categories c
    INNER JOIN Products p
     ON c.CategoryID = p.CategoryID
    INNER JOIN

                 (SELECT  c.CategoryID,
                         NoOfProducts = count(* )
                 FROM     Categories c
                   INNER JOIN Products p1
                       ON c.CategoryID = p1.CategoryID
                 GROUP BY c.CategoryID)                         AS CAT

     ON c.CategoryID = CAT.CategoryID
ORDER BY Category;
-- (77 row(s) affected)  - Partial results.
```

Category	ProductName	UnitPrice
Dairy Products	Raclette Courdavault	55.00
Dairy Products	Camembert Pierrot	34.00
Dairy Products	Gudbrandsdalsost	36.00
Dairy Products	Flotemysost	21.50
Dairy Products	Mozzarella di Giovanni	34.80
Grains/Cereals	Gustaf's Knäckebröd	21.00
Grains/Cereals	Tunnbröd	9.00
Grains/Cereals	Singaporean Hokkien Fried Mee	14.00
Grains/Cereals	Filo Mix	7.00
Grains/Cereals	Gnocchi di nonna Alice	38.00
Grains/Cereals	Ravioli Angelo	19.50

Results from the subquery (derived table).

CategoryID	NoOfProducts
1	12
2	12
3	13
4	10
5	7
6	6
7	5
8	12

CHAPTER 9: Subqueries in SELECT Statements

The UNION & UNION ALL Set Operators

UNION (distinct, duplicates eliminated) and UNION ALL (duplicates allowed) merge two or more sets of data into one set. Important points to remember about UNION:

➢ First SELECT column list establishes column names and data types; if INTO used it goes here

➢ Subsequent SELECTs must match the column structure; column names can be any; NULL if no data

➢ ORDER BY goes at the very end with the last SELECT

T-SQL UNION query merges data from different countries into a single result set.

```
USE NorthWind;
SELECT  ContactName,
        CompanyName,
        City,
        Country,
        Phone
FROM   Customers
WHERE  Country IN ( 'USA', 'Canada' )
-- (16 row(s) affected)
UNION
SELECT  ContactName,
        CompanyName             AS Company,
        City,      Country,
        Phone                   AS Telephone
FROM   Customers
WHERE  Country IN ( 'Germany', 'France' )
-- (22 row(s) affected)
UNION
SELECT  ContactName             AS Contact,
        CompanyName,   City,   Country,
        Phone                   AS Telephone
FROM   Customers
WHERE  Country IN ( 'Brazil', 'Spain' )
-- (14 row(s) affected)
ORDER  BY CompanyName,   ContactName ASC;
-- (52 row(s) affected)  - Partial results.
```

ContactName	CompanyName	City	Country	Phone
Maria Anders	Alfreds Futterkiste	Berlin	Germany	030-0074321
Hanna Moos	Blauer See Delikatessen	Mannheim	Germany	0621-08460
Frédérique Citeaux	Blondesddsl père et fils	Strasbourg	France	88.60.15.31
Martín Sommer	Bólido Comidas preparadas	Madrid	Spain	(91) 555 22 82

CHAPTER 9: Subqueries in SELECT Statements

CTE: Common Table Expression for Structured Coding

Common Table Expression is new in SQL Server 2005. It is similar to derived tables in one aspect with a difference: it is defined at the very beginning of a the query, above the main(outer) query. In addition, CTEs can be nested and defined as recursive.

```
USE AdventureWorks;

WITH CTE(ManagerID, StaffCount)
AS
(
    SELECT ManagerID, COUNT(*)
    FROM HumanResources.Employee AS e
    GROUP BY ManagerID
)

SELECT          CONCAT(LEFT(FirstName,1), '. ', LastName)          AS Manager,
                e.Title, StaffCount
FROM CTE s
        INNER JOIN HumanResources.Employee e
    ON s.ManagerID = e.EmployeeID
        INNER JOIN Person.Contact c
    ON c.ContactID = e.ContactID
ORDER BY Manager;
-- (47 row(s) affected) - Partial results.
```

Manager	Title	StaffCount
A. Alberts	European Sales Manager	3
A. Hill	Production Supervisor - WC10	7
A. Wright	Master Scheduler	4
B. Diaz	Production Supervisor - WC40	12
B. Welcker	Vice President of Sales	3
C. Kleinerman	Maintenance Supervisor	4
C. Petculescu	Production Supervisor - WC10	5
C. Randall	Production Supervisor - WC30	6
D. Bradley	Marketing Manager	8
D. Hamilton	Production Supervisor - WC40	6
D. Liu	Accounts Manager	7
D. Miller	Research and Development Manager	3
E. Gubbels	Production Supervisor - WC20	10
G. Altman	Facilities Manager	2
H. Abolrous	Quality Assurance Manager	2

Multiple CTEs Query

A query can have multiple CTEs, they can even be nested (CTE has reference to previous CTE). The two CTEs in the following query are first name and last name frequencies.

```
USE AdventureWorks2012;

WITH cteLastNameFreq

    AS (SELECT     LastName          AS [LastNames],
                   count(* )         AS [LNFrequency]
        FROM    Person.Person
        GROUP BY LastName),

    cteFirstNameFreq
    AS (SELECT     FirstName         AS [FirstNames],
                   count(* )         AS [FNFrequency]
        FROM    Person.Person
        GROUP BY FirstName)

SELECT   CONCAT(rtrim(FirstName), ' ', rtrim(LastName))     AS [Name],
                   isnull(Title,'')                         AS [Title] ,
                   f.FNFrequency,
                   l.LNFrequency
FROM    Person.Person c
        INNER JOIN cteFirstNameFreq AS f
        ON c.FirstName = f.FirstNames
        INNER JOIN cteLastNameFreq AS l
        ON c.LastName = l.LastNames
WHERE    LastName LIKE 'P%' ORDER BY [Name];
-- (1187 row(s) affected) - Partial results;
```

Name	Title	FNFrequency	LNFrequency
Aaron Patterson		56	117
Aaron Perez		56	170
Aaron Perry		56	122
Aaron Phillips		56	80
Aaron Powell		56	116
Abby Patel		19	86
Abby Perez		19	170
Abigail Patterson		76	117
Abigail Patterson		76	117
Abigail Perry		76	122
Abigail Peterson		76	92
Abigail Powell		76	116

Testing Common Table Expressions

A CTE can be tested independently of the main query if it does not have nesting (reference to a previous CTE). The following screen snapshot displays the execution of the first CTE SELECT query.

Nested CTEs Queries

CTEs can be nested by reference to a previous CTE like a table.

```
;WITH CTE1
   AS (SELECT 1 AS NUMBER
       UNION ALL
       SELECT 1),
   CTE2
   AS (SELECT 1 AS NUMBER
       FROM   CTE1 x,
            CTE1 y),
   CTE3
   AS (SELECT 1 AS NUMBER
       FROM   CTE2 x,
            CTE2 y),
   CTE4
   AS (SELECT 1 AS NUMBER
       FROM   CTE3 x,
            CTE3 y),
   CTE8BIT
   AS (SELECT ROW_NUMBER()
             OVER(ORDER BY NUMBER) AS INTSequence
       FROM   CTE4)
SELECT *
FROM   CTE8BIT
ORDER BY INTSequence;
-- (256 row(s) affected) - Partial results.
```

INTSequence
241
242
243
244
245
246
247
248
249
250
251
252
253
254
255
256

CTE nesting: cteLastSalary has a nested reference to cteLastSalaryChange

```
USE AdventureWorks2012;

WITH cteLastSalaryChange
    AS (SELECT     BusinessEntityID          AS EmployeeID,
                   Max(RateChangeDate)            AS ChangeDate
        FROM   HumanResources.EmployeePayHistory    GROUP BY BusinessEntityID),

    cteLastSalary
    AS (SELECT    eph.BusinessEntityID            AS EmployeeID,    Rate
        FROM  HumanResources.EmployeePayHistory eph
            INNER JOIN cteLastSalaryChange lsc
            ON lsc.EmployeeID = eph.BusinessEntityID
               AND lsc.ChangeDate = eph.RateChangeDate)

-- SELECT * FROM cteLastSalary  -- for testing & debugging

SELECT TOP 1 FORMAT( Rate, 'c', 'en-US') AS SecondHighestPayRate
FROM    (SELECT  TOP 2 Rate     FROM    cteLastSalary    ORDER BY Rate DESC) a    -- Derived table
ORDER BY Rate ASC;
```

SecondHighestPayRate
$84.13

Testing Nested CTEs

Nested CTEs can be tested independently of the main query the following way.

```
USE AdventureWorks2012;
WITH cteLastSalaryChange
    AS (SELECT     BusinessEntityID          AS EmployeeID,
                   Max(RateChangeDate)            AS ChangeDate
        FROM   HumanResources.EmployeePayHistory
        GROUP BY BusinessEntityID),
    cteLastSalary
    AS (SELECT    eph.BusinessEntityID             AS EmployeeID,
                  Rate
        FROM  HumanResources.EmployeePayHistory eph
            INNER JOIN cteLastSalaryChange lsc
            ON lsc.EmployeeID = eph.BusinessEntityID
               AND lsc.ChangeDate = eph.RateChangeDate)
SELECT * FROM cteLastSalary  -- for testing & debugging
```

In Query Editor, uncomment the testing line, select (highlight) the top part of the query and execute it

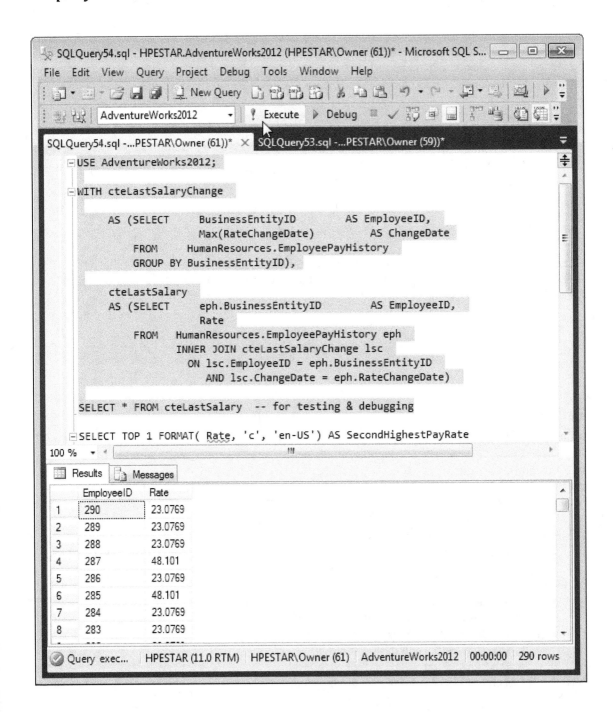

Recursive CTEs for Tree Hierarchy Processing

Recursive CTEs are one of the most exciting new features introduced with SQL Server 2005. They allow tree processing, such as organizational charts or bill of materials parts assembly, as well as generating sets of data without tables. The following recursive CTE generates 1 million integers all by itself. The query execution time is 10 seconds as it can be seen in the lower right.

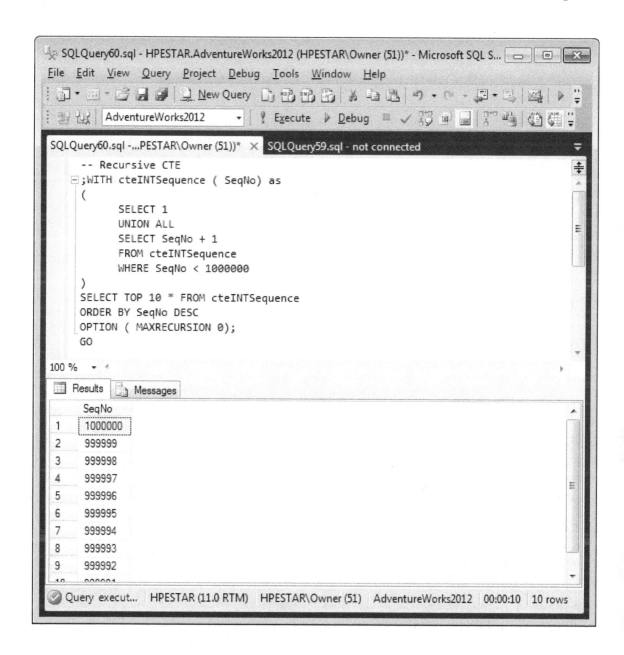

Recursive Generation of Date & Month Sequences

Date sequence can be generated without a calendar table (Note: generally it is helpful to have a calendar table in the database) using recursive CTE.

```
DECLARE @StartDate date = '20160701', @Range smallint = 1000;

WITH cteSEQ ( SeqNo) as
(
    SELECT 0                                        -- Anchor member
    UNION ALL                                       -- Assemble set
    SELECT SeqNo + 1                                -- Recursive member
    FROM cteSEQ
    WHERE SeqNo < @Range
)
SELECT TOP 10 [DATE]=DATEADD(day, SeqNo, @StartDate)
FROM cteSEQ
OPTION ( MAXRECURSION 0);
GO
```

DATE
2016-07-01
2016-07-02
2016-07-03
2016-07-04
2016-07-05
2016-07-06
2016-07-07
2016-07-08
2016-07-09
2016-07-10

```
-- Month sequence generation
DECLARE @StartDate date = '20160701', @Range smallint = 100;
WITH cteSEQ ( SeqNo) as
(
    SELECT 0                                        -- Anchor member
    UNION ALL                                       -- Assemble set
    SELECT SeqNo + 1                                -- Recursive member
    FROM cteSEQ
    WHERE SeqNo < @Range
)
SELECT TOP 3 [DATE]=DATEADD(month, SeqNo, @StartDate)
FROM cteSEQ  OPTION ( MAXRECURSION 0);
```

CHAPTER 9: Subqueries in SELECT Statements

Generate Month Names in Different Languages

The following query can be used to generate month names in any of the SQL Server 2012 supported languages.

```
SET language Spanish;  -- Se cambió la configuración de idioma a Español.
;WITH CTE AS
(   SELECT    1 MonthNo, CONVERT(DATE, '19000101') MonthFirst
    UNION ALL
    SELECT    MonthNo+1, DATEADD(Month, 1, MonthFirst)
    FROM  CTE
    WHERE Month(MonthFirst) < 12    )
SELECT  MonthNo AS MonthNumber,  DATENAME(MONTH, MonthFirst) AS MonthName
FROM  CTE
ORDER BY MonthNo;
SET language English; -- Changed language setting to us_english.
```

```
SET language Hungarian;  -- Nyelvi beállítás átállítva a következőre: magyar.
;WITH CTE AS
(   SELECT    1 MonthNo, CONVERT(DATE, '19000101') MonthFirst
    UNION ALL
    SELECT    MonthNo+1, DATEADD(Month, 1, MonthFirst)
    FROM  CTE
    WHERE Month(MonthFirst) < 12    )
SELECT  MonthNo AS MonthNumber,  DATENAME(MONTH, MonthFirst) AS MonthName
FROM  CTE
ORDER BY MonthNo;
SET language English; -- Changed language setting to us_english.
```

MonthNumber	MonthName	MonthNumber	MonthName
1	Enero	1	január
2	Febrero	2	február
3	Marzo	3	március
4	Abril	4	április
5	Mayo	5	május
6	Junio	6	június
7	Julio	7	július
8	Agosto	8	augusztus
9	Septiembre	9	szeptember
10	Octubre	10	október
11	Noviembre	11	november
12	Diciembre	12	december

CHAPTER 9: Subqueries in SELECT Statements

Graphical Organizational Chart of AdventureWorks Cycles

T-SQL recursive CTE query generates the entire company chart of AdventureWorks Cycles. The anchor term is Ken Sanchez CEO with ManagerID as NULL. Everybody else in the company has a ManagerID which is not NULL.

```
USE AdventureWorks;

WITH cteEmployeeTree
    AS (SELECT      Root.EmployeeName, Root.ManagerName,
                    Root.EmployeeId, Root.ManagerId,
                    CONVERT(VARCHAR(MAX),Root.PathSequence) AS PathLabel
        FROM   (SELECT EmployeeName = CONCAT(c.FirstName, SPACE(1), c.LastName),
                    ManagerName = convert(VARCHAR(128),''),
                    e.EmployeeId,
                    e.ManagerId,
                    char(64 + ROW_NUMBER() OVER(ORDER BY e.EmployeeId)) AS PathSequence
            FROM   HumanResources.Employee e
                INNER JOIN Person.Contact c
                ON e.ContactID = c.ContactID
            WHERE  e.ManagerId IS NULL) Root            -- Anchor/root term (above)
        UNION ALL                                       -- Build a set
        SELECT      Branch.EmployeeName,                -- Recursive term (below)
                    Branch.ManagerName,
                    Branch.EmployeeId, Branch.ManagerId,
                    PathLabel = Branch.PathLabel + CONVERT(VARCHAR(MAX), Branch.PathSequence)
        FROM   (SELECT EmployeeName = CONCAT(c.FirstName, SPACE(1), c.LastName),
                ManagerName = CONVERT(VARCHAR(128),CONCAT(cm.FirstName, SPACE(1), cm.LastName)),
                    e.EmployeeId,
                    e.ManagerId,
                    cte.PathLabel,
                    PathSequence = char(64 + ROW_NUMBER() OVER(ORDER BY e.EmployeeId))
            FROM   cteEmployeeTree cte
                INNER JOIN HumanResources.Employee e
                ON e.ManagerId = cte.EmployeeId
                INNER JOIN Person.Contact c
                ON e.ContactID = c.ContactID
                INNER JOIN HumanResources.Employee em
                ON em.EmployeeID = e.ManagerID
                INNER JOIN Person.Contact cm
                ON em.ContactID = cm.ContactID) Branch)
-- Outer / main query
SELECT   CONCAT(REPLICATE(CHAR(9), LEN(PathLabel)-1),   -- tabs for indenting
            EmployeeName) AS EmployeeName
FROM     cteEmployeeTree  ORDER BY PathLabel;
```

The resulting organizational chart was generated by Word as tabs (CHAR(9)) were converted to table columns (partial results).

EmployeeName				
Ken Sánchez				
	David Bradley			
		Kevin Brown		
		Sariya Harnpadoungsataya		
		Mary Gibson		
		Jill Williams		
		Terry Eminhizer		
		Wanida Benshoof		
		John Wood		
		Mary Dempsey		
	Terri Duffy			
		Roberto Tamburello		
			Rob Walters	
			Gail Erickson	
			Jossef Goldberg	
			Dylan Miller	
				Diane Margheim
				Gigi Matthew
				Michael Raheem
			Ovidiu Cracium	
				Thierry D'Hers
				Janice Galvin
			Michael Sullivan	
			Sharon Salavaria	
	Jean Trenary			
		Janaina Bueno		
		Dan Bacon		
		François Ajenstat		
		Dan Wilson		
		Ramesh Meyyappan		
		Stephanie Conroy		
			Ashvini Sharma	
			Peter Connelly	
		Karen Berg		
	Laura Norman			
		Paula Barreto de Mattos		
			Willis Johnson	
			Mindy Martin	
			Vidur Luthra	
			Hao Chen	
			Grant Culbertson	
		Wendy Kahn		
			Sheela Word	
				Mikael Sandberg
				Arvind Rao
				Linda Meisner
				Fukiko Ogisu
				Gordon Hee
				Frank Pellow
				Eric Kurjan
				Erin Hagens
				Ben Miller
				Annette Hill
				Reinout Hillmann
		David Barber		
		David Liu		
			Deborah Poe	
			Candy Spoon	
			Bryan Walton	
			Dragan Tomic	
			Barbara Moreland	
			Janet Sheperdigian	
			Mike Seamans	
	James Hamilton			
		Peter Krebs		
			JoLynn Dobney	
				Simon Rapier
				James Kramer
				Nancy Anderson
				Bryan Baker
				Eugene Kogan
				Thomas Michaels
			Taylor Maxwell	
				Kendall Keil
				Bob Hohman
				Pete Male
				Diane Tibbott
				Denise Smith

Chain of Command Recursive Query

Find all ancestors (superiors) of a tree node(employee), all the up to the root of the tree (CEO in this instance).

```
USE AdventureWorks; DECLARE @EmployeeID INT = 100;
WITH CTE(Name, EmployeeID, ManagerID, Level)
    AS (SELECT     CONCAT(FirstName,' ', LastName),
                   EmployeeID,   ManagerID,  0 AS Level
       FROM  HumanResources.Employee AS E
           INNER JOIN Person.Contact AS C
               ON C.ContactID = E.ContactID
       WHERE  EmployeeID = @EmployeeID
       UNION ALL
       SELECT      CONCAT(C.FirstName,' ',C.LastName),
                   HRE.EmployeeID,  HRE.ManagerID,  Level + 1
       FROM  HumanResources.Employee AS HRE
           INNER JOIN Person.Contact AS C
               ON C.ContactID = HRE.ContactID
           INNER JOIN CTE AS E
               ON E.ManagerID = HRE.EmployeeID)
SELECT STUFF((SELECT CONCAT(', ', Name)
         FROM   CTE       ORDER  BY Level
         FOR XML path('')), 1, 2, '') AS [Chain of Command];
```

Chain of Command
Lane Sacksteder, Yuhong Li, Peter Krebs, James Hamilton, Ken Sánchez

Graphical Bill of Materials for Mountain-100 Silver, 44 Bike

T-SQL query will generate bill of materials (assembly) listing for Mountain-100 Silver, 44 mountain bike. The AdventureWorks2012 database image for Mountain-100 Silver, 44 in Production.ProductPhoto table.

```
USE AdventureWorks2012;
DECLARE          @StartProductID int      = 773,              -- Mountain-100 Silver, 44
                 @CheckDate datetime      = '20080201';

 WITH cteBOM(ProductAssemblyID, ComponentID, ComponentName,  RecursionLevel)
 AS (
   SELECT b.ProductAssemblyID, b.ComponentID, p.Name,  0
        FROM Production.BillOfMaterials b
        INNER JOIN Production.Product p
        ON b.ComponentID = p.ProductID
   WHERE          b.ProductAssemblyID = @StartProductID
                  AND @CheckDate >= b.StartDate
                  AND @CheckDate <= ISNULL(b.EndDate, @CheckDate)        -- Anchor/root member (above)
   UNION ALL                                                            -- Build a set
   SELECT         b.ProductAssemblyID, b.ComponentID, p.Name,           -- Recursive member (below)
                  RecursionLevel + 1
   FROM cteBOM c
     INNER JOIN Production.BillOfMaterials b
     ON b.ProductAssemblyID = c.ComponentID
     INNER JOIN Production.Product p
     ON b.ComponentID = p.ProductID
   WHERE          @CheckDate >= b.StartDate           AND @CheckDate <= ISNULL(b.EndDate, @CheckDate)   )
-- Outer/main query
   SELECT CONCAT(REPLICATE(CHAR(9), RecursionLevel),  -- Generate indents with tab character
                  (SELECT Name FROM Production.Product WHERE ProductID=ProductAssemblyID)) AS PartName,
                  ComponentName
         FROM cteBOM    GROUP BY  RecursionLevel,ProductAssemblyID,ComponentName
   ORDER BY        RecursionLevel, ProductAssemblyID,ComponentName    OPTION (MAXRECURSION 10);
-- (87 row(s) affected)
```

CHAPTER 9: Subqueries in SELECT Statements

The resulting graphical bill of materials for the mountain bike.

PartName	ComponentName			
Mountain-100 Silver, 44	Chain			
Mountain-100 Silver, 44	Front Brakes			
Mountain-100 Silver, 44	Front Derailleur			
Mountain-100 Silver, 44	HL Bottom Bracket			
Mountain-100 Silver, 44	HL Crankset			
Mountain-100 Silver, 44	HL Headset			
Mountain-100 Silver, 44	HL Mountain Frame - Silver, 44			
Mountain-100 Silver, 44	HL Mountain Front Wheel			
Mountain-100 Silver, 44	HL Mountain Handlebars			
Mountain-100 Silver, 44	HL Mountain Pedal			
Mountain-100 Silver, 44	HL Mountain Rear Wheel			
Mountain-100 Silver, 44	HL Mountain Seat Assembly			
Mountain-100 Silver, 44	Rear Brakes			
Mountain-100 Silver, 44	Rear Derailleur			
	HL Mountain Seat Assembly	HL Mountain Seat/Saddle		
	HL Mountain Seat Assembly	Pinch Bolt		
	HL Mountain Seat Assembly	Seat Lug		
	HL Mountain Seat Assembly	Seat Post		
	HL Mountain Frame - Silver, 44	Chain Stays		
	HL Mountain Frame - Silver, 44	Decal 1		
	HL Mountain Frame - Silver, 44	Decal 2		
	HL Mountain Frame - Silver, 44	Down Tube		
	HL Mountain Frame - Silver, 44	Head Tube		
	HL Mountain Frame - Silver, 44	HL Fork		
	HL Mountain Frame - Silver, 44	Paint - Silver		
	HL Mountain Frame - Silver, 44	Seat Stays		
	HL Mountain Frame - Silver, 44	Seat Tube		
	HL Mountain Frame - Silver, 44	Top Tube		
	HL Headset	Adjustable Race		
	HL Headset	Crown Race		
	HL Headset	Headset Ball Bearings		
	HL Headset	Keyed Washer		
	HL Headset	Lock Nut 19		
	HL Headset	Lower Head Race		
	HL Mountain Handlebars	Handlebar Tube		
	HL Mountain Handlebars	HL Grip Tape		
	HL Mountain Handlebars	Mountain End Caps		
	HL Mountain Handlebars	Stem		
	HL Mountain Front Wheel	HL Hub		
	HL Mountain Front Wheel	HL Mountain Rim		
	HL Mountain Front Wheel	HL Mountain Tire		
	HL Mountain Front Wheel	HL Nipple		
	HL Mountain Front Wheel	Mountain Tire Tube		
	HL Mountain Front Wheel	Reflector		
	HL Mountain Front Wheel	Spokes		
	HL Mountain Rear Wheel	HL Hub		
	HL Mountain Rear Wheel	HL Mountain Rim		
	HL Mountain Rear Wheel	HL Mountain Tire		
	HL Mountain Rear Wheel	HL Nipple		
	HL Mountain Rear Wheel	Mountain Tire Tube		
	HL Mountain Rear Wheel	Reflector		
	HL Mountain Rear Wheel	Spokes		
	Rear Derailleur	Guide Pulley		
	Rear Derailleur	Rear Derailleur Cage		
	Rear Derailleur	Tension Pulley		
	Front Derailleur	Front Derailleur Cage		
	Front Derailleur	Front Derailleur Linkage		
	HL Crankset	Chainring		
	HL Crankset	Chainring Bolts		

HL Crankset	Chainring Nut		
HL Crankset	Freewheel		
HL Crankset	HL Crankarm		
HL Bottom Bracket	BB Ball Bearing		
HL Bottom Bracket	HL Shell		
	BB Ball Bearing	Bearing Ball	
	BB Ball Bearing	Cone-Shaped Race	
	BB Ball Bearing	Cup-Shaped Race	
	BB Ball Bearing	Lock Ring	
	Chain Stays	Metal Sheet 5	
	Down Tube	Metal Sheet 3	
	Mountain End Caps	Metal Sheet 2	
	Handlebar Tube	Metal Sheet 6	
	Head Tube	Metal Sheet 4	
	HL Hub	HL Shell	
	HL Hub	HL Spindle/Axle	
	Stem	Metal Bar 1	
	Seat Stays	Metal Sheet 7	
	Seat Tube	Metal Bar 2	
	Top Tube	Metal Sheet 2	
	HL Fork	Blade	
	HL Fork	Fork Crown	
	HL Fork	Fork End	
	HL Fork	Steerer	
		Blade	Metal Sheet 5
		Fork End	Metal Sheet 2
		Fork Crown	Metal Sheet 5
		Steerer	Metal Sheet 6

CHAPTER 9: Subqueries in SELECT Statements

PIVOT Operator to Transform Rows Into Columns

The PIVOT operator, new to SQL Server 2005, can be used to create pivot table also called cross tabulation (crosstab). The data to be PIVOTed is generated by a CTE.

```
USE AdventureWorks2012;
;WITH CTE    AS (SELECT   YEAR              = YEAR(orderDate),
                          QUARTER           = DatePart(qq,OrderDate),
                          Sales             = Sum(TotalDue)
        FROM    Sales.SalesOrderHeader   GROUP BY YEAR(OrderDate), DatePart(qq,OrderDate))
SELECT * FROM CTE;
```

YEAR	QUARTER	Sales
2007	4	14886562.6775
2006	3	11555907.1472
2007	1	7492396.3224
2007	2	9379298.7027
2006	1	6562121.6796
2006	4	9397824.1785
2008	3	56178.9223
2007	3	15413231.8434
2005	3	5203127.8807
2008	1	12744940.3554
2005	4	7490122.7457
2008	2	16087078.2305
2006	2	6947995.43

PIVOT operator takes the data from the CTE source, aggregates it and transforms it to columns.

```
;WITH CTE    AS (SELECT   YEAR              = YEAR(orderDate),
                          QUARTER           = DatePart(qq,OrderDate),
                          Sales             = Sum(TotalDue)
        FROM    Sales.SalesOrderHeader   GROUP BY YEAR(OrderDate), DatePart(qq,OrderDate)     )
SELECT   YEAR
              ,FORMAT ([1], 'c','en-US') AS Q1
              ,FORMAT ([2], 'c','en-US') AS Q2
              ,FORMAT ([3], 'c','en-US') AS Q3
              ,FORMAT ([4], 'c','en-US') AS Q4
FROM    (SELECT * FROM CTE) AS PivotInput
    PIVOT     (SUM(Sales)  FOR QUARTER IN ( [1],[2],[3],[4] ) ) AS PivotOutput  ORDER BY YEAR;
```

YEAR	Q1	Q2	Q3	Q4
2005	NULL	NULL	$5,203,127.88	$7,490,122.75
2006	$6,562,121.68	$6,947,995.43	$11,555,907.15	$9,397,824.18
2007	$7,492,396.32	$9,379,298.70	$15,413,231.84	$14,886,562.68
2008	$12,744,940.36	$16,087,078.23	$56,178.92	NULL

UNPIVOT Crosstab View Results

The vSalesPersonSalesByFiscalYears view is a crosstab listing of sales person (rows) and sales by year (columns). The UNPIVOT operation transforms the year columns into rows.

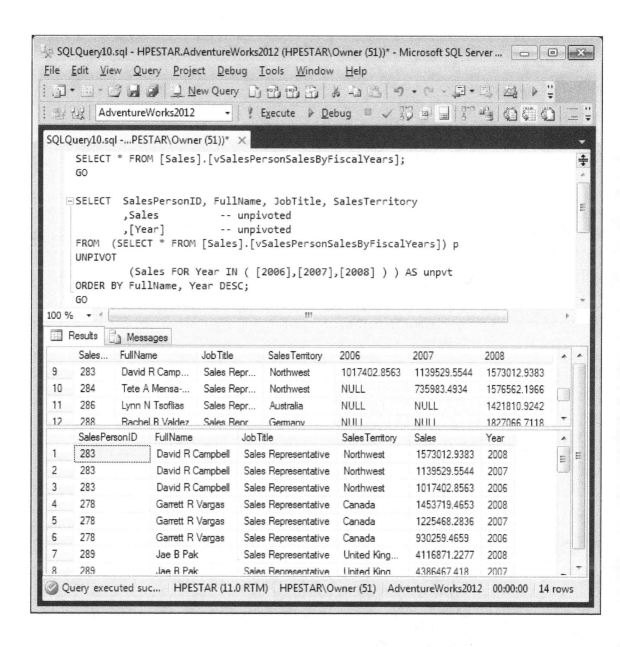

Using Subquery in Column List of SELECT

A subquery can be used in the column list of a SELECT statement.

```
USE Northwind;
GO


;WITH CTE AS
(
  SELECT ShipCity,
         CONVERT(DATE, OrderDate)                              AS OrderDate,
         (SELECT CONVERT(DATE, MAX(OrderDate))  FROM dbo.Orders)   AS CurrentOrderDate,
         DATEDIFF(dd,OrderDate,(SELECT MAX(OrderDate) FROM dbo.Orders)) AS DeltaDays,
         ROW_NUMBER() OVER (PARTITION BY ShipCity
                             ORDER BY OrderDate DESC)           AS RN
  FROM dbo.Orders
)

SELECT TOP 20 ShipCity, OrderDate, CurrentOrderDate, DeltaDays
FROM CTE
WHERE RN=1      ORDER BY DeltaDays DESC;
GO
```

ShipCity	OrderDate	CurrentOrderDate	DeltaDays
Walla Walla	1997-05-22	1998-05-06	349
Elgin	1997-09-08	1998-05-06	240
Montréal	1997-10-30	1998-05-06	188
Reims	1997-11-12	1998-05-06	175
Caracas	1997-12-18	1998-05-06	139
Lille	1997-12-22	1998-05-06	135
Vancouver	1998-01-01	1998-05-06	125
Kirkland	1998-01-08	1998-05-06	118
Strasbourg	1998-01-12	1998-05-06	114
Lyon	1998-01-23	1998-05-06	103
San Francisco	1998-02-12	1998-05-06	83
Luleå	1998-03-04	1998-05-06	63
Barcelona	1998-03-05	1998-05-06	62
Cowes	1998-03-06	1998-05-06	61
Resende	1998-03-09	1998-05-06	58
Leipzig	1998-03-12	1998-05-06	55
Bergamo	1998-03-16	1998-05-06	51
Münster	1998-03-23	1998-05-06	44
Nantes	1998-03-24	1998-05-06	43
Versailles	1998-03-24	1998-05-06	43

CHAPTER 10: SELECT INTO Table Creation & Population

Simple SELECT INTO Statement Variations

SELECT INTO is an easy way to create a table for ad-hoc purposes in database development and administration. **An added benefit is minimal logging, therefore good performance.** INSERT SELECT is logged, although with special setup minimal logging can be achieved in some cases.

```
-- Create and populate copy of the product table in tempdb
SELECT *
INTO   tempdb.dbo.Product
FROM   AdventureWorks2012.Production.Product;
-- (504 row(s) affected)
```

```
SELECT TableRows = count(*)  FROM tempdb.dbo.Product;  -- 504
```

```
-- Copy all persons into new table with last name starting with 'A'
SELECT   BusinessEntityID               AS ID,
         CONCAT(FirstName, ' ', LastName)  AS FullName,
         PersonType
INTO   ListA
FROM   AdventureWorks2012.Person.Person
WHERE  LEFT(LastName, 1) = 'A'
ORDER BY LastName, FirstName;
-- (911 row(s) affected)
```

```
SELECT TOP (10) ID, FullName, PersonType FROM ListA ORDER BY ID;
```

ID	FullName	PersonType
38	Kim Abercrombie	EM
43	Nancy Anderson	EM
67	Jay Adams	EM
121	Pilar Ackerman	EM
207	Greg Alderson	EM
211	Hazem Abolrous	EM
216	Sean Alexander	EM
217	Zainal Arifin	EM
227	Gary Altman	EM
270	François Ajenstat	EM

SELECT TOP(0) Creates an Empty Table

```
USE AdventureWorks2012;

-- Create a copy of table in a different schema, same name
-- The WHERE clause predicate with >=, < comparison is better performing than the YEAR function
SELECT *
INTO   dbo.SalesOrderHeader
FROM   Sales.SalesOrderHeader
WHERE  OrderDate >= '20080101' AND OrderDate < '20090101';  -- YEAR(OrderDate)=2008
-- (13951 row(s) affected)


-- Create a table without population
SELECT TOP (0)   SalesOrderID,      OrderDate
INTO   SOH
FROM   Sales.SalesOrderHeader;
-- (0 row(s) affected)


-- SELECT INTO cannot be used to target an existing table
SELECT * INTO   SOH FROM   Sales.SalesOrderHeader;
/* Msg 2714, Level 16, State 6, Line 1
There is already an object named 'SOH' in the database.  */
```

```
                                    NOTE
              IDENTITY column is automatically populated.
    Direct insert into IDENTITY column requires using of SET IDENTITY_INSERT.
```

```
INSERT SOH (SalesOrderID, OrderDate)
SELECT SalesOrderID, OrderDate
FROM   Sales.SalesOrderHeader ORDER BY SalesOrderID;
GO
/* ERROR due to SalesOrderID in SOH inherited the IDENTITY property.
Msg 544, Level 16, State 1, Line 1
Cannot insert explicit value for identity column in table 'SOH' when IDENTITY_INSERT is set to OFF.  */


-- Turn on forced IDENTITY insert
SET IDENTITY_INSERT dbo.SOH ON;
GO


INSERT SOH(SalesOrderID, OrderDate)
SELECT SalesOrderID, OrderDate  FROM   Sales.SalesOrderHeader ORDER BY SalesOrderID;
GO
-- (31465 row(s) affected)


SET IDENTITY_INSERT dbo.SOH OFF;
```

Any Kind of SELECT Result Set Can Be Turned into a Table

```
-- Filter on date
SELECT *
INTO   SOH1
FROM   Sales.SalesOrderHeader WHERE  OrderDate >= '20080101' AND OrderDate < '20090101';
-- (13951 row(s) affected)
```

```
-- Descending sort for population
SELECT *
INTO   SOH2
FROM   Sales.SalesOrderHeader
ORDER  BY SalesOrderID DESC
-- (31465 row(s) affected)
```

```
-- 3 columns only
SELECT   SalesOrderID,
         OrderDate,
         SubTotal
INTO   SOH3
FROM   Sales.SalesOrderHeader;
-- (31465 row(s) affected)
```

```
-- SELECT INTO with GROUP BY query source
SELECT   [Year]=YEAR(OrderDate),
         Orders=COUNT(*)
INTO   SOH4
FROM   Sales.SalesOrderHeader
GROUP  BY YEAR(OrderDate)
-- (4 row(s) affected)
```

```
SELECT * FROM SOH4 ORDER BY Year DESC;
```

Year	Orders
2008	13951
2007	12443
2006	3692
2005	1379

```
-- All source columns, and a new populated datetime column
SELECT   *,        [CreateDate]=getdate()
INTO   SOH5
FROM   Sales.SalesOrderHeader ;
-- (31465 row(s) affected)
```

CHAPTER 10: SELECT INTO Table Creation & Population

SELECT INTO Can Create Temporary Tables or Tables in tempdb

```
-- SELECT INTO temporary table
SELECT TotalOrders = COUNT(*)
INTO   #TotalOrders
FROM   Sales.SalesOrderHeader ;
-- (1 row(s) affected)
```

```
SELECT * FROM #TotalOrders;
```

TotalOrders
31465

```
-- Empty table create with one NULL row
SELECT   Name=CONVERT(VARCHAR(45), NULL),
         Age=CONVERT(INT, NULL)
INTO   tempdb.dbo.Person;
```

```
INSERT tempdb.dbo.Person (Name, Age)
SELECT 'Roger Bond', 45;
-- (1 row(s) affected)
```

```
SELECT * FROM tempdb.dbo.Person;
```

Name	Age
NULL	NULL
Roger Bond	45

```
DELETE tempdb.dbo.Person WHERE Name is NULL;
-- (1 row(s) affected)
```

```
SELECT * FROM tempdb.dbo.Person;
```

Name	Age
Roger Bond	45

```
-- Create gaps in ID sequence; increment by 2:  2, 4, 6, 8 instead of 1, 2, 3, 4
SELECT   2 * [BusinessEntityID]             AS BusinessEntityID
         ,[PhoneNumber]
         ,[PhoneNumberTypeID]
         ,[ModifiedDate]
 INTO dbo.Phone
 FROM [AdventureWorks2012].[Person].[PersonPhone] pp    ORDER BY pp.BusinessEntityID;
-- (19972 row(s) affected)
```

CHAPTER 10: SELECT INTO Table Creation & Population

The SELECT INTO Created Table is a "Regular" Table

```
-- Populate with 100 random rows
SELECT TOP (100) *
INTO   POH
FROM   Purchasing.PurchaseOrderHeader ORDER  BY NEWID(); -- (100 row(s) affected)
```

```
SELECT        PurchaseOrderID,
              CONVERT(date, OrderDate)        AS OrderDate,
              FORMAT(SubTotal, 'c', 'en-US')   AS SubTotal
FROM POH;
```

PurchaseOrderID	OrderDate	SubTotal
3553	2008-08-03	$9,948.33
1637	2008-02-07	$25,531.28
2796	2008-05-31	$97.97
684	2007-09-26	$270.81
3478	2008-07-28	$28,072.28
1904	2008-03-09	$43,878.45
755	2007-10-01	$50,860.43
2660	2008-05-19	$944.37
2787	2008-05-31	$34,644.23
601	2007-09-19	$146.29

```
-- SELECT INTO with data transformation
SELECT   CultureID
        ,UPPER(Name)                    AS Name
        ,CONVERT(date,ModifiedDate)      AS ModifiedDate
INTO dbo.Culture
FROM [AdventureWorks2012].[Production].[Culture]
ORDER BY CultureID;
-- (8 row(s) affected)
```

```
SELECT * FROM dbo.Culture WHERE CultureID != '' ORDER BY CultureID;  -- exclude empty ID
```

CultureID	Name	ModifiedDate
ar	ARABIC	2002-06-01
en	ENGLISH	2002-06-01
es	SPANISH	2002-06-01
fr	FRENCH	2002-06-01
he	HEBREW	2002-06-01
th	THAI	2002-06-01
zh-cht	CHINESE	2002-06-01

CHAPTER 10: SELECT INTO Table Creation & Population

SELECT INTO with IDENTITY Column

The column data types are inherited in SELECT INTO table create. The IDENTITY property is also inherited in a SELECT INTO unless it is prevented with special coding. No other constraint is inherited.

```
-- IDENTITY property of ProductID is inherited
SELECT TOP (0) ProductID, ProductNumber, ListPrice, Color
INTO tempdb.dbo.Product
FROM AdventureWorks2012.Production.Product;  -- (0 row(s) affected)
```

```
INSERT tempdb.dbo.Product (ProductID, ProductNumber, ListPrice, Color)
SELECT 20001, 'FERRARI007RED', $400000, 'Red';
GO
/* Msg 544, Level 16, State 1, Line 1
Cannot insert explicit value for identity column in table 'Product'
when IDENTITY_INSERT is set to OFF. */
```

```
-- The following is one way to check for IDENTITY property
USE tempdb;
EXEC sp_help 'dbo.Product';
```

Identity	Seed	Increment	Not For Replication
ProductID	1	1	0

```
USE AdventureWorks2012;
DROP TABLE tempdb.dbo.Product;
GO
```

```
-- The following construct will prevent IDENTITY inheritance
SELECT TOP (0)    CAST(ProductID AS INT) AS ProductID,  -- Cast/Convert the identity column
                 ProductNumber,
                 ListPrice,
                 Color
INTO tempdb.dbo.Product  FROM AdventureWorks2012.Production.Product;
-- (0 row(s) affected)
```

```
INSERT tempdb.dbo.Product (ProductID, ProductNumber, ListPrice, Color)
SELECT 20001, 'FERRARI007RED', $400000, 'Firehouse Red';
GO
```

```
SELECT * FROM tempdb.dbo.Product;
```

ProductID	ProductNumber	ListPrice	Color
20001	FERRARI007RED	400000.00	Firehouse Red

CHAPTER 10: SELECT INTO Table Creation & Population

SELECT INTO From Multiple-Table Queries

SELECT INTO works with any query with some restrictions such as XML data type columns cannot be included.

```
SELECT   JobCandidateID
        ,BusinessEntityID
        ,Resume
        ,ModifiedDate
 INTO dbo.Resume
  FROM AdventureWorks2012.HumanResources.JobCandidate;
/* ERROR MESSAGE
Msg 458, Level 16, State 0, Line 2
Cannot create the SELECT INTO target table "dbo.Resume" because the xml column "Resume"
is typed with a schema collection "HRResumeSchemaCollection" from database "AdventureWorks2012".
Xml columns cannot refer to schemata across databases.
*/
```

```
-- SELECT INTO from joined tables
 SELECT          soh.SalesOrderID,
                 OrderDate,
                 OrderQty,
                 ProductID
INTO   SalesOrder
FROM   Sales.SalesOrderHeader soh
    INNER JOIN Sales.SalesOrderDetail sod
        ON soh.SalesOrderID = sod.SalesOrderID ;
-- (121317 row(s) affected)
```

```
SELECT TOP(5) * FROM SalesOrder ORDER BY SalesOrderID DESC;
```

SalesOrderID	OrderDate	OrderQty	ProductID
75123	2008-07-31 00:00:00.000	1	878
75123	2008-07-31 00:00:00.000	1	879
75123	2008-07-31 00:00:00.000	1	712
75122	2008-07-31 00:00:00.000	1	878
75122	2008-07-31 00:00:00.000	1	712

```
-- Check column types - partial results
EXEC sp_help SalesOrder;
```

Column_name	Type	Computed	Length	Prec	Scale
SalesOrderID	int	no	4	10	0
OrderDate	datetime	no	8		
OrderQty	smallint	no	2	5	0
ProductID	int	no	4	10	0

SELECT INTO with Sorted Table Population

We can create ordering in a new temporary table by using the IDENTITY function. **There is no guarantee though that the IDENTITY sequence will be the same as the ORDER BY clause specifications**. Unique identity values on the other hand are guaranteed.

```
SELECT  ID=IDENTITY(int, 1, 1),
        ProductNumber,
        ProductID=CAST(ProductID AS INT),
        ListPrice,
        COALESCE(Color, 'N/A') AS Color
INTO   #Product
FROM   Production.Product WHERE  ListPrice > 0.0 ORDER BY ProductNumber;
GO -- (304 row(s) affected)
```

```
SELECT TOP 10 * FROM #Product  ORDER BY ID;
```

ID	ProductNumber	ProductID	ListPrice	Color
1	BB-7421	994	53.99	N/A
2	BB-8107	995	101.24	N/A
3	BB-9108	996	121.49	N/A
4	BC-M005	871	9.99	N/A
5	BC-R205	872	8.99	N/A
6	BK-M18B-40	989	539.99	Black
7	BK-M18B-42	990	539.99	Black
8	BK-M18B-44	991	539.99	Black
9	BK-M18B-48	992	539.99	Black
10	BK-M18B-52	993	539.99	Black

```
-- Permanent table create
SELECT * INTO ProductByProdNo FROM #Product ORDER BY ID;
GO -- (304 row(s) affected)
```

```
SELECT TOP (6) * FROM ProductByProdNo ORDER BY ID;
```

ID	ProductNumber	ProductID	ListPrice	Color
1	BB-7421	994	53.99	N/A
2	BB-8107	995	101.24	N/A
3	BB-9108	996	121.49	N/A
4	BC-M005	871	9.99	N/A
5	BC-R205	872	8.99	N/A
6	BK-M18B-40	989	539.99	Black

SELECT INTO with Random Population

We can create a random population by sorting with the NEWID() function.

```
USE tempdb;

SELECT TOP(5)    ID           = ContactID,
                 FullName     = CONCAT(FirstName, ' ', LastName),
                 Email        = EmailAddress
INTO   dbo.Person
FROM   AdventureWorks.Person.Contact
WHERE  EmailPromotion = 2
ORDER  BY NEWID();
-- (5 row(s) affected)
```

```
SELECT * FROM  dbo.Person;
GO
```

ID	FullName	Email
1075	Diane Glimp	diane0@adventure-works.com
15739	Jesse Mitchell	jesse36@adventure-works.com
5405	Jose Patterson	jose33@adventure-works.com
1029	Wanida Benshoof	wanida0@adventure-works.com
8634	Andrea Collins	andrea26@adventure-works.com

```
-- Rerun the script again after dropping the table
DROP TABLE tempdb.dbo.Person;
GO
-- Command(s) completed successfully.
```

```
SELECT TOP(5) ID        = ContactID,
       FullName         = CONCAT(FirstName, ' ', LastName),
       Email            = EmailAddress
INTO   dbo.Person
FROM   AdventureWorks.Person.Contact
WHERE  EmailPromotion = 2 ORDER  BY NEWID();
```

```
SELECT * FROM  dbo.Person;
```

ID	FullName	Email
9984	Sydney Clark	sydney81@adventure-works.com
15448	Denise Raman	denise13@adventure-works.com
12442	Carson Jenkins	carson5@adventure-works.com
1082	Mary Baker	mary1@adventure-works.com
18728	Emma Kelly	emma46@adventure-works.com

Combining SELECT INTO with INSERT SELECT

First we create an empty table with identity property using SELECT INTO, then we populate it with INSERT SELECT.

```
-- Following will fail - only one IDENTITY column per table
SELECT TOP (0)    IDENTITY(int, 1, 1)              AS ID,
        ProductID,
        Name                                        AS ProductName,
        ListPrice,
        COALESCE(Color, 'N/A')                      AS Color
INTO  #Product  FROM  Production.Product;
GO
/* ERROR Msg 8108, Level 16, State 1, Line 1
Cannot add identity column, using the SELECT INTO statement, to table '#Product',
which already has column 'ProductID' that inherits the identity property.  */
```

```
SELECT TOP (0)    IDENTITY(int, 1, 1)         AS ID,
        CAST(ProductID AS INT)                AS ProductID, -- IDENTITY will not be inherited
        Name                                  AS ProductName,
        ListPrice,
        COALESCE(Color, 'N/A')                AS Color
INTO  #Product  FROM  Production.Product;
GO
-- (0 row(s) affected)
```

```
DECLARE @Rows tinyint = 5;
INSERT INTO #Product   (ProductID, ProductName,  ListPrice,  Color)
SELECT TOP (@Rows)        ProductID,
                Name,
                ListPrice,
                Color
FROM  Production.Product
WHERE  ListPrice > 0.0    AND Color IS NOT NULL  ORDER BY ListPrice DESC;
-- (5 row(s) affected)
```

```
SELECT * FROM #Product;
```

ID	ProductID	ProductName	ListPrice	Color
1	749	Road-150 Red, 62	3578.27	Red
2	750	Road-150 Red, 44	3578.27	Red
3	751	Road-150 Red, 48	3578.27	Red
4	752	Road-150 Red, 52	3578.27	Red
5	753	Road-150 Red, 56	3578.27	Red

Copy Table into Different Database with SELECT INTO

It requires 3-part name referencing to operate between databases (cross database). The current database requires only 2-part object name referencing.

```
USE tempdb;
SELECT *, CopyDate = CONVERT(DATE,GETDATE())
INTO Department
FROM AdventureWorks.HumanResources.Department  ORDER BY DepartmentID;
GO
```

```
SELECT TOP (5) DepartmentID, Department=Name, CopyDate  FROM Department ORDER BY DepartmentID;
```

DepartmentID	Department	CopyDate
1	Engineering	2016-07-19
2	Tool Design	2016-07-19
3	Sales	2016-07-19
4	Marketing	2016-07-19
5	Purchasing	2016-07-19

```
-- SQL drop table - full referencing of table for mistake reduction
DROP TABLE tempdb.dbo.Department;
```

Combining SELECT INTO with UPDATE

After creating a populated table with SELECT INTO, we perform UPDATE to change a column.

```
USE tempdb;
SELECT TOP 100 * INTO   PurchaseOrderHeader
FROM   AdventureWorks.Purchasing.PurchaseOrderHeader  ORDER  BY NEWID();
GO
```

```
-- The following logic updates dates to different values - multiple value assignment operator
DECLARE @OrderDate DATETIME = CURRENT_TIMESTAMP;
UPDATE PurchaseOrderHeader  SET    @OrderDate = OrderDate = dateadd(day, -1, @OrderDate);
GO
```

```
SELECT TOP (5) PurchaseOrderID,   VendorID,  OrderDate  FROM  PurchaseOrderHeader;
```

PurchaseOrderID	VendorID	OrderDate
631	39	2016-07-18 09:03:18.193
759	32	2016-07-17 09:03:18.193
2652	33	2016-07-16 09:03:18.193
769	80	2016-07-15 09:03:18.193
949	30	2016-07-14 09:03:18.193

```
DROP TABLE tempdb.dbo.PurchaseOrderHeader;
```

CHAPTER 10: SELECT INTO Table Creation & Population

SELECT INTO Table Create from Complex Query

SELECT INTO table create works from simple to very complex queries.

```
USE AdventureWorks;

SELECT          SalesStaff       = CONCAT(C.LastName, ', ', C.FirstName),
                ZipCode          = A.PostalCode,
                TotalSales       = FORMAT(SUM(SOD.LineTotal),'c', 'en-US'),
                PercentOfTotal   = FORMAT( SUM(SOD.LineTotal) /
                                   SUM(SUM(SOD.LineTotal)) OVER (PARTITION BY 1, 2 ),'p')
INTO   tempdb.dbo.SalesSummary
FROM   Person.Contact C
   INNER JOIN Person.[Address] A
       ON A.AddressID = C.ContactID
   INNER JOIN Sales.SalesOrderHeader SOH
       ON SOH.SalesPersonID = C.ContactID
   INNER JOIN Sales.SalesOrderDetail SOD
       ON SOD.SalesOrderID = SOH.SalesOrderID
WHERE  TerritoryID IS NOT NULL
GROUP  BY C.FirstName,    C.LastName,    A.PostalCode,    C.ContactID
ORDER  BY SalesStaff,    ZipCode;
-- (17 row(s) affected)


-- SELECT 10 rows random, then sort them by name (SalesStaff) - derived table construct
SELECT * FROM
(
        SELECT TOP (10) *
        FROM   tempdb.dbo.SalesSummary ORDER  BY NEWID()
) x         -- x is called a derived table; also dubbed SELECT FROM SELECT
ORDER BY SalesStaff;
```

SalesStaff	ZipCode	TotalSales	PercentOfTotal
Dusza, Maciej	98027	$9,293,903.00	11.55 %
Dyck, Shelley	98027	$10,367,007.43	12.88 %
Ecoffey, Linda	98027	$10,065,803.54	12.51 %
Eldridge, Carla	98027	$3,609,447.21	4.48 %
Elliott, Carol	98027	$7,171,012.75	8.91 %
Emanuel, Michael	98055	$5,926,418.36	7.36 %
Erickson, Gail	98055	$8,503,338.65	10.56 %
Estes, Julie	98055	$172,524.45	0.21 %
Esteves, Janeth	98055	$1,827,066.71	2.27 %
Evans, Twanna	98055	$1,421,810.92	1.77 %

```
DROP TABLE tempdb.dbo.SalesSummary ;
```

CHAPTER 10: SELECT INTO Table Creation & Population

SELECT INTO Table Create from System Procedure Execution

Using OPENROWSET and OPENQUERY, we can make the result sets of system procedures and user stored procedures table-like.

```
SELECT * INTO  #spwho
FROM  OPENROWSET ( 'SQLOLEDB',
          'SERVER=.;Trusted_Connection=yes',
          'SET FMTONLY OFF EXEC sp_who');
GO -- (64 row(s) affected) - it varies, depends on the number server connections
```

```
SELECT TOP (5) *  FROM  #spwho  ORDER BY spid;
```

spid	ecid	status	loginame	hostname	blk	dbname	cmd	request_id
1	0	background	sa		0	NULL	LOG WRITER	0
2	0	background	sa		0	NULL	RECOVERY WRITER	0
3	0	background	sa		0	NULL	LAZY WRITER	0
4	0	background	sa		0	NULL	LOCK MONITOR	0
5	0	background	sa		0	master	SIGNAL HANDLER	0

```
/* Requirement for OPENQUERY operation on current instance.

DATA ACCESS to current SQL Server named instance can be setup the following way:

exec sp_serveroption @server = 'PRODSVR\SQL2008'  -- computer name for default instance
    ,@optname = 'DATA ACCESS'
    ,@optvalue = 'TRUE' ;

This way, OPENQUERY can be used against current instance. Usually OPENQUERY is used to access linked
servers.  */
```

```
SELECT  DB_NAME(dbid) AS DB, *
INTO  #splock FROM  OPENQUERY(HPESTAR, 'EXEC sp_lock');
GO
-- (156 row(s) affected)  - it varies, depends how busy is the system with OLTP activities
```

```
SELECT TOP(2) * FROM  #splock ;
```

DB	spid	dbid	ObjId	IndId	Type	Resource	Mode	Status
ReportServer	52	5	0	0	DB		S	GRANT
msdb	54	4	0	0	DB		S	GRANT

System procedure to list all tables in a database. Corresponding procedure for linked server: sp_tables_ex.

```
EXEC pubs..sp_tables @table_type = "'TABLE'";
```

CHAPTER 10: SELECT INTO Table Creation & Population

SELECT INTO from OPENQUERY Stored Procedure Execution

The following is the only way to make stored procedure results table-like. The bill-of-materials stored procedure is recursive.

```
USE AdventureWorks2012;
GO
SELECT Name FROM Production.Product
WHERE ProductID = 900;   -- LL Touring Frame - Yellow, 50


-- First we test the query execution
DECLARE @RC int;  DECLARE @StartProductID int; DECLARE @CheckDate datetime;

EXECUTE @RC = [dbo].[uspGetBillOfMaterials]     @StartProductID = 900 , @CheckDate = '20080216';
GO
-- 24 rows returned


-- Transform query into SELECT INTO table create  - Single quotes (around date literal) must be doubled
SELECT * INTO BOM900
FROM OPENQUERY(HPESTAR, 'EXECUTE [AdventureWorks2012].[dbo].[uspGetBillOfMaterials]
900,"20080216"');
GO
-- (1 row(s) affected)          -- create table
-- (24 row(s) affected)         -- inserts


SELECT * FROM BOM900;
```

ProductAssemblyID	ComponentID	ComponentDesc	TotalQuantity	StandardCost	ListPrice	BOMLevel	RecursionLevel
900	324	Chain Stays	2.00	0.00	0.00	2	0
900	325	Decal 1	2.00	0.00	0.00	2	0
900	326	Decal 2	1.00	0.00	0.00	2	0
900	327	Down Tube	1.00	0.00	0.00	2	0
900	399	Head Tube	1.00	0.00	0.00	2	0
900	496	Paint - Yellow	8.00	0.00	0.00	2	0
900	532	Seat Stays	4.00	0.00	0.00	2	0
900	533	Seat Tube	1.00	0.00	0.00	2	0
900	534	Top Tube	1.00	0.00	0.00	2	0
900	802	LL Fork	1.00	65.8097	148.22	2	0
324	486	Metal Sheet 5	1.00	0.00	0.00	3	1
327	483	Metal Sheet 3	1.00	0.00	0.00	3	1
399	485	Metal Sheet 4	1.00	0.00	0.00	3	1
532	484	Metal Sheet 7	1.00	0.00	0.00	3	1
533	478	Metal Bar 2	1.00	0.00	0.00	3	1
534	482	Metal Sheet 2	1.00	0.00	0.00	3	1
802	316	Blade	2.00	0.00	0.00	3	1
802	331	Fork End	2.00	0.00	0.00	3	1
802	350	Fork Crown	1.00	0.00	0.00	3	1
802	531	Steerer	1.00	0.00	0.00	3	1
316	486	Metal Sheet 5	1.00	0.00	0.00	4	2
331	482	Metal Sheet 2	1.00	0.00	0.00	4	2
350	486	Metal Sheet 5	1.00	0.00	0.00	4	2
531	487	Metal Sheet 6	1.00	0.00	0.00	4	2

Execution of SELECT INTO from Dynamic SQL

T-SQL script demonstrates SELECT INTO execution within a dynamic SQL. Biggest challenge is to get the single quotes right. CHAR(39) use is an option.

```
-- SQL Server 2008 new feature: instant assignment to a localvariable
DECLARE @DynamicQuery nvarchar(max) =
    'SELECT *
    INTO BOM400
    FROM OPENQUERY(' + QUOTENAME(CONVERT(sysname, @@SERVERNAME))+ ',
    ''EXECUTE [AdventureWorks2012].[dbo].[uspGetWhereUsedProductID] 400,
    ""2007-11-21""""")' ;
```

```
PRINT @DynamicQuery;     -- test query;  this is the static query which will be executed
/*
SELECT *
    INTO BOM400
    FROM OPENQUERY([HPESTAR],
    'EXECUTE [AdventureWorks2012].[dbo].[uspGetWhereUsedProductID] 400,
    "2007-11-21"')
*/
```

```
EXEC sp_executeSQL @DynamicQuery;
GO -- (64 row(s) affected)
```

```
SELECT TOP ( 5 ) * FROM BOM400 ORDER BY NEWID() ;
GO
```

ProductAssemblyID	ComponentID	ComponentDesc	TotalQuantity	StandardCost	ListPrice	BOMLevel	RecursionLevel
761	818	Road-650 Red, 62	1.00	486.7066	782.99	1	1
987	823	Mountain-500 Silver, 48	1.00	308.2179	564.99	1	1
990	823	Mountain-500 Black, 42	1.00	294.5797	539.99	1	1
765	826	Road-650 Black, 58	1.00	486.7066	782.99	1	1
770	818	Road-650 Black, 52	1.00	486.7066	782.99	1	1

```
-- Cleanup
DROP TABLE BOM400;
```

CHAPTER 10: SELECT INTO Table Creation & Population

SELECT INTO Table Create from View

Transact-SQL script demonstrates how to import view query results into a table.

```
SELECT [FullName],
    [SalesPersonID]                         AS StaffID,
    [SalesTerritory],
    COALESCE(FORMAT([2006], 'c','en-US'), '')    AS [2006],
    COALESCE(FORMAT([2007], 'c','en-US'), '')    AS [2007],
    COALESCE(FORMAT([2008], 'c','en-US'), '')    AS [2008]
INTO   #Sales
FROM   [AdventureWorks2012].[Sales].[vSalesPersonSalesByFiscalYears]
ORDER  BY SalesTerritory, FullName;
GO
```

```
SELECT *
FROM   #Sales
ORDER  BY SalesTerritory, FullName;
GO
```

FullName	StaffID	SalesTerritory	2006	2007	2008
Lynn N Tsoflias	286	Australia			$1,421,810.92
Garrett R Vargas	278	Canada	$930,259.47	$1,225,468.28	$1,453,719.47
José Edvaldo Saraiva	282	Canada	$2,088,491.17	$1,233,386.47	$2,604,540.72
Jillian Carson	277	Central	$2,737,537.88	$4,138,847.30	$3,189,418.37
Ranjit R Varkey Chudukatil	290	France		$1,388,272.61	$3,121,616.32
Rachel B Valdez	288	Germany			$1,827,066.71
Michael G Blythe	275	Northeast	$1,602,472.39	$3,928,252.44	$3,763,178.18
David R Campbell	283	Northwest	$1,017,402.86	$1,139,529.55	$1,573,012.94
Pamela O Ansman-Wolfe	280	Northwest	$1,226,461.83	$746,063.63	$1,352,577.13
Tete A Mensa-Annan	284	Northwest		$735,983.49	$1,576,562.20
Tsvi Michael Reiter	279	Southeast	$2,645,436.95	$2,210,390.19	$2,315,185.61
Linda C Mitchell	276	Southwest	$2,260,118.45	$3,855,520.42	$4,251,368.55
Shu K Ito	281	Southwest	$1,593,742.92	$2,374,727.02	$2,458,535.62
Jae B Pak	289	United Kingdom		$4,386,467.42	$4,116,871.23

SELECT INTO Data Import from Excel

T-SQL OPENROWSET query imports data into a temporary table from Excel. Your Excel library maybe different than the one in the example. SQL Server Import and Export Wizard is the best way to exchange date between SS database and Excel.

```
SELECT * INTO ContactList  FROM OPENROWSET('Microsoft.Jet.OLEDB.4.0',
        'Excel 8.0;Database=D:\data\excel\Contact.xls', 'SELECT * FROM [Contact$]')
-- (19972 row(s) affected)
```

CHAPTER 11: Modify Data - INSERT, UPDATE, DELETE & MERGE

INSERT VALUES - Table Value Constructor

T-SQL scripts illustrate the use of INSERT VALUES with Table Value Constructor (a list of values).
Because the text columns are defined as nvarchar the string literals are prefixed with "N"
indicating UNICODE literal. Since only Latin letters used, the "N" can be omitted.

```
USE tempdb;
SELECT TOP 0 * INTO dbo.Department FROM AdventureWorks2012.HumanResources.Department;
-- This is necessary because IDENTITY property was inherited in the SELECT INTO
SET IDENTITY_INSERT dbo.Department ON;
GO
INSERT dbo.Department (DepartmentID, Name, GroupName, ModifiedDate) VALUES
(1, N'Engineering', N'Research and Development', getdate()),
(2, N'Tool Design', N'Research and Development', getdate()),
(3, N'Sales', N'Sales and Marketing', getdate()),
(4, N'Marketing', N'Sales and Marketing', getdate()),
(5, N'Purchasing', N'Inventory Management', getdate()),
(6, N'Research and Development', N'Research and Development', getdate()),
(7, N'Production', N'Manufacturing', getdate()),
(8, N'Production Control', N'Manufacturing', getdate()),
(9, N'Human Resources', N'Executive General and Administration', getdate()),
(10, N'Finance', N'Executive General and Administration', getdate()),
(11, N'Information Services', N'Executive General and Administration', getdate()),
(12, N'Document Control', N'Quality Assurance', getdate()),
(13, N'Quality Assurance', N'Quality Assurance', getdate()),
(14, N'Facilities and Maintenance', N'Executive General and Administration', getdate()),
(15, N'Shipping and Receiving', N'Inventory Management', getdate()),
(16, N'Executive', N'Executive General and Administration',getdate());
GO
SET IDENTITY_INSERT dbo.Department OFF;
GO
SELECT TOP 4 * FROM dbo.Department ORDER BY DepartmentID;
```

DepartmentID	Name	GroupName	ModifiedDate
1	Engineering	Research and Development	2016-08-02 06:35:44.623
2	Tool Design	Research and Development	2016-08-02 06:35:44.623
3	Sales	Sales and Marketing	2016-08-02 06:35:44.623
4	Marketing	Sales and Marketing	2016-08-02 06:35:44.623

INSERT VALUES - Ye Olde Way

T-SQL scripts illustrate the INSERT VALUES for single row insert, the only available method prior to SQL Server 2008.

```
USE AdventureWorks2012;
GO

CREATE TABLE Shift(
        ShiftID tinyint IDENTITY(1,1) NOT NULL,
        Name dbo.Name NOT NULL,
        StartTime time(7) NOT NULL,
        EndTime time(7) NOT NULL,
        ModifiedDate datetime NOT NULL,
        CONSTRAINT PK_Shift_ShiftID PRIMARY KEY CLUSTERED (ShiftID ASC) );
GO

SET IDENTITY_INSERT Shift ON;              -- To force insert into ShiftID

INSERT Shift (ShiftID, Name, StartTime, EndTime, ModifiedDate)
VALUES (1, N'Day', CAST(0x0700D85EAC3A0000 AS Time), CAST(0x07001882BA7D0000 AS Time),
CAST(0x0000921E00000000 AS DateTime))
INSERT Shift (ShiftID, Name, StartTime, EndTime, ModifiedDate)
VALUES (2, N'Evening', CAST(0x07001882BA7D0000 AS Time), CAST(0x070058A5C8C00000 AS Time),
getdate());
INSERT Shift (ShiftID, Name, StartTime, EndTime, ModifiedDate)
VALUES (3, N'Night', CAST(0x070058A5C8C00000 AS Time), CAST(0x0700D85EAC3A0000 AS Time),
CURRENT_TIMESTAMP);
GO

SET IDENTITY_INSERT Shift OFF;

ALTER TABLE Shift ADD  CONSTRAINT DF_Shift_ModifiedDate  DEFAULT (getdate()) FOR ModifiedDate
GO

SELECT * FROM Shift ORDER BY ShiftID;
GO
```

ShiftID	Name	StartTime	EndTime	ModifiedDate
1	Day	07:00:00.0000000	15:00:00.0000000	2002-06-01 00:00:00.000
2	Evening	15:00:00.0000000	23:00:00.0000000	2018-08-20 19:31:02.293
3	Night	23:00:00.0000000	07:00:00.0000000	2018-08-20 19:31:02.293

```
DROP TABLE Shift;
GO
```

CHAPTER 11: Modify Data - INSERT, UPDATE, DELETE & MERGE

INSERT SELECT

INSERT SELECT Literal List

T-SQL scripts demonstrate the insertion of literal records (rows) using INSERT SELECT.

```
USE tempdb;
GO
SELECT TOP 0 * INTO dbo.Department FROM AdventureWorks2012.HumanResources.Department;
GO
-- This is necessary because IDENTITY property was inherited in the SELECT INTO
SET IDENTITY_INSERT dbo.Department ON;
GO
INSERT dbo.Department (DepartmentID, Name, GroupName, ModifiedDate)
SELECT 1, N'Engineering', N'Research and Development', CURRENT_TIMESTAMP  UNION
SELECT 2, N'Tool Design', N'Research and Development', CURRENT_TIMESTAMP  UNION
SELECT 3, N'Sales', N'Sales and Marketing', CURRENT_TIMESTAMP  UNION
SELECT 4, N'Marketing', N'Sales and Marketing', CURRENT_TIMESTAMP  UNION
SELECT 5, N'Purchasing', N'Inventory Management', CURRENT_TIMESTAMP  UNION
SELECT 6, N'Research and Development', N'Research and Development', CURRENT_TIMESTAMP  UNION
SELECT 7, N'Production', N'Manufacturing', CURRENT_TIMESTAMP  UNION
SELECT 8, N'Production Control', N'Manufacturing', CURRENT_TIMESTAMP  UNION
SELECT 9, N'Human Resources', N'Executive General and Administration', CURRENT_TIMESTAMP  UNION
SELECT 10, N'Finance', N'Executive General and Administration', CURRENT_TIMESTAMP  UNION
SELECT 11, N'Information Services', N'Executive General and Administration', CURRENT_TIMESTAMP
UNION
SELECT 12, N'Document Control', N'Quality Assurance', CURRENT_TIMESTAMP  UNION
SELECT 13, N'Quality Assurance', N'Quality Assurance', CURRENT_TIMESTAMP  UNION
SELECT 14, N'Facilities and Maintenance', N'Executive General and Administration',
CURRENT_TIMESTAMP  UNION
SELECT 15, N'Shipping and Receiving', N'Inventory Management', CURRENT_TIMESTAMP  UNION
SELECT 16, N'Executive', N'Executive General and Administration', CURRENT_TIMESTAMP;
GO
SET IDENTITY_INSERT dbo.Department OFF;
GO
SELECT TOP 4 * FROM dbo.Department ORDER BY DepartmentID;
GO
```

DepartmentID	Name	GroupName	ModifiedDate
1	Engineering	Research and Development	2016-08-02 06:35:44.623
2	Tool Design	Research and Development	2016-08-02 06:35:44.623
3	Sales	Sales and Marketing	2016-08-02 06:35:44.623
4	Marketing	Sales and Marketing	2016-08-02 06:35:44.623

```
-- Cleanup
DROP TABLE tempdb.dbo.Department;
```

CHAPTER 11: Modify Data - INSERT, UPDATE, DELETE & MERGE

INSERT SELECT from Table

T-SQL script demonstrates table population with table SELECT.

```
USE tempdb;
SELECT TOP 0 * INTO dbo.Department FROM AdventureWorks2012.HumanResources.Department;
GO
-- This is necessary because IDENTITY property was inherited in the SELECT INTO
SET IDENTITY_INSERT dbo.Department ON;
GO
INSERT dbo.Department (DepartmentID, Name, GroupName, ModifiedDate)
SELECT TOP 15 DepartmentID, Name, GroupName, ModifiedDate
FROM AdventureWorks2012.HumanResources.Department  ORDER BY DepartmentID;
GO
-- (15 row(s) affected)
SELECT TOP 4 * FROM dbo.Department ORDER BY DepartmentID;
```

DepartmentID	Name	GroupName	ModifiedDate
1	Engineering	Research and Development	2016-08-02 06:35:44.623
2	Tool Design	Research and Development	2016-08-02 06:35:44.623
3	Sales	Sales and Marketing	2016-08-02 06:35:44.623
4	Marketing	Sales and Marketing	2016-08-02 06:35:44.623

SCOPE_IDENTITY() for Last-Inserted IDENTITY Value

The last inserted IDENTITY value can be returned with the SCOPE_IDENTITY() or @@IDENTITY system function (variable). SCOPE_IDENTITY() is better choice since it is within the current connection scope. @@IDENTITY is at server level. The best choice though is the OUTPUT clause.

```
INSERT dbo.Department (DepartmentID, Name, GroupName, ModifiedDate)
SELECT TOP 1 DepartmentID, Name, GroupName, ModifiedDate
FROM AdventureWorks2012.HumanResources.Department  ORDER BY DepartmentID DESC;
GO
-- (1 row(s) affected)
```

Alternate is SELECT @@IDENTITY; @@ variables are system variables.

```
DECLARE @LastID INT = SCOPE_IDENTITY();
SELECT @LastID;   -- 16
```

```
SET IDENTITY_INSERT dbo.Department OFF;
GO
```

```
-- Cleanup
DROP TABLE tempdb.dbo.Department;
```

CHAPTER II: Modify Data - INSERT, UPDATE, DELETE & MERGE

INSERT with Subset of Columns

Only the required columns must be present in the INSERT column list. A column with default or NULL property can be omitted. In the next T-SQL script, ModifiedDate is filled by default with getdate().

```
USE tempdb;
SELECT TOP 0 * INTO dbo.Department FROM AdventureWorks2012.HumanResources.Department;
GO
ALTER TABLE dbo.Department ADD CONSTRAINT DF_Dept_ModDate
DEFAULT getdate() FOR ModifiedDate;
GO
SET IDENTITY_INSERT dbo.Department ON;
GO
INSERT dbo.Department (DepartmentID, Name, GroupName)
SELECT DepartmentID, Name, GroupName  FROM AdventureWorks2012.HumanResources.Department;
GO  -- (16 row(s) affected)
SELECT TOP 4 * FROM dbo.Department ORDER BY DepartmentID;
```

DepartmentID	Name	GroupName	ModifiedDate
1	Engineering	Research and Development	2016-08-02 06:35:44.623
2	Tool Design	Research and Development	2016-08-02 06:35:44.623
3	Sales	Sales and Marketing	2016-08-02 06:35:44.623
4	Marketing	Sales and Marketing	2016-08-02 06:35:44.623

Capturing Last-Inserted IDENTITY Set Values with OUTPUT

When more than one row is inserted with one statement, the OUTPUT clause can be used to capture the list of just inserted IDENTITY values.

```
DECLARE @LastInserted TABLE (ID INT);
INSERT dbo.Department (DepartmentID, Name, GroupName)
      OUTPUT inserted.DepartmentID INTO @LastInserted
SELECT DepartmentID+1000, Name, GroupName  FROM
AdventureWorks2012.HumanResources.Department;
SELECT TOP 5 * FROM @LastInserted ORDER BY ID;
GO
```

ID
1001
1002
1003
1004
1005

```
SET IDENTITY_INSERT dbo.Department OFF;
DROP TABLE tempdb.dbo.Department;
```

CHAPTER 11: Modify Data - INSERT, UPDATE, DELETE & MERGE

INSERT EXEC Stored Procedure

Data can be directly inserted from the execution of a user-defined stored procedure or system procedure. We create a table and a stored procedure, then perform INSERT EXEC.

```
USE AdventureWorks2012;
IF OBJECT_ID ('dbo.EmployeeSales', 'U') IS NOT NULL   DROP TABLE dbo.EmployeeSales;
IF OBJECT_ID ('dbo.uspGetEmployeeSales', 'P') IS NOT NULL   DROP PROCEDURE uspGetEmployeeSales;
CREATE TABLE dbo.EmployeeSales
 (
   BusinessEntityID       VARCHAR(11) NOT NULL PRIMARY KEY,
   LastName               VARCHAR(40) NOT NULL,
   SalesDollars           MONEY NOT NULL,
   DataSource             VARCHAR(20) NOT NULL
 );
GO


CREATE PROCEDURE dbo.uspGetEmployeeSales AS
 BEGIN
   SELECT         e.BusinessEntityID, c.LastName, sp.SalesYTD, 'PROCEDURE'
   FROM   HumanResources.Employee AS e
      INNER JOIN Sales.SalesPerson AS sp
          ON e.BusinessEntityID = sp.BusinessEntityID
      INNER JOIN Person.Person AS c
          ON e.BusinessEntityID = c.BusinessEntityID
   WHERE  e.BusinessEntityID > 280    ORDER  BY   e.BusinessEntityID,  c.LastName;
 END;
GO

--INSERT...EXECUTE user-defined stored procedure
INSERT EmployeeSales EXECUTE uspGetEmployeeSales;

SELECT * FROM   EmployeeSales;
```

BusinessEntityID	LastName	SalesDollars	DataSource
281	Ito	2458535.6169	PROCEDURE
282	Saraiva	2604540.7172	PROCEDURE
283	Campbell	1573012.9383	PROCEDURE
284	Mensa-Annan	1576562.1966	PROCEDURE
285	Abbas	172524.4512	PROCEDURE
286	Tsoflias	1421810.9242	PROCEDURE
287	Alberts	519905.932	PROCEDURE
288	Valdez	1827066.7118	PROCEDURE
289	Pak	4116871.2277	PROCEDURE
290	Varkey Chudukatil	3121616.3202	PROCEDURE

Insert Into A Table Via The Direct Execution Of An SQL Query With The EXEC Command

SELECT Population = count(*) FROM   dbo.EmployeeSales;

Population
10

```
--INSERT...EXECUTE('string') example
INSERT EmployeeSales
EXECUTE ('      SELECT e.BusinessEntityID, c.LastName,     sp.SalesYTD, ''EXEC SQL STRING''
                FROM HumanResources.Employee AS e       INNER JOIN Sales.SalesPerson AS sp
                ON e.BusinessEntityID = sp.BusinessEntityID      INNER JOIN Person.Person AS c
                ON e.BusinessEntityID = c.BusinessEntityID
                WHERE e.BusinessEntityID BETWEEN 270 and 280
                ORDER BY e.BusinessEntityID, c.LastName ');
GO
-- (7 row(s) affected)
```

Inserted number of rows can be captured for later use. **Capture must be done immediately after the monitored statement.** Any following statement will change @@ROWCOUNT value.

```
DECLARE @InsertCount int = @@ROWCOUNT;
SELECT @InsertCount;   -- 7
GO
```

SELECT * FROM   dbo.EmployeeSales ORDER BY BusinessEntityID ;

BusinessEntityID	LastName	SalesDollars	DataSource
274	Jiang	559697.5639	EXEC SQL STRING
275	Blythe	3763178.1787	EXEC SQL STRING
276	Mitchell	4251368.5497	EXEC SQL STRING
277	Carson	3189418.3662	EXEC SQL STRING
278	Vargas	1453719.4653	EXEC SQL STRING
279	Reiter	2315185.611	EXEC SQL STRING
280	Ansman-Wolfe	1352577.1325	EXEC SQL STRING
281	Ito	2458535.6169	PROCEDURE
282	Saraiva	2604540.7172	PROCEDURE
283	Campbell	1573012.9383	PROCEDURE
284	Mensa-Annan	1576562.1966	PROCEDURE
285	Abbas	172524.4512	PROCEDURE
286	Tsoflias	1421810.9242	PROCEDURE
287	Alberts	519905.932	PROCEDURE
288	Valdez	1827066.7118	PROCEDURE
289	Pak	4116871.2277	PROCEDURE
290	Varkey Chudukatil	3121616.3202	PROCEDURE

CHAPTER 11: Modify Data - INSERT, UPDATE, DELETE & MERGE

INSERT EXEC System Procedure

Data can be inserted into a table by the execution of a system procedure. We create a test table with SELECT INTO FROM OPENQUERY. We can also create the table manually if we know the data type of columns.

```
-- DATA ACCESS must be turned on at YOURSERVER SQL Server instance
SELECT TOP(0) * INTO #SPWHO
FROM OPENQUERY(YOURSERVER, 'exec sp_who');        -- will not work with sp_who2 due to duplicate
column name
```

```
/*  Table created
CREATE TABLE [dbo].[#SPWHO](
        [spid] [smallint] NOT NULL,
        [ecid] [smallint] NOT NULL,
        [status] [nchar](30) NOT NULL,
        [loginame] [nvarchar](128) NULL,
        [hostname] [nchar](128) NOT NULL,
        [blk] [char](5) NULL,
        [dbname] [nvarchar](128) NULL,
        [cmd] [nchar](16) NOT NULL,
        [request_id] [int] NOT NULL
); */
```

```
INSERT #SPWHO   EXEC sp_who
```

The blk column contains blocking spid if any. A large update for example may block other queries until it completes. The spid of the current session is @@SPID.

```
SELECT * FROM  #SPWHO
GO -- (42 row(s) affected) - Partial results.
```

spid	ecid	status	loginame	hostname	blk	dbname	cmd	request_id
21	0	background	sa		0	master	TASK MANAGER	0
22	0	background	sa		0	master	CHECKPOINT	0
23	0	sleeping	sa		0	master	TASK MANAGER	0
24	0	background	sa		0	master	BRKR TASK	0
25	0	sleeping	sa		0	master	TASK MANAGER	0
26	0	sleeping	sa		0	master	TASK MANAGER	0
27	0	sleeping	sa		0	master	TASK MANAGER	0
28	0	sleeping	sa		0	master	TASK MANAGER	0
29	0	sleeping	sa		0	master	TASK MANAGER	0
30	0	sleeping	sa		0	master	TASK MANAGER	0
40	0	background	sa		0	master	BRKR TASK	0
42	0	background	sa		0	master	BRKR TASK	0
43	0	background	sa		0	master	BRKR TASK	0
51	0	sleeping	YOURSERVER \Owner	YOURSERVER	0	AdventureWorks2012	AWAITING COMMAND	0
52	0	sleeping	NT SERVICE\SQLSERVERAGENT	YOURSERVER	0	msdb	AWAITING COMMAND	0

```
DROP TABLE #SPWHO
GO
```

INSERT Only New Rows Omit the Rest

INSERT only new records. If record exists, do nothing. Note: DELETE will not rollback IDENTITY current value. Therefore with repeated testing, the IDENTITY current value will roll ahead.

```
USE AdventureWorks2012;
SELECT COUNT(*) FROM HumanResources.Department;             -- 16
```

```
-- All rows exists, no new row insertion
INSERT HumanResources.Department (Name, GroupName)
SELECT Name, GroupName
FROM AdventureWorks2008.HumanResources.Department D
WHERE NOT EXISTS (      SELECT * FROM HumanResources.Department DD  -- Correlated subquery
                 WHERE D.Name = DD.Name
                    AND D.GroupName = DD.GroupName);
GO -- (0 row(s) affected)
```

```
-- Prefix Name with "ZZZ", 16 successful new inserted rows
INSERT HumanResources.Department (Name, GroupName)
SELECT CONCAT('ZZZ', Name), GroupName
FROM AdventureWorks2008.HumanResources.Department D
WHERE NOT EXISTS (      SELECT * FROM HumanResources.Department DD
          WHERE DD.Name = CONCAT('ZZZ', D.Name)    AND DD.GroupName = D.GroupName);
GO -- (16 row(s) affected)
```

```
DELETE TOP ( 7 ) HumanResources.Department WHERE Name LIKE ('ZZZ%');     -- (7 row(s) affected)
```

Only 7 rows will be inserted since the rest are duplicates.

```
INSERT HumanResources.Department (Name, GroupName)
SELECT CONCAT('ZZZ', Name), GroupName
FROM AdventureWorks2008.HumanResources.Department D
WHERE NOT EXISTS (      SELECT * FROM HumanResources.Department DD
             WHERE DD.Name = CONCAT('ZZZ', D.Name)    AND DD.GroupName = DD.GroupName);
GO
-- (7  row(s) affected)
```

```
SELECT * FROM HumanResources.Department;   -- (32 row(s) affected) -- Partial results;
```

DepartmentID	Name	GroupName	ModifiedDate
16	Executive	Executive General and Administration	2002-06-01 00:00:00.000
65	ZZZEngineering	Research and Development	2018-08-13 08:32:43.133

```
DELETE HumanResources.Department
WHERE Name LIKE ('ZZZ%');          -- (16 row(s) affected)
SELECT COUNT(*) FROM HumanResources.Department;             -- 16
```

CHAPTER 11: Modify Data - INSERT, UPDATE, DELETE & MERGE

DELETE - A Dangerous Operation

DELETE is a logged operation. DELETE may be slow from large table with indexes due to index reorganization. Warning: **DELETE is a dangerous operation since it removes data. Protection: regular database backup and/or creating a copy of the table prior to DELETE with SELECT INTO.**

```
USE [AdventureWorks2012]
GO
-- Create test table with SELECT INTO
SELECT [SalesOrderID]
    ,CONVERT(INT,[SalesOrderDetailID]) AS SalesOrderDetailID
    ,[CarrierTrackingNumber]
    ,[OrderQty]
    ,[ProductID]
    ,[SpecialOfferID]
    ,[UnitPrice]
    ,[UnitPriceDiscount]
    ,[LineTotal]
    ,[rowguid]
    ,[ModifiedDate]
INTO tempdb.dbo.SOD
FROM [Sales].[SalesOrderDetail];
GO -- (121317 row(s) affected)
```

```
-- Increase table population 64 fold
INSERT  tempdb.dbo.SOD  SELECT * FROM tempdb.dbo.SOD;
GO 6
/* Beginning execution loop
(121317 row(s) affected)
(242634 row(s) affected)
(485268 row(s) affected)
(970536 row(s) affected)
(1941072 row(s) affected)
(3882144 row(s) affected)
Batch execution completed 6 times.
Execution time - 00:01.27 */
```

```
CREATE INDEX idxSOD on tempdb.dbo.SOD (SalesOrderID, ProductID);
-- Command(s) completed successfully. Time: 00:00:06
```

```
SELECT COUNT(*) FROM tempdb.dbo.SOD;  -- 7764288
```

```
-- Delete even SalesOrderID records
DELETE FROM tempdb.dbo.SOD WHERE SalesOrderID % 2 = 0;
-- (3925184 row(s) affected)  - Execution time - 00:01:30
```

CHAPTER 11: Modify Data - INSERT, UPDATE, DELETE & MERGE

TRUNCATE TABLE & DBCC CHECKIDENT

TRUNCATE TABLE command is very fast since it is minimally logged. It also resets IDENTITY column to (1,1). Warning: **TRUNCATE is a dangerous operation since it removes all the data in a table**. Protection: regular database backup and/or creating a copy of the table prior to TRUNCATE with SELECT INTO.

```
SELECT COUNT(*) FROM tempdb.dbo.SOD;  -- 3839104

TRUNCATE TABLE tempdb.dbo.SOD;
-- Command(s) completed successfully.  Execution time: 00:00:00

SELECT COUNT(*) FROM tempdb.dbo.SOD;  -- 0
GO

DROP TABLE tempdb.dbo.SOD;
GO
-- Command(s) completed successfully

-- Create new test table with SELECT INTO
USE tempdb;

SELECT * INTO SOD FROM AdventureWorks2012.Sales.SalesOrderDetail;
GO -- (121317 row(s) affected)

-- Next IDENTITY value will be 121318.
DBCC CHECKIDENT ("dbo.SOD");
/* Checking identity information: current identity value '121317', current column value '121317'.
DBCC execution completed. If DBCC printed error messages, contact your system administrator.  */

TRUNCATE TABLE SOD;
GO
-- Command(s) completed successfully.

-- IDENTITY is reset
DBCC CHECKIDENT ("dbo.SOD");
/* Checking identity information: current identity value 'NULL', current column value 'NULL'.
DBCC execution completed. If DBCC printed error messages, contact your system administrator. */

EXEC sp_help SOD;
GO
-- Partial results.
```

Identity	Seed	Increment	Not For Replication
SalesOrderDetailID	1	1	0

CHAPTER II: Modify Data - INSERT, UPDATE, DELETE & MERGE

Reseeding IDENTITY

```
-- Without this command, it may not start at 1
DBCC CHECKIDENT ("SOD", RESEED, 1);


-- Populate the table with 5 rows
INSERT INTO SOD
       ([SalesOrderID]
       ,[CarrierTrackingNumber]
       ,[OrderQty]
       ,[ProductID]
       ,[SpecialOfferID]
       ,[UnitPrice]
       ,[UnitPriceDiscount]
       ,[LineTotal]
       ,[rowguid]
       ,[ModifiedDate])
SELECT   TOP (5)
       [SalesOrderID]
       ,[CarrierTrackingNumber]
       ,[OrderQty]
       ,[ProductID]
       ,[SpecialOfferID]
       ,[UnitPrice]
       ,[UnitPriceDiscount]
       ,[LineTotal]
       ,[rowguid]
       ,[ModifiedDate]
FROM AdventureWorks2012.Sales.SalesOrderDetail;
GO
-- (5 row(s) affected)
```

```
-- Next value assigned is 6
DBCC CHECKIDENT ("dbo.SOD");
/*Checking identity information: current identity value '5', current column value '5'.
DBCC execution completed. If DBCC printed error messages, contact your system administrator. */
```

```
SELECT * FROM SOD;
-- (5 row(s) affected) - Partial results.
```

SalesOrderID	SalesOrderDetailID	CarrierTrackingNumber	OrderQty	ProductID	SpecialOfferID	UnitPrice	UnitPriceDiscount	LineTotal
43659	1	4911-403C-98	1	776	1	2024.994	0.00	2024.994000
43659	2	4911-403C-98	3	777	1	2024.994	0.00	6074.982000
43659	3	4911-403C-98	1	778	1	2024.994	0.00	2024.994000
43659	4	4911-403C-98	1	771	1	2039.994	0.00	2039.994000
43659	5	4911-403C-98	1	772	1	2039.994	0.00	2039.994000

CHAPTER 11: Modify Data - INSERT, UPDATE, DELETE & MERGE

UPDATE - A Complex Operation

UPDATE changes data content at a row and column level (cell). It is a logged operation: deleted row contains previous data, inserted row contains new data. Warning: UPDATE is a dangerous operation since it changes the data in a table. Protection: regular database backup and/or creating a copy of the table prior to UPDATE with SELECT INTO.

Some UPDATEs are reversible, such as some calculated UPDATE, others may be irreversible.

Checking Cardinality & Changes by UPDATE Prior to Execution

Since UPDATE is replaces previous data, it is very important to check prior to execution that is works correctly. It is quite simple to convert UPDATE into a checking SELECT. We intend to UPDATE the SalesYTD column with the last day sales for each salesperson.

```
USE AdventureWorks2012;
SELECT   sp.BusinessEntityID, SalesYTD,
            [NewSalesYTD]=SalesYTD
        + (SELECT SUM(SODa.SubTotal)
          FROM   Sales.SalesOrderHeader AS SODa
          WHERE  CONVERT(date,SODa.OrderDate) = CONVERT(date,(SELECT MAX(OrderDate)
          FROM   Sales.SalesOrderHeader AS SODb
          WHERE
             SODb.SalesPersonID = SODa.SalesPersonID))
            AND sp.BusinessEntityID =  SODa.SalesPersonID
          GROUP  BY SODa.SalesPersonID)
FROM Sales.SalesPerson sp  ORDER BY sp.BusinessEntityID;
GO
```

BusinessEntityID	SalesYTD	NewSalesYTD
274	559697.5639	597350.4859
275	3763178.1787	4133185.161
276	4251368.5497	4534079.5941
277	3189418.3662	3527404.588
278	1453719.4653	1599132.4735
279	2315185.611	2548077.4756
280	1352577.1325	1503691.0098
281	2458535.6169	2678660.7921
282	2604540.7172	3030519.8258
283	1573012.9383	1714964.9067
284	1576562.1966	1719945.1917
285	172524.4512	176721.5652
286	1421810.9242	1649155.9058
287	519905.932	520578.226
288	1827066.7118	1962768.1658
289	4116871.2277	4556655.2802
290	3121616.3202	3240852.6195

ANSI Style UPDATE

T-SQL supports ANSI UPDATE, in addition T-SQL supports the FROM clause in UPDATE.

```
USE AdventureWorks2012;
UPDATE Sales.SalesPerson
SET   SalesYTD = SalesYTD
          + (SELECT SUM(SODa.SubTotal)
            FROM   Sales.SalesOrderHeader AS SODa
            WHERE  CONVERT(date,SODa.OrderDate) =
                  CONVERT(date,(SELECT MAX(OrderDate)
            FROM   Sales.SalesOrderHeader AS SODb
            WHERE
                SODb.SalesPersonID = SODa.SalesPersonID))
                AND Sales.SalesPerson.BusinessEntityID =   SODa.SalesPersonID
            GROUP  BY SODa.SalesPersonID);
GO
-- (17 row(s) affected)
```

```
SELECT BusinessEntityID, SalesQuota, SalesYTD, SalesLastYear
FROM Sales.SalesPerson
ORDER BY BusinessEntityID;
GO
```

BusinessEntityID	SalesQuota	SalesYTD	SalesLastYear
274	NULL	597350.4859	0.00
275	300000.00	4133185.161	1750406.4785
276	250000.00	4534079.5941	1439156.0291
277	250000.00	3527404.588	1997186.2037
278	250000.00	1599132.4735	1620276.8966
279	300000.00	2548077.4756	1849640.9418
280	250000.00	1503691.0098	1927059.178
281	250000.00	2678660.7921	2073505.9999
282	250000.00	3030519.8258	2038234.6549
283	250000.00	1714964.9067	1371635.3158
284	300000.00	1719945.1917	0.00
285	NULL	176721.5652	0.00
286	250000.00	1649155.9058	2278548.9776
287	NULL	520578.226	0.00
288	250000.00	1962768.1658	1307949.7917
289	250000.00	4556655.2802	1635823.3967
290	250000.00	3240852.6195	2396539.7601

UPDATE from Table in Another Database

UPDATE can be performed with data from a second database. ZorigAdventureWorks2012 is an original read-only copy of the AdventureWorks2012 database. The "Z" prefix is to force it to the end of alphabetical database list in SSMS Object Explorer.

```
UPDATE Sales.SalesPerson
      SET SalesYTD = (
                      SELECT SalesYTD
                      FROM ZorigAdventureWorks2012.Sales.SalesPerson sp
                      WHERE sp.BusinessEntityID =
Sales.SalesPerson.BusinessEntityID
                      );
GO
```

```
SELECT  BusinessEntityID,
        SalesQuota,
        SalesYTD,
        SalesLastYear
FROM Sales.SalesPerson
ORDER BY BusinessEntityID;
GO
```

BusinessEntityID	SalesQuota	SalesYTD	SalesLastYear
274	NULL	559697.5639	0.00
275	300000.00	3763178.1787	1750406.4785
276	250000.00	4251368.5497	1439156.0291
277	250000.00	3189418.3662	1997186.2037
278	250000.00	1453719.4653	1620276.8966
279	300000.00	2315185.611	1849640.9418
280	250000.00	1352577.1325	1927059.178
281	250000.00	2458535.6169	2073505.9999
282	250000.00	2604540.7172	2038234.6549
283	250000.00	1573012.9383	1371635.3158
284	300000.00	1576562.1966	0.00
285	NULL	172524.4512	0.00
286	250000.00	1421810.9242	2278548.9776
287	NULL	519905.932	0.00
288	250000.00	1827066.7118	1307949.7917
289	250000.00	4116871.2277	1635823.3967
290	250000.00	3121616.3202	2396539.7601

UPDATE Syntax Challenges

The UPDATE statement in SQL has perplexing and potentially confusing syntax. Typically mastered by expert DBA-s and SQL developers, and the rest of the database community uses it in an insecure manner: never sure if it works as intended. Simple T-SQL examples demonstrate some of the issues with the UPDATE syntax and offer solutions.

First we create a new table for experimentation from the AdventureWorks2012 database and perform a demo inner join UPDATE on the new table.

```
USE tempdb;

SELECT ProductID,
    ProductName = Name,
    StandardCost AS Cost,
    ListPrice,
    Color,
    CONVERT(date, ModifiedDate) AS ModifiedDate
INTO   Product
FROM   AdventureWorks2012.Production.Product
WHERE  ListPrice > 0.0
        AND Color IS NOT NULL;
GO
-- (245 row(s) affected)
```

```
SELECT TOP 5 * FROM Product
ORDER BY ProductID DESC;
GO
```

ProductID	ProductName	Cost	ListPrice	Color	ModifiedDate
999	Road-750 Black, 52	343.6496	539.99	Black	2008-03-11
998	Road-750 Black, 48	343.6496	539.99	Black	2008-03-11
997	Road-750 Black, 44	343.6496	539.99	Black	2008-03-11
993	Mountain-500 Black, 52	294.5797	539.99	Black	2008-03-11
992	Mountain-500 Black, 48	294.5797	539.99	Black	2008-03-11

We shall proceed and update ALL (no WHERE clause) the rows in the Product table. We increase the ListPrice by 5%.

```
UPDATE Product     SET ListPrice = ListPrice * 1.05;  -- (245 row(s) affected)
```

In this instance a reversible UPDATE. But not always.

```
UPDATE Product     SET ListPrice = ListPrice / 1.05;
-- (245 row(s) affected)
```

UPDATE with INNER JOIN
The UPDATE uses a table alias from the FROM clause.

```
SELECT TOP 2 * FROM Product  WHERE Color = 'Yellow' ORDER BY ProductID DESC;
```

ProductID	ProductName	Cost	ListPrice	Color	ModifiedDate
976	Road-350-W Yellow, 48	1082.51	1700.99	Yellow	2008-03-11
975	Road-350-W Yellow, 44	1082.51	1700.99	Yellow	2008-03-11

```
UPDATE p  SET   p.ModifiedDate = DATEADD(HH,1,awp.ModifiedDate)
FROM   Product p   INNER JOIN AdventureWorks2012.Production.Product awp
                   ON p.ProductID = awp.ProductID  AND  p.Size LIKE '4%' ;
-- (91 row(s) affected)
```

Capturing Affected Rows with @@ROWCOUNT
When we have to know the number of updated rows, it is best to capture it into local variable
and use it from there in the program logic.

```
DECLARE @UpdatedRows  int;   -- capture @@ROWCOUNT for subsequent  use in the program

UPDATE p  SET    p.ModifiedDate = DATEADD(mm,1,awp.ModifiedDate)
FROM   Product p
    INNER JOIN AdventureWorks2012.Production.Product awp    ON p.ProductID = awp.ProductID
WHERE  p.Color = 'Yellow' ;
-- (36 row(s) affected)

SET @UpdatedRows = @@ROWCOUNT;

SELECT @@ROWCOUNT;              -- @@ROWCOUNT already changed
-- 1
SELECT TOP 5 * FROM Product  WHERE Color = 'Yellow' ORDER BY ProductID DESC;

SELECT @@ROWCOUNT;              -- @@ROWCOUNT changed again
-- 5
SELECT @UpdatedRows;           -- local variable kept the UPDATE count
-- 36
```

ProductID	ProductName	Cost	ListPrice	Color	ModifiedDate
976	Road-350-W Yellow, 48	1082.51	1700.99	Yellow	2008-04-11
975	Road-350-W Yellow, 44	1082.51	1700.99	Yellow	2008-04-11
974	Road-350-W Yellow, 42	1082.51	1700.99	Yellow	2008-04-11
973	Road-350-W Yellow, 40	1082.51	1700.99	Yellow	2008-04-11
965	Touring-3000 Yellow, 62	461.4448	742.35	Yellow	2008-04-11

UPDATE with Common Table Expression

UPDATE can be issued through a CTE to UPDATE the underlying table, Product in this case. Prices are increased 5% for products with over $1,000.00 list price.

```
SELECT TOP 5 * FROM Product  WHERE ListPrice > 1000.0 ORDER BY ProductID DESC;
GO
```

ProductID	ProductName	Cost	ListPrice	Color	ModifiedDate
976	Road-350-W Yellow, 48	1082.51	1700.99	Yellow	2008-04-11
975	Road-350-W Yellow, 44	1082.51	1700.99	Yellow	2008-04-11
974	Road-350-W Yellow, 42	1082.51	1700.99	Yellow	2008-04-11
973	Road-350-W Yellow, 40	1082.51	1700.99	Yellow	2008-04-11
972	Touring-2000 Blue, 54	755.1508	1214.85	Blue	2008-03-11

```
;WITH CTE
   AS (SELECT Price = ListPrice
      FROM   Product
      WHERE  ListPrice > 1000.0)
UPDATE CTE
SET   Price = Price * 1.05
GO
-- (86 row(s) affected)
```

```
SELECT TOP 5 * FROM Product  WHERE ListPrice > 1000.0 ORDER BY ProductID DESC;
```

ProductID	ProductName	Cost	ListPrice	Color	ModifiedDate
976	Road-350-W Yellow, 48	1082.51	1786.0395	Yellow	2008-04-11
975	Road-350-W Yellow, 44	1082.51	1786.0395	Yellow	2008-04-11
974	Road-350-W Yellow, 42	1082.51	1786.0395	Yellow	2008-04-11
973	Road-350-W Yellow, 40	1082.51	1786.0395	Yellow	2008-04-11
972	Touring-2000 Blue, 54	755.1508	1275.5925	Blue	2008-03-11

Similar data modification with ANSI SQL UPDATE.

```
UPDATE Product
SET   ListPrice = (SELECT p8.ListPrice * 1.05
         FROM  AdventureWorks2012.Production.Product p8   WHERE  Product.ProductID =
p8.ProductID)
WHERE  EXISTS (SELECT * FROM  AdventureWorks2012.Production.Product p8
      WHERE  Product.ProductID = p8.ProductID   AND Product.ListPrice > 1000.0);
```

Four Methods of UPDATE with GROUP BY Query

UPDATE can be done a few ways with GROUP BY aggregates.

```
USE tempdb;
SELECT Color=ISNULL(Color,'N/A'), ItemCount=0 INTO ProductColor
FROM AdventureWorks2008.Production.Product
GROUP BY Color
GO
-- (10 row(s) affected)
```

```
SELECT * FROM ProductColor
GO
```

Color	ItemCount
N/A	0
Black	0
Blue	0
Grey	0
Multi	0
Red	0
Silver	0
Silver/Black	0
White	0
Yellow	0

ANSI UPDATE

```
UPDATE ProductColor
SET ItemCount = (SELECT ProductColorCount FROM  (SELECT Color=ISNULL(Color, 'N/A'),
            ProductColorCount=COUNT(*)
             FROM AdventureWorks2008.Production.Product
             GROUP BY Color) cg WHERE  ProductColor.Color = cg.Color)
GO -- (10 row(s) affected)
```

FROM Clause UPDATE with Derived Table

```
UPDATE pc   SET pc.ItemCount = cg.ProductColorCount
FROM ProductColor pc
INNER JOIN (SELECT Color=ISNULL(Color, 'N/A'), ProductColorCount=COUNT(*)
     FROM AdventureWorks2008.Production.Product GROUP BY Color) cg
ON pc.Color = cg.Color;
-- (10 row(s) affected)
```

FROM Clause UPDATE with CTE

```
;WITH CTE AS (SELECT Color=ISNULL(Color, 'N/A'), ProductColorCount=COUNT(*)
       FROM AdventureWorks2008.Production.Product
       GROUP BY Color)
UPDATE pc
SET pc.ItemCount = CTE.ProductColorCount
FROM ProductColor pc
INNER JOIN CTE
ON pc.Color = CTE.Color;
GO
-- (10 row(s) affected)
```

CTE UPDATE

```
;WITH CTE AS (SELECT * FROM ProductColor pc
       INNER JOIN (SELECT ColorPrd=ISNULL(Color, 'N/A'), ProductColorCount=COUNT(*)
       FROM AdventureWorks2008.Production.Product
       GROUP BY Color) cg
                     ON pc.Color = cg.ColorPrd)
UPDATE CTE SET CTE.ItemCount = CTE.ProductColorCount;
GO
-- (10 row(s) affected)
```

```
SELECT * FROM ProductColor;
GO
```

Color	ItemCount
N/A	248
Black	93
Blue	26
Grey	1
Multi	8
Red	38
Silver	43
Silver/Black	7
White	4
Yellow	36

```
DROP TABLE tempdb.dbo.ProductColor;
```

CHAPTER 11: Modify Data - INSERT, UPDATE, DELETE & MERGE

MERGE for Combination INSERT, UPDATE or DELETE

The MERGE statement can be used to INSERT, UPDATE and/or DELETE all in one statement.

```
USE tempdb;
go


-- Setup 2 test tables
SELECT TOP (5000) ResellerKey,
        OrderDateKey,
        ProductKey,
        OrderQuantity,
        SalesAmount
INTO   FactResellerSales
FROM   AdventureWorksDW2012.dbo.FactResellerSales
ORDER BY OrderDateKey ;
go
-- (5000 row(s) affected)


SELECT TOP (8000) ResellerKey,
        OrderDateKey,
        ProductKey,
        OrderQuantity,
        SalesAmount
INTO   ResellerSalesTransaction
FROM   AdventureWorksDW2012.dbo.FactResellerSales ;
go
-- (8000 row(s) affected)


DELETE rsc
FROM   ResellerSalesTransaction rsc
    JOIN (SELECT TOP 1000 *
       FROM   ResellerSalesTransaction
       ORDER  BY ResellerKey DESC) x
    ON x.ResellerKey = rsc.ResellerKey ;
go
-- (1010 row(s) affected)


UPDATE TOP (6000) ResellerSalesTransaction
SET   SalesAmount = SalesAmount * 1.1 ;
go
-- (6000 row(s) affected)
```

CHAPTER 11: Modify Data - INSERT, UPDATE, DELETE & MERGE

MERGE is a very powerful statement

```
SELECT TOP (10) *
FROM   FactResellerSales
ORDER  BY ResellerKey,          OrderDateKey,          ProductKey ;
go
```

ResellerKey	OrderDateKey	ProductKey	OrderQuantity	SalesAmount
1	20050801	270	1	183.9382
1	20050801	275	1	356.898
1	20050801	285	1	178.5808
1	20050801	314	2	4293.924
1	20050801	317	1	874.794
1	20050801	319	2	1749.588
1	20050801	324	2	838.9178
1	20050801	326	1	419.4589
1	20050801	328	1	419.4589
1	20050801	332	2	838.9178

```
SELECT BeforeFactCount=COUNT(*)
FROM   FactResellerSales ;
-- 5000
```

```
-- Ready for the MERGE (update if exists,  insert otherwise)
MERGE FactResellerSales AS fact
USING (SELECT *
    FROM   ResellerSalesTransaction) AS feed
ON ( fact.ProductKey = feed.ProductKey
   AND fact.ResellerKey = feed.ResellerKey
   AND fact.OrderDateKey = feed.OrderDateKey )
WHEN MATCHED THEN
 UPDATE SET fact.OrderQuantity += feed.OrderQuantity,
       fact.SalesAmount += feed.SalesAmount
WHEN NOT MATCHED THEN
 INSERT (ResellerKey,
     OrderDateKey,
     ProductKey,
     OrderQuantity,
     SalesAmount)
 VALUES (feed.ResellerKey,
     feed.OrderDateKey,
     feed.ProductKey,
     feed.OrderQuantity,
     feed.SalesAmount);
go   -- (6990 row(s) affected)
```

CHAPTER 11: Modify Data - INSERT, UPDATE, DELETE & MERGE

Checking results after MERGE

```
SELECT TOP (10) *
FROM  FactResellerSales ORDER  BY        ResellerKey,   OrderDateKey,   ProductKey;
```

ResellerKey	OrderDateKey	ProductKey	OrderQuantity	SalesAmount
1	20050801	270	2	386.2702
1	20050801	275	2	749.4858
1	20050801	285	2	375.0197
1	20050801	314	4	9017.2404
1	20050801	317	2	1837.0674
1	20050801	319	4	3674.1348
1	20050801	324	4	1761.7274
1	20050801	326	2	880.8637
1	20050801	328	2	880.8637
1	20050801	332	4	1761.7274

```
SELECT AfterFactCount=COUNT(*)  FROM  FactResellerSales ;
go
-- 7658

DROP TABLE ResellerSalesTransaction;  DROP TABLE FactResellerSales;
go
```

CHAPTER 11: Modify Data - INSERT, UPDATE, DELETE & MERGE

Using MERGE Instead of UPDATE

MERGE statement can be used in the UPDATE only mode to replace UPDATE.

```
-- Prepare 2 test tables
USE tempdb;
SELECT TOP (5000) ResellerKey, OrderDateKey, ProductKey, OrderQuantity, SalesAmount
INTO  FactResellerSales FROM  AdventureWorksDW2012.dbo.FactResellerSales;
GO -- (5000 row(s) affected)
SELECT TOP (8000) ResellerKey, OrderDateKey, ProductKey, OrderQuantity, SalesAmount
INTO  ResellerSalesTransaction FROM  AdventureWorksDW2012.dbo.FactResellerSales;
GO -- (8000 row(s) affected)
```

```
-- Alter the test data
DELETE rsc
FROM  ResellerSalesTransaction rsc
    INNER JOIN (SELECT TOP 1000 * FROM  ResellerSalesTransaction
       ORDER BY ResellerKey DESC) x  -- subquery inner join
    ON x.ResellerKey = rsc.ResellerKey;
GO --(1010 row(s) affected)
UPDATE TOP (6000) ResellerSalesTransaction SET SalesAmount = SalesAmount * 1.1;
GO -- (6000 row(s) affected)
```

```
SELECT BeforeFactCount=COUNT(*) FROM  FactResellerSales;
GO -- 5000
```

```
-- Ready for the MERGE UPDATE only mode
MERGE FactResellerSales AS fact
USING (SELECT * FROM  ResellerSalesTransaction) AS feed
ON ( fact.ProductKey = feed.ProductKey
   AND fact.ResellerKey = feed.ResellerKey
   AND fact.OrderDateKey = feed.OrderDateKey )
WHEN MATCHED THEN
  UPDATE SET fact.OrderQuantity = fact.OrderQuantity + feed.OrderQuantity,
       fact.SalesAmount = fact.SalesAmount + feed.SalesAmount;
GO -- 4332 row(s) affected)
```

```
SELECT AfterFactCount=COUNT(*) FROM  FactResellerSales;
GO -- 5000
```

```
DROP TABLE ResellerSalesTransaction;  DROP TABLE FactResellerSales;
```

CHAPTER 12: The Magic of Transact-SQL Programming

IF...ELSE Conditional

IF... ELSE is a step toward a bona fide programming language.

```
DECLARE @StringNumber varchar(32) ;
SET @StringNumber = '12,000,000';
IF EXISTS( SELECT * WHERE ISNUMERIC(@StringNumber) = 1)
        PRINT 'VALID NUMBER: ' + @StringNumber
ELSE    PRINT 'INVALID NUMBER: ' + @StringNumber;
GO
-- VALID NUMBER: 12,000,000
```

```
DECLARE @StringNumber varchar(32) = '12,000:000';

IF EXISTS( SELECT * WHERE ISNUMERIC(@StringNumber) = 1)
        PRINT CONCAT('VALID NUMBER: ' , @StringNumber)
ELSE    PRINT CONCAT('INVALID NUMBER: ', @StringNumber);
GO
-- INVALID NUMBER: 12,000:000
```

```
DECLARE @StringDate varchar(32);

SET @StringDate = '2017-03-15 18:50';

IF EXISTS( SELECT * WHERE ISDATE(@StringDate) = 1)
        PRINT 'VALID DATE: ' + @StringDate
ELSE    PRINT 'INVALID DATE: ' + @StringDate;
GO
-- Result: VALID DATE: 2017-03-15 18:50
```

```
DECLARE @StringDate varchar(32) = '20116-03-15 18:50';
IF EXISTS( SELECT * WHERE ISDATE(@StringDate) = 1)
        PRINT CONCAT('VALID DATE: ', @StringDate)
ELSE    PRINT CONCAT('INVALID DATE: ', @StringDate);
-- Result: INVALID DATE: 20116-03-15 18:50
```

WHILE Looping - UPDATE in Batches

WHILE looping can be used to break down large transaction to small batches. Executing in small batches is safer and does not block other OLTP transactions for a long time. Blocking can be seen by running sp_who system stored procedure

```
EXEC sp_who;
```

UPDATE of 121,317 rows is batched to 13 batches of 10,000 or less.

```
USE tempdb;
SELECT * INTO SOD
FROM AdventureWorks2012.Sales.SalesOrderDetail ORDER BY SalesOrderDetailID;
GO
--(121317 row(s) affected)
```

```
WHILE (2 > 1)   -- Infinite loop until BREAK is issued
  BEGIN
   UPDATE TOP ( 10000 ) SOD
   SET   UnitPriceDiscount = 0.08,  ModifiedDate = CONVERT(DATE, getdate())
   WHERE  ModifiedDate < CONVERT(DATE, getdate());

   IF @@ROWCOUNT = 0
    BEGIN
     BREAK;
    END
   -- 1 second delay - Very important for other OLTP transactions execution
   WAITFOR DELAY '00:00:01'
 END; -- WHILE
GO
```

(10000 row(s) affected)
(10000 row(s) affected)
(10000 row(s) affected)
(10000 row(s) affected)
(10000 row(s) affected)
(10000 row(s) affected)
(10000 row(s) affected)
(10000 row(s) affected)
(10000 row(s) affected)
(10000 row(s) affected)
(10000 row(s) affected)
(10000 row(s) affected)
(1317 row(s) affected)
(0 row(s) affected)

```
DROP TABLE tempdb.dbo.SOD
```

WHILE Loop Usage in Cursors

Transact-SQL logic will visit all databases on the current SQL Server instance using a cursor. NOTE: **cursor solutions do not scale well, first choice is set-based logic if appropriate.**

```
DECLARE @CurrentDB sysname;
DECLARE AllDBCursor CURSOR  STATIC LOCAL FOR
        SELECT  name FROM    MASTER.dbo.sysdatabases
        WHERE   name NOT IN ('master','tempdb','model','msdb') ORDER BY name;
OPEN AllDBCursor;
FETCH  AllDBCursor INTO @CurrentDB;
WHILE (@@FETCH_STATUS = 0) -- loop through all db-s
  BEGIN
/***** PROCESSING (like BACKUP database)  *****/
        PRINT @CurrentDB;
        FETCH  AllDBCursor   INTO @CurrentDB;
  END; -- while
CLOSE AllDBCursor; DEALLOCATE AllDBCursor;
```

```
/*.... AdventureWorks
AdventureWorks2008
AdventureWorks2012
AdventureWorksDW2012 .... */
```

Transact-SQL script demonstrates a subcategory cursor.

```
USE AdventureWorks2012;
DECLARE curSubcategory CURSOR STATIC LOCAL  FOR          -- declare cursor
        SELECT ProductSubcategoryID, Subcategory=Name
        FROM Production.ProductSubcategory ORDER BY Subcategory;
DECLARE @Subcategory varchar(40), @PSID int
OPEN curSubcategory
FETCH NEXT FROM curSubcategory INTO @PSID, @Subcategory  -- fetch cursor
WHILE (@@fetch_status = 0)              -- cursor fetch_status
BEGIN -- begin cursor loop
/***** USER DEFINED PROCESSING CODE HERE  *****/
        DECLARE @Msg varchar(128);
  SELECT @Msg = CONCAT('ProductSubcategory info: ', @Subcategory,' ',CONVERT(varchar, @PSID));
        PRINT @Msg;
FETCH NEXT FROM curSubcategory INTO @PSID, @Subcategory;  -- fetch cursor
END; -- end cursor loop
CLOSE curSubcategory;   DEALLOCATE curSubcategory;
```

```
/* ... ProductSubcategory info: Bike Stands 27
ProductSubcategory info: Bottles and Cages 28
ProductSubcategory info: Bottom Brackets 5   ... */
```

CHAPTER 12: The Magic of Transact-SQL Programming

T-SQL Transaction

Transact-SQL language has been extended with features beyond ANSI SQL such as variables, IF... ELSE and WHILE. **"Transact" refers to the capability to execute business transactions which require the synchronized update of tables as one or none at all.**

DELETE from 2 Tables with TRANSACTION Control

DELETE PRIMARY KEY rows from PK table and related FOREIGN KEY rows from FK table in a single transaction. NOTE: Deleting lots of rows may interfere with online access in an ecommerce database.

Alternate method: define tables with CASCADE ON DELETE action.

```
BEGIN TRANSACTION
```

```
-- First delete from FOREIGN KEY table
DELETE OmegaFK
FROM Omega AS OmegaFK
  INNER JOIN Delta AS DeltaPK
    ON DeltaPK.ColApk = OmegaFK.ColBfk
WHERE DeltaPK.ColApk = {single value A} ;
```

```
IF @@ERROR <> 0
BEGIN
        ROLLBACK TRANSACTION;
        RAISERROR('FK delete failed.', 10, 1);
END
-- if no error, delete from PRIMARY KEY table
ELSE
        DELETE
        FROM Delta
        WHERE ColApk = = {single value A};
```

```
-- Commit transaction only if both DELETE-s succeeded
IF @@ERROR <> 0
BEGIN
        ROLLBACK TRANSACTION;
        RAISERROR('PK delete failed.', 10, 1);
ELSE
        COMMIT TRANSACTION;
```

Stored Procedure with Input & Output Parameters

A stored procedure usually returns a table-like result set from the SELECT(s) in the stored procedure. Scalar value can also be returned with the OUTPUT option.

```
USE AdventureWorks2012;
GO
CREATE PROCEDURE uspQuarterSales     @StartYear INT,     @TotalSales MONEY OUTPUT
AS
 BEGIN -- sproc definition
  SET NOCOUNT ON -- turn off rows affected messages
  SELECT @TotalSales = SUM(SubTotal)
  FROM Sales.SalesOrderHeader   WHERE OrderDate >= DATEADD(YY,@StartYear-1900,'19000101')

  SELECT  YEAR = YEAR(OrderDate),
      COALESCE(FORMAT(SUM(CASE
          WHEN DATEPART(QQ,OrderDate) = 1 THEN SubTotal
                END),'c','en-US'),'') AS 'Q1',
      COALESCE(FORMAT(SUM(CASE
          WHEN DATEPART(QQ,OrderDate) = 2 THEN SubTotal
                END),'c','en-US'),'') AS 'Q2',
      COALESCE(FORMAT(SUM(CASE
          WHEN DATEPART(QQ,OrderDate) = 3 THEN SubTotal
                END),'c','en-US'),'') AS 'Q3',
      COALESCE(FORMAT(SUM(CASE
          WHEN DATEPART(QQ,OrderDate) = 4 THEN SubTotal
                END),'c','en-US'),'') AS 'Q4'
  FROM    Sales.SalesOrderHeader soh
  WHERE   OrderDate >= DATEADD(YY,@StartYear-1900,'19000101')
   GROUP BY YEAR(OrderDate)    ORDER BY YEAR(OrderDate);
 END; -- sproc definition
GO
```

```
-- Execute stored procedure with INPUT/OUTPUT parameters
DECLARE @TotSales money
EXEC uspQuarterSales 2007, @TotSales OUTPUT;
SELECT TotalSales = @TotSales;
```

YEAR	Q1	Q2	Q3	Q4
2007	$6,679,873.80	$8,357,874.88	$13,681,907.05	$13,291,381.43
2008	$11,398,376.28	$14,379,545.19	$50,840.63	

TotalSales
67839799.2669

Dynamic SQL Stored Procedure to REBUILD Indexes

The following dynamic SQL stored procedure uses database metadata to loop through all tables in the database, assemble and execute the index REBUILD command.

```
USE AdventureWorks2012;
GO

CREATE PROC sprocAllTablesIndexREBUILD @FILLFACTOR INT = 90
AS
 BEGIN
   DECLARE @DatabaseName SYSNAME = DB_NAME(),
       @TableName   VARCHAR(256);
   DECLARE @DynamicSQL NVARCHAR(max) = CONCAT('DECLARE cursorForAllTables CURSOR FOR
            SELECT CONCAT(TABLE_SCHEMA,''.'', TABLE_NAME) AS TABLENAME    FROM ',
@DatabaseName,
       '.INFORMATION_SCHEMA.TABLES WHERE   TABLE_TYPE = ''BASE TABLE''');
   BEGIN
     EXEC sp_executeSQL
      @DynamicSQL; -- create tables cursor
     OPEN cursorForAllTables;

     FETCH NEXT FROM cursorForAllTables INTO @TableName;
     WHILE ( @@FETCH_STATUS = 0 )
      BEGIN
        SET @DynamicSQL = CONCAT('ALTER INDEX ALL ON ', @TableName,
             ' REBUILD WITH ( FILLFACTOR = ',
                  CONVERT(VARCHAR, @FILLFACTOR), ')'  );
        PRINT @DynamicSQL;  -- test & debug
        EXEC sp_executeSQL
         @DynamicSQL;
        FETCH NEXT FROM cursorForAllTables INTO @TableName;
      END; -- cursor WHILE
     CLOSE cursorForAllTables;   DEALLOCATE cursorForAllTables;
   END;
 END; -- sproc
GO
-- Command(s) completed successfully.


-- Reindex tables with 85% fill factor leaving 15% free space for growth
EXEC sprocAllTablesIndexREBUILD 85;
/*
ALTER INDEX ALL ON Production.ScrapReason REBUILD WITH ( FILLFACTOR = 85)
ALTER INDEX ALL ON HumanResources.Shift REBUILD WITH ( FILLFACTOR = 85)
 ....  */
```

User-Defined Functions

Table-Valued Functions

A table-valued function returns a table variable, therefore, it has to be invoked like it were a table in a query. T-SQL table-valued function creates a table from a delimited string of values.

```
CREATE FUNCTION dbo.ufnSplitDelimitedString ( @StringList VARCHAR(MAX),    @Delimiter CHAR(1))
RETURNS @TableList TABLE(ID int identity(1,1), StringLiteral VARCHAR(128))
BEGIN
   IF @StringList = '' RETURN;
   IF @Delimiter = ''
   BEGIN
     WITH Split AS                             -- Recursive CTE
       ( SELECT CharOne=LEFT(@StringList,1),R=RIGHT(@StringList,len(@StringList)-1)
         UNION ALL
         SELECT LEFT(R,1), R=RIGHT(R, len(R)-1)
         FROM Split    WHERE LEN(R)>0  )          -- End of CTE
     INSERT @TableList
     SELECT CharOne FROM Split    OPTION ( MAXRECURSION 0);
     RETURN;
   END; -- IF
   DECLARE @XML xml=CONCAT('<root><csv>',replace(@StringList,@Delimiter,'</csv><csv>'),
                            '</csv></root>');
   INSERT @TableList
   SELECT rtrim(ltrim(replace(Word.value('.','nvarchar(128)'),char(10),'')))    AS ListMember
     FROM @XML.nodes('/root/csv') AS WordList(Word);
RETURN;
END; -- FUNCTION
GO
```

```
SELECT * FROM dbo.ufnSplitDelimitedString ('New York, California, Arizona, Texas, Toronto, Grand
Canyon, Yosemite,  Yellowstone, Niagara Falls, Belgium, Denmark, South Africa, Sweden', ',');
```

ID	StringLiteral
1	New York
2	California
3	Arizona
4	Texas
5	Toronto
6	Grand Canyon
7	Yosemite
8	Yellowstone
9	Niagara Falls
10	Belgium
11	Denmark
12	South Africa
13	Sweden

Table-Valued Function for PRIME Numbers Generation

Transact-SQL table-valued function generates prime numbers up to the input parameter limit.

```
USE AdventureWorks2012;
GO

CREATE FUNCTION ufnPrimeNumbers ( @Stop INT)
RETURNS @Result TABLE  (Prime INT)
BEGIN
WITH CTE ( SeqNo)
  AS (SELECT 0
       UNION ALL
       SELECT SeqNo + 1
       FROM   CTE
       WHERE  SeqNo < @Stop)
INSERT @Result
SELECT PrimeNo = N2.SeqNo
FROM   CTE N1
    INNER JOIN CTE N2
  ON  N2.SeqNo % N1.SeqNo > 0
    AND N2.SeqNo % 2 > 0
    AND N1.SeqNo < N2.SeqNo
    AND N2.SeqNo > 1
    AND N1.SeqNo >= 1
GROUP  BY N2.SeqNo
HAVING ( N2.SeqNo - COUNT(*) ) = 2
OPTION ( MAXRECURSION 0);
RETURN ;
END;
GO
```

```
SELECT * FROM dbo.ufnPrimeNumbers (1000);
GO
-- (167 row(s) affected) - Partial results.
```

Prime
3
5
7
11
13
17
19
23
29
31

Inline Functions

An inline user-defined function, returns table, can be used as a parameterized view.

```
USE AdventureWorks2012
GO


CREATE FUNCTION Sales.ufnStaffSalesByFiscalYear (@OrderYear INT)
RETURNS TABLE  AS
RETURN
SELECT
     CONVERT(date, soh.OrderDate)                                              AS OrderDate
    ,CONCAT(p.FirstName, ' ', COALESCE(p.MiddleName, ''), ' ', p.LastName)    AS FullName
    ,e.JobTitle
    ,st.Name                                                                  AS SalesTerritory
    ,FORMAT(soh.SubTotal, 'c', 'en-US')                                       AS SalesAmount
    ,YEAR(DATEADD(mm, 6, soh.OrderDate))                                      AS FiscalYear
FROM Sales.SalesPerson sp
    INNER JOIN Sales.SalesOrderHeader soh
        ON sp.BusinessEntityID = soh.SalesPersonID
    INNER JOIN Sales.SalesTerritory st
        ON sp.TerritoryID = st.TerritoryID
    INNER JOIN HumanResources.Employee e
        ON soh.SalesPersonID = e.BusinessEntityID
    INNER JOIN Person.Person p
        ON p.BusinessEntityID = sp.BusinessEntityID
WHERE           soh.OrderDate >= datefromparts(@OrderYear, 1, 1)
         AND soh.OrderDate < dateadd(yy,1, datefromparts(@OrderYear, 1, 1));
GO
-- Command(s) completed successfully.


SELECT * FROM Sales.ufnStaffSalesByFiscalYear (2007)
ORDER BY FullName, CONVERT(money, SalesAmount) DESC;   --   SalesAmount (string) does not sort
correctly
--( 1476  row(s) affected)  -- Partial results.
```

OrderDate	FullName	JobTitle	SalesTerritory	SalesAmount	FiscalYear
2007-08-01	David R Campbell	Sales Representative	Northwest	$101,609.29	2008
2007-07-01	David R Campbell	Sales Representative	Northwest	$93,397.64	2008
2007-04-01	David R Campbell	Sales Representative	Northwest	$75,104.65	2007
2007-07-01	David R Campbell	Sales Representative	Northwest	$74,149.95	2008
2007-04-01	David R Campbell	Sales Representative	Northwest	$73,963.26	2007
2007-08-01	David R Campbell	Sales Representative	Northwest	$71,283.24	2008
2007-09-01	David R Campbell	Sales Representative	Northwest	$66,871.84	2008
2007-01-01	David R Campbell	Sales Representative	Northwest	$63,864.71	2007
2007-11-01	David R Campbell	Sales Representative	Northwest	$63,339.26	2008
2007-10-01	David R Campbell	Sales Representative	Northwest	$60,519.95	2008

Scalar Functions

A scalar user-defined function returns a scalar value. It can be used in a query wherever a single value is required.

```
USE AdventureWorks2012;
GO
CREATE FUNCTION dbo.ufnNumberToEnglish (@Number INT)
RETURNS VARCHAR(1024)  AS
 BEGIN
   DECLARE @Below20 TABLE    ( ID  INT IDENTITY ( 0, 1 ),   Word VARCHAR(32) );
   DECLARE @Tens TABLE  ( ID   INT IDENTITY ( 2, 1 ),    Word VARCHAR(32) );
   INSERT @Below20 (Word)
   VALUES('Zero'), ('One'),('Two'), ('Three'), ('Four'), ('Five'), ('Six'), ('Seven'), ('Eight'),
       ('Nine'), ('Ten'), ('Eleven'), ('Twelve'), ('Thirteen'), ('Fourteen'), ('Fifteen'),
       ('Sixteen'), ('Seventeen'), ('Eighteen'), ('Nineteen');
   INSERT @Tens
   VALUES('Twenty'),   ('Thirty'),  ('Forty'),  ('Fifty'),  ('Sixty'),  ('Seventy'),  ('Eighty'), ('Ninety');
   DECLARE @English VARCHAR(1024) = (SELECT CASE
         WHEN @Number = 0 THEN ''
         WHEN @Number BETWEEN 1 AND 19
               THEN (SELECT Word FROM   @Below20 WHERE  ID = @Number)
         WHEN @Number BETWEEN 20 AND 99 THEN
     CONCAT((SELECT Word FROM   @Tens
WHERE  ID = @Number / 10), '-', dbo.ufnNumberToEnglish(@Number%10))
      WHEN @Number BETWEEN 100 AND 999 THEN CONCAT((
         dbo.ufnNumberToEnglish(@Number / 100) ), ' Hundred ',
dbo.ufnNumberToEnglish(@Number%100))
      WHEN @Number BETWEEN 1000 AND 999999 THEN CONCAT((
         dbo.ufnNumberToEnglish(@Number / 1000) ), ' Thousand ',
dbo.ufnNumberToEnglish(@Number%1000))
     WHEN @Number BETWEEN 1000000 AND 999999999 THEN CONCAT((
         dbo.ufnNumberToEnglish(@Number / 1000000) ), ' Million ',
dbo.ufnNumberToEnglish(@Number%1000000))
      ELSE ' INVALID INPUT'  END);
    SELECT @English = RTRIM(@English);
    SELECT @English = RTRIM(LEFT(@English, len(@English) - 1))   WHERE  RIGHT(@English, 1) = '-';
    RETURN ( @English );                         END;
GO -- Command(s) completed successfully.

SELECT dbo.ufnNumberToEnglish (9999);   -- Nine Thousand Nine Hundred Ninety-Nine

SELECT dbo.ufnNumberToEnglish (1000001); -- One Million One

SELECT dbo.ufnNumberToEnglish (7777777);
-- Seven Million Seven Hundred Seventy-Seven Thousand Seven Hundred Seventy-Seven
```

CHAPTER 12: The Magic of Transact-SQL Programming

Dynamic PIVOT Script

Static PIVOT has pretty limited role since it has to be changed when data changes effects the PIVOT range. Dynamic SQL makes PIVOT data driven. Instead of hard-wired columns, dynamic PIVOT builds the columns from the data dynamically.

```
USE AdventureWorks;
GO


DECLARE @OrderYear AS TABLE
 (
   YYYY INT NOT NULL PRIMARY KEY
 ) ;
DECLARE @DynamicSQL AS NVARCHAR(4000) ;

INSERT INTO @OrderYear
SELECT DISTINCT YEAR(OrderDate)
FROM   Sales.SalesOrderHeader;

DECLARE @ReportColumnNames AS NVARCHAR(MAX),  @IterationYear   AS INT;

SET @IterationYear = (SELECT MIN(YYYY)     FROM   @OrderYear);
SET @ReportColumnNames = N'';

-- Assemble pivot list dynamically
WHILE ( @IterationYear IS NOT NULL )
 BEGIN
   SET @ReportColumnNames = @ReportColumnNames + N','
             + QUOTENAME(CAST(@IterationYear AS NVARCHAR(10)));
   SET @IterationYear = (SELECT MIN(YYYY)
            FROM   @OrderYear
            WHERE  YYYY > @IterationYear);
 END;

SET @ReportColumnNames = SUBSTRING(@ReportColumnNames, 2,
          LEN(@ReportColumnNames));

PRINT @ReportColumnNames; -- [2001],[2002],[2003],[2004]

SET @DynamicSQL = CONCAT(N'SELECT * FROM (SELECT [Store (Freight Summary)]=s.Name,
       YEAR(OrderDate) AS OrderYear,  Freight = convert(money, convert(varchar, Freight))
       FROM Sales.SalesOrderHeader soh
       INNER JOIN Sales.Store s
       ON soh.CustomerID = s.CustomerID) as Header
       PIVOT (SUM(Freight)   FOR OrderYear IN(', @ReportColumnNames,N')) AS Pvt ORDER BY 1;');
-- T-SQL script continued
```

```
PRINT @DynamicSQL; -- Testing & debugging
/* SELECT * FROM (SELECT [Store (Freight Summary)]=s.Name,
      YEAR(OrderDate) AS OrderYear,  Freight = convert(money, convert(varchar, Freight))
      FROM Sales.SalesOrderHeader soh
      INNER JOIN Sales.Store s    ON soh.CustomerID = s.CustomerID) as Header
      PIVOT (SUM(Freight)    FOR OrderYear IN([2001],[2002],[2003],[2004]))  AS Pvt ORDER BY 1;*/

-- Execute dynamic sql
EXEC sp_executesql  @DynamicSQL;
GO  -- (633 row(s) affected) - Partial results.
```

Store (Freight Summary)	2001	2002	2003	2004
A Bike Store	921.55	1637.24	NULL	NULL
A Great Bicycle Company	142.08	114.34	15.24	NULL
A Typical Bike Shop	976.61	1529.08	NULL	NULL
Acceptable Sales & Service	12.58	25.17	NULL	NULL

INSERT, UPDATE & DELETE through a View

Underlying table can be modified through a view, thus adding flexibility to security access since a view can be permissioned independently of the table.

```
USE tempdb;
SELECT CONVERT(INT, ProductID) AS ID, Name AS ProductName, ListPrice, ModifiedDate INTO
Product
FROM AdventureWorks2012.Production.Product;
GO -- (504 row(s) affected)
CREATE VIEW vProduct AS SELECT * FROM Product;
GO
UPDATE vProduct SET ModifiedDate = '2018-01-01';
GO -- (504 row(s) affected)
INSERT vProduct VALUES (2000, 'Three-Wheeler Bike', $999.99, getdate());
GO -- (1 row(s) affected)
DELETE TOP (10) FROM vProduct;
GO -- (1 row(s) affected)
SELECT TOP (1) * FROM Product;  -- 322 Chainring      0.00    2018-01-01 00:00:00.000
GO
DROP VIEW dbo.vProduct;
DROP TABLE tempdb.dbo.Product;
GO
```

Sensitive Data Audit Trigger

Triggers can be used to track sensitive data changes into an audit table. The OUTPUT clause is an alternative, but not exactly equivalent.

```
USE Payroll;
GO

CREATE TRIGGER uTrgEmployeeUpdate
ON Employee
AFTER UPDATE
AS
  IF ( Update(Salary)
     OR Update(SSN) )
   BEGIN
     INSERT INTO CorpSecurityEmployeeAudit
            (auditlogtype,
             auditEmployeeDeptID,
             auditEmployeeID,
             auditEmployeeSalary,
             auditEmployeeSSN,
             auditUpdatedBy)
     SELECT 'PREVIOUSDATA',
         DeptID,
         EmployeeID,
         Salary,
         SSN,
         User_name()
     FROM   DELETED

     INSERT INTO CorpSecurityEmployeeAudit
            (auditlogtype,
             auditEmployeeDeptID,
             auditEmployeeID,
             auditEmployeeSalary,
             auditEmployeeSSN,
             auditUpdatedBy)
     SELECT 'NEWDATA',
         DeptID,
         EmployeeID,
         Salary,
         SSN,
         User_name()
     FROM   INSERTED
   END;
GO
```

Automatic Timestamp Trigger

Whenever the Person.Contact is updated, the ModifiedDate will be updated to current time by the update after trigger. NOTE: disable/drop other update triggers on this table, if any, for the test.

```
USE AdventureWorks;
GO

CREATE TRIGGER uTrgContactTimestamp
ON Person.Contact
FOR UPDATE
AS
 BEGIN
 IF TRIGGER_NESTLEVEL() > 1      RETURN;
  UPDATE Person.Contact  SET    Person.Contact.ModifiedDate = CURRENT_TIMESTAMP
  FROM   Person.Contact c
      INNER JOIN INSERTED i
        ON c.ContactID = i.ContactID
 END
GO
-- (1 row(s) affected)

SELECT *
FROM   Person.Contact
WHERE  FirstName = 'Kim'   AND MiddleName = 'B'      AND LastName = 'Abercrombie'
GO
-- ModifiedDate: 2000-02-10 00:00:00.000

-- Updating a column will automatically update the ModifiedDate
UPDATE Person.Contact          SET   Phone = '299 484-3924'
WHERE  FirstName = 'Kim'   AND MiddleName = 'B'      AND LastName = 'Abercrombie'
GO

SELECT *
FROM   Person.Contact WHERE  FirstName = 'Kim'   AND MiddleName = 'B'   AND LastName =
'Abercrombie'
GO
-- ModifiedDate: 2018-08-11 07:22:01.157

-- Cleanup
DROP TRIGGER Person.uTrgContactTimestamp
```

CHAPTER 12: The Magic of Transact-SQL Programming

Recursive Product Assembly

Recursive Common Table Expression (CTE) is used to assemble a bike frame based on the BillOfMaterials table.

```
USE AdventureWorks2012;

DECLARE @ProductID int = 831;
WITH CTE(AssemblyID, ComponentID, PerAssemblyQty,  AssemblyLevel) AS
(        SELECT bom0.ProductAssemblyID, bom0.ComponentID, bom0.PerAssemblyQty,
                0 AS AssemblyLevel
        FROM Production.BillOfMaterials AS bom0
        WHERE bom0.ProductAssemblyID = @ProductID
                AND bom0.EndDate is null
        UNION ALL
        SELECT bom.ProductAssemblyID, bom.ComponentID, p.PerAssemblyQty,
                AssemblyLevel + 1
        FROM Production.BillOfMaterials AS bom
                INNER JOIN CTE AS p
                        ON bom.ProductAssemblyID = p.ComponentID   AND bom.EndDate is null   )
SELECT pp.Name AS ProductName, AssemblyID, ComponentID,
        p.Name AS AssemblyName, PerAssemblyQty, AssemblyLevel
FROM CTE
        INNER JOIN Production.Product AS p
                ON CTE.ComponentID = p.ProductID
        INNER JOIN Production.Product AS pp
                ON CTE.AssemblyID = pp.ProductID
ORDER BY AssemblyLevel, AssemblyID, ComponentID;
```

ProductName	AssemblyID	ComponentID	AssemblyName	PerAssemblyQty	AssemblyLevel
ML Mountain Frame - Black, 44	831	324	Chain Stays	2.00	0
ML Mountain Frame - Black, 44	831	325	Decal 1	2.00	0
ML Mountain Frame - Black, 44	831	326	Decal 2	1.00	0
ML Mountain Frame - Black, 44	831	327	Down Tube	1.00	0
ML Mountain Frame - Black, 44	831	399	Head Tube	1.00	0
ML Mountain Frame - Black, 44	831	492	Paint - Black	8.00	0
ML Mountain Frame - Black, 44	831	532	Seat Stays	4.00	0
ML Mountain Frame - Black, 44	831	533	Seat Tube	1.00	0
ML Mountain Frame - Black, 44	831	534	Top Tube	1.00	0
ML Mountain Frame - Black, 44	831	803	ML Fork	1.00	0
Chain Stays	324	486	Metal Sheet 5	2.00	1
Down Tube	327	483	Metal Sheet 3	1.00	1
Head Tube	399	485	Metal Sheet 4	1.00	1
Seat Stays	532	484	Metal Sheet 7	4.00	1
Seat Tube	533	478	Metal Bar 2	1.00	1
Top Tube	534	482	Metal Sheet 2	1.00	1
ML Fork	803	316	Blade	1.00	1
ML Fork	803	331	Fork End	1.00	1
ML Fork	803	350	Fork Crown	1.00	1
ML Fork	803	531	Steerer	1.00	1
Blade	316	486	Metal Sheet 5	1.00	2
Fork End	331	482	Metal Sheet 2	1.00	2
Fork Crown	350	486	Metal Sheet 5	1.00	2
Steerer	531	487	Metal Sheet 6	1.00	2

Percent on Base Calculation

When deriving percent on base, we need to calculate the overall total in a single value subquery to use it as denominator in the percentile calculation.

```
USE AdventureWorks2012;


SELECT YEAR(OrderDate) AS [Year],
    FORMAT(SUM(TotalDue),'c0','en-US') AS YearTotal,
    FORMAT(SUM(TotalDue) /
        (SELECT SUM(TotalDue) FROM Sales.SalesOrderHeader),'p0') AS Percentile
FROM Sales.SalesOrderHeader
GROUP BY YEAR(OrderDate)
ORDER BY YEAR ASC;
```

Year	YearTotal	Percentage
2005	$12,693,251	10 %
2006	$34,463,848	28 %
2007	$47,171,490	38 %
2008	$28,888,198	23 %

Adding a Grand Total line with ROLLUP.

```
SELECT COALESCE(CONVERT(varchar,YEAR(OrderDate)), 'Grand Total') AS [Year],
    FORMAT(SUM(TotalDue),'c0','en-US') AS [SalesTotal],
    FORMAT(SUM(TotalDue) /
        (SELECT SUM(TotalDue) FROM Sales.SalesOrderHeader),'p0') AS Percentage
FROM Sales.SalesOrderHeader
GROUP BY YEAR(OrderDate)
        WITH ROLLUP
ORDER BY YEAR ASC;
```

Year	SalesTotal	Percentage
2005	$12,693,251	10 %
2006	$34,463,848	28 %
2007	$47,171,490	38 %
2008	$28,888,198	23 %
Grand Total	$123,216,786	100 %

CHAPTER 13: Exporting & Importing Data

Saving a T-SQL Script as .sql File

Any T-SQL script can be saved as .sql file. One easy way is saving from Management Studio Query Editor. Here is the script we will save.

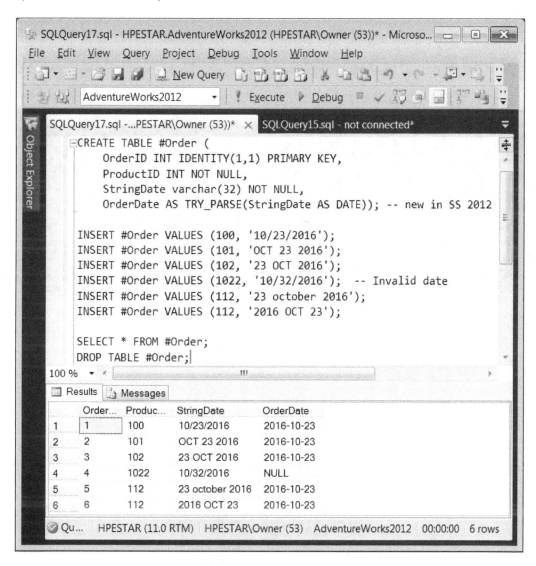

Click on File, click on Save .. As, choose a path and enter the file name for the script.

To load it back: click on File, click on Open File, locate file in Open File dialog pop-up.

Executing a .sql Script File Using SQLCMD

The SQLCMD command line utility can be used to execute a .sql script file typically with the -i (input) and -o (output) options. **Note: with any of the Command Prompt utilities the command line should not be broken with carriage return or line feed (CR/LF), it has to be one long line.**

SQLCMD -S"HPESTAR" -Uyourlogin -Psecret007 -i "f:\data\sql\tryparsedemo.sql" -o"f:\data\result\tryparsedemo.txt"

"HPESTAR" is the name of the SQL Server. With Windows authentication:

SQLCMD -S"HPESTAR" -i "f:\data\sql\tryparsedemo.sql" -o"f:\data\result\tryparsedemo.txt"

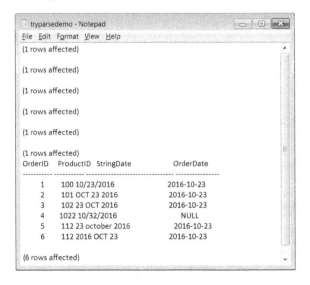

The output file collects warnings, messages, errors and results.

Making a T-SQL Script Rerunnable

It takes special attention to make a T-SQL script re-executable as many times as desired. A CREATE VIEW script can only be executed once.

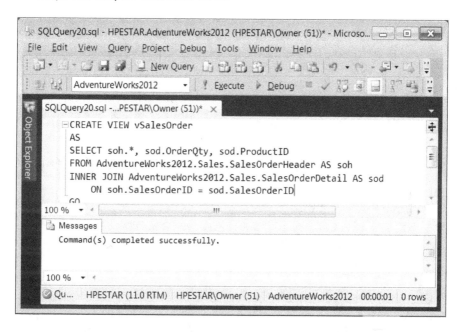

Repeat execution gives an error.

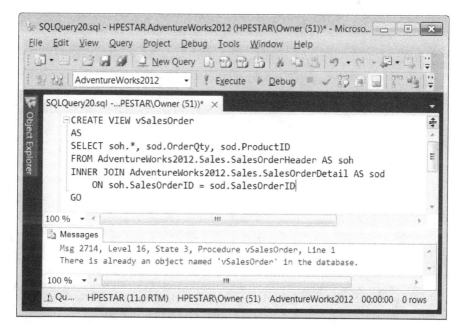

IF...ELSE Conditional Way to Make a Script Rerunnable

IF...ELSE is frequently the solution to prepare a rerunnable script. In this instance, first we check if the view exists. If it doesn't exist, we just go ahead and create it. If indeed it exists, we drop it first, then create it again.

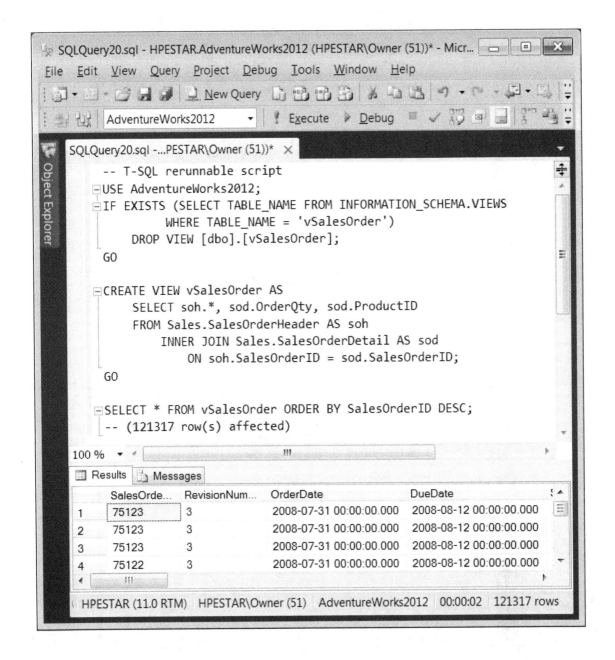

bcp Usage for Exporting & Importing Data

bcp (Bulk Copy Program) is a command line utility for moving data. The Production.Product table is exported to a flat file with bcp using Windows authentication.

For SQL Server authentication, add the "-Uyourlogin -Pyourpasswrd" parameters. **Note: the command must be one long line without breaks.**

```
Command Prompt

Microsoft Windows [Version 6.1.7601]
Copyright (c) 2009 Microsoft Corporation.   All rights reserved.

C:\Users\Owner>bcp AdventureWorks2012.Production.Product out F:\data\export\prod
uctz.txt -w -T -S"HPESTAR"

Starting copy...
SQLState = S1000, NativeError = 0
Error = [Microsoft][SQL Server Native Client 11.0]Warning: BCP import with a for
mat file will convert empty strings in delimited columns to NULL.

504 rows copied.
Network packet size (bytes): 4096
Clock Time (ms.) Total      : 125     Average : (4032.00 rows per sec.)

C:\Users\Owner>
```

The **results of a query execution** can be exported with bcp as well using the queryout option. Rule is the same, no carriage return or line feed in the command no matter how long is it. The command can be edited in SSMS Query Editor and pasted into Command Prompt with Right Mouse Click Paste. CTRL-V does not work.

```
Command Prompt

C:\Users\Owner>bcp "SELECT * from AdventureWorks2012.HumanResources.Department"
queryout F:\data\export\departmentz.txt -w -T -S"HPESTAR"

Starting copy...

16 rows copied.
Network packet size (bytes): 4096
Clock Time (ms.) Total      : 453     Average : (35.32 rows per sec.)

C:\Users\Owner>
```

Importing Data with the bcp Utility

Importing is very similar to exporting. For better control though it is necessary to use a format file. First we create an empty table for the data.

```
use tempdb;
select  TOP 0 * into product1 from AdventureWorks2012.Production.Product;
go
```

We are ready to execute the bcp import command.

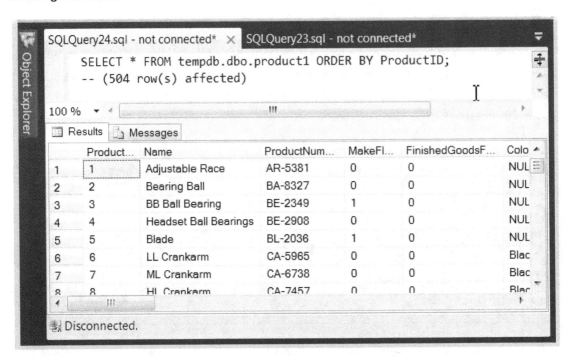

Checking the results.

CHAPTER 13: Exporting & Importing Data

Exporting Data with SQL Server Import and Export Wizard

We will export a view query results to a new Excel worksheet. The SELECT query returns 8,914 rows from the vPersonDemographics view.

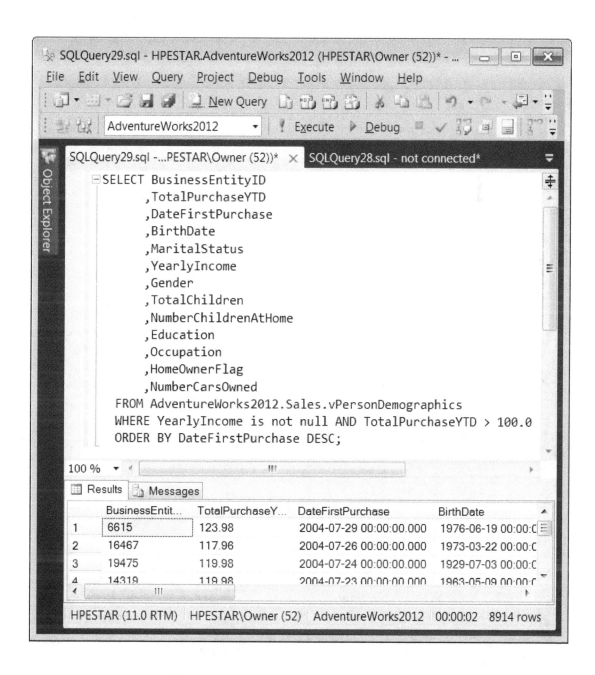

Starting the SSIS Import and Export Wizard

We start the SSIS Import/Export Wizard by a Right Click on the database in Object Explorer. It does not matter much if we choose Import Data or Export data since it only presets the destination or source pages respectively.

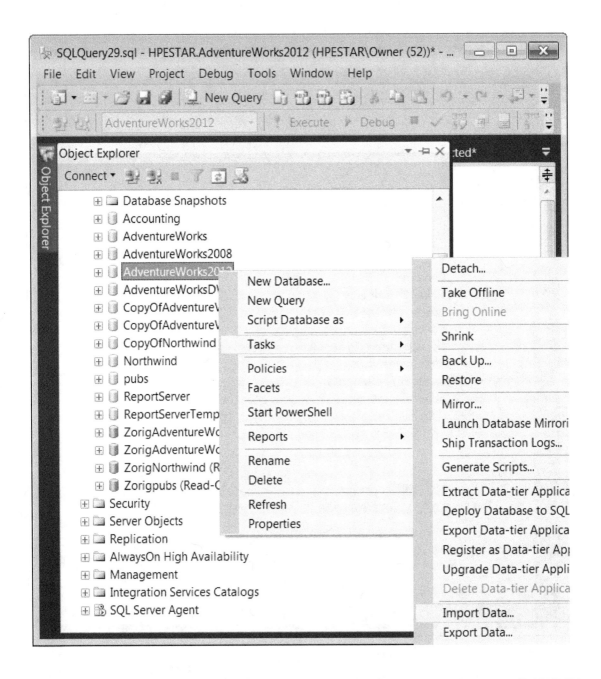

Optional Wizard Starting Welcome Screen

There is a checkmark option on the bottom to turn it off.

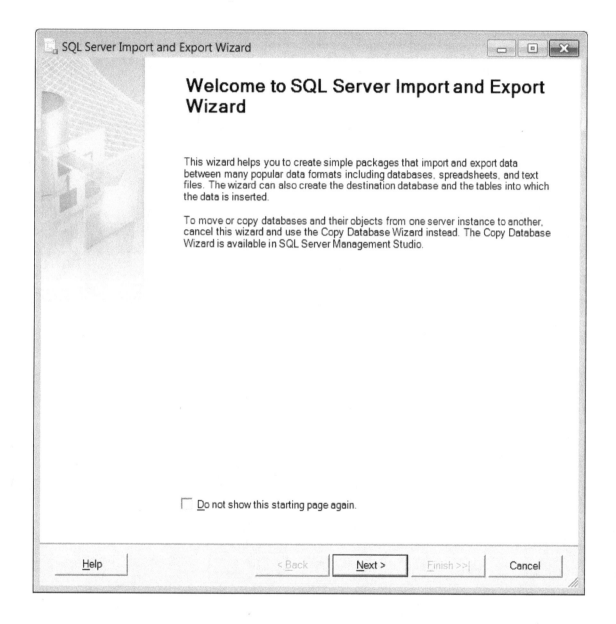

Configuring the Data Source Page

The data source is a database, therefore the server and database must be set up on this page.

Configuring the Destination Page

The destination is a new Excel worksheet. Path & name must be given.

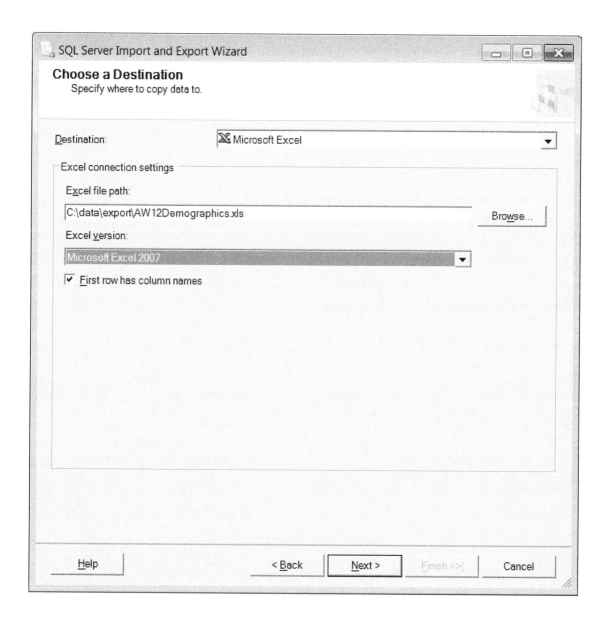

Specifying Table/View or Query Source

The Wizard logic branches based on what radio button we choose. If the choose table/view source, the next dialog box offers the entire list of tables/views in the database for checkmark selection.

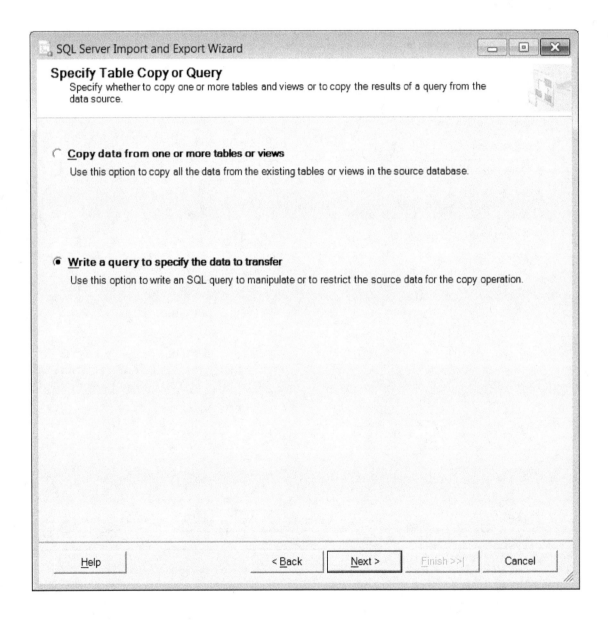

Entering the Query Source

We should use a tested query in order to avoid a failure in the execution of the generated SSIS package. Parse option is available for syntax checking.

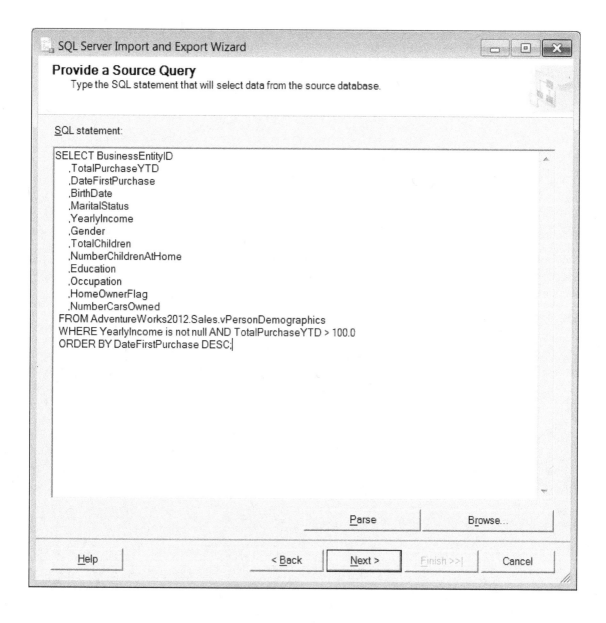

Option to Edit Mappings & Review Data

If you trust the Wizard, you can just click "Next". Otherwise, you can edit column mappings and review the data.

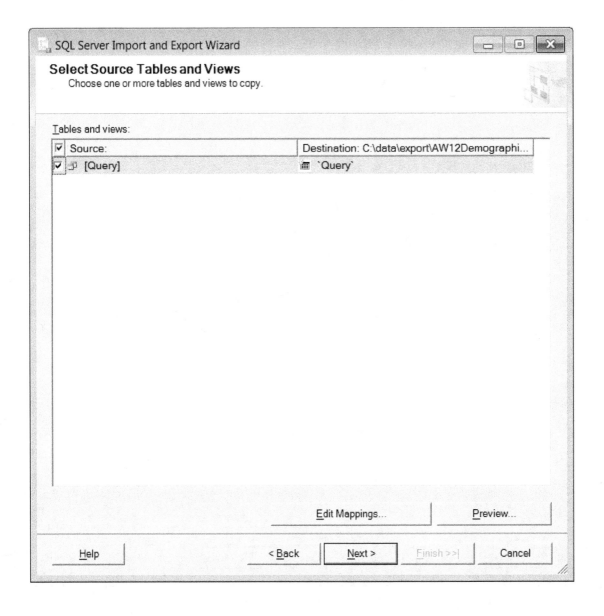

Edit Mappings & Preview

The next Wizard screen offers popup windows for editing the column mappings, changing the CREATE TABLE SQL and preview the data. We don't perform any change.

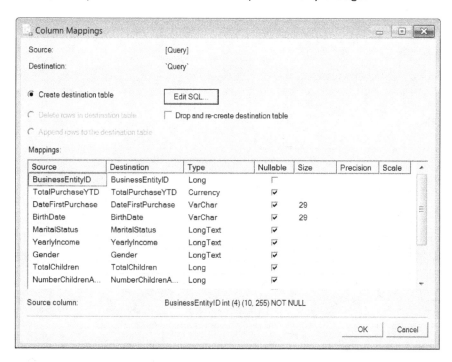

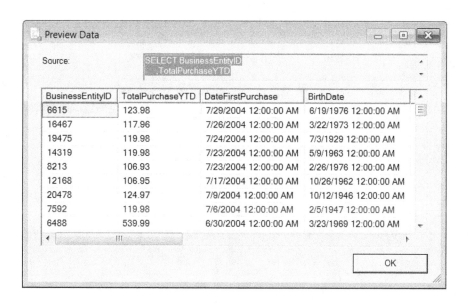

Review Data Type Mappings

Column data mappings can be reviewed in detail on this dialog box.

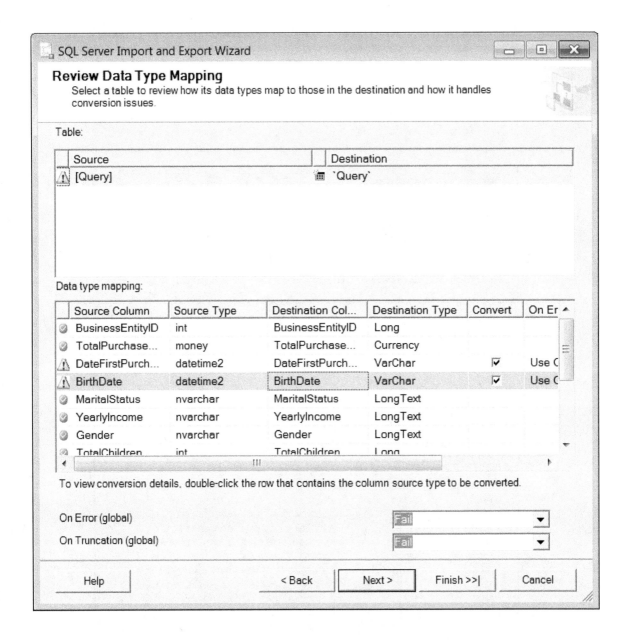

Save and/or Run Package

The Wizard generated SSIS package can be saved for future use or enhancements. If we run it immediately without saving, it will just go away after execution.

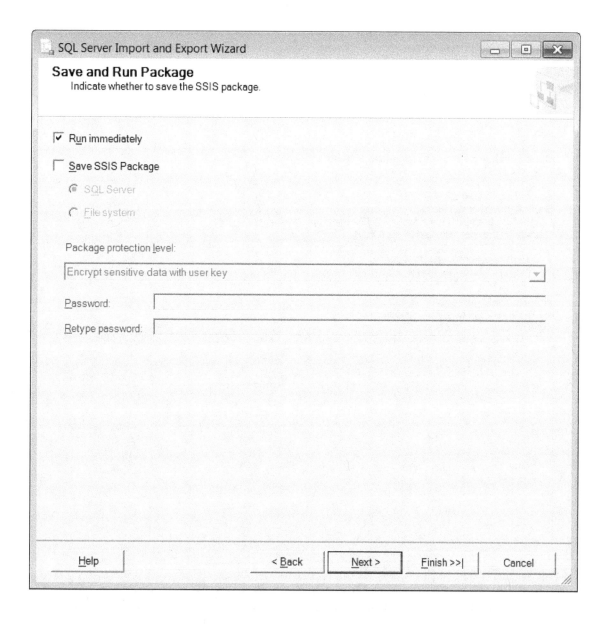

Verification Screen before Execution

At this point we still can go back and make changes should it be necessary. Once we click on Finish and we did not checkmark Save, the package will execute and goes away on success or failure.

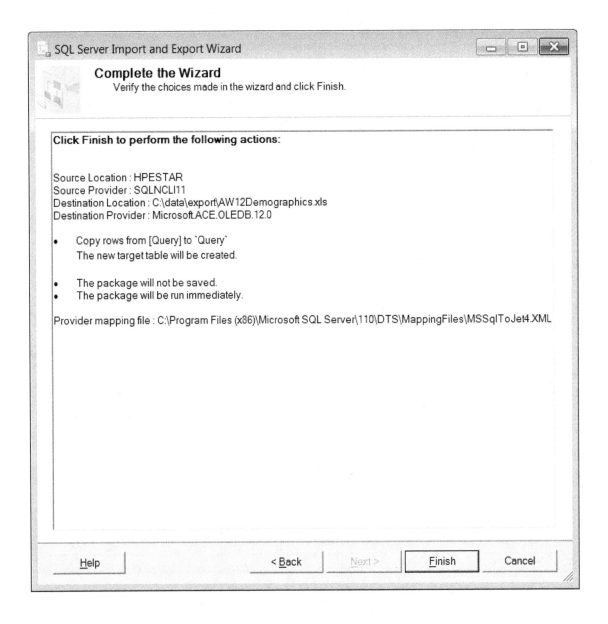

Execution Results Screen

If there are errors in the execution of the package, they will show in this window. The current Wizard generated SSIS package executed successfully.

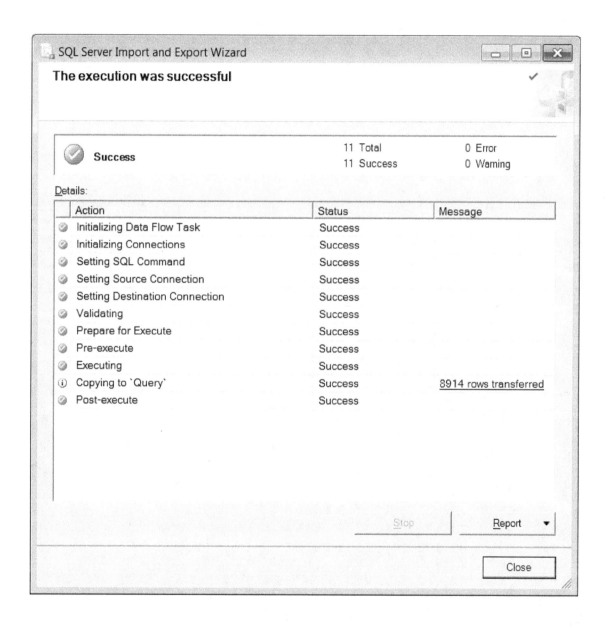

Checking Results in Excel

If the double click on the destination filename, the transferred data is displayed by Excel.

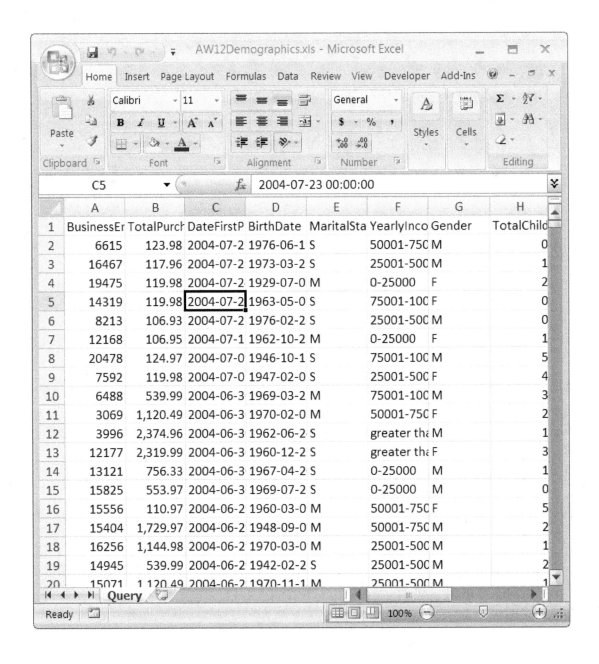

Importing Data with SQL Server Import and Export Wizard

Importing with the Wizard is very similar to the exporting process. We are going to import the just created AW12Demographics.xls Excel worksheet into a new database table. We start the Wizard the same as for export. First we configure the source as Excel worksheet.

Specify Data Source

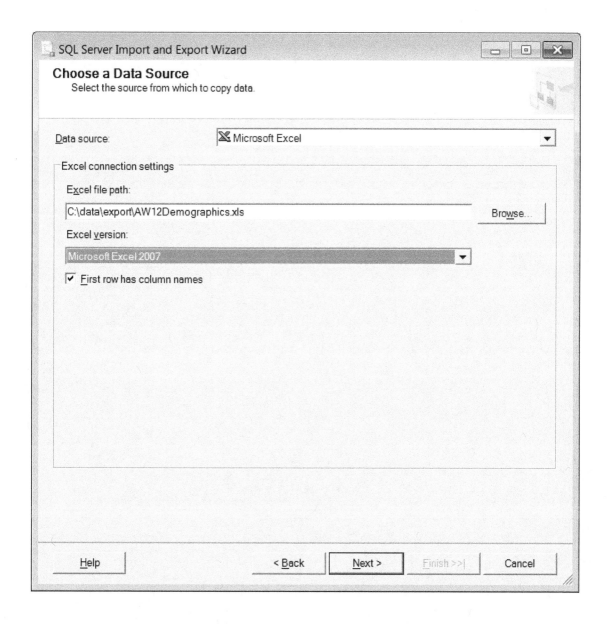

Specify Data Destination as Database

AdventureWorks2012 is the destination for the data movement.

Excel Worksheet Source Is Considered a Table

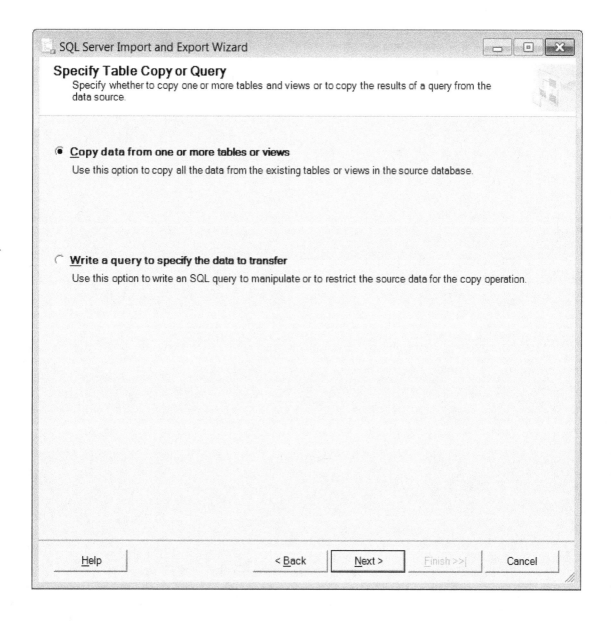

Select Excel Sheet and Assign Database Table Name

All the data is on the 'Query' sheet.

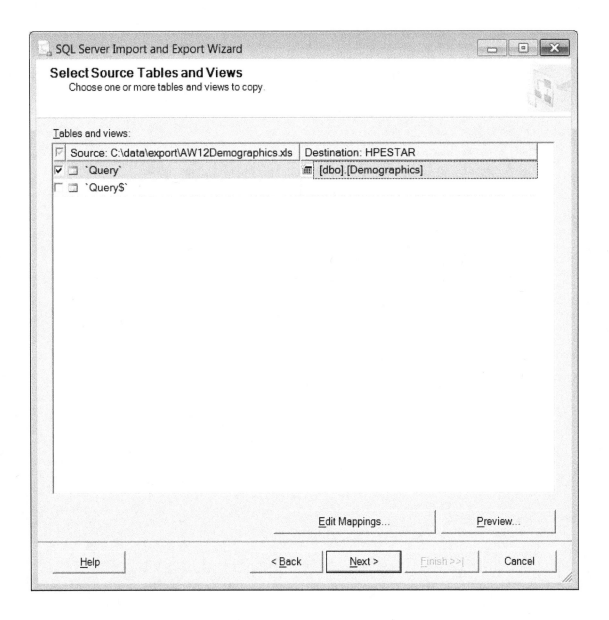

Column Mappings & CREATE TABLE Edit Panels

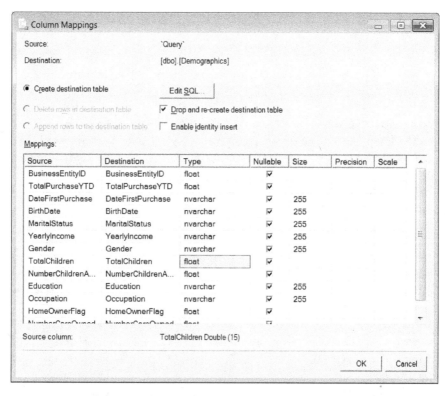

Source Data Inspection with Preview Data

This is a very important step. If the data does not look correct here, it will not be correct in the database table either.

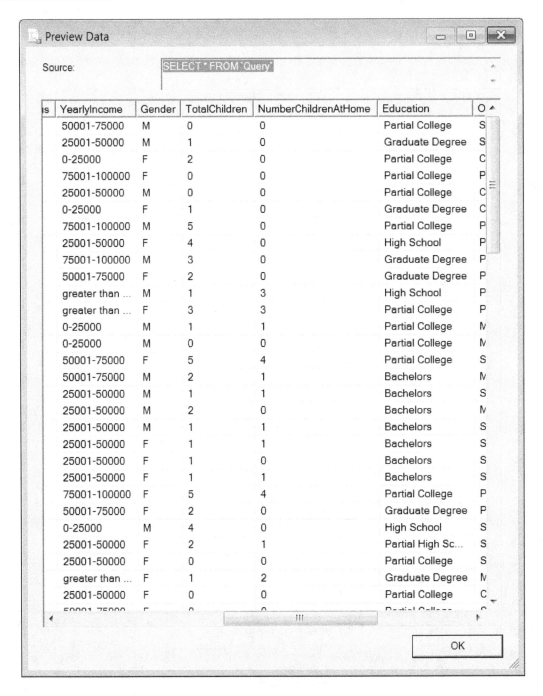

Indicate Saving and/or Run the SSIS Package

The Final Release Screen for Execution

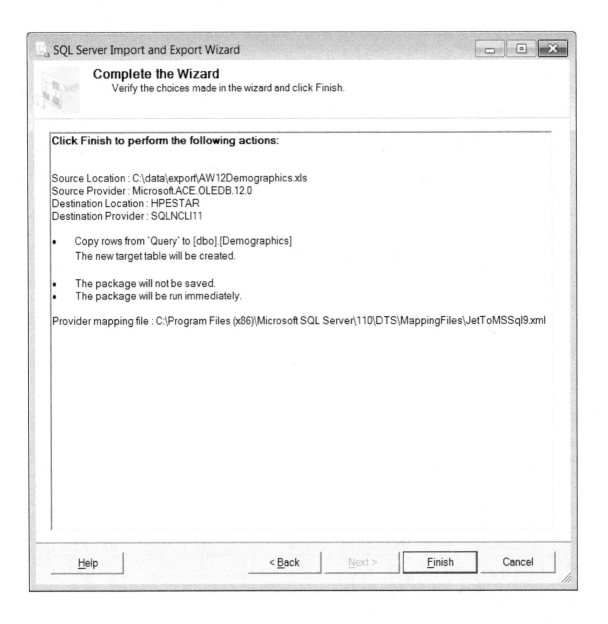

Successful Execution Screen
In case of errors, hyperlink to errors will display.

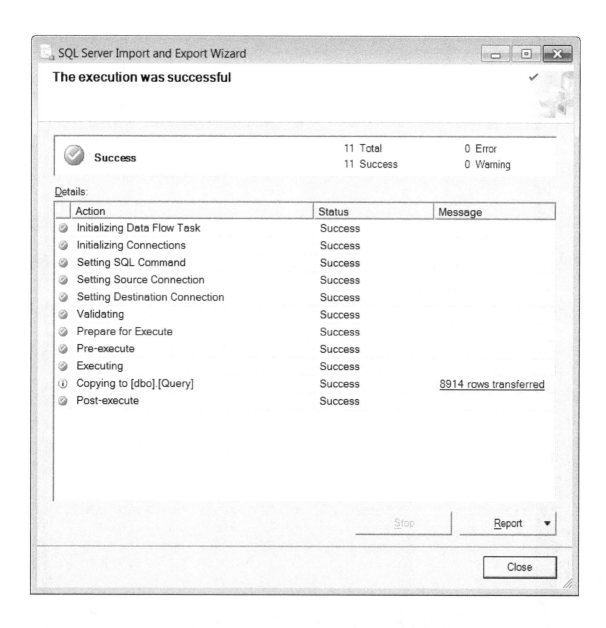

Check New Table in Database

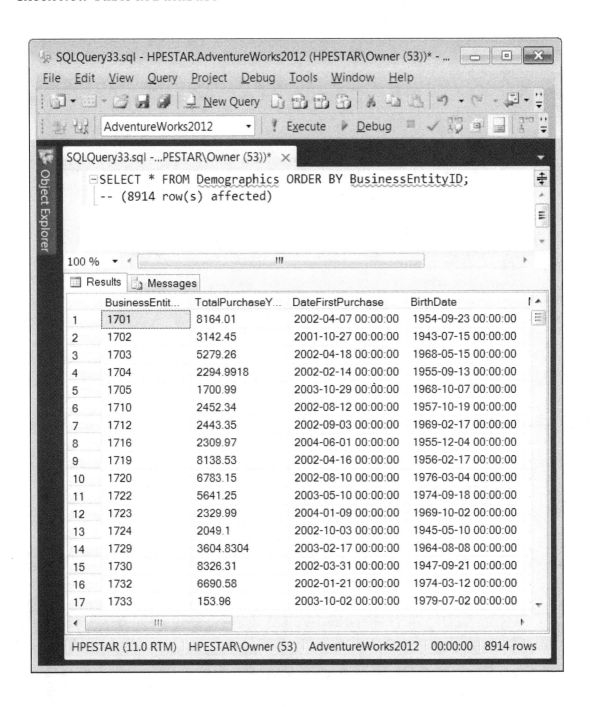

Exporting Database Table to Excel

The Wizard sequence is very similar to exporting query results. We shall export Sales.SalesOrderHeader table.

Specify Destination

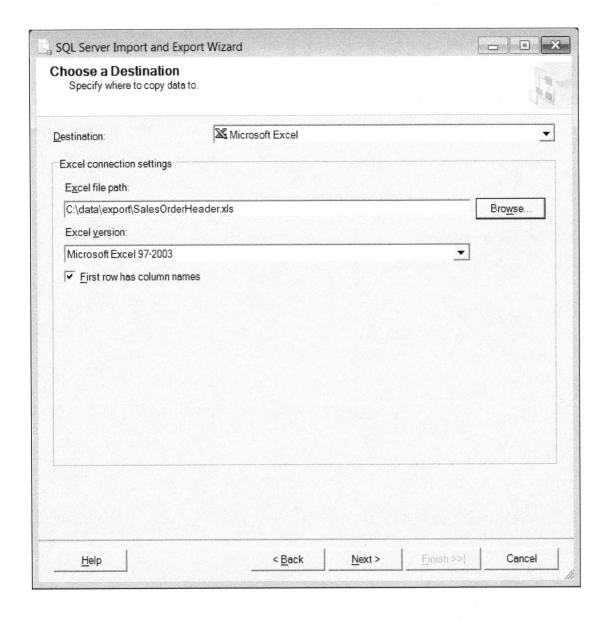

Choose Table Copy or Query

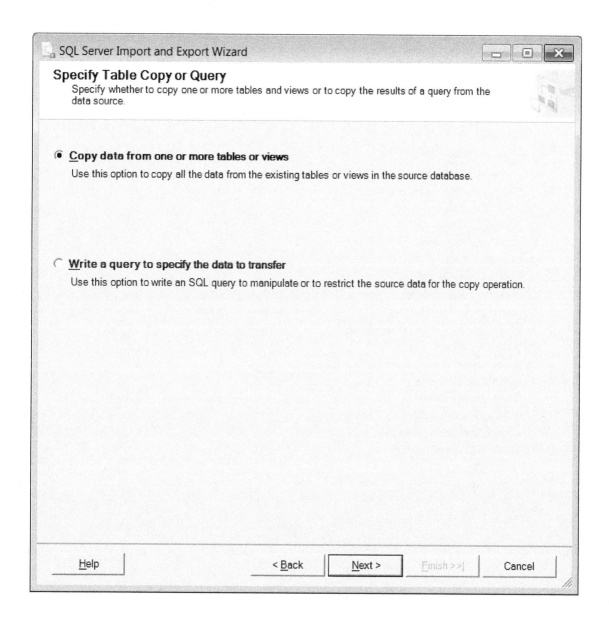

Checkmark Source Table

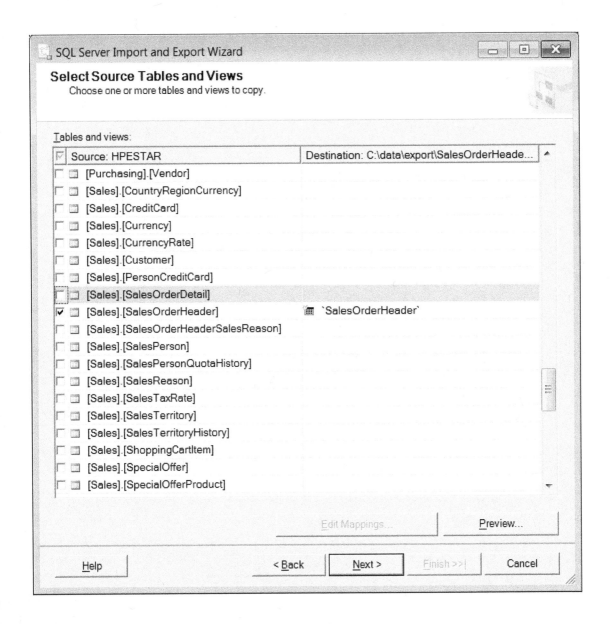

Check Data Type Mapping

Save and/or Run Package

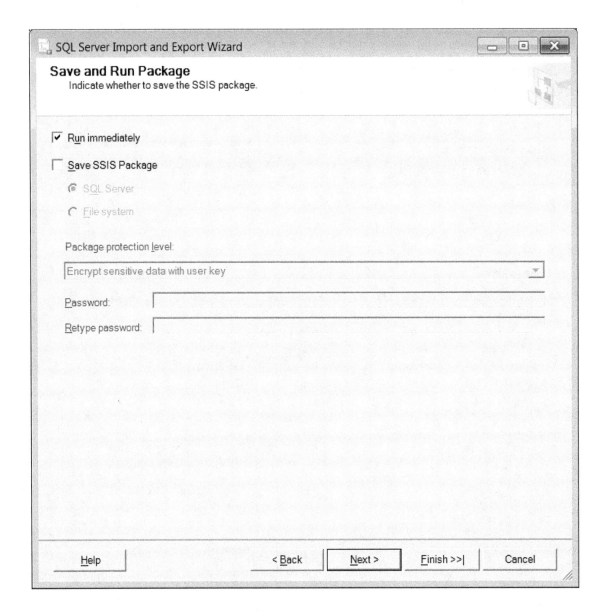

Complete the Wizard

Successful Execution Screen

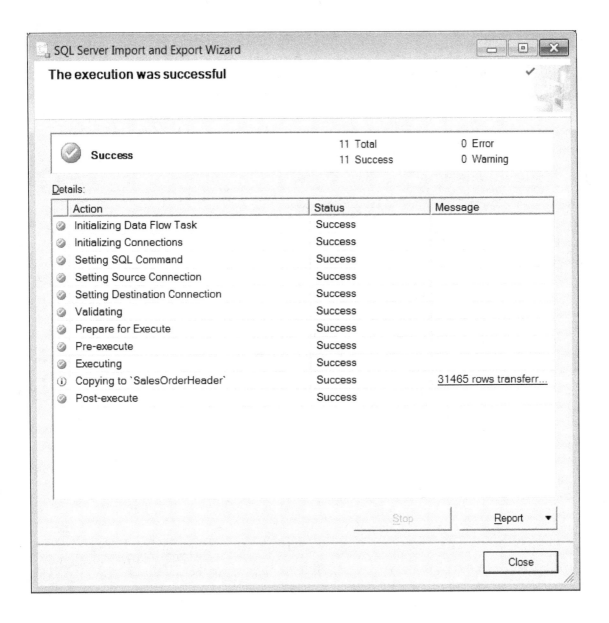

Check File in Folder and Data in Excel

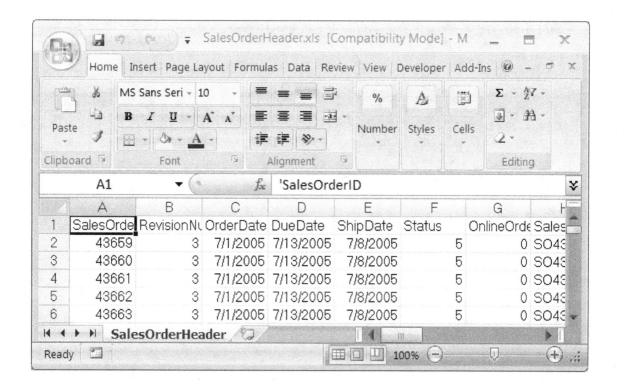

Exporting Data Directly into a Flat File

There is no equivalent of BULK INSERT, however, with xp_cmdshell & ECHO commands we can export data directly into a flat file.

> Security blog on xp_cmdshell (usually disabled on production server):
> http://blogs.msdn.com/b/sqlsecurity/archive/2008/01/10/xp-cmdshell.aspx .

```
USE AdventureWorks;
GO
CREATE PROC uspWeeklySupplierSummary  @FilePath VARCHAR(100) AS  BEGIN
   DECLARE  @Line NVARCHAR(1000), @Command NVARCHAR(2000) ,@Return INT;
   DECLARE  @VendorID  INT,  @VendorName NVARCHAR(50), @ProductName NVARCHAR(50);
   SET @Line = '******** SUPPLIERS PRODUCTS REPORT ********';
   SET @Command = CONCAT('echo ', @Line , ' >>', @FilePath);
   EXEC @Return = master..xp_cmdshell  @Command, no_output;
   DECLARE curVendor CURSOR FAST_FORWARD FOR
   SELECT  VendorID, Name  FROM  Purchasing.Vendor  WHERE   CreditRating = 1   ORDER BY VendorID;
   OPEN curVendor  FETCH NEXT FROM curVendor  INTO @VendorID,  @VendorName;
   WHILE @@FETCH_STATUS = 0      BEGIN
      SET @Line = '. '; SET @Command = CONCAT('echo ', @Line,' >>', @FilePath);
      EXEC @Return = master..xp_cmdshell  @Command, no_output;
      SET @Line = '***** Products From Supplier: ' + @VendorName;
      SET @Command = CONCAT('echo ', @Line, ' >>', @FilePath);
      EXEC @Return = master..xp_cmdshell  @Command, no_output
      DECLARE curProduct CURSOR FAST_FORWARD FOR
      SELECT v.Name  FROM   Purchasing.ProductVendor pv INNER JOIN Production.Product v
      ON  pv.ProductID = v.ProductID   AND pv.VendorID = @VendorID;
      OPEN curProduct; FETCH NEXT FROM curProduct INTO @ProductName;
      IF @@FETCH_STATUS <> 0    BEGIN
         SET @Line = '*** NO PRODUCTS AVAILABLE AT THIS TIME *** ';
         SET @Command = CONCAT('echo ', @Line,' >>', @FilePath);
         EXEC @Return = master..xp_cmdshell  @Command, no_output;
      END;
      WHILE @@FETCH_STATUS = 0  BEGIN
         SET @Line = CONCAT( SPACE(1), @ProductName );
         SET @Command = CONCAT('echo ', @Line,' >>',@FilePath);
         EXEC @Return = master..xp_cmdshell  @Command, no_output;
         FETCH NEXT FROM curProduct  INTO @ProductName;
      END;   CLOSE curProduct; DEALLOCATE curProduct;
     FETCH NEXT FROM curVendor  INTO @VendorID, @VendorName;
   END ;  CLOSE curVendor;   DEALLOCATE curVendor;
 END
GO


EXEC uspWeeklySupplierSummary  'F:\data\export\SUPPWeek31.txt' ;
```

CHAPTER 13: Exporting & Importing Data

Command Prompt Commands List by HELP

Command Prompt commands can be used for data transport as well including COPY & XCOPY. We can get the entire command list by typing the "HELP" command. It is like a time machine back to the programming style of 1960-s.

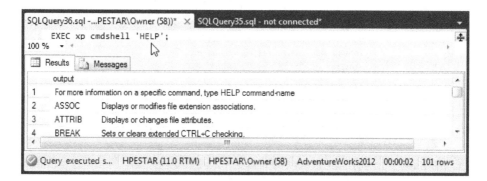

Command List

ASSOC	Displays or modifies file extension associations.
ATTRIB	Displays or changes file attributes.
BREAK	Sets or clears extended CTRL+C checking.
BCDEDIT	Sets properties in boot database to control boot loading.
CACLS	Displays or modifies access control lists (ACLs) of files.
CALL	Calls one batch program from another.
CD	Displays the name of or changes the current directory.
CHCP	Displays or sets the active code page number.
CHDIR	Displays the name of or changes the current directory.
CHKDSK	Checks a disk and displays a status report.
CHKNTFS	Displays or modifies the checking of disk at boot time.
CLS	Clears the screen.
CMD	Starts a new instance of the Windows command interpreter.
COLOR	Sets the default console foreground and background colors.
COMP	Compares the contents of two files or sets of files.
COMPACT	Displays or alters the compression of files on NTFS partitions.
CONVERT	Converts FAT volumes to NTFS. You cannot convert the current drive.
COPY	Copies one or more files to another location.
DATE	Displays or sets the date.
DEL	Deletes one or more files.
DIR	Displays a list of files and subdirectories in a directory.
DISKCOMP	Compares the contents of two floppy disks.
DISKCOPY	Copies the contents of one floppy disk to another.
DISKPART	Displays or configures Disk Partition properties.
DOSKEY	Edits command lines, recalls Windows commands, and creates macros.
DRIVERQUERY	Displays current device driver status and properties.
ECHO	Displays messages, or turns command echoing on or off.
ENDLOCAL	Ends localization of environment changes in a batch file.
ERASE	Deletes one or more files.
EXIT	Quits the CMD.EXE program (command interpreter).
FC	Compares two files or sets of files, and displays the differences between them.
FIND	Searches for a text string in a file or files.

FINDSTR	Searches for strings in files.
FOR	Runs a specified command for each file in a set of files.
FORMAT	Formats a disk for use with Windows.
FSUTIL	Displays or configures the file system properties.
FTYPE	Displays or modifies file types used in file extension associations.
GOTO	Directs the Windows command interpreter to a labeled line in a batch program.
GPRESULT	Displays Group Policy information for machine or user.
GRAFTABL	Enables Windows to display an extended character set in graphics mode.
HELP	Provides Help information for Windows commands.
ICACLS	Display, modify, backup, or restore ACLs for files and directories.
IF	Performs conditional processing in batch programs.
LABEL	Creates, changes, or deletes the volume label of a disk.
MD	Creates a directory.
MKDIR	Creates a directory.
MKLINK	Creates Symbolic Links and Hard Links
MODE	Configures a system device.
MORE	Displays output one screen at a time.
MOVE	Moves one or more files from one directory to another directory.
OPENFILES	Displays files opened by remote users for a file share.
PATH	Displays or sets a search path for executable files.
PAUSE	Suspends processing of a batch file and displays a message.
POPD	Restores the previous value of the current directory saved by PUSHD.
PRINT	Prints a text file.
PROMPT	Changes the Windows command prompt.
PUSHD	Saves the current directory then changes it.
RD	Removes a directory.
RECOVER	Recovers readable information from a bad or defective disk.
REM	Records comments (remarks) in batch files or CONFIG.SYS.
REN	Renames a file or files.
RENAME	Renames a file or files.
REPLACE	Replaces files.
RMDIR	Removes a directory.
ROBOCOPY	Advanced utility to copy files and directory trees
SET	Displays, sets, or removes Windows environment variables.
SETLOCAL	Begins localization of environment changes in a batch file.
SC	Displays or configures services (background processes).
SCHTASKS	Schedules commands and programs to run on a computer.
SHIFT	Shifts the position of replaceable parameters in batch files.
SHUTDOWN	Allows proper local or remote shutdown of machine.
SORT	Sorts input.
START	Starts a separate window to run a specified program or command.
SUBST	Associates a path with a drive letter.
SYSTEMINFO	Displays machine specific properties and configuration.
TASKLIST	Displays all currently running tasks including services.
TASKKILL	Kill or stop a running process or application.
TIME	Displays or sets the system time.
TITLE	Sets the window title for a CMD.EXE session.
TREE	Graphically displays the directory structure of a drive or path.
TYPE	Displays the contents of a text file.
VER	Displays the Windows version.
VERIFY	Tells Windows whether to verify that your files are written correctly to a disk.
VOL	Displays a disk volume label and serial number.
XCOPY	Copies files and directory trees.
WMIC	Displays WMI information inside interactive command shell.

CHAPTER 13: Exporting & Importing Data

CHAPTER 14: Maintaining Data Integrity in the Enterprise

Why is Data Integrity Paramount

A business or organization can only operate efficiently with good quality data. Computers were the real engine of economic progress since the 1950-s. Without computers, we would pretty much be at post Second World War level. Computers work with data and produce data. As the saying goes: garbage in, garbage out. Therefore it is our job as database designers, database developers and database administrators to ensure the data integrity in a database. What are the sources of the bad data? They can be data feeds received from various sources, data entry by people, and bugs in database or application programming. The best way to minimize bugs is putting each piece of new software through rigorous quality assurance (QA) process. To prevent bad data getting into the database there are a number of possibilities: table design, constraints, stored procedures, triggers and application software.

At the lowest level, constraints make up the guarding force over data integrity. The default constraint is different from the rest: it provides predefined default value if no value is provided for a cell (a column in a row), it does not give an error message.

```
USE AdventureWorks2012;
SELECT          ConstraintType = type_desc,  [Count] = COUNT(*)
FROM sys.objects
WHERE type_desc in     (
                        'CHECK_CONSTRAINT',
                        'DEFAULT_CONSTRAINT',
                        'FOREIGN_KEY_CONSTRAINT',
                        'PRIMARY_KEY_CONSTRAINT',
                        'UNIQUE_CONSTRAINT'
                        )
GROUP BY type_desc  ORDER BY type_desc;
```

ConstraintType	Count
CHECK_CONSTRAINT	89
DEFAULT_CONSTRAINT	152
FOREIGN_KEY_CONSTRAINT	90
PRIMARY_KEY_CONSTRAINT	71
UNIQUE_CONSTRAINT	1

Entity Integrity

Entity Integrity defines a row as a unique entity for a particular table. The main enforcing mechanisms are: NOT NULL constraint and unique index. PRIMARY KEY implies not null, and unique index automatically created. In the Production.Product table ProductID is the INT IDENTITY PRIMARY KEY, Name & ProductNumber are NATURAL KEYs and rowguid is a system generated unique key. All four keys are not null and all have unique index defined. The implication is that we can use any of 4 columns for row identification. However, ProductID INT (4 bytes) column is the most efficient row (record) identifier.

How to Remove Duplicates in a Table

The best way to prevent duplicates is by placing a UNIQUE KEY or unique index on the unique column(s). PRIMARY KEY & UNIQUE KEY constraints automatically create a unique index on the key column(s). If the entire row is a duplicate, removal is real simple with the DISTINCT clause.

```
SELECT DISTINCT * INTO T2 FROM T1;
GO
```

If duplicates are only in one or more columns, then duplicates removal is fairly easy with the ROW_NUMBER method, it is more involved with the GROUP BY method (prior to SQL Server 2005).

```
-- Create test table
USE tempdb;
SELECT        ProductID=CONVERT(int, ProductID),
              ProductName = Name,  ProductNumber,
              ListPrice = ListPrice + 1.00
INTO Product
FROM AdventureWorks2012.Production.Product   WHERE ListPrice > 0.0;
GO  -- (304 row(s) affected)
```

```
-- Unique index prevents duplicates
CREATE UNIQUE INDEX idxProd ON Product(ProductName, ProductNumber);
GO
```

```
 -- Try to insert  duplicates on ProductName & ProductNumber
INSERT INTO Product
SELECT        TOP (100) ProductID=CONVERT(int, ProductID) + 1000,
              ProductName = Name, ProductNumber,
              ListPrice = ListPrice + 2.00
FROM AdventureWorks2008.Production.Product
WHERE ListPrice > 0.0 ORDER BY NEWID();
GO
/*  Msg 2601, Level 14, State 1, Line 2
Cannot insert duplicate key row in object 'dbo.Product' with unique index 'idxProd'.
The duplicate key value is (Fender Set - Mountain, FE-6654).
The statement has been terminated.  */
```

```
DROP INDEX Product.idxProd;
GO
```

Rows with Duplicates Can Be Numbered in Ordered or Random Manner

```
-- Insert  100 duplicates on ProductName & ProductNumber
INSERT INTO Product
SELECT          TOP (100) ProductID=CONVERT(int, ProductID) + 1000,
                ProductName = Name, ProductNumber,   ListPrice = ListPrice + 2.00
FROM AdventureWorks2008.Production.Product
WHERE ListPrice > 0.0
ORDER BY NEWID();
GO
```

```
-- Quantify duplicates with GROUP BY query
SELECT ProductName, ProductNumber, [Count] = count(*)
FROM Product
GROUP BY ProductName, ProductNumber
        HAVING count(*) > 1
ORDER BY ProductName, ProductNumber;
GO -- (100 row(s) affected) - Partial results.
```

ProductName	ProductNumber	Count
Bike Wash - Dissolver	CL-9009	2
Classic Vest, L	VE-C304-L	2
Classic Vest, S	VE-C304-S	2
Front Brakes	FB-9873	2
Full-Finger Gloves, M	GL-F110-M	2

```
-- Quantify duplicates with ROW_NUMBER OVER - we don't care about duplicates ordering
;WITH CTE AS (
    SELECT RN=ROW_NUMBER() OVER (PARTITION BY ProductName, ProductNumber
    ORDER BY NEWID() ),  ProductName, ProductNumber
    FROM Product)
SELECT * FROM CTE WHERE RN > 1
ORDER BY ProductName, ProductNumber;
GO -- (100 row(s) affected) - Partial results.
```

RN	ProductName	ProductNumber
2	Bike Wash - Dissolver	CL-9009
2	Classic Vest, L	VE-C304-L
2	Classic Vest, S	VE-C304-S
2	Front Brakes	FB-9873
2	Full-Finger Gloves, M	GL-F110-M

Remove Duplicates with CTE & ROW_NUMBER OVER PARTITION BY

```
-- To removal of duplicates is real easy with CTE & ROW_NUMBER
;WITH CTE AS (
    SELECT RN=ROW_NUMBER() OVER (PARTITION BY ProductName, ProductNumber
    ORDER BY NEWID()),  ProductName, ProductNumber    FROM Product)
DELETE CTE  WHERE RN > 1;
GO -- (100 row(s) affected)
```

```
-- Test for duplicates again
SELECT ProductName, ProductNumber, [Count] = count(*)
FROM Product  GROUP BY ProductName, ProductNumber  HAVING count(*) > 1
ORDER BY ProductName, ProductNumber;
GO -- (0 row(s) affected)
```

```
SELECT COUNT(*) FROM Product;  -- 304
GO
```

Remove Duplicates with GROUP BY

```
-- Insert  duplicates on ProductName & ProductNumber
INSERT INTO Product    SELECT    TOP (100) ProductID=CONVERT(int, ProductID) + 1000,
                ProductName = Name, ProductNumber,    ListPrice = ListPrice + 2.00
FROM AdventureWorks2008.Production.Product  WHERE ListPrice > 0.0  ORDER BY NEWID();
GO
```

```
-- Sample of conflicting data - It is a business decision what to keep
SELECT TOP (4) * FROM Product WHERE ProductNumber IN
    ( SELECT ProductNumber FROM Product   GROUP BY ProductNumber HAVING count(*) > 1    )
ORDER BY ProductNumber;
```

ProductID	ProductName	ProductNumber	ListPrice
992	Mountain-500 Black, 48	BK-M18B-48	540.9900
1992	Mountain-500 Black, 48	BK-M18B-48	541.9900
993	Mountain-500 Black, 52	BK-M18B-52	540.9900
1993	Mountain-500 Black, 52	BK-M18B-52	541.9900

```
-- Assume it does not matter which duplicate to keep: any ProductID and any ListPrice OK
SELECT ProductID=MIN(ProductID), ProductName, ProductNumber, ListPrice=MIN(ListPrice)
INTO Product1 FROM Product GROUP BY ProductName, ProductNumber ORDER BY ProductID;
GO  -- (304 row(s) affected)
```

CHAPTER 14: Maintaining Data Integrity in the Enterprise

Domain Integrity

A domain defines the possible values for a column. Domain Integrity rules enforce the validity data in a column:

Data type	table design
Data length	table design
Nullability	table design
Collation	table design
Allowable values	check constraints - table design
Default value	default constraints - table design

CHECK constraint is used for simple rules such as OrderQty > 0. UDF CHECK constraints can be used for complex rules. In addition, at the development phase, triggers, stored procedures and client-side application software can be developed to enforce Domain Integrity.

Server-side CHECK constraints are the most desirable. Client-side Domain Integrity enforcement is the least desirable. However, it may happen that there is no database expert on the project and developers feel more confident programming data validity rules in the application software. Ultimately what counts is valid data in the database. Usually big-budget projects can do everything the right way due to the availability of expert-level resources in all areas of the software development project. Basic table definition data from INFORMATION_SCHEMA views.

```
SELECT       COLUMN_NAME, ORDINAL_POSITION, DATA_TYPE, IS_NULLABLE,
             CHARACTER_MAXIMUM_LENGTH, COLLATION_NAME, COLUMN_DEFAULT
FROM INFORMATION_SCHEMA.COLUMNS WHERE TABLE_NAME = 'SalesOrderHeader';
```

COLUMN_NAME	ORDINAL_POSITION	DATA_TYPE	IS_NULLABLE	CHARACTER_MAXIMUM_LENGTH	COLLATION_NAME	COLUMN_DEFAULT
SalesOrderID	1	int	NO	NULL	NULL	NULL
RevisionNumber	2	tinyint	NO	NULL	NULL	((0))
OrderDate	3	datetime	NO	NULL	NULL	(getdate())
DueDate	4	datetime	NO	NULL	NULL	NULL
ShipDate	5	datetime	YES	NULL	NULL	NULL
tatus	6	tinyint	NO	NULL	NULL	((1))
OnlineOrderFlag	7	bit	NO	NULL	NULL	((1))
SalesOrderNumber	8	nvarchar	NO	25	SQL_Latin1_General_CP1_CI_AS	NULL
PurchaseOrderNumber	9	nvarchar	YES	25	SQL_Latin1_General_CP1_CI_AS	NULL
AccountNumber	10	nvarchar	YES	15	SQL_Latin1_General_CP1_CI_AS	NULL
CustomerID	11	int	NO	NULL	NULL	NULL
SalesPersonID	12	int	YES	NULL	NULL	NULL
TerritoryID	13	int	YES	NULL	NULL	NULL
BillToAddressID	14	int	NO	NULL	NULL	NULL
ShipToAddressID	15	int	NO	NULL	NULL	NULL
ShipMethodID	16	int	NO	NULL	NULL	NULL
CreditCardID	17	int	YES	NULL	NULL	NULL
CreditCardApprovalCode	18	varchar	YES	15	SQL_Latin1_General_CP1_CI_AS	NULL
CurrencyRateID	19	int	YES	NULL	NULL	NULL
SubTotal	20	money	NO	NULL	NULL	((0.00))
TaxAmt	21	money	NO	NULL	NULL	((0.00))
Freight	22	money	NO	NULL	NULL	((0.00))
TotalDue	23	money	NO	NULL	NULL	NULL
Comment	24	nvarchar	YES	128	SQL_Latin1_General_CP1_CI_AS	NULL
rowguid	25	uniqueidentifier	NO	NULL	NULL	(newid())
ModifiedDate	26	datetime	NO	NULL	NULL	(getdate())

Domain Integrity Summary Display with sp_help

The sp_help system procedure provides a convenient way to display a summary of Domain Integrity definitions for a table.

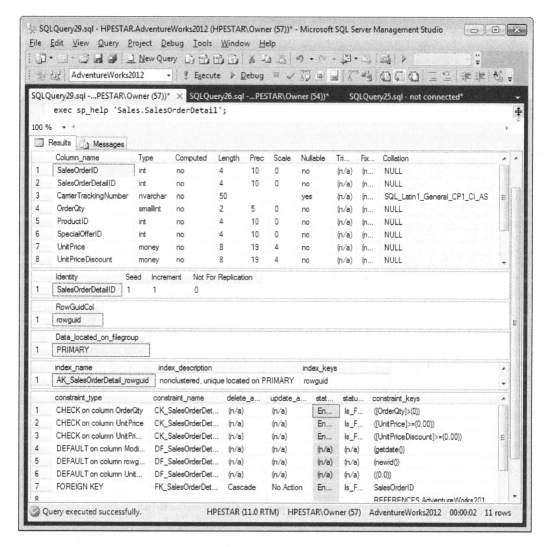

We can query "sys" system views metadata for column definition as well.

```
SELECT * FROM sys.columns
WHERE object_name(object_id) = 'PurchaseOrderHeader'  ORDER BY column_id;
-- (13 row(s) affected) - Partial results.
```

object_id	name	column_id	system_type_id	user_type_id	max_length	precision	scale	collation_name
946102411	PurchaseOrderID	1	56	56	4	10	0	NULL

CHAPTER 14: Maintaining Data Integrity in the Enterprise

THE COLUMNPROPERTY() Function

The COLUMNPROPERTY() function can be used for programmatic discovery of column properties. Script to generate SELECT queries for all properties.

```
USE AdventureWorks2012;
GO

DECLARE @Parms TABLE (Property varchar(32))
INSERT  @Parms VALUES
('AllowsNull'), ('ColumnId'),
('FullTextTypeColumn'), ('IsComputed'),
('IsCursorType'), ('IsDeterministic'),
('IsFulltextIndexed'), ('IsIdentity'),
('IsIdNotForRepl'), ('IsIndexable'),
('IsOutParam'), ('IsPrecise'),
('IsRowGuidCol'), ('IsSystemVerified'),
('IsXmlIndexable'), ('Precision'),
('Scale'), ('StatisticalSemantics'),
('SystemDataAccess'), ('UserDataAccess'),
('UsesAnsiTrim'), ('IsSparse'),
('IsColumnSet')
SELECT CONCAT('SELECT COLUMNPROPERTY( OBJECT_ID("Person.Person"), "LastName", "",
              Property, "") AS [', Property, '];')
FROM @Parms
GO  -- Partial results.
```

```
SELECT COLUMNPROPERTY( OBJECT_ID('Person.Person'), 'LastName', 'AllowsNull') AS [AllowsNull];
SELECT COLUMNPROPERTY( OBJECT_ID('Person.Person'), 'LastName', 'ColumnId') AS [ColumnId];
SELECT COLUMNPROPERTY( OBJECT_ID('Person.Person'), 'LastName', 'FullTextTypeColumn') AS [FullTextTypeColumn];
SELECT COLUMNPROPERTY( OBJECT_ID('Person.Person'), 'LastName', 'IsComputed') AS [IsComputed];
SELECT COLUMNPROPERTY( OBJECT_ID('Person.Person'), 'LastName', 'IsCursorType') AS [IsCursorType];
```

Executing the queries, the column properties are returned one by one.

AllowsNull
1 0

ColumnId
1 7

FullTextTypeColumn
1 0

IsComputed
1 0

IsCursorType
1 0

CHAPTER 14: Maintaining Data Integrity in the Enterprise

Column List Using System Views & Data Dictionary

We can combine sys. system views with data dictionary description to get a valuable list when working with domain integrity.

```
USE AdventureWorks2012;
SELECT SCHEMA_NAME(T.schema_id)    AS SchemaName,
    T.name                         AS TableName,
    C.name                         AS ColumnName,
    TP.name                        AS ColumnType,
    C.max_length                   AS ColumnLength,
    COALESCE(EP.value, Space(1))   AS ColumnDesc
FROM   sys.tables AS T
    INNER JOIN sys.columns AS C
        ON T.object_id = C.object_id
    INNER JOIN sys.types AS TP
        ON  C.system_type_id = TP.user_type_id
    LEFT JOIN sys.extended_properties AS EP
        ON EP.major_id = T.object_id
            AND EP.minor_id = C.column_id
ORDER  BY SchemaName,  TableName,  ColumnName;
GO  -- (643 row(s) affected) - Partial Results.
```

Purchasing	PurchaseOrderHeader	EmployeeID	int	4	Employee who created the purchase order. Foreign key to Employee.BusinessEntityID.
Purchasing	PurchaseOrderHeader	Freight	money	8	Shipping cost.
Purchasing	PurchaseOrderHeader	ModifiedDate	datetime	8	Date and time the record was last updated.
Purchasing	PurchaseOrderHeader	OrderDate	datetime	8	Purchase order creation date.
Purchasing	PurchaseOrderHeader	PurchaseOrderID	int	4	Primary key.
Purchasing	PurchaseOrderHeader	PurchaseOrderID	int	4	Clustered index created by a primary key constraint.
Purchasing	PurchaseOrderHeader	RevisionNumber	tinyint	1	Incremental number to track changes to the purchase order over time.
Purchasing	PurchaseOrderHeader	RevisionNumber	tinyint	1	Nonclustered index.
Purchasing	PurchaseOrderHeader	ShipDate	datetime	8	Estimated shipment date from the vendor.
Purchasing	PurchaseOrderHeader	ShipMethodID	int	4	Shipping method. Foreign key to ShipMethod.ShipMethodID.
Purchasing	PurchaseOrderHeader	Status	tinyint	1	Order current status. 1 = Pending; 2 = Approved; 3 = Rejected; 4 = Complete
Purchasing	PurchaseOrderHeader	Status	tinyint	1	Nonclustered index.
Purchasing	PurchaseOrderHeader	SubTotal	money	8	Purchase order subtotal. Computed as SUM(PurchaseOrderDetail.LineTotal)for the appropriate PurchaseOrderID.
Purchasing	PurchaseOrderHeader	TaxAmt	money	8	Tax amount.
Purchasing	PurchaseOrderHeader	TotalDue	money	8	Total due to vendor. Computed as Subtotal + TaxAmt + Freight.
Purchasing	PurchaseOrderHeader	VendorID	int	4	Vendor with whom the purchase order is placed. Foreign key to Vendor.BusinessEntityID.

Declarative Referential Integrity

Referential Integrity refers to ensuring that relationships between tables remain consistent. Declarative means it is part of table setup, not in programming objects like stored procedure. When one table attempts to create a FOREIGN KEY to another (PK) table, Referential Integrity requires that the primary key value exists in the referenced (PK) table. The optional cascading update & cascading delete ensure that changes made to the primary table are reflected in the linked referencing (FK) table. For example, if a row is deleted in the primary table, then all referencing rows are automatically deleted in the linked (FK) table when ON DELETE CASCADE is set. All three Referential Integrity constraint actions are demonstrated by the following script.

```
USE tempdb;

-- Create 2 test tables with PK-FK relationship
CREATE TABLE Product (
        ProductID INT PRIMARY KEY,
        ProductName varchar(50) UNIQUE,
        ProductNumber varchar(20) UNIQUE,
        ListPrice MONEY);
GO
```

```
-- First we test without the DELETE CASCADE action
CREATE TABLE OrderDetail (
        SalesOrderID INT,
        SalesOrderDetailID INT,
        PRIMARY KEY (SalesOrderID, SalesOrderDetailID),
        OrderQty INT ,
        ProductID INT REFERENCES Product(ProductID)  -- ON DELETE CASCADE  );
GO
```

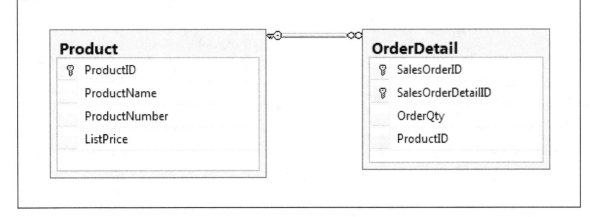

FOREIGN KEY Constraint Protects Two Ways

```
-- Populate test tables
INSERT Product
SELECT ProductID, Name, ProductNumber, ListPrice
FROM AdventureWorks2012.Production.Product
ORDER BY ProductID;
GO
--(504 row(s) affected)
```

```
INSERT OrderDetail
SELECT          SalesOrderID,
                SalesOrderDetailID,
                OrderQty,
                ProductID
FROM AdventureWorks2012.Sales.SalesOrderDetail
ORDER BY SalesOrderID, SalesOrderDetailID;
GO
-- (121317 row(s) affected)
```

```
-- Attempting to insert into FK table a reference to a non-existing (PK) ProductID
INSERT OrderDetail
SELECT          SalesOrderID = 100000,
                SalesOrderDetailID = 1000000,
                OrderQty = 5,
                ProductID = 2000
GO
/* Msg 547, Level 16, State 0, Line 1
The INSERT statement conflicted with the FOREIGN KEY constraint
"FK__OrderDeta__Produ__59FA5E80". The conflict occurred in database "tempdb", table
"dbo.Product", column 'ProductID'.
The statement has been terminated.   */
```

```
-- Attempting to delete from  PK table a ProductID which is referenced from the FK table
DELETE Product WHERE ProductID = 800;
GO
/* Msg 547, Level 16, State 0, Line 1
The DELETE statement conflicted with the REFERENCE constraint
"FK__OrderDeta__Produ__59FA5E80". The conflict occurred in database "tempdb", table
"dbo.OrderDetail", column 'ProductID'.
The statement has been terminated.  */
```

ON DELETE CASCADE Action Causes DELETE Chain Reaction

```
-- Change FOREIGN KEY: specify ON DELETE  CASCADE  option
-- Lookup FK constraints name
SELECT * FROM INFORMATION_SCHEMA.REFERENTIAL_CONSTRAINTS;
```

CONSTRAINT_ CATALOG	CONSTRAINT _SCHEMA	CONSTRAINT_NAME	UNIQUE_CONSTRAI NT_CATALOG	UNIQUE_CONSTRAI NT_SCHEMA	UNIQUE_CONSTRAIN T_NAME	MATCH_ OPTION	UPDATE _RULE	DELETE _RULE
tempdb	dbo	FK__OrderDeta__Prod u__0A9D95DB	tempdb	dbo	PK__Product__B40CC 6ED66641298	SIMPLE	NO ACTION	NO ACTION

```
BEGIN TRANSACTION
GO
ALTER TABLE dbo.OrderDetail  DROP CONSTRAINT FK__OrderDeta__Produ__0A9D95DB;
GO
ALTER TABLE dbo.Product SET (LOCK_ESCALATION = TABLE)
GO
COMMIT TRANSACTION -- Command(s) completed successfully.
```

```
BEGIN TRANSACTION;
GO
ALTER TABLE dbo.OrderDetail  ADD CONSTRAINT FK__OrderDeta__Produ__0A9D95DB
FOREIGN KEY (ProductID)  REFERENCES dbo.Product (ProductID) ON DELETE  CASCADE;
GO
ALTER TABLE dbo.OrderDetail SET (LOCK_ESCALATION = TABLE);
GO
COMMIT TRANSACTION;  -- Command(s) completed successfully.
```

```
SELECT * FROM INFORMATION_SCHEMA.REFERENTIAL_CONSTRAINTS;
```

CONSTRAINT_ CATALOG	CONSTRAINT _SCHEMA	CONSTRAINT_NAME	UNIQUE_CONSTRAI NT_CATALOG	UNIQUE_CONSTRAI NT_SCHEMA	UNIQUE_CONSTRAIN T_NAME	MATCH_ OPTION	UPDATE _RULE	DELETE _RULE
tempdb	dbo	FK__OrderDeta__Prod u__0A9D95DB	tempdb	dbo	PK__Product__B40CC 6ED66641298	SIMPLE	NO ACTION	CASCAD E

```
SELECT COUNT(*) FROM OrderDetail;
GO  -- 121317
```

```
-- Cascading DELETE: first DELETE all referencing FK records, then DELETE PK record
DELETE Product WHERE ProductID = 800;
GO
-- (1 row(s) affected)
```

```
SELECT COUNT(*) FROM OrderDetail;
GO  -- 120822
```

FOREIGN KEY Constraints Represent the Only Connections Among Tables

While we talk about linked tables in functional terms such as master/header-detail, parent-child, dimension-fact, junction, etc., **there is only a single way to connect tables: FOREIGN KEY references PRIMARY KEY in another table**. We are going to demonstrate it in a grand manner: we will create 290 tables with the names of all the employees of AdventureWorks Cycles (fictional) company in a new test database. We shall connect all of them with FOREIGN KEY constraints: employee (FK table) references manager (PK table).

```
USE master;
GO
CREATE DATABASE AWOrgChart;
GO
USE AWOrgChart;
GO


DECLARE @SQL NVARCHAR(max) = '';

WITH CTE (ID, Emp, Mgr, MgrNode)  -- CTE with column names
    AS
(    SELECT E.BusinessEntityID,
          Emp=CONCAT(P.FirstName, SPACE(1), P.LastName),
          NULL,
          NULL
     FROM   AdventureWorks2012.HumanResources.Employee E
          INNER JOIN AdventureWorks2012.Person.Person P
             ON E.BusinessEntityID = P.BusinessEntityID
     WHERE  E.OrganizationNode = 0x                        -- Root node
     UNION
     SELECT E.BusinessEntityID,
         CONCAT(P.FirstName, SPACE(1), P.LastName)              AS Emp,
         CONCAT(PP.FirstName, SPACE(1), PP.LastName)            AS Mgr,
         E.OrganizationNode.GetAncestor(1)                     AS SuperNode
     FROM   AdventureWorks2012.HumanResources.Employee E
          INNER JOIN AdventureWorks2012.Person.Person P
             ON E.BusinessEntityID = P.BusinessEntityID
          INNER JOIN AdventureWorks2012.HumanResources.Employee EE
             ON ( EE.OrganizationNode = E.OrganizationNode.GetAncestor(1) )
          INNER JOIN AdventureWorks2012.Person.Person PP
             ON EE.BusinessEntityID = PP.BusinessEntityID)
```

```
SELECT @SQL = CONCAT(@SQL, CONCAT('CREATE TABLE ', QUOTENAME(Emp),
                '( ID INT PRIMARY KEY ,',
                    ' MgrID INT ',
                        CASE
            WHEN Mgr IS NOT NULL THEN CONCAT(' REFERENCES ',
                        QUOTENAME(Mgr),   '(ID)')
            ELSE ''  END, '); '))
FROM   CTE;

PRINT @SQL;  -- Partial text.
```

```
CREATE TABLE [Ken Sánchez]( ID INT PRIMARY KEY , MgrID INT );
CREATE TABLE [Terri Duffy]( ID INT PRIMARY KEY , MgrID INT  REFERENCES [Ken Sánchez](ID));
CREATE TABLE [Roberto Tamburello]( ID INT PRIMARY KEY ,
MgrID INT  REFERENCES [Terri Duffy](ID));
CREATE TABLE [Rob Walters]( ID INT PRIMARY KEY ,
MgrID INT  REFERENCES [Roberto Tamburello](ID));
CREATE TABLE [Gail Erickson]( ID INT PRIMARY KEY ,
MgrID INT  REFERENCES [Roberto Tamburello](ID));
CREATE TABLE [Jossef Goldberg]( ID INT PRIMARY KEY ,
MgrID INT  REFERENCES [Roberto Tamburello](ID));
CREATE TABLE [Dylan Miller]( ID INT PRIMARY KEY ,
MgrID INT  REFERENCES [Roberto Tamburello](ID));
CREATE TABLE [Diane Margheim]( ID INT PRIMARY KEY ,
MgrID INT  REFERENCES [Dylan Miller](ID));
CREATE TABLE [Gigi Matthew]( ID INT PRIMARY KEY , MgrID INT  REFERENCES [Dylan Miller](ID));
CREATE TABLE [Michael Raheem]( ID INT PRIMARY KEY ,
MgrID INT  REFERENCES [Dylan Miller](ID));
CREATE TABLE [Ovidiu Cracium]( ID INT PRIMARY KEY ,
MgrID INT  REFERENCES [Roberto Tamburello](ID));
CREATE TABLE [Thierry D'Hers]( ID INT PRIMARY KEY ,
MgrID INT  REFERENCES [Ovidiu Cracium](ID));
```

The functional meaning of Terry Duffy "references" Ken Sanchez: Duffy reports to Sanchez.

```
EXEC sp_executeSQL @SQL; -- Dynamic SQL execution: create 290 linked tables
GO
```

```
-- USE master;
DROP DATABASE AWOrgChart;
```

CHAPTER 14: Maintaining Data Integrity in the Enterprise

Diagram Tool Can Be Used for Organizational Charts

We can use the diagram tool in the AWOrgChart database as an orgchart tool. We add a chosen table to the diagram, for example, [Ken Sanchez]. With the right click menu, we add related tables, set view to table name only & arrange selection. The result is orgchart with the CEO and executive managers.

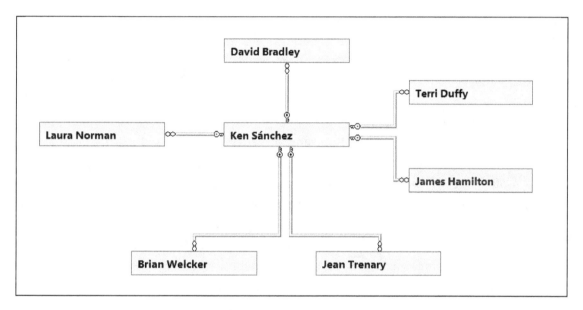

Orgchart starting with [David Hamilton]. Hamilton reports to Krebs (Gold Key).

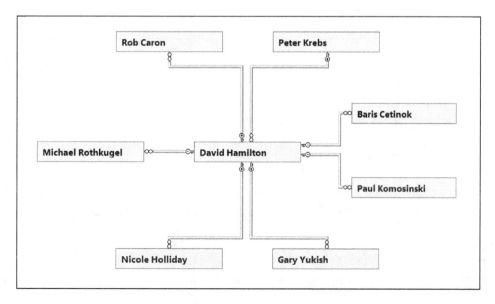

Enterprise-Level Business Rules Enforcement

Enterprise-Level Business Rules can be enforced by stored procedures & triggers on the server-side and application programs on the client-side. While stored procedures & application programs can be used to implement a complex set of business rules, they can only effect the current application. Stored procedure or application cannot catch an UPDATE transaction, for example, coming from a legacy application nobody dares to touch at the IT department. In a way stored procedure can be configured to perform after-the-fact near-real-time updates for recently posted data: configure the stored procedure as SQL Server Agent job and schedule it to run each minute.

Special Role of Triggers

Triggers, on the other hand, can catch, for example, an INSERT to the ProductPrice table, wherever it is coming from; current in-house application software, old in-house application, another profit-center of the enterprise application or 3rd party software package. An example for an enterprise business rule: convert foreign currency pricing to USD in the INSERT record to ProductPrice using the latest conversion rates from the ForeignExchange table. A constraint cannot be used to implement such a rule, a trigger can. Trigger code almost as flexible as stored procedure code. Triggers can also be used for cross-database referential integrity enforcement. While triggers are compiled into one database, they can access tables in another database. Because of their omnipotent nature, triggers are frequently misapplied as fix-it-all tools.

WARNING
Triggers are high maintenance database objects. Triggers are not for junior staff. Dropped/disabled triggers do not "COMPLAIN": stealth behavior.

Triggers are just like silent workhorses. They can be forgotten after months of operation since they don't have to be called explicitly from the client-side application programs, they are event launched on the server-side. DDL trigger can be applied to guard DML triggers, but then someone or something has to guard the DDL trigger as well. On the other hand, a dropped stored procedure causes user error ("complains"). Dropped trigger can cause user error also, but the error cannot easily be traced back the trigger.

The following update trigger will prevent last name update from new software, old software, other department's software or even 3rd party software package.

```
CREATE TRIGGER trgEmployee  ON Employee FOR UPDATE AS
   IF (UPDATE(LastName))                BEGIN
      RAISERROR ('Last name cannot be changed', 16, 1);  ROLLBACK TRAN;  RETURN;   END
GO
```

Product Reorder Trigger

The UPDATE trigger is attached to the Products table. It fires whenever there is an UPDATE for the table, no matter what kind of software application from what part of the world executed the UPDATE statement. **A trigger should never return a result set**. However, there is no error if we try to return a result set with a SELECT statement just like in a stored procedure. For testing & debugging purposes we can return results.

```
USE Northwind
GO


-- Logging table for product reorder notices
CREATE TABLE Reorder (
        ID INT IDENTITY(1,1) PRIMARY KEY,
        Message varchar(256),
        CreateDate datetime default (CURRENT_TIMESTAMP));
GO


IF EXISTS (select * from sys.objects where type='TR' and name = 'trgProductReorder')
        DROP TRIGGER trgProductReorder
GO


CREATE TRIGGER trgProductReorder
ON Products FOR UPDATE
AS
 BEGIN
   SET NOCOUNT ON;
   DECLARE @MsgText    varchar(128),    @QtyOnHand   int, @ReorderLevel int;
   SELECT @MsgText = CONCAT('Please place a reorder  for ', Rtrim(ProductName))
   FROM   inserted;

   SELECT @QtyOnHand = UnitsInStock,   @ReorderLevel = ReorderLevel   FROM   inserted;

   IF @QtyOnHand < @ReorderLevel
        INSERT Reorder  (Message)      SELECT @MsgText;

 --select * from deleted -- for testing &debugging only
 --select * from inserted
 --select @MsgText
 END
GO
```

A Trigger Should Never Return A Result Set Like A Stored Procedure
Check Data Manipulation Language (DML) trigger existence with sp_helptrigger system procedure.

```
EXEC sp_helptrigger Products ;
GO
```

trigger_name	trigger_owner	isupdate	isdelete	isinsert	isafter	isinsteadof	trigger_schema
trgProductReorder	dbo	1	0	0	1	0	dbo

```
-- Test trigger
/* For demonstration purposes, the debugging statements in trigger were uncommented */
UPDATE Products
        SET   UnitsInStock = 10
        WHERE  ProductID = 77;
GO
```

SQL Server UPDATE is implemented as complete deleted (old) and inserted (new) rows. Even if 1 byte updated, a complete row deleted and complete row inserted generated for logging.

deleted table row:

Product ID	ProductNa me	Supplier ID	Category ID	QuantityPer Unit	UnitPri ce	**UnitsInSt ock**	UnitsOnOr der	ReorderLe vel	Discontinu ed
77	Original Frankfurter grüne Soße	12	2	12 boxes	13.00	**50**	0	15	0

inserted table row:

Product ID	ProductNa me	Supplier ID	Category ID	QuantityPer Unit	UnitPri ce	**UnitsInSt ock**	UnitsOnOr der	ReorderLe vel	Discontinu ed
77	Original Frankfurter grüne Soße	12	2	12 boxes	13.00	**10**	0	15	0

```
SELECT * FROM  Reorder;
GO
```

ID	Message	CreateDate
1	Please place a reorder for Original Frankfurter grüne Soße	2016-11-25 06:06:45.043

```
DROP TRIGGER trgProductReorder;
DROP TABLE Reorder;
```

CHAPTER 14: Maintaining Data Integrity in the Enterprise

Trigger Examples In AdventureWorks2012

List of triggers in the sample database. parent_object_id is the object_id of the trigger parent table. SELF-JOIN is required to get the parent information.

```
USE AdventureWorks2012;
SELECT
  o.name                                            AS TriggerName,
  SCHEMA_NAME(po.schema_id)                          AS TableSchema,
  OBJECT_NAME(o.parent_object_id)                    AS TableName,
  OBJECTPROPERTY( o.object_id, 'ExecIsUpdateTrigger')    AS [isupdate],
  OBJECTPROPERTY( o.object_id, 'ExecIsDeleteTrigger')    AS [isdelete],
  OBJECTPROPERTY( o.object_id, 'ExecIsInsertTrigger')    AS [isinsert],
  OBJECTPROPERTY( o.object_id, 'ExecIsAfterTrigger')     AS [isafter],
  OBJECTPROPERTY( o.object_id, 'ExecIsInsteadOfTrigger') AS [isinsteadof],
  OBJECTPROPERTY( o.object_id, 'ExecIsTriggerDisabled')  AS [disabled]
FROM sys.objects AS o
        INNER JOIN sys.objects AS po     ON o.parent_object_id = po.object_id
WHERE o.[type] = 'TR'  ORDER BY TableSchema, TableName, TriggerName;
```

TriggerName	TableSchema	TableName	isupdate	isdelete	isinsert	isafter	isinsteadof	disabled
dEmployee	HumanResources	Employee	0	1	0	0	1	0
iuPerson	Person	Person	1	0	1	1	0	0
iWorkOrder	Production	WorkOrder	0	0	1	1	0	0
uWorkOrder	Production	WorkOrder	1	0	0	1	0	0
iPurchaseOrderDetail	Purchasing	PurchaseOrderDetail	0	0	1	1	0	0
uPurchaseOrderDetail	Purchasing	PurchaseOrderDetail	1	0	0	1	0	0
uPurchaseOrderHeader	Purchasing	PurchaseOrderHeader	1	0	0	1	0	0
dVendor	Purchasing	Vendor	0	1	0	0	1	0
iduSalesOrderDetail	Sales	SalesOrderDetail	1	1	1	1	0	0
uSalesOrderHeader	Sales	SalesOrderHeader	1	0	0	1	0	0

Alternate method of obtaining all triggers information.

```
SELECT * FROM sys.triggers ORDER BY name; -- Partial results.
```

name	object_id	parent_class	parent_class_desc	parent_id	type	type_desc
ddlDatabaseTriggerLog	261575970	0	DATABASE	0	TR	SQL_TRIGGER
dEmployee	1739153241	1	OBJECT_OR_COLUMN	1237579447	TR	SQL_TRIGGER
dVendor	1851153640	1	OBJECT_OR_COLUMN	766625774	TR	SQL_TRIGGER
iduSalesOrderDetail	1819153526	1	OBJECT_OR_COLUMN	1154103152	TR	SQL_TRIGGER
iPurchaseOrderDetail	1771153355	1	OBJECT_OR_COLUMN	850102069	TR	SQL_TRIGGER
iuPerson	1755153298	1	OBJECT_OR_COLUMN	1765581328	TR	SQL_TRIGGER
iWorkOrder	1867153697	1	OBJECT_OR_COLUMN	846626059	TR	SQL_TRIGGER
uPurchaseOrderDetail	1787153412	1	OBJECT_OR_COLUMN	850102069	TR	SQL_TRIGGER
uPurchaseOrderHeader	1803153469	1	OBJECT_OR_COLUMN	946102411	TR	SQL_TRIGGER
uSalesOrderHeader	1835153583	1	OBJECT_OR_COLUMN	1266103551	TR	SQL_TRIGGER
uWorkOrder	1883153754	1	OBJECT_OR_COLUMN	846626059	TR	SQL_TRIGGER

Trigger Can Be Modified in Object Explorer
When the Modify Trigger option is picked, Object Explorer loads it as ALTER TRIGGER script.

Programmatic way to get trigger definition.

SELECT OBJECT_DEFINITION(object_id('Person.iuPerson'));

CREATE TRIGGER [Person].[iuPerson] ON [Person].[Person]
AFTER INSERT, UPDATE NOT FOR REPLICATION AS
BEGIN
DECLARE @Count int;
SET @Count = @@ROWCOUNT;
IF @Count = 0   RETURN;
SET NOCOUNT ON;
IF UPDATE([BusinessEntityID]) OR UPDATE([Demographics])

CHAPTER 14: Maintaining Data Integrity in the Enterprise

Business Intelligence in the Enterprise

SQL Server Analysis Services (SSAS), SQL Server Integration Services (SSIS) & SQL Server Reporting Services (SSRS) are the server side Business Intelligence software components. Easy to remember associations: SSAS: OLAP cubes and more, SSIS: ETL (extract, transform, load) data transfer system & SSRS: traditional reports, interactive & OLAP reports. SQL Server Data Tools (SSDT) provides 3 customized templates as design environments.

SSRS: Designing Complex Interactive Reports

SSDT report design environment: product catalog in the report design editor.

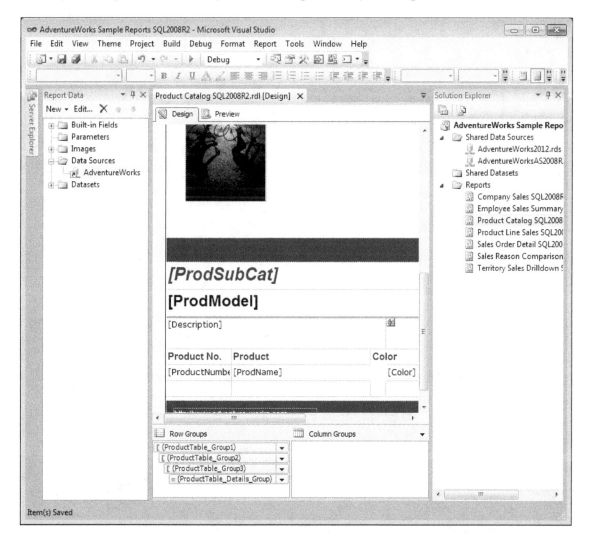

Previewing the Report Design

The product catalog is interactive with a drill down directory on the left which is based on the Production.ProductCategory and Production.ProductSubcategory tables. The Product, ProductSubcategory & ProductCategory tables form a hierarchy which is neatly exploited in the product catalog report. What makes the report design environment extremely powerful that you can try the look & feel of a report just by clicking a tab and staying in the studio environment. The product images are from the ProductPhoto table(in Management Studio we cannot see the images, only the binary code).

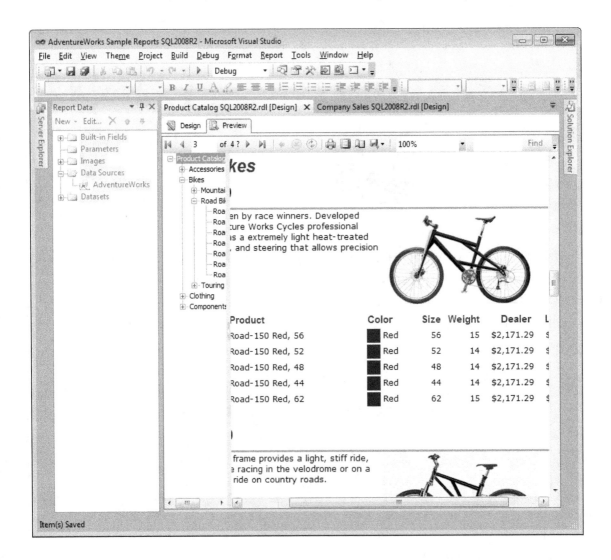

Detailed Preview of AWC Product Catalog

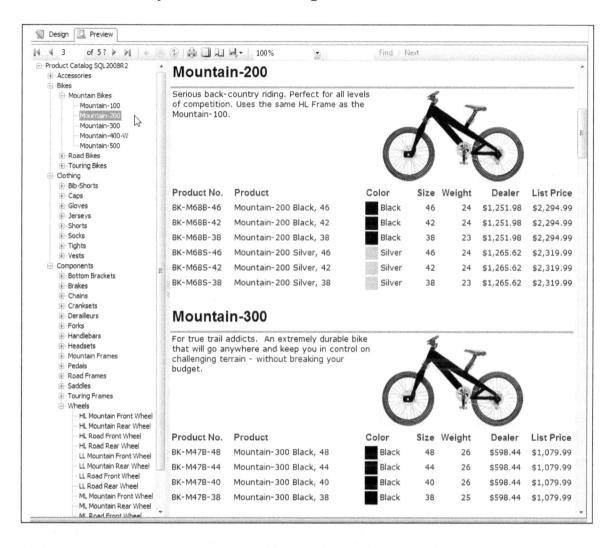

SSAS: Designing Multi-Dimensional Cubes

SSAS cubes contain millions of pre-calculated answers just waiting for the question like: what was the net revenue in Florida for the 3rd Quarter of 2016? Since the answer is ready, the response time is sub-second. AS cubes are derived from dimension tables and fact tables in a data warehouse database.

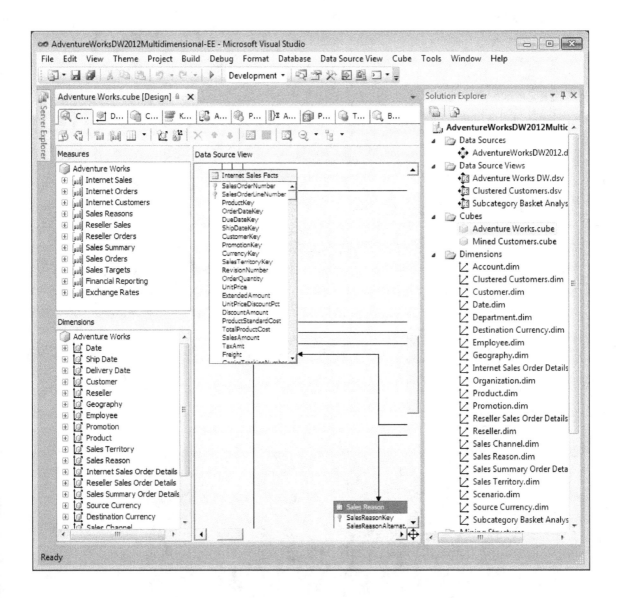

Test OLAP Analysis Services Cube Design with Browser

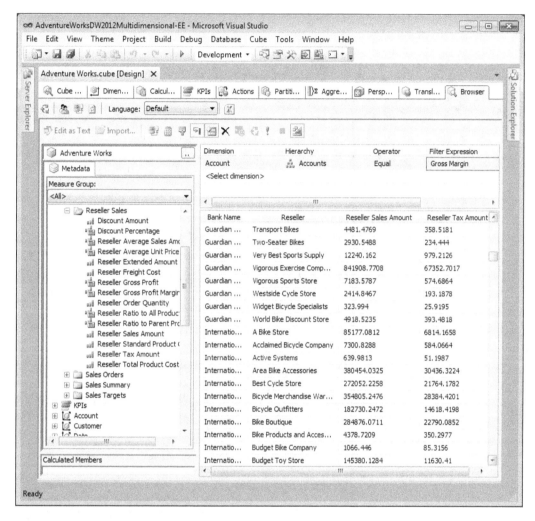

Dimension Usage Display

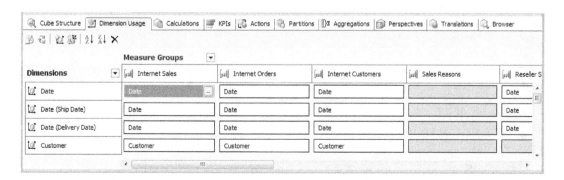

CHAPTER 14: Maintaining Data Integrity in the Enterprise

Browsing Multidimensional Cube in Management Explorer

In Object Explorer we can connect to Analysis Server and browse the available multidimensional cubes.

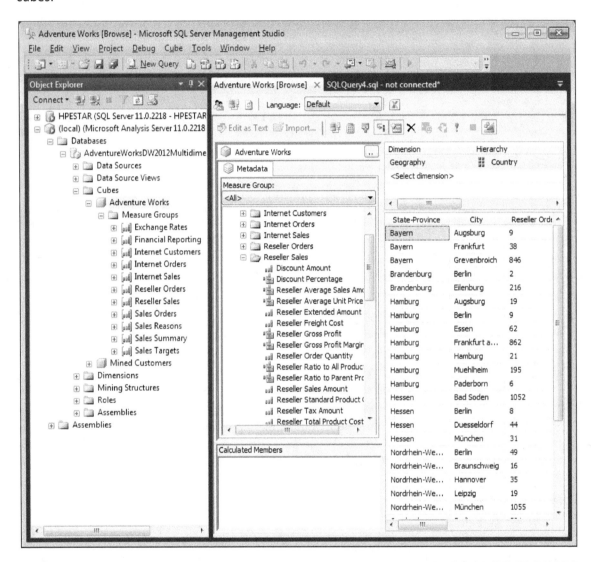

```
USE AdventureWorksDW2012;
-- Searching data warehouse database metadata for table objects
SELECT  CONCAT(schema_name(O.schema_id),'.', O.NAME) AS ObjectName,
        O.TYPE AS ObjectType,      C.NAME AS ColumnName
FROM sys.objects O INNER JOIN sys.columns C ON O.OBJECT_ID = C.OBJECT_ID
WHERE  O.type='U' AND O.NAME LIKE '%sales%' AND C.NAME LIKE '%price%'
ORDER BY ObjectName, ColumnName;  -- Partial results.
-- dbo.FactInternetSales     U         UnitPrice
```

CHAPTER 14: Maintaining Data Integrity in the Enterprise

Excel PivotTable Report Using AS Cube Datasource

Excel can use as datasource SQL Server database and Analysis Services database(bottom image). Actually PivotTable is a very good match for browsing multidimensional cubes since the underlying concepts are very similar: summary data tabulations by dimensions.

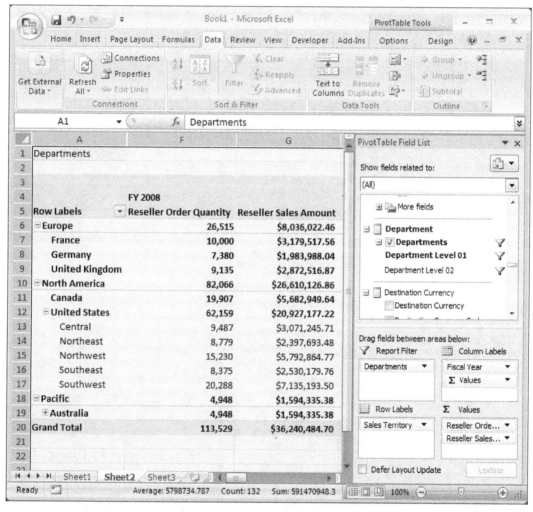

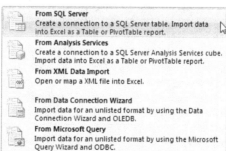

Sales Reason Comparison Report Based on AS Cube

The Sales Reason Comparison report (converted to 2012) is based on the multidimensional AdventureWorksAS AS cube. Design mode and report segment in preview mode.

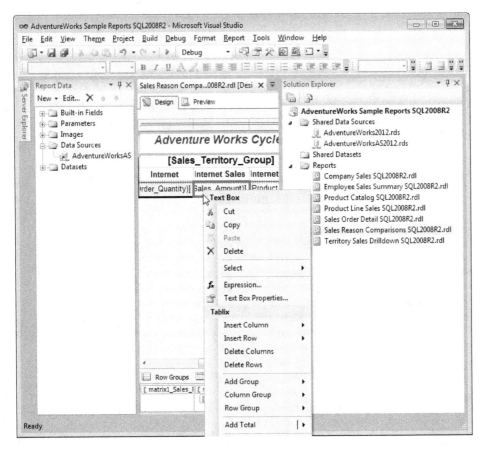

Sales Reason	Europe			North America		
	Internet Orders	Internet Sales Amount	Internet Total Product Cost	Internet Orders	Internet Sales Amount	Interr Prod
Manufacturer	$352	$1,206,594	$733,050	$803	$2,765,552	$
On Promotion	$1,118	$2,009,804	$1,182,740	$1,298	$2,217,191	$
Other	$111	$65,666	$39,932	$109	$62,743	
Price	$2,275	$3,586,028	$2,120,140	$2,630	$4,158,322	$
Quality	$316	$1,130,733	$686,129	$718	$2,569,198	$
Review	$226	$436,477	$250,168	$319	$578,245	

SSIS: Enterprise Level Data Integration

SSIS is an enterprise level data integration and data transformation software tool. Transmit (clean, transformed) data from different data sources to the database and vice versa. The Data Flow editor in SSDT for an SSIS sample project.

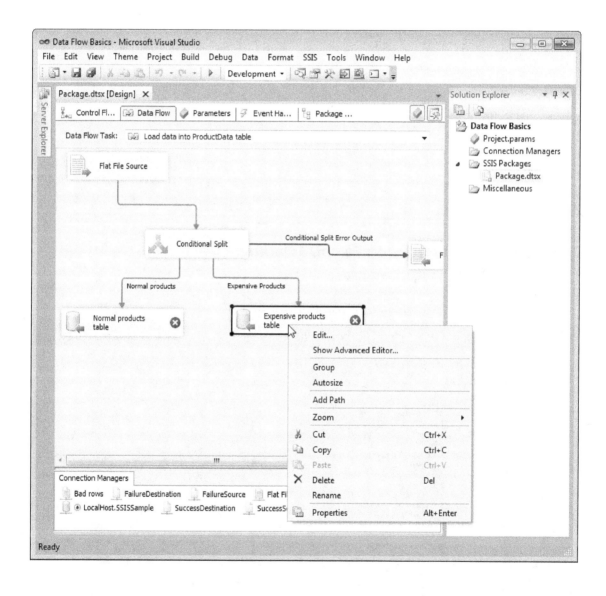

SSAS, SSIS, SSRS in Configuration Manager

SSIS is shared for all instances. SSAS & SSRS are per instance. MSSQLSERVER means the default instance, HPESTAR. SQL12 means the names instance HPESTAR\SQL12.

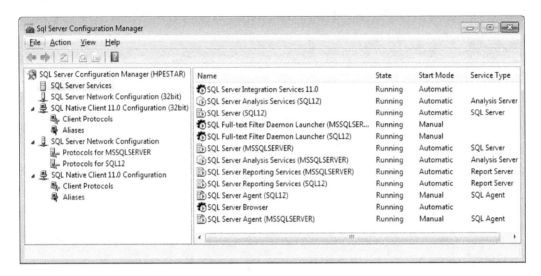

ReportServer & ReportServerTempDB Databases

Each Reporting Services instance is supported by two databases.

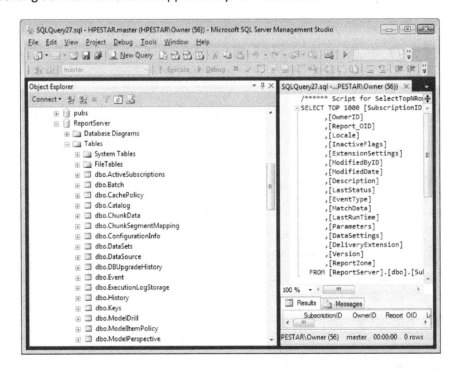

Full-Text Index & Full-Text Search

Full-Text Search in SQL Server 2012 allows users and application programs, such as C#, to execute Full-Text Search queries against text-based data in SQL Server 2012 tables. Prior to running full-text search queries on a table, full-text catalog and full-text indexes on table text column(s) must be created.

```
USE AdventureWorks2012;
SELECT * INTO dbo.JobCandidate FROM HumanResources.JobCandidate; ; -- (13 row(s) affected)
GO
CREATE UNIQUE INDEX idxHRJC ON JobCandidate(JobCandidateID);
CREATE FULLTEXT CATALOG HRFullText AS DEFAULT;
CREATE FULLTEXT INDEX ON JobCandidate(Resume) KEY INDEX idxHRJC WITH STOPLIST = SYSTEM;
GO
```

```
SELECT JobCandidateID FROM JobCandidate WHERE CONTAINS(Resume, ' "production line" ');     -- 2
```

```
SELECT JobCandidateID FROM JobCandidate WHERE CONTAINS(Resume, ' "C#" ');                  -- 3
```

```
SELECT JobCandidateID FROM JobCandidate WHERE CONTAINS (Resume, ' "machin*" ' );           -- 1, 7
```

```
SELECT * FROM CONTAINSTABLE(JobCandidate, Resume, 'ISABOUT ("mach*",
    tool WEIGHT(0.9), automatic WEIGHT(0.1)  ) ' );
```

KEY	RANK
1	51
7	22

```
SELECT jc.JobCandidateID, x.* FROM JobCandidate jc
        INNER JOIN CONTAINSTABLE(JobCandidate, Resume, 'ISABOUT ("mach*",
                tool WEIGHT(0.9), automatic WEIGHT(0.1) ) ' ) x  ON x.[KEY] = jc.JobCandidateID;
```

JobCandidateID	KEY	RANK
1	1	51
7	7	22

```
SELECT JobCandidateID FROM JobCandidate WHERE CONTAINS(Resume, '(ingénierie NEAR expérimenté)');  -- 7
```

```
SELECT JobCandidateID FROM JobCandidate WHERE CONTAINS(Resume, '(visual and basic)'); -- 3
```

```
SELECT JobCandidateID FROM JobCandidate WHERE CONTAINS(Resume, '(visual or basic)'); -- 2, 3
```

```
SELECT JobCandidateID FROM JobCandidate WHERE CONTAINS (Resume,'FORMSOF(INFLECTIONAL,"computer")'); -- 1
GO
```

```
DROP TABLE dbo.JobCandidate;
DROP FULLTEXT CATALOG HRFullText;
GO
```

SQL Azure - Enterprise in the Clouds

Microsoft Windows Azure account is available at:

http://www.windowsazure.com/en-us/ .

There is a 90-day free trial package available which includes an SQL database. Credit card is required for an Azure account. One form of verification: a code is sent to your mobile phone.

Creating an SQL database in the "clouds".

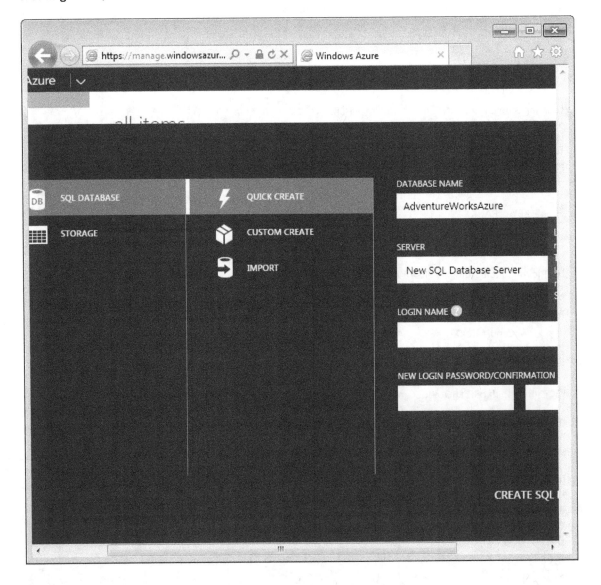

Getting Started with SQL Azure Database

Basic configuration has to be done online such as setting SQL Azure server login & password, and setting up firewall rules so you can use Management Studio and other client software from your computer. The configuration processes are automated to a large degree and user-friendly. The best part: once you are finished with configuration, you can continue with the "friendly skies" from the friendly Management Studio environment.

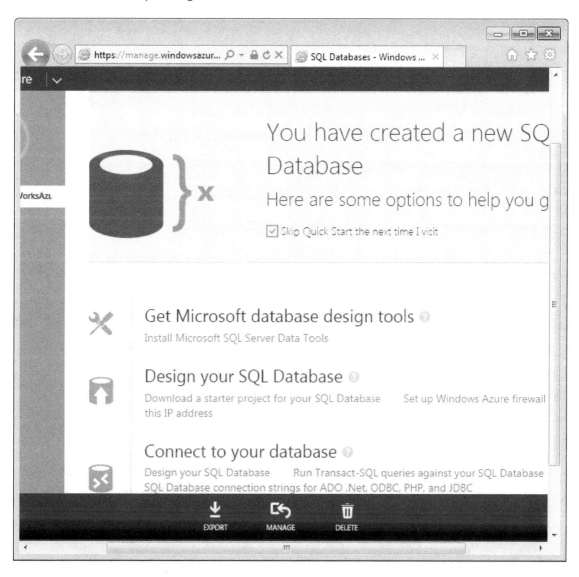

Connecting Azure SQL Server from Management Studio

You can connect to the Azure SQL Server after setting up a firewall rule for your computer IP using the regular dialog box with SQL Server authentication. The server name is: yourazureserver.database.windows.net. The login & password is what you configured on Azure. Some server & login information has been blanked out on the following screenshot. The Azure T-SQL is different from SQL Server 2012 T-SQL

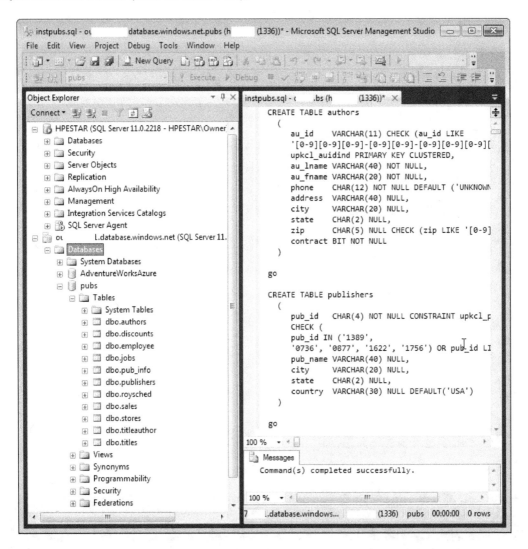

We can get SQL Azure version information by a SELECT:

select @@version -- Microsoft SQL Azure (RTM) - 11.0.2065.0 Aug 29 2012 18:41:07

CHAPTER 15: Query & Stored Procedure Optimization

Optimization Basics

Optimization revolves around techniques for the reduction of the resource requirements to carry out an operation such as a SELECT query. There are two ways to do optimization:

> ➢ Engineering the query / script the optimal way
> ➢ Creating indexes on the tables

In both instances the usual objective is "reads" (logical 8K page reads) reduction. While the final objective is the "duration" reduction, that measure involves blocking as well so it is not as reliable as the "reads" measure. Using the first software engineering technique, we aim to eliminate unneeded operations or find a replacement which is less resource intensive. The second indexing technique is purely "reads" reduction in focus, we are not changing the query or the script. T-SQL has 2 statistics commands for taking basic performance measures. For even tests, we don't want to use cache memory (fast), but only disk (slow). A "cold" execute of a query may take 8 seconds, while the next (using cache) 1 second only.

```
USE AdventureWorks2012;
DBCC DROPCLEANBUFFERS;  -- Forces reload of data pages (forces disk io) in cache buffer memory
SET STATISTICS IO ON; SET STATISTICS TIME ON;
       EXEC uspGetBillOfMaterials 801, '2008-01-05';
SET STATISTICS TIME OFF; SET STATISTICS IO OFF;  -- Messages
```

DBCC execution completed. If DBCC printed error messages, contact your system administrator.
SQL Server parse and compile time:
CPU time = 0 ms, elapsed time = 0 ms.
SQL Server Execution Times:
CPU time = 0 ms, elapsed time = 0 ms.
Table 'Product'. Scan count 0, logical reads 178, physical reads 3, read-ahead reads 0, lob logical reads 0, lob physical reads 0, lob read-ahead reads 0.
Table 'BillOfMaterials'. Scan count 90, logical reads 181, physical reads 4, read-ahead reads 0, lob logical reads 0, lob physical reads 0, lob read-ahead reads 0.
Table 'Worktable'. Scan count 2, logical reads 510, physical reads 0, read-ahead reads 0, lob logical reads 0, lob physical reads 0, lob read-ahead reads 0.
SQL Server Execution Times:
CPU time = 16 ms, elapsed time = 6 ms.
SQL Server Execution Times:
CPU time = 16 ms, elapsed time = 6 ms.

No Disk IO Needed When All Pages for a Query Are in Buffer Cache

When we execute a query shortly after the previous execution, most pages may still be on cache memory, thus reduction in the need for (slow) disk io.

```
USE AdventureWorks2012;
SET STATISTICS IO ON;
SET STATISTICS TIME ON;
        EXEC uspGetBillOfMaterials 801, '2008-01-05';
SET STATISTICS TIME OFF;  SET STATISTICS IO OFF;
GO -- Messages
```

SQL Server parse and compile time:
   CPU time = 0 ms, elapsed time = 0 ms.

 SQL Server Execution Times:
   CPU time = 0 ms, elapsed time = 0 ms.
Table 'Product'. Scan count 0, logical reads 178, **physical reads 0**, read-ahead reads 0, lob logical reads 0, lob physical reads 0, lob read-ahead reads 0.
Table 'BillOfMaterials'. Scan count 90, logical reads 181, **physical reads 0,** read-ahead reads 0, lob logical reads 0, lob physical reads 0, lob read-ahead reads 0.
Table 'Worktable'. Scan count 2, logical reads 510, physical reads 0, read-ahead reads 0, lob logical reads 0, lob physical reads 0, lob read-ahead reads 0.

 SQL Server Execution Times:
   CPU time = 0 ms, elapsed time = 2 ms.

 SQL Server Execution Times:
   CPU time = 0 ms, elapsed time = 2 ms.

We can see that physical reads have been eliminated, hence the faster execution. Note, however, timing will vary due to server activities. Therefore, to obtain good measurements we should average over multiple executions, for example 3, 11 or 31. When we monitor a similar execution sequence in SQL Server Profiler, we can see that the logical reads (Reads) were the same but the execution was faster (2 milliseconds) the second time due to the lack of disk io (physical reads). Note: STATISTICS IO and Profiler are 2 different piece of software, hence the difference in figures.

CPU	Reads	Writes	Duration
0	1096	0	7
0	1096	0	2

Optimizing a Query by Reengineering

Less fancy way of saying is rewriting the query. Consider an INNER JOIN query with a view which may look simple until we look at the view underlying code. The database engine has to expand the view definition "on the fly" and develop a plan for the more complex query.

```
USE [AdventureWorks2012]
GO
DBCC DROPCLEANBUFFERS;
SET STATISTICS IO ON;
SET STATISTICS TIME ON;
SELECT  LTRIM(CONCAT(ISNULL(Title,''),SPACE(1), FullName))          AS SalesPerson,
        JobTitle, SalesTerritory, FORMAT([2008],'c0','en-US')        AS [2008]
FROM [Sales].[vSalesPersonSalesByFiscalYears] VSP
  INNER JOIN Person.Person P
    ON CONCAT(FirstName, ' ', MiddleName, ' ', LastName) = VSP.FullName
ORDER BY [2008] DESC;
SET STATISTICS TIME OFF;  SET STATISTICS IO OFF;
GO
```

SalesPerson	JobTitle	SalesTerritory	2008
Linda C Mitchell	Sales Representative	Southwest	$4,251,369
Jae B Pak	Sales Representative	United Kingdom	$4,116,871
Michael G Blythe	Sales Representative	Northeast	$3,763,178
Jillian Carson	Sales Representative	Central	$3,189,418
Ranjit R Varkey Chudukatil	Sales Representative	France	$3,121,616
José Edvaldo Saraiva	Sales Representative	Canada	$2,604,541
Shu K Ito	Sales Representative	Southwest	$2,458,536
Tsvi Michael Reiter	Sales Representative	Southeast	$2,315,186
Rachel B Valdez	Sales Representative	Germany	$1,827,067
Mr. Tete A Mensa-Annan	Sales Representative	Northwest	$1,576,562
David R Campbell	Sales Representative	Northwest	$1,573,013
Garrett R Vargas	Sales Representative	Canada	$1,453,719
Lynn N Tsoflias	Sales Representative	Australia	$1,421,811
Pamela O Ansman-Wolfe	Sales Representative	Northwest	$1,352,577

DBCC execution completed. If DBCC printed error messages, contact your system administrator.

(14 row(s) affected)
Table 'Worktable'. Scan count 0, logical reads 0, physical reads 0, read-ahead reads 0, lob logical reads 0, lob physical reads 0, lob read-ahead reads 0.
Table 'SalesOrderHeader'. Scan count 5, logical reads 865, physical reads 2, read-ahead reads 784, lob logical reads 0, lob physical reads 0, lob read-ahead reads 0.
Table 'Employee'. Scan count 0, logical reads 28, physical reads 1, read-ahead reads 0, lob logical reads 0, lob physical reads 0, lob read-ahead reads 0.
Table 'Person'. Scan count 5, logical reads 4240, physical reads 2, read-ahead reads 3817, lob logical reads 0, lob physical reads 0, lob read-ahead reads 0.
Table 'SalesTerritory'. Scan count 0, logical reads 28, physical reads 1, read-ahead reads 0, lob logical reads 0, lob physical reads 0, lob read-ahead reads 0.
Table 'SalesPerson'. Scan count 0, logical reads 34, physical reads 1, read-ahead reads 0, lob logical reads 0, lob physical reads 0, lob read-ahead reads 0.
Table 'Worktable'. Scan count 0, logical reads 0, physical reads 0, read-ahead reads 0, lob logical reads 0, lob physical reads 0, lob read-ahead reads 0.

SQL Server Execution Times:
  CPU time = 172 ms, elapsed time = 1162 ms.

JOIN on INT Columns Faster Than on nvarchar Strings

Our suspicion is that JOINing on nvarchar fields may be improved if we replace it with JOIN on INT columns (4 bytes). Actually, we are in luck, it is just an easy rewrite of the query.

```
USE [AdventureWorks2012]
GO
DBCC DROPCLEANBUFFERS;
SET STATISTICS IO ON;
SET STATISTICS TIME ON;
SELECT  LTRIM(CONCAT(ISNULL(Title,''),SPACE(1), FullName))         AS SalesPerson,
        JobTitle, SalesTerritory, FORMAT([2008],'c0','en-US')      AS [2008]
FROM [Sales].[vSalesPersonSalesByFiscalYears] VSP
  INNER JOIN Person.Person P
    ON P.BusinessEntityID = VSP.SalesPersonID  ORDER BY [2008] DESC;
SET STATISTICS TIME OFF;  SET STATISTICS IO OFF;
GO
```

DBCC execution completed. If DBCC printed error messages, contact your system administrator.

(14 row(s) affected)
Table 'Person'. Scan count 0, logical reads 90, physical reads 2, read-ahead reads 0, lob logical reads 0, lob physical reads 0, lob read-ahead reads 0.
Table 'SalesOrderHeader'. Scan count 14, logical reads 12333, physical reads 9, read-ahead reads 352, lob logical reads 0, lob physical reads 0, lob read-ahead reads 0.
Table 'Employee'. Scan count 0, logical reads 28, physical reads 2, read-ahead reads 0, lob logical reads 0, lob physical reads 0, lob read-ahead reads 0.
Table 'SalesTerritory'. Scan count 0, logical reads 28, physical reads 1, read-ahead reads 0, lob logical reads 0, lob physical reads 0, lob read-ahead reads 0.
Table 'SalesPerson'. Scan count 1, logical reads 2, physical reads 1, read-ahead reads 0, lob logical reads 0, lob physical reads 0, lob read-ahead reads 0.

SQL Server Execution Times:
  CPU time = 16 ms, elapsed time = 68 ms.

When we compare the statistics we observe the elimination of 2 worktables and we reduced the "reads" on the Person table by the more efficient JOIN. The low CPU in the Profiler comparison screenshot indicative of the simpler JOIN. Even though the total "reads" are higher, the indexed INT JOIN proves to be quite advantageous over varchar JOIN as reflected in the lower CPU figure.

CPU	Reads	Writes	Duration
0	0	0	0
236	5314	0	1144
0	0	0	0
78	14194	0	302

Examining the Actual Execution Plan

There are two execution plan which can be turned by clicking on the corresponding icons: estimated and actual. The execution plan can be helpful with missing indexes and improvement considerations. Understanding a complex execution plan requires extensive studying and experience.

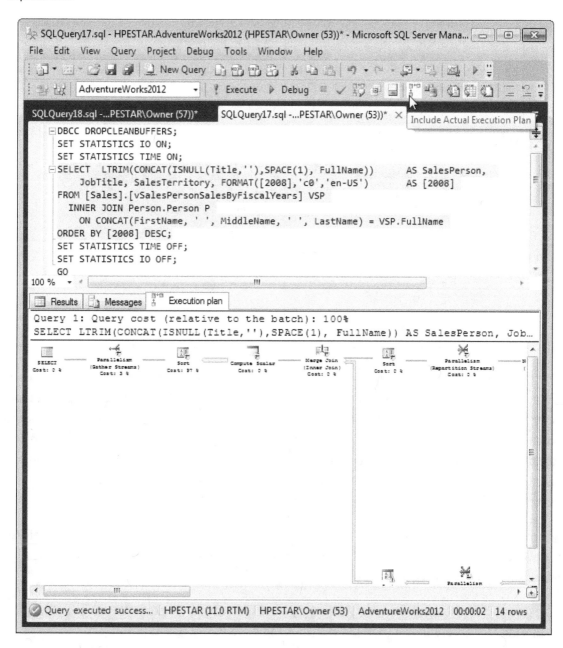

Comparing Execution Plan Cost Summary Pop-ups

When hovering with the mouse over the SELECT on the left side of the execution plan, a cost summary panel pops up.

SELECT	
Cached plan size	120 KB
Degree of Parallelism	4
Estimated Operator Cost	0 (0%)
Memory Grant	1018816
Estimated Subtree Cost	15132.9
Estimated Number of Rows	2608890

Statement

SELECT LTRIM(CONCAT(ISNULL
(Title,''),SPACE(1), FullName)) AS
SalesPerson,
JobTitle, SalesTerritory, FORMAT
([2008],'c0','en-US') AS [2008]
FROM [Sales].
[vSalesPersonSalesByFiscalYears] VSP
  INNER JOIN Person.Person P
    ON CONCAT(FirstName, ' ',
MiddleName, ' ', LastName) =
VSP.FullName
ORDER BY [2008] DESC;

SELECT	
Cached plan size	96 KB
Degree of Parallelism	1
Estimated Operator Cost	0 (0%)
Estimated Subtree Cost	1.60204
Memory Grant	7352
Estimated Number of Rows	1306.27

Statement

SELECT LTRIM(CONCAT(ISNULL
(Title,''),SPACE(1), FullName)) AS
SalesPerson,
JobTitle, SalesTerritory, FORMAT
([2008],'c0','en-US') AS [2008]
FROM [Sales].
[vSalesPersonSalesByFiscalYears] VSP
  INNER JOIN Person.Person P
    ON P.BusinessEntityID =
VSP.SalesPersonID
ORDER BY [2008] DESC;

Side by side comparison of the cost panels shows dramatic differences. Cost of 15,132 versus 1.6 are simply shocking. The example powerfully illustrates the challenges in query optimization whereby relatively simple rewrite may result in huge performance improvement. We cannot say much about the optimization state of a query just by looking at cost. Only when we compare it to a different version of the query we can say if worsened, improved or much improved. We can also notice the huge difference in rows: 2.6 million vs. 1,300. Memory requirement for the nvarchar JOIN is over a million grants, while only 7 thousands for the INT JOIN.

Poorly written query not only slow in execution but very resource intensive as well, therefore it slows down other queries executing simultaneously. Hence the need to optimize queries especially frequently executed ones.

An extreme bad query can bring down the mightiest server to its "knees". We can see why just by looking at this very simple example with bad and good INNER JOINs.

Optimizing with Multi Statements Query Using Temporary Tables

Assume that the fast INT JOIN is not available. Another technique: instead of a single statement query multi statements since we have more control over the execution plan. In the current example we are forcing the optimizer to evaluate the view query first and store the results into a temporary table. Note: messages shows the long (real) name of #VSP temporary table, personalized to this connection.

```
DBCC DROPCLEANBUFFERS;
SET STATISTICS IO ON;
SET STATISTICS TIME ON;
SELECT * INTO #VSP FROM [Sales].[vSalesPersonSalesByFiscalYears];


SELECT  LTRIM(CONCAT(ISNULL(Title,''),SPACE(1), FullName))        AS SalesPerson,
        JobTitle, SalesTerritory, FORMAT([2008],'c0','en-US')     AS [2008]
FROM #VSP
  INNER JOIN Person.Person P
   ON CONCAT(FirstName, ' ', MiddleName, ' ', LastName) = #VSP.FullName
ORDER BY [2008] DESC;
SET STATISTICS TIME OFF;
SET STATISTICS IO OFF;
GO
DROP TABLE #VSP
```

Messages

```
DBCC execution completed. If DBCC printed error messages, contact your system administrator.
Table 'SalesOrderHeader'. Scan count 14, logical reads 12452, physical reads 9, read-ahead reads 352, lob logical reads 0, lob physical reads 0, lob read-ahead reads 0.
Table 'Person'. Scan count 0, logical reads 42, physical reads 2, read-ahead reads 0, lob logical reads 0, lob physical reads 0, lob read-ahead reads 0.
Table 'Employee'. Scan count 0, logical reads 28, physical reads 2, read-ahead reads 0, lob logical reads 0, lob physical reads 0, lob read-ahead reads 0.
Table 'SalesTerritory'. Scan count 0, logical reads 28, physical reads 1, read-ahead reads 0, lob logical reads 0, lob physical reads 0, lob read-ahead reads 0.
Table 'SalesPerson'. Scan count 1, logical reads 2, physical reads 1, read-ahead reads 0, lob logical reads 0, lob physical reads 0, lob read-ahead reads 0.


(14 row(s) affected)


(1 row(s) affected)


SQL Server Execution Times:
  CPU time = 94 ms,  elapsed time = 362 ms.
SQL Server parse and compile time:
  CPU time = 0 ms, elapsed time = 70 ms.
SQL Server parse and compile time:
  CPU time = 0 ms, elapsed time = 236 ms.


(14 row(s) affected)
Table 'Person'. Scan count 1, logical reads 3826, physical reads 0, read-ahead reads 3817, lob logical reads 0, lob physical reads 0, lob read-ahead reads 0.
Table 'Worktable'. Scan count 1, logical reads 42166, physical reads 0, read-ahead reads 0, lob logical reads 0, lob physical reads 0, lob read-ahead reads 0.
Table '#VSP_____000000000074'. Scan count
1, logical reads 1, physical reads 0, read-ahead reads 0, lob logical reads 0, lob physical reads 0, lob read-ahead reads 0.


(1 row(s) affected)


SQL Server Execution Times:
  CPU time = 266 ms,  elapsed time = 832 ms.
```

Obstacle: Worktable 42K "reads" Cannot Be Decreased

This course of action is not as good as the JOIN on the INT (integer) keys. Yet the combination of costs came down to 6, a reasonable figure relatively speaking. The Estimated Number of Rows are "reasonable" as well, just like the Memory Grants.

CPU	Reads	Writes	Duration
125	15849	3	1155
203	42536	123	356

SELECT INTO		SELECT	
Cached plan size	120 KB	Cached plan size	32 KB
Degree of Parallelism	1	Degree of Parallelism	1
Estimated Operator Cost	0 (0%)	Estimated Operator Cost	0 (0%)
Estimated Subtree Cost	1.6378	Memory Grant	1024
Estimated Number of Rows	1306.27	Estimated Subtree Cost	4.18429
		Estimated Number of Rows	19972

Statement
SELECT * INTO #VSP FROM [Sales].
[vSalesPersonSalesByFiscalYears];

Statement

SELECT LTRIM(CONCAT(ISNULL
(Title,''),SPACE(1), FullName)) AS
SalesPerson,
JobTitle, SalesTerritory, FORMAT
([2008],'c0','en-US') AS [2008]
FROM #VSP
  INNER JOIN Person.Person P
    ON #VSP.FullName = CONCAT
(FirstName, ' ', MiddleName, ' ',
LastName)
ORDER BY [2008] DESC;

The 42K "reads" is huge, in this case on an internal work table which is outside our direct control, however, indirectly we may be able to influence it. The common goal of optimization is "reads" reduction usually with indexing if the query is engineered correctly. With indexing we may be able to bring down the reads to 500 or even 50.

Optimizing with Covering Index

We can achieve miracles in query optimization with indexing but at a cost: index represents an overhead since it slows down some operations such as INSERT or DELETE and it has to be maintained. First we add a computed column to the Person.Person table, them create a "covering" index on it which includes the Title used in the SELECT clause. Note: computed column and covering index are "luxury" items which are used to support **business critical queries** only. In a covering index all columns are present in the index for the query as keys or included column. **Note: there is no "free lunch" with indexing only tradeoff**. Covering index tends to be wide and may slow down other than the target queries.

```
ALTER TABLE Person.Person ADD FullName
        AS CONCAT(FirstName, ' ', MiddleName, ' ', LastName)         PERSISTED;
GO
--Command(s) completed successfully.
```

```
CREATE INDEX idxFullName
                on Person.Person(FullName) INCLUDE (Title);
GO
-- Command(s) completed successfully.
```

```
-- DROP INDEX Person.Person.idxFullName;
```

The new query using the new column in the INNER JOIN:

```
SELECT  LTRIM(CONCAT(ISNULL(Title,''),SPACE(1), #VSP.FullName))     AS SalesPerson,
        JobTitle, SalesTerritory, FORMAT([2008],'c0','en-US')       AS [2008]
FROM #VSP
 INNER JOIN Person.Person P
  ON P.FullName = #VSP.FullName
```

The result is simply amazing: the 42K "reads" on the work table is gone. The 123 "writes" are gone as well. Duration is not a stable measure because it includes blocking as well. If there is no blocking duration is proportionally higher with higher CPU, Reads & Writes.

CPU	Reads	Writes	Duration
140	15802	1	551
16	81	0	117

Optimizing with Indexing

The general rule is that all JOIN keys and WHERE condition columns should be indexed. Since PRIMARY KEY is automatically indexed, the rule means that all FOREIGN KEYs should be indexed since that is not automatic.

```
USE tempdb;
GO
SELECT [SalesOrderID]
    ,CONVERT(INT,[SalesOrderDetailID]) AS [SalesOrderDetailID] -- inhibit identity inheritence
    ,[CarrierTrackingNumber]
    ,[OrderQty]
    ,[ProductID]
    ,[SpecialOfferID]
    ,[UnitPrice]
    ,[UnitPriceDiscount]
    ,[LineTotal]
    ,[rowguid]
    ,[ModifiedDate]
INTO SOD
FROM [AdventureWorks2012].[Sales].[SalesOrderDetail];
GO
-- (121317 row(s) affected)
INSERT SOD SELECT * FROM SOD;   -- increase size of table by duplicating itself
GO 5
/* Beginning execution loop
(121317 row(s) affected)
(242634 row(s) affected)
(485268 row(s) affected)
(970536 row(s) affected)
(1941072 row(s) affected)
Batch execution completed 5 times. */
SELECT FORMAT(COUNT(*), '###,###,###') FROM SOD;  -- 3,882,144


SELECT * INTO Product FROM AdventureWorks2012.Production.Product;
GO
```

The Larger the Table the More Benefits of Indexing

```
DBCC DROPCLEANBUFFERS;  SET STATISTICS IO ON; SET STATISTICS TIME ON;
        SELECT * FROM SOD INNER JOIN Product P
                ON SOD.ProductID = P.ProductID      WHERE P.ProductID = 800;
SET STATISTICS TIME OFF;   SET STATISTICS IO OFF;
GO
```

DBCC execution completed. If DBCC printed error messages, contact your system administrator.

(15840 row(s) affected)
Table 'SOD'. Scan count 5, logical reads 54796, physical reads 0, read-ahead reads 1719, lob logical reads 0, lob physical reads 0, lob read-ahead reads 0.
Table 'Product'. Scan count 1, logical reads 14, physical reads 0, read-ahead reads 0, lob logical reads 0, lob physical reads 0, lob read-ahead reads 0.
Table 'Worktable'. Scan count 0, logical reads 0, physical reads 0, read-ahead reads 0, lob logical reads 0, lob physical reads 0, lob read-ahead reads 0.

SQL Server Execution Times:
  CPU time = 483 ms, elapsed time = 845 ms.

```
CREATE CLUSTERED INDEX idxPrd ON SOD(ProductID);
CREATE UNIQUE INDEX idxPrd ON Product(ProductID);
GO
```

```
DBCC DROPCLEANBUFFERS; SET STATISTICS IO ON;  SET STATISTICS TIME ON;
        SELECT * FROM SOD INNER JOIN Product P
                ON SOD.ProductID = P.ProductID      WHERE P.ProductID = 800;
SET STATISTICS TIME OFF;   SET STATISTICS IO OFF;
GO
```

DBCC execution completed. If DBCC printed error messages, contact your system administrator.
SQL Server parse and compile time:
  CPU time = 0 ms, elapsed time = 2 ms.

(15840 row(s) affected)
Table 'SOD'. Scan count 1, logical reads 210, physical reads 0, read-ahead reads 206, lob logical reads 0, lob physical reads 0, lob read-ahead reads 0.
Table 'Product'. Scan count 0, logical reads 3, physical reads 0, read-ahead reads 0, lob logical reads 0, lob physical reads 0, lob read-ahead reads 0.

(1 row(s) affected)

SQL Server Execution Times:
  CPU time = 47 ms, elapsed time = 517 ms.

Clustered Index for Business Critical Query Support

Clustered index is another "luxury" item in optimization since there can only be one on a table and 0 to many nonclustered indexes. In this example nonclustered index does some improvement, but not significant. Cleanup commands for the indexing example script.

-- DROP INDEX SOD.idxPrd; DROP INDEX Product.idxPrd;
DROP TABLE SOD; DROP TABLE Product;

SQL Profiler statistics on the sequence of batches we sent to the server from SSMS Query Editor.

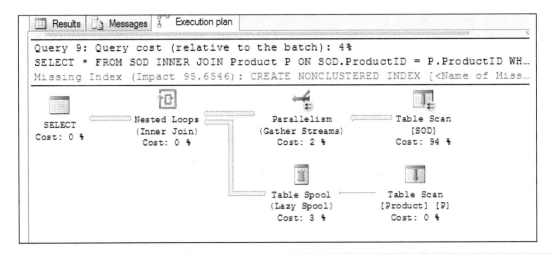

```
SQL Server Profiler - [Untitled - 1 (HPESTAR)]
File  Edit  View  Replay  Tools  Window  Help
```

TextData	CPU	Reads	Writes	Duration	SPID	EventClass
USE tempdb;	0	0	0	0	53	SQL:BatchCompleted
SELECT [SalesOrderID] ,CONVE...	218	3327	672	782	53	SQL:BatchCompleted
INSERT SOD SELECT * FROM SOD; -...	796	496577	2968	832	53	SQL:BatchCompleted
INSERT SOD SELECT * FROM SOD; -...	1685	1026720	3103	1700	53	SQL:BatchCompleted
INSERT SOD SELECT * FROM SOD; -...	3354	2086787	6433	3505	53	SQL:BatchCompleted
INSERT SOD SELECT * FROM SOD; -...	6645	4207017	12832	6709	53	SQL:BatchCompleted
INSERT SOD SELECT * FROM SOD; -...	13229	8447507	25504	13339	53	SQL:BatchCompleted
/* Beginning execution loop (121...	719	55189	9	249	53	SQL:BatchCompleted
DBCC DROPCLEANBUFFERS; SET STATI...	732	57035	1	1182	53	SQL:BatchCompleted
CREATE CLUSTERED INDEX idxPrd ON ...	15398	133236	51211	13607	53	SQL:BatchCompleted
DBCC DROPCLEANBUFFERS; SET STATI...	109	225	0	497	53	SQL:BatchCompleted
-- DROP INDEX SOD.idxPrd -- DROP...	16	480	0	147	53	SQL:BatchCompleted

We can see the reads of 57,035 decreased to 225 after creating the indexes. Not only we speeded up this query but other queries as well by decreasing the load on the server. The execution plan displays **table scan** prior to index creation.

```
Results    Messages    Execution plan

Query 9: Query cost (relative to the batch): 4%
SELECT * FROM SOD INNER JOIN Product P ON SOD.ProductID = P.ProductID WH...
Missing Index (Impact 95.6546): CREATE NONCLUSTERED INDEX [<Name of Miss...

   SELECT  <---- Nested Loops  <---- Parallelism       <---- Table Scan
   Cost: 0 %      (Inner Join)        (Gather Streams)       [SOD]
                  Cost: 0 %           Cost: 2 %              Cost: 94 %

                               Table Spool  <----  Table Scan
                               (Lazy Spool)        [Product] [P]
                               Cost: 3 %           Cost: 0 %
```

Execution Plan after Index Creation & Cost Comparison

The execution plan shows clustered index seek instead of table scan after index creation. Generally our aim with indexing is to replace table scan or index scan with index seek.

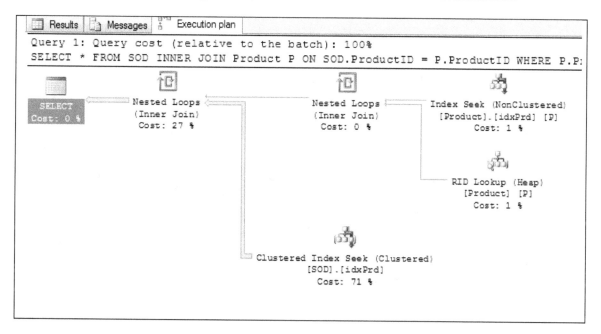

Cost comparison before and after index create reflects a very significant improvement in cost, roughly 200 fold.

SELECT		SELECT	
Cached plan size	56 KB	Cached plan size	56 KB
Degree of Parallelism	4	Degree of Parallelism	1
Estimated Operator Cost	0 (0%)	Estimated Operator Cost	0 (0%)
Estimated Subtree Cost	45.4362	Estimated Subtree Cost	0.247049
Memory Grant	72	Estimated Number of Rows	15840
Estimated Number of Rows	15513.1		

Statement

SELECT * FROM SOD INNER JOIN
Product P
    ON SOD.ProductID = P.ProductID
    WHERE P.ProductID = 800;

Statement

SELECT * FROM SOD INNER JOIN Product
P
    ON SOD.ProductID = P.ProductID
    WHERE P.ProductID = 800;

Non-SARGable Predicates Force Index Scan

The term SARGable stands for Search ARGument ABLE. It means the WHERE clause OR join ON clause predicate written such a way that the database engine can use the index on the column. Basically means if we form an expression with the indexed column, index scan will be performed instead of index seek, in other words, index will not be used to speed up the query. The (SOD.ProductID +1 - 1) expression in the ON clause causes clustered index scan. The relative query costs are 1% (SARGable) and 99% (non-SARGable) in the batch of 2 queries.

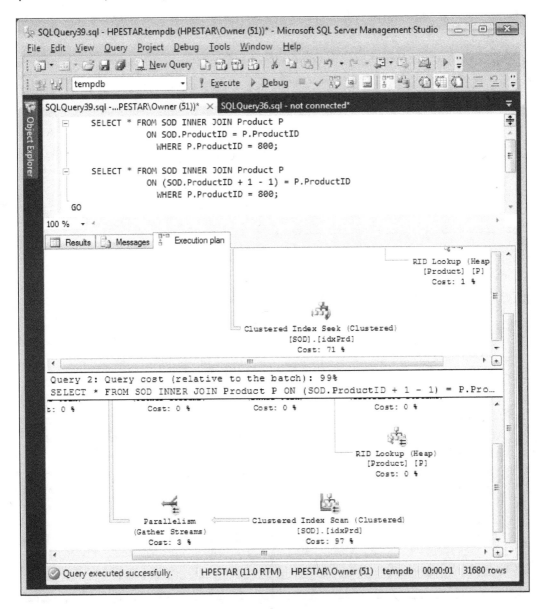

SARGable Predicate Construction

It is a challenge to remember all the time to make the predicate SARGable. Frequently, so much easier to make it non-SARGable.

```
YEAR(OrderDate) = 2016 AND MONTH(OrderDate) = 10              -- non-SARGable
OrderDate >= '2016-10-01' AND OrderDate < DATEADD(MM,1, '2016-10-01') -- SARGable
```

The payoff can be great as shown by the previous SARGable & non-SARGable examples, duration in msec.

CPU	Reads	Writes	Duration
125	223	0	668
1527	51451	0	11497

Clustered Index Seek (Clustered)		Clustered Index Scan (Clustered)	
Scanning a particular range of rows from a clustered index.		Scanning a clustered index, entirely or only a range.	
Physical Operation	Clustered Index Seek	**Physical Operation**	Clustered Index Scan
Logical Operation	Clustered Index Seek	**Logical Operation**	Clustered Index Scan
Actual Execution Mode	Row	**Actual Execution Mode**	Row
Estimated Execution Mode	Row	**Estimated Execution Mode**	Row
Storage	RowStore	**Actual Number of Rows**	15840
Actual Number of Rows	15840	**Actual Number of Batches**	0
Actual Number of Batches	0	**Estimated I/O Cost**	37.8224
Estimated Operator Cost	0.174279 (71%)	**Estimated Operator Cost**	39.9576 (97%)
Estimated I/O Cost	0.156698	**Estimated CPU Cost**	2.13526
Estimated CPU Cost	0.017581	**Estimated Subtree Cost**	39.9576
Estimated Subtree Cost	0.174279	**Number of Executions**	4
Number of Executions	1	**Estimated Number of Executions**	1
Estimated Number of Executions	1	**Estimated Number of Rows**	15840
Estimated Number of Rows	15840	**Estimated Row Size**	112 B
Estimated Row Size	112 B	**Actual Rebinds**	0
Actual Rebinds	0	**Actual Rewinds**	0
Actual Rewinds	0	Ordered	False
Ordered	True	Node ID	58
Node ID	54		

Object
[tempdb].[dbo].[SOD].[idxPrd]
Output List
[tempdb].[dbo].[SOD].SalesOrderID, [tempdb].[dbo].
[SOD].SalesOrderDetailID, [tempdb].[dbo].
[SOD].CarrierTrackingNumber, [tempdb].[dbo].
[SOD].OrderQty, [tempdb].[dbo].[SOD].ProductID, [tempdb].
[dbo].[SOD].SpecialOfferID, [tempdb].[dbo].[SOD].UnitPrice,
[tempdb].[dbo].[SOD].UnitPriceDiscount, [tempdb].[dbo].
[SOD].LineTotal, [tempdb].[dbo].[SOD].rowguid, [tempdb].
[dbo].[SOD].ModifiedDate
Seek Predicates
Seek Keys[1]: Prefix: [tempdb].[dbo].[SOD].ProductID =
Scalar Operator((800))

Predicate
([tempdb].[dbo].[SOD].[ProductID]+(1)-(1))=(800)
Object
[tempdb].[dbo].[SOD].[idxPrd]
Output List
[tempdb].[dbo].[SOD].SalesOrderID, [tempdb].[dbo].
[SOD].SalesOrderDetailID, [tempdb].[dbo].
[SOD].CarrierTrackingNumber, [tempdb].[dbo].
[SOD].OrderQty, [tempdb].[dbo].[SOD].ProductID, [tempdb].
[dbo].[SOD].SpecialOfferID, [tempdb].[dbo].[SOD].UnitPrice,
[tempdb].[dbo].[SOD].UnitPriceDiscount, [tempdb].[dbo].
[SOD].LineTotal, [tempdb].[dbo].[SOD].rowguid, [tempdb].
[dbo].[SOD].ModifiedDate

CHAPTER 15: Query & Stored Procedure Optimization

Stored Procedure Parameter Sniffing & Prevention

When SQL Server database engine compiles a stored procedure, it may use the actual parameters supplied to prepare an execution plan. If the parameters are atypical, the plan may be slow for typical parameters. For consistent stored procedure performance parameter sniffing should be eliminated. A telltale sign of parameter sniffing when suddenly a stored procedure executes in 2 minutes, as an example, instead of the usual 10 seconds. *This is different when the first (cold from disk) execution of a stored procedure is much longer than the second & on (warm since pages in buffer memory) execution.* Parameter sniffing may show up also as 5 minutes execution in one environment (like application) and 2 seconds in another (like SSMS).

> Technet Article
> Batch Compilation, Recompilation, and Plan Caching Issues in SQL Server 2005
> http://technet.microsoft.com/en-us/library/cc966425.aspx

Here are the most popular two ways of preventing parameter sniffing.

First prevention method: remap parameters to local variables and use those only.

```
USE AdventureWorks2012;
GO
CREATE PROCEDURE uspProductByColor @pcolor varchar(20)   AS BEGIN
        DECLARE @color varchar(20) = @pcolor;          -- remapping
        SET NOCOUNT ON;
        SELECT * FROM Production.Product WHERE Color = @color  ORDER BY name;
END
GO
```

```
EXEC uspProductByColor 'Red';  -- 38 rows returned
```

Second prevention method: RECOMPILE stored procedure at each execution (for large procedure compilation time may be significant).

```
CREATE PROCEDURE uspProductByColor @pcolor varchar(20)
WITH RECOMPILE AS BEGIN  SET NOCOUNT ON;
   SELECT * FROM Production.Product WHERE Color = @pcolor   ORDER BY name; END
```

Stress Testing a View with Include Client Statistics Feature

Client Statistics feature can be turned by icon or right click drop-down menu option. It calculates averages for up to 10 trials. DBCC DROPCLEANBUFFERS equalizes the tests by purging thecached data pages from buffer memory. Note: server load will influence timings. Query drop-down has option to Reset Client Statistics.

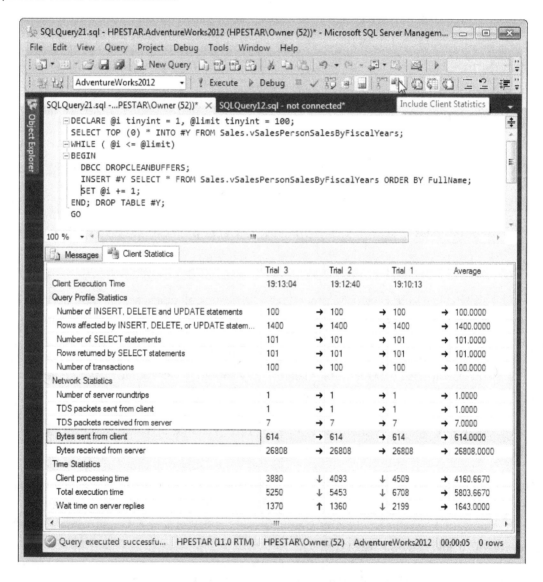

```
DECLARE @i tinyint = 1, @limit tinyint = 100;
SELECT TOP (0) * INTO #Y FROM Sales.vSalesPersonSalesByFiscalYears;
WHILE ( @i <= @limit)
BEGIN
    DBCC DROPCLEANBUFFERS;
    INSERT #Y SELECT * FROM Sales.vSalesPersonSalesByFiscalYears ORDER BY FullName;
    SET @i += 1;
END; DROP TABLE #Y;
GO
```

	Trial 3	Trial 2	Trial 1	Average
Client Execution Time	19:13:04	19:12:40	19:10:13	
Query Profile Statistics				
Number of INSERT, DELETE and UPDATE statements	100	→ 100	→ 100	→ 100.0000
Rows affected by INSERT, DELETE, or UPDATE statem...	1400	→ 1400	→ 1400	→ 1400.0000
Number of SELECT statements	101	→ 101	→ 101	→ 101.0000
Rows returned by SELECT statements	101	→ 101	→ 101	→ 101.0000
Number of transactions	100	→ 100	→ 100	→ 100.0000
Network Statistics				
Number of server roundtrips	1	→ 1	→ 1	→ 1.0000
TDS packets sent from client	1	→ 1	→ 1	→ 1.0000
TDS packets received from server	7	→ 7	→ 7	→ 7.0000
Bytes sent from client	614	→ 614	→ 614	→ 614.0000
Bytes received from server	26808	→ 26808	→ 26808	→ 26808.0000
Time Statistics				
Client processing time	3880	↓ 4093	↓ 4509	→ 4160.6670
Total execution time	5250	↓ 5453	↓ 6708	→ 5803.6670
Wait time on server replies	1370	↑ 1360	↓ 2199	→ 1643.0000

Maximum Capacity Specifications for SQL Server
http://msdn.microsoft.com/en-us/library/ms143432.aspx

10 Point Optimization Guide

Performance tuning and optimization are a huge topic. We only touch the tip of the iceberg. Nonetheless, the important elements of optimization can be summarized quite easily. It starts with prioritizing what is business critical, what is not. If 500 users are unhappy with a stored procedure, that is business critical. If one user is unhappy with a slow report, that is not business critical, unless that user is the CEO.

1. REBUILD indexes every weekend. Use FILLFACTOR for dynamic tables with lots of INSERTs. FILLFACTOR 70 means 70% data and 30% empty space. Free database maintenance scripts at http://ola.hallengren.com/ - SQL Server Backup, Integrity Check, and Index and Statistics Maintenance.

2. UPDATE STATISTICS every night. The database engine query optimizer uses the statistics to prepare efficient execution plans.

3. Eliminate missing indexes. All FOREIGN KEY & WHERE condition columns should be indexed.

4. Optimize all business critical queries. WHERE & ON clause predicates should be SARGable.

5. Examine execution plan for business critical queries to make sure they are efficient.

6. Optimize all business critical stored procedures. In a sproc all queries should be optimized and looping should be kept at an absolute minimum. Non-scalable cursors should be avoided.

7. Server memory max should be set in server properties. That is quite a challenge with 32-bit OS. For 64 bit OS with 65GB of memory, max memory should be set to 55GB, as a general guideline, to leave enough room for SS and other program operations.

8. Disk configuration should be optimized. Article: http://technet.microsoft.com/en-us/library/cc966412.aspx .

9. Operational solutions for performance problems which cannot be readily resolved due to lack of resources. For example, external feed arrives 11AM every day and promptly uploaded in 1/2 hour thus slowing down the system and annoying users. Instead schedule uploading with SQL Server Agent to low use time like 11pm.

10. Database design should be efficient. Narrow and fixed row size tables are the best performant. Note: frequently database design is frozen, "as is" , for budget reasons or a 3rd party package. Even in a such a case, index & statistics maintenance can improve performance.

Object Explorer GUI REBUILD Indexes

The indexes can be rebuilt in SSMS Object Explorer using Graphical User Interface. REBUILD indexes updates statistics as well. T-SQL command syntax example:

ALTER INDEX ALL ON [Sales].[SalesOrderDetail] REBUILD WITH (FILLFACTOR = 90);

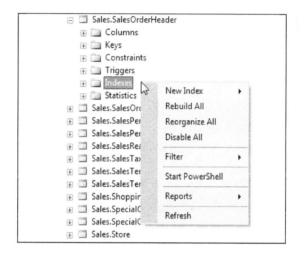

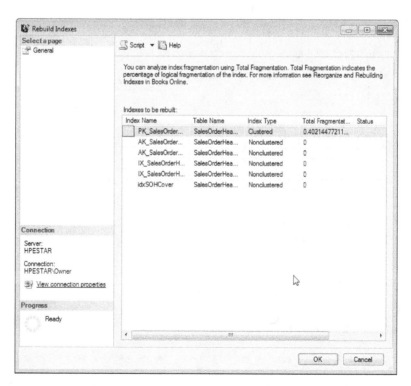

UPDATE STATISTICS on All Tables Stored Procedure

The UPDATE STATISTICS on all tables stored procedure has one parameter: the sample percent for scanning. Lower the number, faster the update. WITH FULLSCAN option does 100% sampling, it may be slow for large tables. Create & execute stored procedure script.

```
CREATE PROCEDURE sprocUpdateAllStats (@Sample int)  AS
BEGIN
DECLARE @SQL AS NVARCHAR(1024), @Table sysname, @Schema sysname;
DECLARE curAllTables CURSOR FOR
        SELECT TABLE_SCHEMA, TABLE_NAME
        FROM INFORMATION_SCHEMA.TABLES
        WHERE TABLE_TYPE='BASE TABLE'
        ORDER BY TABLE_SCHEMA, TABLE_NAME;
OPEN curAllTables;
FETCH NEXT FROM curAllTables
        INTO @Schema, @Table;

WHILE (@@FETCH_STATUS = 0)
BEGIN
 SET @SQL =    CONCAT('UPDATE STATISTICS ',
                QUOTENAME( @Schema),'.', QUOTENAME( @Table),
                ' WITH SAMPLE ', CONVERT(char(3), @sample), ' PERCENT;');
--              ' WITH FULLSCAN; ');
 PRINT @SQL;
 -- UPDATE STATISTICS [Sales].[Store] WITH SAMPLE 10 PERCENT;

 EXEC sp_executesql @SQL;

 FETCH NEXT FROM curAllTables
        INTO @Schema, @Table;
END -- while
 CLOSE curAllTables;  DEALLOCATE curAllTables;
END
GO
```

```
EXEC sprocUpdateAllStats 10;
```

Blocking of a Query by Another Query

SQL Server applies locks at the row, page and table level in order to maintain data integrity. If another query tries to operate on the locked part, it may get blocked. It is easy to see how blocking can degrade the performance of the server. We can simulate blocking. In connection 1 we execute and leave open a transaction. In connection 2 we execute a query which intends to operate on the locked table. The result is blocking of connection 2 query by connection 1 query.

```
-- Connection 1
BEGIN TRAN;
UPDATE HumanResources.Shift SET ModifiedDate = convert(datetime, ModifiedDate);
-- ROLLBACK TRAN;
```

```
-- Connection 2
BEGIN TRAN;
UPDATE HumanResources.Shift SET ModifiedDate = convert(datetime, ModifiedDate);
COMMIT TRAN;
```

Checking blocking by **sp_who** system procedure (exec sp_who in a 3rd connection) and **Activity Monitor** (right click on server menu). The Activity Monitor chart even shows the Head Blocker which is very helpful to trace the source of a blocking chain. A quick resolution is killing the head blocker (kill 55). Long term fix is making the blocking query efficient.

	spid	ecid	status	loginame	hostname	blk	dbname	cmd
36	52	0	runnable	HPES...	HPEST...	0	master	SELECT
37	53	0	sleeping	NT SE...	HPEST...	0	ReportServer	AWAITING COMMAND
38	54	0	sleeping	HPES...	HPEST...	0	master	AWAITING COMMAND
39	55	0	sleeping	HPES...	HPEST...	0	AdventureWorks2012	AWAITING COMMAND
40	56	0	sleeping	NT SE...	HPEST...	0	ReportServer	AWAITING COMMAND
41	57	0	suspended	HPES...	HPEST...	55	AdventureWorks2012	UPDATE

S...	U...	Login	Dat...	Tas...	Com...	Appl...	Wait Tim...	Wait...	Wait...	Blocked By	Head Blocker	Me...
51	1	HPESTA...	master			Microsoft...	0					
52	1	HPESTA...	master			Microsoft...	0					
53	1	NT SER...	ReportS...			Report S...	0					
54	1	HPESTA...	master	RUNNING	SELECT	Microsoft...	0					
55	1	HPESTA...	Adventur...			Microsoft...	0				1	
56	1	NT SER...	ReportS...			Report S...	0					
57	1	HPESTA...	Adventur...	SUSPEN...	UPDATE	Microsoft...	172568	LCK_M_U	keylock ...	55		

Activity Monitor

The Activity Monitor provides real time operational information in list and graphical chart formats based on operational DMV-s.

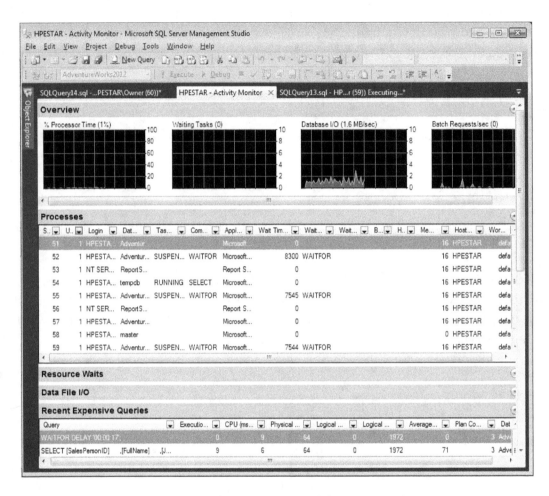

Operational Solutions for Performance Problems

Frequently real fix cannot be carried out quickly or at all for a performance issue due to software complexities and limited expert-level resources. In such a case we have to think about implementing operational solutions:

> Users complain about slow online reports. Setup reports as night jobs with automatic email distribution.

> Reports slow OLTP activities. Restore last night DB backup under new name as reporting DB. Usually, only a small fraction of reports need to be real-time.

CHAPTER 15: Query & Stored Procedure Optimization

Server & Database Standard Reports

The Server Standard Reports can be accessed via the right click on server drop-down menu in SSMS Object Explorer (top left). The Database Standard Reports can be accessed via the right click on database drop down menu (top right). The reports are based on Dynamic Management Views (DMV-s). They represent operational data since the last restart of the server. At the bottom, partial display of the Index Usage Statistics report.

Server Dashboard	Disk Usage
Configuration Changes History	Disk Usage by Top Tables
Schema Changes History	Disk Usage by Table
Scheduler Health	Disk Usage by Partition
Memory Consumption	Backup and Restore Events
Activity - All Blocking Transactions	All Transactions
Activity - All Cursors	All Blocking Transactions
Activity - Top Cursors	Top Transactions by Age
Activity - All Sessions	Top Transactions by Blocked Transactions Count
Activity - Top Sessions	Top Transactions by Locks Count
Activity - Dormant Sessions	Resource Locking Statistics by Objects
Activity - Top Connections	Object Execution Statistics
Top Transactions by Age	Database Consistency History
Top Transactions by Blocked Transactions Count	Index Usage Statistics
Top Transactions by Locks Count	Index Physical Statistics
Performance - Batch Execution Statistics	Schema Changes History
Performance - Object Execution Statistics	User Statistics
Performance - Top Queries by Average CPU Time	
Performance - Top Queries by Average IO	
Performance - Top Queries by Total CPU Time	
Performance - Top Queries by Total IO	
Service Broker Statistics	
Transaction Log Shipping Status	

HumanResources.Employee

Index Name	Index Type	# User Seeks	# User Scans	# User Updates
PK_Employee_BusinessEntityID	CLUSTERED	697	0	0

HumanResources.Shift

Index Name	Index Type	# User Seeks	# User Scans	# User Updates
PK_Shift_ShiftID	CLUSTERED	0	5	5

Person.Person

CHAPTER 15: Query & Stored Procedure Optimization

Server Dashboard

The Server Dashboard contains important high-level information about the server.

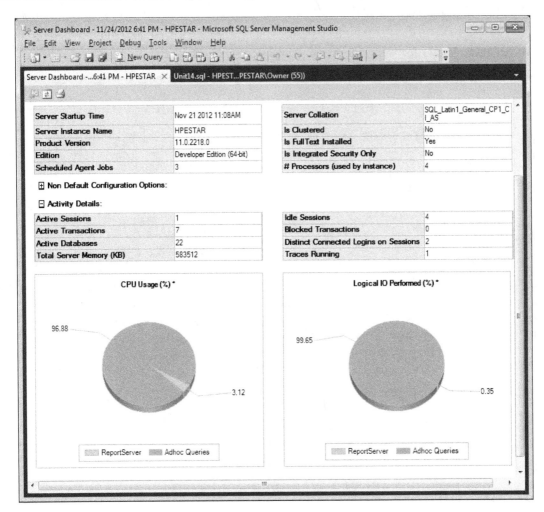

Segment from Performance - Top Queries by Total CPU Time report.

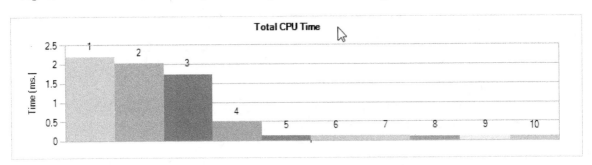

Batching Large INSERT, UPDATE & DELETE

Batch processing jobs best executed at low use time like night or weekend. Frequently, however, we may not have a choice, we have to run them during transactional activities. We can minimize conflict by breaking down a large job to small batches and providing 1 second or so wait time for other queries to execute. During that 1 second hundreds of short transactions may execute. DELETE from large tables may prove to be very slow due to restructuring of the index pages.

```
USE tempdb;
SELECT  ProductID=CONVERT(int, ProductID), ProductName=Name,
        ProductNumber, ListPrice, Color, Size
INTO Product FROM AdventureWorks2008.Production.Product;
```

```
INSERT Product SELECT * FROM Product;  -- Double table rows at each execution
GO 16
/* .....   (16515072 row(s) affected)
Batch execution completed 16 times.   */
SELECT FORMAT(COUNT(*),'###,###,###') FROM Product;   -- 33,030,144
GO
CREATE CLUSTERED INDEX idxProductID
             on Product(ProductID);
GO -- 12 minutes 44 seconds
```

```
DECLARE @BatchSize int = 10000;
WHILE (@@ROWCOUNT > 0)  BEGIN    WAITFOR DELAY '00:00:01';
        DELETE TOP (@BatchSize) FROM Product    WHERE ProductNumber = 'CA-5965';
END
GO   -- 3 minutes 8 seconds
/*(10000 row(s) affected)
(10000 row(s) affected)
(10000 row(s) affected)
(10000 row(s) affected)
(10000 row(s) affected)
(10000 row(s) affected)
(5536 row(s) affected)
(0 row(s) affected)*/
```

```
SELECT FORMAT(COUNT(*),'###,###,###') FROM Product;   -- 32,964,608  -- 5 seconds
GO
DROP TABLE tempdb.dbo.Product;
```

CHAPTER 15: Query & Stored Procedure Optimization

Database Engine Tuning Advisor

The Database Engine Tuning Advisor (DETA or DTA) provides indexing & statistics recommendations based on the supplied workload. A single query can be analyzed as well, right click Query drop-down menu.

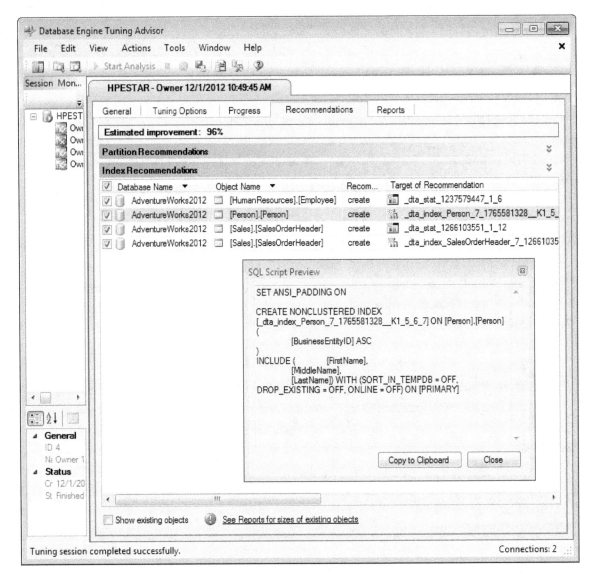

DBCC HELP Command

Withe the DBCC HELP command you can get syntax assistance with any of the DBCC commands.

```
DBCC HELP (checkdb);
```

CHAPTER 16: Advanced T-SQL Programming Topics

String Pattern Matching & Parsing

The CHARINDEX() function, PATINDEX() function and LIKE operator offer substring search in string functionality with some differences. Frequently, all 3 can be used for the same result.

The LIKE Operator

LIKE operator usage for numeric and alphanumeric differentiation.

```
USE AdventureWorks2012;
SELECT AddressID, City, StateProvinceID, PostalCode
FROM Person.Address WHERE PostalCode LIKE '%[^0-9]%';
-- (3644 row(s) affected) - Partial results.
```

AddressID	City	StateProvinceID	PostalCode
532	Ottawa	57	K4B 1S2
497	Burnaby	7	V5A 4X1
15272	Haney	7	V2W 1W2
14068	Cambridge	14	CB4 4BZ

```
SELECT AddressID, City, StateProvinceID, PostalCode
FROM Person.Address WHERE PostalCode NOT LIKE '%[^0-9]%';
-- (15970 row(s) affected) - Partial results.
```

AddressID	City	StateProvinceID	PostalCode
26916	Dunkerque	145	59140
28885	Lille	145	59000
708	Paris	161	75017
23902	Lieusaint	163	77127

Elaborate patterns can be formed from regular characters and wildcard characters. Underscore (_) matches any character.

```
DECLARE @Pattern varchar(20) = '[CFPS]___[eo]n'
SELECT DISTINCT LastName FROM Person.Person WHERE LastName  LIKE @Pattern;
-- Campen, Cannon, Carson, Fulton, Patten, Slaven, Sutton
```

The CHARINDEX() Function

The CHARINDEX() function locates a substring within a string. A string with 2 hyphens (-) is split into 3 parts.

```
SELECT          ProductNumber,
                [Part1] = LEFT(ProductNumber,CHARINDEX('-',ProductNumber) - 1),
                [Part2] = SUBSTRING(ProductNumber,CHARINDEX('-',ProductNumber) + 1,
                          CHARINDEX('-',ProductNumber,CHARINDEX('-',
                          ProductNumber) + 1) - (CHARINDEX('-',ProductNumber) + 1)),
                [Part3] = RIGHT(ProductNumber,CHARINDEX('-',REVERSE(ProductNumber)) - 1)
FROM AdventureWorks2012.Production.Product
WHERE LEN(ProductNumber) - LEN(REPLACE(ProductNumber, '-','')) = 2;   -- 2 hyphens in string
-- (213 row(s) affected) - Partial results.
```

ProductNumber	Part1	Part2	Part3
BK-M18B-40	BK	M18B	40
BK-M18B-42	BK	M18B	42
BK-M18B-44	BK	M18B	44
BK-M18B-48	BK	M18B	48
BK-M18B-52	BK	M18B	52

Find the left part of a string before the comma. We get an error without the NULLIF function due to subtracting 1 from the LEN() result which may be 0 (zero).

```
SELECT Name, LEFT(Name,CHARINDEX(',',Name)-1) AS NamePrefix
FROM AdventureWorks2012.Production.Product ORDER BY Name;
/* Msg 537, Level 16, State 3, Line 1
Invalid length parameter passed to the LEFT or SUBSTRING function. */
```

```
SELECT  ProductNumber,
        NamePrefix=LEFT(Name,COALESCE(NULLIF(CHARINDEX(',',Name)-1,-1),LEN(Name))),
        ProductName=Name
FROM AdventureWorks2012.Production.Product ORDER BY ProductName;
-- (504 row(s) affected) - Partial results;
```

ProductNumber	NamePrefix	ProductName
FR-T67Y-58	LL Touring Frame - Yellow	LL Touring Frame - Yellow, 58
FR-T67Y-62	LL Touring Frame - Yellow	LL Touring Frame - Yellow, 62
HB-T721	LL Touring Handlebars	LL Touring Handlebars
SA-T467	LL Touring Seat Assembly	LL Touring Seat Assembly

The PATINDEX() Function

The PATINDEX() function can be used for complex pattern searches.

```
use AdventureWorks2012;
```

```
select          [Name]                        AS ProductName,
                ProductNumber,
                [Description],
                ListPrice
from [Production].[Product] p
  inner join [Production].[ProductModelProductDescriptionCulture] pmpdc
    on p.ProductModelID = pmpdc.ProductModelID
  inner join  [Production].[ProductDescription] pd
    on pmpdc.ProductDescriptionID = pd.ProductDescriptionID
where patindex( '%mountain%innovative%', pd.[Description]) > 0
order by ProductNumber DESC;
-- (8 row(s) affected) - Partial results.
```

ProductName	ProductNumber	Description	ListPrice
Mountain-100 Silver, 48	BK-M82S-48	Top-of-the-line competition mountain bike. Performance-enhancing options include the innovative HL Frame, super-smooth front suspension, and traction for all terrain.	3399.99

Searching UNICODE Chinese text.

```
select [Name] AS ProductName, ProductNumber, [Description], ListPrice
from [Production].[Product] p
  inner join [Production].[ProductModelProductDescriptionCulture] pmpdc
    on p.ProductModelID = pmpdc.ProductModelID
  inner join  [Production].[ProductDescription] pd
    on pmpdc.ProductDescriptionID = pd.ProductDescriptionID
where patindex( N'%量的%快速%', pd.[Description]) > 0
order by ProductNumber DESC;
```

ProductName	ProductNumber	Description	ListPrice
HL Headset	HS-3479	高质量的一英寸无螺纹车头碗组具有油口，可确保快速润滑。	124.73

Complex pattern match with wildcards.

```
SELECT PATINDEX('%[A-T,0-9]%[Q,0-9]%[0-9]%','ZQZQXYZABC123'); --2
```

CHAPTER 16: Advanced T-SQL Programming Topics

Composable DML - INSERT into 2 Tables with One Statement

Composable DML is new to SQL Server 2012. It expands the concept of SELECT subquery to
INSERT/UPDATE/DELETE/MERGE operation using the OUTPUT clause with some restrictions.

```
USE tempdb;
CREATE TABLE PurchaseOrderDetail(              -- Create 2 empty tables for testing
        PurchaseOrderID int NOT NULL,
        PurchaseOrderDetailID int NOT NULL,
        DueDate datetime NOT NULL,
        OrderQty smallint NOT NULL,
        ProductID int NOT NULL,
        UnitPrice money NOT NULL,
        LineTotal  money,
        ReceivedQty decimal(8, 2) NOT NULL,
        RejectedQty decimal(8, 2) NOT NULL,
        StockedQty  int,
        ModifiedDate datetime NOT NULL);
```

```
SELECT * INTO POD FROM PurchaseOrderDetail;
```

```
INSERT PurchaseOrderDetail  OUTPUT inserted.*          -- Test query with OUTPUT
SELECT * FROM AdventureWorks2012.Purchasing.PurchaseOrderDetail
GO
-- (8845 row(s) affected)
```

```
TRUNCATE TABLE PurchaseOrderDetail;
GO
-- Command(s) completed successfully.
```

```
INSERT POD                                         -- Composable DML
SELECT *  FROM (
        INSERT PurchaseOrderDetail    OUTPUT inserted.*
        SELECT * FROM AdventureWorks2012.Purchasing.PurchaseOrderDetail ) X ;
GO
```

```
SELECT COUNT(*) FROM POD;                          -- 8845
SELECT COUNT(*) FROM PurchaseOrderDetail;          -- 8845
GO
```

```
DROP TABLE POD;  DROP TABLE PurchaseOrderDetail;
```

Double Assignment Operator

The multiple value assignment operator allows more than one assignment for the same value.

```
USE tempdb;

SELECT       CONVERT(int, SalesOrderID)          AS ID,
             CONVERT(date, ModifiedDate)         AS TestDate
INTO   DateSequence
FROM   AdventureWorks2012.Sales.SalesOrderHeader ;
go
--(31465 row(s) affected)

SELECT TOP 5 *
FROM   DateSequence ;
go
```

ID	TestDate
43659	2005-07-08
43660	2005-07-08
43661	2005-07-08
43662	2005-07-08
43663	2005-07-08

```
-- Multiple assignment UPDATE
DECLARE @Date date = dateadd(day, 1, CURRENT_TIMESTAMP),
        @id   int = 0 ;

UPDATE DateSequence
       SET    @id = ID = @id + 1,
              @Date = TestDate = dateadd (Day, -1, @Date);
go

SELECT TOP 5 * FROM   DateSequence ORDER BY TestDate DESC;
go
```

ID	TestDate
1	2012-10-21
2	2012-10-20
3	2012-10-19
4	2012-10-18
5	2012-10-17

Running Total & Average Calculation with the OVER Clause

Running total support is a new feature of SQL Server 2012. OVER clause makes the RT calculation a breeze.

```
USE AdventureWorks2012;
GO

SELECT SalesOrderID,
    FORMAT(TotalDue,'c0','en-US')                                    AS TotalDue,
    FORMAT(COUNT(TotalDue) OVER( ORDER BY SalesOrderID), '###,###') AS RunningCount,
    FORMAT(SUM(TotalDue) OVER( ORDER BY SalesOrderID), 'c0','en-US')  AS RunningTotal,
    FORMAT(AVG(TotalDue) OVER( ORDER BY SalesOrderID), 'c0','en-US')  AS RunningAvg
FROM Sales.SalesOrderHeader
WHERE OrderDate >='20080201'
        AND OrderDate < DATEADD(mm,1,'20080201')
ORDER BY SalesOrderID;
GO
-- (2032 row(s) affected) - Partial results.
```

SalesOrderID	TotalDue	RunningCount	RunningTotal	RunningAvg
63119	$247	1	$247	$247
63120	$234	2	$481	$240
63121	$187	3	$668	$223
63122	$213	4	$881	$220
63123	$16,320	5	$17,201	$3,440
63124	$36,462	6	$53,663	$8,944
63125	$9,603	7	$63,266	$9,038
63126	$2,298	8	$65,564	$8,196
63127	$8,870	9	$74,435	$8,271
63128	$21,805	10	$96,240	$9,624
63129	$1,691	11	$97,930	$8,903
63130	$4,355	12	$102,285	$8,524
63131	$97,929	13	$200,214	$15,401
63132	$38,158	14	$238,372	$17,027
63133	$36,926	15	$275,298	$18,353
63134	$8,597	16	$283,896	$17,743
63135	$1,872	17	$285,768	$16,810
63136	$41,760	18	$327,528	$18,196
63137	$987	19	$328,515	$17,290
63138	$5,344	20	$333,859	$16,693

Running Total with Subquery - Ye Olde Way

Calculating cumulative totals with subquery is quite inefficient, but it works.

```
USE AdventureWorks2012;
GO


DECLARE @Year INT = 2005, @Month INT = 7;
SELECT   RN = ROW_NUMBER()
            OVER(ORDER BY SalesOrderID),
      OrderDate = convert(CHAR(10),OrderDate,111), -- date formatting
      SalesOrderId,
      TotalDue = '$' + convert(VARCHAR,TotalDue,1), -- Currency formatting
      [Running Total] = '$' + convert(VARCHAR,
      (SELECT sum(TotalDue)
       FROM   Sales.SalesOrderHeader
       WHERE  SalesOrderID <= soh.SalesOrderID    -- Key predicate in the process
         AND year(OrderDate) = @Year
         AND month(OrderDate) = @Month),
                   1)
FROM     Sales.SalesOrderHeader soh
WHERE    year(OrderDate) = @Year
      AND month(OrderDate) = @Month
ORDER BY RN;
GO
-- (184 row(s) affected) - Partial results.
```

RN	OrderDate	SalesOrderId	TotalDue	Running Total
1	2005/07/01	43659	$23,153.23	$23,153.23
2	2005/07/01	43660	$1,457.33	$24,610.56
3	2005/07/01	43661	$36,865.80	$61,476.36
4	2005/07/01	43662	$32,474.93	$93,951.30
5	2005/07/01	43663	$472.31	$94,423.61
6	2005/07/01	43664	$27,510.41	$121,934.02
7	2005/07/01	43665	$16,158.70	$138,092.71
8	2005/07/01	43666	$5,694.86	$143,787.57
9	2005/07/01	43667	$6,876.36	$150,663.94
10	2005/07/01	43668	$40,487.72	$191,151.66
11	2005/07/01	43669	$807.26	$191,958.92
12	2005/07/01	43670	$6,893.25	$198,852.17
13	2005/07/01	43671	$9,153.61	$208,005.78
14	2005/07/01	43672	$6,895.41	$214,901.19
15	2005/07/01	43673	$4,216.03	$219,117.21

Running Total with Multiple Assignment UPDATE

Cumulative total can be generated a fast way using double assignment SET in UPDATE command. There are some restrictions such as no table partitioning. It should not be used in production unless there is a serious performance problem.

```
USE AdventureWorks2012;
```

```
DECLARE  @RunningTotal MONEY;
DECLARE  @Result  TABLE(
            SalesOrderID INT   NOT NULL   PRIMARY KEY,
            TotalDue    MONEY,
            RunningTotal MONEY
            );
SET @RunningTotal = 0.0;
INSERT INTO @Result
     (SalesOrderID,
      TotalDue)
SELECT  SalesOrderID,      TotalDue
FROM    Sales.SalesOrderHeader
ORDER BY SalesOrderID
-- (31465 row(s) affected)


UPDATE @Result
SET   @RunningTotal = RunningTotal = @RunningTotal + TotalDue;
-- (31465 row(s) affected)


SELECT  SalesOrderId,
        FORMAT(TotalDue,'c0','en-US')        AS TotalDue,
        FORMAT(RunningTotal, 'c0','en-US')   AS RunningTotal
FROM    @Result ORDER BY SalesOrderID;
GO
-- (31465 row(s) affected) -- Partial results.
```

SalesOrderId	TotalDue	RunningTotal
43659	$23,153	$23,153
43660	$1,457	$24,611
43661	$36,866	$61,476
43662	$32,475	$93,951
43663	$472	$94,424
43664	$27,510	$121,934
43665	$16,159	$138,093

Subtotal, Total & Grand Total GROUPING Function

It is a challenge to generate multi-level totals in T-SQL. The GROUPING() function tells us what level we are on in the GROUP BY summary.

```
USE AdventureWorks2012;
```

```
SELECT *
FROM  (SELECT COALESCE(CONVERT(VARCHAR, YEAR(OrderDate)), '')          AS YYYY,
              COALESCE(LEFT(CONVERT(VARCHAR, OrderDate, 111), 7), '')   AS MM,
              FORMAT(COUNT(*), '###,###')                               AS ORDERS,
              FORMAT(SUM(TotalDue), 'c0', 'en-US')                      AS SALES,
              CASE   WHEN GROUPING(LEFT(CONVERT(VARCHAR, OrderDate, 111), 7)) = 0
                 AND GROUPING(YEAR(OrderDate)) = 1 THEN 'SUBTOTAL'
                 ELSE ''
              END                                                       AS GRPMM,
              CASE   WHEN GROUPING(YEAR(OrderDate)) = 0
                 AND GROUPING(LEFT(CONVERT(VARCHAR, OrderDate, 111), 7)) = 1 THEN 'TOTAL'
                 ELSE ''
              END                                                       AS GRPYY,
              CASE   WHEN GROUPING(LEFT(CONVERT(VARCHAR, OrderDate, 111), 7)) = 1
                 AND GROUPING(YEAR(OrderDate)) = 1 THEN 'GRAND TOTAL'
                 ELSE ''
              END                                                       AS GRPALL
       FROM  Sales.SalesOrderHeader
     GROUP  BY YEAR(OrderDate), LEFT(CONVERT(VARCHAR, OrderDate, 111), 7) WITH CUBE) rpt
WHERE  GRPMM != '' OR GRPYY != ''  OR GRPALL != ''
ORDER  BY CASE  WHEN GRPALL != '' THEN 3  WHEN GRPYY != '' THEN 2  ELSE 1 END,
       YYYY, MM ;
```

YYYY	MM	ORDERS	SALES	GRPMM	GRPYY	GRPALL
	2008/01	1,946	$3,359,927	SUBTOTAL		
	2008/02	2,032	$4,662,656	SUBTOTAL		
	2008/03	2,109	$4,722,358	SUBTOTAL		
	2008/04	2,128	$4,269,365	SUBTOTAL		
	2008/05	2,386	$5,813,557	SUBTOTAL		
	2008/06	2,374	$6,004,156	SUBTOTAL		
	2008/07	976	$56,179	SUBTOTAL		
2005		1,379	$12,693,251		TOTAL	
2006		3,692	$34,463,848		TOTAL	
2007		12,443	$47,171,490		TOTAL	
2008		13,951	$28,888,198		TOTAL	
		31,465	$123,216,786			GRAND TOTAL

The GROUP BY Clause with GROUPING SETS

A GROUP BY clause that uses GROUPING SETS is equivalent to multiple GROUP BY queries combined with UNION ALL operator.

```
USE AdventureWorks2012;
```

```
SELECT T."Group"                        AS N'Continent',
       T.CountryRegionCode              AS N'Country',
       S.Name                           AS N'Dealer',
       CN.LastName                      AS N'SalesStaff',
       FORMAT(SUM(TotalDue), 'c0','en-US')   AS N'TotalSales'
FROM   AdventureWorks.Sales.Customer C
       INNER JOIN AdventureWorks.Sales.Store S
           ON C.CustomerID = S.CustomerID
       INNER JOIN AdventureWorks.Sales.SalesTerritory T
           ON C.TerritoryID = T.TerritoryID
       INNER JOIN AdventureWorks.Sales.SalesOrderHeader H
           ON S.CustomerID = H.CustomerID
       INNER JOIN AdventureWorks.Person.Contact CN
           ON H.SalesPersonID = CN.ContactID
GROUP  BY GROUPING SETS( CUBE(T."Group", T.CountryRegionCode), S.Name, CN.LastName )
ORDER  BY Continent, Country, Dealer, SalesStaff;
-- (664 row(s) affected) - Partial results.
```

Continent	Country	Dealer	SalesStaff	TotalSales
NULL	NULL	Year-Round Sports	NULL	$197,777
NULL	NULL	Yellow Bicycle Company	NULL	$102,699
NULL	AU	NULL	NULL	$2,185,110
NULL	CA	NULL	NULL	$19,316,294
NULL	DE	NULL	NULL	$2,741,548
NULL	FR	NULL	NULL	$6,215,065
NULL	GB	NULL	NULL	$5,758,606
NULL	US	NULL	NULL	$72,049,624
Europe	NULL	NULL	NULL	$14,715,219
Europe	DE	NULL	NULL	$2,741,548
Europe	FR	NULL	NULL	$6,215,065
Europe	GB	NULL	NULL	$5,758,606
North America	NULL	NULL	NULL	$91,365,917
North America	CA	NULL	NULL	$19,316,294
North America	US	NULL	NULL	$72,049,624
Pacific	NULL	NULL	NULL	$2,185,110
Pacific	AU	NULL	NULL	$2,185,110

SELECT Top N from Each Group

Top 3 in each group is a very popular interview question.

USE AdventureWorks2012;

```
DECLARE @TopN tinyint = 3;
WITH cteBestSalesByProduct
    AS (SELECT ROW_NUMBER() OVER( PARTITION BY sod.ProductID
                ORDER BY Sum(sod.LineTotal) DESC)              AS   SeqNo,
        CONCAT(FirstName, SPACE(1), LastName)                  AS   [Name],
        p.Name                                                 AS   ProductName,
        FORMAT(CONVERT(MONEY, Sum(sod.LineTotal)), 'c', 'en-US')  AS   TotalBySalesPerson,
        p.ProductNumber,
        sod.ProductID
      FROM   Sales.SalesOrderDetail AS sod
        INNER JOIN Production.Product AS p
            ON sod.ProductID = p.ProductID
        INNER JOIN Sales.SalesOrderHeader AS soh
            ON sod.SalesOrderID = soh.SalesOrderID
        INNER JOIN Person.Person AS pe
            ON soh.SalesPersonID = pe.BusinessEntityID
      WHERE  soh.SalesPersonID IS NOT NULL
      GROUP  BY          CONCAT(FirstName, SPACE(1), LastName),
                         sod.ProductID,
                         p.ProductNumber,
                         p.Name )
SELECT *
FROM   cteBestSalesByProduct cte
WHERE  SeqNo <= @TopN
ORDER  BY      ProductID,
               SeqNo;
-- (749 row(s) affected) - Partial results.
```

SeqNo	Name	ProductName	TotalBySalesPerson	ProductNumber	ProductID
1	Jae Pak	Women's Mountain Shorts, L	$19,385.51	SH-W890-L	869
2	Linda Mitchell	Women's Mountain Shorts, L	$15,371.85	SH-W890-L	869
3	Michael Blythe	Women's Mountain Shorts, L	$11,411.44	SH-W890-L	869
1	Jillian Carson	Water Bottle - 30 oz.	$936.04	WB-H098	870
2	Linda Mitchell	Water Bottle - 30 oz.	$833.59	WB-H098	870
3	Rachel Valdez	Water Bottle - 30 oz.	$758.01	WB-H098	870
1	Jillian Carson	Patch Kit/8 Patches	$163.51	PK-7098	873
2	Jae Pak	Patch Kit/8 Patches	$120.91	PK-7098	873
3	Ranjit Varkey Chudukatil	Patch Kit/8 Patches	$104.42	PK-7098	873

SELECT Top N from Each Group Ye Olde Way

SQL Server 2005 has introduced revolutionary enhancements including the OVER clause and recursive CTE-s. It was a bit cumbersome to program certain tasks prior to SS 2005. TOP N products in each subcategory.

```
USE AdventureWorks2012;
GO

DECLARE @Top TINYINT = 3;
SELECT Subcategory,
    ProductName,
        ProductID
FROM  (
  SELECT PSC.Name                                          AS SubCategory,
        P1.Name                                            AS ProductName,
        P1.ProductID,
            (SELECT COUNT(*)
            FROM   Production.ProductSubcategory PSC
                LEFT JOIN Production.Product P2
                    ON P2.ProductSubcategoryID =
                    PSC.ProductSubcategoryID
            WHERE  P2.ProductSubcategoryID = P1.ProductSubcategoryID
                AND P2.ProductID <= P1.ProductID)           AS RN
    FROM   Production.ProductSubcategory PSC
        LEFT JOIN Production.Product P1
            ON P1.ProductSubcategoryID = PSC.ProductSubcategoryID
        ) AS   X -- derived table
WHERE  RN <= @Top
ORDER  BY Subcategory,  ProductID;
GO
-- (90 row(s) affected) - Partial results.
```

Subcategory	ProductName	ProductID
Pumps	Minipump	844
Pumps	Mountain Pump	845
Road Bikes	Road-150 Red, 62	749
Road Bikes	Road-150 Red, 44	750
Road Bikes	Road-150 Red, 48	751
Road Frames	HL Road Frame - Black, 58	680
Road Frames	HL Road Frame - Red, 58	706
Road Frames	HL Road Frame - Red, 62	717

Table-Valued Parameters

Table-valued parameters were introduced with SQL Server 2008. They can be used to send parameters to SQL statement, stored procedure or function as next demonstrated.

```
USE AdventureWorks2012;
GO
```

```
-- Create new user-defined table data type
CREATE TYPE dbo.utpProdInfo AS TABLE(
        ProdID          int,
        ProdNbr         char(12),
        StandardCost    money,
        ListPrice       money,
        Color    char(16));
GO
```

```
-- Create user- defined table-valued function(UDF) with table-valued parameter
CREATE FUNCTION ufnColorGrouping (@Input dbo.utpProdInfo READONLY)
        RETURNS @Result TABLE (Color char(16), AvgListPrice money)
AS
BEGIN
 INSERT @Result
 SELECT Color, avg(ListPrice) FROM @Input
 GROUP BY Color
 RETURN
END;
GO
```

```
-- Create stored procedure with table-valued parameter
CREATE PROCEDURE uspPriceRange
                    @Input dbo.utpProdInfo READONLY
AS
BEGIN
 SELECT Color,  MinPrice=format(min(ListPrice), 'c0','en-US'),
            MaxPrice=format(max(ListPrice), 'c0','en-US')
 FROM @Input
 GROUP BY Color
 ORDER BY MAX(ListPrice)  DESC
END;
GO
```

Among the TVP's Benefits: Simple but Powerful Modular Programming

```
-- Test TVF with table-valued parameter
DECLARE @PriceDetail dbo.utpProdInfo
INSERT @PriceDetail SELECT ProductID, ProductNumber, StandardCost, ListPrice, Color
        FROM Production.Product WHERE Color is not null;
```

```
SELECT * FROM ufnColorGrouping (@PriceDetail)
ORDER BY AvgListPrice DESC
```

Color	AvgListPrice
Red	1401.95
Yellow	959.0913
Blue	923.6792
Silver	850.3053
Black	725.121
Grey	125.00
Silver/Black	64.0185
Multi	59.865
White	9.245

```
-- Test stored procedure with table-valued parameter
DECLARE @PriceDetail dbo.utpProdInfo;
INSERT @PriceDetail SELECT ProductID, ProductNumber, StandardCost, ListPrice, Color
        FROM Production.Product WHERE Color is not null;
```

```
EXEC uspPriceRange @PriceDetail;
GO
```

Color	MinPrice	MaxPrice
Red	$35	$3,578
Silver	$0	$3,400
Black	$0	$3,375
Blue	$35	$2,384
Yellow	$54	$2,384
Grey	$125	$125
Multi	$9	$90
Silver/Black	$40	$81
White	$9	$10

```
-- Cleanup
DROP FUNCTION ufnColorGrouping;
DROP PROC uspPriceRange;
DROP TYPE dbo.utpProdInfo;
```

Creating Comma Delimited String from a Column

XML PATH is the most popular way of accomplishing it, but other methods available as well.

```
;WITH CTE AS (
SELECT   ps.[Name]                                               AS Subcategory,
      Stuff((SELECT ', ' + Color AS [text()]
            FROM AdventureWorks2012.Production.Product p
            WHERE p.ProductSubcategoryID = ps.ProductSubcategoryID
                        AND Color is not null
            GROUP BY Color ORDER BY Color
            FOR XML PATH ('')),1,1,'')                           AS ColorList,
      Stuff((SELECT ', ' + Size AS [text()]
            FROM AdventureWorks2012.Production.Product p
            WHERE p.ProductSubcategoryID = ps.ProductSubcategoryID
                        AND Size is not null
            GROUP BY Size ORDER BY Size
            FOR XML PATH ('')),1,1,'')                           AS SizeList
FROM    AdventureWorks2012.Production.ProductSubcategory ps  )
SELECT * FROM CTE WHERE ColorList is not null AND SizeList is not null  ORDER BY Subcategory;
```

Subcategory	ColorList	SizeList
Bib-Shorts	Multi	L, M, S
Gloves	Black	L, M, S
Hydration Packs	Silver	70
Jerseys	Multi, Yellow	L, M, S, XL
Mountain Bikes	Black, Silver	38, 40, 42, 44, 46, 48, 52
Mountain Frames	Black, Silver	38, 40, 42, 44, 46, 48, 52
Road Bikes	Black, Red, Yellow	38, 40, 42, 44, 48, 52, 56, 58, 60, 62
Road Frames	Black, Red, Yellow	38, 40, 42, 44, 48, 52, 56, 58, 60, 62
Shorts	Black	L, M, S, XL
Socks	White	L, M
Tights	Black	L, M, S
Touring Bikes	Blue, Yellow	44, 46, 50, 54, 58, 60, 62
Touring Frames	Blue, Yellow	44, 46, 50, 54, 58, 60, 62
Vests	Blue	L, M, S

```
DECLARE @CSVList VARCHAR(MAX) = '';    -- Multiple variable assignment method
SELECT @CSVList = CONCAT(Color, ', ', @CSVList)
FROM (SELECT DISTINCT Color FROM AdventureWorks2012.Production.Product
                        WHERE Color is not null) x;
SELECT CommaDelimitedList=@CSVList;
-- Yellow, White, Silver/Black, Silver, Red, Multi, Grey, Blue, Black,
```

Configuring Comma Delimited Result Sets in SSMS

It requires special setup for CSV result sets when using Management Studio. This feature is applicable for the Results to Text mode.

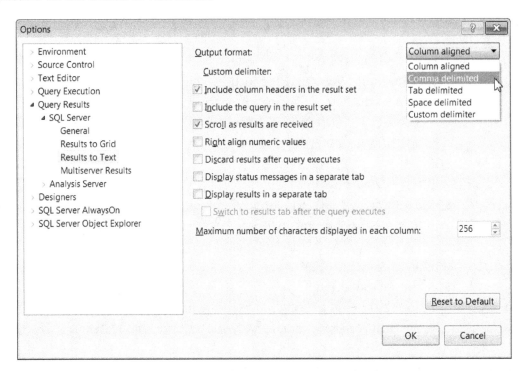

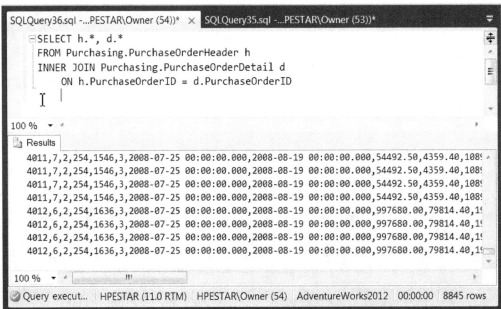

Nesting Cursors

Cursors should be avoided with a few exceptions: better performance (rare but happens) or cannot be done by set-based statements. Being new to set-based logic is not a good excuse for using cursors because they do not scale well. Single-level cursor example.

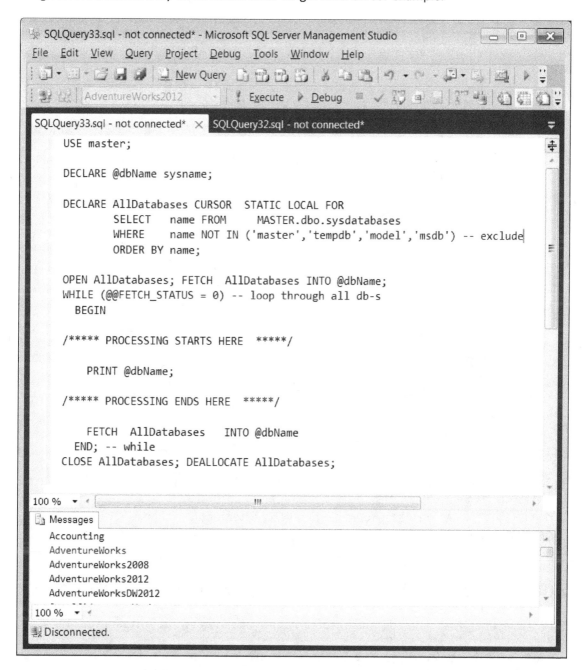

```
USE master;

DECLARE @dbName sysname;

DECLARE AllDatabases CURSOR  STATIC LOCAL FOR
        SELECT    name FROM      MASTER.dbo.sysdatabases
        WHERE     name NOT IN ('master','tempdb','model','msdb') -- exclude
        ORDER BY name;

OPEN AllDatabases; FETCH  AllDatabases INTO @dbName;
WHILE (@@FETCH_STATUS = 0) -- loop through all db-s
  BEGIN

/***** PROCESSING STARTS HERE  *****/

    PRINT @dbName;

/***** PROCESSING ENDS HERE  *****/

    FETCH  AllDatabases   INTO @dbName
  END; -- while
CLOSE AllDatabases; DEALLOCATE AllDatabases;
```

Messages

```
Accounting
AdventureWorks
AdventureWorks2008
AdventureWorks2012
AdventureWorksDW2012
```

Nested Cursors

Outer cursor over period Purchase Orders. Inner cursor over products ordered for each PO.

```sql
USE AdventureWorks2012;
DBCC DROPCLEANBUFFERS;  -- Preparation for performance timing - empty memory buffers
DECLARE @StartTime datetime = Getdate();
DECLARE @IterationID INT,  @OrderDetail VARCHAR(max),  @ProductName VARCHAR(10);
DECLARE @Result TABLE ( PurchaseOrderID INT, ProductList VARCHAR(max) ) ;

DECLARE PurchaseOrdersInPeriod CURSOR STATIC LOCAL FOR    -- OUTER CURSOR declaration
 SELECT PurchaseOrderID  FROM  Purchasing.PurchaseOrderHeader
 WHERE  Year(OrderDate) = 2008  AND Month(OrderDate) = 2  ORDER  BY PurchaseOrderID;

OPEN PurchaseOrdersInPeriod; FETCH NEXT FROM PurchaseOrdersInPeriod INTO @IterationID;
PRINT 'OUTER LOOP START';
WHILE ( @@FETCH_STATUS = 0 ) -- sql cursor fetch_status
 BEGIN     SET @OrderDetail = SPACE(0);

   DECLARE POLineItems CURSOR STATIC LOCAL FOR              -- INNER CURSOR declaration
    SELECT p.productNumber  FROM  Purchasing.PurchaseOrderDetail pd
      INNER JOIN Production.Product p  ON pd.ProductID = p.ProductID
    WHERE  pd.PurchaseOrderID = @IterationID ORDER  BY PurchaseOrderDetailID;

   OPEN POLineItems;  FETCH NEXT FROM POLineItems INTO @ProductName;
   PRINT 'INNER LOOP START';
   WHILE ( @@FETCH_STATUS = 0 )
    BEGIN         SET @OrderDetail = CONCAT(@OrderDetail, @ProductName,', ');
      FETCH NEXT FROM POLineItems INTO @ProductName;     PRINT 'INNER LOOP' ;
     END -- inner while
   CLOSE POLineItems;  DEALLOCATE POLineItems;

   SET @OrderDetail = LEFT(@OrderDetail, Len(@OrderDetail) - 1);  -- Truncate trailing comma
   INSERT INTO @Result  VALUES     (@IterationID,@OrderDetail);
    FETCH NEXT FROM PurchaseOrdersInPeriod INTO @IterationID ;   PRINT 'OUTER LOOP';
  END -- outer while
CLOSE PurchaseOrdersInPeriod; DEALLOCATE PurchaseOrdersInPeriod;

SELECT * FROM  @Result ORDER  BY PurchaseOrderID;  -- Results  (268 row(s) affected)

SELECT ExecutionMsec = Datediff(millisecond, @StartTime, Getdate());  -- Timing  653 msec
GO
```

Nested Cursor Loops Processing Partial Results

PurchaseOrderID	ProductList
1573	CR-7833
1574	RA-2345
1575	PB-6109
1576	CR-9981
1577	SD-2342, SD-9872
1578	PA-187B, PA-361R, PA-529S, PA-632U, PA-823Y
1579	SE-R581, SE-R908, SE-R995, SE-T312, SE-T762
1580	RF-9198
1581	RC-0291
1582	RM-M464, RM-M692
1583	TP-0923
1584	FC-3982, FL-2301
1585	RM-M464, RM-M692
1586	NI-9522
1587	FW-5160, FW-5800, FW-7160, FW-9160
1588	PD-M282, PD-M340
1589	HN-5400, HN-5811, HN-5818, HN-6320, HN-7161
1590	MS-2348, MS-6061, MT-1000
1591	KW-4091
1592	RM-R436, RM-R600

Set Based Operations Equivalent Code

```
DBCC DROPCLEANBUFFERS;
DECLARE @StartTime datetime = CURRENT_TIMESTAMP;
SELECT poh.PurchaseOrderID,OrderDetail = Stuff((
                    -- correlated subquery
                    SELECT CONCAT(', ', ProductNumber) AS [text()]
                    FROM  Purchasing.PurchaseOrderDetail pod
                         INNER JOIN Production.Product p
                         ON pod.ProductID = p.ProductID
                    WHERE  pod.PurchaseOrderID =  poh.PurchaseOrderID
                    ORDER  BY PurchaseOrderDetailID
                    FOR XML PATH ('')), 1, 1, '')
FROM   Purchasing.PurchaseOrderHeader poh
WHERE  Year(OrderDate) = 2004 AND Month(OrderDate) = 2
ORDER  BY PurchaseOrderID;
SELECT ExecutionMsec = Datediff(millisecond, @StartTime, Getdate()) -- Timing: 33 msec
```

Advanced Graphical Query Designer

While SSMS GUI query / view designer cannot handle very complex queries, it does a pretty good job with "normal" relational database queries.

Aliasing Tables in the Diagram Pane

We start with right click on the top table frame in the Diagram Pane.

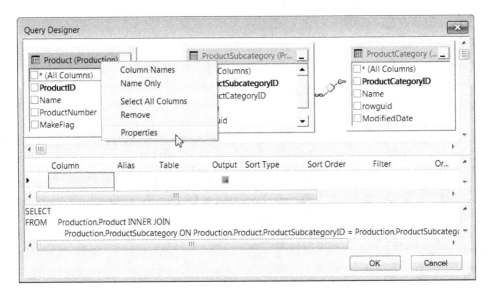

In the pop-up dialog box we enter the alias for the table.

Specifying OUTER JOIN in Diagram Pane

To change the INNER JOIN to RIGHT JOIN, right click on the connection square in the middle and click on Properties.

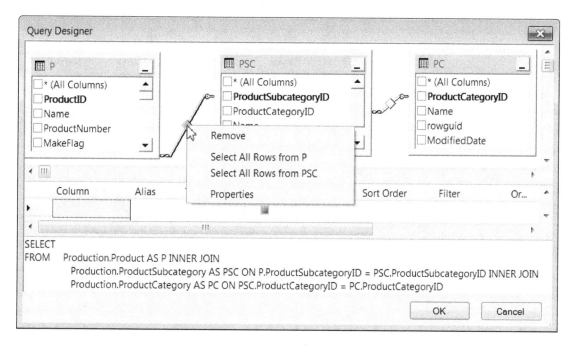

With checkmark selection we can specify LEFT JOIN, RIGHT JOIN or FULL JOIN.

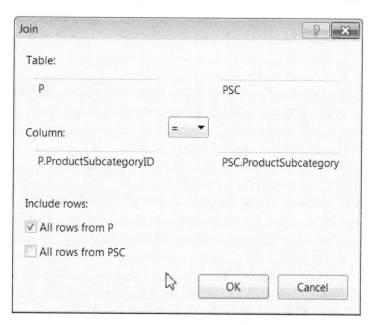

Query Designer Generated Query

This is the final graphical image in Query Designer prior to the exiting to Query Editor.

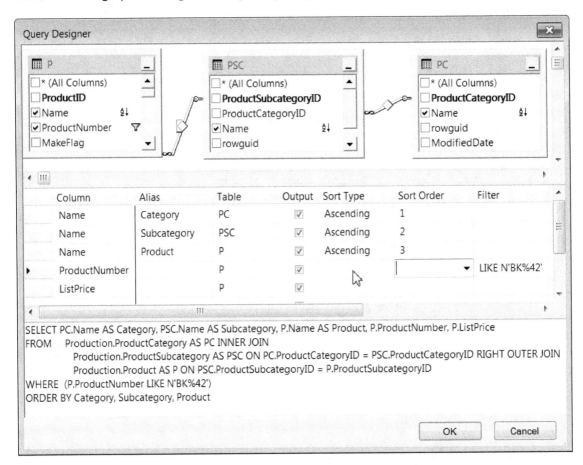

```
SELECT  PC.Name AS Category, PSC.Name AS Subcategory, P.Name AS Product,
            P.ProductNumber, P.ListPrice
FROM    Production.ProductCategory AS PC
        INNER JOIN Production.ProductSubcategory AS PSC
            ON PC.ProductCategoryID = PSC.ProductCategoryID
        RIGHT OUTER JOIN Production.Product AS P
            ON PSC.ProductSubcategoryID = P.ProductSubcategoryID
WHERE  (P.ProductNumber LIKE N'BK%42') ORDER BY Product, Subcategory, Category;
-- (9 row(s) affected) - Partial results.
```

Category	Subcategory	Product	ProductNumber	ListPrice
Bikes	Mountain Bikes	Mountain-500 Silver, 42	BK-M18S-42	564.99
Bikes	Road Bikes	Road-350-W Yellow, 42	BK-R79Y-42	1700.99

Template Explorer & Browser

The Template Explorer & Browser helps to start coding by providing a framework code with optional parameter replacements.

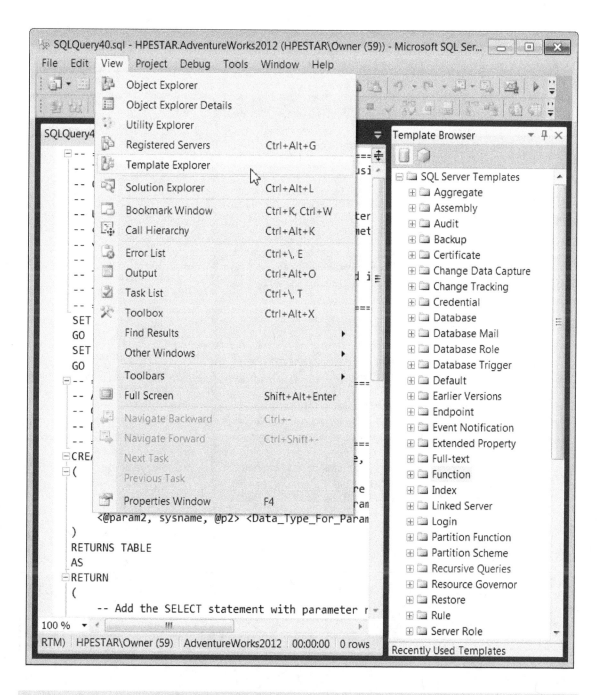

Create Inline Function Template

Double on the template name to get the starter code in a new Query Editor window.

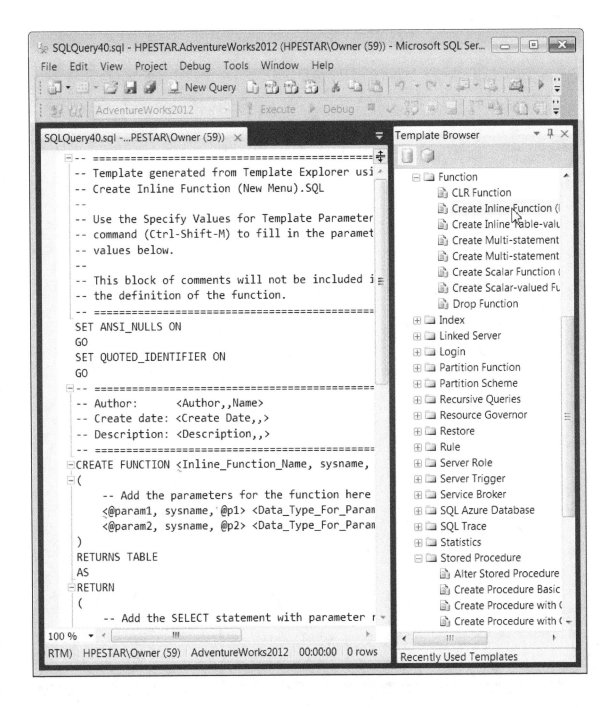

Template Parameters Specifications

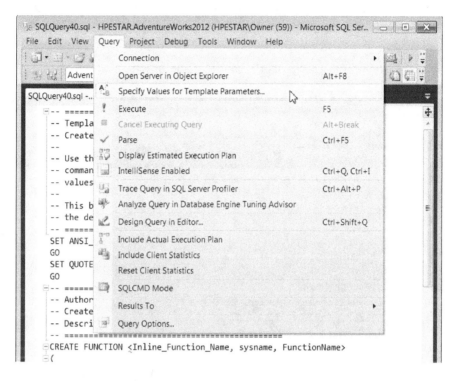

The values must be filled in for the parameter in the dialog box.

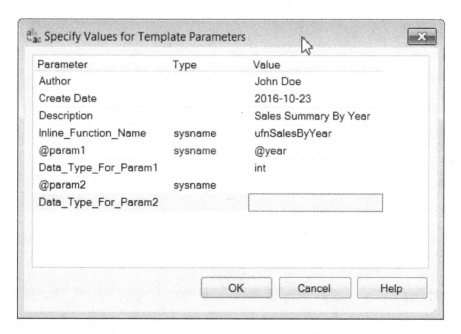

Completion of the Function by Entering the SELECT Query with Parameter
Inline user-defined function can be used as a make over for a view with accepting parameters feature.

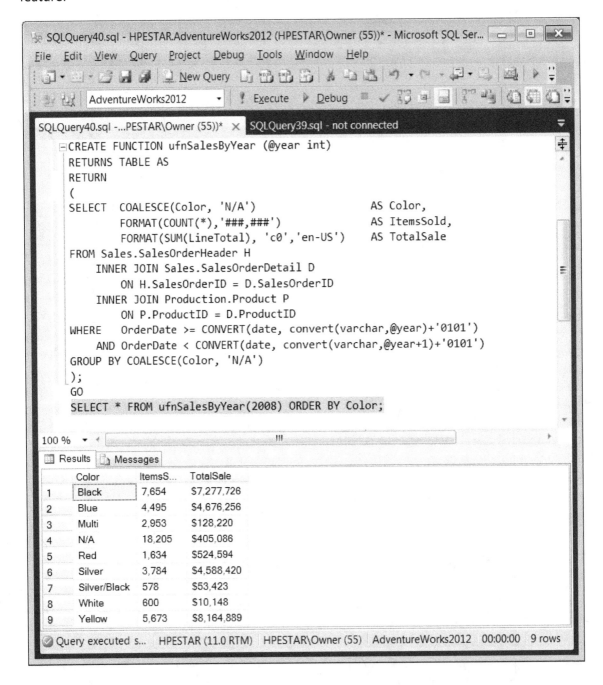

```sql
CREATE FUNCTION ufnSalesByYear (@year int)
RETURNS TABLE AS
RETURN
(
SELECT   COALESCE(Color, 'N/A')                  AS Color,
         FORMAT(COUNT(*),'###,###')              AS ItemsSold,
         FORMAT(SUM(LineTotal), 'c0','en-US')    AS TotalSale
FROM Sales.SalesOrderHeader H
    INNER JOIN Sales.SalesOrderDetail D
        ON H.SalesOrderID = D.SalesOrderID
    INNER JOIN Production.Product P
        ON P.ProductID = D.ProductID
WHERE   OrderDate >= CONVERT(date, convert(varchar,@year)+'0101')
    AND OrderDate < CONVERT(date, convert(varchar,@year+1)+'0101')
GROUP BY COALESCE(Color, 'N/A')
);
GO
SELECT * FROM ufnSalesByYear(2008) ORDER BY Color;
```

	Color	ItemsS...	TotalSale
1	Black	7,654	$7,277,726
2	Blue	4,495	$4,676,256
3	Multi	2,953	$128,220
4	N/A	18,205	$405,086
5	Red	1,634	$524,594
6	Silver	3,784	$4,588,420
7	Silver/Black	578	$53,423
8	White	600	$10,148
9	Yellow	5,673	$8,164,889

Query executed s...   HPESTAR (11.0 RTM)   HPESTAR\Owner (55)   AdventureWorks2012   00:00:00   9 rows

Entering PowerShell from Object Explorer

In addition to executing sqlps in Command Prompt, we can enter PowerShell from SSMS Object Explorer via the right click drop-down menu. Entering the get-childitem command will list all the views in the path (directory).

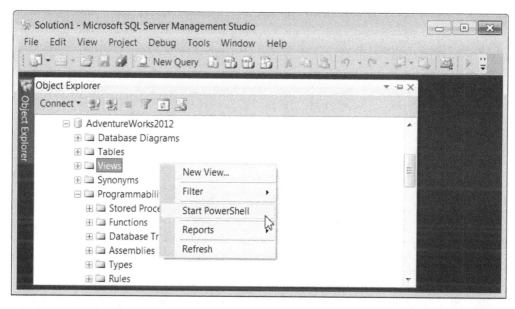

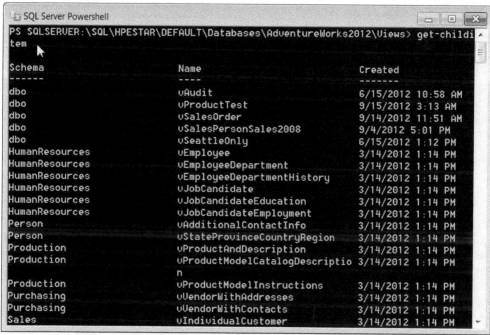

PowerShell Command List

The following command will list all the PowerShell commands.

```
get-command | out-file 'f:\temp\command.txt'
```

CommandType	Name	Definition
Alias	%	ForEach-Object
Alias	?	Where-Object
Function	A:	Set-Location A:
Alias	ac	Add-Content
Cmdlet	Add-Computer	Add-Computer [-DomainName] <...
Cmdlet	Add-Content	Add-Content [-Path] <String[...
Cmdlet	Add-History	Add-History [[-InputObject] ...
Cmdlet	Add-Member	Add-Member [-MemberType] <PS...
Cmdlet	Add-PSSnapin	Add-PSSnapin [-Name] <String...
Cmdlet	Add-RoleMember	Add-RoleMember [-MemberName]...
Cmdlet	Add-SqlAvailabilityDatabase	Add-SqlAvailabilityDatabase ...
Cmdlet	Add-SqlAvailabilityGroupList...	Add-SqlAvailabilityGroupList...
Cmdlet	Add-Type	Add-Type [-TypeDefinition] <...
Alias	asnp	Add-PSSnapIn
Function	B:	Set-Location B:
Cmdlet	Backup-ASDatabase	Backup-ASDatabase [-BackupFi...
Cmdlet	Backup-SqlDatabase	Backup-SqlDatabase [-Databas...
Function	C:	Set-Location C:
Alias	cat	Get-Content
Alias	cd	Set-Location
Function	cd..	Set-Location ..
Function	cd\	Set-Location \
Alias	chdir	Set-Location
Cmdlet	Checkpoint-Computer	Checkpoint-Computer [-Descri...
Alias	clc	Clear-Content
Alias	clear	Clear-Host
Cmdlet	Clear-Content	Clear-Content [-Path] <Strin...
Cmdlet	Clear-EventLog	Clear-EventLog [-LogName] <S...
Cmdlet	Clear-History	Clear-History [[-Id] <Int32[...
Function	Clear-Host	$space = New-Object System.M...
Cmdlet	Clear-Item	Clear-Item [-Path] <String[]...
Cmdlet	Clear-ItemProperty	Clear-ItemProperty [-Path] <...
Cmdlet	Clear-Variable	Clear-Variable [-Name] <Stri...
Alias	clhy	Clear-History
Alias	cli	Clear-Item
Alias	clp	Clear-ItemProperty
Alias	cls	Clear-Host
Alias	clv	Clear-Variable
Alias	compare	Compare-Object
Cmdlet	Compare-Object	Compare-Object [-ReferenceOb...
Cmdlet	Complete-Transaction	Complete-Transaction [-Verbo...
Cmdlet	Connect-WSMan	Connect-WSMan [[-ComputerNam...
Cmdlet	ConvertFrom-Csv	ConvertFrom-Csv [-InputObjec...
Cmdlet	ConvertFrom-SecureString	ConvertFrom-SecureString [-S...
Cmdlet	ConvertFrom-StringData	ConvertFrom-StringData [-Str...
Cmdlet	Convert-Path	Convert-Path [-Path] <String...
Cmdlet	ConvertTo-Csv	ConvertTo-Csv [-InputObject]...
Cmdlet	ConvertTo-Html	ConvertTo-Html [[-Property] ...
Cmdlet	ConvertTo-SecureString	ConvertTo-SecureString [-Str...
Cmdlet	ConvertTo-Xml	ConvertTo-Xml [-InputObject]...
Cmdlet	Convert-UrnToPath	Convert-UrnToPath [-Urn] <St...
Alias	copy	Copy-Item
Cmdlet	Copy-Item	Copy-Item [-Path] <String[]>...
Cmdlet	Copy-ItemProperty	Copy-ItemProperty [-Path] <S...
Alias	cp	Copy-Item
Alias	cpi	Copy-Item
Alias	cpp	Copy-ItemProperty
Alias	cvpa	Convert-Path
Function	D:	Set-Location D:
Alias	dbp	Disable-PSBreakpoint
Cmdlet	Debug-Process	Debug-Process [-Name] <Strin...

Cmdlet	Decode-SqlName	Decode-SqlName [-SqlName] <S...
Alias	del	Remove-Item
Alias	diff	Compare-Object
Alias	dir	Get-ChildItem
Cmdlet	Disable-ComputerRestore	Disable-ComputerRestore [-Dr...
Cmdlet	Disable-PSBreakpoint	Disable-PSBreakpoint [-Break...
Function	Disable-PSRemoting	...
Cmdlet	Disable-PSSessionConfiguration	Disable-PSSessionConfigurati...
Cmdlet	Disable-SqlAlwaysOn	Disable-SqlAlwaysOn [[-Path]...
Cmdlet	Disable-WSManCredSSP	Disable-WSManCredSSP [-Role]...
Cmdlet	Disconnect-WSMan	Disconnect-WSMan [[-Computer...
Function	E:	Set-Location E:
Alias	ebp	Enable-PSBreakpoint
Alias	echo	Write-Output
Cmdlet	Enable-ComputerRestore	Enable-ComputerRestore [-Dri...
Cmdlet	Enable-PSBreakpoint	Enable-PSBreakpoint [-Id] <I...
Cmdlet	Enable-PSRemoting	Enable-PSRemoting [-Force] [...
Cmdlet	Enable-PSSessionConfiguration	Enable-PSSessionConfiguratio...
Cmdlet	Enable-SqlAlwaysOn	Enable-SqlAlwaysOn [[-Path] ...
Cmdlet	Enable-WSManCredSSP	Enable-WSManCredSSP [-Role] ...
Cmdlet	Encode-SqlName	Encode-SqlName [-SqlName] <S...
Cmdlet	Enter-PSSession	Enter-PSSession [-ComputerNa...
Alias	epal	Export-Alias
Alias	epcsv	Export-Csv
Alias	epsn	Export-PSSession
Alias	erase	Remove-Item
Alias	etsn	Enter-PSSession
Cmdlet	Exit-PSSession	Exit-PSSession [-Verbose] [-...
Cmdlet	Export-Alias	Export-Alias [-Path] <String...
Cmdlet	Export-Clixml	Export-Clixml [-Path] <Strin...
Cmdlet	Export-Console	Export-Console [[-Path] <Str...
Cmdlet	Export-Counter	Export-Counter [-Path] <Stri...
Cmdlet	Export-Csv	Export-Csv [-Path] <String> ...
Cmdlet	Export-FormatData	Export-FormatData [-InputObj...
Cmdlet	Export-ModuleMember	Export-ModuleMember [[-Funct...
Cmdlet	Export-PSSession	Export-PSSession [-Session] ...
Alias	exsn	Exit-PSSession
Function	F:	Set-Location F:
Alias	fc	Format-Custom
Alias	fl	Format-List
Alias	foreach	ForEach-Object
Cmdlet	ForEach-Object	ForEach-Object [-Process] <S...
Cmdlet	Format-Custom	Format-Custom [[-Property] <...
Cmdlet	Format-List	Format-List [[-Property] <Ob...
Cmdlet	Format-Table	Format-Table [[-Property] <O...
Cmdlet	Format-Wide	Format-Wide [[-Property] <Ob...
Alias	ft	Format-Table
Alias	fw	Format-Wide
Function	G:	Set-Location G:
Alias	gal	Get-Alias
Alias	gbp	Get-PSBreakpoint
Alias	gc	Get-Content
Alias	gci	Get-ChildItem
Alias	gcm	Get-Command
Alias	gcs	Get-PSCallStack
Alias	gdr	Get-PSDrive
Cmdlet	Get-Acl	Get-Acl [[-Path] <String[]>]...
Cmdlet	Get-Alias	Get-Alias [[-Name] <String[]...
Cmdlet	Get-AuthenticodeSignature	Get-AuthenticodeSignature [-...
Cmdlet	Get-ChildItem	Get-ChildItem [[-Path] <Stri...
Cmdlet	Get-Command	Get-Command [[-ArgumentList]...
Cmdlet	Get-ComputerRestorePoint	Get-ComputerRestorePoint [[-...
Cmdlet	Get-Content	Get-Content [-Path] <String[...
Cmdlet	Get-Counter	Get-Counter [[-Counter] <Str...
Cmdlet	Get-Credential	Get-Credential [-Credential]...
Cmdlet	Get-Culture	Get-Culture [-Verbose] [-Deb...
Cmdlet	Get-Date	Get-Date [[-Date] <DateTime>...
Cmdlet	Get-Event	Get-Event [[-SourceIdentifie...
Cmdlet	Get-EventLog	Get-EventLog [-LogName] <Str...
Cmdlet	Get-EventSubscriber	Get-EventSubscriber [[-Sourc...
Cmdlet	Get-ExecutionPolicy	Get-ExecutionPolicy [[-Scope...
Cmdlet	Get-FormatData	Get-FormatData [[-TypeName] ...
Cmdlet	Get-Help	Get-Help [[-Name] <String>] ...

CHAPTER 16: Advanced T-SQL Programming Topics

Cmdlet	Get-History	Get-History [[-Id] <Int64[]>...
Cmdlet	Get-Host	Get-Host [-Verbose] [-Debug]...
Cmdlet	Get-HotFix	Get-HotFix [[-Id] <String[]>...
Cmdlet	Get-Item	Get-Item [-Path] <String[]> ...
Cmdlet	Get-ItemProperty	Get-ItemProperty [-Path] <St...
Cmdlet	Get-Job	Get-Job [[-Id] <Int32[]>] [-...
Cmdlet	Get-Location	Get-Location [-PSProvider <S...
Cmdlet	Get-Member	Get-Member [[-Name] <String[...
Cmdlet	Get-Module	Get-Module [[-Name] <String[...
Cmdlet	Get-PfxCertificate	Get-PfxCertificate [-FilePat...
Cmdlet	Get-Process	Get-Process [[-Name] <String...
Cmdlet	Get-PSBreakpoint	Get-PSBreakpoint [[-Script] ...
Cmdlet	Get-PSCallStack	Get-PSCallStack [-Verbose] [...
Cmdlet	Get-PSDrive	Get-PSDrive [[-Name] <String...
Cmdlet	Get-PSProvider	Get-PSProvider [[-PSProvider...
Cmdlet	Get-PSSession	Get-PSSession [[-ComputerNam...
Cmdlet	Get-PSSessionConfiguration	Get-PSSessionConfiguration [...
Cmdlet	Get-PSSnapin	Get-PSSnapin [[-Name] <Strin...
Cmdlet	Get-Random	Get-Random [[-Maximum] <Obje...
Cmdlet	Get-Service	Get-Service [[-Name] <String...
Cmdlet	Get-TraceSource	Get-TraceSource [[-Name] <St...
Cmdlet	Get-Transaction	Get-Transaction [-Verbose] [...
Cmdlet	Get-UICulture	Get-UICulture [-Verbose] [-D...
Cmdlet	Get-Unique	Get-Unique [-InputObject <PS...
Cmdlet	Get-Variable	Get-Variable [[-Name] <Strin...
Function	Get-Verb	...
Cmdlet	Get-WinEvent	Get-WinEvent [[-LogName] <St...
Cmdlet	Get-WmiObject	Get-WmiObject [-Class] <Stri...
Cmdlet	Get-WSManCredSSP	Get-WSManCredSSP [-Verbose] ...
Cmdlet	Get-WSManInstance	Get-WSManInstance [-Resource...
Alias	ghy	Get-History
Alias	gi	Get-Item
Alias	gjb	Get-Job
Alias	gl	Get-Location
Alias	gm	Get-Member
Alias	gmo	Get-Module
Alias	gp	Get-ItemProperty
Alias	gps	Get-Process
Alias	group	Group-Object
Cmdlet	Group-Object	Group-Object [[-Property] <O...
Alias	gsn	Get-PSSession
Alias	gsnp	Get-PSSnapIn
Alias	gsv	Get-Service
Alias	gu	Get-Unique
Alias	gv	Get-Variable
Alias	gwmi	Get-WmiObject
Alias	h	Get-History
Function	H:	Set-Location H:
Function	help	...
Alias	history	Get-History
Function	I:	Set-Location I:
Alias	icm	Invoke-Command
Alias	iex	Invoke-Expression
Alias	ihy	Invoke-History
Alias	ii	Invoke-Item
Cmdlet	Import-Alias	Import-Alias [-Path] <String...
Cmdlet	Import-Clixml	Import-Clixml [-Path] <Strin...
Cmdlet	Import-Counter	Import-Counter [-Path] <Stri...
Cmdlet	Import-Csv	Import-Csv [-Path] <String[]...
Cmdlet	Import-LocalizedData	Import-LocalizedData [-Bindi...
Cmdlet	Import-Module	Import-Module [-Name] <Strin...
Cmdlet	Import-PSSession	Import-PSSession [-Session] ...
Function	ImportSystemModules	...
Cmdlet	Invoke-ASCmd	Invoke-ASCmd [-Verbose] [-De...
Cmdlet	Invoke-Command	Invoke-Command [-ScriptBlock...
Cmdlet	Invoke-Expression	Invoke-Expression [-Command]...
Cmdlet	Invoke-History	Invoke-History [[-Id] <Strin...
Cmdlet	Invoke-Item	Invoke-Item [-Path] <String[...
Cmdlet	Invoke-PolicyEvaluation	Invoke-PolicyEvaluation [-Po...
Cmdlet	Invoke-ProcessCube	Invoke-ProcessCube [-Name] <...
Cmdlet	Invoke-ProcessDimension	Invoke-ProcessDimension [-Na...
Cmdlet	Invoke-ProcessPartition	Invoke-ProcessPartition [-Na...
Cmdlet	Invoke-Sqlcmd	Invoke-Sqlcmd [[-Query] <Str...

Cmdlet	Invoke-WmiMethod	Invoke-WmiMethod [-Class] <S...
Cmdlet	Invoke-WSManAction	Invoke-WSManAction [-Resourc...
Alias	ipal	Import-Alias
Alias	ipcsv	Import-Csv
Alias	ipmo	Import-Module
Alias	ipsn	Import-PSSession
Alias	ise	powershell_ise.exe
Alias	iwmi	Invoke-WMIMethod
Function	J:	Set-Location J:
Cmdlet	Join-Path	Join-Path [-Path] <String[]>...
Cmdlet	Join-SqlAvailabilityGroup	Join-SqlAvailabilityGroup [-...
Function	K:	Set-Location K:
Alias	kill	Stop-Process
Function	L:	Set-Location L:
Cmdlet	Limit-EventLog	Limit-EventLog [-LogName] <S...
Alias	lp	Out-Printer
Alias	ls	Get-ChildItem
Function	M:	Set-Location M:
Alias	man	help
Alias	md	mkdir
Alias	measure	Measure-Object
Cmdlet	Measure-Command	Measure-Command [-Expression...
Cmdlet	Measure-Object	Measure-Object [[-Property] ...
Cmdlet	Merge-Partition	Merge-Partition [-Name] <Str...
Alias	mi	Move-Item
Function	mkdir	...
Function	more	param([string[]]$paths)...
Alias	mount	New-PSDrive
Alias	move	Move-Item
Cmdlet	Move-Item	Move-Item [-Path] <String[]>...
Cmdlet	Move-ItemProperty	Move-ItemProperty [-Path] <S...
Alias	mp	Move-ItemProperty
Alias	mv	Move-Item
Function	N:	Set-Location N:
Alias	nal	New-Alias
Alias	ndr	New-PSDrive
Cmdlet	New-Alias	New-Alias [-Name] <String> [...
Cmdlet	New-Event	New-Event [-SourceIdentifier...
Cmdlet	New-EventLog	New-EventLog [-LogName] <Str...
Cmdlet	New-Item	New-Item [-Path] <String[]> ...
Cmdlet	New-ItemProperty	New-ItemProperty [-Path] <St...
Cmdlet	New-Module	New-Module [-ScriptBlock] <S...
Cmdlet	New-ModuleManifest	New-ModuleManifest [-Path] <...
Cmdlet	New-Object	New-Object [-TypeName] <Stri...
Cmdlet	New-PSDrive	New-PSDrive [-Name] <String>...
Cmdlet	New-PSSession	New-PSSession [[-ComputerNam...
Cmdlet	New-PSSessionOption	New-PSSessionOption [-Maximu...
Cmdlet	New-RestoreFolder	New-RestoreFolder [-Original...
Cmdlet	New-RestoreLocation	New-RestoreLocation [-File <...
Cmdlet	New-Service	New-Service [-Name] <String>...
Cmdlet	New-SqlAvailabilityGroup	New-SqlAvailabilityGroup [-N...
Cmdlet	New-SqlAvailabilityGroupList...	New-SqlAvailabilityGroupList...
Cmdlet	New-SqlAvailabilityReplica	New-SqlAvailabilityReplica [...
Cmdlet	New-SqlHADREndpoint	New-SqlHADREndpoint [-Name] ...
Cmdlet	New-TimeSpan	New-TimeSpan [[-Start] <Date...
Cmdlet	New-Variable	New-Variable [-Name] <String...
Cmdlet	New-WebServiceProxy	New-WebServiceProxy [-Uri] <...
Cmdlet	New-WSManInstance	New-WSManInstance [-Resource...
Cmdlet	New-WSManSessionOption	New-WSManSessionOption [-Pro...
Alias	ni	New-Item
Alias	nmo	New-Module
Alias	nsn	New-PSSession
Alias	nv	New-Variable
Function	O:	Set-Location O:
Alias	ogv	Out-GridView
Alias	oh	Out-Host
Cmdlet	Out-Default	Out-Default [-InputObject <P...
Cmdlet	Out-File	Out-File [-FilePath] <String...
Cmdlet	Out-GridView	Out-GridView [-InputObject <...
Cmdlet	Out-Host	Out-Host [-Paging] [-InputOb...
Cmdlet	Out-Null	Out-Null [-InputObject <PSOb...
Cmdlet	Out-Printer	Out-Printer [[-Name] <String...
Cmdlet	Out-String	Out-String [-Stream] [-Width...

CHAPTER 16: Advanced T-SQL Programming Topics

Function	P:	Set-Location P:
Alias	popd	Pop-Location
Cmdlet	Pop-Location	Pop-Location [-PassThru] [-S...
Function	prompt	$(if (test-path variable:/PS...
Alias	ps	Get-Process
Alias	pushd	Push-Location
Cmdlet	Push-Location	Push-Location [[-Path] <Stri...
Alias	pwd	Get-Location
Function	Q:	Set-Location Q:
Alias	r	Invoke-History
Function	R:	Set-Location R:
Alias	rbp	Remove-PSBreakpoint
Alias	rcjb	Receive-Job
Alias	rd	Remove-Item
Alias	rdr	Remove-PSDrive
Cmdlet	Read-Host	Read-Host [[-Prompt] <Object...
Cmdlet	Receive-Job	Receive-Job [-Job] <Job[]> [...
Cmdlet	Register-EngineEvent	Register-EngineEvent [-Sourc...
Cmdlet	Register-ObjectEvent	Register-ObjectEvent [-Input...
Cmdlet	Register-PSSessionConfiguration	Register-PSSessionConfigurat...
Cmdlet	Register-WmiEvent	Register-WmiEvent [-Class] <...
Cmdlet	Remove-Computer	Remove-Computer [[-Credentia...
Cmdlet	Remove-Event	Remove-Event [-SourceIdentif...
Cmdlet	Remove-EventLog	Remove-EventLog [-LogName] <...
Cmdlet	Remove-Item	Remove-Item [-Path] <String[...
Cmdlet	Remove-ItemProperty	Remove-ItemProperty [-Path] ...
Cmdlet	Remove-Job	Remove-Job [-Id] <Int32[]> [...
Cmdlet	Remove-Module	Remove-Module [-Name] <Strin...
Cmdlet	Remove-PSBreakpoint	Remove-PSBreakpoint [-Breakp...
Cmdlet	Remove-PSDrive	Remove-PSDrive [-Name] <Stri...
Cmdlet	Remove-PSSession	Remove-PSSession [-Id] <Int3...
Cmdlet	Remove-PSSnapin	Remove-PSSnapin [-Name] <Str...
Cmdlet	Remove-RoleMember	Remove-RoleMember [-MemberNa...
Cmdlet	Remove-SqlAvailabilityDatabase	Remove-SqlAvailabilityDataba...
Cmdlet	Remove-SqlAvailabilityGroup	Remove-SqlAvailabilityGroup ...
Cmdlet	Remove-SqlAvailabilityReplica	Remove-SqlAvailabilityReplic...
Cmdlet	Remove-Variable	Remove-Variable [-Name] <Str...
Cmdlet	Remove-WmiObject	Remove-WmiObject [-Class] <S...
Cmdlet	Remove-WSManInstance	Remove-WSManInstance [-Resou...
Alias	ren	Rename-Item
Cmdlet	Rename-Item	Rename-Item [-Path] <String>...
Cmdlet	Rename-ItemProperty	Rename-ItemProperty [-Path] ...
Cmdlet	Reset-ComputerMachinePassword	Reset-ComputerMachinePasswor...
Cmdlet	Resolve-Path	Resolve-Path [-Path] <String...
Cmdlet	Restart-Computer	Restart-Computer [[-Computer...
Cmdlet	Restart-Service	Restart-Service [-Name] <Str...
Cmdlet	Restore-ASDatabase	Restore-ASDatabase [-Restore...
Cmdlet	Restore-Computer	Restore-Computer [-RestorePo...
Cmdlet	Restore-SqlDatabase	Restore-SqlDatabase [-Databa...
Cmdlet	Resume-Service	Resume-Service [-Name] <Stri...
Cmdlet	Resume-SqlAvailabilityDatabase	Resume-SqlAvailabilityDataba...
Alias	ri	Remove-Item
Alias	rjb	Remove-Job
Alias	rm	Remove-Item
Alias	rmdir	Remove-Item
Alias	rmo	Remove-Module
Alias	rni	Rename-Item
Alias	rnp	Rename-ItemProperty
Alias	rp	Remove-ItemProperty
Alias	rsn	Remove-PSSession
Alias	rsnp	Remove-PSSnapin
Alias	rv	Remove-Variable
Alias	rvpa	Resolve-Path
Alias	rwmi	Remove-WMIObject
Function	S:	Set-Location S:
Alias	sajb	Start-Job
Alias	sal	Set-Alias
Alias	saps	Start-Process
Alias	sasv	Start-Service
Alias	sbp	Set-PSBreakpoint
Alias	sc	Set-Content
Alias	select	Select-Object
Cmdlet	Select-Object	Select-Object [[-Property] <...

CHAPTER 16: Advanced T-SQL Programming Topics

Cmdlet	Select-String	Select-String [-Pattern] <St...
Cmdlet	Select-Xml	Select-Xml [-XPath] <String>...
Cmdlet	Send-MailMessage	Send-MailMessage [-To] <Stri...
Alias	set	Set-Variable
Cmdlet	Set-Acl	Set-Acl [-Path] <String[]> [...
Cmdlet	Set-Alias	Set-Alias [-Name] <String> [...
Cmdlet	Set-AuthenticodeSignature	Set-AuthenticodeSignature [-...
Cmdlet	Set-Content	Set-Content [-Path] <String[...
Cmdlet	Set-Date	Set-Date [-Date] <DateTime> ...
Cmdlet	Set-ExecutionPolicy	Set-ExecutionPolicy [-Execut...
Cmdlet	Set-Item	Set-Item [-Path] <String[]> ...
Cmdlet	Set-ItemProperty	Set-ItemProperty [-Path] <St...
Cmdlet	Set-Location	Set-Location [[-Path] <Strin...
Cmdlet	Set-PSBreakpoint	Set-PSBreakpoint [-Script] <...
Cmdlet	Set-PSDebug	Set-PSDebug [-Trace <Int32>]...
Cmdlet	Set-PSSessionConfiguration	Set-PSSessionConfiguration [...
Cmdlet	Set-Service	Set-Service [-Name] <String>...
Cmdlet	Set-SqlAvailabilityGroup	Set-SqlAvailabilityGroup [[-...
Cmdlet	Set-SqlAvailabilityGroupList...	Set-SqlAvailabilityGroupList...
Cmdlet	Set-SqlAvailabilityReplica	Set-SqlAvailabilityReplica [...
Cmdlet	Set-SqlHADREndpoint	Set-SqlHADREndpoint [[-Path]...
Cmdlet	Set-StrictMode	Set-StrictMode -Version <Ver...
Cmdlet	Set-TraceSource	Set-TraceSource [-Name] <Str...
Cmdlet	Set-Variable	Set-Variable [-Name] <String...
Cmdlet	Set-WmiInstance	Set-WmiInstance [-Class] <St...
Cmdlet	Set-WSManInstance	Set-WSManInstance [-Resource...
Cmdlet	Set-WSManQuickConfig	Set-WSManQuickConfig [-UseSS...
Cmdlet	Show-EventLog	Show-EventLog [[-ComputerNam...
Alias	si	Set-Item
Alias	sl	Set-Location
Alias	sleep	Start-Sleep
Alias	sort	Sort-Object
Cmdlet	Sort-Object	Sort-Object [[-Property] <Ob...
Alias	sp	Set-ItemProperty
Alias	spjb	Stop-Job
Cmdlet	Split-Path	Split-Path [-Path] <String[]...
Alias	spps	Stop-Process
Alias	spsv	Stop-Service
Function	SQLSERVER:	Set-Location SQLSERVER:
Alias	start	Start-Process
Cmdlet	Start-Job	Start-Job [-ScriptBlock] <Sc...
Cmdlet	Start-Process	Start-Process [-FilePath] <S...
Cmdlet	Start-Service	Start-Service [-Name] <Strin...
Cmdlet	Start-Sleep	Start-Sleep [-Seconds] <Int3...
Cmdlet	Start-Transaction	Start-Transaction [-Timeout ...
Cmdlet	Start-Transcript	Start-Transcript [[-Path] <S...
Cmdlet	Stop-Computer	Stop-Computer [[-ComputerNam...
Cmdlet	Stop-Job	Stop-Job [-Id] <Int32[]> [-P...
Cmdlet	Stop-Process	Stop-Process [-Id] <Int32[]>...
Cmdlet	Stop-Service	Stop-Service [-Name] <String...
Cmdlet	Stop-Transcript	Stop-Transcript [-Verbose] [...
Cmdlet	Suspend-Service	Suspend-Service [-Name] <Str...
Cmdlet	Suspend-SqlAvailabilityDatabase	Suspend-SqlAvailabilityDatab...
Alias	sv	Set-Variable
Cmdlet	Switch-SqlAvailabilityGroup	Switch-SqlAvailabilityGroup ...
Alias	swmi	Set-WMIInstance
Function	T:	Set-Location T:
Function	TabExpansion	...
Alias	tee	Tee-Object
Cmdlet	Tee-Object	Tee-Object [-FilePath] <Stri...
Cmdlet	Test-ComputerSecureChannel	Test-ComputerSecureChannel [...
Cmdlet	Test-Connection	Test-Connection [-ComputerNa...
Cmdlet	Test-ModuleManifest	Test-ModuleManifest [-Path] ...
Cmdlet	Test-Path	Test-Path [-Path] <String[]>...
Cmdlet	Test-SqlAvailabilityGroup	Test-SqlAvailabilityGroup [[...
Cmdlet	Test-SqlAvailabilityReplica	Test-SqlAvailabilityReplica ...
Cmdlet	Test-SqlDatabaseReplicaState	Test-SqlDatabaseReplicaState...
Cmdlet	Test-WSMan	Test-WSMan [[-ComputerName] ...
Cmdlet	Trace-Command	Trace-Command [-Name] <Strin...
Alias	type	Get-Content
Function	U:	Set-Location U:
Cmdlet	Undo-Transaction	Undo-Transaction [-Verbose] ...
Cmdlet	Unregister-Event	Unregister-Event [-SourceIde...

CHAPTER 16: Advanced T-SQL Programming Topics

Cmdlet	Unregister-PSSessionConfigur...	Unregister-PSSessionConfigur...
Cmdlet	Update-FormatData	Update-FormatData [[-AppendP...
Cmdlet	Update-List	Update-List [[-Property] <St...
Cmdlet	Update-TypeData	Update-TypeData [[-AppendPat...
Cmdlet	Use-Transaction	Use-Transaction [-Transacted...
Function	V:	Set-Location V:
Function	W:	Set-Location W:
Cmdlet	Wait-Event	Wait-Event [[-SourceIdentifi...
Cmdlet	Wait-Job	Wait-Job [-Id] <Int32[]> [-A...
Cmdlet	Wait-Process	Wait-Process [-Name] <String...
Alias	where	Where-Object
Cmdlet	Where-Object	Where-Object [-FilterScript]...
Alias	wjb	Wait-Job
Alias	write	Write-Output
Cmdlet	Write-Debug	Write-Debug [-Message] <Stri...
Cmdlet	Write-Error	Write-Error [-Message] <Stri...
Cmdlet	Write-EventLog	Write-EventLog [-LogName] <S...
Cmdlet	Write-Host	Write-Host [[-Object] <Objec...
Cmdlet	Write-Output	Write-Output [-InputObject] ...
Cmdlet	Write-Progress	Write-Progress [-Activity] <...
Cmdlet	Write-Verbose	Write-Verbose [-Message] <St...
Cmdlet	Write-Warning	Write-Warning [-Message] <St...
Function	X:	Set-Location X:
Function	Y:	Set-Location Y:
Function	Z:	Set-Location Z:

We can access help for a command just by typing "help" and the command name. "help" example for format-list.

help format-list

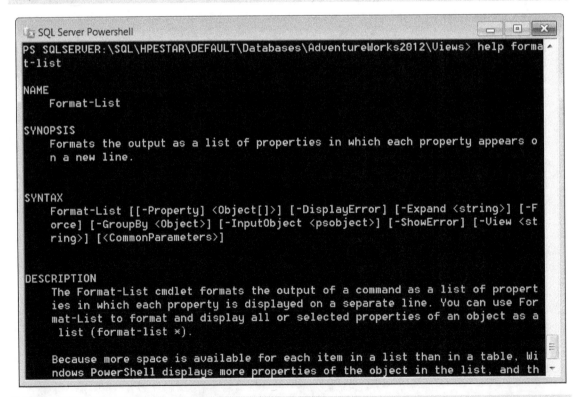

TRY...CATCH Block With TRANSACTION

If the TRY is successful the transaction is committed, otherwise the transaction (previous statements if any) is rolled back and the error is logged into an errorlog table.

```
USE tempdb; -- Create & configure table for testing
IF OBJECT_ID ('dbo.Product', 'U') IS NOT NULL DROP TABLE dbo.Product ;
SELECT ID=CONVERT(INT,ProductID), ProductName=Name, ListPrice, ModifiedDate
INTO Product FROM AdventureWorks2012.Production.Product WHERE ListPrice > 0;  -- (304 row(s) affected)
ALTER TABLE PRODUCT ADD CONSTRAINT uqProd UNIQUE (ProductName);
ALTER TABLE PRODUCT ADD CONSTRAINT dfProd DEFAULT (CURRENT_TIMESTAMP) FOR ModifiedDate;
ALTER TABLE PRODUCT ADD rowguid UNIQUEIDENTIFIER default(newsequentialid());
GO -- Command(s) completed successfully.
```

```
IF OBJECT_ID ('dbo.ErrorLogForTransactions', 'U') IS NOT NULL  DROP TABLE dbo.ErrorLogForTransactions ;
CREATE TABLE ErrorLogForTransactions( ID INT IDENTITY(1,1) PRIMARY KEY,
     UserName sysname, TableName sysname, ErrorNumber sysname,  ErrorSeverity sysname,
     ErrorState sysname, ErrorMessage nvarchar(1024),  rowguid UNIQUEIDENTIFIER default(newid()),
     ModifiedDate datetime default (getdate()));
GO -- Command(s) completed successfully.
```

```
IF OBJECT_ID ('dbo.uspInsertNewProduct', 'P') IS NOT NULL DROP PROC dbo.uspInsertNewProduct ;
GO
CREATE PROCEDURE uspInsertNewProduct ( @NewProduct NVARCHAR(64), @Price  SMALLMONEY) AS
BEGIN    DECLARE @TableName   SYSNAME, @ErrorMessage NVARCHAR(1024);
 BEGIN TRY;    BEGIN TRANSACTION;
  SELECT @ErrorMessage = 'Duplicate insert failed', @TableName = 'Product';
  INSERT dbo.Product (ID, ProductName, ListPrice)
        SELECT max(ID)+1, @NewProduct,  @Price FROM Product;    COMMIT TRANSACTION;
 END TRY
 BEGIN CATCH    ROLLBACK TRANSACTION;    INSERT dbo.ErrorLogForTransactions
         (UserName, TableName, ErrorNumber, errorSeverity, errorState, ErrorMessage)
         VALUES(suser_sname(),@TableName,ERROR_NUMBER(),ERROR_SEVERITY(),
         ERROR_STATE(),ERROR_MESSAGE());    RAISERROR (@ErrorMessage,16,1);  END CATCH
END
GO
```

```
EXEC uspInsertNewProduct  'xDelta SmartPhone', 999.99;               -- Valid INSERT
DECLARE @NewProduct varchar(64) = (SELECT TOP(1) ProductName FROM Product), @Price SMALLMONEY = 999.99;
EXEC uspInsertNewProduct  @NewProduct, @Price;               -- Invalid INSERT - duplicate name
GO
```

SELECT * FROM ErrorLogForTransactions;

ID	UserName	TableName	ErrorNumber	ErrorSeverity	ErrorState	ErrorMessage	ModifiedDate
1	HPESTAR\Owner	Product	2627	14	1	Violation of UNIQUE KEY constraint 'uqProd'. Cannot insert duplicate key in object 'dbo.Product'. The duplicate key value is (All-Purpose Bike Stand).	2016-12-09 13:35:23.687

CHAPTER 16: Advanced T-SQL Programming Topics

SET TRANSACTION ISOLATION LEVEL Command

The syntax for the command:

SET TRANSACTION ISOLATION LEVEL

   { READ UNCOMMITTED

   | READ COMMITTED

   | REPEATABLE READ

   | SNAPSHOT

   | SERIALIZABLE

   } [;]

Preparation for demonstrating levels. We have to use 2 connections to represent 2 users of the database. First we create a test table.

```
USE tempdb;
SELECT * INTO Product FROM AdventureWorks2012.Production.Product;
-- (504 row(s) affected)
```

In connection 1 we simulate a large (slow) transaction on the Product table.

```
BEGIN TRAN;
SELECT StartTime = CURRENT_TIMESTAMP;
UPDATE Product SET ListPrice=ListPrice * 1.05;
WAITFOR DELAY '00:00:20'; -- 20 sec delay to keep transaction pending
ROLLBACK TRAN;
SELECT FinishTime = CURRENT_TIMESTAMP;
```

In connection 2 we test the isolation levels. We start execution after connection 1 started. Code for the first test.

```
SET TRANSACTION ISOLATION LEVEL READ UNCOMMITTED
SELECT StartTime = CURRENT_TIMESTAMP;
SELECT TOP (2) * FROM Product ORDER BY ListPrice DESC;
SELECT FinishTime = CURRENT_TIMESTAMP;
```

READ UNCOMMITTED Isolation Level - Dirty Reads

The SELECT with TOP started 4 seconds later after the UPDATE, yet it finished immediately without waiting for the UPDATE transaction to come to a conclusion (ROLLBACK or COMMIT).

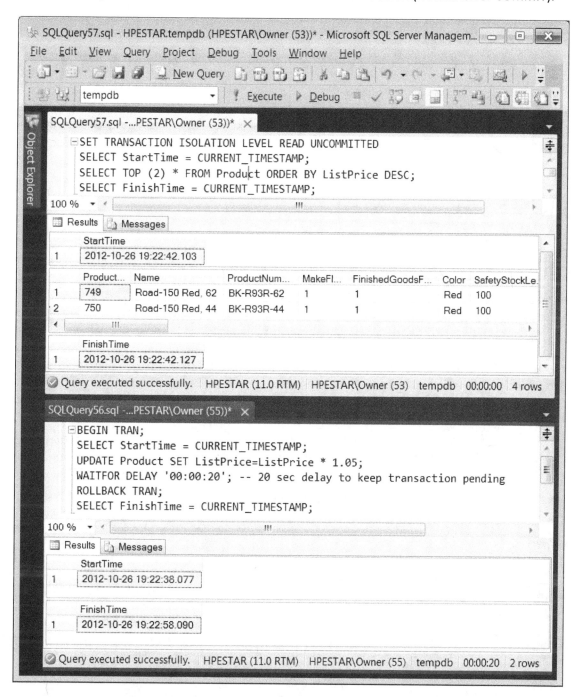

READ COMMITTED Isolation Level - Default for SQL Server

The SELECT query waits until the exclusive lock is removed by the UPDATE transaction. To prevent such a wait, frequently the NOLOCK hint (dirty reads) is used.

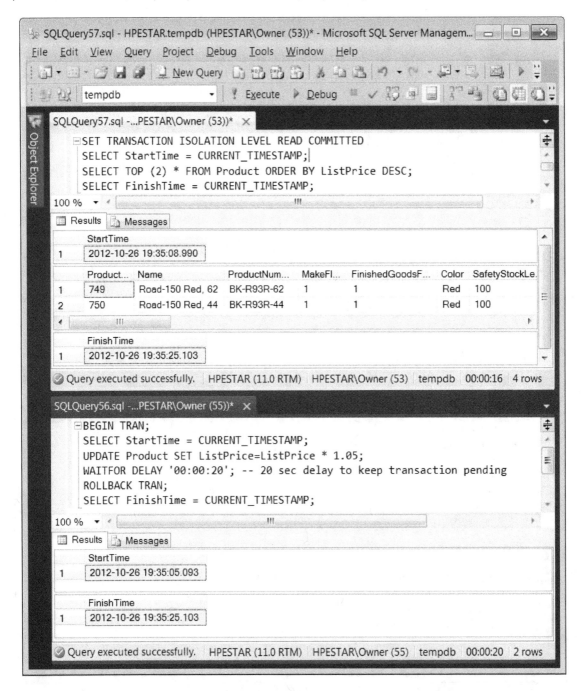

REPEATABLE READ Isolation Level

The UPDATE (transaction by itself) must wait until the exclusive lock is released by the 2 SELECT statements transaction. The ListPrice changed after the COMMIT transaction.

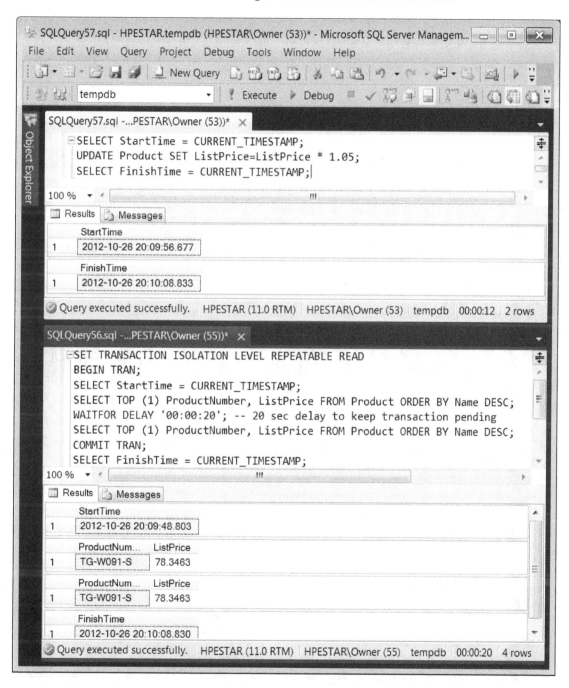

Redefining the Product table without IDENTITIY & testing it

```
DROP TABLE tempdb.dbo.Product;
SELECT ID = CONVERT(INT, ProductID), Name, ProductNumber, ListPrice, Color
INTO tempdb.dbo.Product FROM AdventureWorks2012.Production.Product;
```

REPEATABLE READ blocks UPDATE & DELETE, but not INSERT. The row counts differ.

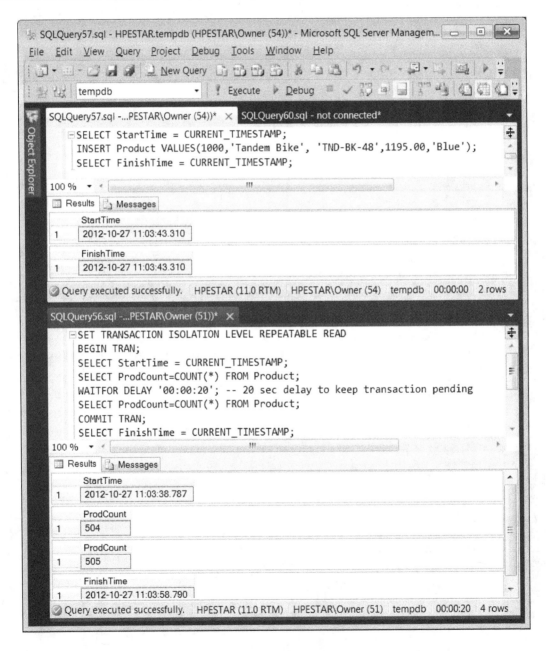

SERIALIZABLE Isolation Level

SERIALIZABLE isolation level blocks INSERT as well in addition to blocking UPDATE & DELETE. The row counts are the same.

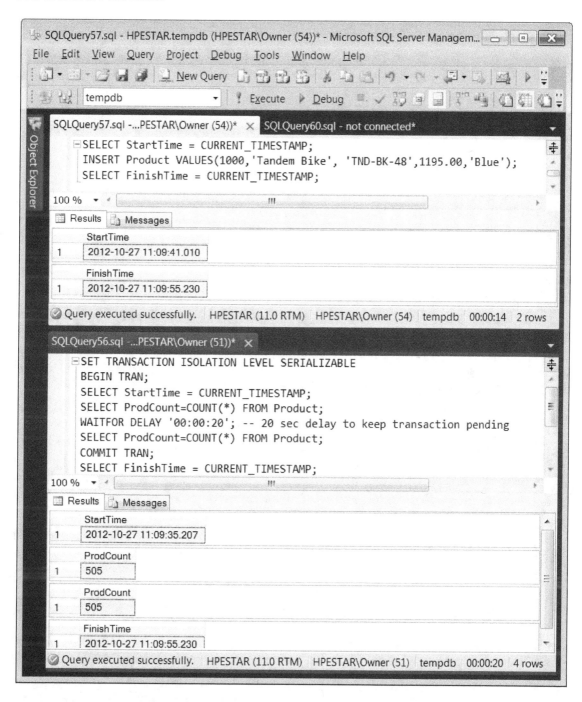

SNAPSHOT Isolation Level

SNAPSHOT isolation produces the same results as SERIALIZABLE without blocking INSERT (same for UPDATE &DELETE).

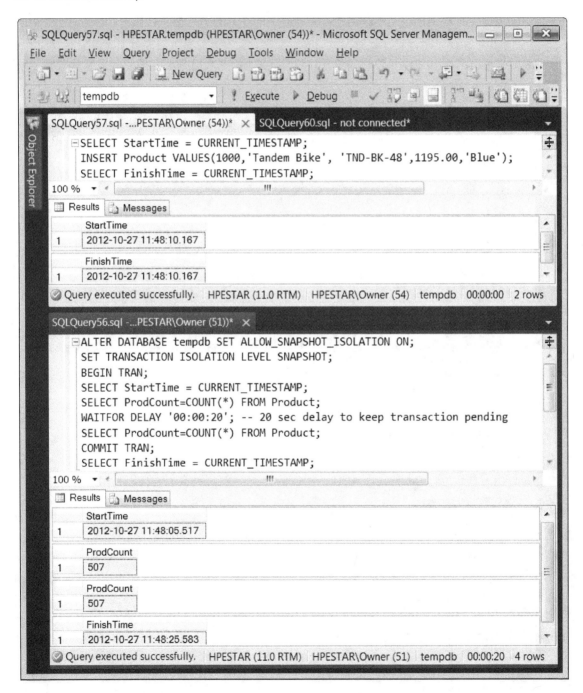

Tabular Summary of Isolation Levels

DBCC command returns the isolation level property for the database among other database options.

```
USE tempdb;
DBCC USEROPTIONS;
/* (13 row(s) affected)
DBCC execution completed. If DBCC printed error messages,
contact your system administrator. */
```

Set Option	Value
textsize	2147483647
language	us_english
dateformat	mdy
datefirst	7
lock_timeout	-1
quoted_identifier	SET
arithabort	SET
ansi_null_dflt_on	SET
ansi_warnings	SET
ansi_padding	SET
ansi_nulls	SET
concat_null_yields_null	SET
isolation level	**read committed**

Dirty Reads & Phantom Reads

Dirty Reads: reading uncommitted data; there is no guarantee that data read will ever be committed.

Phantom Reads: data working with in the first connection changed by another transaction in the second connection since first read. Subsequent reads of the data in the first connection same transaction could be different.

Isolation level	Dirty read	Nonrepeatable read	Phantom read
Read uncommitted	Yes	Yes	Yes
Read committed	No	Yes	Yes
Repeatable read	No	No	Yes
Serializable	No	No	No
Snapshot	No	No	No

INSERT Data Into Parent-Child Tables in One Transaction

The business meaning of transaction: either insert successfully to both tables or do nothing, return an error. First we prepare the test data to be inserted in two temporary tables by SELECT INTO table create and populate.

```
USE AdventureWorks2012
GO
```

```
DECLARE @SourceSOID int = 50701;
SELECT OrderDate
       ,DueDate ,ShipDate,Status,OnlineOrderFlag,PurchaseOrderNumber
       ,AccountNumber,CustomerID,SalesPersonID,TerritoryID,BillToAddressID
       ,ShipToAddressID,ShipMethodID,CreditCardID,CreditCardApprovalCode
       ,CurrencyRateID,SubTotal,TaxAmt,Freight,Comment
INTO #SOH
FROM Sales.SalesOrderHeader
WHERE SalesOrderID = @SourceSOID;    -- (1 row(s) affected)
```

```
SELECT SalesOrderID,
       CarrierTrackingNumber,OrderQty,ProductID,SpecialOfferID,UnitPrice,UnitPriceDiscount
INTO #SOD
FROM Sales.SalesOrderDetail
WHERE SalesOrderID = @SourceSOID;
GO   -- (6 row(s) affected)
```

```
SELECT * FROM #SOH;
```

Orde rDat e	Due Date	Ship Date	St at us	Online Order Flag	Purchase OrderNu mber	Accou ntNu mber	Cust ome rID	Sales Perso nID	Terr itor yID	BillTo Addre ssID	ShipTo Addre ssID	Ship Meth odID	Cred itCar dID	CreditCar dApprova lCode	Curre ncyRa teID	Sub Tot al	Ta xA mt	Fre igh t	Co mm ent
2007 -06- 01 00:0 0:00. 000	2007 -06- 13 00:0 0:00. 000	2007 -06- 08 00:0 0:00. 000	5	0	PO24071 99018	10- 4020- 00022 5	298 82	279	5	933	933	5	1280 8	56789Vi6 6226	NULL	777 .29 02	73. 47 48	22. 96 09	NU LL

```
SELECT * FROM #SOD;
GO
```

CarrierTrackingNumber	OrderQty	ProductID	SpecialOfferID	UnitPrice	UnitPriceDiscount
B67A-4C0A-B3	1	843	1	15.00	0.00
B67A-4C0A-B3	1	726	1	202.332	0.00
B67A-4C0A-B3	1	722	1	183.9382	0.00
B67A-4C0A-B3	4	855	1	53.994	0.00
B67A-4C0A-B3	2	813	1	65.6018	0.00
B67A-4C0A-B3	1	716	1	28.8404	0.00

CHAPTER 16: Advanced T-SQL Programming Topics

ROLLBACK Does Not Roll Back Everything

ROLLBACK has no effect on IDENTITY seed, table variable or writing to a flat file. The implication is that IDENTITY column will have gaps where ROLLBACKs happened. With RAISERROR we return an error flag to the calling application program.

```
BEGIN TRANSACTION

DECLARE @Insert TABLE(ID INT); DECLARE @Error INT; DECLARE @ID INT;

INSERT INTO Sales.SalesOrderHeader(OrderDate
        ,DueDate ,ShipDate,Status,OnlineOrderFlag,PurchaseOrderNumber
        ,AccountNumber,CustomerID,SalesPersonID,TerritoryID,BillToAddressID
        ,ShipToAddressID,ShipMethodID,CreditCardID,CreditCardApprovalCode
        ,CurrencyRateID,SubTotal,TaxAmt,Freight,Comment )
OUTPUT inserted.SalesOrderID INTO @Insert(ID)  -- This is the PRIMARY KEY value
SELECT * FROM #SOH; -- (1 row(s) affected)


SET @Error = @@ERROR;
IF @Error <>0 BEGIN
        ROLLBACK TRANSACTION;
        RAISERROR ('An error occured inserting Sales.SalesOrderHeader',12,1);   END
ELSE BEGIN

SELECT * FROM @Insert; -- debugging   -- 75124

SELECT @ID = ID FROM @Insert;  -- FOREIGN KEY value

INSERT Sales.SalesOrderDetail ( SalesOrderID,
        CarrierTrackingNumber, OrderQty, ProductID, SpecialOfferID,
        UnitPrice, UnitPriceDiscount)
SELECT @ID, * FROM #SOD;  -- (6 row(s) affected)

SET @Error = @@ERROR;
IF @Error <>0 BEGIN
  ROLLBACK TRANSACTION;
  RAISERROR ('An error occured inserting Sales.SalesOrderDetail',12,1);
  END
ELSE
        COMMIT TRAN;
END
GO
```

Optimistic Concurrency Control

A table can have only one rowversion(formerly timestamp) column which is used for version-stamping rows. The value in the rowversion column is updated automatically every time a row in the table inserted or updated. Of course this means we cannot use it as a PRIMARY KEY, because we may get many FK orphans quickly if updates are performed on other columns. When a row is modified in a table, the timestamp is updated with the current database timestamp value obtained from the @@DBTS function.

Rowversion is the synonym for timestamp starting with SQL Server 2005. It is an 8 bytes unique binary key within the database. A quick demo of rowversion data type follows. **Rowversion values may not be consecutive.** Since all the columns in the demo table have default values, we can use the DEFAULT VALUES clause for INSERT.

```
USE tempdb;
GO


CREATE TABLE Alpha ( ID int IDENTITY(1,1) PRIMARY KEY,
       Number int default(datepart(ss,CURRENT_TIMESTAMP)),
       String varchar(16) default(datename(dw, CURRENT_TIMESTAMP)),
       ModifiedDate date default(CURRENT_TIMESTAMP),
       RowStamp rowversion);
GO


INSERT Alpha DEFAULT VALUES;
GO 100


SELECT TOP(5) * FROM Alpha ORDER BY ID;
GO
```

ID	Number	String	ModifiedDate	RowStamp
1	43	Sunday	2012-10-28	0x0000000000000840
2	43	Sunday	2012-10-28	0x0000000000000841
3	43	Sunday	2012-10-28	0x0000000000000842
4	43	Sunday	2012-10-28	0x0000000000000843
5	43	Sunday	2012-10-28	0x0000000000000844

The rowversion (timestamp) starts changing as soon as the transaction begins. If the transaction is rolled back, it returns to the original value.

The main purpose is row versioning in multi user environment, in other words concurrency checking. The users may be humans or computer programs.

CHAPTER 16: Advanced T-SQL Programming Topics

Pessimistic Concurrency Control vs. Optimistic

Pessimistic concurrency means locking the data at the row, page, or table level and don't allow anyone to modify it until the target user is done modifying the data and saving it back into the database. Trouble with this method: it may take a few minutes for the target user to update a record during which period other users may be prevented from doing their work (locked out from the table by blocking). If the target user called away for a meeting for example in the middle of data entry, you need to unlock the table by a timeout mechanism in order to prevent damaging disruption to data access by other users.

Optimistic concurrency means reading a record in a table and displaying it for the target user, but not locking it. Other users can read and modify the record at anytime while the target user is performing the manual update on the computer screen. When the target user releases the record for database update you need to check if someone changed it in between the initial read and the release (like 1-5 minutes). Usually this is not a problem due to the work distribution among staff (business process organization), nevertheless you have to program for it to avoid conflicting updates and damage to database integrity.

Assume you are a developer and developing a program in Visual Basic to update the name and address table of customers. There will be 100 staff member who can perform this application function. How can you be sure that while target staff Alpha typing in the change, staff Beta is not changing the same row?

Here is what you can do:

- ➢ Read the name and address table including the rowversion. You display the info to the user for update and save the rowversion.
- ➢ Certain amount of time later, like 2 minutes, the user presses the submit button after changes were typed in.
- ➢ You open a transaction with Begin Transaction.
- ➢ You read the rowversion of the name and address row.
- ➢ You compare the current rowversion to the saved rowversion.
- ➢ If the rowversions are same, you update the row and commit the transaction.
- ➢ If rowversions are different, you roll back the transaction and notify the user about the fact that the data was changed by someone else. You can let then the user decide what to do or follow the appropriate company business rule for data entry conflict resolution.

This is pretty common practice in multi-user environment. The alternate would be to examine a datetime column, or the entire row which is more processing intensive and less reliable as well due to potential blocking.

Example Showing rowversion (formerly timestamp) in Action

```
USE tempdb;

CREATE TABLE Star
(
       StarID                INT IDENTITY PRIMARY KEY,          -- SURROGATE PK
       FirstName             VARCHAR(25),
       LastName              VARCHAR(30),
       UNIQUE (LastName, FirstName),                            -- NATURAL KEY
       ModifiedDate          DATE default( CURRENT_TIMESTAMP),
       VERSIONSTAMP          ROWVERSION
);
go

-- Populate table
INSERT Star     (FirstName, LastName)
VALUES          ('Tom', 'Jones'),
                ('Jessica', 'Simpson'),
                ('Luciano', 'Pavarotti'),
                ('Stevie',  'Brock'),
                ('Christina', 'Aguilera'),
                ('Frank', 'Sinatra'),
                ('Doris', 'Day'),
                ('Elvis', 'Presley');
go

SELECT * FROM   Star ORDER BY StarID;
go
```

StarID	FirstName	LastName	ModifiedDate	VERSIONSTAMP
1	Tom	Jones	2018-11-07	0x00000000000007E0
2	Jessica	Simpson	2018-11-07	0x00000000000007E1
3	Luciano	Pavarotti	2018-11-07	0x00000000000007E2
4	Stevie	Brock	2018-11-07	0x00000000000007E3
5	Christina	Aguilera	2018-11-07	0x00000000000007E4
6	Frank	Sinatra	2018-11-07	0x00000000000007E5
7	Doris	Day	2018-11-07	0x00000000000007E6
8	Elvis	Presley	2018-11-07	0x00000000000007E7

Simulation of Conflicting Updates of the Same Record

```
-- Temporary table to store current record version
CREATE TABLE #semaphore
 (
   ID                     INT IDENTITY(1, 1) PRIMARY KEY,
   StartVersion           BIGINT,
   PK                     INT
 );
```

```
INSERT INTO #semaphore (StartVersion, PK)
SELECT VERSIONSTAMP, StarID
FROM   Star
WHERE  StarID = 1;
```

```
SELECT * FROM #semaphore;
```

ID	StartVersion	PK
1	2016	1

```
-- We send the info to "our" application user;  user is making changes on the app form;
SELECT StarID, FirstName, LastName
FROM Star
WHERE StarID = 1;
```

```
-- SIMULATION: somebody else updating the same record meanwhile
-- Execute the following UPDATE statement in a different SSMS connection
/*********************************************************
UPDATE Star
SET     FirstName = 'Celine',
        LastName = 'Dion'
WHERE  StarID = 1
*********************************************************/
```

```
SELECT StarID, FirstName, LastName FROM Star WHERE StarID = 1;
```

StarID	FirstName	LastName
1	Celine	Dion

We Envelope the UPDATE Attempt into a Transaction

```
-- We are attempting to update, but cannot because current version is different
BEGIN TRANSACTION

IF (SELECT StartVersion
    FROM    #semaphore
    WHERE PK=1 )
      =
   (SELECT VERSIONSTAMP
    FROM    Star
    WHERE   StarID = 1)
  BEGIN
     UPDATE Star
     SET    FirstName = 'Julia',
            LastName = 'Roberts'
     WHERE  StarID = 1
     COMMIT TRANSACTION
  END
ELSE
  BEGIN
     ROLLBACK TRANSACTION
     PRINT 'ROLLBACK - UPDATE CONFLICT'
     RAISERROR ('Star update conflict.',10,0)
  END;
```

```
/* Messages
ROLLBACK - UPDATE CONFLICT
Star update conflict.    */
```

RAISERROR returns error flag to application. The application will follow a business rule to handle the exception.

Xquery Examples

The XML data type has the following methods for exposing the data: Query, Value, Exist, Modify, and Nodes.

The query() Method

The query() method takes an XQuery expression that evaluates to a list of XML nodes and allows the extraction of fragments of an XML document. The result is an instance of untyped XML. First we create xml data with the FOR XML AUTO clause, then query it.

The query() Method Retrieves Assembly Instructions from XML Column

inst is a derived table representing the inner query which retrieves information from the ProductModel table XML column. The outer query formats and filters the data to return the final result set.

```
USE AdventureWorks2012;
SELECT  ProductModelID,
        rtrim(ltrim(convert(nvarchar(max),[Procedure]))) AS [Procedure]
FROM
(SELECT ProductModelID,Instructions.query(
' declare namespace AWPMMI="http://schemas.microsoft.com/sqlserver/2004/07/adventure-works/ProductModelManuInstructions";
  for $Step in /AWPMMI:root/AWPMMI:Location[1]/AWPMMI:step
    return string($Step)'
) AS [Procedure]
FROM Production.ProductModel WHERE Instructions is not null) inst
WHERE ProductModelID = 53;
GO
```

ProductModelID	Procedure
53	
	Visually examine the pedal spindles to determine left and right pedals. The left and right pedals have different threading directions. It is important you identify them correctly.
	Apply a small amount of grease to the left pedal and thread the pedal onto the left crank arm by hand.
	If the threads do not turn easily, back the spindle out and re-start.
	Securely tighten the spindle against the crank arm using a small wrench.
	Apply a small amount of grease to the right pedal and thread the pedal onto the right crank arm by hand. If the threads do not turn easily, back the spindle out and re-start. Securely tighten the spindle against the crank arm using a small wrench.
	Inspect per specification FI-520.

When we examine the Procedure string with convert(varbinary(max), ...), we can see that it has next line (hex 0A) an leading spaces (hex 20) imbedded for formatting purposes. We can check the size of XML data with the DATALENGTH() function:

```
select   MinLen = min(datalength(resume)),  MaxLen = max(datalength(resume)),
      AvgLen = avg(datalength(resume))
from AdventureWorks2012.HumanResources.JobCandidate;
-- 3931        9080         6241
```

value() Method

The value() method performs an XQuery against the XML and returns a scalar value.

```
DECLARE @xmlDoc xml =' <root><MP3List><MP3ListID>99</MP3ListID></MP3List> </root>';
SELECT @xmlDoc.value('(/root//MP3List/MP3ListID/text())[1]','nvarchar(32)' );   -- 99
```

nodes() Method

The nodes() method shreds an XML data type instance into relational data. It returns a rowset.
In the XML resume example, each column returned as scalar value.

exist() Method

The exist() method returns bit 1 (true) if the XQuery expression returns at least one XML node.

Bike models are listed if <Summary> element is included in XML ProductDescription.

```
SELECT          Name                                    AS ModelName,
                CatalogDescription.query('
declare namespace pd="http://schemas.microsoft.com/sqlserver/2004/07/adventure-
works/ProductModelDescription";
   <Product
      ProductModelID= "{ sql:column("ProductModelID") }"
      />
')                                                      AS ProductModelID
FROM AdventureWorks2012.Production.ProductModel
WHERE CatalogDescription.exist('
   declare namespace  pd="http://schemas.microsoft.com/sqlserver/2004/07/adventure-
works/ProductModelDescription";
   /pd:ProductDescription[(pd:Summary)]'
   ) = 1
ORDER BY ModelName;
GO
```

ModelName	ProductModelID
Mountain-100	<Product ProductModelID="19" />
Mountain-500	<Product ProductModelID="23" />
Road-150	<Product ProductModelID="25" />
Road-450	<Product ProductModelID="28" />
Touring-1000	<Product ProductModelID="34" />
Touring-2000	<Product ProductModelID="35" />

The CatalogDescription XML data for ProductModelID 23

```
<?xml-stylesheet href="ProductDescription.xsl" type="text/xsl"?>
<p1:ProductDescription
xmlns:p1="http://schemas.microsoft.com/sqlserver/2004/07/adventure-
works/ProductModelDescription"
xmlns:wm="http://schemas.microsoft.com/sqlserver/2004/07/adventure-
works/ProductModelWarrAndMain" xmlns:wf="http://www.adventure-
```

```
works.com/schemas/OtherFeatures" xmlns:html="http://www.w3.org/1999/xhtml"
ProductModelID="23" ProductModelName="Mountain-500">
 <p1:Summary>
  <html:p>Suitable for any type of riding, on or off-road.
                      Fits any budget. Smooth-shifting with a comfortable ride.
           </html:p>
 </p1:Summary>
 <p1:Manufacturer>
  <p1:Name>AdventureWorks</p1:Name>
  <p1:Copyright>2002</p1:Copyright>
  <p1:ProductURL>HTTP://www.Adventure-works.com</p1:ProductURL>
 </p1:Manufacturer>
 <p1:Features>Product highlights include:
        <wm:Warranty><wm:WarrantyPeriod>1
year</wm:WarrantyPeriod><wm:Description>parts and
labor</wm:Description></wm:Warranty><wm:Maintenance><wm:NoOfYears>3
years</wm:NoOfYears><wm:Description>maintenance contact available through
dealer</wm:Description></wm:Maintenance><wf:wheel>Stable, durable wheels suitable for
novice riders.</wf:wheel><wf:saddle>Made from synthetic leather and features gel padding for
increased comfort.</wf:saddle><wf:pedal><html:b>Expanded platform</html:b> so you can
ride in any shoes; great for all-around riding.</wf:pedal><wf:crankset> Super rigid spindle.
</wf:crankset><wf:BikeFrame>Our best value frame utilizing the same, ground-breaking
technology as the ML aluminum frame.</wf:BikeFrame></p1:Features>
 <!-- add one or more of these elements... one for each specific product in this product model --
>
 <p1:Picture>
  <p1:Angle>front</p1:Angle>
  <p1:Size>small</p1:Size>
  <p1:ProductPhotoID>1</p1:ProductPhotoID>
 </p1:Picture>
 <!-- add any tags in <specifications> -->
 <p1:Specifications> These are the product specifications.
        <Height>Varies</Height> Centimeters.
        <Material>Aluminum Alloy</Material><Color>Available in all
colors.</Color><ProductLine>Mountain
bike</ProductLine><Style>Unisex</Style><RiderExperience>Novice to Intermediate
riders</RiderExperience></p1:Specifications>
</p1:ProductDescription>
```

modify() Method

The modify() method modifies the contents of an XML document. It can only be used in the SET statement or the SET clause of an UPDATE statement for tables with XML columns.

```
DECLARE @XML xml = '<Root>
 <Picture>
  <Angle>front</Angle>
  <Size>small</Size>
  <ProductPhotoID>1</ProductPhotoID>
 </Picture>     </Root>';        SELECT @XML;
```

```
<Root><Picture><Angle>front</Angle><Size>small</Size><ProductPhotoID>1</ProductPhotoID
></Picture></Root>
```

```
-- update angle
SET @XML.modify('
 replace value of (/Root/Picture/Angle[1]/text())[1]
 with    "side" ');        SELECT @XML;
```

```
<Root><Picture><Angle>side</Angle><Size>small</Size><ProductPhotoID>1</ProductPhotoID>
</Picture></Root>
```

```
-- update size
SET @XML.modify('
 replace value of (/Root/Picture/Size[1]/text())[1]
 with    "medium" ');    SELECT @XML;
```

```
<Root><Picture><Angle>side</Angle><Size>medium</Size><ProductPhotoID>1</ProductPhotoI
D></Picture></Root>
```

```
-- update productphotoid
SET @XML.modify('
 replace value of (/Root/Picture/ProductPhotoID[1]/text())[1]
 with    "99" ');        SELECT @XML;
```

```
<Root><Picture><Angle>side</Angle><Size>medium</Size><ProductPhotoID>99</ProductPhot
oID></Picture></Root>
```

Insert (XML DML)

Insert(XML DML) inserts one or more nodes as child nodes or siblings of the target node.

```
DECLARE @XML xml = '<Root>
 <Picture ID = "4">
  <Angle>front</Angle>
  <Size>small</Size>
  <ProductPhotoID>1</ProductPhotoID>
 </Picture>      </Root>';
SELECT @XML;
```

```
<Root>
 <Picture ID="4">
  <Angle>front</Angle>
  <Size>small</Size>
  <ProductPhotoID>1</ProductPhotoID>
 </Picture>
</Root>
```

```
SET @XML.modify('insert  <Picture ID = "1">
  <Angle>front</Angle>
  <Size>large</Size>
  <ProductPhotoID>45</ProductPhotoID>
 </Picture> as first   into  (/Root)[1] ');
SELECT @XML;
```

```
<Root>
 <Picture ID="1">
  <Angle>front</Angle>
  <Size>large</Size>
  <ProductPhotoID>45</ProductPhotoID>
 </Picture>
 <Picture ID="4">
  <Angle>front</Angle>
  <Size>small</Size>
  <ProductPhotoID>1</ProductPhotoID>
 </Picture>
</Root>
```

Delete (XML DML)

The delete(XML DML) deletes nodes from an XML instance.

```
DECLARE @XML xml = '<Root>
<Picture ID = "1">
  <Angle>front</Angle>
  <Size>large</Size>
  <ProductPhotoID>45</ProductPhotoID>
</Picture>
<Picture ID = "4">
  <Angle>front</Angle>
  <Size>small</Size>
  <ProductPhotoID>1</ProductPhotoID>
</Picture>
 <Picture ID = "8">
  <Angle>above</Angle>
  <Size>small</Size>
  <ProductPhotoID>12</ProductPhotoID>
</Picture>      </Root>';
```

```
SET @XML.modify('
 delete /Root/Picture[@ID=4] ');
```

```
SELECT @XML;
```

```
<Root>
 <Picture ID="1">
  <Angle>front</Angle>
  <Size>large</Size>
  <ProductPhotoID>45</ProductPhotoID>
 </Picture>
 <Picture ID="8">
  <Angle>above</Angle>
  <Size>small</Size>
  <ProductPhotoID>12</ProductPhotoID>
 </Picture>
</Root>
```

Working with hierarchyid Data Type

Orgchart Based on AdventureWorks2012

Let's take a look at the hierarchyid and related data in the Employee table first.

```
USE AdventureWorks2012;

SELECT TOP(20) BusinessEntityID, NationalIdNumber, OrganizationNode, OrganizationLevel,
        OrgNodeText=CONVERT(varchar, OrganizationNode),  JobTitle
FROM HumanResources.Employee  ORDER BY OrganizationNode;
```

BusinessEntityID	NationalIdNumber	OrganizationNode	OrganizationLevel	OrgNodeText	JobTitle
1	295847284	0x	0	/	Chief Executive Officer
2	245797967	0x58	1	/1/	Vice President of Engineering
3	509647174	0x5AC0	2	/1/1/	Engineering Manager
4	112457891	0x5AD6	3	/1/1/1/	Senior Tool Designer
5	695256908	0x5ADA	3	/1/1/2/	Design Engineer
6	998320692	0x5ADE	3	/1/1/3/	Design Engineer
7	134969118	0x5AE1	3	/1/1/4/	Research and Development Manager
8	811994146	0x5AE158	4	/1/1/4/1/	Research and Development Engineer
9	658797903	0x5AE168	4	/1/1/4/2/	Research and Development Engineer
10	879342154	0x5AE178	4	/1/1/4/3/	Research and Development Manager
11	974026903	0x5AE3	3	/1/1/5/	Senior Tool Designer
12	480168528	0x5AE358	4	/1/1/5/1/	Tool Designer
13	486228782	0x5AE368	4	/1/1/5/2/	Tool Designer
14	42487730	0x5AE5	3	/1/1/6/	Senior Design Engineer
15	56920285	0x5AE7	3	/1/1/7/	Design Engineer
16	24756624	0x68	1	/2/	Marketing Manager
17	253022876	0x6AC0	2	/2/1/	Marketing Assistant
18	222969461	0x6B40	2	/2/2/	Marketing Specialist
19	52541318	0x6BC0	2	/2/3/	Marketing Assistant
20	323403273	0x6C20	2	/2/4/	Marketing Assistant

```
-- Convert text node to hierarchyid
SELECT CONVERT(hierarchyid, '/3/1/22/4/');   -- 0x7AF07610
```

hierarchyid Based Organizational Chart with Recursive CTE

TAB (CHAR(9)) is used to create the indentation using OrganizationLevel.

```
;WITH cteOrgChart(ManagerID, EmployeeID, EmployeeLevel)
    AS (SELECT   OrganizationNode,                        -- anchor member
                 OrganizationNode, OrganizationLevel
        FROM   HumanResources.Employee
        WHERE  OrganizationLevel = 0
        UNION ALL
        SELECT   e.OrganizationNode.GetAncestor(1),        -- recursive member
                 e.OrganizationNode, OrganizationLevel
        FROM   HumanResources.Employee e
            INNER JOIN cteOrgChart d
            ON e.OrganizationNode.GetAncestor(1) = d.EmployeeID)

-- SELECT * FROM   cteOrgChart  -- for testing & debugging

SELECT  Employee = CONCAT(replicate(CHAR(9),(EmployeeLevel)), P.LastName, ', ',
P.FirstName)
FROM    cteOrgChart OC
    INNER JOIN HumanResources.Employee E
        ON OC.EmployeeID = E.OrganizationNode
    INNER JOIN Person.Person P
        ON E.BusinessEntityID = P.BusinessEntityID
ORDER BY E.OrganizationNode;
-- (290 row(s) affected)  - Partial Results.
```

Employee				
Sánchez, Ken				
	Duffy, Terri			
		Tamburello, Roberto		
			Walters, Rob	
			Erickson, Gail	
			Goldberg, Jossef	
			Miller, Dylan	
				Margheim, Diane
				Matthew, Gigi
				Raheem, Michael
			Cracium, Ovidiu	
				D'Hers, Thierry
				Galvin, Janice
			Sullivan, Michael	
			Salavaria, Sharon	
	Bradley, David			

Inline User-Defined Function OrgChart at Any Level

We can easily wrap the company orgchart logic into a parameterized function to get the orgchart for any executive or manager in the company.

```
CREATE FUNCTION ufnOrgChart ( @OrganizationNode hierarchyid )
RETURNS TABLE AS RETURN
(WITH cteOrgChart(ManagerID, EmployeeID, EmployeeLevel)
   AS (SELECT OrganizationNode,
         OrganizationNode,
         0
     FROM   HumanResources.Employee
     WHERE  OrganizationNode = @OrganizationNode
     UNION ALL
     SELECT e.OrganizationNode.GetAncestor(1),
         e.OrganizationNode,
         EmployeeLevel+1
     FROM   HumanResources.Employee e
         INNER JOIN cteOrgChart d
         ON e.OrganizationNode.GetAncestor(1) = d.EmployeeID)
SELECT   Employee = CONCAT(replicate(CHAR(9),(EmployeeLevel)), P.LastName, ', ',
                         P.FirstName)
FROM    cteOrgChart OC
     INNER JOIN HumanResources.Employee E
      ON OC.EmployeeID = E.OrganizationNode
     INNER JOIN Person.Person P
      ON E.BusinessEntityID = P.BusinessEntityID  );
GO
```

SELECT * FROM ufnOrgChart (0x84); -- (29 row(s) affected) - Partial Results.

Employee			
Norman, Laura			
	Barreto de Mattos, Paula		
	Liu, David		
	Kahn, Wendy		
	Barber, David		
		Word, Sheela	
			Sandberg, Mikael
			Rao, Arvind
			Meisner, Linda
			Ogisu, Fukiko

hierarchyid System Functions

Specialized system hierarchyid functions available to deal with hierarchyid data.

```
SELECT          BusinessEntityID, JobTitle,
                OrganizationNode,
                OrganizationLevel,
                OrganizationNode.ToString()           AS TextOrgNode,
                OrganizationNode.GetLevel()            AS NodeLevel,
                OrganizationNode.GetAncestor(1)        AS Ancestor,
                OrganizationNode.IsDescendantOf(0x58)  AS [0x58 Descendant]
FROM HumanResources.Employee
ORDER BY TextOrgNode;
-- (290 row(s) affected) - Partial results.
```

BusinessEntityID	JobTitle	OrganizationNode	OrganizationLevel	TextOrgNode	NodeLevel	Ancestor	0x58 Descendant
1	Chief Executive Officer	0x	0	/	0	NULL	0
2	Vice President of Engineering	0x58	1	/1/	1	0x	1
3	Engineering Manager	0x5AC0	2	/1/1/	2	0x58	1
4	Senior Tool Designer	0x5AD6	3	/1/1/1/	3	0x5AC0	1
5	Design Engineer	0x5ADA	3	/1/1/2/	3	0x5AC0	1
6	Design Engineer	0x5ADE	3	/1/1/3/	3	0x5AC0	1
7	Research and Development Manager	0x5AE1	3	/1/1/4/	3	0x5AC0	1
8	Research and Development Engineer	0x5AE158	4	/1/1/4/1/	4	0x5AE1	1
9	Research and Development Engineer	0x5AE168	4	/1/1/4/2/	4	0x5AE1	1
10	Research and Development Manager	0x5AE178	4	/1/1/4/3/	4	0x5AE1	1
11	Senior Tool Designer	0x5AE3	3	/1/1/5/	3	0x5AC0	1
12	Tool Designer	0x5AE358	4	/1/1/5/1/	4	0x5AE3	1
13	Tool Designer	0x5AE368	4	/1/1/5/2/	4	0x5AE3	1
14	Senior Design Engineer	0x5AE5	3	/1/1/6/	3	0x5AC0	1
15	Design Engineer	0x5AE7	3	/1/1/7/	3	0x5AC0	1
16	Marketing Manager	0x68	1	/2/	1	0x	0
17	Marketing Assistant	0x6AC0	2	/2/1/	2	0x68	0
18	Marketing Specialist	0x6B40	2	/2/2/	2	0x68	0
19	Marketing Assistant	0x6BC0	2	/2/3/	2	0x68	0
20	Marketing Assistant	0x6C20	2	/2/4/	2	0x68	0
21	Marketing Specialist	0x6C60	2	/2/5/	2	0x68	0
22	Marketing Specialist	0x6CA0	2	/2/6/	2	0x68	0
23	Marketing Specialist	0x6CE0	2	/2/7/	2	0x68	0
24	Marketing Specialist	0x6D10	2	/2/8/	2	0x68	0

Sort Outline Numbering with hierarchyid

Certain sorts which are obvious to us, due to our Human Intelligence, are a challenge in traditional SQL programming due to lack of tree/hierarchy structure processing. Such a case is outline numbers which are easily convertible to hierarchyid, hence the simple solution.

```
CREATE TABLE #OutlineNumber  (Nbr Varchar(64));
INSERT #OutlineNumber Values
 ('1'), ('1.1'), ('1.1.1'), ('1.1.9'), ('1.1.10'), ('1.1.11'), ('2'), ('2.1'), ('2.1.1'), ('10.1.2'), ('11.1.9');
SELECT * FROM #OutlineNumber ORDER BY Nbr;
```

Nbr	
1	
1.1	
1.1.1	
1.1.10	
1.1.11	
1.1.9	out of order
10.1.2	out of order
11.1.9	out of order
2	
2.1	
2.1.1	

```
-- Sorting on hierarchyid by converting outline string with "/" replaces "."  & "/" prefix, suffix
SELECT *, [HierarchyID].ToString() AS TextHierarchyID FROM
  (SELECT *, CONVERT(hierarchyid, CONCAT('/',REPLACE(Nbr, '.', '/') ,'/')) AS [HierarchyID]
    FROM #OutlineNumber) x /* derived table */ ORDER BY HierarchyID;
```

Nbr	HierarchyID	TextHierarchyID
1	0x58	/1/
1.1	0x5AC0	/1/1/
1.1.1	0x5AD6	/1/1/1/
1.1.9	0x5AE980	/1/1/9/
1.1.10	0x5AEA80	/1/1/10/
1.1.11	0x5AEB80	/1/1/11/
2	0x68	/2/
2.1	0x6AC0	/2/1/
2.1.1	0x6AD6	/2/1/1/
10.1.2	0xAAB680	/10/1/2/
11.1.9	0xAEBA60	/11/1/9/

Dynamic SQL PIVOT

Dynamic SQL PIVOT transposes rows into columns based on dynamic data. Dynamic PIVOT contrasts hard-wired PIVOT. Prior to coding the dynamic SQL, write out & test the static query.

> Database security article: Dynamic SQL & SQL Injection:
> http://blogs.msdn.com/b/raulga/archive/2007/01/04/dynamic-sql-sql-injection.aspx

We need the following data-driven column header list of years:

[2005], [2006], [2007], [2008]

We need the following static PIVOT query to be generated dynamically:

```
SELECT * FROM (SELECT [Store (Freight Summary)] = S.Name,
                YEAR(OrderDate) AS OrderYear,  Freight
FROM    Sales.SalesOrderHeader SOH
INNER JOIN Sales.Customer C ON SOH.CustomerID = C.CustomerID
INNER JOIN Sales.Store S ON C.StoreID = S.BusinessEntityID) as Header
PIVOT (SUM(Freight) FOR OrderYear IN( [2005], [2006], [2007], [2008])) AS Pvt ORDER BY 1;
-- (633 row(s) affected) - Partial results.
```

Store (Freight Summary)	2005	2006	2007	2008
Sensible Sports	NULL	NULL	364.2076	472.8672
Separate Parts Corporation	1243.1035	4883.5698	2493.3725	NULL
Serious Cycles	4868.9888	3511.0184	354.9403	NULL
Seventh Bike Store	831.2495	4329.8166	4866.4755	2024.7107
Sharp Bikes	912.9061	549.7834	NULL	NULL
Sheet Metal Manufacturing	NULL	6050.2523	9169.2709	3328.5167
Shipping Specialists	NULL	NULL	NULL	12.9692
Showcase for Cycles	NULL	NULL	35.2509	6.2386
Simple Bike Parts	87.9217	100.5808	31.1732	29.8886
Sixth Bike Store	426.1619	1346.1144	79.9409	NULL
Sleek Bikes	NULL	NULL	3407.692	2364.0185
Small Bike Accessories Shop	NULL	NULL	1116.6658	992.0197
Small Bike Shop	2359.1319	5277.5806	3681.3405	2216.5242
Small Cycle Store	152.3481	989.9408	801.0264	553.2965
Social Activities Club	177.3895	52.9214	9.7198	29.8886
Solid Bike Parts	1134.6482	1535.374	372.4571	NULL
Some Discount Store	2499.3443	733.0964	38.0211	1.1373
South Bike Company	NULL	NULL	1043.9713	837.2011
Spa and Exercise Outfitters	NULL	94.3411	3777.5336	2441.4004

Dynamic SQL PIVOT: Dealer Freight Cost by Year

```
USE AdventureWorks2012;

DECLARE @OrderYear AS TABLE( YYYY INT   NOT NULL   PRIMARY KEY )
DECLARE @DynamicSQL AS NVARCHAR(MAX)

INSERT INTO @OrderYear
SELECT DISTINCT YEAR(OrderDate) FROM  Sales.SalesOrderHeader

DECLARE @ReportColumnNames AS NVARCHAR(MAX),   @IterationYear   AS INT
SET @IterationYear = (SELECT MIN(YYYY) FROM  @OrderYear)
SET @ReportColumnNames = N''

-- Assemble pivot list dynamically
WHILE (@IterationYear IS NOT NULL)
 BEGIN
  SET @ReportColumnNames = CONCAT(@ReportColumnNames, N', ',
   QUOTENAME(CAST(@IterationYear AS NVARCHAR(10))))
  SET @IterationYear = (SELECT MIN(YYYY)
          FROM  @OrderYear   WHERE  YYYY > @IterationYear)
 END

SET @ReportColumnNames =
SUBSTRING(@ReportColumnNames,2,LEN(@ReportColumnNames))

PRINT @ReportColumnNames

-- Assemble final code
SET @DynamicSQL = CONCAT(N'SELECT * FROM (SELECT [Store (Freight Summary)]=S.Name,
                    YEAR(OrderDate) AS OrderYear,  Freight
FROM    Sales.SalesOrderHeader SOH
INNER JOIN Sales.Customer C ON SOH.CustomerID = C.CustomerID
INNER JOIN Sales.Store S ON C.StoreID = S.BusinessEntityID) as Header
PIVOT (SUM(Freight)
FOR OrderYear IN(', @ReportColumnNames, N')) AS Pvt ORDER BY 1;')

PRINT @DynamicSQL; -- Testing & debugging

EXEC sp_executesql @DynamicSQL;
GO
```

CHAPTER 16: Advanced T-SQL Programming Topics

Date Range Programming with Datetime Column

The time portion of a datetime column presents a big problem ("midnight bug") when looking for a time range of records (rows). The equal operator picks up only the midnight records, nothing beyond as demonstrated. Similar issue for the BETWEEN operator. Best solution is to use DATE (SQL Server2008) if time portion is of no interest. With datetime we cannot assume that the time portion is 00:00:00.000 since it may have been changed unintentionally.

```
USE tempdb;
SELECT * INTO SOH FROM AdventureWorks2012.Sales.SalesOrderHeader; -- Create test table
GO
-- (31465 row(s) affected)
SELECT COUNT(SalesOrderID), MAX(OrderDate) FROM SOH WHERE OrderDate = '2008-02-01';
-- 244   2008-02-01 00:00:00.000
SELECT COUNT(SalesOrderID), MAX(OrderDate) FROM SOH
WHERE OrderDate BETWEEN '2008-02-01' AND '2008-02-01';
-- 244   2008-02-01 00:00:00.000
-- Advance order date 1 second passed midnight
UPDATE SOH SET OrderDate = dateadd(ss, 1, OrderDate) WHERE OrderDate = '2008-02-01';
-- (244 row(s) affected)
-- Due to the non-zero time portion, no equal match
SELECT COUNT(SalesOrderID), MAX(OrderDate) FROM SOH WHERE OrderDate = '2008-02-01';
-- 0     NULL
-- The BETWEEN operator also fails
SELECT COUNT(SalesOrderID), MAX(OrderDate) FROM SOH
WHERE OrderDate BETWEEN '2008-02-01' AND '2008-02-01';
-- 0     NULL
-- A safe way to get all the sales - not the best performant if there is index on OrderDate
SELECT COUNT(SalesOrderID), MAX(OrderDate) FROM SOH
WHERE YEAR(OrderDate)=2008 AND MONTH(OrderDate) = 2 AND DAY(OrderDate) = 1;
--244   2008-02-01 00:00:01.000
-- Another way to get all sales - no performance issue in case of index on OrderDate
SELECT COUNT(SalesOrderID), MAX(OrderDate) FROM SOH
WHERE OrderDate >= '2008-02-01' AND OrderDate < DATEADD(dd,1,'2008-02-01');
-- 244   2008-02-01 00:00:01.000
-- Using the BETWEEN operator - performance issue in case of index on OrderDate
SELECT COUNT(SalesOrderID), MAX(OrderDate) FROM SOH
WHERE CONVERT(DATE, OrderDate) BETWEEN '2008-02-01' AND '2008-02-01';
-- 244   2008-02-01 00:00:01.000
GO
DROP TABLE tempdb.dbo.SOH;
```

The BETWEEN Operator for DATE & DATETIME Ranges

```
-- BETWEEN dates implementation for datetime OrderDate
DECLARE @StartDate datetime ='20080201', @EndDate datetime = '20080205';
SELECT OrderCount=COUNT(*) FROM AdventureWorks2012.Sales.SalesOrderHeader
WHERE OrderDate >= @StartDate and OrderDate < DATEADD(DD,1,@EndDate);
GO
-- 502
```

```
-- BETWEEN dates implementation for datetime OrderDate using DATE data type
DECLARE @StartDate date ='20080201', @EndDate date = '20080205';
SELECT OrderCount=COUNT(*) FROM AdventureWorks2012.Sales.SalesOrderHeader
WHERE OrderDate >= @StartDate and OrderDate < DATEADD(DD,1,@EndDate);
GO
-- 502
```

```
-- Past midnight and next midnight
SELECT  dateadd(dd, datediff(dd, 0, CURRENT_TIMESTAMP)+0, 0),
        dateadd(dd, 1+datediff(dd, 0, CURRENT_TIMESTAMP)+0, 0)
-- 2016-10-23 00:00:00.000   2016-10-24 00:00:00.000
```

```
-- Orders for today (date range 1 day)
SELECT * FROM AdventureWorks2012.Sales.SalesOrderHeader
WHERE OrderDate >= dateadd(dd, datediff(dd, 0, CURRENT_TIMESTAMP)+0, 0)
 AND OrderDate <  dateadd(dd, 1+datediff(dd, 0, CURRENT_TIMESTAMP)+0, 0)
GO
```

```
-- Create a copy of the PurchaseOrderHeader (similar to SalesOrderHeader) table
USE tempdb;
SELECT * INTO POH FROM AdventureWorks2012.Purchasing.PurchaseOrderHeader
GO
-- (4012 row(s) affected)
```

```
-- Purchase order count for the entire month of MARCH 2008
SELECT COUNT(*) FROM POH WHERE OrderDate >='2008-03-01  00:00:00.000'
             AND OrderDate < '2008-04-01  00:00:00.000'
-- 313
```

```
-- Equivalent datetime or date comparison queries
SELECT COUNT(*) FROM POH WHERE OrderDate >='2008-03-01' AND OrderDate < '2008-04-01'
-- 313
```

CHAPTER 16: Advanced T-SQL Programming Topics

BETWEEN for Date Ranges cont.

```
-- SQL date between - performance issue due to CAST if OrderDate is indexed
SELECT COUNT(*) FROM POH WHERE
        CAST(OrderDate AS DATE) BETWEEN '2008-03-01' AND '2008-03-31';
-- 313
```

```
-- SQL datetime between with explicit inclusive lower and upper limits
/***** WORKS BUT NOT BEST PRACTICES *****/
SELECT COUNT(*) FROM POH WHERE OrderDate
BETWEEN '2008-03-01 00:00:00.000' AND '2008-03-31 23:59:59.997'; -- 313
```

```
/***** NOT BEST PRACTICES - WRONG RESULT IF TIME PART IS NOT 12:00AM *****/
SELECT COUNT(*) FROM POH WHERE OrderDate
        BETWEEN '2008-03-01 00:00:00.000' AND '2008-03-31 00:00:00.000' ; --313
SELECT COUNT(*) FROM POH WHERE OrderDate BETWEEN '2008-03-01' AND '2008-03-31';
-- 313
/*****************************************************************/
```

```
-- TIME PART assumed to be 12:00AM = 00:00:00.000 if not specified
SELECT COUNT(*) FROM POH WHERE OrderDate BETWEEN '2008-01-02' AND '2008-01-07';
-- 60
UPDATE TOP(1) POH SET OrderDate = DATEADD (second, 1, OrderDate)
        WHERE  OrderDate='2008-01-07';        -- (1 row(s) affected)
-- The 1 second passed midnight record is no longer included in the BETWEEN range
SELECT COUNT(*) FROM POH WHERE OrderDate BETWEEN '2008-01-02' AND '2008-01-07';
-- 59
```

```
-- BETWEEN is inclusive operator - it includes the limits
SELECT COUNT(*) FROM POH WHERE OrderDate
        BETWEEN '2008-01-02 00:00:00.000' AND '2008-01-07 00:00:00.000';   -- 59
```

```
-- Include midnight and midnight+1 sec records for 2008-01-07
SELECT COUNT(*) FROM POH WHERE OrderDate
        BETWEEN '2008-01-02 00:00:00.000' AND '2008-01-07 00:00:01.000';   -- 60
```

```
-- Date range query - good performance if OrderDate indexed ( SARGABLE)
SELECT [Sales]=COUNT(*) FROM Purchasing.PurchaseOrderHeader
WHERE OrderDate >= CONVERT(DATE,'20080301')
        AND OrderDate < CONVERT(DATE,'20080316');
-- 137
```

4-Week 13 Month Calendar

The Christian (Gregorian, Western) calendar, used in most parts of the World, has been introduced by Pope Gregory in 1582. It appears to be irregular due to using 12 months instead of 13 months. While 13 month calendars were proposed in the past, its urgency rapidly increasing due to the expansion of Business Intelligence. 4 weeks 13 months calendar totals to 364 days, almost on the mark!

SELECT 4 * 7 * 13 -- 364

To include the remaining 1 or 2 (leap year) days, we have to make the last week of the year longer with 1 or 2 days, tentatively named **Earthday** and **Starday**. Each month starts with Monday. Therefore, each year starts with Monday. The new month is tentatively called **Undecimber** after undecim, Latin for 11. This naming follows the Latin number sequence starting with September (septem Latin for 7). The year ends two ways:

- ➢ Friday, Saturday, Sunday, Earthday (Undecimber 29)
- ➢ Friday, Saturday, Sunday, Earthday, Starday (Undecimber 30) - leap year
- ➢ January 1 is Monday in each year
- ➢ Each month calendar identical with Undecimber having an extra day or two

```
DECLARE @4week13month TABLE( ID INT IDENTITY(1,1),
 Mon char(3), Tue char(3), Wed char(3), Thu char(3), Fri char(3), Sat char(3), Sun char(3));
INSERT @4week13month VALUES ('MON', 'TUE', 'WED', 'THU', 'FRI', 'SAT', 'SUN'),
('1','2','3','4','5','6','7'), ('8','9','10','11','12','13','14'),
('15','16','17','18','19','20','21'),('22','23','24','25','26','27','28');
SELECT * FROM @4week13month ORDER BY ID;
```

MON	TUE	WED	THU	FRI	SAT	SUN
1	2	3	4	5	6	7
8	9	10	11	12	13	14
15	16	17	18	19	20	21
22	23	24	25	26	27	28

The SQL significance of such a calendar is immense: week can be used in GROUP BY summaries just like month. Currently week-based analysis is misaligned with month-based analysis. Some businesses do use 13-month calendars for business analysis and reporting.

> The **benefits of 13 month calendar** are presented at:
> http://en.wikipedia.org/wiki/International_Fixed_Calendar

CHAPTER 16: Advanced T-SQL Programming Topics

DDL Trigger on DATABASE CREATE

DDL trigger carries out action, in this instance just sending a message, when a new database is created. The screenshot segment shows the DDL trigger listing in SSMS Object Explorer.

```
USE master;
GO
CREATE TRIGGER trgNewDatabase
ON ALL SERVER  FOR CREATE_DATABASE  AS
BEGIN
DECLARE @database sysname, @event_data XML = EVENTDATA()
 SET @database = @event_data.value('(/EVENT_INSTANCE/DatabaseName)[1]', 'sysname')
 RAISERROR( 'trgNewDatabase DDL trigger message: %s DB has been created', 16,1, @database)
END
GO -- Command(s) completed successfully.
```

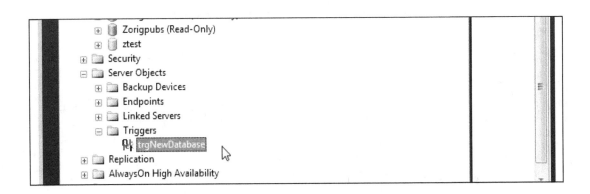

```
CREATE DATABASE zTest1;
GO  /* Messages
Msg 50000, Level 16, State 1, Procedure trgNewDatabase, Line 10
trgNewDatabase DDL trigger message: zTest1 DB has been created */
```

```
DROP DATABASE zTest1;
GO -- Command(s) completed successfully.
```

```
DROP TRIGGER [trgNewDatabase] ON ALL SERVER
GO -- Command(s) completed successfully.
```

Spatial Data Types: Geometry & Geography

The POLYGON & STLength() Functions

The geometry data type and geography data type are used for spatial and mapping applications. The geometry data type can store polygons. The perimeter of a polygon can be calculated by the STLength() spatial function and the polygon itself can be visualized in Management Studio Spatial results.

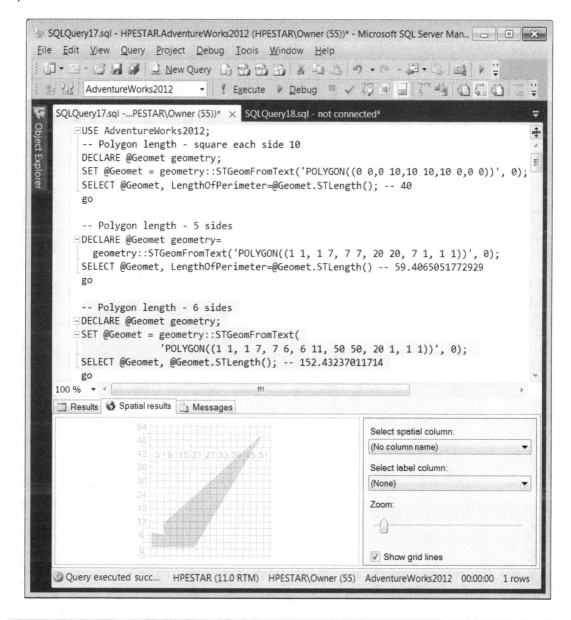

Polygon Difference & Intersection

The STDifference() and STIntersection functions will calculate the difference and intersection of two polygons. The example is for a small square inside a bigger square. The difference is displayed in Spatial results which is the dark area. The intersection coincidentally is the white small square.

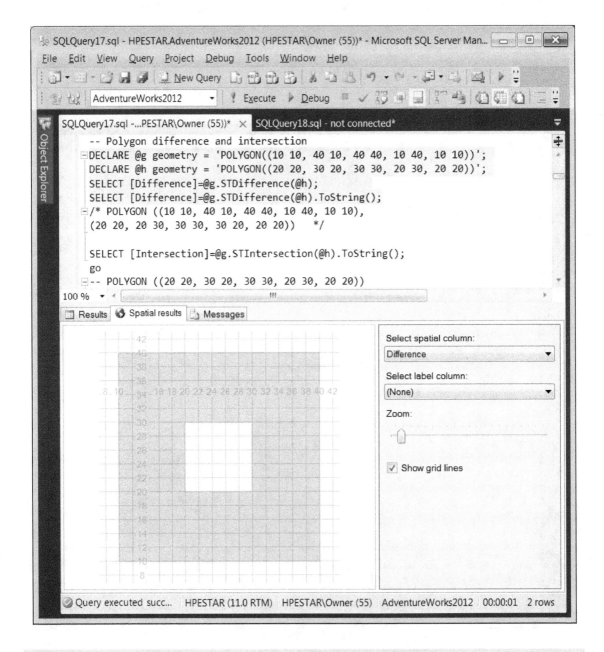

Geometry Area & CIRCULARSTRING Functions

```
-- Area of a polygon - triangle
DECLARE @Geomet geometry;
SET @Geomet = geometry::STGeomFromText('POLYGON((3 3,40 40, 80 3, 3 3))', 0);
SELECT @Geomet, AreaOfPolygon=@Geomet.STArea();
GO
-- 1424.5
```

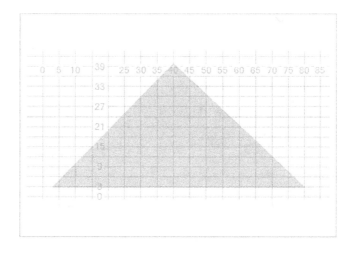

The STBuffer() function "draws" the thick border.

```
SELECT geometry::Parse('CIRCULARSTRING(-2 2, 2 -2, 4 2, 2 4, -2 2)').STBuffer(.3);
```

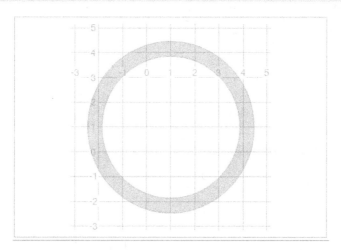

Working with geometry Data in Tables

```
IF OBJECT_ID ( 'dbo.GeometryTest', 'U' ) IS NOT NULL     DROP TABLE dbo.GeometryTest;
go
```

```
create table GeometryTest
(
        GeometryTestID int identity(1,1) primary key,
        Geom geometry ,
        GeomText as Geom.STAsText(),              -- computed column
        GeomDim as Geom.STDimension());           -- computed column
go
```

```
insert GeometryTest (Geom) values
        (geometry::STPointFromText ( 'POINT (85 115)',0)),
        (geometry::STPointFromText ( 'POINT (100 100)',0)),
        (geometry::STGeomFromText ('LINESTRING (70 70, 30 150,  150 150)', 0)),
        (geometry::STGeomFromText ('POLYGON ((0 0, 300 0, 300 300, 0 300, 0 0))', 0));
```

```
select * from GeometryTest
go
```

GeometryTestID	Geom	GeomText	GeomDim
1	0x00000000010C00000000004055400000000000C05C40	POINT (85 115)	0
2	0x00000000010C00000000000059400000000000005940	POINT (100 100)	0
3	0x00000000010403000000000000000000008051400000000000008051400000000000003E400000000000C06240000000000000C0624000000000000C0624001000000010000000001000000FFFFFFFF000000000002	LINESTRING (70 70, 30 150, 150 150)	1
4	0x0000000001040500000000000000000000000000000000000000000000000000C072400000000000000000000000000000C0724000000000000C0724000000000000000000000000000C0724000000000000000000000000000000000000000000001000000020000000001000000FFFFFFFF0000000003	POLYGON ((0 0, 300 0, 300 300, 0 300, 0 0))	2

```
declare @gmtry1 geometry,  @gmtry2 geometry, @combo geometry;
select @gmtry1 = Geom from GeometryTest where GeometryTestID=3
select @gmtry2 = Geom from GeometryTest where GeometryTestID=4
select @combo = @gmtry1.STIntersection(@gmtry2)
select Intersection = @Combo.STAsText();
go
```

Intersection
LINESTRING (150 150, 30 150, 70 70)

CHAPTER 16: Advanced T-SQL Programming Topics

The geography Data Type in Map Application

Locating address in a rectangular Earth region based on the Person.Address table geo SpatialLocation column data.

```
USE AdventureWorks2012;

DECLARE @Rectangle geography;
SET @Rectangle = geography::STGeomFromText(
        'POLYGON((-50.0 50.0, -90.0 50.0, -90.0 25.0, -50.0 25.0, -50.0 50.0))',
                4326);
SELECT          s.BusinessEntityID
                ,s.Name                         AS Dealer
                ,a.AddressLine1
                ,a.City
                ,sp.StateProvinceCode
                ,a.PostalCode
 FROM Sales.Store s
        INNER JOIN Person.BusinessEntityAddress bea
                ON s.BusinessEntityID =bea.BusinessEntityID
        INNER JOIN Person.Address a
                ON bea.AddressID = a.AddressID
        INNER JOIN Person.StateProvince sp
                ON a.StateProvinceID = sp.StateProvinceID
WHERE  a.SpatialLocation.STIntersects(@Rectangle) = 1
        ORDER BY Dealer;
GO  -- (240 row(s) affected) - Partial results.
```

BusinessEntityID	Dealer	AddressLine1	City	StateProvinceCode	PostalCode
2051	A Bicycle Association	6405 Erie Blvd. Hills Plaza	De Witt	NY	13214
354	Acclaimed Bicycle Company	830 Highway 499 So	Mcdonough	GA	30253
836	Active Cycling	Indian Mound Mall	Heath	OH	43056
1916	Active Life Toys	55 Standish Court	Mississauga	ON	L5B 3V4
1936	Active Transport Inc.	225200 Miles Ave.	North Randall	OH	44128
366	Activity Center	Factory Stores Of America	Crossville	TN	38555
1046	Better Bike Shop	42525 Austell Road	Austell	GA	30106
878	Bicycle Outfitters	Cherry Grove Plaza	Cincinnati	OH	45202
422	Bike Boutique	Polaris Town Center	Columbus	OH	43215
1924	Bike Products and Accessories	Regency Hilltop Shopping Cntr	Virginia Beach	VA	23451
698	Bike Rims Company	Edgewater Mall	Biloxi	MS	39530
622	Bikes and Motorbikes	22580 Free Street	Toronto	ON	M4B 1V7
424	Bikes Anyone?	Ames Plaza	Saugus	MA	01906
1162	Bikes for Kids and Adults	9900 Ronson Drive	Etobicoke	ON	M9W 3P3
510	Bikes for Two	63 West Beaver Creek	Richmond Hill	ON	L4E 3M5

Surveying Spatial Locations in Person.Address with TABLESAMPLE

Since the limit is 5000 for Spatial results graphics, we use TABLESAMPLE random sampling. The outline of the Unites States is clearly visible in the spatial graphics. 4810 dots and partial results.

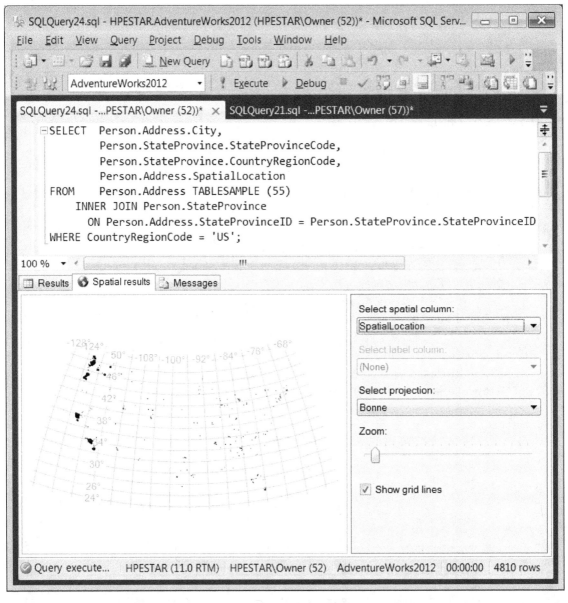

City	StateProvinceCode	CountryRegionCode	SpatialLocation
Concord	CA	US	0xE6100000010CA18642EB19FF4240E84C0794157B5EC0
Seattle	WA	US	0xE6100000010CCC2A6CCDCBCA474094427543D1995EC0
Torrance	CA	US	0xE6100000010C943F7FEBB1E440402956F3FF52A05DC0
Woodburn	OR	US	0xE6100000010CBF692502648C4640839FE7AD54AB5EC0
Puyallup	WA	US	0xE6100000010C827BF9CD1598474096246A5843935EC0

Data Encryption & Decryption

Data encryption is an important part of keeping sensitive data, such as credit card numbers, safe. When we encrypt successively, the encrypted string varies.

```
USE AdventureWorks2012;
CREATE CERTIFICATE CertQ  ENCRYPTION BY PASSWORD = '007SkyFall$'
WITH SUBJECT ='CertQ',  START_DATE = '2012/01/01', EXPIRY_DATE = '2016/01/01';


DECLARE  @CypherText VARBINARY(MAX);
SET @CypherText = EncryptByCert(Cert_ID('CertQ'),'United States of America');
SELECT  @CypherText;
/*
0xDFAD2CABDDD07E75A74722CECF799B4AADBFE704D29F366DBF6F22C229E7EB6D94BC082BB2DFC7795C1AA92F7452D0AE2EF91
A2356B22F8508E37F7BC440CF926BC89C0FFCBBB04DF75206F2C6282FE87756D2003F40D738F92499674749BA8C9204A3BCAC9A7
8366939786A8D4E421DC71289E9D9D8140678EFD329BB5D7822
*/
SELECT Decyphered = CONVERT(VARCHAR(256),DecryptByCert(Cert_ID('CertQ'),
@CypherText,N'007SkyFall$'));
GO -- United States of America


DECLARE  @CypherText VARBINARY(MAX);
SET @CypherText = EncryptByCert(Cert_ID('CertQ'),'United States of America');
SELECT  @CypherText;
/*
0x77E17C2A7B30E68B3AA5792400842FBDA19E121F8BEFCF787F3C6F68D720CC6B992BBF1C27168CC7B5592359437494BF1F719FF
67A1B5131C5AA69EEEA539DC5AA261BBAEDC12201BDC2EC1E31280FD0B76E8773CDB57582BE857F24FD86997582ACFAE07028A9
0A0FA9D29A69FB53FC24261828F53884636A4452597A18A908
*/
SELECT Decyphered = CONVERT(VARCHAR(256), DecryptByCert(Cert_ID('CertQ'),
@CypherText,N'007SkyFall$'));
GO -- United States of America


 DECLARE  @CypherText VARBINARY(MAX), @cleartext varchar(256)='Yellowstone National Park
ID, MT ,WY';
SET @CypherText = EncryptByCert(Cert_ID('CertQ'), @cleartext);  SELECT  @CypherText;
/*
0x386D15B848B3200CA2F0FD1341550AD16C61A19B71D2A14256B8C281249B5F9471EEB9C81DE9FA21CBE4602E099E1F7F363923
B8E0BF2960CAF13824D5EE0E852BA0B156532D50B336377648C6580BDFEB85453F34D722038FF6F7BD695343617E39E68259B05D
65F686CE63A68CFC795D86F94ADC75D0974882721A5083842C
*/
SELECT Decyphered = CONVERT(VARCHAR(256),DecryptByCert(Cert_ID('CertQ'),
@CypherText,N'007SkyFall$'));
GO -- Yellowstone National Park ID, MT ,WY
```

Database Backup

Full Database Backup with Verification

Full database backup and verify script for the AdventureWorks2012 database.

```
USE master;
GO
-- Backup database
BACKUP DATABASE [AdventureWorks2012] TO  DISK = N'F:\data\backup\AW2012.bak' WITH
NAME = N'AdventureWorks2012-Full DB Backup', STATS = 5;
GO
-- Verify database backup
DECLARE @backupSetId as int;
SELECT @backupSetId = position from msdb..backupset where
database_name=N'AdventureWorks2012' and backup_set_id=(select max(backup_set_id) from
msdb..backupset where database_name=N'AdventureWorks2012' );

IF @backupSetId is null begin raiserror(N'Verify failed. Backup info for DB
''AdventureWorks2012'' not found.', 16, 1) end;

RESTORE VERIFYONLY FROM  DISK = N'F:\data\backup\AW2012.bak' WITH  FILE =
@backupSetId,  NOUNLOAD,  NOREWIND;
GO
```

```
/* Messages
5 percent processed.
10 percent processed.
15 percent processed.
.......
95 percent processed.
Processed 27920 pages for database 'AdventureWorks2012', file 'AdventureWorks2012_Data' on file 1.
Processed 80 pages for database 'AdventureWorks2012', file 'FSAlpha' on file 1.
Processed 2 pages for database 'AdventureWorks2012', file 'AdventureWorks2012_Log' on file 1.
100 percent processed.
BACKUP DATABASE successfully processed 28002 pages in 7.931 seconds (27.582 MB/sec).

The backup set on file 1 is valid.   */
```

Full Database Backup with Datestamp in Filename

```
DECLARE @BackupPathFile nvarchar(256)
 = N'f:\data\backup\AW2012_' + CONVERT(varchar, CURRENT_TIMESTAMP, 112) + '.BAK'
PRINT @BackupPathFile -- f:\data\backup\AW2012_20121114.BAK
BACKUP DATABASE [AdventureWorks2012] TO  DISK = @BackupPathFile
```

Backup of a Single Table

Here is the list of options available.

- ➤ SELECT * INTO table2 FROM table1
- ➤ SSMS Script Wizard generates script with INSERTs
- ➤ SSMS execute SELECT query & the save the output to a file
- ➤ bcp table to a file
- ➤ SS Import/Export Wizard - export table to a table or file

The first one is the easiest, the last one is the most flexible. We have to pay attention that the export is reversible. For example, if we use CSV format then the strings should be enclosed in double quotes for example in order not to conflict with commas used for column separation. Execute the query.

SELECT * FROM Production.Product ORDER BY ProductNumber;

On upper left corner in results, right click, save results as, .csv (comma delimited). Sounds safe. But it is not because the some product names contain commas. That makes the data export irreversible, and probably useless for any application.

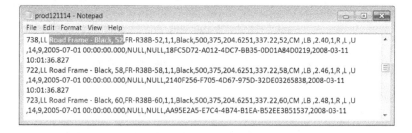

The SS Import & Export Wizard has option to specify Text qualifier for flat file destination.

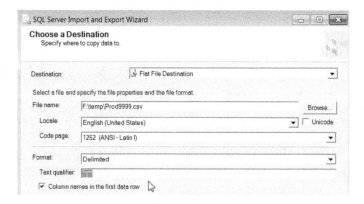

CHAPTER 16: Advanced T-SQL Programming Topics

Setting SSMS Query Options to Include Double Quotes with Strings

There is a query option in SSMS setting to set double quote as text qualifier when saving in csv format. Click on Query, click on Query Options. Configure as shown.

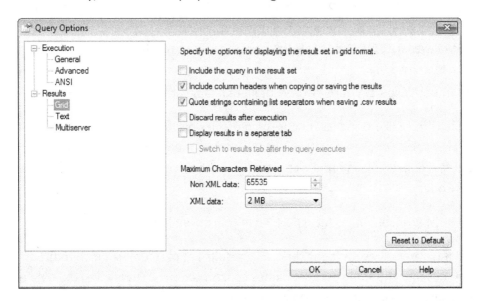

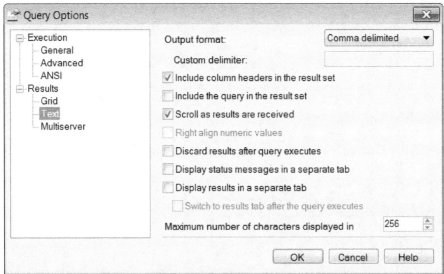

The output will be proper csv file.

793,"Road-250 Black, 44",BK-R89B-44,1,1,Black,100,75,1554.9479,2443.35,44,CM ,LB ,14.77,4,R ,H ,U ,2,26,2006-07-01 00:00:00.000,NULL,NULL,1FF419B5-52AF-4F7E-AEAE-4FEC5E99DE35,2008-03-11 10:01:36.827

Database Restore

To restore a database backup to a new database we have to indicate the location (path & name) of the database files. FILE=1 refers to the first backup set in AW2012.BAK. A backup file can contain more than one backup.

```
USE [master]
RESTORE DATABASE [rptAdventureWorks2012] FROM  DISK = N'f:\data\backup\AW2012.BAK'
WITH  FILE = 1,
MOVE N'FSAlpha' TO N'F:\data\db\data\FSAlpha',
MOVE N'AdventureWorks2012_Data' TO N'F:\data\db\data\AdventureWorks2012_Data.mdf',
MOVE N'AdventureWorks2012_Log' TO N'F:\data\db\log\AdventureWorks2012_log.ldf',
NOUNLOAD,  STATS = 5
GO


/* Messages
5 percent processed.
10 percent processed.
15 percent processed.
.....
55 percent processed.
60 percent processed.
65 percent processed.
70 percent processed.
75 percent processed.
80 percent processed.
85 percent processed.
90 percent processed.
95 percent processed.
100 percent processed.
Processed 27920 pages for database 'rptAdventureWorks2012', file
'AdventureWorks2012_Data' on file 1.
Processed 2 pages for database 'rptAdventureWorks2012', file 'AdventureWorks2012_Log' on
file 1.
Processed 81 pages for database 'rptAdventureWorks2012', file 'FSAlpha' on file 1.

RESTORE DATABASE successfully processed 28002 pages in 25.375 seconds (8.621 MB/sec). */
```

Restore of a Single Table

Restoring a table can be tricky. When exporting a table, basically the data content goes, and some metadata such as column names. SELECT INTO copies the data, column names, data types, sizes and the IDENTITY property if any. Constraints and indexes are not exported. Before restoring, the current table should be emptied. DELETE and TRUNCATE are not exactly the same. TRUNCATE is faster due to minimal logging. TRUNCATE also resets the IDENTITY SEED.

```
SELECT * INTO tempdb.dbo.Product
FROM Adventureworks2012.Production.Product;
GO   - (504 row(s) affected)
```

```
use tempdb;
CREATE UNIQUE INDEX idxProd on Product(Name);
GO
```

```
DELETE Product;  -- (504 row(s) affected)
DBCC CHECKIDENT(Product);
/*Checking identity information: current identity value '999', current column value 'NULL'.
DBCC execution completed. If DBCC printed error messages, contact your system
administrator.*/
```

```
TRUNCATE TABLE Product;
GO
DBCC CHECKIDENT(Product);
GO
/*Checking identity information: current identity value 'NULL', current column value 'NULL'.
DBCC execution completed. If DBCC printed error messages, contact your system
administrator.*/
```

```
-- Restore the content of table
INSERT Product
SELECT *
FROM Adventureworks2012.Production.Product;
/*Msg 8101, Level 16, State 1, Line 1
An explicit value for the identity column in table 'Product' can only be specified when a column
list is used and IDENTITY_INSERT is ON.*/
```

Repopulating Table with IDENTITY Column

IDENTITY is an obstacle in moving back the original data. We have to set the IDENTITY_INSERT flag and we have to specify all the columns in the INSERT statement. After repopulating we have to check if IDENTITY is seeded at the right value and rebuild the out-of-shape index.

```
SET IDENTITY_INSERT Product ON;
GO
INSERT INTO [dbo].[Product]
      ([ProductID],[Name]
      ,[ProductNumber],[MakeFlag]
      ,[FinishedGoodsFlag],[Color]
      ,[SafetyStockLevel],[ReorderPoint]
      ,[StandardCost],[ListPrice]
      ,[Size],[SizeUnitMeasureCode]
      ,[WeightUnitMeasureCode],[Weight]
      ,[DaysToManufacture],[ProductLine]
      ,[Class] ,[Style]
      ,[ProductSubcategoryID],[ProductModelID]
      ,[SellStartDate],[SellEndDate]
      ,[DiscontinuedDate],[rowguid],[ModifiedDate])
SELECT *
FROM Adventureworks2012.Production.Product;
GO
-- (504 row(s) affected)
SET IDENTITY_INSERT Product OFF;


DBCC CHECKIDENT(Product) ;
GO
/*Checking identity information: current identity value '999', current column value '999'.
DBCC execution completed. If DBCC printed error messages, contact your system
administrator.*/


ALTER INDEX [idxProd] ON [dbo].[Product] REBUILD;
```

A good strategy is to save the table script with all related item scripts onto a disk .sql file.

That way we isolate table definition with constraints, defaults and indexes from table content.

The Database Maintenance Plan Wizard

The SQL Server Maintenance Plan Wizard is an SSMS Object Explorer GUI tool to prepare a partial or complete maintenance plan for a database(s).

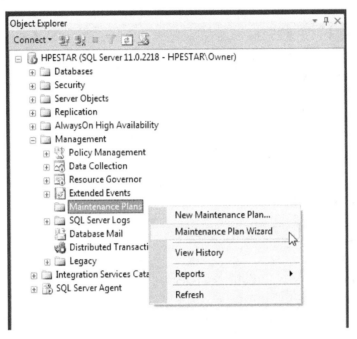

Follow the Plan Wizard Step by Step

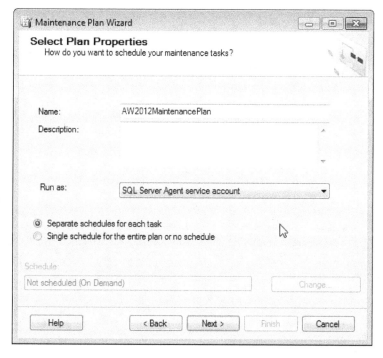

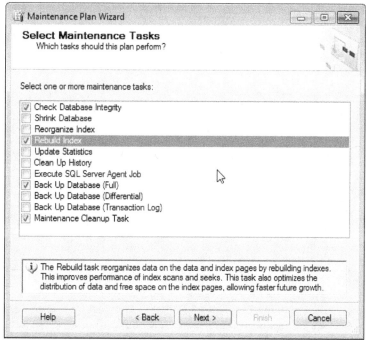

One or More Databases Can Be Specified, Schedule Setup

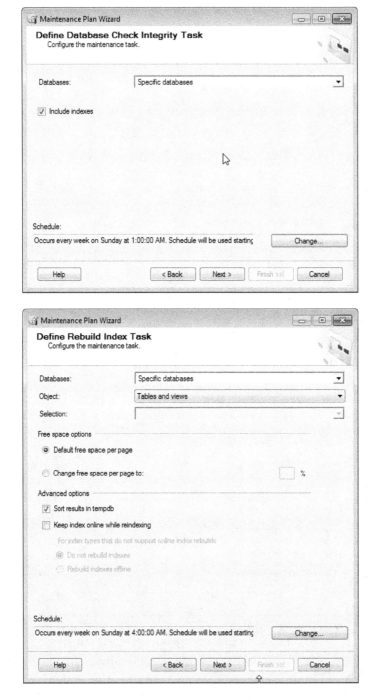

Full Database Backup Specifications

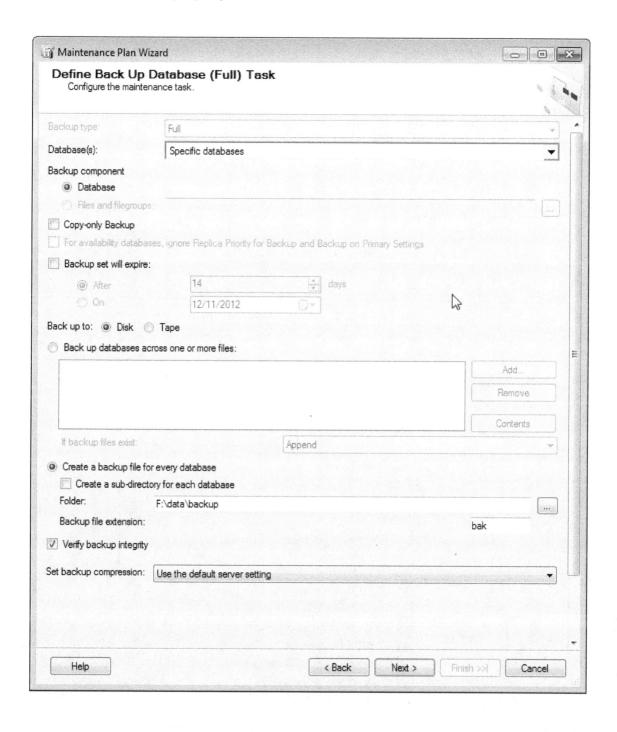

Create the Maintenance Plan & Schedule the Jobs

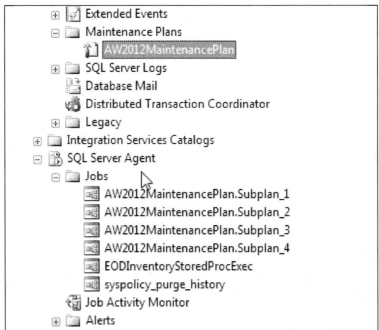

Configure Stored Procedure As SS Agent Job & Schedule

SSMS Object Explorer GUI editor can be used to setup a new job with schedule. It can also be done programmatically. The EOWBatchProcessing job scripted.

```
USE [msdb];
GO

BEGIN TRANSACTION
DECLARE @ReturnCode INT;  SELECT @ReturnCode = 0;
IF NOT EXISTS (SELECT name FROM msdb.dbo.syscategories WHERE name=N'Database Maintenance' AND category_class=1)
BEGIN

EXEC @ReturnCode = msdb.dbo.sp_add_category @class=N'JOB', @type=N'LOCAL', @name=N'Database Maintenance'
IF (@@ERROR <> 0 OR @ReturnCode <> 0) GOTO QuitWithRollback
END

DECLARE @jobId BINARY(16)

EXEC @ReturnCode = msdb.dbo.sp_add_job @job_name=N'EOWBatchProcessing',
                @enabled=1,                    @notify_level_eventlog=0,
                @notify_level_email=0,         @notify_level_netsend=0,
                @notify_level_page=0,          @delete_level=0,
                @description=N'Process all end of week jobs.',      @category_name=N'Database Maintenance',
                @owner_login_name=N'HPESTAR\Owner',         @job_id = @jobId OUTPUT
IF (@@ERROR <> 0 OR @ReturnCode <> 0) GOTO QuitWithRollback

EXEC @ReturnCode = msdb.dbo.sp_add_jobstep @job_id=@jobId, @step_name=N'EOWInventory',
                @step_id=1,                    @cmdexec_success_code=0,
                @on_success_action=1,          @on_success_step_id=0,
                @on_fail_action=2,             @on_fail_step_id=0,
                @retry_attempts=0,             @retry_interval=0,
                @os_run_priority=0, @subsystem=N'TSQL',         @command=N'exec uspInventoryEOW;',
                @database_name=N'AdventureWorks2018',       @flags=0
IF (@@ERROR <> 0 OR @ReturnCode <> 0) GOTO QuitWithRollback

EXEC @ReturnCode = msdb.dbo.sp_update_job @job_id = @jobId, @start_step_id = 1
IF (@@ERROR <> 0 OR @ReturnCode <> 0) GOTO QuitWithRollback

EXEC @ReturnCode = msdb.dbo.sp_add_jobschedule @job_id=@jobId, @name=N'EOWProcessingSATAM',
                @enabled=1,                    @freq_type=8,
                @freq_interval=65,             @freq_subday_type=1,
                @freq_subday_interval=0,       @freq_relative_interval=0,
                @freq_recurrence_factor=1,     @active_start_date=20181127,
                @active_end_date=99991231,     @active_start_time=40000,
                @active_end_time=235959,       @schedule_uid=N'0610654b-da58-46ff-9a96-39d69a0686a1'
IF (@@ERROR <> 0 OR @ReturnCode <> 0) GOTO QuitWithRollback

EXEC @ReturnCode = msdb.dbo.sp_add_jobserver @job_id = @jobId, @server_name = N'(local)'
IF (@@ERROR <> 0 OR @ReturnCode <> 0) GOTO QuitWithRollback
COMMIT TRANSACTION
GOTO EndSave
QuitWithRollback:
  IF (@@TRANCOUNT > 0) ROLLBACK TRANSACTION
EndSave:
GO
```

BULK INSERT Command

BULK INSERT is a T-SQL command which corresponds to bcp "in" action for uploading a file into a database table. The command includes an optional format file. Generally it is a good idea to use format file with BULK INSERT and bcp for more reliable and successful data transfer.

Format File Generation with bcp

Format file can be created manually by an editor or automatically by bcp. Execute at Command Prompt as one line with no breaks to create a non-XML format file:

bcp AdventureWorks2012.HumanResources.Department format nul -T -n -f f:\data\bcpdemo\hrdept.fmt

The generated format file:

```
11.0
4
1    SQLSMALLINT    0    2      ""  1   DepartmentID        ""
2    SQLNCHAR       2    100    ""  2   Name                SQL_Latin1_General_CP1_CI_AS
3    SQLNCHAR       2    100    ""  3   GroupName           SQL_Latin1_General_CP1_CI_AS
4    SQLDATETIME    0    8      ""  4   ModifiedDate        ""
```

11.0 refers to SQL Server 2012 internal version number.

Export Data with bcp Format File Option

We use the format file for exporting the data at Command Prompt.

bcp AdventureWorks2012.HumanResources.Department out f:\data\bcpdemo\hrdept.txt -f f:\data\bcpdemo\hrdept.fmt -T

This is how the exported data looks in Notepad:

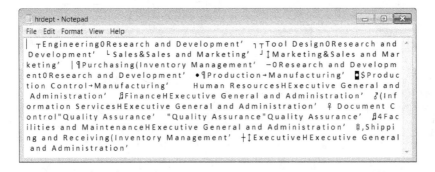

Import Data with BULK INSERT Format File Option

The same format file can be used to import the data into the database with BULK INSERT. First we create an empty table for the data import.

```
USE tempdb;
SELECT TOP(0)
        [DepartmentID] = CONVERT(INT, DepartmentID) --prevent IDENTITY inheritance
        ,[Name]
        ,[GroupName]
        ,[ModifiedDate]
INTO Department
FROM [AdventureWorks2012].[HumanResources].[Department];
GO
-- (0 row(s) affected)
```

```
BULK INSERT Department
        FROM 'f:\data\bcpdemo\hrdept.txt'
        WITH (FORMATFILE = 'f:\data\bcpdemo\hrdept.fmt');
GO
-- (16 row(s) affected)
```

```
SELECT TOP (3) * FROM Department ORDER BY NEWID();
GO
```

DepartmentID	Name	GroupName	ModifiedDate
14	Facilities and Maintenance	Executive General and Administration	2002-06-01 00:00:00.000
15	Shipping and Receiving	Inventory Management	2002-06-01 00:00:00.000
3	Sales	Sales and Marketing	2002-06-01 00:00:00.000

We can use the -n native mode for exporting data and DATAFILETYPE for importing.

```
bcp AdventureWorks2012.HumanResources.Shift out f:\temp\shift.txt -n -T
```

```
CREATE TABLE [Shift](
        [ShiftID] [tinyint]  NOT NULL,
        [Name] [dbo].[Name] NOT NULL,
        [StartTime] [time](7) NOT NULL,
        [EndTime] [time](7) NOT NULL,
        [ModifiedDate] [datetime] NOT NULL,
);
```

```
BULK INSERT Shift    FROM 'f:\temp\shift.txt'    WITH (DATAFILETYPE='native');
```

CHAPTER 16: Advanced T-SQL Programming Topics

Importing & Exporting Images

Importing & exporting images and other binary large objects (BLOB) requires special techniques. We use OPENROWSET BULK method to import an image.

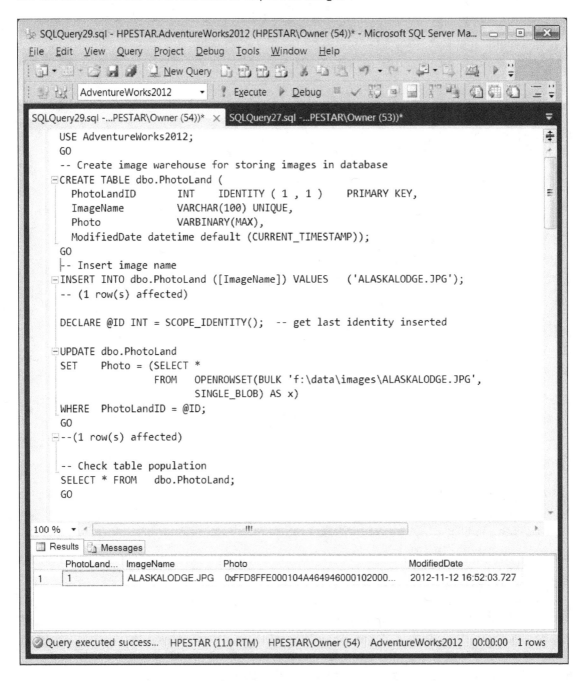

Exporting Image with bcp

The bcp command can be used to export an image. In the following demo, it is executed from xp_cmdshell. **NOTE: on most production servers the xp_cmdshell option is disabled due to security concerns.**

```
DECLARE  @Command NVARCHAR(4000);

-- Keep the command on ONE LINE - here it wraps around
SET @Command = 'bcp "SELECT Photo FROM AdventureWorks2012.dbo.PhotoLand WHERE
PhotoLandID=1"  queryout "F:\temp\ALASKALODGE.jpg" -T -n' ;

PRINT @Command -- debugging

EXEC xp_cmdshell  @Command;
GO
/*NULL
Starting copy...
NULL
1 rows copied.
Network packet size (bytes): 4096
Clock Time (ms.) Total    : 203   Average : (4.93 rows per sec.)
NULL */
```

Building a bcp Format File Interactively for Image Export

Exporting All Images from Table

The content of the previously created bcp format file.

```
11.0
1
1    SQLBINARY    0    0    ""    1    LargePhoto        ""
```

T-SQL script for exporting all images to the file system from Production.ProductPhoto table LargePhoto column.

```
USE AdventureWorks2012;
GO


DECLARE @Command  VARCHAR(4000), @PhotoID  INT,  @ImageFileName VARCHAR(128) ;
DECLARE PHOTOcursor CURSOR  FOR
        SELECT ProductPhotoID,   LargePhotoFileName  FROM   Production.ProductPhoto
        WHERE  LargePhotoFileName != 'no_image_available_large.gif';


OPEN PHOTOcursor FETCH NEXT FROM PHOTOcursor INTO @PhotoID,  @ImageFileName;


WHILE (@@FETCH_STATUS = 0) -- Cursor loop
 BEGIN
-- No carriage return or new line in bcp command string!
  SET @Command = CONCAT('bcp "SELECT LargePhoto FROM
AdventureWorks2012.Production.ProductPhoto WHERE ProductPhotoID = ',
  convert(VARCHAR,@PhotoID) + '" queryout "f:\data\images\productphoto\',
  @ImageFileName,'" -T -f "f:\data\images\bcpimage.fmt" ');


  PRINT @Command -- debugging
  EXEC xp_cmdshell @Command, no_output;


  FETCH NEXT FROM PHOTOcursor  INTO @PhotoID,     @ImageFileName;
 END;  -- cursor loop


CLOSE PHOTOcursor; DEALLOCATE PHOTOcursor;
GO
```

Product Photo Icons in the ProductPhoto Folder

The folder contains 100 exported product photos. The photos cannot be visualized in SSMS. but in the file system or SSRS reports. The following is a partial list of image icons.

In SSIS the Export Column & Import Column Transformations can be used for exporting and importing a set of images to and from folders.

CHAPTER 16: Advanced T-SQL Programming Topics

FOR XML Clause

A SELECT query returns results as a table-like rowset. With a FOR XML clause the results are returned in XML format.

FOR XML RAW

The FOR XML RAW mode generates a single <row> element per row in the rowset that is returned by the SELECT statement. Tree structure can be generated by nesting queries.

```
SELECT *
FROM HumanResources.Shift
ORDER BY ShiftID
FOR XML RAW;
```

```
<row ShiftID="1" Name="Day" StartTime="07:00:00" EndTime="15:00:00" ModifiedDate="2002-06-01T00:00:00" />
<row ShiftID="2" Name="Evening" StartTime="15:00:00" EndTime="23:00:00" ModifiedDate="2002-06-01T00:00:00" />
<row ShiftID="3" Name="Night" StartTime="23:00:00" EndTime="07:00:00" ModifiedDate="2002-06-01T00:00:00" />
```

FOR XML AUTO

The FOR XML AUTO mode generates nesting in the resulting XML by using heuristics based on the way the SELECT statement is specified. You have minimal control over the shape of the XML generated. Tree structure can be generated by nesting queries.

```
SELECT *
FROM HumanResources.Shift
ORDER BY ShiftID
FOR XML AUTO;
```

```
<HumanResources.Shift ShiftID="1" Name="Day" StartTime="07:00:00" EndTime="15:00:00" ModifiedDate="2002-06-01T00:00:00" />
<HumanResources.Shift ShiftID="2" Name="Evening" StartTime="15:00:00" EndTime="23:00:00" ModifiedDate="2002-06-01T00:00:00" />
<HumanResources.Shift ShiftID="3" Name="Night" StartTime="23:00:00" EndTime="07:00:00" ModifiedDate="2002-06-01T00:00:00" />
```

FOR XML EXPLICIT

The FOR XML EXPLICIT mode allows extensive control over the shape of the XML document. Attributes and elements can be freely combined in deciding the shape of the XML document. One of the options with XML EXPLICIT is the ELEMENT directive. The UNION ALL operator is used to assemble the tag and data information.

```
SELECT        1              AS Tag,
              NULL           AS Parent,
              ProductNumber AS [ProductHeader!1!ProdNo],
              NULL            AS [ProductDetail!2!ProductName!ELEMENT],
              NULL           AS [ProductDetail!2!ListPrice!ELEMENT],
              NULL           AS [ProductDetail!2!Color!ELEMENT],
              NULL           AS [ProductDetail!2!Size!ELEMENT]
FROM   AdventureWorks2012.Production.Product P WHERE ProductSubcategoryID is not NULL
UNION ALL
SELECT        2,
              1,
              ProductNumber,
              Name,
              ListPrice,
              Color,
              Size
FROM   AdventureWorks2012.Production.Product P  WHERE ProductSubcategoryID is not NULL
ORDER BY [ProductHeader!1!ProdNo], Tag   FOR XML EXPLICIT;
-- (590 row(s) affected) - Partial results.

<ProductHeader ProdNo="BK-M68B-46">
 <ProductDetail>
  <ProductName>Mountain-200 Black, 46</ProductName>
  <ListPrice>2294.9900</ListPrice>
  <Color>Black</Color>
  <Size>46</Size>
 </ProductDetail>
</ProductHeader>
<ProductHeader ProdNo="BK-M68S-38">
 <ProductDetail>
  <ProductName>Mountain-200 Silver, 38</ProductName>
  <ListPrice>2319.9900</ListPrice>
  <Color>Silver</Color>
  <Size>38</Size>
 </ProductDetail>
</ProductHeader>
```

FOR XML PATH

The FOR XML PATH mode together with the nested FOR XML query capability provides the flexibility of the EXPLICIT mode in a simpler manner. The example lists sales orders with detail line and header information.

Concatenation Loop With XML PATH

The FOR XML PATH clause makes it possible to do program looping within a query without requiring multiple statements. One way is to implement it as a correlated subquery.

```
Use AdventureWorks2012;
Go
```

```
SELECT  PM.Name AS Model
       ,(SELECT CONCAT(P.Name, ', ')
         FROM Production.Product AS P   WHERE P.ProductModelID = PM.ProductModelID
         ORDER BY P.Name FOR XML PATH('') ) AS ProductLineup
FROM Production.ProductModel AS PM ORDER BY Model;
-- (128 row(s) affected) - Partial result.
```

Model	ProductLineup
All-Purpose Bike Stand	All-Purpose Bike Stand,
Bike Wash	Bike Wash - Dissolver,
Cable Lock	Cable Lock,
Chain	Chain,
Classic Vest	Classic Vest, L, Classic Vest, M, Classic Vest, S,
Cycling Cap	AWC Logo Cap,
Fender Set - Mountain	Fender Set - Mountain,
Front Derailleur	Front Derailleur,
Full-Finger Gloves	Full-Finger Gloves, L, Full-Finger Gloves, M, Full-Finger Gloves, S,

A popular solution for the trailing comma issue is making it leading comma and taking it out from the first position with the STUFF function. Since the product name may contain commas, we use "|" as string list delimiter.

```
SELECT  PM.Name AS Model
       ,LTRIM(RTRIM(STUFF((SELECT CONCAT('| ', P.Name)
         FROM Production.Product AS P   WHERE P.ProductModelID = PM.ProductModelID
         ORDER BY P.Name FOR XML PATH('') ), 1, 1, ''))) AS ProductLineup
FROM Production.ProductModel AS PM
ORDER BY Model;
-- (128 row(s) affected) - Partial result.
```

Model	ProductLineup
ML Mountain Frame	ML Mountain Frame - Black, 40| ML Mountain Frame - Black, 44| ML Mountain Frame - Black, 48

CHAPTER 16: Advanced T-SQL Programming Topics

Interesting T-SQL Scripts

Challenging String Manipulations

```
-- Displaying hidden characters (whitespace) in a string; TAB character appears as space;
DECLARE @text varchar(64) = 'New'+char(9)+'York'+char(9)+'City'+char(9);
SELECT @text, CONVERT(varbinary(64), @text);
-- New York City 0x4E657709596F726B094369747909
```

```
-- Working with SUBSTRING & ASCII functions
SELECT       TOP (5)
             ProductNumber,
             MiddleOfString    =    SUBSTRING(ProductNumber,4,5),
             SecondChar        =    SUBSTRING(ProductNumber,2,1),
             ASCIIValue        =    ASCII(SUBSTRING(ProductNumber,2,1))
FROM AdventureWorks2012.Production.Product  ORDER BY NEWID();
```

ProductNumber	MiddleOfString	SecondChar	ASCIIValue
FR-R72R-44	R72R-	R	82
BK-R89B-48	R89B-	K	75
HN-4402	4402	N	78
LJ-1220	1220	J	74
BA-8327	8327	A	65

```
-- Compare empty string and NULL string
DECLARE @NullString varchar(32) = NULL, @EmptyString varchar(32)= '';

SELECT LEN(@EmptyString); SELECT LEN(@NullString);   -- 0  NULL

SELECT DATALENGTH(@EmptyString); SELECT DATALENGTH(@NullString); -- 0  NULL

-- Testing for empty string and null string
SELECT 'Miami' WHERE @EmptyString = '';  SELECT 'Miami' WHERE @NullString is null;
-- Miami Miami

SELECT 'Miami' WHERE LEN(@EmptyString)=0;  SELECT 'Miami' WHERE LEN(@NullString) = 0;
-- Miami  (0 row(s) affected)

SELECT @EmptyString + @NullString+'Vegas';                -- NULL

SELECT CONCAT(@EmptyString,@NullString, 'Vegas');         -- Vegas
```

Date & Datetime Manipulations

```
-- Count business days for a date range
CREATE FUNCTION ufnWeekDaysCount ( @DateStart DATETIME, @DateEnd  DATETIME)
RETURNS INT AS  BEGIN
   IF ( @DateStart IS NULL OR @DateEnd IS NULL )
    RETURN ( 0 )
   DECLARE @i INT = 0;
   WHILE ( @DateStart <= @DateEnd )  BEGIN
     SET @i = @i + CASE
              WHEN datename(dw, @DateStart) IN ( 'Saturday', 'Sunday' )
              THEN 0   ELSE 1    END
     SET @DateStart = @DateStart + 1
   END -- while
   RETURN ( @i )
 END -- function
GO
```

```
SELECT dbo.ufnWeekDaysCount('2016-01-01', '2016-12-31');     -- 261
```

```
-- YEAR(), MONTH(), DATENAME() functions in aggregate query
SELECT  YEAR          = YEAR(OrderDate),
        MONTH         = MONTH(OrderDate),
        MMM           = UPPER(left(DATENAME(MONTH,OrderDate),3)),
        Sales         = FORMAT(sum(TotalDue),'c0','en-US'),
        OrderCount    = COUNT(* )
FROM    AdventureWorks2012.Sales.SalesOrderHeader
GROUP BY      YEAR(OrderDate), MONTH(OrderDate), DATENAME(MONTH,OrderDate)
ORDER BY      YEAR, MONTH;
GO -- (37 row(s) affected) - Partial results.
```

YEAR	MONTH	MMM	Sales	OrderCount
2008	5	MAY	$5,813,557	2386
2008	6	JUN	$6,004,156	2374

```
-- Month start/end is easy with EOMONTH() - Find month ending weekday
SELECT  DATEADD(DD,1,EOMONTH(GETDATE(),-2) )        AS FirstDayOfPreviousMonth,
        EOMONTH(GETDATE(),-1)                       AS LastDayOfPreviousMonth
-- 2016-11-01   2016-11-30
```

```
SELECT DATENAME(DW, EOMONTH(CURRENT_TIMESTAMP)) -- Monday
```

CHAPTER 16: Advanced T-SQL Programming Topics

Find Sprocs, Triggers, Functions & Views Where Column is Used

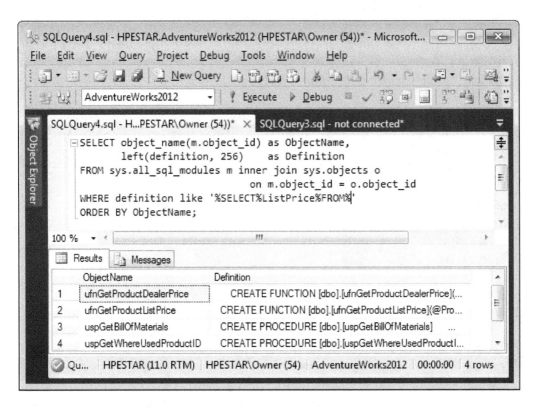

Designing the Query in GUI Query Designer

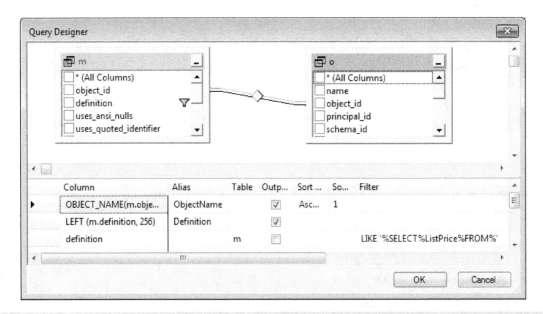

Transforming Dynamic SQL Result Set into a View

A view is "clean", a dynamic SQL script can be pretty "messy". By wrapping dynamic SQL into a view, we get the best of both worlds: the power of dynamic SQL and the table-like access to a view.

```
USE AdventureWorks2012;
GO
CREATE PROC sprocListDepartment AS   BEGIN
DECLARE @SQL nvarchar(max) =
 'SELECT DepartmentID, Name, GroupName FROM HumanResources.Department ORDER BY
DepartmentID DESC';
EXEC sp_executeSQL @SQL;
END
GO
```

```
CREATE VIEW vDepartment AS
SELECT * FROM OPENQUERY( HPESTAR, 'exec AdventureWorks2012.dbo.sprocListDepartment
WITH RESULT SETS  ((ID int, Department varchar(50), GroupName varchar(50)))');
GO
```

```
SELECT * FROM vDepartment;    -- (16 row(s) affected)
```

Accessing a View from Excel

A view can be accessed from Excel by logging in to SQL Server, choosing a database and picking the view.

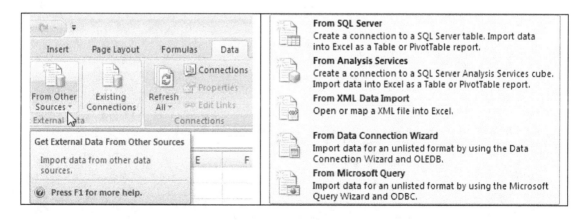

After Login the Data Connection Wizard Guides Us Through

The Data Connection Wizard requires network access and login to SQL Server.

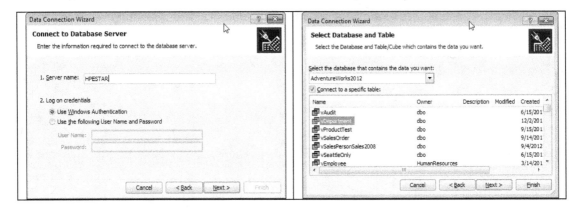

The next popop window offers radio button selection for: Table, PivotTable and PivotChart & PivotTable; choosing Table.

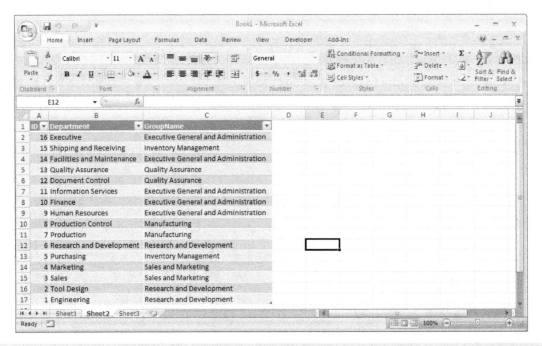

Querying the Database from a Client C# Program

The general program logic for SQL Server database access is very similar for other languages such as C++, VB or Java. First connection has to be established to SQL Server and the database, then a SQL query or stored procedure execution command is sent to the server, and finally the server returns a result set which has to be processed in a C# loop.

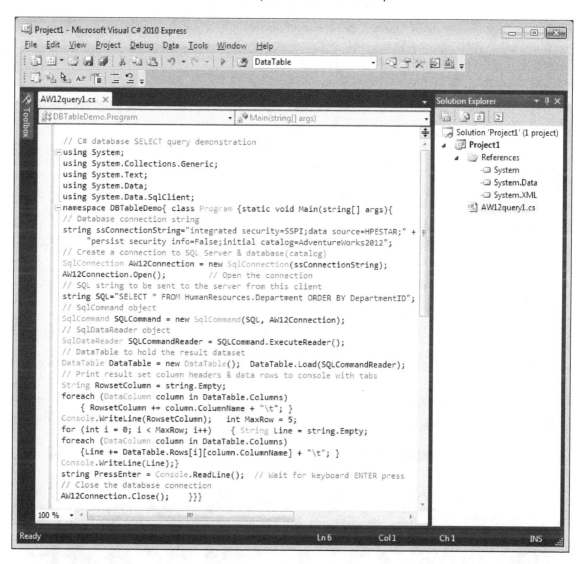

C# Code Listing

```
// C# database SELECT query demonstration
using System;
using System.Collections.Generic;
```

```
using System.Text;
using System.Data;
using System.Data.SqlClient;
namespace DBTableDemo{ class Program {static void Main(string[] args){
// Database connection string
string ssConnectionString="integrated security=SSPI;data source=HPESTAR;" +
    "persist security info=False;initial catalog=AdventureWorks2012";
// Create a connection to SQL Server & database(catalog)
SqlConnection AW12Connection = new SqlConnection(ssConnectionString);
AW12Connection.Open();      // Open the connection
// SQL string to be sent to the server from this client
string SQL="SELECT * FROM HumanResources.Department ORDER BY DepartmentID";
// SqlCommand object
SqlCommand SQLCommand = new SqlCommand(SQL, AW12Connection);
// SqlDataReader object
SqlDataReader SQLCommandReader = SQLCommand.ExecuteReader();
// DataTable to hold the result dataset
DataTable DataTable = new DataTable();  DataTable.Load(SQLCommandReader);
// Print result set column headers & data rows to console with tabs
String RowsetColumn = string.Empty;
foreach (DataColumn column in DataTable.Columns)
   { RowsetColumn += column.ColumnName + "\t"; }
Console.WriteLine(RowsetColumn);   int MaxRow = 5;
for (int i = 0; i < MaxRow; i++)   { String Line = string.Empty;
foreach (DataColumn column in DataTable.Columns)
   {Line += DataTable.Rows[i][column.ColumnName] + "\t"; }
Console.WriteLine(Line);}
string PressEnter = Console.ReadLine();  // Wait for keyboard ENTER press
// Close the database connection
AW12Connection.Close();   }}}
```

Console Image with Data Display from HumanResources.Department

```
file:///C:/Users/Owner/AppData/Local/Temporary Projects/Project1/bin/Debug/Project1.EXE        _  ▢  ✕
DepartmentID    Name      GroupName          ModifiedDate
1          Engineering     Research and Development          6/1/2002 12:00:00 AM
2          Tool Design     Research and Development          6/1/2002 12:00:00 AM
3          Sales    Sales and Marketing      6/1/2002 12:00:00 AM
4          Marketing       Sales and Marketing      6/1/2002 12:00:00 AM
5          Purchasing      Inventory Management     6/1/2002 12:00:00 AM
```

CHAPTER 16: Advanced T-SQL Programming Topics

APPENDIX A: Job Interview Questions

Selected Database Design Questions

D1. What is your approach to database design?

D2. Some of our legacy databases are far from 3NF. Can you work in such an environment?

D3. Can UNIQUE KEY be used instead of PRIMARY KEY?

D4. Can a FOREIGN KEY be NULL?

D5. Can a PRIMARY KEY be NULL?

D6. Can a PRIMARY KEY be based on non-clustered unique index?

D7. Do you implement OrderQty > 0 condition as a CHECK constraint or in the application software?

D8. What is a heap?

D9. Can a table have 2 IDENTITY columns, 2 FOREIGN KEYs, 2 PRIMARY KEYs and 2 clustered indexes?

D10. Should each table have a NATURAL KEY or is INT IDENTITY PK sufficient?

D11. How can you prevent entry of "U.S", "USA", etc. instead of "United States" into Country column?

D12. How would you implement ManagerID in an Employee table with EmployeeID as PRIMARY KEY?

D13. How would you implement the relationship between OrderMaster and OrderDetail tables?

D14. Product table has the Color column. Would you create a Color table & change column to ColorID FK?

D15. Can you insert directly into an IDENTITY column?

D16. Which one is better? Composite PRIMARY KEY on NATURAL KEY, or INT IDENTITY PRIMARY KEY & UNIQUE KEY on NATURAL KEY?

D17. What is the lifetime of a regular table created in tempdb?

D18. How many different ways can you connect tables in a database?

D19. How would you connect the Vehicle and Owner tables?

D20. Can you have the same table names in different schemas?

Selected Database Programming Questions

P1. Write a query to list all departments with employee count based on the Department column of Employee table.

P2. Same as above but the Employee table has the DepartmentID column.

P3. Write an INSERT statement for a new "Social Technology" department with GroupName "Sales & Marketing".

P4. Same query es in P2, but the new department should be included even though no employees yet.

P5. Write a query to generate 1000 sequential numbers without a table.

P6. Write a query with SARGable predicate to list all orders from OrderMaster received on 2016-10-23. OrderDate is datetime.

P7. Write a query to add a header record DEPARTMENTNAME to the departments listing from the Department table. If there are 20 departments, the result set should have 21 records.

P8. Make the previous query a derived table in an outer SELECT * query

P9. Write an ORDER BY clause for the previous query with CASE expression to sort DEPARTMENTNAME as first record and alphabetically descending from there on.

P10. Same as above with the IIF conditional.

P11. The table-valued dbo.ufnSplitCSV splits a comma delimited string (input parameter). The Product table has some ProductName-s with comma(s). Write a CROSS APPLY query to return ProductName-s with comma and each split string value from the UDF as separate line. ProductName should repeat for each split part.

ProductName	SplitPart
Full-Finger Gloves, L	Full-Finger Gloves
Full-Finger Gloves, L	L

P12. You need the inserted lines count 10 lines down following the INSERT statement. What should be the statement immediately following the INSERT statement?

P13. What is the result of the second query? What is it called?

SELECT COUNT_BIG(*) FROM Sales.SalesOrderDetail;   -- 121317

SELECT COUNT_BIG(*) FROM Sales.SalesOrderDetail x, Sales.SalesOrderDetail y;

P14. Declare & Assign the string variable @Text varchar(32) the literal '2016/10/23 10:20:12' without the "/" and ":".

P15. You want to add a parameter to a frequently used view. What is the workaround?

P16. When converting up to 40 characters string, can you use varchar instead of varchar(40)?

P17. Can you roll back IDENTITY seeds and table variables with ROLLBACK TRANSACTION?

P18. How do you decide where to place the clustered index?

P19. What is the simplest solution for the collation error: "Cannot resolve collation conflict..."?

P20. Which system table can be used for integer sequence up to 2^12 values?

This page is intentionally left blank.

This page is intentionally left blank.

APPENDIX B: Job Interview Answers

Selected Database Design Answers

D1. I prefer 3NF design due to high database developer productivity and low maintenance cost.

D2. I did have such projects in the past. I can handle them. Hopefully, introduce some improvements.

D3. Partially yes since UNIQUE KEYs can be FK referenced, fully no. Every table should a PRIMARY KEY.

D4. Yes.

D5. No.

D6. Yes. The default is clustered unique index. Only unique index is required.

D7. CHECK constraint. A server-side object solution is more reliable than code in application software.

D8. A table without clustered index. Database engine generally works better if a table has clustered index.

D9. No, yes, no, no.

D10. A table should be designed with NATURAL KEY(s). INT IDENTITY PK is not a replacement for NK.

D11. Lookup table with UDF CHECK Constraint. UDF checks the Lookup table for valid entries.

D12. ManagerID as a FOREIGN KEY referencing the PRIMARY KEY of the same table; self-referencing.

D13. OrderID PRIMARY KEY of OrderMaster. OrderID & LineItemID composition PK of OrderDetail. OrderID of OrderDetail FK to OrderID of OderMaster.

D14. Yes. It makes sense for color to be in its own table.

D15. No. Only if you SET IDENTITY_INSERT tablename ON.

D16. Meaningless INT IDENTITY PRIMARY KEY with UNIQUE KEY ON NATURAL KEY is better.

D17. Until SQL Server restarted. tempdb starts empty as copy of model database.

D18. There is only one way: FOREIGN KEY constraint.

D19. With the OwnerVehicleXref junction table reflecting many-to-many relationship.

D20. Yes. A table is identified by SchemaName.TableName . dbo is the default schema.

Selected Database Programming Answers

P1. SELECT Department, Employees=COUNT(*) FROM Employee
    GROUP BY Department ORDER BY Department;

P2. SELECT d.Department, Employees = COUNT(EmployeeID) FROM Employee e
    INNER JOIN Department d ON e.DepartmentID = d.DepartmentID
    GROUP BY d.Department ORDER BY Department;

P3. INSERT Department (Name, GroupName) VALUES ('Social Technology', 'Sales & Marketing');

P4. SELECT d.Department, Employees = COUNT(EmployeeID) FROM Employee e
    RIGHT JOIN Department d ON e.DepartmentID = d.DepartmentID
    GROUP BY d.Department ORDER BY Department;

P5. ;WITH Seq AS (SELECT SeqNo = 1 UNION ALL SELECT SeqNo+1 FROM Seq WHERE SeqNo < 100)
    SELECT * FROM Seq;

P6. SELECT * FROM OrderMaster WHERE OrderDate >='20161023'
    AND OrderDate < DATEADD(DD,1,'20161023');

P7. SELECT AllDepartments = 'DEPARTMENTNAME' UNION SELECT Department FROM Department;

P8. SELECT * FROM (SELECT AllDepartments = 'DEPARTMENTNAME' UNION SELECT Name
     FROM HumanResources.Department) x

P9. ORDER BY CASE WHEN AllDepartments = 'DEPARTMENTNAME' THEN 1 ELSE 2 END,
     AllDepartments DESC;

P10. ORDER BY IIF(AllDepartments = 'DEPARTMENTNAME', 1 , 2), AllDepartments DESC;

P11. SELECT ProductName, S.SplitPart FROM Product P CROSS APPLY dbo.ufnSplitCSV (Name) S
     WHERE ProductName like '%,%';

P12. DECLARE @InsertedCount INT = @@ROWCOUNT;

P13. 121317*121317; Cartesian product.

P14. DECLARE @Text varchar(32) =
     REPLACE(REPLACE ('2016/10/23 10:20:12', '/', SPACE(0)), ':', SPACE(0));

P15. Table-valued INLINE user-defined function.

P16. varchar(40). It is a good idea to specify the length always. The default is 30.

P17. No. ROLLBACK has no effect on IDENTITY seeds or table variables. If an INSERT advanced the
IDENTITY seed by 5 during the rollbacked transaction, it will stay that way after the ROLLBACK. It means a
gap in the IDENTITY sequence.

P18. Business critical queries are the determining factor in placing the clustered index. Clustered index
speeds up range queries.

P19. Place "COLLATE DATABASE_DEFAULT" on the right side of the expression.

P20. spt_values table.
SELECT N = number FROM master.dbo.spt_values WHERE type='P' ORDER BY N;

INDEX of SQL Server 2012 Programming

Index of the Most Important Topics

E

T

U

---

www.ingramcontent.com/pod-product-compliance
Lightning Source LLC
LaVergne TN
LVHW062258060326
832902LV00013B/1950